THE MARRIAGE FEAST

By Alice Brown

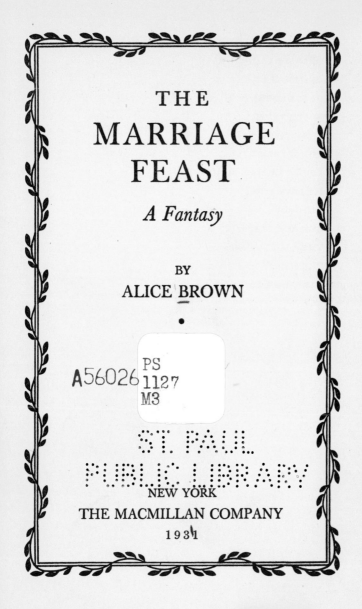

THE
MARRIAGE
FEAST

A Fantasy

BY
ALICE BROWN

•

NEW YORK
THE MACMILLAN COMPANY
1931

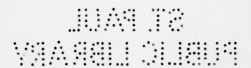

PRINTED IN THE UNITED STATES OF AMERICA
BY THE STRATFORD PRESS, INC., NEW YORK

THE MARRIAGE FEAST

THE MARRIAGE FEAST

The scene is a woodland glade where the sun lies sweetly upon a small rustic house standing on an upward rise of green. On this sward the SOUL *and* BODY, *both young, both beautiful, are playing, running and leaping in excess of spirits, and just now tossing a ball, one to the other, of iridescent colors that catch the sun. We may say that the* SOUL, *from her unbound hair and her more flowing garments, is feminine, and the* BODY, *from his rougher build and deeper voice, is a youth soon to be a man; but one does not know. And it hardly matters, since both have beauty, though not of the same sort. The* SOUL *has just caught the ball and clasps it to her breast before throwing it. She calls out, in ecstasy.*

THE SOUL

Bubble of joy!

THE BODY
Fling higher. Oh, fling high!

[*As she is about to fling the ball, a majestic* PRESENCE *stands near them, a man's figure dressed in a robe of soft mist-like gray falling in lovely lines, as it might be the marching gear of an ancient Greek. And yet he is not Greek, but a stranger from scarce imagined regions, and the* SOUL, *bewildered, keeps her arm in air for a moment, at the sight of him. To her, he is a thing of brightness, despite the mist-like effect of the subduing violet gray, and she is not only bewildered by his appearance but by its suggestion that sometime, somewhere, she has seen him before. There is a circlet of gold about his head, so like a line of light that it might almost be a part of his hair, on which it lies as if it were not for ornament, or any indication of rank, but the design of keeping the hair in place. This effect may come from the certainty one has that he is not more a personage of heavenly degree than one of strength and good intent who chooses, (as it were being consecrated) to serve some higher power.*]

THE SOUL

[*in awe*]. Look who has come. [*The ball drops from her lowered hand.*]

[4]

The Marriage Feast

THE BODY

       Heedless! You've lost the ball.

THE SOUL

See! see! what wonder in the shadows there.
[*to the* PRESENCE, *timidly*]. An angel art thou?

THE BODY

             [*barely glancing
that way*]. Only a shaft of sun.
Look for the ball. It may be rolling yet.

THE SOUL

A radiance, a whiteness dressed in light
And hair that flames and flames like its own crown.
[*to the* PRESENCE, *wistfully*]. Who are you—lord?

THE BODY

       No mortal thing is there.

THE SOUL

Not mortal, no! but look, O playmate, look!
He moves a pace toward us, as he would speak.

THE BODY

Only a sun-shaft quivering in the breeze.
If you're bemused by such a thing of naught
I'll walk apart, or sleep, to wake again
When your imaginings have spent themselves,

And you are fain to laugh and toss the ball.
You'll find yourself as lone as a maimed bird:
For without me, the body of your bliss,
You do not live.

> [*He turns about and feigns to be interested in the tall fringing shrubbery near. The* PRESENCE *approaches the* SOUL *and speaks.*]

THE PRESENCE

Not live? not you, the Soul
That dwelt in the bright west'ring place of stars
Before you habited with mortal flesh?
You, the keen breath of the one puissant One
Blown out in stress of His creativeness?
Not you, the Soul? You lived in empery
Before you chose this heavy partnership.
Again, when time moves round, you'll live alone
In light, and he—[*The* PRESENCE *pauses in pity of them.*]

THE SOUL

[*troubled*]. Oh, must he be alone?

THE BODY

[*turning to her briefly*]. Don't stand there babbling to the empty air.
The ball's a hundred leagues away, by this.

[6]

The Marriage Feast

It is an angel, and he seems to know
The past—my past—and things that are to come.

THE BODY

[*scoffingly*]. An angel! daytime visions!

THE SOUL

                    [*eagerly*]. See the sun
Upon his baldric.

THE BODY

[*swaggering and pretending to draw a sword*].
        See it upon my steel.
[*He walks away, making passes at the air in a
braggart display.*]

THE PRESENCE

Ask what you will that may advantage him.
His pride will need assuagement ere he dies,
That so his flesh rot gently into earth,
Not shrieking back defiance to its Lord
And triply bound by its own froward will.

THE SOUL

[*cries out*]. Ah, then he needs must die, this
    miracle,
This springtime loveliness of earthborn grace.

[7]

THE MARRIAGE FEAST

THE PRESENCE

[*tenderly*]. You knew it.

THE SOUL

   [*despairingly*]. Yes, but still I do forget
While we are dancing down the illusive hours
And the sphered wonder of this whirling earth,
All green and gold and blue, so dazzling bright,
Seems like a heaven enwrapt in ecstasy.
When must he die?

THE PRESENCE

     Let him not think of that,
But dwell on ways to live heroical.
And teach him, thou: for all the runes of God
Are open to thee, thou who art the Soul.

THE SOUL

[*timidly*]. I think he thinks this earth belongs to
   him.

THE PRESENCE

[*with a grave emphasis*]. The earth belongs to
   God, the heavens also,
And he is of the earth, but you of God.
Let him beware lest in his love of earth
He bind you to its wheel. And you, the Soul,
Take heed. The Body is your servitor.

[8]

THE MARRIAGE FEAST

THE SOUL

[*in a despairing outburst*]. My mate, my darling,
    let it be!

THE PRESENCE

                                        [*in a sad*
tenderness]. Your child
To yield obedience, not your mate alone.
Your servitor to do your highest will,
And make the wilding earth bloom out in flowers.

THE SOUL

[*eagerly*]. I said so: flowers for him to dance upon.

THE PRESENCE

For all to walk upon: God's tiniest child.

THE SOUL

But shall there be no dancing any more?

THE PRESENCE

Yes, and the sound of flutes, and merry ways
To bring the vintage in. But it must be
Not his nor yours, but a processional
Home to the doorway of the hidden house
Whose windows front the rays of Paradise.
You may not see me more. But hold your cup,
Your little cup of prayerful emptiness

Up to the sky, and God will fill it full.
Do not forget. I say you are of God,
And all your ways and all the Body's walk
Must be of God. See to it straitly, thou,
Since he is of the earth, and cannot see.

    [*The* SOUL *looks bewildered at the place where he was, for he is no longer there.*]

THE SOUL

[*amazed*]. He is gone.

    [*The* BODY *returns his imaginary sword to its scabbard and comes back to her.*]

THE BODY

    [*teasingly*]. So is the moonshine of last night.

THE SOUL

[*troubled, pointing to the grassy bank*]. Sit here,
and let me tell you what he said.

THE BODY

[*dancing a few steps and singing*].

        Moonshine and madness!
        Madness and the moon!
        Fill the horn of gladness!
        Run with magic shoon!

[10]

THE MARRIAGE FEAST

THE SOUL

[*trying to remember*]. We talked—you saw us
    talk—surely you heard?
'Twas all of us and the dear earth. It ebbs,
The message thins away from me like mist,
Wind-driven mist before the rising sun.
I think he meant—

THE BODY

[*mocking her*]. She thinks the moonshine meant—

THE SOUL

[*still painfully trying to remember*]. Oh, I must
    spell it out from hour to hour
As time shall serve. He said I'd lived before—

THE BODY

[*roughly*]. What's that to tell? I am alive to-day.

THE SOUL

[*groping for words*]. At least, if you're to die,
    surely I may
Come after you.

THE BODY

    [*shuddering*]. Die! curse that obscene word.
We are alive, I say.

[11]

The Marriage Feast

THE SOUL

[*persisting*]. If you're to die
And I to live, shall I remember you?

THE BODY

[*defiantly*]. But I am you.

THE SOUL

[*in despair*]. No. I shall be alone.

THE BODY

[*insisting hotly*]. And you are I, and the bright
    quickening dawn
Calls each to raptures never to be wrought
Without the other.

THE SOUL

[*in growing anguish*]. Nay, I am the Soul.
The Angel says I am the quickening soul.

THE BODY

[*proudly*]. I am the body, and no messenger
Of moonshine generate need tell me that.
Is she not mine, this earth? I tread on her
As godhead treading clouds. I rive the plough
Into her bosom, and she wraps herself
In vesture woven to conceal the scar.
She gives me nurture, half unwillingly,

[12]

And yet she gives it, for I am her god,
And though she hate me I can conquer her,
Destroy her children, gay four-footed things
That range wild pastures on the mountain side,
And steal her sport of killing them herself
When they are old and their small dancing hoofs
No more can wake a thrill in her dull breast.

THE SOUL

[*in troubled questioning*]. But do you never hear
    the myriad voice
Of some great ally that is not the earth,
Some call, some high compulsion from a land—
Oh, farther than the sun and moon, and bright,
Brighter than sun or moon?

THE BODY

        [*indifferently*]. I have my ears,
Yet I hear nothing.

THE SOUL

    [*forgetting him*]. Where can that land be?

THE BODY

This land is ours, this day. We'll laugh and dance
And throw our bubble to the reddening sky,
And call down satyrs from the mountain side
To sport with us.

THE MARRIAGE FEAST

THE SOUL

[*shrinking with a remembered
fear*]. The satyrs frighten me.

THE BODY

[*jovially*]. They are the best of fellows, they that
live
Where turbid rivers born of melting snows
Rush to the valleys and the summoning sea.

THE SOUL

Rivers that sweep down houses in their track
And leave a hearthstone in a mountain cleft,
Or strand a roof-tree on a hindering pine.
And houses, dear, are homes.

THE BODY

[*kindled by his love
of earth*]. Yes, hearths and homes
With all their chaffer of the common life
And brutish plodding to the sty and field.
But satyrs are the impish spawn of chance,
Not, as mankind, reigning by privilege
And vaunted license from creation's Lord,
But tricksy folk, sprung from the loins of earth
Without her careless mothering, and wild,
From innocent malignancy, to set

THE MARRIAGE FEAST

The ball of motion rolling up the hill,
And turn things here and yon and counterwise.
They flout at miracles of dawn and dark,
They grin and gesture at the growing moon,
And when the moon's away they play a game
With stars for counters from a velvet purse,
Dropped in blind pools, to gleam and eddy there.

THE SOUL

[*waking to the wonder of earthly beauty*]. What
     things they know, the strange, bright, silent
     stars,
Bestudding the cold arch of sunless night:
The patterned anadem of the great Crown,
The four gold nails of Pegasus, to hold
The firmament in place, the silver clash
Of Pleiades. The things of earth and sky
Are known of them.

THE BODY

           And as they read the sky
My satyrs read the earth. They know the rain
That washes all aglow, the wild wet dawn
That turns to fire, and the red sun in spate,
Flooding at length the vales. The cloistered snow
Who holds her maiden vigils near the sky,
Locking her crystalline cold wreaths away

In chasms where no foot may penetrate,
Is theirs, to work their impish will upon,
And leave her, slain like bridal innocence,
With all her damaskry of whorling stars,
Dissolved into their gay buffoonery.
And she is glad, as the spring flowers are glad
When April lets them lend their honied breath
To quicken little hoofs that dance and turn
And dance again, so witless, they destroy
The things they love, yet leave the ruin sweet.
They are the wild high note in harmony,
Thrilling the shaken air by dissonance
And dying with its echoes, briefly born.
Oh, let them play with us and dance with us
And speed the languor of our crawling day!

THE SOUL

Dance with us? No, they shall not. I have heard
How they lead mortals by a breathless lure,
How mortal blood may catch the flow of theirs
And mortal hearts fall into hurried time
With their wild trampling. How they touch your
    hand
And you must go, and how they call to you
And you must answer.

[16]

THE BODY

[*suddenly on fire*]. Listen. I hear their feet,
My satyrs' from the mountain.

THE SOUL

[*apprehensively*]. Hark! the horn.

THE BODY

[*in delight*]. They mock the huntsmen on the outer
peaks.

THE SOUL

[*trying desperately to urge him to the house*].
Come! come! we'll bolt the door.
[*The disorderly rout of* SATYRS *sweeps up, and
they dance wildly on the green. Waiting in the
background is a* WOMAN, *a fillet of gold on her
golden head. She is diaphanously dressed and is
lovely with the loveliness of all the provocative
legends touching the Venus of mortal memories.
She waits and listens in the removed manner of
one who knows her time is to come and she need
not hasten it.*]

THE BODY

[*going from one to another of the
satyrs and greeting them with a wild delight*].
Welcome, old fox,

Old bear, old wolf! is't you that lead the chase,
And find us here, your quarry run to earth?

A SATYR

[*slyly*]. A man and wench, the Body and his trull.

THE SOUL

[*still trying to draw the* BODY *away*]. No! no! I
 am the Soul. The Angel said—

THE BODY

[*not heeding her*]. 'Tis view hallo indeed. Old wolf,
 you've found,
And having found, now dance and sport with us,
And snatch us straightway up and carry us
Home to the needles of the farther peaks,
And dash us down, and bid our racing blood
Be quickened of the earth that mothered it,
And catch us up again and make us reel
Like motes that live a day and then are gone.
 [*A* SATYR *rushes to the* SOUL *and snatches at her*
 hand.]

THE SATYR

He gives us leave. Come and be mad with us.

THE SOUL

[*in terror*]. I will not. No!

[18]

The Marriage Feast

THE BODY

        Dance with him, as he bids.
[*Another* SATYR *approaches, with the* WOMAN
we may call the SORCERESS, *who understands
that this is her moment and advances with sinu-
ous steps. She extends her hand to the* BODY, *and
he takes it, in a tremulous awe, and carries it to
his lips.*]

THE SOUL

[*to the Body, in desperate warning*]. Let go her
    hand. It is a lethal cup
Filled full with wine of poisoned berries pressed,
The nightshade of the will, the desperate draught
Lean hags and harpies brew their enemies.

THE BODY

[*bemused*]. O rare sweet wonder of a snowflake
    hand!
What delicate ichor courses in these veins
Converting moulded snow to liquid fire?

THE SOUL

[*passionately*]. Let go her hand, I say.

THE BODY

        Let go this hand,
Alive with merry blood, and rounded o'er

Here in the palm, there at the finger tips,
With sweet lascivious beguilement? Come,
Take it in yours, and feel its languid spell
Creep through your veins and stir your tepid
    blood.
How could there be a hand so coldly white,
Yet feeding fires that burn men to the bone?
Take it, I say, and stroke and fondle it
As I do now, for the hand bids me so.
And these three kisses, this—and this—and this—
Dropped in the burning palm, are tribute paid
To the dark ritual of her hidden house.

THE SOUL

[*stricken*]. If she is then your love, why, what
    am I?

THE BODY

Sweet fool, she needs you, needs your artlessness
To start the working of her yeasty brew.
She is too far removed in heaven's delight
To be a moment's mate of clods like me;
And even as the crafty alchemist
Can blend no wonders out of empty air
Without his elements and crucibles,
So she, great Love, needs mortal ministrants

To fan her creeping fires into flame
And burn the world up, if she bids it so.

THE SOUL

[*doubtingly*]. But I? What has the hesitant Soul
    to do
With orgiac tumult in the mountain wastes?

THE BODY

Then learn from her how, seeming to forbid,
You beckon, and the lure of your retreat
The Body needs must follow, like the wind
Unleashed to blow the pollen from the flowers
And wreak his maddened will on earth herself
Who bids him mirror her productiveness.

THE SOUL

[*perplexed*]. I love the earth, and loving you, I
    serve
Her also in her deep maternal aims.
But this strange Sorceress from the mountain side,
This lewd familiar of goat-footed men,—
How should she bid me beckon or deny,
I who love all things here, but only so
As in the glass of heaven's loveliness,
And when I see you thirst, would give you drink
From the deep grail of holy benison:

Wine out of grapes grown here on earth, yet old
In tinctured sacring from the sun above?

THE BODY

Give me no drink then, nor to eat the bread
Mixed for pale priests, the consecrated host.
Fill me deep draughts of wine ambrosial
Splashed on a damask muddied o'er with lees
Stained of old time by tipsy acolytes
Who learned her magic and acclaimed her lore,
But could not cease, being mad with flagoned rage,
Short of destruction though it touched her shrine.
Bow down to her, and she will teach you, too,
How best to give, and giving, seem to stint
Man's hunger, and so quicken it: for no kiss
But is more burning if it be denied,
No natural ardor but is feebler grown
Without the fiction of fair unconsent,
The hesitant breath of the unravished mind.
What mad conceits of dalliance she knows!
And she will whisper thee, and thou must start
And frown and halt, and seemingly deny,
Drowned in thy blushes, and then yield thee, loath
To understand, yet pure and dutiful.
For she is Love, and so must be obeyed.

The Marriage Feast

The Soul

[*passionately*]. Not Love! another name is written
    there
On that white silken brow that shames the gleam
Of the bold eyes beneath.

The Body

                  She is Love, I say,
And I will so enjoy her, but through thee
To make our bliss ineffable.

The Soul

                  The soul,
The body, and the body's lust? Shall I
Stoop from my empery—he said that word—
To make a triune bond with her and thee,
And so flout all the mysteries of heaven
And all the sanities of earth, and all
The great reprisals written in her star?
Ah, but I love thee! Never doubt—

The Body

                  Then come,
Dance, dance until the hot blood surges up
To flood the lips with tang of salt and fire,
And learn how sacramental lees run dry
When body's ancient bliss froths o'er the brim.

THE SOUL

Since then I may not have thee undefiled,
And she is ministrant of the only draught
Commensurate with your lust—then, O my love,
What if I will not? Would you leave me here
And go wherever this wild goat-like herd
Commands, so long as she is yours and theirs?

[*The* SATYRS *fall into an inarticulate chant, and
dance grotesquely about the* SORCERESS, *who is
advancing toward the* SOUL *with a fixed gaze, as
if casting a spell. She quiets the* SATYRS *by a
glance and they are silent, after a broken note
or two, and watch her curiously. The* SOUL *regards her, at first in questioning and then an
unwilling and maddened submission. The* SORCERESS, *as if that submission were what she
desired and her errand is accomplished, waves
back the* SATYRS *and retreats with them, leaving
the* BODY *and the* SOUL *to fulfil their destiny.*]

THE SOUL

[*turns to the* BODY *and chants piercingly*]. The
    world's aflame! a million suns
Are rising o'er the brim of night.
The tide of being swifter runs.
I am blinded by excess of light.

[24]

THE MARRIAGE FEAST

My heart is gushing gouts of blood,
A torrent swelling to a sea,
And I a mote, swept on the flood,
Die in a swooning ecstasy.

THE BODY

[*antiphonally*]. And she, the goddess of our rite,
Purveyor of all dark delight,
Is she not mine as thine, my bride,
A flaming cresset at my side,
Burning and yet consuming not,
But lighting this one destined spot
That is the matrix of desire
For thee, for me, the fostering fire
Built by Old Mystery, the Lord
Who made the earth and sky His Word,
Creating all for man and mate,
Themselves created, to create?

THE SOUL

[*moved by that one name*]. The Lord? you say the
        Lord, you who deny
That bright dark Mystery sitting in the sky,
Save when His tumults shake the unfriended
        ground?
And then you raise to Him the whimpering sound
Of frightened children in the lonely night;

But when day sheds her mild accustomed light,
Shake your gay, tinkling bauble in the face
Of Majesty unseen, since neither place
Nor time nor Tables of the Law can swear:
"Behold your God. Here is He, or is there."

THE BODY

I know not all this talk of hidden powers,
Of quaking ground and firmament that lowers,
And how a man may shrink when death and night
Are on him, and he goes to earth, till light
Fills up his cup of courage. Drink and food
And breath, mere wanton breath, seem to him good.
And when she, daughter of the mystic name,
She, waiting here with us, a torch of flame
To light us on our way of joy unguessed,
Would drink with us at earth's mad marriage
    feast,
Then shall he heap her altar with his fears,
His dull obedience to the trampling years,
His caitiff shrinking from a Power above.
For she is God.

THE SOUL

      [*wistfully*]. Is her name truly Love?

The Marriage Feast

THE BODY

Love and Delight. She has a million names
As men have seen her through transfiguring eyes,
Vile names, and names of lyric loveliness,
Names the hot midnight beats upon the ear
Like brazen clangor of a marching host,
Or names like bird notes echoing through a wood
And moonlit ripples murmuring on the shore.

THE SOUL

[*in doubt and anguish*]. And yet she looks to me
    an evil thing,
Not like the sweet mild goddess who, by day,
Sits at our table and adorns our bed
With woven sheets of exquisite content
Spun from the thread of April hearts-in-bloom.
O Love, she will not bind our spirits close
In an unstained communion! She is big
With a strange lore of evil known to man
Through immemorial heritage. And the earth,
In a sad patience, bears the weight of it,
And God Himself, in a sad patience, stays
His hand while some last word shall be fulfilled,
And you and I, the Body and the Soul,
Drink of the spell the others who have gone,
Millions and millions of bewildered men,

Have drunk of, and the burdened earth is still,
And God says naught. How strange it is and long,
This dragging length of dreary destiny.

THE BODY

[*fretfully*]. You are bemused with all these wan-
      dering thoughts
Of days and hours and what was meant by them,
While here is day, not night, and flooding sun,
Not caverned dusk to hide and whimper in,
And there stands light incarnate, beckoning us
With that white hand, the wonder of the world.
And all her satyrs, listening, round her wait
The call of Pan and our quick answering,
And her rewarding smile. Give me your hand.

THE SOUL

[*despairingly*]. I cannot bring you hand or lips
      unspoiled,
While her rank breath subdues my every sense
And blinding lustre shuts me out from light.

THE BODY

Behold her. How imperial she grows,
Bidding you bring your gifts to me. Come, dance
And rain your rigorous-hoarded fragrance down
On the dry fallow of your niggard will,

And see how all our mad attunéd steps
Will set themselves to the wild mountain side
Where we shall be as gods and one with her.

THE SOUL

[*wildly*]. And if I come, and if I bring my gifts
Such only as I can, being myself
And meant for some dear far-off destiny,
You cannot see them, and you cannot hear
My supplications to the unseen God,
Nor my thin childish echoing of the song
Forever sounding from that fabled land
Where being lives unveiled.

> [*The* PRESENCE *appears at a little distance, and
> the* SORCERESS *retreats still further into the
> background with the* SATYRS *whom her out-
> stretched hands hush into silence.*]

THE BODY

          She has withdrawn
A pace, like twilight presaging the night.
Choose thou between us now.

THE SOUL

          I look on thee
And hear the birds. I feel the warm bright spell
Of June in promise of benignant calm,

[29]

With brooks and apple orchards and the airs
That stir the pictured arras of this world.
Oh, thou art mine! I needs must follow thee.
Without me, thou wouldst be forspent and sad
In the dim frozen nights when no sun is.
Yet if I stay, perhaps thou wilt return
To the lone hearth, the bees and violets.

THE BODY

[*startled*]. Oh, hark! the horn upon the mountain
    side.

THE SOUL

[*apprehensively*]. Pan is it, think you?

THE BODY

                  Ay, it should be Pan.
None else that wild cascade of echoing notes.
The satyrs hear it, every muscle tensed
For play, and she, their leader, turns a pace,
As she would leave us to our lethargy.
He comes, and all the merry goatherd rout
Wait for him, as for us.

THE SOUL

          And must we go?
See, dearest one, the heaven we leave behind,
The vine-drest walls, the hive and the dear bees,

The Marriage Feast

The violets I planted yesterday.
If I should go, who'd keep the hearthstone warm?

THE BODY

A hearthstone is like any other stone,
Save that it sprawls there flat, and hugs itself,
Sucking the fatness of the drowsy fire.
The satyrs, they and I, know jollier stones,
Brown dripping imps, sib to the rushing brook,
Cold as March water, ever jostling,
With ripply noises like to plangent words
On faerie anvils in the echoing glen.

THE SOUL

Who'd water our young violets?

THE BODY

The rain.

THE SOUL

The rain! God's merciful abounding rain.
And yet, will God do all we shirk ourselves?

THE BODY

[*excitedly*]. Aha! I hear them now. Aha! aha!
A fall of feet like hail, a million drops,
So do they come, a million hoof-beats strong.

[31]

The Marriage Feast

I hear their beat, and I do yield myself
To the mere multitude of corporate wills.
And I will go with them, if you would go,
Though I must bend me to your goddess even.

THE BODY

[*in a wild exaltation*]. I swear to you by the great
    arch of heaven,
By the sun and the moon and the Pleiades seven,
By the leaves of the trees and the roots of the hills,
By the water that runs and the sea basin fills,
That she is thy love and my love, as thine,
And the deeps gave her birth, but we crown her
    divine.
She is old, like the harlots of Babylon's day,
She is young as a flower sprung the firstling of
    May.
She is great Aphrodite redeemed from the sea,
To be temptress of men in the days yet to be.
Love, Love is her name, and the body's desire
Is the blood on her altar, the smoke and the fire.
   [*The* PRESENCE *is now standing beside them,
   and they are amazed.*]
But who art thou?

[32]

The Marriage Feast

THE PRESENCE

I come to claim this house.

THE BODY

This is the house of love, for dance and song
And flooding pipes of wine.

THE PRESENCE

I claim thy house
In the name of the helpless, the unhoused, the
unfed.
I bid thee sow wheat in thy garden for bread.

THE BODY

[*carelessly*]. Our garden is to roses given o'er.

THE SOUL

I scarcely know thee since thou cam'st before,
Thou art so sad.

THE PRESENCE

[*gently*]. Mine is the House of Love.
And I am sent to thee to bid thee move
In willing service to my Lord and thine.

THE SOUL

[*timidly*]. Who is thy Lord?

The Marriage Feast

THE PRESENCE

He is the One divine,
The One for whom thou shalt all things forsake.

THE BODY

[*angrily*]. And never lead the dance, nor merry
make?

THE PRESENCE

[*not heeding him*]. There are who need thee, and
so I am sent
And, finding thee with revelry forspent,
I haste to tell thee what my mission is
Lest some sweet solemn ritual thou should'st miss.

THE BODY

[*to the* SOUL, *remindingly*]. They wait for us. Bid
him begone.

THE SOUL

[*to the* PRESENCE]. Thy name
Is Love? Yet her name, too—

THE PRESENCE

He calls her Love,
And you, through love of him, will call her so.

THE BODY

We call her Love because she brings us bliss,

[34]

And lust of further bliss and gay belief
In the eternal spring of joys processional.

THE SOUL

[*to the* PRESENCE]. What dost thou bring? [*To
the* BODY, *who would silence her*]. Nay, let me
hear.

THE PRESENCE

   I bring
A million tender ecstasies: The Soul
And Body wedded, with divine consent,
To spend themselves in daily benison,
To be the sun to pallid youngling shoots,
To tend the earth with an unweakened will
Claiming slight portion for their own, save one,—
To share the Godhead's own divine employ,
He Who first made and daily gives, as then,
The rivers and the sea and earth to love.

THE SOUL

[*in anguish*]. And yet we cannot act unscathed
    like Him,
For we must suffer, and His regal path
Is like the moon's bright highway on the sea,
A splendor of foreknowledge lit by Him;
And we,—our being may sweep on like His,

But in the dark. We have no radiance.
And if we give as He has given to us,
Shall we not starve our hearts? Must God starve
    His?

THE PRESENCE

[*gently*]. Think on these things and thinking,
    dwell with Him.
He is less lonely in His boundless room
If little thoughts fly toward Him like bright sparks
Blown from the wasteful fire of circumstance
Earth generates, here and there, to pleasure Him.
For earth works for Him, in her blundering way,
To keep His heart warm through her heavy nights.

THE SOUL

[*seeking painfully*]. You think He knows, you
    think He feels our woe,
He Who is Holy and thrice Holy hailed
By sinless children round about His throne?
And yet He must know all, since He is God.
But can He feel our sharp reflective pangs
When the dear body, like my playmate here,
Seeks beauty only and yet never sees,
With holden eyes, what manner beauty is?
God is all-wise, but does He comprehend
That we call evil, which is not of Him,

[36]

The Marriage Feast

Because He did not make it? There it cowers
Outside His door, a wandering, homeless thing.
And yet it has to wander, being lone
And outcast in a trivial-minded world.
Tell me what evil is, and what God is,
Or I must perish in a sea of dread.

THE PRESENCE

[*always gently*]. Then ask Him and Him only. If
    I tell
The simple-syllabled lore I have spelled out
Through spaceless time of waiting on His will,
You could not understand: for every soul
Has its own language 'twixt itself and God.
But this I say, lest He should seem to you
A dazzling star, hung by Himself aloft,
And not the sum of all things, dark and bright,
What you must think He hates, yet does not hate,
What He must bear, yet ever bears alone:
He must forever share in our distress.
Since He created, He must die with us,
Die and be born like the recurrent sun.

THE SOUL

Be patient lest I never understand
These strange mutations of the less and more.
I know the sun, existing, seems to die

Only to prank himself and shine anew;
But God Who glows within him cannot die
Nor seem to die, even to wake again.

THE PRESENCE

Yet, being God, He must not only die
With what He has created, when it dies:
He must be what He is and what He seems
To every atomy that seems—and is.
As He fulfils Himself in grass and stone
And makes them grass and stone by quickening
    them,
So He must live in your imaginings
Of grass and stone, and every angled shaft
Shot in the eye-beams that have sped from you
And back into the lens He also made.
And though He move in an unhindered light,
He dwells within the shadow that is death.

THE SOUL

I have strange thoughts of Him: that He is far
Beyond all seeking, save one found the way
To halls of purest light where beings dwell
I have not seen, nor may I ever see.
Then, on a morning when the sun is kind
And a bird sings—careless, as if he knew
God would not rob him of his nested pride—

And halcyon breezes sigh in madrigals,
He seems to me a neighbor visitant,
Talking with me about my trivial cares:
Whether the lilies might withstand a drought,
And promising He'd think to send them rain.
Then I start back at my effrontery,
My arrogance toward God omnipotent.

THE PRESENCE

Yet if you will, you may with reverence dwell
—Reverence that is a child's simplicity—
On the kind features of a pictured God
Wrought, in your need, from all benign delights
Your hands have gathered on the shores of time.
And that is God also, a whimsical
Droll Father, who made funny creeping things
(When He made beauty, in the dawn of days)
A wilful smile upon the face of earth,
Mummery He lends you, that you also smile
And call Him Father, though His panoply
Might blind your eyes, being too splendor-bright
When you are wrought on by the press of things.
You are a child, such as we all must be
To Him, and if your dawn-like innocence
Breed childish terror before phantom shapes,
You needs must be assuaged and comforted

By childish baubles, apples of delight
That are the food for childish hungering.
For these are also God: ungarnered seed
Sown by wild hap, and purple flowering.
And I—smile with me at my hardihood!—
Though I come here to you accredited
His eager messenger, I bear also
My own poor pack of truth remedial.
This tinctured hope, this homely lenitive,
I have myself compounded from the herbs
He lets me snatch as I fly here and yon,
Serving His cup of grace. And since He knows
My passionate will to paint the radiant flower
And rich enduring fruitage of His state,
(Not frowning Godhead but divine delight
In being Himself as young as dawn and hoar
With age out-dating starry galaxies)
He will not smite me, but will smile at me
And you also, at your dear childish games
In gardens with the birds and lovesome breeze:
Because, being God, He comprehends us both,
And where we will to seek Him, He is there.

THE SOUL

Then—I! what shall I do to pleasure Him?
Follow my playmate here, who is my self,

The Marriage Feast

Into the raging sea of body's lust
—For he will go before the moment's gone—
And watch o'er him and tend his earthborn ails?
Or shall I stay here by the hearth, and wait
Lest sometime, spent with sin and smeared by sloth,
He may come back to crave my company?
Or shall I, like a child, cry out on God
To show me the dark way: how to return
To Him and that bright place I seem to know
As home, when happy dreams hark back to Him?

THE PRESENCE

Choose how you will. It is your privilege,
The gift enclosed in every hand at birth,
Spirit as body.

THE SOUL

Yet you will not say
What He would have me do to bend myself
To fit His pattern that is beauty's own?

THE PRESENCE

Ask Him. Or wonder, in the sacristy
Of your desires, what small humilities
Toward Him might fill your eager hands withal
Unbidden of high chartered servitors
Vowed to observance of His kinglihood.

THE MARRIAGE FEAST

For He must count quick laughter and its tears
Dearer than incense and rich vestured state.
Think! mid the shadows of a moonlit sea
When vagrant clouds are idling overhead,
Reflected light pursues its lovely way
Through that vast welter of almightiness,
Like wilful runnels in a boundless plain.
So might your nameless worship be to God
A line of light in All Immensity.

THE SOUL

Then may it be that when I love Him most
My hands are quicker to work out His will?
For I would fain be instant at His call.
What shall I do to be God's ministrant?

THE PRESENCE

There is some idle speech, from time to time,
In what the earthborn call the courts of heaven,
When servitors like me sit down and prose
About the wistful deeds done here and there
To bring us nearer God's creativeness:
How, if we muse upon the shapes of things,
A flower's petal as it might be made
More pointed or more lovely in a line,
And how the game of riding on a cloud
—A game made out of nothing but our wits,

THE MARRIAGE FEAST

A folly like an earth-child's "Let's pretend"—
Could be less perilous when the cloud melts down,
And how we could do much for musty hearts
With fragrant concepts God would deign to smell.
And I do know—it is well known to all—
That when a spirit's heart has furniture
Of tender ruth for bodies wayward grown,
A flower of hope, a face of innocence,
A bed of peace where one may lay him down
And wake up purged of baneful fantasies,—
That spot is sanctuary to the good
And evil also, whom God loves to heal.

THE SOUL

Go on. Be patient. Let me grave your words
On the dim tablets of my tarnished mind.

THE PRESENCE

I do not say these things are actual.
They are the bruited tales that go the rounds
Of that delighted spot, the courts of heaven.
Nor may I guess whether one might redeem
His body there, drenched with mad revelry,
By keeping holy house in his own mind,
And letting hospitable casements gleam
And open doors stand wide in welcoming.
These things are dark and can be only conned

By each lone pilgrim at the postern gate.
I am myself a pilgrim, but I know
There are remedial herbs bloomed out in heaven
You would not note, except you were a child,
Or that untainted soul, a child of God
Who seeks for nothing save to keep his mind
With open door, that God may enter in.

> [*Now the* SOUL *looks about her in bewilderment for, upon the last words, the* PRESENCE *is no longer there. Nor is the* BODY *within sight, nor the* SATYRS, *but the sound of their pipes and singing is heard, ever diminishing in the distance. The* SOUL *hurries a few steps on the way they have gone. Then she halts, looks at the ground and seems sadly to reflect. She returns slowly toward the house, touching a leaf or flower by the way, as if assuring them of care in their need of her. She has made her choice, as the* BODY *has made his; but before we have time to note more than the beginning of the shadow stealing over her face, the dark begins to fall and we cannot see. Yet, though the darkness has wholly fallen, she remains a slender pillar of brightness in the night.*]

EPILOGUE

The scene is the woodland glade where we first saw the SOUL *and the* BODY *tossing their bubble of joy. The rustic house is there, a little changed by time, perhaps more softly brown and the vines about it more luxuriant; but everything is in peaceful order, as if tended by wise hands. The indefinable atmosphere is that of spring at the exquisite moment when the world, locked in by frost, is now released and can scarcely bear the fragrant load of her own ecstasy, compounded of memories and her present bliss.*

The door of the house is open, and in the doorway appears the SOUL, *looking eagerly forward as if she expected some one. She is more beautiful than when we saw her before, and, in a radiant way, as young. She does not see what she is expecting. Or perhaps she does not expect, but tremulously hopes. A shade of seriousness falls over her face, but only as if she had awaited the same thing many times before, only to accept denial. She steps out and stands there on the rise*

[45]

*of green, looking about her as if she loved the
sylvan scene she has so long been mothering,
and suddenly raises her arms to the sky, throws
back her head and silently invokes the day. She
lowers her arms and is about to turn away to her
tasks; but the* PRESENCE *is beside her and she
stops short in welcome, yet in fear.*

THE PRESENCE

Do not dismiss me, though I come in ruth
For your foreboding heart.

THE SOUL

[*cries out sharply*]. Ah! he is dead!

THE PRESENCE

You knew?

THE SOUL

I have been listening to-day
As well as all the days of all the years
For fear the ministrant voices of the air
Might bring me news: for fear and yet in hope.

THE PRESENCE

I knew the voices would have thought of you,
And yet I came, bearing medicinal balm
From far away where consolation grows

[46]

And is distilled into an unguent joy
Like spikenard tinct with rose and strengthening
    rue.
I come to say—[*pausing*].

THE SOUL

        [*quietly*]. And so you come to say
Though leaves are opening on the mountain side
And hylas fluting, my dear playmate there
Grown old in gay communion with the earth,
Has sunk on her warm bosom at the last,
Beseeching her to hide and mother him.
[*wistfully*]. He had grown old?

THE PRESENCE

        He has grown old—in death.

THE SOUL

[*wonderingly*]. And I—I am not old. How could
    I keep
My April freshness through the envious years
While he was bearing nature's buffeting?

THE PRESENCE

You, by your will, were dedicate to life,
And he, through the mad hungers of the flesh,
To death. Yet at the last he knew the last
Had come, and, knowing, heard the sacring bell

Of a divine compassion, and the sound
Of elfin voices, chanting: Be at rest.
Faint voices of the sentient earth alone
May oft besiege the ears grown deaf to heaven.
And since high heaven is heaven and earth also,
It is permitted that the ritual
The earth has wrought out for her votaries
Be chanted for them in extremest need.
And so perhaps a starveling patch of green
Might whisper to him, in his body's stress:
"A many years ago you danced o'er me,
And I do not forget." A listening pine
Might murmur: "In that twilight when you
    mourned
Your old defection from the Soul you left,
I wafted it across the vale below,
And bending flowers felt it, and the breeze
Took it up mournfully and carried it
Down to the shores of the resounding sea
Whose tide-wash straight conveyed it to the moon
And—who shall say?—the moon mayhap to God.
And God might shed it, like a holy chrism,
Of dew and fragrance on the Soul you left,
Never to seek again from shame or fear,
The earthborn fear of being unforgiven."

[48]

The Marriage Feast

THE SOUL

But I had no such cancerous vengefulness,
No thought that I might judge him and condemn
His dancing progress through the world he loved.
What had I to condemn, save the sad wounds
He wrought upon himself, in love's despite?
I could have bled my heart out and believed
The turbulent red torrent all divine,
A river risen in God's own intent,
If he might float thereon to faerie isles;
Or if, being fed by love, a mystic stream
Returning on itself to its own source,
Flowing and flowing while his earthly barque
Moved with it, to find port in paradise.
And he has died! and is he not to be
In that sweet silvery boskage which is heaven?

THE PRESENCE

He is not there, but has beta'en himself
To kind small pensioners of the slumbrous earth:
A stunted flower waiting for his dust
To nourish it, a slender runnel made
More musical for tears of his lament.
Now you may hear his voice in stream and wind
Because he was at one with earth herself
And gave her heirdom of his bones and blood.

The Marriage Feast

THE SOUL

And I be left to brood and agonise
And know, since he is fettered deep in mold,
I cannot wrap him round with welcomings
Such as are given to one who travels far
And yet, by grace of God, fares home at last?

THE PRESENCE

[*kindly*]. Nothing can ever be as it has been.
This hour, this place, can never lift again
An unchanged visage to the glass of time.
All things are passing as the planets pass
And turn, in their grave course, to pass again,
Obedient to the orbits of the air.
But who shall say they may not thrill with life
When they approach some dear uncharted space
Where hands Divine first cast them to the void,
To roam their ordered way and come again?
Being is but a palimpsest of change,
Life overgrown with life. But under all,
In all and to our eyes the end of all,
Is the one Heart where all hearts come to rest.

THE SOUL

But I am but a little homesick soul,
And I am frightened in the singing void.

[50]

The Marriage Feast

The earth is turning, so I think, and I
Turning with it, am dizzy with dismay
Lest I should come to no remembered place
Such as the slumbering planets wake to hail,
Nor find unchanged my playmate whom I love.

THE PRESENCE

It is not all mischance, this doom of change.
As the earth turns, the uneasy mind of man
Turns with it to new concepts of its end.
So you and he, the Body and the Soul,
May find yourselves abloom with ecstasy,
You that you live, and he that he has risen
To put on raiment he has never worn,
Woven by earth, in her dumb fealty:
The sombre cloak of late humility,
Sandals of speed, to bear him to the shrine
His heart has hungered for since that poor heart
Learned the sad ritual of the common tongue,
And learned it late, too late to spread the feast
Bidding his brother mendicants come in.

THE SOUL

And shall they come, and will you come with them
To teach us the new tongue we are to learn
And fain would swell to hymns of choric praise,

THE MARRIAGE FEAST

Whirlwinds of worship, and low antiphone
Like birds awakening to the flaming dawn?

THE PRESENCE

I do not know. My quests are dim and far.
Nor know I whether I have told you aught
To guide you on your endless pilgrimage,
Or whether God told all when you went forth
Like the young planets in their orbéd way,
Or if this lore of travelers come to rest
Is printed on your own forereaching mind,
By anguish sensitised. But he will rise,
That I do know. The Body will rise in power,
Out of corruption, like to earth herself
Eating putrescence and aflame with bloom,—
Earth whom he loved and who has drawn him in
To be anhousel'd at her mystic shrine,
Before she gives him back to God again.

THE SOUL

She gives him back and I may meet him there
Somewhere—I know not—in the house of God,
Sit by his side at the great marriage feast
Perpetually renewed in memory
Of earth's restored community with heaven?
Where shall it be? this earth, or there on high?
And will he know me, as I rush to him

[52]

THE MARRIAGE FEAST

Striking glad hands of welcome in his own,
Seeing him mine, the Body of my love?

THE PRESENCE

He will be yours, the Body of your love.
Yet not the one who scaled the mountain side,
The while you kept his hearth inviolate,—
Not he, and yet so wondrous like to him
I cannot trace the change from dust to flower,
Nor in what beauty he is clothed withal.

THE SOUL

But if he come, and if we laugh and sing,
And toss the ball of joyance to the skies,
Will all be as before, and yet again
The satyrs lure him to their dark delights,
And the wheel turn and turn, and we be drawn
Into the dread abysm where God is not—
[*recalling herself painfully*]. Nay, nay, you tried
    to teach me all is God,
And God being all, there is no void of Him.
And I will heed, and never speak so rash.
But will it be as it has been before,
A long, long road in darkness home to Heaven?
    [*As she speaks, the darkness falls, or perhaps
    not darkness, but a dimness like a veil, and when
    it lifts she is still standing there, enraptured,*

[53]

holding her hands out to another who is not her PLAYMATE *of old but like him, as it were his earthly* BODY *transmuted to a heavenly shape. He is young and beautiful and, being aware of her as she is of him, happy with the happiness of dreams fulfilled.*]

THE SOUL

[*in awe*]. Are you the Body of my dear lost love?
And may I take your hand and go with you?

THE PRESENCE

[*softly*]. It is the body he has made himself
By loving earth, and you have made with him
From your foreshadowing memories of heaven.

[*The darkness falls again, and when it lifts, as it does quickly, the* PRESENCE *is standing there alone, a look of exquisite contentment on his face. We shall not see the* SOUL *and the* BODY *again upon this earth. They are off and away, and he, bent upon quests beyond the morning star, may not yet follow them.*]

ACTA UNIVERSITATIS UPSALIENSIS
Studia Slavica Upsaliensia 46
Editors: Ingrid Maier & Juhani Nuorluoto

Tradition and Translation

Maciej Stryjkowski's Polish Chronicle in
Seventeenth-Century Russian Manuscripts

Christine Watson

UPPSALA
UNIVERSITET

Dissertation presented at Uppsala University to be publicly examined in Ihresalen, Engelska parken, Thunbergsvägen 3L, Uppsala. Saturday, May 5, 2012 at 10:15 for the degree of Doctor of Philosophy. The examination will be conducted in English.

Abstract
Watson, C. 2012. Tradition and Translation: Maciej Stryjkowski's Polish Chronicle in Seventeenth-Century Russian Manuscripts. Acta Universitatis Upsaliensis. *Studia Slavica Upsaliensia* 46. 356 pp. Uppsala. ISBN 978-91-554-8308-1.

The object of this study is a translation from Polish to Russian of the Polish historian Maciej Stryjkowski's *Kronika Polska, Litewska, Żmódzka i wszystkiej Rusi*, made at the Diplomatic Chancellery in Moscow in 1673–79. The original of the chronicle, which relates the origin and early history of the Slavs, was published in 1582. This Russian translation, as well as the other East Slavic translations that are also discussed here, is preserved only in manuscripts, and only small excerpts have previously been published.

In the thesis, the twelve extant manuscripts of the 1673–79 translation are described and divided into three groups based on variant readings. It also includes an edition of three chapters of the translation, based on a manuscript kept in Uppsala University Library.

There was no standardized written language in 17th-century Russia. Instead, there were several co-existing norms, and the choice depended on the text genre. This study shows that the language of the edited chapters contains both originally Church Slavonic and East Slavic linguistic features, distributed in a way that is typical of the so-called hybrid register. Furthermore, some features vary greatly between manuscripts and between scribes within the manuscripts, which shows that the hybrid register allowed a certain degree of variation.

The translation was probably the joint work of several translators. Some minor changes were made in the text during the translation work, syntactic structures not found in the Polish original were occasionally used to emphasize the bookish character of the text, and measurements, names etc. were adapted to Russian norms. Nevertheless, influence from the Polish original can sometimes be noticed on the lexical and syntactic levels. All in all, this thesis is a comprehensive study of the language of the translated chronicle, which is a representative 17th-century text.

Keywords: Slavic philology, history of the Russian language, 17th century, Polish historiography, chronicles, Polish-Russian translation, Maciej Stryjkowski

Christine Watson, Uppsala University, Department of Modern Languages, Slavic Languages, Box 636, SE-751 26 Uppsala, Sweden.

ISSN 0562-3030
ISBN 978-91-554-8308-1
urn:nbn:se:uu:diva-171395 (http://urn.kb.se/resolve?urn=urn:nbn:se:uu:diva-171395)

Printed in Sweden by Edita Västra Aros, Västerås 2012

Acknowledgements

If I remember correctly, the first person to suggest that I should apply for a PhD position was Professor Ulla Birgegård, then my teacher in Russian at the undergraduate level, now – for the last five and a half years – my advisor. Therefore, my first thanks go to her for her help and encouragement.

My co-advisor Professor Ingrid Maier has also been of great help. She has always read my thesis drafts very carefully and paid attention to both contents and form. I also thank Professor Juhani Nuorluoto for his comments in the final stages of my work.

I am very grateful to Professor Per Ambrosiani, Umeå University, who was the opponent at my final seminar and gave me many valuable suggestions, from which my thesis has benefited greatly. Of course, I also wish to thank my fellow Slavists at the Department of Modern Languages for attending my seminars, commenting on my text, discussing different aspects of research and in general creating a good atmosphere.

I have made regular visits to Russia, the longest of which was for nearly two months in the fall of 2009. During this visit, I had the opportunity to participate in Professor Vadim Krys'ko's seminars, which was a very interesting and rewarding experience. Professor Krys'ko has also been helpful in answering questions and suggesting literature.

In the spring of 2010, I spent three months as a visiting scholar at UC Berkeley, where Professor Viktor Živov was kind enough to discuss my thesis with me. I owe him thanks for inviting me to Berkeley and for his comments on my work.

I can't count the hours I have spent in libraries – especially in manuscript departments – and archives: Uppsala University Library, of course, but also Russian libraries and archives. In Moscow, I have visited the Russian State Library, the manuscript department at the State Historical Museum, the Russian State Archive of Ancient Acts and the State Public Historical Library; in St. Petersburg, the Library of the Russian Academy of Sciences, the National Library of Russia and the Central State Historical Archive of St. Petersburg; in Jaroslavl', the library of the Jaroslavl' State Pedagogical University. I have always met with helpful staff and wish to thank them all. Dr. Stepan Šamin in Moscow and Dr. Varvara Vovina-Lebedeva in St. Petersburg have assisted me at times when it was impossible for me to visit the libraries and archives in person, which I appreciate very much.

I want to thank Professor Ewa Teodorowicz-Hellman for helping me with Polish matters, Moa Ekbom and Dr. Karin W. Tikkanen for helping me with Latin and Greek, and Dr. Donald MacQueen for checking my English.

The first two years of my doctoral studies were funded by a grant from Knut och Alice Wallenbergs stiftelse, for which I am very grateful. My longest visit to Russia and my stay in Berkeley were funded by Sederholms stipendium för utrikes resor and Birgit och Gad Rausings stiftelse för humanistisk forskning. Shorter trips for collecting material or participating in conferences have been funded by Rektors resebidrag från Wallenbergstiftelsen, Sven och Dagmar Saléns stiftelse, Kungl. Vitterhetsakademien (Wallenbergstiftelsens fond), Kungl. Humanistiska Vetenskaps-Samfundet i Uppsala and Håkanssons resestipendium.

I have many good friends who have been very supportive and made my life more enjoyable. Some of them have also spent their days at the English Park Campus, such as Moa, Susanna, Daniel, Johan, Camilla and Karin. Thank you for all the lunches, coffee breaks, late nights, serious discussions and laughs! Others have given me a reason to leave the four walls of my office now and then, such as Lisa, Frida, Ingrid and Kajsa. Thank you for your company and encouragement!

I want to thank my parents for encouraging me, feeding me, taking an interest in my work and bragging about me to everyone they know. My father has also helped me with the illustrations to the thesis and other manuscript pictures, and proofread parts of the text. My sister and her family have been very supportive, and I look forward to spending more time with my nephews.

Last but not least: Olof, thank you for always being there for me.

Uppsala, March 2012

Christine Watson

Contents

Abbreviations

BAN	Biblioteka Akademii nauk
CGIA SPb	Central'nyj gosudarstvennyj istoričeskij archiv Sankt-Peterburga
f.	fond
fol., fols.	folio, folios
GIM	Gosudarstvennyj istoričeskij muzej
HSBM	Histaryčny sloŭnik belaruskaj movy
JaGPU	Jaroslavskij gosudarstvennyj pedagogičeskij universitet
ms., mss.	manuscript, manuscripts
NB SPbGU	Naučnaja biblioteka im. Gor'kogo Sankt-Peterburgskogo gosudarstvennogo universiteta
NBUV	Nacional'na biblioteka Ukraïny im. V. I. Vernads'koho
NPL	Novgorodskaja pervaja letopis'
OCS	Old Church Slavonic
PSB	Polski słownik biograficzny
PSRL	Polnoe sobranie russkich letopisej
PVL	Povest' vremennych let
RGADA	Rossijskij gosudarstvennyj archiv drevnich aktov
RGB	Rossijskaja gosudarstvennaja biblioteka
RNB	Rossijskaja nacional'naja biblioteka
SDJa	Slovar' drevnerusskogo jazyka (XI–XIV vv.)
SKK	Slovar' knižnikov i knižnosti
SP XVI	Słownik polszczyzny XVI wieku
SRJa	Slovar' russkogo jazyka XI–XVII vv.
SSP	Słownik staropolski
SUM	Slovnyk ukraïns'koï movy XVI–peršoï polovyny XVII st.
TODRL	Trudy otdela drevnerusskoj literatury
UUB	Uppsala universitetsbibliotek

1 Introduction

The language situation in late 17th-century Russia has received quite some attention from scholars. There was not yet a standardized literary language[1] in Russia (cf. Chapter 4), and the various text genres could be grouped into four registers, which had their own traditions with different proportions of bookish and non-bookish lingustic features.

This was a time of intense contact with the Polish language, and many translations from Polish were made, of scientific works as well as literary texts. One of these translations is the object of the present study: the Polish historical text *Kronika Polska Litewska/ Zmodźka/ y wszystkiey Rusi* by Maciej Stryjkowski, printed in 1582 and translated into Russian several times in the late 17th century. One of the translations, made in 1673–79, will be in focus for reasons explained further on (cf. Section 3.4).

Through its combination of rich information on Russian history and methodical comparison of sources, this text has influenced Russian history writing for centuries, which has been well documented by scholars. Its language, however, has not been studied. During a time such as the late 17th century, with high translation activity and a growth of new genres, this translation was, one might say, at the intersection between an old tradition and new influence from foreign literature through translation.

Tradition played an important role since the register system was maintained through text orientation, i.e. scribes modeled their texts on earlier texts of a similar kind. This could show in the choice of words and phrases as well as of bookish or non-bookish linguistic features, and in the extent of the variation between them. Therefore, studying the language of this text as compared to other texts of the period will show not only where in the register system it was placed, but also how it related to different genres.

Since it is preserved in quite a few copies and since we know that its subject matter was influential, one may suppose that the language had an impact on later writings as well, again through text orientation. Therefore it deserves to be studied not only for its own sake, but as a contribution to our knowledge of the history of the Russian language.

---

[1] Although a more accurate translation of the Russian term *литературный язык* may be 'standard language,' I will follow the practice of Slavists writing in English and use the term 'literary language.'

This is one of many Russian texts from that period that have not been published, and therefore an important part of the thesis is an edition of a portion of the text.

1.1 Aim and outline of the study

The aim of the thesis is to give as full a picture as possible of the 1673–79 translation of Stryjkowski's chronicle, especially its language. The first two chapters give background information. Chapter 1, the introduction, presents the material and method, defines some important terms and introduces some literature that will be used for reference throughout the thesis. Chapter 2 is about the author of the chronicle, Maciej Stryjkowski, and the original Polish text. This chapter also sketches the background of the historical context in which the chronicle was written and mentions some of the major tendencies in the historiography of the period.

The aim of Chapter 3 is to establish the manuscript situation and history of the 1673–79 translation. This chapter also gives the historical and cultural background for the East Slavic translations, provides information on those translators who are known by name and lists the manuscripts belonging to the other translations.

Chapter 4 contains a commentary on some morphological and syntactic features of the edited text against the background of the language situation in Russia in the 17th century. Focus is on those aspects that show variation between bookish and non-bookish forms and constructions. The aim is on the one hand to describe this particular text, and on the other hand to contribute to the knowledge of the language by setting the results in relation to previous studies on texts from that period.

To properly judge the language of the text, the relationship between the source text and the target text must be taken into account, and the translation technique is also an important field of study considering the great amount of translations made from Polish at this time. Therefore, Chapter 5 discusses translation theory in Russia during this period and comments on some aspects of the translation with the aim of identifying the norms by which the translators were guided. Through these translations, and through translators of Ruthenian[2] or Polish origin (cf. Section 5.1), the Polish language exerted

---

[2] The name 'Ruthenia' will be used in this thesis for the lands historically connected with Kievan Rus': parts of present-day Ukraine and Belarus. This term was in use until the 19th century (Niendorf 2006: 97). The name 'Ukraine' was first applied to the area around the Dnepr in the 16th century, and in the 17th century it was quite widely used about that area, although it was at this time not yet a sovereign state or a well-defined province. It was also applied to the Cossack Hetmanate (cf. Myl'nikov 1999: 77–81; Plokhy 2006: 316–320). I will use 'Ukraine' and 'Ukrainian' to refer to the area from the 17th century onwards, when my

influence on Russian. The study of lexical and syntactic polonisms in the text aims to determine their role and degree of integration in this text as well as their status in the Russian language of the time.

Naturally, different individuals would make different choices when translating. This particular text offers a chance to compare parts that were probably translated by different people. Chapter 6 attempts to determine the division of the text between them and at the same time to test criteria that in the future may help identify translators of 17th-century texts. For this purpose, the edited part of the text is compared with samples from other parts of the chronicle.

Chapter 7 contains a comparison of the text with original Russian chronicles from the same period and tries to determine what characterizes this translation as opposed to original chronicles. This is an attempt to contribute to the more general picture of the relationship between translated texts and existing genres.

Chapter 8 gives the editorial principles and describes the manuscripts used in the critical apparatus in more detail. Chapter 9 consists of a summary and conclusions, and the edition concludes the thesis as an appendix.

1.2 Editions of the *Kronika*: Polish and Russian

The original of the studied text, Maciej Stryjkowski's *Kronika Polska Litewska/ Zmodźka/ y wszystkiey Rusi*, was printed in 1582 in Königsberg (hereafter called "the *Kronika*" or "the chronicle" – the latter only in unambiguous contexts, when it cannot be confused with Russian chronicles).

It was written in Polish with some dedications and quotes in Latin. The main part of it is written in prose, but some chapters or parts of chapters are written in verse, especially descriptions of battles.[3] The text of the printed chronicle is paginated from 1 to 790, but as so often in early printed books, there are errors in the pagination. Only one of these will be mentioned here, since it falls within the chapters that are in focus in this study: there are two pages numbered 92, and they will be referred to as 92_1 and 92_2, respectively.

The chronicle proper is preceded by 42 unnumbered pages containing a list of sources, several dedications, a portrait of the author, his rhymed autobiography and a preface. References to these pages will be made using their signatures, e.g. A1r, where A refers to signature A, 1 to its first leaf and r to

---

sources do so. For earlier periods, and when a less specific area is referred to, I will speak of 'Ruthenia.' For the corresponding language terminology, cf. Section 1.6.

[3] Typical examples of the topics for verse sections can be found in headings such as *O Bitwie pod Haliczem z Xiążęty Ruskimi/ y poráźeniu ich od Polakow* (chapter VI: 2, Stryjkowski 1582: 229) and *O sławney woynie/ y szczęsliwey bitwie Iágiełowey y Witołdowey z Krziżaki Pruskimi/ y Xiążęty Niemieckiey Rzesze/ Roku 1410* (chapter XV: 1, Stryjkowski 1582: 521).

the recto side of the leaf.[4] After the main text, there is an index of people, places and events (*Reyestr/ álbo krotkie náznáczenie mieysc osobliwszych/ dla rychleyszego y snádnieyszego ználazienia*). The chronicle is divided into 25 books with a varying number of chapters. The contents of the chronicle and the dedications are discussed in more detail in Section 2.3. Roman numerals will be used to designate the books of the chronicle, and Arabic numerals for the chapters. For instance, IV: 1 means book four, chapter one.

The next edition was printed in Warsaw in 1766 by Franciszek Bohomolec, who published it in the series *Zbiór dziejopisów polskich* (Stryjkowski 1766; cf. also *Nowy Korbut* 3: 297). Here, the punctuation has been modernized, and the orthography is slightly changed; for instance, the diacritical mark has been removed from *á* (*a jasne*) in most cases. Capitalization follows the 1582 edition closely in that not only proper names but also some other nouns were capitalized. The *Kronika* is followed by a history of Russia, *Historia odmian w panstwe Rossyiskim*, which deals with 18th-century events.

The latest edition of the Polish chronicle is a two-volume set published in 1846 and reprinted in 1985 (Stryjkowski [1846] 1985). It also has modernized punctuation and some changes in orthography, including the loss of the diacritical mark from *á* and the introduction of *ó* according to modern usage. Furthermore, *y* 'and' has been changed to modern *i*. Spellings with *j* have been introduced according to modern usage, e.g. *ieden* has been changed to *jeden* and *Litewskiey* to *Litewskiéj* (with *é* for *e pochylone*). In the 1846 edition and the 1985 reprint, the text is preceded by two articles, one by Mikołaj Malinowski (Malinowski [1846] 1985) and one by Ignac Daniłowicz (Daniłowicz [1846] 1985). After the text of the chronicle, a few of Stryjkowski's minor works are also published (cf. Section 2.2.2).

Quotes and references in this thesis will be made to the original edition from 1582, since some scholars have pointed out the shortcomings of the 1846 edition (e.g. Rothe 1983: 73; Wojtkowiak 1990: 21, 75). Since early prints can show individual peculiarities, four copies have been consulted: a microfilm version of a copy kept in the Bibliothèque Nationale in Paris, a copy kept in the Cathedral Library in Strängnäs, Sweden, a copy kept in Wojewódzka Biblioteka Publiczna in Opole and one kept in Zakład Narodowy im. Ossolińskich (the Ossolinski National Institute) in Wrocław. The latter two are accessible online on the digital library web sites www.obc.opole.pl and www.dbc.wroc.pl, respectively. No differences have been found between the copies that influence the reasoning in the thesis.

In some cases it has been desirable to be able to conduct a computer search for specific words, and for this purpose the 1846 edition has been

---

[4] The chronicle does not follow the common practice of beginning with signature A. Instead, it begins with)(and)()(, which will here be cited as X and XX, and A is the third signature.

used. The first volume is searchable on the site *Polska biblioteka inter-netowa* (www.pbi.edu.pl). The second volume is to some extent searchable on Google Books, and certain parts of it have been converted to text files with the help of an OCR tool (www.newocr.com). The converted texts are not perfect, but have been considered sufficient for this purpose.

In the 17th century, the Polish text (in whole or in part) was translated into Ruthenian once and into Russian several times (for the terms 'Ruthenian' and 'Russian,' cf. Section 1.6). All these translations will be discussed in greater detail in Section 3.2. They are all preserved only in manuscripts, but parts of some of them have been published.

András Zoltán has published one small excerpt each from two of the Russian translations according to the manuscripts GIM Muzejskoe sobranie, no. 1391 (the 1673–79 translation, two folios) and GIM Uvarovskoe sobranie, no. 4 (the 1688 translation, three folios), once as diplomatic editions (Zoltán 2003) and later with variants from other manuscripts: RGB Egorovskoe so-branie, f. 98, no. 243 and BAN 31.4.32 for the 1673–79 translation and BAN 32.11.4, RGB Piskarëvskoe sobranie, f. 228, no. 171 and RGADA f. 181, no. 59 for the 1688 translation (Zoltán 2006).[5]

R. I. Avanesaŭ (1961: 387–397) has published excerpts (approximately seven folios) from what he considered to be a Belorussian translation of the chronicle. Although the manuscript on which he based his edition is actually a copy of the Ukrainian Chronograph (cf. Section 3.2.6), Avanesaŭ's claim makes it justified to mention it here, as well as the fact that large parts are verbatim quotes from the Ruthenian translation of the *Kronika*.

According to the Polish biographical dictionary PSB (44: 540), the *Obščestvo ljubitelej drevnej pis'mennosti* in St. Petersburg and *Komissija po izdaniju gosudarstvennych gramot i dogovorov* in Moscow planned in the 1870s and 1880s to publish a bilingual edition of the Polish chronicle and its Russian translation, which never came to pass. The source of this informa-tion is not specified.

Aside from the editions, one of the most important titles among the sec-ondary literature will be introduced here: the historian A. I. Rogov's mono-graph *Russko-pol'skie kul'turnye svjazi v ėpochu vozroždenija. Stryjkovskij i ego chronika* (Rogov 1966). It is one of the major works on Stryjkowski's sources, the reception of his chronicle in Russia and the manuscripts of the Russian translations and incorporates the results from earlier articles by the same scholar (Rogov 1963, 1965).

---

[5] Cf. Sections 3.5 and 3.7 for more information on the different translations and manuscripts.

1.3 Material and method

As has already been mentioned, this thesis contains an edition of a portion of Stryjkowski's chronicle in Russian translation, which is meant to contribute to the knowledge about the Russian language of the late 17th century. The edition aims at philologists and linguists, and great detail has therefore been observed on all linguistic levels (cf. Chapter 8).

Different aspects of the language in the translated chronicle have been studied. The Russian text in ms. U (UUB Slav 26–28), which is also the main manuscript of the edition (cf. Section 3.6.2), has served as the basis for the study. Depending on the nature of the various research questions, different portions of the text have been chosen as material.

The chapters that are the object of the edition, chapters IV: 1–3 (cf. Section 3.4), have been studied in detail. They will be described against the background of the language situation of the late 17th century, based on the assumption that there were several genre-dependent text traditions that were formed through the use of model texts (cf. Chapter 4). The description covers some morphological and syntactic features that display, or could be expected to display, variation, and the findings are set in relation to other 17th-century texts.

In other parts of the study, it is not sufficient to study only chapters IV: 1–3. Certain signs lead us to assume that the translation was the joint work of several people, and therefore some aspects of the language at the time are best described by comparing different parts of the text. These parts have been selected in the following way.

An estimate of the whole chronicle based on the distribution of verbal tenses referring to past events shows that some parts are dominated by the aorist and imperfect, some by the perfect tense. They alternate as illustrated by Table 1. The segments will be labeled A, B, C and D. This criterion alone does not reveal if there were two translators who worked on two parts each (A+C and B+D), three translators, one of whom worked on two parts (A+C, B and D or A, B+D and C), four who translated one part each, or even more (cf. Section 6.3).

Table 1. Division of the chronicle into segments according to dominant tenses

Books	Dominant tenses	Segment label
I–VI	Aorist/imperfect	A
VII–X	Perfect	B
XI–XIV	Aorist/imperfect	C
XV–XXV	Perfect	D

Since the *Kronika* is a large text and it is difficult and time-consuming to work with such large amounts of manuscript text, sample chapters from each of the four segments have been chosen and compared. One set of sample

18

chapters is IV: 1–3, the chapters that are the object of the edition. For comparison, three consecutive chapters from each of the other segments have been chosen. The only criterion was that they had to be written in prose in the Polish original, since the translation of verse seems to differ from the translation of prose, at least as far as verbal tenses for past events are concerned (cf. Section 5.3.1). Table 2 shows the selected sample chapters and the approximate number of words they contain in the Russian translation according to ms. U.

Table 2. The sample chapters

Segment	Sample chapters	No. of words
A	IV: 1–3	18,160
B	VIII: 3–5	5,390
C	XII: 3–5	5,120
D	XXIV: 3–5	7,380

These sample chapters have been used as material primarily in Chapter 6, where the validity of this preliminary division has been tested. Lexical and syntactic features – in comparison with the Polish original – have been chosen as criteria to distinguish between translators. It should be added that although the hypothesis of the different translators is not tested until Chapter 6, I will assume that it holds true and speak of "the translators" throughout the thesis, to avoid bulky constructions such as "the translator or translators".

Special attention has been paid to the relationship between the Polish original, as found in the 1582 edition, and the translation. The existence of polonisms, lexical as well as syntactic, has been noted. These have been identified partly with the help of earlier studies, partly by observing glosses, alterations and varying translations in the text (cf. Chapter 5). All the sample chapters have been searched for polonisms, and the very fact that they were probably translated by different people has been helpful when characterizing lexical polonisms as more or less integrated into the Russian language (cf. Section 5.4.1).

Although ms. U is the main manuscript in the edition and provides the material for most of the thesis, some things could only be studied on the basis of another manuscript, ms. B (BAN 31.4.32). In this manuscript, corrections and alterations have been made throughout the text (cf. Section 3.6.1). Thus, in order to study the nature of these alterations, a different manuscript has been used as material than in other parts of the thesis, and examples have been taken from the whole text, not only the sample chapters.

The text has been compared with a variety of original chronicles in search of similarities and differences. Attempts have been made to identify syntactic constructions known to be typical for chronicles, and also fixed formulas and expressions (cf. Chapter 7).

Since this thesis views one text from several aspects, no single method has been applied, but in every part of the study, previous studies of a similar kind have been used and this text has been compared with their findings.

Cyrillic script is transliterated according to the recommendations of the journal Scando-Slavica, which are similar to the International Scholarly System. When discussing Ruthenians who were active in Muscovy, I use the Russian forms of their names. Longer passages from manuscripts are quoted according to the principles used in the edition, but accents and *paerok* have been omitted for greater legibility. Isolated words or short phrases quoted in the text have been slightly simplified with regard to graphical variation. Biblical quotes and names in English are given according to the King James Bible.

1.4 Historical interest

The Russian translations of the *Kronika* were held in high esteem in their time. One sign of this is that a manuscript containing the text was in the possession of tsar Fëdor Alekseevič, and passed on from him to Peter I (Zabelin 1915: 604; Luppov 1970: 115–116; Lukičev 2004: 340). Catherine II had a copy made for her when she studied Russian history (Rogov 1966: 276–277). Muscovite noble families turned to the chronicle to establish links between themselves and Polish nobility, and it served as an inspiration in the development of Russian heraldry (Sedov 2006: 401–402, 477).[6]

This may say something about the status of the text, but its popularity is perhaps best determined by charting its influence on later historiography. The extent of that influence, primarily on Russian and Ukrainian historiography, has been well studied, for instance by Rogov (1967) and by G. N. Moiseeva (1970). The authors and works mentioned below do not give the full picture of its influence, but serve as representative examples.

In Russia, the *Kronika* was used in chronicle compilations as well as by historiographers. Among the first historiographers to use it was Andrej Lyzlov, who often referred to it in his *Skifskaja istorija* (finished 1692), and who also translated a part of it (cf. Section 3.3.1) (SKK 1993: 305–306). A. I. Mankiev, a man of Polish origin who worked as the secretary of the Russian resident in Sweden and spent many years in Swedish captivity, used it as a source for his *Jadro rossijskoj istorii*, which he finished in 1715, al-

---

[6] Sedov (2006: 477) speaks of a copy of the translated *Kronika* with sketches of Polish and Lithuanian coats-of-arms in the margins, and refers to Rogov as his source, but I have not found this information in Rogov's monograph.

though it was not printed until 1770 (Rogov 1967: 146–147; Moiseeva 1970: 85–86).[7]

V. N. Tatiščev used the chronicle as a source for his *Istorija rossijskaja* (published posthumously between 1768 and 1784), partly because it offered information from sources to which Tatiščev did not have access. He also held Stryjkowski in high esteem as a historian, even though he pointed out some shortcomings. In some respects, Tatiščev's way of presenting facts was similar to Stryjkowski's, which may indicate that Stryjkowski served as a model for history writing (Rogov 1966: 8; 1967: 150–152). It is not known, however, if Tatiščev used the printed Polish edition or a manuscript of one of the Russian translations as his source. When he quotes Stryjkowski, the quotes do not coincide with the known Russian translations, and since he knew Polish, he himself may have translated these fragments (Rogov 1967: 154–156; Moiseeva 1970: 87–88).

M. V. Lomonosov also studied the *Kronika* in connection with the preparations for his *Drevnjaja rossijskaja istorija*, published posthumously in 1766. He may have come in contact with the Polish original, but according to Moiseeva (1970: 90–98), the penciled notes in the margins of ms. R are of his hand (cf. Section 3.5.2).

Late chronicles from Russian territory often used Stryjkowski as a source, either directly or through intermediate sources, e.g. other chronicles. One example of a chronicle that made use of the *Kronika* is the *Mazurinskij letopisec* from the 1680s (PSRL XXXI: 3).

Stryjkowski's popularity in Russia can to some extent be explained by his own attention towards the country (Radziszewska 1978: 97). A remark by the *d'jak* Timofej Kudrjavcev, who in the 1650s was head of the *Zapisnoj prikaz*, the institution that at that time was in charge of official Muscovite historiography, implies that Stryjkowski was appreciated for his positive view on the Russian people and for the prominent position of the Russians in his explanation of the origin of the Slavic peoples, as seen in Section 2.4 (Rogov 1966: 266–267). G. Brogi Bercoff (2003: 215) claims that Stryjkowski was translated because he wrote in a manner reminiscent of East Slavic tradition. She also points out that of all the historiographical works available during that period, the only one that was translated into Russian apart from Stryjkowski was Bielski's chronicle, which was close to the medieval, annalistic way of presenting history. This, she says, can be related to the fact that Russia was never really a part of Renaissance culture.

It is remarkable that in Russia, Polish historical works were used not only to learn about the history of the neighboring countries Poland and Lithuania,

---

[7] Some scholars believe that the text was written not by Mankiev, but by the Russian resident himself, A. Ja. Chilkov (cf. Kozlov 2011: 213–216).

but also about Russia's own history. This may be explained by the fact that historiography developed later in Russia (Rogov 1966: 265).

Stryjkowski, together with other Polish authors, also had a great influence on historiography in Ruthenia, since even the parts that were under Muscovite rule (cf. Section 3.1.1) had close contact with Poland (Rogov 1965; 1966: 292–303). According to Rogov, Stryjkowski's influence there may have been greater than in Russia, because historiography developed earlier in Ruthenia, and fewer early sources were available there. Old chronicles, for instance, were scarce and could only be used as a complement to the Polish historiographers. When Russian historiography began to take shape, Ruthenian texts became the main source of information, making Stryjkowski secondary. Moreover, Russian historiographers had easy access to old chronicles.

The best-known and most widely spread Ruthenian work for which Stryjkowski's *Kronika* served as a source was the Kievan *Synopsis* (1st edition 1674), printed in the Cave monastery under the supervision of Innokentij Gizel' (cf. Rothe 1983; Moser 2007). It was reprinted 11 times during the 17th century and the first half of the 18th, and manuscript copies were also made from the printed editions to meet the demand (Robinson 1963: 118; Rothe 1983: 46–49, 126–127). It was one of the few historical treaties of its time to be printed; most printed books were religious ones, whereas secular works were usually spread in manuscript (Myl'nikov 1996: 15–16). There are numerous references to and quotes from Stryjkowski in the *Synopsis*, and to some extent, his influence is seen in the dating of events, the method of comparing different sources, the order of the chapters, etc. (Rogov 1965: 328–329; 1966: 300–303; Rothe 1983: 76–78). The *Synopsis* also quotes a number of other sources straight from Stryjkowski (Rothe 1983: 72–73). Some scholars believe that the Polish printed edition of the *Kronika* was used (Rothe 1983: 76), others claim the source was rather the Ukrainian Chronograph, but that the Polish edition served as reference in some cases (Toločko 1996: 175–176).

The Ukrainian Chronograph is based on Stryjkowski's *Kronika*, alongside the *Synopsis* and Guagnini's *Sarmatiae Europeae Descriptio* (cf. Section 2.2.2), in some places following the text so closely that it has been mistaken for a translation (cf. Section 3.2.6) (Ulaščik 1968; PSRL XXXII: 4–5). The *Letopis' Račinskogo* also used the *Kronika* as a source (Rogov 1966: 233).

Stryjkowski's information was also used on the Orthodox side in the conflicts between the Orthodox and Uniate churches in Ruthenia. Although Stryjkowski himself was Catholic, he quoted Russian, i.e. Orthodox, sources and stressed Russia's Orthodox history, which became an important argument (Rogov 1965: 312; 1966: 293; Rothe 1983: 36–37).

Among Lithuanian historiographers, the Jesuit Albert Wijuk Kojałowicz (1609–77) made extensive use of Stryjkowski in his *Historia Lithuaniae*, printed in two parts in 1650 and 1669, perhaps the first major work to focus exclusively on Lithuanian history (Niendorf 2006: 56).

1.5 Linguistic interest

Against this background, it is understandable that historians have been interested in the *Kronika* and its translations. This thesis, however, deals with the language of the 1673–79 translation, which is suitable for such a study for several reasons.

In the 17th century, genetically Church Slavonic and East Slavic language elements still co-existed in Russian writing tradition, in different proportions depending on the text genre. Some kinds of texts were regulated by norms, whereas others allowed great variation. As a result of normalizing efforts, the 18th century saw the emergence of a literary language (cf. Chapter 4) and the disappearance of the genre-dependent variations (Živov 2004: 21–28). Publishing and examining part of yet another 17th-century text, and such an influential one as this, will hopefully contribute to our knowledge of the language situation.

At the time when the chronicle was translated, Polish was one of the most common source languages for book translations made in Russia, second only to Latin (Sobolevskij 1903: 49–50). It is therefore of interest to examine the mechanisms that were at work when such translations were made. Translating between two similar languages, such as Polish and Russian, increases the probability of interference, which leads to two main areas of research: one is which of these elements of interference left their imprint on the Russian language, and the other is what the translators' strategies were for avoiding interference that would have been unacceptable. It has been suggested in connection with this very chronicle that the differences and similarities between the original and the translation may reveal interesting facts about the rules by which 17th-century translators were guided (Davidsson 1975: 74–75).

Besides the generally interesting aspects of studying a translated text, this chronicle offers even more possibilities since it may be the joint work of several translators (cf. Chapter 6). By comparing segments translated by different people, we may come to conclusions regarding the mechanisms and strategies they applied; that is, we may be able to compare how different people chose to interpret and translate parts of the same text, and thus identify individual and collective norms. A later task could be a comparison with the other translations that were made during a period of a few decades, which would add a dimension of diachrony.

Because of its historical theme, the text stands in an interesting relationship to Russian chronicle tradition. Stryjkowski himself used Russian chronicles as sources (cf. Section 2.3.1), and then again, as mentioned above (Section 1.4), later Russian chronicle compilations could use Stryjkowski as a source in turn. Thus, the language of the *Kronika* may contain traces of earlier chronicle tradition. A comparison of the text with original Russian chronicles may reveal to what degree these earlier texts were present in the translators' minds.

1.6 Terminology: Russian and Ruthenian

As will be explained in Chapter 4, scholars differ in their views on the language situation in 17th-century Russia, and consequently use different words for the language varieties found in texts from that time. In the terminology I will use, the translation of Stryjkowski's chronicle is in part written in Hybrid Church Slavonic and in part in a non-bookish register of Russian. However, to avoid having to use the term Hybrid Church Slavonic when speaking of some chapters and Russian when speaking of others, I will simply call it a Russian translation, since it was made in Moscow and in a manner found in many other texts written in Russia in the same period. This does not mean that every linguistic feature mentioned as occurring in the "Russian translation" was characteristic of vernacular Russian.

The language varieties spoken and written in the western parts of Muscovy and the eastern parts of the Polish-Lithuanian Commonwealth, i.e. in Ruthenia, are also of interest, since many translators in Moscow came from those areas and since influence from Polish often came by that route. The spoken language showed a variety of dialects that could roughly be divided into Ukrainian, Belorussian and Polissian (Shevelov 1974: 149).

As for the written language, there are two main ways of describing the situation: either modern Ukrainian and Belorussian each had a predecessor in the period under discussion, or they had one in common (cf. Pugh 1996: 2–5). G. Y. Shevelov (1974: 147–150) speaks of a standard secular language that he calls Ruthenian, mainly containing elements found in Belorussian dialects, but in which Ukrainian features could also appear more or less regularly. In the 16th century, there was no written language that was entirely based on Ukrainian dialects, but Ukrainian and Belorussian features can nevertheless be distinguished from each other in texts from a quite early date. S. Pugh (1996: 6–7), however, points out that using the modern standard languages as starting points for identifying such features may give an inaccurate picture of the situation in the 16th or 17th century, since the situation at that time was that of a dialect continuum rather than two emerging languages.

J. Besters-Dilger (2005: 239–242) uses the word Ruthenian to cover the non-Russian East Slavic written language in the 14th–17th centuries, and the more specific term *prosta mova* for the language used in written texts, including religious ones, from the mid-16th and throughout the 17th century. According to Uspenskij (2002: 386–408), the *prosta mova* existed in a Ukrainian and a Belorussian variety, of which the Ukrainian variety was more influenced by Church Slavonic and the Belorussian one by Polish. Evidence from texts shows that it was clearly recognized as a written language with bookish syntax, distinct from the spoken dialects, and that it was to some extent codified.

Some previous scholars have used the term West-Russian (mainly in Russian: *zapadnorusskij*); others use the terms Ruthenian and Old Belorussian interchangeably (Niendorf 2006: 101).

In this thesis, unless my sources specify the Ukrainian or Belorussian provenance of a certain linguistic element, text or person, or characterize a text or feature as belonging to the *prosta mova*, I will use the term 'Ruthenian,' by virtue of its being the most general one, neutral with regard to later nationalities and applicable to both the spoken and written varieties. This general term is especially useful when discussing the influence of this language on the Russian spoken and written in Moscow, since the distinction between Ukrainian and Belorussian is even more difficult when seen through the prism of Russian.

When referring to the historical dictionaries SUM and HSBM, I will accept their definition of sources as Ukrainian and Belorussian, respectively, although I am quite aware that the distinction is problematic. However, no major conclusions in this thesis are based on that distinction.

1.7 Earlier studies on chronicle language

As explained above, this study consists of several parts, and I have chosen to present previous research on the different aspects in connection with each chapter, e.g. literature about Polish influence on Russian in Chapter 5 and about authorship attribution in Chapter 6. Previous studies on chronicle language, however, will be used for comparison throughout the thesis, and therefore some important contributions to this field will be presented here.

Several studies have focused on the verbal system, especially the use of the simplex preterites (aorist and imperfect).[8] V. M. Živov (1995) has studied the *Mazurinskij letopisec* from the 17th century, which was written by a scribe who did not fully command the bookish language. The mistakes made by the scribe give hints as to what he considered to be characteristic of bookishness and chronicle language. He has also studied the *Stepennaja kniga*,

---

[8] Cf. Matthews (1995); this corresponds to *prostye preterity* in e.g. Živov (1995) and Petruchin (2003).

which, like Stryjkowski's chronicle, is not annalistic and only to some extent a part of chronicle tradition (Živov 2011).

P. V. Petruchin (1996; 2003) has examined the use of verbal tenses referring to past events in both early and late chronicles. His dissertation (Petruchin 2003) deals with the use of the imperfect in early chronicles, the use of the perfect and the pluperfect in the First Novgorod Chronicle and the use of verbal tenses in the 17th-century *Piskarëvskij letopisec*. One of his observations regarding the *Piskarëvskij letopisec* concerned the relation between the verbal aspect and the choice between the aorist and the imperfect. The hybrid norm (cf. Section 4.1.3) dictated that the imperfect be formed from imperfective verbs and the aorist from perfective verbs, but in a number of cases, this balance is disturbed for different reasons (Petruchin 2003: 147–167).

O. N. Kijanova has studied the language norms in late chronicle writing. Her results were first published in a monograph (Kijanova 2006), then defended as a dissertation (Kijanova 2007), which was later published as yet another monograph (Kijanova 2010).[9] One of the aims of her study, based on a large number of chronicles of different types – monastic and provincial chronicles and family chronicles kept by the nobility – was to find out if the appearance of new types of chronicles led to a change in language usage as well (Kijanova 2010: 28). In some cases, chronicles written close to the administrative center in Moscow showed more archaic linguistic traits than those further from power (Kijanova 2010: 74). She also took into consideration the new type of texts that arose in the 17th century, which are something in between chronicles and historical texts of a more narrative type (Kijanova 2010: 120). In her study, Kijanova used a number of characteristics to determine to what extent a chronicle was written according to the old standards. One of these was the use of verb forms for the past, since the use of simplex preterites was a sign of bookish language. Another such sign of bookishness was the use of the dative absolute, and yet another was the use of dual forms of nouns and verbs (Kijanova 2010: 34, 47–48).

---

[9] These three works basically contain the same information, although they all have different titles. The dissertation and the 2010 monograph share a conclusion that is more substantial than the one in the 2006 monograph, and I will therefore refer to the 2010 monograph.

2 The author and the Polish original

The reason for the popularity of Stryjkowski's chronicle in Russia can perhaps be found in the views it expressed on different peoples and states. It seems to have been more popular in the eastern parts of Poland than in the western ones, and the opinion of the author in Russia has been more decidedly positive than in Poland (Wojtkowiak 1990: 6–7). Polish writers who were influenced by him tended to emphasize the ties between Polish, Lithuanian and Ruthenian history, whereas Lithuanian and Ruthenian authors increasingly stressed the differences in origins and background between their lands and Poland (Plokhy 2006: 175).

The historical context, society and cultural ideas of the Poland-Lithuanian Commonwealth in the late 16th century are important to the understanding of the chronicle and can also partly explain why it became so popular in Muscovy and had such a great influence on Russian history writing. This chapter aims to give that historical background, as well as to introduce the author, the Polish printed original of the chronicle and a few of its most important topics.

2.1 Polish-Lithuanian society and culture in the late 16th century

The country in which Stryjkowski published his chronicle was a large and diverse one. Besides most of present-day Poland and Lithuania, it also included Ruthenia, the lands historically connected with Kievan Rus'.

This section is mainly based on three monographs with slightly different perspectives. D. Stone's *The Polish-Lithuanian state, 1386–1795* (Stone 2001) is a thorough historical study that also contains reflections on economics, society and culture during the indicated period. S. Plokhy's *The origins of the Slavic nations. Premodern identities in Russia, Ukraine, and Belarus* (Plokhy 2006) focuses on national identities in the East Slavic realm, from Kievan Rus' to late 18th-century Russia and Ukraine or Little Russia. M. Niendorf's *Das Großfürstentum Litauen. Studien zur Nationsbildung in der Frühen Neuzeit (1569–1795)* (Niendorf 2006) studies Lithuania from various angles, containing chapters about ethnogenetic myths, the role of religion and language, and a chapter about Samogitia.

Through the formation of the Union of Lublin in 1569, the Kingdom of Poland and the Grand Duchy of Lithuania went from an originally personal and then dynastic to a full union, forming the Polish-Lithuanian Commonwealth. This meant that the King of Poland was also to be the Grand Duke of Lithuania, elected jointly by the two parts of the Commonwealth. There was to be a common Sejm and other joint functions. There was firm Lithuanian opposition to the union, led by the Radziwiłł family and the magnates who did not want to be restricted by stricter Polish laws, but at the same time, Lithuania needed Polish support in its dealings with Muscovy (Stone 2001: 59–63; Plokhy 2006: 114–116). Wars between Lithuania and Muscovy concerning the Ruthenian lands had escalated in the beginning of the 16th century (Plokhy 2006: 108–109). Through the union, Poland also became involved in these conflicts. Stefan Batory, who reigned from 1575 to 1586, saw war against Russia as an important part of his foreign policy (Stone 2001: 122–127).

Because of the territorial overlap between Lithuania and Kievan Rus', the Lithuanian dukes could call themselves Grand Princes, as the Ruthenian princes had, or *Rex Letvinorum et Ruthenorum*, and see themselves as the successors of the Kievan princes. Although the relations between Lithuanians and Ruthenians had not always been good and local loyalties were often of higher priority than regional or national ones, the people of the Grand Duchy seem to have kept a sense of unity when faced with external threats (Myl'nikov 1999: 301–303; Stone 2001: 3–5; Plokhy 2006: 85–89, 114–121). In the 16th century, 40% of the nobility in the Grand Duchy of Lithuania was ethnically Ruthenian rather than Lithuanian, but all the same, the term 'Lithuania' was used for them all, rather than '[terrae] Litwaniae et Russiae' used in the beginning of the 15th century (Niendorf 2006: 33).

To this can be added Samogitia, set aside especially by Stryjkowski in the title of his work. This duchy, sometimes called Lower Lithuania, was a region with a distinct dialect of Lithuanian and a separate status within the Grand Duchy that set it on the same level as Lithuania and Rus', and it was identified both by its inhabitants and its neighbors as a separate entity (cf. Niendorf 2006: 179–199). Thus, its status in Stryjkowski's writings is partly explained by the fact that this was where he lived (cf. Section 2.2.1), but he was not the only one to treat it separately from the rest of Lithuania.

There were social and cultural differences between the various parts of the Commonwealth, but as time went by, Lithuanian gentry tended to adopt Polish culture, while they still kept their feeling of Lithuanian identity. The use of the Polish language spread particularly quickly in Ruthenian areas, and even the peasants in Lithuania acquired at least passive knowledge of the language, since nobles and priests spoke Polish to them (Stone 2001: 63–64). Many people were probably multilingual, and the major languages spoken in the Grand Duchy influenced each other as well as the minority languages, such as Yiddish (Niendorf 2006: 96–100).

Humanism had gained entry into Polish culture already in the 15th century and left its imprint on many aspects of society. The Jagellonian University in Cracow ensured that Poland developed in the same direction as the rest of Europe. Lithuania lagged behind somewhat. In political treatises, the division of power between monarch, aristocracy and people was defended. In religion, humanism inspired reforms and thoughts about a national church. Secular literature, especially poetry, developed, and with it a set of genres. During the 16th century, Polish took shape as a literary language, although many authors still wrote in Latin as well. Lithuanian was also used in printed books (Stone 2001: 94–107).[10]

Religious tolerance was pledged by all Polish-Lithuanian kings starting with Henri Valois in 1573 (Stone 2001: 120). With the growth of Sarmatism (cf. Section 2.4) and in connection with the wars against the Lutheran Swedes, the Orthodox Russians and Cossacks and the Moslem Turks and Tatars, the position of Catholicism was strengthened (Stone 2001: 212). Freedom of religion seems to have been greater in the Lithuanian part than in Poland, at least until the second half of the 17th century, when the conditions for non-Catholics began to change for the worse (Niendorf 2006: 124–125).

This diversity means, among other things, that when Stryjkowski wrote the history of the Polish-Lithuanian Commonwealth, he needed to trace the origins of Polish, Lithuanian and Ruthenian territories, which in the latter case meant Kievan Rus'. This explains why he turned to Russian chronicles for information, and hence the interest his writings evoked in Russia.

2.2 Maciej Stryjkowski's life and works

2.2.1 Stryjkowski's life

Most of what is known about Stryjkowski has been drawn from his own texts. The chronicle is preceded by a rhymed autobiography, and his other major work, *O początkach* (cf. Section 2.2.2), is followed by an appeal to his readers (Stryjkowski 1978: 588–591) that also contains some information about his life. In addition to this, there are numerous references to his life and travels in the main text of the chronicle and *O początkach*.

Several scholars have extracted information from these sources and discussed their authenticity. Mikołaj Malinowski, in his introduction to the 1846 edition (Malinowski [1846] 1985), was among the first to attempt to

---

[10] During the period 1553–1660, 20 books were printed in Lithuanian (Niendorf 2006: 104).

unite them into a biography and bibliography. He was especially concerned with Stryjkowski's travels, describing them elaborately based on information from the chronicle. Julia Radziszewska has written about his life and works in a monograph (Radziszewska 1978) and in connection with the publication of *O początkach* (Stryjkowski 1978: 5–25). Zbysław Wojtkowiak's monograph (Wojtkowiak 1990) is the latest major work to have been devoted to Stryjkowski's biography and bibliography. The following information is mainly based on Wojtkowiak, since his monograph is more recent and more detailed than the others, and since he seems to have been more conscientious in critically examining the reliability of Stryjkowski's information about himself (cf. Wojtkowiak 1990: 14, 52).

The name Stryjkowski (which is the accepted form, although the spelling Striykowski is more frequent in the chronicle) is derived from the town of Stryków in Łódź voivodeship, Poland, where the author was born in 1547 (Wojtkowiak 1990: 15–21). He also used the name Osostevicius or Ososte-wiciusz. He himself traced this from his ancestors, "od [...] Osostow z Herbu Leliwá" (Stryjkowski 1582: XX1r), thereby implying that he was a nobleman. Who they were and where the name comes from has not been firmly established, and his relation to other known figures of the name Stryjkowski is also uncertain. No other noble families of the name Osostevicius are known from that time, and the secrecy and uncertainty surrounding Stryjkowski's descent may indicate that he was, in fact, not a nobleman at all.[11] His father's name, as can be gathered from the patronymic *Iacobi*, which he added to his name (in its Latin form) in one instance, was Jacob or Jakub, but nothing else is known for sure about him (Wojtkowiak 1990: 22–24; cf. Stryjkowski 1582: 23).

Stryjkowski received his education at a parochial school in Brzeziny, close to his hometown. He probably never studied at the university. In his texts, he does not mention higher education, but, on the contrary, in the rhymed autobiography he calls Brzeziny his Padua and Bologna.[12] Still, he prided himself on his knowledge of languages and on his ability to write poetry and draw portraits and maps (Radziszewska 1978: 19–20; Wojtkowiak 1990: 40–51).

At the age of 16 or 18 he left for Lithuania, where he served in the army.[13] The chronicle does not tell very much about his time in the military. The author mentions battles but does not explicitly claim to have taken part in

---

[11] Cf. Wojtkowiak (1990: 24–35) for a discussion of this.

[12] Some scholars, such as Rogov (1966: 21–22), believe he studied in Cracow, but the registers of the University of Cracow speak of a Mathias Stanislai de Strykoff – the son of a Stanisław, and therefore not "our" Stryjkowski (Wojtkowiak 1990: 36–40).

[13] There are two contradicting statements in the chronicle regarding his age at the time of his first journey to Lithuania (Stryjkowski 1582: 372 vs. Stryjkowski 1582: A3v). Cf. Wojtkowiak (1990: 20–22).

them. That, and the fact that he describes a lot of places that were on Russian territory, may, according to Wojtkowiak, imply that he worked as some kind of spy. He claims to have seen many places along the Russian border in 1573, which was the last year he spent in that area. One of his duties in the military may have been that of a cartographer (Wojtkowiak 1990: 58–69).[14] In 1574, he joined Andrzej Taranowski's embassy to Turkey, which later allowed him to add his own observations when he wrote about Constantinople in his chronicle (Radziszewska 1978: 21–27; Wojtkowiak 1990: 71–75).

As can be gathered from his dedications and from the text of the chronicle, Stryjkowski spent the following years as the client of different noblemen, as discussed further in Section 2.3.2. After the death of one of his patrons, Jerzy (Jurij) Olelkowicz, in 1578, he sought the protection of the bishop of Samogitia, Melchior Giedrojć, and during the time of their connection he became a priest. In a list from 1579, he is mentioned as one of the canons in Giedrojć's diocese (Radziszewska 1978: 38; Wojtkowiak 1990: 81–86).

After 1582, when the chronicle – Stryjkowski's last known text – appeared, we have to rely on archival material for information. In a letter from 1586, he is called "canonic zmodzki plieban jurborski," ('canon of Samogitia and curate of Jurbork,' present-day Jurbarkas), which meant that he had risen in the ranks of the church since 1579 (Wojtkowiak 1990: 89–91). In May of 1592, another man is mentioned as canon of Samogitia, which may mean that Stryjkowski was dead and this was his successor. Wojtkowiak (1990: 94–97) puts forth the hypothesis that he may have fallen victim to the plague that raged in Lithuania in 1590. Other scholars date his death to before or around 1593 (Radziszewska 1978: 38).

2.2.2 Stryjkowski's works

The *Kronika* was Stryjkowski's largest piece of work and the one he is best known for, but he also wrote other texts in prose and verse. However, as is the case with his biography, the bibliography is also largely based on his own information, rather than on extant texts. Therefore, scholars have reached very different results.

Malinowski ([1846] 1985: 19–30) listed eight printed texts and eleven manuscripts by Stryjkowski and believed that he may have written another four texts. The two main Polish bibliographies, Estreicher's *Bibliografia polska* and *Nowy Korbut*, disagree with each other: Estreicher (29: 350–357)

---

[14] Cf. also the map in Wojtkowiak (1990) between pp. 56 and 57.

lists eight certain and eleven possible titles,[15] *Nowy Korbut* (3: 296–299) 17 titles all in all. Radziszewska (1978: 145) puts down 21 titles on her list, of which 9 survive at least in part, and in the cases where the text is not preserved, she indicates where Stryjkowski refers to them in his extant works. Wojtkowiak (1990: 180–191) lists ten extant texts (printed or in manuscript) and discusses some texts that may since have been destroyed, without making a definite list of them.

Besides the *Kronika*, Stryjkowski's other major text was *O początkach, dzielnościach, sprawach rycerskich i domowych sławnego narodu litewskiego, żemojdzkiego i ruskiego, przedtym nigdy od żadnego ani kuszone, ani opisane, z natchnienia Bożego a uprzejmie pilnego doświadczenia*, usually called *O początkach*, which was not printed during his lifetime but has been published in modern times by Julia Radziszewska (Stryjkowski 1978). It is preserved in one manuscript, kept in the Biblioteka Narodowa (the National Library) in Warsaw.[16] For several years, Stryjkowski worked on them simultaneously (*O początkach* was written 1571–78, the *Kronika* 1574–82). It deals with basically the same subjects as the chronicle, and some scholars do not see the two as distinct pieces of work, but rather as two versions of the same thing. They differ in form, however: the *Kronika* is written mainly in prose, *O początkach* mainly in verse, although verse and prose alternate in both. The *Kronika* consists of books and chapters, whereas *O początkach* is divided into unnumbered sections (Radziszewska 1978: 67). Wojtkowiak (1990: 191–211) has discussed the relationship between the two texts and tried to reconstruct how they came into being. He sees one main difference in content, namely that the *Kronika* had the ambition to be the history of the Slavic peoples in general, or at least of most of Eastern Europe, whereas *O początkach* concentrated on the Lithuanian nobility. Radziszewska (1978: 67–68) also points out the lack of information on the origin of the Poles in *O początkach*.

New editions of two of Stryjkowski's other texts, printed in his lifetime, were included in the 1846 edition together with the chronicle: *Przesławnego wjazdu do Krakowa* [...] *Henryka Walezyusa* and *Goniec cnothy*, both from 1574 (Stryjkowski [1846] 1985, II: 439–563). A manuscript text that was listed by bibliographers but considered perished has lately attracted the attention of scholars, but no complete edition has as yet been published (Wojtkowiak 2010).

Stryjkowski also claimed to have written another important historical text. He complained in the introduction to his chronicle, in his rhymed autobiog-

---

[15] Wojtkowiak (1990: 175) counts nine titles in Estreicher; perhaps he counted the 1766 edition of the *Kronika* as a separate title.

[16] For a description of the manuscript cf. Radziszewska (1978: 54–56), Stryjkowski (1978: 22–23).

raphy and in hints elsewhere in the chronicle that "an Italian" had stolen or plagiarized his work, *Sarmatiae Europeae Descriptio*, and published it (Stryjkowski 1582: XX2r, A3v; Wojtkowiak 1990: 177–178). This Italian was Alexander Guagnini, who had been his superior in the army (cf. SKK 2004: 205–207). Guagnini was born in Verona but had been in Polish service since 1561, and he was a captain of the cavalry at the fortress of Vicebsk (Vitebsk) (Radziszewska 1978: 71). The text was printed in Latin in 1578 (there is also a Polish translation, printed in 1611). Stryjkowski complained to the king about the suspected plagiarism, and in 1580, king Stefan Batory decided the case in Stryjkowski's favor, which did not change the fact that the popular text was still published under Guagnini's name (Radziszewska 1978: 73). Given the fact that Guagnini does not seem to have written anything else, and given the similarities between *Sarmatiae Europeae Descriptio* and Stryjkowski's other texts, the question of whether the latter's claims were true is usually decided in his favor. However, it is not certain if Guagnini, in that case, reworked the manuscript and to what extent (Rogov 1966: 24–25; Wojtkowiak 1990: 179–180).

2.3   Contents of the *Kronika*, sources and ideology

The chronicle deals with the history of Poland, Lithuania, Samogitia and Muscovy from the creation of the world until 1580, when the text appears to have been handed over to the printer (Wojtkowiak 1990: 88). It concerns the relations of these countries to each other and their struggle against Turks and Tatars.

Preceding the chronicle itself in the printed edition from 1582 (several copies of which have been consulted, cf. Section 1.2), we find the following:

1) a title page
2) a list of sources (one page)
3) a dedication in Latin to Stefan Batory (five pages)
4) a dedication in Latin to Jerzy Radziwiłł (two pages)
5) a dedication in Latin to Jerzy, Szymon and Aleksander Olelkowicz (three pages)
6) a portrait of the author, and below it, beginning on the same page
7) his rhymed autobiography in Polish (nine pages)
8) various shorter dedications in Polish and Latin to Stryjkowski from other people (six pages)
9) a letter of privilege in Latin from Stefan Batory (one page)
10) a preface (*przedmowa*) in Polish (fifteen pages).

The chronicle proper begins on page 1 and ends on page 791 (unnumbered), and is followed by a list of corrections (one page) and an index (17 pages). It is divided into 25 books, which in turn are divided into a varying number of chapters, ranging from book III, which consists of only one chapter, to books VI and XV, with 16 chapters each. Many chapters are subdivided into smaller units with separate headings.

2.3.1 Stryjkowski's sources

Stryjkowski used a number of sources, which he listed in the beginning of the *Kronika*. He referred to Greek and Roman historians, but most of his account was based on Polish historians, primarily Maciej Miechowita (1457–1523) and Marcin Kromer (1512–89), but also Jan Długosz (1415–80), Bernard Wapowski (ca. 1450–1535) and Marcin Bielski (ca. 1495–1575).[17] He also made great use of Siegmund von Herberstein's (1486–1566) *Rerum Moscoviticarum Commentarii* (Rogov 1966: 44–46).

However, he also used old chronicles and annals of different origin that are mentioned in his list, usually with no more detailed reference than e.g. "Kijowskie Kroniki stare 4," "Litewskich Latopisczów 12," "Ruskie Kroniki stare" (Stryjkowski 1582: X1v). Sometimes he repeated information that his Polish predecessors had quoted from chronicles, but often when he found discrepancies he either quoted both the Polish historiographers and the chronicles on equal footing or gave priority to the version found in the chronicles. Rogov (1966: 41–44) gives several examples of how Stryjkowski compared the sources he had at hand. The following is an example of such a comparison:

> A s tey przyczyny stoczył bitwę z Izasławem Synem Wołodimirzowym Xiążęciá Pereasławskiego nie Kiiowskiego/ iak Miechouius fol. 62 pisze/ bo ná ten czás był Swatopelk Kijowskim (Stryjkowski 1582: 195–196).

Rogov (1966: 123–258) has made an important contribution to the research on Stryjkowski's sources about Lithuania, but also on the Russian chronicles that provided information on Kievan Rus' (Rogov 1966: 35–122). With the help of Stryjkowski's own comments on the contents of his sources, Rogov came to the conclusion that Stryjkowski used the Primary Chronicle, probably in versions close to the *Novgorodsko-Sofijskij svod* from the 1430s (sometimes dated 1448), the *Tverskaja letopis'* and the *Letopisec Perejaslavlja Suzdal'skogo*. Short versions of the *Novgorodsko-Sofijskij svod* were frequent in Ruthenia, as were the other two chronicles (Rogov 1966: 108–114).

Stryjkowski had access to a fragment of a chronicle that he chose to quote in its entirety in Polish translation (Stryjkowski 1582: 184–186). Rogov

---

[17] Cf. Appendix IV in Wojtkowiak (1990: 236–238).

(1966: 83–90, 115–122) tried to trace its origins and connected it with the Cave Monastery in Kiev, partly on account of the detailed information it gives on important church events. He dated it to the 16th century, but the events it tells about occurred between 1093 and 1146. D. Aleksandrov and D. Volodichin also turned their attention to this text and published it in a modern Russian translation (Aleksandrov & Volodichin 1993).

Another category of chronicles, one that has raised some discussion, consists of what Stryjkowski sometimes calls "latopisce ruskie," i.e. Ruthenian chronicles, sometimes "latopisce litewskie."[18] These chronicles were written on Lithuanian territory and deal with early Lithuanian history, but their language is Ruthenian, sometimes called Old Belorussian (cf. Section 1.6). Therefore, they are usually called Belorussian-Lithuanian chronicles, although some scholars have used other names for them, such as Lithuanian or West-Russian chronicles (Ulaščik 1985: 3).

Daniłowicz ([1846] 1985) was among the first to recognize the existence of chronicles written on Lithuanian territory and to try to establish the relationships between them. He wished to separate Lithuanian chronicles, which explained the origin of the Grand Duchy and were not annalistic, from Ruthenian ones, i.e. chronicles about Rus', but stated that Stryjkowski did not do so and that they were all written in Ruthenian. N. N. Ulaščik, in his monograph about these very chronicles, included a summary of the discussions about their nature (Ulaščik 1985: 9–28). Later scholars have divided the existing Belorussian-Lithuanian chronicles into two main groups according to what they contain, especially regarding the origins of the Lithuanians (cf. Section 2.5).

Among them, the *Chronika* (or *Letopis'*) *Bychovca* (Polish: *Kronika Bychowca*), which was written in Ruthenian, but using the Latin alphabet with Polish orthography, is usually singled out as being the most complete (Ulaščik 1985: 18, 23, 25–26). It is now lost but was published by T. Narbutt (1846) and has been reprinted several times (PSRL XVII: IX, 473–572; PSRL XXXII: 8, 128–173). Stryjkowski seems to have had access to several chronicles that were similar to it, but more extensive in their presentation of events, and sometimes differing in facts (Rogov 1966: 250–251; Ulaščik 1985: 94). In general, however, Stryjkowski's chronicle and the *Chronika Bychovca* coincide so closely that Stryjkowski's text is used to fill in the missing parts in the edition of the *Chronika Bychovca* (PSRL XXXII: 128).

---

[18] Cf. Stryjkowski (1582: 47): "To własna rzecz Latopiszczow Litewskich po Rusku pissanych," Stryjkowski (1582: 384): "Látopiszce też wszystki Litewskie po Rusku pisane/ ktorych Litwá z stárodawná zá Kronikę używa […]," cf. also Ulaščik (1985: 91). Ulaščik (1985: 83–84) provides a list of the instances where Stryjkowski refers to these sources.

2.3.2 Connections and ideology

Many of the chapters in the chronicle are preceded by dedications. Attempts have been made to extract information about Stryjkowski's sympathies and political views – especially on the subject of the Polish-Lithuanian union – from the text of the chronicle, its dedications and information about his patrons. A few conclusions made by other scholars on this topic will be summarized here.

2.3.2.1 Connections

Wojtkowiak (1990: 140–174) discusses the people mentioned in dedications and also lists them along with their titles and religious affiliation in Appendix III (Wojtkowiak 1990: 233–234). J. Bardach (1970: 70) also discusses some of those mentioned. He notes that there are many dedications to people connected with Samogitia and Ruthenia. The people to whom dedications were written are too numerous to discuss here, but those who can be believed to have been Stryjkowski's patrons at some point will be mentioned.

As can be gathered from Stryjkowski's writings, he was connected to the Chodkiewicz family. He mentions three members of the family in his texts and dedications (Wojtkowiak 1990: 126–128). Aleksander Chodkiewicz, *starosta* of Hrodna (Grodno), who died in 1578, was most certainly one of his patrons, since he dedicated a poem from 1574 to "Panu Alexandrowi Chodkiewicowi […] panu memu miłosciwemu" (Wojtkowiak 1990: 128–129; cf. Stryjkowski [1846] 1985, II: 441). Both Aleksander and his cousin Jan Chodkiewicz, *starosta* of Samogitia and castellan of Vilnius (from 1574), supplied Stryjkowski with chronicles as sources.[19] This family seems to have been important to Stryjkowski, since people connected to them by marriage can also be found in his dedications (Wojtkowiak 1990: 129–131).

The Olelkowicz family, princes of Słuck, was related by marriage to the Chodkiewicz family. Stryjkowski spent some time at the court of Jerzy (Jurij) Olelkowicz before the latter's death in 1578, perhaps after Stryjkowski's return from the embassy to Turkey in 1575. *O początkach* is dedicated to Jerzy Olelkowicz, and in the *Kronika*, which, as we know, was printed a few years later, Stryjkowski wrote an extensive dedication to his three sons Jerzy, Szymon and Aleksander (cf. Section 2.3). Stryjkowski seems to have received some help in his historical research from the family. Jerzy Olelkowicz belonged to the Orthodox church, but two of his sons later converted

---

[19] Cf. Stryjkowski (1582: 288): "dwu dowodnych Látopiszczow/ ktory káżdy náleść może w Grodku w skárbie sławney pámięći Páná Chodkiewicá Alexandrá Stárosty Grodzienskiego/ y ktorego ieszcze u mnie iest Exemplarz," "tę przerzeczoną Kronikę Pruską stároswieckimi literámi ku wyczytániu trudnymi pissáną/ nálazł sławney pámięći Pan Ian Chodkiewic ná Zamku Rumborku w Kośćiele […] A ten potym mnie użyczył."

to Catholicism, and the household was characterized by religious tolerance (Malinowski [1846] 1985: 12–13; Wojtkowiak 1990: 81–82, 131–136).

Stryjkowski also had connections to the Samogitian bishop Melchior Giedrojć, to whom he wrote a large dedication as an introduction to chapter II: 1 (Stryjkowski 1582: 21–23). He was an ardent Catholic and Jesuit (Bardach 1970: 69; Radziszewska 1978: 38; Wojtkowiak 1990: 138–140) and notable for promoting Lithuanian interests in education and publishing (Stone 2001: 107).

Even though there are many dedications to members of the Radziwiłł family in the chronicle, it is improbable that Stryjkowski was particularly close to them, since they were adversaries to his protectors, the Chodkiewicz family. Most of the members of the Radziwiłł family were Calvinists, but there were also Catholics among them (Radziszewska 1978: 31, 35; Wojtkowiak 1990: 142–144; cf. Niendorf 2006: 130). They belonged to the most active separatists before the union was concluded.

2.3.2.2 Ideology

Stryjkowski's views on the Union of Lublin have been of interest to several scholars. Some have considered him to belong to a kind of separatist camp (Zachara-Wawrzyńczyk 1963: 29; Rogov 1966: 30–31). Others have claimed that he was in favor of the union, but promoted Lithuania's rights within it and its equality with Poland (Bardach 1970: 69–71; Kulicka 1980: 14). Radziszewska (1978: 12, 31) calls him a Polish patriot who took it upon him to write about the less well-known history of Lithuania.

Wojtkowiak (1990: 140–141) points out the need to be careful when announcing the affiliations of Stryjkowski's patrons, since mostly it is known what their positions were around the time of the union, but it is uncertain how their views might have changed in the years that passed until Stryjkowski wrote his chronicle. The same can be said about the religious affiliation of the magnates. Bardach (1970: 70–71) also stresses that many of those who were originally opposed to the union adopted another point of view after its realization, one that concentrated more on the rights of Lithuania within the union. Separatism would, according to him, have been an anachronism at this time, and in the 1570s, the existence of the union was not debated in the Sejms, only the conditions of it. Stone (2001: 63, 148), on the other hand, states that separatism remained in Polish-Lithuanian life for as long as the Commonwealth existed. The attempt of Janusz Radziwiłł the Younger in 1655 to replace the Union of Lublin with a union with Sweden must be counted as an expression of separatism, even though it was mainly the initiative of a few people and not a widespread desire (Niendorf 2006: 51). The question of Stryjkowski's attitude towards the union may deserve a new study.

In religious matters, not much can be gathered from the dedications. Although Stryjkowski himself was a Catholic priest and his patron Giedrojć was active in the counterreformation, some of the names belong to Orthodox persons, Lutherans or Calvinists (Wojtkowiak 1990: 141–142, 233–234).

However interesting Stryjkowski's dedications may be, it is not certain that they reveal much about his political views. Wojtkowiak (1990: 174) believes that they are only signs of whom he was indebted to for the financial means to print the *Kronika*. It may therefore be more fruitful to conclude something about Stryjkowski's views from what he says in his chronicle.

Although he was born in Poland, Stryjkowski apparently identified with Lithuania, as can be seen from many details in his chronicle, as well as from the very fact that he wrote it, and the manner in which he wrote it. Expressions such as *u nas w Zmodzi* (Stryjkowski 1582: 298) show that he felt at home in Samogitia, and he sometimes used similar expressions about Lithuania as well (Wojtkowiak 1990: 216–218), although phrases such as *my Polacy* or *Polacy nászy* (e.g. Stryjkowski 1582: 87, 149) are also found. According to F. Sielicki, who studied the reception of Russian chronicles in Poland, Stryjkowski was the first Polish author to describe Lithuania in a positive way, as his own country, instead of using neutral or negative expressions (Sielicki 1965: 151–152). In his interpretation of events, he often chose a Lithuanian version of the story over a Polish one, or judged them as equal (cf. Rogov 1966: 153–154, 192–194).

As previously mentioned, Stryjkowski devoted much attention to the early history of Kievan Rus', as the predecessor of Ruthenia. Further on in the chronicle, he did not give as much attention to the Muscovite state, other than as a neighbor or enemy of the Commonwealth (Rogov 1966: 36–37, 243). When reporting on Muscovite struggles with Tatars and the Teutonic Order, however, Stryjkowski did show some sympathy for Russia (Bardach 1970: 73).

Stryjkowski's writings betray his aversion to the Turks, especially *O wolności Korony Polskiej i Wielkiego Księstwa Litewskiego*, a versed text comprising 43 leaves, written shortly after the author's return from Turkey and printed in Cracow in 1575 (Malinowski [1846] 1985: 20; Radziszewska 1978: 44–47).

As mentioned above, Stryjkowski had connections with people of different religious affiliations. In the text of the chronicle, he also adopted a tolerant view on the Orthodox Eastern Slavs, emphasizing the common provenance and related languages of all Slavs, as well as the fact that they all were Christians, without placing too much judgment in the fact that some were Orthodox and some Catholic (Myl'nikov 1996: 120; cf. Niendorf 2006: 79). This may be related to the fact that he saw the Ottoman Empire as a common enemy of all Christian peoples.

2.4 Sarmatism and the origins of the Slavs

Early historiographers often saw it as their task to search for the roots of their people or nation, and to give them as prominent a place in history as possible. These theories were very important in their time, and Stryjkowski's *Kronika* is frequently mentioned as having a special place in that tradition. The most thorough study of the ethnogenic myths among the Slavic peoples is A. S. Myl'nikov's *Kartina slavjanskogo mira: vzgljad iz Vostočnoj Evropy* (Myl'nikov 1996). It will be the main point of reference in this section.

One way of giving a people ancient and noble roots was to search for biblical ancestry. Many peoples attempted to trace their roots to Noah's sons Shem, Ham and Japheth, primarily referring to Genesis, where the division of the earth between them is described. These claims were often supported by quotes from Herodotus and other antique or Byzantine writers.

In the case of the Slavic peoples, such attempts had been made ever since Eastern Slavic chronicle writing began. Chronicle writers incorporated the legends in their texts, and the Primary Chronicle, for instance, begins by describing this division of the earth (PVL 2007: 7–8). As we will see, these myths still circulated in the 16th and 17th centuries.

According to biblical tradition, Noah's son Japheth was the ancestor of all peoples in the northern and western parts of the world, among which were the Slavs (Myl'nikov 1996: 21; Kohut 2004: 59–60).[20] Most chroniclers and historiographers agreed on this and it was an accepted truth among Polish historiographers, but they differed in their views on which one of Japheth's sons was to be considered the ancestor of the Slavs. Maciej Miechowita, for instance, followed a medieval tradition in claiming that the Slavs stemmed from Japheth's fourth son Javan and Javan's son Elishah (Myl'nikov 1996: 22–23). Ukrainian Cossack chronicles, on the other hand, preferred a version about Japheth's eldest son, Gomer. Being a descendant of the eldest son was of course the most prestigious (Kohut 2004: 76–77).

The most widely spread version and the most important one in this context was introduced by Bernard Wapowski and further promoted by Marcin Bielski. It claimed Japheth's sixth son Meshech as the ancestor of the Muscovites, based on the similarity of the words *Mosoch* (i.e. Meshech) and *Moskva* (Myl'nikov 1996: 25; Kohut 2004: 63). This connection between Meshech and Moscow gained popularity with time, and Stryjkowski is often mentioned in connection with it. An important trait of the Meshech-theory is that it emphasized the common ancestry of all the Slavs, despite confessional differences. As explained above, Stryjkowski also seems to have harbored such ideals (Robinson 1963: 103–105; Myl'nikov 1996: 36–37).

---

[20] The Bible itself only says that the lands were divided between Noah's sons, not how this was done, cf. Genesis 10: 1–5.

Stryjkowski also claimed that when Meshech settled the Slavic lands, he was accompanied by "Asarmot [...] álbo Sarmata" (Stryjkowski 1582: 92$_2$), i.e. the biblical Hazarmaveth, descendant of Shem. He associated this name, Asarmot or Sarmata, with the ethnonym Sarmatians, which for Polish historians was synonymous to the ancient Slavs (cf. below). In this way, he united two genealogies into one (Myl'nikov 1996: 26).

Aside from these genealogical discussions, historiographers also had geographically oriented theories. Once they had agreed that the Slavs were descendants of Noah, they had to determine how they had come from Babylon, after the scattering of the languages at the tower of Babel, to the lands they now inhabited. One of the first theories about the origins of the Slavs had its roots in Byzantium, was taken over by the Slavs and can be found in ancient Russian chronicles. It claimed that the Slavs had inhabited the land around the Danube, and is known as the Balkan theory, in the terminology of A. N. Robinson (1963: 101), or the Danube theory, according to Z. Kohut (2004: 59–60).

Another theory, which had its origins in West European, Catholic sources and first won acceptance in Polish and Czech history writing, was based on the assumption that the Slavs had migrated through the Asian area called Sarmatia. Jan Długosz and several other Polish historiographers, among them Stryjkowski, promoted this theory (Kohut 2004: 60–62). As the importance of the Polish state rose, after the Eastern and Southern Slavs had been weakened by Turks and Tatars, the Sarmatian theory gained strength, and in the 15th–16th centuries it became the predominant theory, not only among the Western Slavs, where it had originated, but among all the Slavic peoples (Robinson 1963: 101).

When the Asian Sarmatians, according to the theory, had settled in Europe, their new land was also called Sarmatia. Miechowita, in his *Tractatus de duabus Sarmatis* (1517) and *Chronika Polonorum* (1519, 1520), wrote about the "two Sarmatias," one European and one Asian or Scythian, that were divided by the Don. According to him, Slavic peoples lived in both these areas (Myl'nikov 1996: 97; 1999: 125). Guagnini (or Stryjkowski, if the latter's claims about plagiarism were true, cf. Section 2.2.2) devoted his work *Sarmatiae Europeae descriptio* to this question and emphasized the common Slavic language of the peoples who lived in this area (Myl'nikov 1996: 104). Bielski also distinguished between Scythian Sarmatia and European Sarmatia (Myl'nikov 1996: 102). It was not obvious, however, what was meant by European Sarmatia. Many Polish authors chose to identify it with Poland or the Commonwealth. Others (Kromer, Bielski, Stryjkowski and non-Polish authors) had a wider definition that included Muscovy (Myl'nikov 1996: 129). This variation in usage can be found in the texts of non-Slavic authors as well. It has for instance been documented that Swedish 17th-century writers used the terms *Sarmatae* and *Sarmatia* either for Eastern

Europe and parts of Asia in general, or only for the Poles (Helander 2004: 274–276).

The West-Russian Chronograph from the 16th century presented the same basic thought as the Polish historiographers, but talked about the "two Scythias" (Myl'nikov 1996: 106). The ethnonyms Scythians and Sarmatians were frequently used interchangeably, but according to Stryjkowski, they referred to two distinct peoples with different languages and habits. To him, as can be gathered from the following quote, Scythians were Tatars, and Sarmatians were Slavs (cf. Radziszewska 1978: 97):

> Skąd się też pokázuie/ isz Sarmatowie nászy/ rozni byli y obyczáymi/ i narodem/ y ięzykiem od Scytow álbo Tatarow: Aczkolwiek stárzy Historykowie Greccy y Láćinscy wszystki Narody pułnocne/ y miedzywschodnie/ Scytámi i Sarmatámi zá iedno zwáli/ ták Polaki/ Russaki/ Litwę y Moskwę/ iáko y Tatary iednym być narodem omylnie rozumieiąc (Stryjkowski 1582: 106–107).

This combination of the Sarmatian theory (through Hazarmaveth) with the Meshech-Moscow theory was a way of covering the origins of all the Slavs. Stryjkowski described all Slavs as one people with originally one single language. These ideas were elaborated in the Kievan *Synopsis*, which, because of its many editions and reprints (cf. Section 1.4), helped spread the ideas. In the *Synopsis*, the Slavs are said to have a common language, called *slaveno-rossijskij*: Slavo-Rossian, using the translation of S. Plokhy. Kiev was identified as the core of the Slavo-Rossian nation, but Muscovites were also included, as well as, in certain contexts, the Poles and other Slavs (Kohut 2004: 67–70; Plokhy 2006: 261–263).

In its 16th-century version, the Sarmatian theory served primarily to weld the people of the Commonwealth together, Poles and Lithuanians alike (Kulicka 1980: 10–11). Stryjkowski equated the Sarmatians with all Slavs (Myl'nikov 1996: 263). As time passed, however, the Sarmatians became associated primarily with the Polish nobility, not with Slavs in general, which in the 17th century estranged other Slavic peoples from this idea. This explains why Andrej Lyzlov, in his translation of the *Kronika,* tried to play down the role of the Sarmatians and subordinate Asarmot (Sarmatians) to Meshech (Muscovites), cf. Section 3.2.3 (Das 1986: 348).

When fully developed, the Sarmatian theory served to prove that the Polish nobility, the szlachta, was not of the same descent as the rest of the Polish people. The szlachta was said to have come from the Sarmatians, who, when they came to the Dnieper and Vistula valleys, became the masters of the Slavs who inhabited the land before them. The Sarmatians were hence the ancestors of the szlachta, as opposed to the peasants, who were the descendants of the enslaved Slavs (Myl'nikov 1996: 264). Lithuanian nobility could also be included into this notion of the Sarmatians, as explained further in Section 2.5 (Kulicka 1980: 16).

41

2.5 The origins of the Lithuanians

Stryjkowski was also very much concerned with the origins of the Lithuanians, particularly of the nobility. As was the case with the Slavs, there were legends about the origins of the Lithuanians and attempts to give them as honorable roots as possible. Usually, the Lithuanians were said to have their origins in Rome instead of in biblical tradition.

A connection between the Romans and the Lithuanians was mentioned already by Jan Długosz, who in his chronicle from around 1470 compared the names *Lithuania* and *L'Italia*, drew parallels between Lithuanian and Roman pagan beliefs and saw similarities between the Lithuanian language and Latin. He came to the conclusion that Romans had come to Lithuania during the time of Julius Caesar, but did not name any individuals or families (Zachara-Wawrzyńczyk 1963: 18–21; Kulicka 1980: 4–5; Ulaščik 1985: 135). It is less probable, however, that Długosz, himself a Pole and not overly concerned with Lithuania, invented the legend than that he documented a circulating tale (Niendorf 2006: 59).

Another version of the legend was to be found in Lithuanian chronicles. According to them, the Roman nobleman Palemon left Rome with his family and five hundred other noblemen and came to Lithuania. The chronicles differ as to when and why this happened. Some claimed that he left because of Nero's cruelties in the 1st century A.D., others added that he also may have fled before Attila the Hun in the 5th century (Zachara-Wawrzyńczyk 1963: 24–25; Myl'nikov 1996: 207). The first type of chronicles has survived in for instance the *Evreinskaja letopis'* (PSRL XXXV: 145–172) and the *Letopis' Račinskogo* (PSRL XXXV: 214–238), whereas the second type has a lot in common with the *Chronika Bychovca* (PSRL XXXII: 128–173) and the *Chronika litovskaja i žmojtskaja* (PSRL XXXII: 15–127). All in all, there are six surviving chronicles that tell about Palemon's flight from Rome (Rogov 1966: 123–125; Ulaščik 1985: 130).[21]

Stryjkowski devoted chapter II: 7 of the *Kronika* (Stryjkowski 1582: 47–56) to this legend and related both versions, referring to the chronicles that were his sources with the following words: "To własna rzecz Latopiszczow Litewskich po Rusku pissanych" (Stryjkowski 1582: 47) and "Drugi záś Látopiszec […] tak też Kronikę Litewską y Zmodzską/ poczyna prostymi słowy" (Stryjkowski 1582: 48). Afterwards he retold the legends in verse.

To give the legend a more solid foundation, it was necessary to identify Palemon in Roman sources. Marcin Kromer, in his *De origine et rebus gestis Polonorum* from 1555, derived the name Palemon from Publius Libo, whom he found in the works of the Roman historian Florus (Zachara-Wawrzyńczyk

---

[21] The *Letopis' Račinskogo* is, however, of a later date than Stryjkowski's chronicle and can therefore not be one of his sources, cf. Rogov (1966: 233).

1963: 26).[22] E. Kulicka (1980: 8) points out the contradiction that the closest correspondences to the name Palemon in antique history are in fact Greek: the deity Palaemon and the Pontic kings Polemon I and II.

Stryjkowski followed Kromer's hypothesis. In chapter III: 1, he referred to his sources among classical authors:

> Liuius naprzednieyszy Rzymski Historyk/ y Iulius Florus z niego w księgach 4. w rozdziele 2. Publiussa Libona być morskim Hetmanem Pompeiussowym przećiw Cesarzowi wspomináią.
>
> Trogus też Pompeius niemniey sławny Historyk/ y Iustinus z niego/ iáko Palemoná/ ták Publiussa Liboná częstokroć wspomináią (Stryjkowski 1582: 58).

According to M. Zachara-Wawrzyńczyk (1963: 35), the legend about the Roman origins of the Lithuanians was first employed by the Teutonic Knights to emphasize their own right to power over these lands, and not until Lithuania needed to assert itself against Poland and Russia did they themselves claim it. Most scholars in the field disagree with this theory (Kulicka 1980: 1–4; Niendorf 2006: 59). Kulicka (1980: 5–10) thinks that the legend had its origins among prominent Lithuanian families in the 15th century. However, she also stresses that it filled the function of claiming their status against Poland. It is also possible that these claims were directed towards Muscovy or even aimed at Ruthenian families in an internal conflict within the Grand Duchy (Niendorf 2006: 59–60).

The Lithuanian and the Sarmatian legends were originally opposed to each other, competing for prestige, but in Stryjkowski's interpretation, they were compatible. According to him, when the Roman noblemen arrived in Lithuania, it was already inhabited by the Lithuanians, who were descendants of Japheth and thereby one of the Sarmatian peoples. They mixed with the Romans and together with them formed the people of the Commonwealth. In this way, the two legends were united (Kulicka 1980: 12–14; Niendorf 2006: 61–63).

At a later stage, in the 17th century, Polish magnate families also began tracing their genealogy back to Roman ancestors. This led to a situation where the lesser nobility in both parts of the Commonwealth traced their lineage to the Sarmatians (cf. Section 2.4) and the magnates, likewise in both parts, saw themselves as descendants of the Romans, so that the two myths were used by different social strata rather than by different nationalities (Niendorf 2006: 62).

---

[22] Florus mentions a Libo, but does not call him Publius; instead he is indexed in the Loeb edition as L. Scribonius Libo, cf. Florus (1984: 272–273, 376).

3 The East Slavic translations and the manuscripts

A teras iusz do sámey Historiey Ruskiey w imię
wszech rzeczy początku Bogá przystępuiemy.

Stryjkowski 1582: 110

After this presentation of the author and the Polish original text, it is time to return to the main concern of the thesis, namely the Russian translations of the Polish chronicle, especially the one from 1673–79. The Ukrainian translation and the Ukrainian Chronograph that relies heavily on it will also be discussed here. The aim of the chapter is, however, to determine the relationships between the manuscripts belonging to the 1673–79 translation, since this is of importance to the edition as well as to the reasoning in the remainder of the thesis. Some of these manuscripts are of special interest and are accordingly given more attention. Two identified translators are also introduced here.

3.1 Russian-Polish relations in the late 17th century

Where documentation is absent, it is difficult to know the exact reasons why a particular text was translated and copied. Nevertheless, the situation in Russia, and especially its relations with the Polish-Lithuanian Commonwealth, at the time when Stryjkowski's chronicle was translated, may explain the interest in Polish books in general and, perhaps, this historical work with its emphasis on the common ancestry of the Slavic peoples in particular. There are many aspects to be considered, and this can only be a very general outline of the history and culture of that time.

The monographs by D. Stone (2001) and S. Plokhy (2006), introduced in Section 2.1, will be among the main sources in this section as well. Since they concentrate on the borderlands between Russia and Poland, i.e. Ruthenia, they will be supplemented by *The Cambridge History of Russia* (2006), which also provides an outline of internal Muscovite events. P. V. Sedov (2006) has devoted a monograph to the last years of Aleksej Michajlovič's reign and to that of Fëdor Alekseevič, describing the distribution of power and the events at court in great detail. A classical work on the connections

44

between Ruthenia and Russia from the mid-16th century to 1762, especially – but not exclusively – within the religious sphere, is Charlampovič (1914). The cultural life of this period, especially the expressions of baroque in Russian literature, has been described by L. I. Sazonova (2006).

3.1.1 Historical background

The relations between Russia and the Polish-Lithuanian Commonwealth during the 17th century were complicated. The beginning of the century had seen Poland's intervention in Russian politics during the Time of Troubles, beginning with the Polish support of the first False Dmitrij. After Dmitrij's death, King Sigismund III of Poland attempted to become tsar of Russia, while his son Władysław was invited by some of the Russian boyars to claim the throne, none of which came to pass. Polish troops occupied Moscow. Russia even sought Swedish aid against the Poles, but the credit for liberating Moscow in 1613 goes to Minin and Požarskij. Still, Poland did not give up its claim to the Russian throne until 1634 (Stone 2001: 140–142; *The Cambridge History* 2006: 409–431; Plokhy 2006: 204–206).

The desire to win back the territories around Smolensk that the Commonwealth had taken over from Russia during the Time of Troubles led to Russian involvement in the conflict between Poland and the Ukrainian Cossacks, siding with the Cossack uprising or, as others describe it, the Ukrainian struggle for autonomy, under Bohdan Chmel'nyc'kyj. The Perejaslav agreement between Russia and Chmel'nyc'kyj in 1654, which joined Ukrainian territories to Russia, started the Thirteen Years' War. After Chmel'nyc'-kyj's death in 1657, discontent with Russia grew in the Ukrainian and Lithuanian areas, and there were internal conflicts between those who sought an alliance with the Poles and those who looked to Moscow for support. When the threat arose of the Ukraine breaking free with the support of the Crimean khan, the Commonwealth and Russia finally, in 1667, signed the Treaty of Andrusovo, which meant that Kiev, Smolensk and left-bank Ukraine were turned over to Russia (Stone 2001: 165–166; *The Cambridge History* 2006: 500–506; Plokhy 2006: 303–304). Kiev was supposed to be returned to the Commonwealth in 1669, but this was not done (Izotova 2004: 154–155).

In the second half of the 17th century, ambassadors were sent between Russia and Poland almost every year until they exchanged more permanent representatives in the 1670s (Nikolaev 2004: 86). The relations between the countries were intertwined with internal Russian affairs. A. L. Ordin-Naščokin, who was the head of *Posol'skij prikaz* (the Diplomatic Chancellery) during the years 1667–71 (cf. also Section 5.1), was of the opinion that peace with Poland should be sought even if it meant losing Kiev, and that the main aim in international affairs should be to challenge Sweden for the Baltic lands. Not many people shared this view; instead tsar Aleksej Michajlovič and many others thought it very important to keep Kiev. A. S. Matveev, who replaced Ordin-Naščokin as the head of *Posol'skij prikaz* in 1671, shared the tsar's opinion (Sedov 2006: 119–122).

The conflict between Russia and Poland also had religious implications. When Chmel'nyc'kyj appealed to tsar Aleksej Michajlovič, he did it in the name of Orthodoxy, and the areas taken over by Russia were those with mainly Orthodox population. This left the Commonwealth with a stronger Catholic and Uniate dominance, and increased the Russian notion of being the protector of Orthodoxy with the right to intervene on behalf of Orthodox believers. Another reason why the Orthodox church in Russia was strengthened was because left-bank Ukraine was a cultural center with many well educated clergymen (Skinner 2009: 150–154, 167).

Even after the truce at Andrusovo, all was not calm. Russia felt that its control of the left bank was threatened and feared that the Commonwealth would break the truce and try to reassume control of the area. There was also a fear of an invasion from the Ottoman Empire. The right-bank Cossacks still hoped for a united Ukraine and applied to the Ottoman Empire for help, which led to negotiations between Poland and Russia and the idea of a mutual defense pact against the Ottoman Empire (*The Cambridge History* 2006: 507–516). The conflict with the Ottoman Empire was partly a result of the Russian policy after Ordin-Naščokin's replacement by Matveev, which focused on control over the Ukraine. With the Ottoman Empire as the main enemy, relations with Poland grew friendlier (Sedov 2006: 121–122). During these years it was even suggested that Aleksej Michajlovič or his son Fëdor become king of Poland, but religious differences were an obstacle (Sedov 2006: 182–183). The change towards a more positive Russian view on Poland in the 1660s and 1670s was probably to some extent due to the fact that the older generation that still remembered the Time of Troubles and had a very negative opinion of Poland was succeeded by a younger generation with more experience of Western cultural influence and an attitude towards Poland as a possible ally. This generation shift took place gradually and the positive attitude did not always prevail (Sedov 2006: 346–349).

Russian and Commonwealth diplomats met in Andrusovo in 1669, 1674 and 1678 to discuss the questions that still remained after the Treaty, but not only did they not manage to solve the remaining problems during these meetings, there even arose new ones. In numerous accusations, both sides tried to show that the other party had broken the agreements. For instance, during the meeting in 1674, which took place in the middle of a war between Poland and Turkey that had begun in 1672, Poland complained that Russia had not helped them enough against the Turks and against Cossack troubles in right-bank Ukraine in connection with this war. Muscovy denied these accusations and began to claim all of the Ukraine, even the Polish-controlled right bank, with the motivation that Poland was not doing well in the war and would probably turn those areas over to Turkey (Izotova 2004: 150–160).

In connection with the Russo-Turkish war of 1676–81, Muscovy's position was strengthened. A few years later, the Commonwealth, which had been weakened and was anxious not to stand alone, sought to form an alliance with Russia. The Treaty of Eternal Peace, which brought some advantages to Russia, was signed in 1686 (Izotova 2004: 161–163; *The Cambridge History* 2006: 507–516).

The intensity of Russo-Polish relations can to some extent be measured by the number of books filled with documents on the subject in *Posol'skij prikaz*. For the whole of the 17th century, the number of books filled was 234, almost twice as many as were devoted to Swedish affairs, and far ahead of any other diplomatic area (Kamiński 1993: 98–100; cf. Rogožin 2003: 194–216). The inventory of *Posol'skij prikaz* which was made in 1673 also shows the dominance of Polish-Lithuanian affairs: it lists some 2,100 documents on this topic, which surpasses the number of documents devoted to Crimean and Swedish affairs taken together (Rogožin 2003: 161–163).

3.1.2 Cultural background

As borders changed, people moved in new ways, and political contacts were accompanied by cultural ones. The areas incorporated by Russia in 1654 had until then been part of a Western cultural sphere, and when people instead began to move from there to Moscow and other Russian cities, they brought new influences with them. Many people who later had great impact on Russian cultural life came from these areas, such as Simeon Polockij, Epifanij Slavineckij and Feofan Prokopovič. The influence of the Orthodox but Western-influenced Kiev Mohyla Collegium, founded in 1632, on Russian cultural life is also well attested (Kamiński 1993: 184–185; Plokhy 2006: 253; Sazonova 2006: 36–45).

In Moscow, the end of the 17th century was characterized by tensions between groups with different ideas about the direction society should take. The so-called Latinizers embraced Western influences, mediated by Poland and Ruthenia, and their ideas of reform were to a large extent centered on education. Simeon Polockij and Sil'vestr Medvedev were among the leaders of this group, which was supported by Fëdor Alekseevič and Sof'ja Alekseevna at court. The Graecophiles, led by Epifanij Slavineckij and Evfimij Čudovskij and supported by Patriarch Ioakim, were oriented towards Greek orthodoxy, but rejected other aspects of Greek culture (Uspenskij 2002: 426; Sazonova 2006: 85–112).

Culture and trends at the tsar's court changed during the second half of the 17th century. The changes could be felt in many areas, and they were often connected to Western influence. A new form of church singing was introduced, based on Ukrainian and Polish models and often performed by singers from these areas. Polish clothes became fashionable among Muscovite men in the 1670s – although, because of the Sarmatian ideology (cf. Section 2.4), Polish fashion was in turn inspired by Turkish and Oriental clothing. The women at court began wearing Polish-style hats in the 1680s (Sedov 2006: 494–519).

In the light of the contacts with the West, it is not surprising that the interest in Polish books and history was great in Russia. A number of Polish books and pamphlets were known in Russia in the 17th century. Many of them were bought by *Posol'skij prikaz*, whose library in 1673 contained 17 Polish books, or 14.4%, second only to the number of books in Latin (Luppov 1970: 196–198). The role and importance of *Posol'skij prikaz* will be examined more closely in Chapter 5. Private persons, such as Simeon Polockij, tsar Fëdor Alekseevič, A. S. Matveev and Epifanij Slavineckij, also owned books in Polish, to a lesser or greater extent (Luppov 1970: 148–150).

Polish literature also had a great influence through translations. A. I. Sobolevskij, in his *Perevodnaja literatura moskovskoj Rusi XIV–XVII vekov*, stated that most of the translations in 17th-century Russia were made from Latin, the language of science in "Poland and Western Europe" at that time, followed by Polish as the second most common source language. The geographical origins of the source texts are more varied, but many of them were not translated from the originals, but rather via Polish translations. Sobolevskij points out that the influence by Polish authors was not very large, i.e. even though translations from Polish were common, the share of Polish authors was not as great (Sobolevskij 1903: 49–50).

S. I. Nikolaev, in his bibliography of Russo-Polish relations during the 16th–18th centuries, has listed 60 Polish authors whose texts were translated into Russian during this time, as well as 17 anonymous Polish texts. Twenty-six authors of Antiquity or from Western Europe were translated into Russian via Polish translations. Four translations have been mentioned in documents but cannot now be found, and there are 18 texts that can be assumed for different reasons to be translations from Polish, but the originals are not known (Nikolaev 2008: 244–247).

The Polish books and translations from Polish concerned many different subjects, such as geography, cosmography, astronomy, politics and history. There were also translations of literary works, including poetry of different types (cf. Sobolevskij 1903; Moiseeva 1973; Nikolaev 2008). Polish pamphlets and occasional poetry were translated for diplomatic reasons (Nikolaev 2004: 87).

3.2 The translations of Stryjkowski's *Kronika*

One of the more important historical texts translated was Stryjkowski's *Kronika*. Sobolevskij (1903: 79–80) recognized two translations, the first of which he characterized as Church Slavonic and the second as bad Church Slavonic, written by a person with a tendency to switch into Russian.

A. I. Rogov in his above-mentioned monograph *Russko-pol'skie kul'turnye svjazi v épochu vozroždenija* lists four translations of Stryjkowski into Russian: two partial and two complete ones (Rogov 1966: 269–287). He gives a survey of the manuscripts containing the two complete translations, based on previous descriptions of the manuscripts and completed by his own observations (Rogov 1966: 274–287). A more recent and slightly more complete list has been made by S. I. Nikolaev (2008: 101–102), who, on the other hand, does not describe the manuscripts, but only refers to existing descriptions. These two scholars give no complete list of the manuscripts containing Lyzlov's translation; for that information, one must turn to books about the Kurbskij Collection, such as Keenan (1971), *Perepiska* (1979) and Erusalimskij (2009). Neither of these scholars takes into consideration the Ukrainian translation discussed in Section 3.2.5.

Table 3 shows the history of the chronicle on East Slavic territory, beginning with the earliest translation, the Ukrainian one. The translations will be described in more detail below, and the manuscript situation is accounted for in Sections 3.5 and 3.7, but some parts of the table need a brief explanation here.

Table 3. East Slavic translations of Stryjkowski's Kronika

Year	Parts translated	Known copies	Comments	Section
1608–22	The whole *Kronika*	2	Ukrainian translation	3.2.5
1668–70	IV: 1–3	(9+1)	Preserved in mss. together with1688 translation and parts of 1673–79 translation	3.2.1
1673–79	The whole *Kronika*	11 (12 mss.)	Translated by Čižinskij et al.	3.5
1682	I: 2, part of II: 1, IV: 1–3	7	Translated by Lyzlov	3.2.3, 3.7.1
1688	I–III?	9+1	Preserved in mss. together with 1668–70 translation and parts of 1673–79 translation	3.2.4, 3.7.2

The partial translation from 1668–70 does not exist as separate manuscripts, but is preserved only together with the 1688 translation and parts of the 1673–79 translation, for which reason the number of known copies is set in parentheses.

There are eleven copies of the 1673–79 translation, but one copy is divided into two manuscripts that have different call numbers and are kept in different libraries (cf. Section 3.5.2), and there are therefore twelve manuscripts.

It has not been definitely established what parts of the text were translated in 1688, but it is known that the translation from 1668–70 is incorporated into the mss. containing this translation, and that large parts of the text are very similar to the 1673–79 translation. Nine mss. belong to this translation, and there are references to one more copy that perished in 1812, which is expressed in the table by the figure "9+1".

Nikolaev (2008: 103) listed yet another manuscript, which my studies have shown contains some other historical text, not Stryjkowski's chronicle, although I have not been able to identify the text. The manuscript is RNB f. 659, sobranie Archeologičeskogo obščestva, No. 33 (previously No. 36), from the 17th century. Nikolaev erroneously listed it as BAN sobranie Archeografičeskogo obščestva, No. 36, i.e. he was mistaken in the library and the collection to which it belonged.[23]

Radziszewska (1978: 102) also mentions a Russian translation of IV: 1–2, made in 1688, but without reporting her source. No one else mentions this translation, and it is probably some kind of misunderstanding. Her list contains one more mistake: she claims that Lyzlov's translation was of books I–III, which is incorrect. Therefore, this otherwise unknown translation from 1688 may also be a misunderstanding on her part.

The earliest Russian documents mentioning the chronicle date to the 1680s. One document (RGADA f[ond] 159, op[is'] 1, no. 825, l[isty] 47–50) speaks of the translation of Stryjkowski's chronicle being bound, with gilded edges, by the bookbinder Ostafij Fëdorov for *Posol'skij prikaz*. He was paid for this, and for the binding of another book, which we will return to later (cf. Section 3.3.2), in October 1681.

According to a description of tsar Fëdor Alekseevič's library, it contained a copy of Stryjkowski's chronicle bound in white leather and with marbled edges. A year after Fëdor Alekseevič's death, twelve of his books, among them this copy of the *Kronika*, were delivered to Peter I (on March 19th, 1683),[24] and on April 12th, 1683, they were passed on to the *Masterskaja palata* (Zabelin 1915: 602–607; Luppov 1970: 116).

Besides the translations listed in Table 3, there is another text that has sometimes been referred to as a Belorussian translation of Stryjkowski and will therefore be discussed in Section 3.2.6, even though this attribution is incorrect.

---

[23] Cf. also Prozorovskij (1879: 56–60), who was the first to define this as a translation of Stryjkowski's chronicle in his catalog of the *Sobranie Archeologičeskogo obščestva*.

[24] «Матвѣя Стриковского, въ бѣлой кожѣ, по обрѣзу прыскомъ (и 191 Марта въ 19 день сію книгу Великого Государя Царя и Великого Князя Петра Алексѣевича въ хоромы принялъ околничей Тихонъ Микитичъ Стрѣшневъ)» (Zabelin 1915: 604).

3.2.1 The translation of 1668–70

The first Russian translation was made during the years 1668–70. To begin with, only a part of the chronicle was translated, namely the part that the Russians were supposedly most interested in, i.e. chapters IV: 1–3. They concern the origin of the peoples of the world, particularly the Slavs, and the early history of Kievan Rus'. As already mentioned, this translation has not survived as an independent work, but was included in manuscripts together with later translations, cf. Section 3.2.4 (Rogov 1966: 269–270).

The date 1668 is found in the heading to chapter IV: 1 (RGADA f. 181, no. 59, fol. 127r),[25] and the date 1670 in a passage in chapter IV: 3:

> и отъ лѣта .ѻ҃в. [72][26] до ннѣшнягѡ ., а҃хо. [1670] уже е҃сть ., а҃фчи. [1598] лѣтъ (RGADA 59, fol. 155r)

In this translation, Stryjkowski's name is omitted from the chapter headings, and the comments he made in the Polish original on what he had seen during his travels and the places he had visited were left out. Rogov (1966: 269–271) sees this as an attempt to disguise the fact that he was the author and give him the status of a source among others.

For instance, when describing the weapons hanging on the walls of Adrianople, Stryjkowski refers to his own experience, but this is omitted in the translation:

(1) A ty wszystki dźiwne woienne Instrumenta są záwieszone ná murze […] u wielkiey bramy/ **ktorymem sie ia dobrze przypátrzył.** (Stryjkowski 1582: 88)

a тѣ всѣ дивныя военные орудия повѣшены суть на стене [...] у великои башни (RGADA 59, fol. 129v)

A similar example is found in the beginning of IV: 2, when discussing the origin of the Slavs:

(2) własnymi dziedźicámi Paflagonskiey Ziemie z stárodawnych wiekow być sie powiádáią/ **o czymem ia też sam z niemi miał częste rozmowy/ Roku 1574. gdym tám był w tych kráinach.** (Stryjkowski 1582: 94)

истинными наслѣдники поѳлягонскои земли изъ древнихъ лѣтъ повѣдаются быти (RGADA 59, fol. 137r)

---

[25] Hereafter, for the sake of brevity, called RGADA 59.
[26] In quotes such as this, where numbers are of particular importance, the corresponding Arabic numerals are given in square brackets.

The words left out in example (2) are missing in the 1673–79 translation as well (example (70)), even though there, Stryjkowski was acknowledged as being the author (cf. also Section 5.3.2).

The following is yet another example:

(3)   s stárey Kroniki Moskiewskiey/ **ktorey ia też Exemplarz mam/** opissuie. (Stryjkowski 1582: 128)

во ѡписаниı старого лѣтописца московского ѡписует (RGADA 59, fol. 172v)

In many cases, anything that defines Russians as "them" and the Polish as "us" has been reversed or changed. For example, expressions such as "iák Ruś pisze" have often been left out (e.g. Stryjkowski 1582: 123, cf. RGADA 59, fol. 167r) or altered, so that "ktorego dźiś Ruś używa" (Stryjkowski 1582: 141) turns into «коего мы н̄нѣ россияне употребляемъ» (RGADA 59, fol. 185v), and when Stryjkowski uses expressions such as "naszy polskie," the word "naszy" has often been left out in the translation.

In chapter IV: 2, Stryjkowski quoted the beginning of different passages from Ovid's *Epistulae ex Ponto* and then wrote his own translation of larger parts of the same verses (cf. also Section 5.3.1): two lines in Latin followed by eight in Polish, then two in Latin and twelve in Polish, two in Latin and four in Polish. In the 1668–70 translation, both the Latin and the Polish text have been translated, but with these introductions to the Polish verses, respectively:

Матвеı же Стриковскиı Полскими вещи пишетъ сице (RGADA 59, fol. 148v)

А Стриковскиı сицѣ пишет, (RGADA 59, fol. 148v)

Стриковскиı, (RGADA 59, fol. 149r)

Thus, the only time Stryjkowski's name is mentioned, it gives the impression that he was the translator of the poems from Latin into Polish rather than the author of the whole chronicle. At this time, a translation was often regarded as a separate work by a separate author, so this way of treating translated texts was not considered as deceiving the reader (cf. Nikolaev 1989: 29).

The manuscripts in which this translation is included are listed in Section 3.7.2.

3.2.2   The translation of 1673–79

Shortly after this first, partial translation, the whole chronicle was translated. Rogov (1966: 278) dated this translation to approximately 1673–79. The date 1673 comes from the same passage in chapter IV: 3 of the text that helped date the 1668–70 translation:

и от лѣта .ов̃. [72] до н̃нешняго ҂а҃хог.г̃ [1673] есть ҂а҃х. [1600] с лишком̃ лѣтъ (Slav 26, fol. 186r)

The date 1679 is found in one of the manuscripts, RNB Ėrm. 551, which in itself is a late manuscript, but with a title page (vol. I, fol.₁ 1r) which pronounces it to be a copy of a manuscript from 1679 (cf. Section 3.5.3). It is true that the same title page also claims that the Polish original was printed in 1580, not 1582, so the information might not be entirely trustworthy.

J. E. Šustova (2008: 15–18) refutes Rogov's reasoning and instead dates the translation to 1672–73. The earlier date is based on documents that mention the binding of a Polish chronicle in November of 1672 (cf. Section 5.1). She believes that this refers to the Polish original of Stryjkowski's chronicle that was bound in preparation for translation. Assuming that the text referred to is the *Kronika*, which we do not know for sure, it was bound so late in the year that we cannot be certain that the translation work actually began in the same year.

As for the translation being completed in 1673, Šustova believes that no more than a year was needed for the translation of the chronicle, considering the speed with which books were translated at *Posol'skij prikaz*. This assumption cannot be proved for certain, since too little is known about the time needed for such tasks. For instance, there may have been translations of high and low priority. In any case, she claims, the translation was probably finished before the death of Aleksej Michajlovič in 1676, or else his death would in some way have been mentioned in the note in Slav 26, fol. 5r (cf. Section 3.6.2). However, she assumes that the note was written in connection with the completion of the translation, whereas it was actually made by Johan Gabriel Sparwenfeld, the Swede who received the manuscript as a gift in 1685, and was therefore added long after Aleksej Michajlovič's death anyway.

A weighty argument against Šustova's dating of the translation (and at the same time an argument in favor of the assumption that several translators took part in the work) is that Stepan Čižinskij, who was involved in translating the *Kronika*, did not start working as a translator until 1678 (cf. Section 3.3.2). Therefore, I will use the date suggested by Rogov, which also has the advantage of being the one most widely used by other scholars, which minimizes the risk for misunderstandings.

This is the translation I am primarily concerned with, and the 12 manuscripts belonging to it are described and discussed in Section 3.5.

3.2.3   The translation of 1682

In 1682, the Russian historian Andrej Lyzlov made a translation of I: 2, the beginning of II: 1 and IV: 1–3 (except the end of IV: 3), i.e., IV: 1–3 were translated a third time. Chapter I: 2 is about the division of the earth between the sons of Noah after the flood, and about the peoples that originated from them and their sons. As a whole, the text translated by Lyzlov explained the origin not only of the Slavs, but of other peoples as well. Perhaps he meant in this way to emphasize the position of the Slavs as a part of world history. These parts of the *Kronika* interested him as a sort of introduction or pre-history to later Muscovite chronicles. At the end of his translation, he suggested the *Stepennaja kniga* as further reading (Das 1986: 345–347).

Lyzlov was especially interested in the Slavic peoples' struggle against the Crimean and Ottoman enemy, and this interest was expressed in his translation. The Polish text was accurately rendered, but Lyzlov supplied it with marginal notes that gave the story a Muscovite bias. He especially elaborated on everything that concerned Noah's son Japhet and his sixth son Meshech, who was seen as the forefather of the Slavic peoples (cf. Section 2.4). In his marginal notes, he emphasized the link between biblical past and 17th-century Muscovy through Meshech. He did not, however, stress the connection between Hazarmaveth and the Sarmatians, who by that time had become synonymous with the Poles rather than with all Slavs. Stryjkowski used Rus' and Moscow to signify two different entities, but in Lyzlov's translation – unlike the other ones – Rus' was turned into Rossija, which was more or less the same thing as Muscovy, and thereby Moscow's role in Russia's early history was strengthened, as opposed to Kiev (Das 1986: 346–349).

Lyzlov's translation is preserved in some of the manuscripts belonging to the so-called Kurbskij Collection (*Sbornik Kurbskogo*), cf. Section 3.7.1.

3.2.4   The translation of 1688

There are a number of manuscripts with the year 1688 on the title page that contain a Russian translation of the chronicle (and some without this date, but containing the same translation). Rogov (1966: 280–285) lists nine manuscripts belonging to this translation, one of which perished in 1812. Nikolaev (2008: 102) mentions yet another manuscript.

However, this was not an entirely new translation. As mentioned above (cf. Section 3.2.1), the translation from 1668–70, i.e. IV: 1–3, was incorporated into it. Furthermore, Rogov (1966: 290) put forth the idea that other parts of the 1688 translation were only an edition of the one from 1673–79, and not a separate translation.[27] My comparisons show that the two translations differ mainly in books I–III. From book V onwards, some parts seem to be direct copies from the translation of 1673–79, and some parts are slightly altered. This is only a preliminary conclusion, however, and one of Rogov's text examples, from the very end of book XXV, shows a great difference between the two translations (Rogov 1966: 290). This study does not attempt to solve the question of the relationship between the two translations, but one may safely say that only parts of the chronicle were translated anew in 1688 – perhaps only the first three books.

The manuscripts in which this translation is found are listed in Section 3.7.2.

3.2.5 Two Ukrainian manuscripts

Most scholars have concentrated on these Russian translations, but there are also two manuscripts that have been defined as containing a Ukrainian translation.

One of these manuscripts is kept in the Kiev National Library (NBUV) under the call number f. 1, no. 57487, previously Laz. 48 (Ul'janovs'kyj & Jakovenko 1993: 6; Toločko 1996: 159), although it has also been referred to as VIII 106m/Laz. 52 (SUM 1: 44). Ul'janovs'kyj and Jakovenko (1993: 6–9) explain that the translation of Stryjkowski's chronicle takes up the first 660 folios of a total of 675. The remaining folios contain a Kievan Chronicle (*Kyivs'kyj litopysec'*) from 1618. The scholars have described the manuscript thoroughly and accounted for its history. Among other things, they identified several different watermarks that they dated to the first half of the 17th century. Based on the layout of the text as well as on the degree to which Latin quotes and marginal notes were translated, they reached the conclusion that the text was translated by several people. Toločko (1996: 159–167), who dated the manuscript to some time between 1608 and 1622, studied insertions in the text, made by one of the translators, and traced them to the *Sofijskaja pervaja letopis'* or a chronicle similar to it. This manuscript is used as source material for the Ukrainian historical dictionary, SUM.

The other manuscript is RGADA f. 181, no. 365, which belonged to Petr Mohyla, as is seen from a note in his handwriting. Fols. 1–27 of this manuscript are said to contain excerpts from the Ukrainian translation of the *Kronika*, and have a watermark dated by Ul'janovs'kyj and Jakovenko (1993: 10–11) to 1614–15. The text corresponds to book I of the Polish text, except for the last few phrases. It is written in *poluustav* with initials and occasional marginal notes written in, seemingly, red ink (I have only seen the manu-

---

[27] «[П]еревод 1688 г. производился в какой-то мере с учетом перевода 1673–79 гг., вероятно, даже в отдельных местах редактировался, а не переводился заново».

script in a microfilm copy). In this manuscript, all parts originally written in Latin have been left out, usually with a space in the text, perhaps so that some other person could fill in those parts later, which, however, was not done.

After comparing the manuscripts, Toločko (1996: 167–168), came to the conclusion that they belong to the same translation, although there are minor differences between them. I have not seen the NBUV manuscript, but judging by the articles by Toločko and Ul'janovs'kyj and Jakovenko, I do not, in any case, believe that the text in the RGADA manuscript is a copy of that in the NBUV manuscript. One reason for this is that Ul'janovs'kyj and Jakovenko (1993: 8) claim that Latin quotes are translated faithfully in the first folios of the NBUV manuscript, whereas they, as mentioned, are left out of the RGADA manuscript. There would be no reason to leave blank spaces instead of copying text that had already been translated; it is more probable that a translator who did not master Latin omitted the quotes. There are also some cases where the RGADA manuscript is closer to the Polish text than the NBUV manuscript is, at least if Toločko's transcription of it is to be trusted.

A comparison of these manuscripts with each other and of the Ukrainian translation with one or all of the Russian translations is a project for the future.

3.2.6   The Ukrainian Chronograph

The manuscript RNB F.IV.688 has sometimes been called a West-Russian (Sobolevskij 1903: 80; Ptašickij 1905)[28] or Belorussian translation (Avanesaŭ 1961: 387) of Stryjkowski's chronicle. Therefore, it will be discussed among the translations of the *Kronika* even though it is in fact a copy of the Ukrainian Chronograph (Knjaz'kov 1984). Rogov expressed himself rather contradictorily about this manuscript, once speaking of it as a reworked edition (*pererabotka*) of Stryjkowski's *Kronika*, incorporated into the chronicle of Leontij Bobolinskij (Rogov 1966: 17), once calling it *Slavjanorusskaja krojnika* and saying that it used Stryjkowski as a source (Rogov 1966: 295–297). The latter definition is closest to that expressed by Knjaz'kov.

As a matter of fact, as Toločko (1996: 169–175) shows, the source of this *Ukrainskij chronograf* was not the Polish original of Stryjkowski's chronicle, but the Ukrainian translation, which he bases on the fact that the insertions from other chronicles are found in this text as well. This was also stated by Knjaz'kov (1984: 23, 93, 149).

---

[28] Ptašickij (1905: 381) admitted that it was a translation «с небольшими видоизменениями и сокращениями».

The text in RNB F.IV.688 is divided into two parts, which have been considered to be translations of Bielski's and Stryjkowski's chronicles, respectively. Knjaz'kov (1984: 9–10) instead calls the first part the general part of the chronograph (*obščeistoričeskaja čast'*) and the second the *Slavjano-russkaja krojnika*. The first part is based on Bielski's chronicle and Caesar Baronius' *Annales Ecclesiastici* to almost equal shares (Knjaz'kov 1984: 90). The second part can be divided into a Russian, a Lithuanian and a Polish section. According to Knjaz'kov (1984: 96), 70% of the material in the Russian section is taken from Stryjkowski, and the Lithuanian section is also largely based on his *Kronika* (Knjaz'kov 1984: 116–117), whereas the Polish section relies mainly on Guagnini (Knjaz'kov 1984: 121–122).

Ptašickij (1905: 381) also mentioned RNB F.IV.342 in a footnote as belonging to the "West-Russian translation." RNB F.IV.342, however, is a collection of 18th-century copies of documents from tsar Fëdor Ivanovič's reign. Perhaps Ptašickij was referring to the manuscript RNB F.IV.372, which is a fragment of another copy of the Ukrainian chronograph (PSRL XXXII 5–6; Knjaz'kov 1984: 45).

Although the Ukrainian Chronograph exists in other manuscripts as well (cf. Knjaz'kov 1984: 216–217), only these two have been mentioned in connection with Stryjkowski.

Avanesaŭ (1961: 387) claims that the "Belorussian translation" was made in the first half of the 17th century. Knjaz'kov dates the compilation of the chronograph to some time after 1625 but not later than the early 1630s, judging by the sources used and the watermarks of the earliest manuscript (Knjaz'kov 1984: 32, 61), and dates the manuscript RNB F.IV.688 to the 1670s (Knjaz'kov 1984: 37, 81).

Excerpts from the manuscript RNB F.IV.688 have been published by Avanesaŭ in a textbook of the history of the Belorussian language, where the text is presented as a translation of Stryjkowski's chronicle (cf. Section 1.2). It is used as source material for the Belorussian historical dictionary HSBM. Knjaz'kov (1984: 156), however, characterizes the language as Ukrainian. Leeming (1968: 284) uses Avanesaŭ's edition in his study of polonisms in Ruthenian. Facsimiles of pages from this manuscript can be found in Avanesaŭ (1961: 392) and Knjaz'kov (1984: 232).

3.3 The translators

We do not know the names of all the translators involved in the different translations of the chronicle. All the translations are anonymous, except for the 1682 translation, which was made by Andrej Lyzlov. With the help of archival documents, one name can be connected with the 1673–79 translation, namely that of Stepan Čižinskij.

3.3.1 Andrej Lyzlov

Andrej Ivanovič Lyzlov was born in a noble family in Moscow in the 1650s or 1660s. He participated in several military campaigns during the 1670s–1690s (Das 1992: 502–503; SKK 1993: 305–306). He was a well-educated man, and beside his military duties, he translated a number of texts: the aforementioned parts of Stryjkowski's chronicle, possibly the sections of Alexander Guagnini's *Sarmatiae Europeae Descriptio* that appear in the Kurbskij Collection along with his translation of Stryjkowski, and Szymon Starowolski's *Dwór cesarza tureckiego i rezydencja jego w Konstantyno-polu,* originally printed in 1646 (SKK 1993: 306; Nikolaev 2008: 98–100). He also wrote a historical work of his own, called *Skifskaja istorija* (Lyzlov 1990), which was strongly influenced by Stryjkowski and in which he quoted extensive passages from the *Kronika,* as well as his own translation of *Dwór cesarza tureckiego*, which he included as a final chapter in his book (Čistjakova 1963: 351–354).

In E. M. Isserlin's comparison of the lexical properties of six translations of *Dwór cesarza tureckiego* (cf. also Section 3.3.2), she found Lyzlov's translation to be written in an archaic manner, with a tendency to use abstract words where the others preferred a more concrete wording, to use general expressions instead of specific terminology, and to use one polysemic Russian word for several Polish – more specific – ones (Isserlin 1961: 16–19).

It is sometimes said that Lyzlov introduced to Russian history writing the practice of presenting historical material in parts and chapters, with marginal notes and a table of contents, which he had learned from the Polish sources he used – among them Stryjkowski (Das 1992: 504).

His translation of Stryjkowski's chronicle is discussed in Section 3.2.3.

3.3.2 Stepan Čižinskij

In November 1681, Stepan Čižinskij, a translator at *Posol'skij prikaz* and *Malorossijskij prikaz*, asked for a pay raise because he translated books "day and night and at home."[29] His request was granted because of the large number of books he had translated – among them Stryjkowski.[30] It seems to have been common among translators to take work home (Rogožin 2003: 56–57).

---

[29] «Работаю я холоп твои тебѣ великому гдрю в посолском и малоросиꙵском приказех денно и нощно да и на дому твои великого гдря кнги безпрестанно перевожу» (RGADA f. 138, op. 1, no. 20, l. 418; cf. also Lukičev 2004: 339–340).

[30] «Кнгу о лунѣ с латинскаго на рускоꙵ перевел Стриковского и Баронѣуша переводил же а ннѣ твоя великого гдря на латинском языке дана перевесть на рускоꙵ что о всяких звѣрех» (RGADA f. 138, op. 1, no. 20, l. 418).

Stepan Čižinskij was from the county (*powiat*) of L'viv and came to Moscow in 1675 (Lukičev 2004: 337). He soon became active in the first court theater, which had been founded in 1672. He was in charge of the theater until it was closed down after the death of Aleksej Michajlovič in January of 1676 (Kudrjavcev 1963: 238–239; SKK 2004: 229–232). During that time, four plays were staged, two at the end of 1675 and two in January of 1676, but only two of the four plays have been preserved. Čižinskij is sometimes said to have been the author of these plays, and in any case he was responsible for staging them. Since the main figures at the theater before him, notably the priest Johann Gottfried Gregorii (SKK 1992: 226–229) and the teacher Georg Hübner (SKK 1992: 203–204), had been Germans, some scholars claim that with Čižinskij, the repertoire of the court theater changed from translated plays to original Russian ones (*Istorija russkogo dramatičeskogo teatra* 1977: 71–72). However, the question of the authorship of the plays is disputed, and the language in which they were written has yet to be established.

After the closing of the court theater, Čižinskij was employed at *Posol'skij prikaz* as a translator from Polish and Latin (Kudrjavcev 1963: 238–239; SKK 2004: 229–232). He was employed there from February 1st, 1678 (RGADA f. 138, op. 1, no. 20, l. 385). As already mentioned, he also worked for *Malorossijskij prikaz*.

Besides Stryjkowski's chronicle, he also translated for example Johannes Hevelius' *Selenographia: sive, lunæ descriptio* (which he called книга о лунѣ in his request, cf. note 30) from an edition printed in 1647 (Sobolevskij 1903: 147–148; Nikolaev 2008: 56),[31] Szymon Starowolski's *Dwór cesarza tureckiego* (Sobolevskij 1903: 90–92; Nikolaev 2008: 97–98), Caesar Baronius' *Annales Ecclesiastici* (Баронѣушъ in the request from 1681, which may be the year of the translation, cf. note 30) from the Latin original from 1607 (Sobolevskij 1903: 83–86; Nikolaev 2008: 158), and several other texts. Čižinskij died in 1709 (Kudrjavcev 1963: 238–239; SKK 2004: 229–232).

The translation of Stryjkowski that he worked on must have been the one from 1673–79, since he had not yet come to Moscow when the first translation was made, in 1668–70, and the documents concerning his pay raise are from 1681, i.e. before 1688, when the next anonymous translation was made. His participation also helps to verify the latter date of the 1673–79 translation, since he only began working as a translator in 1678 (cf. also Section 3.2.2). Furthermore, it is an argument in favor of the hypothesis that the text was translated by several people (cf. Chapter 6), since he was not yet em-

---

[31] The lexical properties of the translation have been studied in Sablina & Sacharovskaja (1982).

ployed at *Posol'skij prikaz* in 1673, when the translation work had already begun.

Isserlin stated, in her comparison of the lexical properties of six translations of *Dwór cesarza tureckiego* (cf. Section 3.3.1), that Čižinskij's translation is characterized by great attention to correct Church Slavonic orthography and lexicon, without being unusually archaic. Despite this attempt to maintain a bookish language, he used numerous concrete words and terms, well known from Russian everyday life (Isserlin 1961: 23–24).

In archival documents, Stryjkowski's chronicle and Hevelius' *Selenographia* often occur together, but there is slightly more information to be found about the latter. Both books are mentioned in a document from October 1681 concerning payment for the bookbinder Ostafij Fëdorov (cf. Section 3.2). There it is said that the *книга о лунѣ* was brought to the tsar, but there is no such indication regarding the chronicle (RGADA f. 159, op. 1, no. 825, ll. 47–50). The *pod'jačij* Andrej Ivanov received payment for having written the fair copy of the *книга о лунѣ* alone (ll. 41–43), but we do not know the names of the scribes who wrote the chronicle. In the description of Fëdor Alekseevič's library, also mentioned in Section 3.2, the chronicle is once again found alongside a *книга о лунѣ*.[32]

3.4 The edition: choice of chapters

After this introduction of the different translations, the choice of text for the edition should be explained.

The chapters IV: 1–3 were the first to be translated into Russian and were translated more times than any other part. That makes it fair to assume that this was also the part that was the most interesting for the educated strata of the Russian society, as well as the most widely spread. This is why these chapters have been chosen as the main object of study.

That particular section exists in three Russian versions: the 1668–70 translation, the 1673–79 translation and the 1682 translation, found in the Kurbskij Collection. The choice fell on the 1673–79 version for several reasons.

First of all, it exists in slightly more copies than the others, which might imply that it was more widely spread than the others. Also, as Rogov (1966: 276–277) points out, it seems to have been the officially sanctioned translation, since a copy of it was made especially for Catherine II when she studied Russian history.

---

[32] «О лунѣ и о всѣхъ планетахъ небесныхъ» (Zabelin 1915: 604).

Rogov (1966: 291–292) also suggests that a copy of the 1673–79 translation (BAN 31.4.32) was later prepared for printing, which I, however, wish to argue against (cf. Section 3.6.1).

Moreover, since one aim of this study is to compare different parts of the chronicle, this translation is better suited, since it was, as far as we know, a whole new translation, whereas the manuscripts dated 1688 are a patchwork of old and new parts. Comparing, for instance, books I, IV and VIII of the so-called 1688 translation would actually mean comparing parts translated in 1688, 1668–70, and 1673–79, respectively, which would not suit the purpose of the study.

3.5 The manuscripts of the translation of 1673–79

The 1673–79 translation is in focus for this study. As has already been mentioned, it exists in eleven copies, one of which has been split between two libraries, for which reason there are twelve manuscripts. They can be divided into three different groups based on similarities in the text. Because I needed to study the chapters IV: 1–3 closely in preparation for the edition, the comparison between the manuscripts has been conducted mainly on these chapters. The manuscripts are listed in Table 4, which contains references to sections where they are discussed in more detail.

Table 4. Manuscripts belonging to the 1673–79 translation

Group	No.	Sigla	Library	Call number	Section
1	1	B	BAN	31.4.32	3.5.1, 3.6.1, 3.6.4
	2	G	GIM	Muzejskoe sobranie, no. 1391	3.5.1, 3.6.4
	3		RNB	F.IV.103	3.5.1, 3.6.3, 3.6.4
	4		RNB	F.IV.131	3.5.1, 3.6.3, 3.6.4
	5		JaGPU	B-596	3.5.1
2	6	U	UUB	Slav 26–28	3.5.2, 3.6.2
	7	E	RGB	Egorovskoe sobranie, f. 98, no. 243	3.5.2
	8	R	RGADA	f. 181, no. 58	3.5.2
	9		CGIA SPb	58922	3.5.2
	10		RNB	F.IV.172	3.5.2
3	11	N	RNB	Ėrmitažnoe sobranie, no. 551/1–2	3.5.3
	12		RNB	Pogodinskoe sobranie, no. 1759	3.5.3

The following short characteristic of the manuscripts is partly based on existing descriptions (with Rogov as a starting point), partly on my own observations. The emphasis is on information that is relevant to dating the manuscripts and setting them in relation to each other, as well as the facts on which the choice of manuscripts for the edition has been based. Other information, not found in existing descriptions, is in some cases also included.

For different reasons, I have not been able to study the watermarks of all the manuscripts, and have therefore had to rely on Rogov in many cases. There are, however, several problems with his information about watermarks. To begin with, he often gives countermarks and other letter symbols in the Cyrillic alphabet, even when they are actually in the Latin alphabet, e.g. ДМ instead of DM. More seriously, he sometimes gives inaccurate references to watermark albums, e.g. he describes a watermark as having the countermark CA, but his reference is to a watermark with the countermark CAS, or he describes a Seven Provinces watermark but refers to a watermark with the Amsterdam coat-of-arms. It is of course impossible to know, without turning to the manuscripts for verification, if the descriptions or the references are correct in these cases. Last but not least, he expresses himself very briefly when dating watermarks, which gives the impression that a certain watermark can be dated to a precise year or interval of years, when the correct way to express this would be that the watermark in question has been found in a book or document from that year. If the watermarks are similar but not identical, the dating is of course even more uncertain, and even more so if the countermarks are incorrectly deciphered, as there is reason to believe here. Despite these problems, I have included Rogov's dates below, but have in most cases refrained from repeating his descriptions of the watermarks.

Whenever I have had the opportunity of studying the watermarks myself and made new findings or drawn new conclusions, this information is naturally included in the descriptions of the manuscripts.

3.5.1 Group 1

1. BAN 31.4.32
This is a manuscript in two volumes, written in late 17th-century *skoropis'* in several different hands. Volume I contains books I–XI (except the end), volume II contains books XI (the end) –XXV.

The watermarks were dated by Rogov (1966: 277) to 1676 and 1697, but according to the library's own description, the watermarks in 31.4.32 are only *similar* to the ones found in the albums.[33] Most importantly, the watermark with the double-headed eagle, said to resemble Tromonin's watermark no. 1349 from 1697 (Tromonin 1965: XCIV), is actually more similar to the watermarks no. 1027 and 1028 from GIM's catalog of watermarks. These

---

[33] The expressions used are for example «того же типа, как», «сходен с», «имеет сходство с» (*Opisanie* 1959: 40–41).

are from 1679 and 1677, respectively (*Filigrani XVII veka* 1988: 199). The difference is obvious: Tromonin's eagle has its wings spread out, whereas the eagle in the BAN manuscript, and in GIM's catalog, has the tips of the wings turned down.

A watermark not mentioned in Rogov's or the library's descriptions is the five-pointed Foolscap with the countermark PORE in an oval. This corresponds to no. 353 in GIM's catalog, from 1675 (*Filigrani XVII veka* 1988: 101).

Although precise dating with the help of watermarks is very difficult, the signs point to the end of the 1670s. If the translation is correctly dated, this manuscript may be from the very last years of that decade and is probably the earliest of the extant manuscripts. It will be discussed in more detail in Section 3.6.1.

The text contains many changes and corrections in two different hands, and its wording after the changes corresponds to that in the other manuscripts. Parts of volume I are foliated with Cyrillic alphabetic numerals (cf. Section 3.6.4).

The manuscript has been described in the library's series *Opisanie Rukopisnogo otdela BAN* (*Opisanie* 1959: 40–41).

In the critical apparatus and in the text, this manuscript will hereafter be called B.

2. GIM Muzejskoe sobranie, no. 1391

The manuscript is written in late 17th-century *skoropis'* in several different hands. Rogov (1966: 274) identified watermarks from 1676–82, 1684 (with an incorrect reference to Tromonin (1965)) and 1708 (with a reference to Klepikov (1958)). Nikolaev (2008: 101) dates the manuscript to the 1680s. A few pages in the beginning are missing. On fol. 1r, the text begins:

> ибо внегда тиї высокоумствующе (яко Кенсорин,
> и Корнилиї Агриппа в книгѣ о суетѣ свѣденей въ
> .н͠а.и гл͠вѣ свидѣте́лствуетъ)

This passage is found on fol. 7v of UUB Slav 26 (cf. no. 6 below), which is the verso of the second folio of text, since the text in that manuscript begins on fol. 6r (cf. Section 3.6.2). This leads one to believe that 1–2 folios are missing in the beginning of the GIM manuscript.

Some marginal notes are added in another, perhaps later, hand (hand G6, cf. Section 8.3.2). They do not correspond to marginal notes in the Polish original, although they are sometimes found in similar places. Some of these marginal notes have correspondences in the manuscript JaGPU B-596 (cf. no. 5 below).

As can be seen in the edition, this manuscript has much in common with ms. B and is probably a copy of it. This is confirmed by numbers in the margin, corresponding to the foliation in volume I of ms. B (cf. Section 3.6.4). It is included in the edition to show the development of the text in this group of manuscripts.

In the critical apparatus and in the text, this manuscript will hereafter be called G.

3. RNB F.IV.103

The manuscript is written in late 17th-century *skoropis'* in several different hands. Rogov (1966: 276) identified one watermark that he dated to 1691–1712, but his reference to Klepikov (1959) is inaccurate, and this date is of little use. The manuscript has been described by Stroev (1825: 106).

Many variants found in ms. G can also be found in this manuscript, and it is very closely related to RNB F.IV.131 (cf. Section 3.6.3). It is not included in the critical apparatus, since this group of manuscripts is represented by mss. B and G, from which it derives.

4. RNB F.IV.131

This manuscript is written in late 17th-century *skoropis'* in several different hands. Rogov (1966: 275–276) found one watermark that he identified with one from 1697 in Geraklitov (1963).

It has many readings in common with ms. G, and it is very closely related to RNB F.IV.103 (cf. Section 3.6.3). It is not included in the critical apparatus, since this group is represented by the manuscripts B and G.

5. JaGPU B-596[34]

This is a manuscript in quarto from 1819. It is written on light blue paper, possibly in one single hand. Each of the chronicle's books is bound separately, but the first one is missing, thus leaving 24 books (vol. II–XXV). Each book is paginated, starting anew from 1. A note at the end of vol. XXV says:

Кончено 17 Октября, 1819 года во Сельцѣ Игрищахъ[35]

There are marginal notes, some of which are very similar to the ones in ms. G. Others are not, but occur in approximately the same places as the ones in ms. G. Some marginal notes in this ms. do not have correspondences in ms. G, and and some found in ms. G are missing here.

---

[34] This is the call number given by Luk'janov (1955: 470) and Nikolaev (2008: 103). The number could also be read as B-5961, but the library does not seem to use this number in its records at all.

[35] Igrišči is located south of Jaroslavl', in the province of Ivanovo.

Below are examples of cases where the marginal notes are so similar that it is unlikely that they have been written independently of each other.

Ms. G	JaGPU B-596, vol. IV
Болгары приемлютъ законъ греческиї Премѣна князей их̂ (fol. 121v)	Болгары прїемлютъ законъ Греческїй и премѣна Князей ихъ (p. 64)
Свѣтыї Иеронимъ далмацкиї Кирилъ и Меѳодиї (fol. 122r)	Святый Їеронимъ Далматскїй Кириллъ и Мефодїй (p. 67)
Творение Овидїия Назона (fol. 127r)	Творенїе Овидїя-Назона (p. 87)
М8жество Прок8ло (fol. 128v)	Мужество Прокулово (p. 95)
Ор8жие сарматов (fol. 129v)	Оружїе Сарматовъ (p. 98)
О произведениї р8совъ, или россиянъ (fol. 132r)	О произведенїи Руссовъ, или Россїанъ (p. 108)

Below are a few cases where the marginal notes are found in corresponding places and are similar, but may have been formulated independently of each other.

Ms. G	JaGPU B-596, vol. IV
Константинопо́лский ц̃рь К8рополатъ присла славѧно́ письмена (fol. 108r)	Первыя письмена у Славянъ даннья имъ Греческимъ Царемъ Михаиломъ Куропполатомъ (p. 8)
Начало писmenъ полскихъ (fol. 108v)	Первыя письмена Поляковъ (p. 10)
Ѡр8жїе древних̂ (fol. 109r)	Воинскїя орудїя древнихъ (p. 13)
Древность языка московскаго (fol. 131r)	Древность языка Славянскаго (p. 103)
Осколдъ и Диръ въ Киевѣ Ихъ осада на Ц̃рьгр̃дъ (fol. 141v)	Княженїе Оскольда и Дира въ Кїевѣ Походъ ихъ въ Грецїю и осада Царя-Града (p. 145)
Возвратъ къ Киев8 (fol. 143r)	Возвращенїе Олегово въ Кїевъ (p. 151)

If the JaGPU manuscript is a copy of ms. G, the 19th-century scribe may have recognized that the marginal notes were written in another hand and that they did not belong to the text, so that he felt free to copy some, alter others, leave some out altogether and add some notes of his own. In some cases the notes in the JaGPU manuscript are more substantial, in other cases they are simply phrased differently. As was mentioned above, the marginal notes do not coincide with the ones in the Polish original, i.e. neither scribe translated the Polish marginal notes directly.

Rogov was not aware of the existence of this manuscript, and Nikolaev listed it without having been able to establish which translation it belongs to. It has not been included in the critical apparatus because this group is already represented by two manuscripts.

It has been summarily described by Luk'janov (1955).

3.5.2 Group 2

6. UUB Slav 26–28

This manuscript, written in late 17th-century *skoropis'* in several different hands, consists of three volumes: Slav 26 contains books I–VII, Slav 27 books VIII–XVI, Slav 28 books XVII–XXV. It was a gift to Johan Gabriel Sparwenfeld in 1685 and is described in Nikolaj Glubokovskij's handwritten Russian catalog (Glubokovskij 1918), translated into French by Alexandre de Roubetz (Glubokovskij 1919). It is also discussed in an article about the library's Slavic manuscripts (Davidsson 1975: 71–75), which contains a facsimile of Slav 26, fol. 260r.

The manuscript is described in more detail in Section 3.6.2. This is the main manuscript in the edition, and it will hereafter be called U.

7. RGB Egorovskoe sobranie, f. 98, no. 243

The manuscript is written in late 17th-century *skoropis'* in several different hands. Headings, initials in paragraphs and, in some places, marginal notes are written in red ink. It is foliated in pencil by a modern hand from 1 to 519, but a mistake has been made in the foliation: after fol. 141, the next folio has been numbered 132, and from there the foliation goes on until the end, so that there are actually 529 folios.

Rogov mentions only one watermark: the Amsterdam coat-of-arms, without countermark, and does not date it (Rogov 1966: 275). There are some isolated quires (with the numbers 4, 20 and 21) of lighter and slightly thicker paper with the watermark Seven Provinces without countermark. The letters under the coat-of-arms could possibly be read *&I* (cursive), which would correspond to Klepikov's no 1145, found in a printed book from 1696 (Klepikov 1959: 85). There is a *skrepa* in the manuscript mentioning *Игнатъева с[ы]на Шапкина*.

The order of the chapters seems to have been confused towards the end, possibly in the same way as Rogov observed in RGADA f. 181, no 58 (cf. no. 8 below). The books XXIV and XXV seem, in any case, to be missing. The last words on fol. 519v are the following:

> [...] уст8
> пилъ с литовским воискомъ *от* поляко*в* хитро постави*в* пре*ж*де
> в таины*х* мѣста*х* пѣши*х* ратмистро*в* в [...]

The last few words are hidden under a paper patch.

The manuscript might be a copy of ms. U. The text has much in common with RGADA f. 181, no. 58, which was possibly copied from it.

In the critical apparatus and in the text, this manuscript will hereafter be called E.

8. RGADA f. 181, no. 58

The manuscript is written in late 17th-century *skoropis'* in several different hands. Headings and initials in paragraphs are written in red ink. Rogov (1966: 274–275) identified a watermark which he dated to 1708, but his reference to Klepikov (1959) is inaccurate and the date of little use. The manuscript contains a note from 1707. Nikolaev (2008: 101) dates it to the early 18th century. The order of parts of the text has been confused from book XXII onwards (Rogov 1966: 274–275).

Certain details in the text relate it to mss. U and E, of which it might be a copy. In the critical apparatus and in the text, this manuscript will hereafter be called R.

9. CGIA SPb, library, inventory no. 58922

This manuscript is written in 18th-century *skoropis'*, probably in one single hand. It contains books I–X of the chronicle, although the beginning of I: 1 and the end of X: 6 are missing. Rogov (1966: 277) identified two watermarks: the Amsterdam coat-of-arms with the countermark CA, from 1730 (with an inaccurate reference to Klepikov (1959)), and the Jaroslavl' coat-of-arms, from 1750. I did not find either of these, but instead identified the Amsterdam coat-of-arms with the countermark LVG, similar to Churchill's no. 29, which he dated to 1693 (Churchill 1935: 67), although I have not been able to establish if the watermarks are identical. A scrap of paper in the binding contains the date 1738. The manuscript bears the stamp of the Moscow Archeological Society, which also owned other manuscripts that now belong to this archive (Rogov 1966: 277). There are a few pencilled notes in the text, one of which contains the date 1857, and some changes, made in ink, also in a later hand.

It has been summarily described by Malevanov (1957: 575).

There are some differences between the text in this manuscript and that found in mss. E and R, and it does not seem to derive from them, but forms another branch of this group. It is probably not a direct copy of ms. U, which was brought to Sweden long before this copy was made.

It forms a unity with the manuscript RNB F.IV.172 (cf. below). I have not viewed the manuscripts side by side, since they are kept in two different libraries, but the text portions included in the two manuscripts match, the hand is similar, possibly the same, and quire numbering is continuous throughout the two manuscripts. They do not, however, have any water-marks in common.

10. RNB F.IV.172[36]

The manuscript is written in 18th-century *skoropis'*, probably in one single hand. Rogov (1966: 276) identified two watermarks: the Amsterdam coat-of-arms with the countermark H, from 1720, and with the countermark HK, from 1733, but his references to Klepikov (1958) are inaccurate and at least one of them should instead be to Klepikov (1959). The manuscript contains only the second half of the text, from book XI onwards.

This manuscript forms a unity with the manuscript CGIA SPb no. 58922. The assignment of the text to group 2 has been confirmed by a comparison of chapter XXIV: 3 and half of chapter XXIV: 4 of RNB F.IV.172 with mss. U, B and N (cf. no. 11 below), as the best representatives of the three groups.

The manuscript has been described by Stroev (1825: 157).

3.5.3 Group 3

11. RNB Ėrmitažnoe sobranie, no. 551/1–2

This is a manuscript in two volumes, written in 18th-century *skoropis'*. Rogov (1966: 276–277) identified one watermark, which he dated to 1786, but his reference to Klepikov (1959) is inaccurate. The binding and the index in vol. I suggest that it was made for Catherine II.

As mentioned in Section 3.2.2, the title page of this manuscript is used to date the translation. The text found there is as follows:

> Кроника королевства полскаго великаго княжества литовскаго, русскаго, прусскаго жмудскаго и гд̂рства московскаго, чрезъ Матѳея Стриковскаго Осостовича каноника полскаго на польскомъ языкѣ изданная въ 1580м̂ году и напечатана въ Краковѣ переведена на славенской съ котораго перевода списана въ Москвѣ ҂зрп҃з.го [7187=1678/79] года (vol. I, fol.₁ 1r)[37]

The title page is followed by an index of the books and chapters of the chronicle (vol. I, fol.₁ 2r–19v).

After this, the chronicle begins, and the foliation starts anew with fol. 1. The beginning of the text is slightly modernized. To illustrate this, a sample is given below alongside the corresponding text from ms. U. Relevant differences are set apart in boldface, although there are, as can easily be seen,

---

[36] According to Nikolaev (2008: 101) erroneously RNB F.IV.171.
[37] The title page and index have one foliation and the text itself another, which is here expressed by fol.₁ and fol.₂.

other differences as well. These differences cease after a few folios and are not found in other parts of the text.

Ms. U, Slav 26, fol. 6r	Ms. N, vol. I, fol.₂ 1
О созданїи мира нео*б*ходимагꙍ, земли, н҃ба, и началовъ вещей: **аж***е* на нихъ с҃ть различны **бах**҃, читателю любезный, мнѣнїя, и доводы философовъ и творцевъ еллинскихъ, **инїи** бо **бях**҃ **иже** *от* пропасти [corr. *chao*]³⁸, се есть *от* смѣшенїя веще*и* и стихїи мир҃ сотворен҃ быти **повѣствовах**҃: о се*м* и Овидїи въ .а҃.х книгахъ метамо*р*фосеос, се есть преображе-нїя приводитъ сими **словесы**	О созданїи мира неба и земли, и о началѣ вещей, **что есть** на нихъ различные **были** читателю любезный, мнѣнїя и доводы филозофовъ и творцовъ еллинскихъ, **нѣкоторые** отъ бездны или отъ смешенїя вещей и стихїй мїру сотворѣну быть **повѣствовали**, какъ о томъ и Овидїй въ 1*й* книгѣ метаморфозеосъ (преображенїя) приводитъ сими **словами**:

The manuscript has been described together with the rest of the *Ėrmitažnoe sobranie* (Al'šic 1968: 52).

In the critical apparatus and in the text, this manuscript will be called N.

12. RNB Pogodinskoe sobranie, no. 1759

This manuscript is written in 18th-century *skoropis'*. Rogov (1966: 277) identified one watermark, similar to watermarks from 1754 or 1762–63, but his reference to Klepikov (1959) is inaccurate. The text is very closely related to that in ms. N, but is less carefully written and contains more mistakes. It is therefore not included in the critical apparatus.

3.6 Manuscripts of special interest

Some of the manuscripts listed above deserve special attention for one reason or another. There are also certain points of interest that arise when comparing two or more of these manuscripts.

3.6.1 BAN 31.4.32 (ms. B)

The manuscript BAN 31.4.32 attracted Rogov's attention because of the numerous changes in its text. He interpreted them as an editor's notes in preparation for printing, but I wish to suggest that these changes were made

---

³⁸ This correction has been made by Sparwenfeld.

in connection with the process of translation. There are no known documents that speak of plans to print the *Kronika*, and indeed it would be unusual to choose to print a secular text such as this. The interpretation of the changes as part of the translation work is strengthened by a comparison with other manuscripts, as will be explained below.

Volume I of ms. B is in part foliated with Cyrillic numerals, probably contemporary to the writing of the manuscript (hereafter called the old foliation). A later foliation (the new foliation), probably the library's, includes five empty folios before the text starts, so these numbers (on every tenth folio) differ by five folios from the old foliation. There is a gap in the old foliation, and when the scribe began foliating again, a mistake was made, so that after the gap, the old and new foliation differ only by one folio. Volume II only has the new foliation, beginning again from 1.

In the following, I use the new foliation, but the old foliation plays an important part when determining certain manuscripts' relations to each other (cf. Section 3.6.4). Table 5 shows the relation between the new and old foliation.

Table 5. Foliation in BAN 31.4.32, volume I

New foliation	Old foliation
fols. 6–184	fols. 1–179
fols. 185–192	(no foliation)
fols. 193–205	fols. 192–204

The quires are also numbered, both in Cyrillic and Arabic numerals. Quire 25 (vol. I, fol. 185)[39] bears the numbers .к͞е. и .к͞ѕ. and *25*, and after that the Cyrillic and Arabic quire numbers, when present, differ by one throughout the volume. This quire probably contains the text from two quires in the exemplar from which the copy was made. In volume II, the Cyrillic numeration of quires is continued, but the Arabic numeration begins over again – for instance, we find the numbers .о͞в. [72] together with (probably) *2* (vol. II, fol. 11r).

The text is full of corrections and changes, which Rogov claims to be made in a hand of the early 18th century. Actually, however, changes are made in two different hands: in volume I of the manuscript and sporadically in volume II, they are made in a hand similar and probably contemporary to that of the original text (cf. Illustration 7). It may even be the same hand, but this is difficult to determine. In volume II of the manuscript, many of the changes and especially marginal notes are made in a different, more careless hand (cf. Illustration 8). It is probably also contemporary to the original text,

---

[39] In this section, all manuscript references, unless otherwise stated, are to ms. B.

since it has many superscript letters, characteristic of 17th-century *skoropis'*, and more importantly, since the marginal notes added in this hand are also found in other manuscripts. The changes are more frequent in some parts of the text, but continue throughout.

After the changes, the text corresponds to that of the other manuscripts. This gives the impression of the manuscript being a draft of some sort, which was then corrected before the text was considered to be finished and copies were made. Rogov apparently did not notice that the text in ms. B (before the changes) differs from the other manuscripts. He mentioned that dedications were crossed out (Rogov 1966: 291), but did not reflect on the fact that the other manuscripts do not contain any dedications.

Some remnants of the text as it was before these changes were made can nevertheless be found in other manuscripts. In ms. N, the beginning of chapter XII: 3 is similar to what we find in ms. B before the corrections, and in one ms. belonging to the 1688 translation, Ėrm. 551b, fols. 1–2 contain the beginning of I: 1 as it was in ms. B before the changes were made, but the text then continues in another hand and according to another translation.

Since the changes are so numerous, it is difficult to systematize them and cover them all here. The examples given below are only a small selection, and this manuscript would deserve to be the object of a separate study. The changes concern many different aspects of the text: orthography, morphology, lexicon and syntax, as well as layout. Below are some examples from different parts of the text. In the examples, the parts that have been changed are set in bold face, both before and after the changes. If nothing is set in bold face, it means that the whole example was subject to change (this can apply to single words, such as in example (9), or whole phrases, such as in example (27)). The corresponding expression in the Polish original is in each case provided for comparison.

In some cases, the new letters or words have simply been written on top of the old ones, sometimes the old ones have been crossed out and the new ones added between the lines. These different ways of making changes have not been distinguished here.

Orthographical changes include the correction of misspelled words or names:

(4)   кир**п**елские → кир**ж**елские (vol. I, fol. 165v), Polish: *Kirkielscy* (Stryjkowski 1582: 97)

(5)   Гелес**то**нтом → Гелес**по**нтом (vol. I, fol. 167r), Polish: *Helespontem* (Stryjkowski 1582: 98)

(6) касте л͠лянъ → каштелянъ (vol. II, fol. 9r), Polish: *Castellan* (Stryjkowski 1582: 414[40])

(7) примѣр → Кромѣр (vol. II, fol. 162r), Polish: *Cromer* (Stryjkowski 1582: 502)

There are numerous lexical changes, some of which are also corrections of mistakes:

(8) которая посемъ **одна** бысть в с8пр8жество → которая посемъ **отдана** бысть в с8пр8жество (vol. II, fol. 32r), Polish: *ktora byłá potym wydána w małżeństwo* (Stryjkowski 1582: 427)

In some cases, a word has been replaced by a more or less synonymous one:

(9) зракъ → образ (vol. I, fol. 7r), Latin: *forma* (Stryjkowski 1582: 1)

(10) свѣта → мира (vol. I, fol. 12r), Polish: *Swiátá* (Stryjkowski 1582: 3)

(11) по **правдѣ** → по **истиннѣ** (vol. I, fol. 12r), Polish: *słusznie* (Stryjkowski 1582: 3)

(12) вскоре → абїе (vol. I, fol. 325v), Polish: *wnet* (Stryjkowski 1582: 243)

(13) злоречения → х8л8 (vol. I, fol. 398r), Polish: *bluźnierstwá* (Stryjkowski 1582: 312) (cf. also example (27))

(14) ω кор8нованиї **повторлемой** → ω кор8нованиї **с8г8бом** (vol. I, fol. 413v), Polish: *O Koronáciey dwoiakiey* (Stryjkowski 1582: 330)[41]

Rogov (1966: 291) suggests that these changes may be due to a modernization of the text:

> Некоторые архаические выражения в списке заменены более новыми: «зрак» на «образ» (т. I, л. 7), «потопы» на «наводнения» (т. I, л. 15), «послушные» на «подданные» (т. II, л. 78) и т. п.

I am not convinced that this is the case, since morphology and syntax have not been systematically modernized in the same way, and because it is difficult to judge the connotations of a word for a 17th-century reader. However, I have not tried to resolve this question.

---

[40] The page number is erroneously printed as 314.
[41] This is also a correction of morphology: while Polish *koronácia* is feminine and requires a feminine ending on the adjective, Russian *корунование* is neuter.

Some lexical changes seem to be a matter of avoiding polonisms, since the crossed-out word is closer to the Polish original. Such changes are discussed more closely in Section 5.4.1.1, dealing with lexical polonisms.

(15) от прирождения → естеством (vol. I, fol. 11r), Polish: *s przyrodzenia* (Stryjkowski 1582: 3) (cf. also examples (28) and (97))

(16) твердях8 → гл҃юще (vol. I, fol. 12r), Polish: *twierdzili* (Stryjkowski 1582: 3) (cf. also example (99))

(17) великои **удѣлности** → великои **храбрости** (vol. I, fol. 413v), Polish: *dzielnośći* (Stryjkowski 1582: 330) (cf. also example (100))

(18) **заведения** и пог8бления → **отдачи** и пог8бления (vol. I, fol. 415v), Polish: *záwiedzenia/ y utrácenia* (Stryjkowski 1582: 331) (cf. also example (101))

(19) от крыжаковъ **заложеные** → от крыжаковъ **8строенные** (vol. I, fol. 416v), Polish: *od Krzyżakow záłożone* (Stryjkowski 1582: 332) (cf. also example (102))

In some cases, the translation is more similar to the Polish original after the change:

(20) взятые кн҃зьства р8ские в **предѣлы в 8ѣзды** обратилъ → взятые кн҃зьства р8ские в **повѣты** обратилъ (vol. II, fol. 37r), Polish: *Ruskie Xięstwá podbite w powiáty obroćił* (Stryjkowski 1582: 429)

(21) татарове ж без **супротив̑ления** с великими л8пы 8шли → татарове ж без **отпору** с великими л8пы 8шли (vol. II, fol. 557r), Polish: *á Tátarowie z wielkimi łupy uszli bez odporu* (Stryjkowski 1582: 775)

As for morphological changes, there are some cases of mistakes being corrected, such as case endings of nouns being altered and adjectives or verbs being brought into agreement with their corresponding nouns (cf. also examples (14), (30) and (36)):

(22) мнози н҃ши предки дьянии темномрачн**ыхъ** ночью уд8шенныхъ → мнози н҃ши предки дьянии темномрачн**ою** ночью уд8шенныхъ (vol. I, fol. 149r), Polish: *wiele nászych przodkow dzieiow ćiemnomglistą nocą záduszonych* (Stryjkowski 1582: 87)

(23) от людеи с оч**и**ї ящерчьи → от людеи с оч**мї** ящерчьи (vol. I, fol. 159v), Polish: *od ludźi z Iászczorcimi oczymá* (Stryjkowski 1582: 93)

(24) о [...] князях [...] волынско**и** → о [...] князях [...] волынск**их** (vol. I, fol. 184r), Polish: *O* [...] *Xiążętach* [...] *Wołynskich* (Stryjkowski 1582: 110)

The syntactic changes are of various kinds and affect the text to different degrees. Sometimes, prepositions have been added, crossed out or changed:

(25) **со** отчаяния → **от** отчаяния (vol. I, fol. 150v), Polish: *z desperaciey* (Stryjkowski 1582: 88)

(26) в лѣтописи **в** княжства москѡв҃ского → в лѣтописи княжства москѡв҃ского (vol. I, fol. 153v), Latin: *in Chorographia principatus Moschouiae* (Stryjkowski 1582: 90)

(27) злоречения над Литвою → х8л8 Литвѣ (vol. I, fol. 398r), Polish: *bluźnierstwá nád Litwą* (Stryjkowski 1582: 362) (cf. also example (13))

Sometimes the verbal tense has been changed, a main clause altered into a participle construction or vice versa. It should be noted that there are examples of a seemingly more archaic construction being changed into a more modern one, as well as of the opposite:

(28) Каинъ же **бысть от прирождения** золъ → Каинъ же **сый естеством** золъ (vol. I, fol. 11r), Polish: *A Cain iż był s przyrodzenia zły* (Stryjkowski 1582: 3) (cf. also examples (15) and (97))

(29) Каинъ **ж** в то время при**їде** на мѣт8 → Каину в то время при**шедш8** на мѣт8 (vol. I, fol. 12r), Polish: *á Kain w ten czás tráfił sie ná cel* (Stryjkowski 1582: 3)

(30) Каиновы же с҃нове [...] изобрѣ**ло** → Каиновы же с҃нове [...] изобрѣ**тоша** (vol. I, fol. 12v), Polish: *Kainowi záś Synowie* [...] *wynáleźli* (Stryjkowski 1582: 3)[42]

(31) которые уж в то время к Полше сл8ж**ах8** → которые уж в то время к Полше сл8ж**или** (vol. I, fol. 317v), Polish: *ktore iusz ná ten czás ku Polszcze służyły* (Stryjkowski 1582: 233)[43]

(32) вся грады над рекою С8лою пойма**ша** → вся грады над рекою С8лою пойма**ли** (vol. I, fol. 319r), Polish: *wszystki zamki nád Rzeką Sulą pobráli* (Stryjkowski 1582: 235)

---

[42] This is also a case of morphological correction, from the neuter singular to the correct plural form.

[43] The construction *служити къ* + *dat* is not found in SRJa, but a corresponding construction for Polish is exemplified in SSP.

(33) гсдртвовал͠ и повелѣвал͠ → гсдртвова и повелѣва (vol. I, fol. 414v),
Polish: *pánował y roskázował* (Stryjkowski 1582: 330)

Some of these cases may also have to do with avoiding polonisms, when a
word-by-word translation has been changed into a freer one:

(34) **еже имѣло быти** яко тако есть → **бывшее** яко тако есть (vol. I,
fol. 160v), Polish: *Co musiáło być isz ták iest* (Stryjkowski 1582: 94)

Sometimes a word or a part of a word had originally been inserted in the
wrong place in the text, but the change restored the correct order:

(35) **Анастасию** Софию *ли* → **Аннатазию или** Софию (vol. I, fol.
154r), Polish: *Annotazią/ álbo Zophią* (Stryjkowski 1582: 91)

(36) еп͠скпъ еѵглие, или новыї завѣтъ вверже во огнь, великиï,
невреди, яже в цѣлости [...] **быша** → еп͠скпъ еѵглие, или новыї
завѣтъ вверже во огнь, великиï, **еже** в цѣлости **и невредимо** [...]
пребысть (vol. I, fol. 220v), Polish: *Biskup księgi Ewangeliey álbo No-
wego Testamentu wrzućił w ogień wielki/ ktore namniey nienáruszone w
cále* [...] *zostáły* (Stryjkowski 1582: 142)[44]

(37) римляне **м8ла Квирина** Кастора и Полюꙁа, Зевесака, Вебру
Трясявицу, Арисарь → римляне Кастора и Полюꙁа, Зевеса,
Ѳарт8ну Ѳевр8 или Трясавицу, Ариса **Ромула, и Квирина, и**
проч̃ (vol. I, fol. 223r), Polish: *Rzymiánie Castora y Poluxá/ Jowiszá/
Fortunę/ Febrę álbo Trząscę/ Marsá/ Romulusá/ y Quirinusá etć.*
(Stryjkowski 1582: 145)

In example (35), both readings are possible, but given the Polish original, the
translator had almost certainly intended to use *или*.

Misplacements such as these may indicate that the manuscript is a copy of
an obscure exemplar, where these words were written between the lines or in
the margins and were inserted in the wrong place when the copy was made.
The manuscript from which it was copied, in that case, is not known.

The contents of the manuscript are also affected. The most obvious case is
the question of the dedications. As seen in Section 2.3.2, Stryjkowski dedicated many chapters in his chronicle to different patrons. Judging by this
manuscript, some of them were translated into Russian but later considered
unnecessary and crossed out. Chapters with crossed-out dedications are IV: 4
(vol. I, fol. 222r), VI: 1 (vol. I, fol. 304v), VI: 8 (vol. I, fol. 331r), VI: 10
(vol. I, fol. 340r), VII: 1 (vol. I, fol. 371v), X: 1 (vol. I, fol. 463v) etc. The

---

[44] Note that this correction also changes two words (one reflexive pronoun and one verb) with
plural reference to the singular. The Polish *księgi Ewangeliey* is plural, but the Russian *eѵ︣глие*
is singular.

other manuscripts belonging to this translation do not contain these dedications.

In volume II, the second correcting hand has added marginal notes in many places, of which the ones below are just a few examples. These marginal notes are found in the other manuscripts as well.

(38) крижаки во*и*ну Ли*т*вѣ и поляко*м* сказали (vol. II, fol. 183v)

(39) татары з Ли*т*вою язы*ч*еска*м* обычае*м* разаряю*т* (vol. II, fol. 187v)

(40) Корибута паки прося*т* чехи на короле*в̃*ство (vol. II, fol. 229v)

In the example below, a comment, which was not present in the Polish original, has been added and then crossed out:

(41) но **[яко гл̃е̃тъ ауто*р* сеа книга]** а*з* [...] → но а*з* [...] (vol. I, fol. 167r)

Finally, some changes concern the format of the text, its layout. The word *отставка* is found in several places, of which at least some (vol. I, fol. 220v; vol. II, fol. 33r) correspond to paragraph breaks in other manuscripts (I have not compared all instances to the other manuscripts). In vol. II, fol. 559r, there is the note *страницы бѣлои не оставливат*, after which fols. 559r–559v are left blank.

These notes seem to be instructions for a scribe copying the manuscript: not to leave a blank page, to make a paragraph break etc. Rogov interpreted them as intructions for a printer, but the other facts discussed above make this less probable.

At the bottom of the first page of some quires, someone – probably the person who made the changes – has written *чтена* (vol. I, fol. 93r; vol. I, fol. 101r), as a sign that the text had been read and corrected.

3.6.2 UUB Slav 26–28 (ms. U)

The three-volume manuscript UUB Slav 26–28 has several traits that are missing in the other manuscripts of the 1673–79 translation.

Slav 26, fol. 1r (cf. Illustration 1) contains a note on the provenance of the manuscript, written in J. G. Sparwenfeld's hand:

> Сїею книгою меня пожаловал
> бояри*н̃* и казанскїи воевода
> князъ Ива*н̃* Иванови*ч̃* Голици*н̃* болшо*и*
> Лоб Москвѣ лѣта *ѡт* воплощенїя
> Б̃га слова ҂а҃х̃пе в ї҃юня м̃це.
> Їѡан*н̃* Гаври*л̃* Спа*р*венфелд*т*

Since this note reveals that Sparwenfeld, who spent the years 1684–87 in Russia, received the manuscript in June of 1685 as a gift from the boyar and *voevoda* Ivan Ivanovič Golicyn the elder, it must have been written before that date.

Prince I. I. Golicyn, with the nickname Lob, was promoted from *stol'nik* to boyar on April 19th 1685 (Crummey 1983: 207), or, according to another source, on March 19th of that year (Golicyn 1892: 122). He became a *voevoda* in Kazan' in 1685 (Golicyn 1892: 122) and died on June 8th 1686 (Crummey 1983: 207) or on September 9th 1686 (Golicyn 1892: 122) in Kazan'.

Golicyn is mentioned several times in the diary Sparwenfeld kept during his years in Russia (Birgegård 2002: 169, 179, 183, 189 etc.) and the two men seem to have been fairly well acquainted. It is not known where Golicyn got hold of the chronicle. In the description of Fëdor Alekseevič's library, an Ivan Ivanovič Golicyn is mentioned as having brought books to him,[45] but it is not known if it was Ivan Ivanovič the elder or the younger, who was also a *stol'nik* at that time (Golicyn 1892: 122).

Fol. 2r of Slav 26 (cf. Illustration 2) contains a copy of the first page of the Polish edition, also written in Sparwenfeld's hand. It differs in two ways from the title page of the printed original. In the manuscript, the title begins *KRONIKA Sarmatska, Polska, Litewska*, i.e., the word *Sarmatska* has been added. The rest of the title page is faithfully copied, including the information about the printing of the Polish original, *Drukowano w Krolewcu u Gerzego Osterbergera MDLXXXII*, after which Sparwenfeld has added *Po slawensku perewedena w Moskwe*.

Fol. 2v contains a copy of Stryjkowski's list of sources, also written by Sparwenfeld. Instead of the Polish heading (*Historikowie y Autorowie rozmáići z rożnych Bibliotek...*), he has written *AUCTORES Quibus usus est auctor*.

The list is copied faithfully, except for the fact that the names of the biblical prophets *Esajasz* and *Ezechiel* have been left out. Also, Sparwenfeld often uses the Latin versions of names where Stryjkowski uses the Polish ones or abbreviates the names in a different way. One can also notice that some of the sources are written slightly larger and more distinctly, namely *Olaus Magnus* and *Swedskie kroniki*, testifying to Sparwenfeld's interest in Stryjkowski's Swedish sources.

Fol. 3r contains copies of dedications. It begins with one paragraph of a dedication to the three brothers Jerzy, Szymon and Aleksander Olelkowicz,

---

[45] E.g. «и 192 году Октября въ 30-й день сію книгу одну къ Великому Государю въ хоромы принялъ столникъ князь Иванъ княжъ Ивановъ сынъ Голицынъ» (Zabelin 1915: 599).

found on page X6v in the printed original (cf. Sections 2.3 and 2.3.2). Thereupon follows a Latin dedication, copied from page XX7v in the original, where it also has a Polish translation. The Polish version is left out by Sparwenfeld.

Fol. 3v contains another Latin dedication, which is found on page XX8r in the original. It also has a Polish translation there, but only the Latin version is copied into Slav 26.

Next, also beginning on fol. 3v, there is a copy of the Latin introduction to chapter II: 1 (cf. Stryjkowski 1582: 21–23), which is, as mentioned in Section 2.3.2.1, a dedication to Melchior Giedrojć. Some minor parts are left out in the copy. It ends on fol. 4r. The dedication is left out from the Russian translation of II: 1.

Fol. 5r (cf. Illustration 3) contains a translation into Russian of the title page, written in a calligraphic *poluustav* by an unidentified hand. It is a complete translation of the Polish title page, and here also, just as on the copy of the Polish title page, the title begins *КРОНИКА САРМАТСКАЯ*. At the bottom, Sparwenfeld has added that it was translated

вь поссолскомъ приказѣ, егоже роздныхъ
перевощиковъ власные руки здѣ
обретаются, которые сами сїю
славную кнїгу перевели
по указу цря Алексея
Михаиловичя

The text of the chronicle itself begins on fol. 6r.

This leads to the conclusion that Sparwenfeld had access to the Polish original and that he knew something about where it had been translated and perhaps by whom. We will return to his statement about several translators later (cf. Chapter 6). The addition of the word *Sarmatska* is enigmatic, but probably means that the scribe was familiar with Sarmatism (cf. Section 2.4) and recognized the chronicle as related to that ideology (cf. Myl'nikov 1996: 106). The word was probably added in the Polish original, from which the Polish title page was copied and the Russian one translated. Since the Polish title page was copied by Sparwenfeld and the Russian one written by a professional scribe, it seems improbable that they would both have added it independently of each other. It is likely that Sparwenfeld's notes about the circumstances of the translation were added at the time he heard them, which means that the two title pages were probably written in Moscow.

There are several different watermarks in Slav 26–28. The first two of these are by far the most frequent throughout the three volumes:

1) Amsterdam coat-of-arms with the letters LL/B underneath (B written beneath LL) and with the countermark CATINAVD (?).

2) Foolscap, 7 points, type IV (Klepikov 1963: 408–410) with the letters *AI* in italics underneath, without countermark. Cf. no. 894 in Klepikov (1959: 76; 1963: 419), found in a document from 1682 and a printed book from 1697, and no. 322 in Dianova (1997: 76), found in books from 1678, 1679 and 1680.
3) Foolscap, 7 points, type IV (Klepikov 1963: 408–410) without countermark.
4) Foolscap, 7 points, type IV (Klepikov 1963: 408–410) with the countermark PM. Cf. no. 2645 in Laucevičius (1967b: 366), from 1664–65 (Laucevičius 1967a: 211).
5) Foolscap, 5 points, type I (Klepikov 1963: 408–410) with the countermark PCH written in an oval. Cf. no. 1287 in Klepikov (1959: 91), found in a document from 1682, also listed as no. 218 in Klepikov (1963: 437) with additional reference to a document from 1687.
6) Foolscap, 7 points, type IV (Klepikov 1963: 408–410) with the letters *AI* in italics underneath, with the countermark IV.[46] Cf. no. 11 in Klepikov (1963: 419), found in documents from 1677–79.
7) Amsterdam coat-of-arms without countermark.

The manuscript was donated to Uppsala University Library in 1721, and in connection with this, Sparwenfeld listed all the manuscripts that were part of the donation. His description of Slav 26–28 (which is listed as no. 111) has the following wording:

> NB Mathei Stricowski Chronica Slavorum omnium, &c &c &c Cod. mss, ex cancellaria Russica, pereleganter exscriptam et tribus tomis distractam [?] in folio ipsum Tsaris Theodori Alexeievici autographum, unicum in toto regno Moscovitico (Bibl. Ark. K 52:3).

Tsar Fëdor Alekseevič died in 1682, two years before Sparwenfeld came to Moscow, so the origin of the information that the tsar's handwriting is found in the manuscript is not clear. It is difficult to imagine the tsar fulfilling the duties of a scribe, and moreover, Fëdor Alekseevič was, according to Sedov (2006: 183), not a skilled scribe, which is evident from the strained handwriting in two letters from the tsar to Sil'vestr Medvedev, written in 1682 (RGADA f. 5, op. 1, no. 1). Fëdor Alekseevič's hand as represented by those letters is not found anywhere in ms. U.

The library's description of the donation does not contain this information; it reads as follows:

---

[46] IV stands for Jean Villedary, a French paper-maker who was active from 1668 and made paper for, among others, the Dutch factor Abraham Janssen, who usually placed his initials AI beneath the main watermark in his paper (Churchill 1935: 21–27).

Matthiae Strijkowski Chronicon Sarmaticum Lingua et literis Slaveno-Russicis voll. III. Mscr. nitidissimum (Bibl. Ark. A 7).

3.6.3 The relationship between RNB F.IV.103 and F.IV.131

The manuscripts RNB F.IV.103 and RNB F.IV.131 have been left out of the critical apparatus, since they descend from mss. B and G, which are better representatives of that group of manuscripts. Nevertheless, they have some interesting features that deserve comment.

A comparison of these manuscripts with the others shows clearly that they are closely related to each other and to ms. G. This can be seen in numerous places, where words have been left out or distorted in all three manuscripts. The relationship is confirmed by the existence of numbers in the margins that are connected to the foliation of ms. B (cf. Section 3.6.4). The question of whether they are both independent copies of ms. G or if one is a copy of the other is less easily resolved. In some places, RNB F.IV.103 and F.IV.131 differ from G but coincide with each other. This would seem to speak for one being a copy of the other. Such instances are: *кроники писати начаша писати* (F.IV.103 and F.IV.131, fol. 109r) instead of *кроники писати начаша* (GIM Muz. 1391, fol. 108r; cf. Slav 26, fol. 151r), *родиша* (F.IV.103, fol. 130r; F.IV.131, fol. 131r) instead of *родися* (GIM Muz. 1391, fol. 129r; cf. Slav 26, fol. 180r), *устроши* (F.IV.103, fol. 130v; F.IV.131, fol. 131v) instead of *устраши* (GIM Muz. 1391, fol. 129v; cf. Slav 26, fol. 181v), *зумныхъ* (F.IV.103, fol. 135r; F.IV.131, fol. 136r) instead of *разумныхъ* (GIM Muz. 1391, fol. 134r; cf. Slav 26, fol. 187r) and many more. In several of these instances, however, ms. G bears signs of changes or corrections, so that it may originally also have had the readings found in the other two mss.

In one place, there is a sign of F.IV.103 being copied from F.IV.131. On fol. 185r, something has smudged the text in F.IV.131. In F.IV.103, the scribe has left blank spaces where the smudges are in the other manuscript. This particular part, then, was copied from F.IV.131 to F.IV.103, since the scribe would not have left blank spaces if he had had another exemplar to verify the text by.

However, in an earlier part of the text, approximately in the folios 108–120, where there are different hands in the two manuscripts, the scribe of F.IV.131 has made very many mistakes in spelling, confusing *a* and *o*, *e/ѣ* and *u/ï* more than is usual in the other manuscripts, to such an extent, and often in such a way (in names etc.), that it is not likely that a scribe could reconstruct all the correct readings while copying. Examples of this are: *Дровою и Совою* (F.IV.131, fol. 118v) instead of *Дравою и Савою* (F.IV.103, fol. 117v; cf. Slav 26, fol. 163r), *органаутов* (F.IV.131, fol. 119r) instead of *аргонаутов* (F.IV.103, fol. 118r; cf. Slav 26, fol. 164r), *болгоры или волгоры* (F.IV.131, fol. 120v) instead of *болгары или волгары*

80

(F.IV.103, fol. 119v; cf. Slav 26, fol. 166v). Therefore, in this part of the manuscripts, F.IV.103 can hardly have been copied from F.IV.131, but possibly the other way around. However, the numbers in the margins, explained in the following section, make it more likely that they were both independent copies of ms. G in this part.

A page-by-page comparison of the manuscripts from a codicological and paleographical point of view reveals that similarities can be found here as well. For example, the scribes have gone to great lengths to make the quires begin and end with the same words in both manuscripts. The text has been stretched or compressed, sometimes in one manuscript, sometimes in the other. This suggests that they both are copies of the same exemplar with the same distribution of the text among the quires.

Even more striking is the fact that in parts of the manuscripts, notably in the beginning, the same scribes have written corresponding quires in both manuscripts. Sometimes, not only are the manuscripts written in the same handwriting, but even the flourishes are identical. This may suggest that both copies were made at the same time. It can be added that the two manuscripts do not have any watermarks in common, which may speak against this theory.

As we see, the relationship between these two manuscripts is complicated, but it is certain that they were written partly by the same scribes, probably within a short period of time, and that they interacted closely. For the reasons previously mentioned, however, they will not be included in the edition. Further study could reveal interesting paleographical information about, for instance, the variations that take place in a text copied twice by the same scribe within a short period of time, and similar questions.

3.6.4   Foliation in mss. B, G, RNB F.IV.103 and F.IV.131

As mentioned in the description of ms. B above, there is foliation (in the top right corner of the recto side of the folios) in parts of the manuscript, contemporary with the text itself. There are no other numbers in the margins (cf. Section 3.6.1).

Three other manuscripts contain numbers in the margins, also contemporary with the manuscripts themselves. In ms. G, RNB F.IV.103 and RNB F.IV.131 there are two overlapping series of numbers. They are related in the following way.

An examination of ms. G shows that it is a copy of ms. B. Ms. G has Cyrillic numbers in the margins next to the text in a large part of the manuscript. These numbers are not always in the top right corner of the folios and do not give the actual number of the folio they are on. Instead, they appear next to the same words as does the foliation in ms. B, as if they were copied from B in the belief that they were marginal notes.

When the number 148 was copied in this process, it happened to coincide with the top of fol. 111r in ms. G. This is the last folio of a quire, written by hand G1. The next quire was written by another scribe, hand G2, who evidently glanced at the last sheet of the previous quire and interpreted the number 148 as the number of the folio, since it is at the top of the page. He then continued foliating the pages (as he believed) for as long as he wrote, and the following scribe, G3, also continued with this for as long as he wrote, which was to fol. 140, which, however, he foliated as 177. Fol. 141 is again the first of a new quire, written by a new scribe, hand G4, who copied the number 192 from B but did not continue foliating what he himself wrote.

Table 6 shows the relationship between the incorrect foliation and the actual folio numbers in G.

Table 6. Foliation and marginal notes in ms. G (GIM Muz. 1391)

Actual folios	Incorrect foliation	Comment
to fol. 110	none	hand G1, "marginal notes" from B
fol. 111	fol. 148	hand G1, last folio in quire
fols. 112–140	fols. 149–177	hands G2 and G3, foliation but no "marginal notes"
fol. 141	fol. 192	hand G4, "marginal notes" from B
fols. 142–	none	hand G4, "marginal notes" from B

RNB F.IV.103 and RNB F.IV.131 are copies of ms. G. This can be seen from the fact that in these two manuscripts, the foliation series from *both* B and G have been regarded as marginal notes and copied – though with some omissions – next to the words in the text where they are found in B and G, not in the top right corners of the folios. There are different omissions in the two manuscripts, which points to them each being independent copies of G, not one of the other, in this part of the text, i.e. approximately fols. 108–123 (cf., however, the conclusions in Section 3.6.3).

3.7 The manuscripts of the other Russian translations

The Ukrainian translation is only preserved in two manuscripts, which have already been introduced in Section 3.2.5 and will not be discussed further. The remaining Russian translations, however, are preserved in more copies, which will be listed here.

3.7.1 Lyzlov's 1682 translation

Lyzlov's translation of Stryjkowski can be found in some manuscripts containing the Kurbskij Collection (*Sbornik Kurbskogo*). The core of this collection consists of letters written to Ivan IV by his former vassal Andrej Kurbskij and the tsar's answers during the period 1564–79 (SKK 1988: 496–497). As time went by, other texts were added to copies of these letters, hence the name "collection." The manuscripts are usually grouped according to the redaction of the first letter. The copies of the Kurbskij Collection containing Stryjkowski's *Kronika* all belong to the same group and can be dated from the end of the 17th to the later half of the 18th century (*Perepiska* 1979: 287–289).

There is plenty of literature dealing with Kurbskij's letters and the Kurb-skij Collection,[47] and they also contain information on the contents of the different manuscripts involved. Therefore, the manuscripts containing the translation of Stryjkowski are simply listed below in approximate chrono-logical order. The list is based on Keenan (1971: 193), *Perepiska* (1979: 283–286) and Erusalimskij (2009: 565–635).[48]

1) RNB sobranie Pogodina, no. 1494 (sobranie Stroeva, no. 18)
    Late 17th or early 18th century
2) RGADA f. 181, no. 60/82
    Late 17th century
3) GIM Uvarovskoe sobranie, no. 302
    18th century
4) RGB f. 310, sobranie Undol'skogo, no. 779
    18th century
5) GIM Uvarovskoe sobranie, no. 242/1582
    18th century
6) RGB f. 209, sobranie Ovčinnikova, no. 500
    18th century
7) NB SPbGU Otdel redkich knig i rukopisej, ms. E.IV.47
    18th century

3.7.2 The 1668–70 and 1688 translations

As explained in Section 3.2, the translation dated by its title page to 1688 actually consists of one part translated in that year, one part from 1668–70 and a large part of the 1673–79 translation, slightly reworked. The manu-scripts that contain this compilation of translations have been listed by Ro-gov (1966: 280–287) and by Nikolaev (2008: 102), whose lists have been used as a base for the one below. Information about earlier descriptions of

---

[47] *Poslanija* (1951); Keenan (1971); *Perepiska* (1979); Erusalimskij (2009), cf. also SKK (1988: 501–503).

[48] Keenan (1971: 5–6) is mainly concerned with arguing that the letters were not written by Kurbskij, but by several other persons in the 1620s or 1630s. The majority of scholars do not share this view (cf. *Perepiska* 1979: 222–224; Erusalimskij 2009: 19–63). I do not wish to enter into that discussion, but will nevertheless make use of Keenan's information about the manuscripts, as it is very clear and well arranged.

the manuscripts is, in most cases, not given here, but can be found in Rogov's and Nikolaev's works.

1) GIM Uvarovskoe sobranie, no. 4
Late 17th century

2) RGB Piskarëvskoe sobranie (f. 228), no. 171 (formerly Muzejnoe sobranie, no. 606)
Late 17th century

3) Ul'janovskij Dvorec knigi, Otdel redkich i rukopisnych knig, no. 8
Late 17th century

4) Vladimiro-Suzdal'skij istoriko-chudožestvennyj i architekturnyj muzej-zapovednik, Vladimirskoe otdelenie, no. 405
Late 17th century

5) BAN Archangel'skoe sobranie, C no. 136
Late 17th century

6) RGADA f. 181, no. 620/1130
Late 17th century

7) RGADA f. 181, no. 59/81
Early 18th century

8) RNB Ėrmitažnoe sobranie, no. 551b (1–2)
Early 18th century

9) BAN 32.11.4
Dated 1758

10) Sobranie professora Bauze (perished in 1812) (Moiseeva 1980: 334)

3.8 Chapter summary

Rogov's picture of the history of Stryjkowski's chronicle in East Slavic translations has been updated here to comprise one complete Ruthenian or Ukrainian translation (early 17th century), three partial Russian translations (1668–70, 1682 and 1688) and one complete Russian translation (1673–79). In 1688, the translations from 1668–70 and 1688 were combined with parts of the 1673–79 translation to form a translation of the whole *Kronika*.

Two translators have been identified: Andrej Lyzlov, who made the 1682 translation, and Stepan Čižinskij, who participated in the 1673–79 translation, although he cannot have been involved from the beginning, since he did not begin working at *Posol'skij prikaz* until 1678.

The 1673–79 translation was chosen as the primary object of study because it is a complete translation and not a compilation, as well as because it may have been more widely spread and held in higher esteem than the others. Chapters IV: 1–3 were singled out for the edition and closer study because their subject matter made them especially interesting for Russian readers.

84

The manuscript situation for all the translations has been sketched, with special emphasis on the 1673–79 translation. This is the first time that information on the manuscripts of all the Russian translations of Stryjkowski's chronicle, including that found in the *Sbornik Kurbskogo*, has been published in one place, alongside information about the Ukrainian translation. The alleged Belorussian translation was also discussed, but as some earlier scholars have shown, it cannot be considered an independent translation of the chronicle.

There are eleven copies of the 1673–79 translation, but twelve manuscripts, since one copy of the text has been split up into two manuscripts, kept in different libraries. The manuscripts can be divided into three groups according to the variant readings, marginal notes and other characteristics they display. Group 1 contains five manuscripts, the best of which is ms. B. Group 2 contains five manuscripts (but four copies of the text), the best of which is ms. U. Group 3 contains only two manuscripts, the best of which is ms. N. The main manuscript in the edition is ms. U, and representatives of all three groups have been selected for variant readings.

Ms. B was identified as the earliest extant manuscript. The history of the 1673–79 translation can be reconstructed as follows: the Polish original was divided between at least four translators (cf. Chapter 6), one of whom, according to archival documents, was Stepan Čižinskij. The Polish original was possibly bought and bound in 1672, and the translation may have been begun in the same year, but Čižinskij's part of the work was not done until after 1678. We do not know if the text was immediately divided between translators or if they worked on it in succession. A copy of the translation was bound in 1681.

The original draft of the translation is no longer extant. Possibly, some editorial changes were made in that original draft. Ms. B is a copy of it, and seemingly, the draft was unclear in places, which led to some mistakes in ms. B that later had to be corrected. Mss. U and N, it seems, copied the text correctly from the beginning, or else used a better copy as their exemplar. Ms. N also shows signs of the original draft in one place.

Mss. U and B are the best manuscripts, in the sense that the text in them is more complete and less corrupted than in the others. In most places, the readings in ms. B are better or equal, but in vol. I, fol. 191v, it has a lacuna of three words that are present in Slav 26, fol. 195r. For this reason, ms. B cannot be the original copy of the translation, and we must assume that there was an even earlier draft. Mss. U, B and N together give a picture of what the language of the first draft must have looked like and what the translators had in mind.

4 The language of chapters IV: 1–3

The object of study in this chapter is the text found in the edition, i.e. chapters IV: 1–3 of the translation, based on the main manuscript, ms. U. Whereas the three following chapters aim to shed light upon different aspects of the text and take into account only such features of the language as serve their respective purposes, the intention in this chapter is to describe as many aspects as possible of its morphology and syntax that may be of interest. Contexts where variation occurred, either in this text or in the language of the period in general, have been seen as especially worthy of attention. The text is set in relation to discussions about the language situation of the late 17th century, which involve such concepts as diglossia, literary language and registers. It is also compared with studies of other texts, mainly from the same period.

4.1 The language situation of the late 17th century

The nature of the language situation in pre-Petrine Russia has been the subject of some debate, and scholars disagree as to whether one can speak of a literary language (*literaturnyj jazyk*) during this period.

A. V. Issatchenko's definition of a literary language, cited here according to D. S. Worth (1975: 6), is that it is polyvalent, i.e. "accessible to all members of the given society and serving their various communicatory needs," normalized, obligatory for all members of the given society, and stylistically differentiated (cf. also Živov 1996: 14; 2009: 2). This does not refer only to the language of literature, but rather means 'standard language.'[49] Scholars of Slavic languages writing in English disagree as to which term is preferable, 'literary language' or 'standard language,' but I will use the former, which is well established in the field.

Worth (1975: 1–7) relates the opinions of many earlier scholars on the origins of the Russian literary language. According to one well-known theory, promoted by B. A. Uspenskij and others, Church Slavonic and Russian were in a situation of diglossia, which means that they were two separate

---

[49] Cf. Worth (1975: 8–9): "There was a language of literature [...] but there was no standardized literary language per se."

languages but were not perceived as such by their users. They had wholly different spheres of usage, Church Slavonic assuming the role of literary language, and Russian being the spoken language and the medium of non-bookish written texts (Uspenskij 2002: 23–32).

A modification of this is the view, supported by M. L. Remněva and others, that Church Slavonic was the only literary language in Russia before the 18th century, but that it existed in two varieties, a strict, standardized one and a less strict one that allowed some variation of Church Slavonic and East Slavic forms. Scholars of this opinion recognize that yet another norm existed, based on East Slavic and used for business and law, but unlike the two Church Slavonic varieties, it is not given the status of literary language (Kijanova 2010: 16–19).

Most convincing, however, is the theory that there was no literary language in Russia during that time at all, and that the term cannot be applied to the Russian situation before the 18th century if the criteria listed above are to be fulfilled. Worth (1975: 6–9) argues that a literary language is monocentric, i.e. it has a neutral core, and all stylistic variations are regarded in relation to this core, which is what is meant by stylistic differentiation. The language situation in Russia at this time, however, was polycentric, in the sense that there was not one single neutral norm with stylistic deviations, but several norms or conventions, depending on the type of text.

V. M. Živov, in his monograph *Jazyk i kul'tura Rossii XVIII veka* (1996), which has been translated into English with the title *Language and culture in eighteenth-century Russia* (2009), provides similar arguments, and also points out that the written language as a whole was not codified in the 17th century. Church Slavonic was described in e.g. Smotrickij's grammar, but the other language types, or registers (cf. Section 4.1.1), were not explicitly regulated, although some norms can be deduced from texts. The 16th and 17th centuries saw the appearance of some texts written in a manner not motivated by their genre, but this was only a step towards a literary language. Only in the 18th century, as the result of a conscious language policy, did some of the registers disappear or become marginalized. The language was codified and adopted some features of the former registers, filling them with stylistic connotations, which led to stylistic differentiation and the formation of a literary language (Živov 1996: 14–16).

Since much of what is to follow is hinged on the existence and use of the simplex preterites, aorist and imperfect, it should be pointed out (stating the obvious) that these were no longer in use in the spoken language by the late 17th century. Although some aorist forms, known from religious texts or prayers, could be part of the passive knowledge of Russians of that time, one may assume that only a person with experience of the written language would be able to form this tense independently. In other words, the simplex preterites were wholly a factor of the written language, and without a certain amount of experience, a scribe would not know how to apply them, which can be seen from texts where forms are used incorrectly (e.g. Živov 1995: 53–55). This study, then, concerns the written language, and does not pretend to give a picture of the spoken language of 17th-century Russia.

4.1.1 The registers

The diglossia theory is based on the parallel existence of two languages, Church Slavonic and Russian, covering different spheres of usage. Considering the great variation between texts, and especially the number of texts that present neither pure Church Slavonic nor pure vernacular Russian, it seems appropriate to distinguish between more than two such spheres of usage. A primary division into bookish and non-bookish registers (*knižnye* vs. *neknižnye registry*) can be made – the term 'register' being preferable to 'language.' The registers differed in the structuring of information and by the presence or absence of markers of bookishness (*priznaki knižnosti*). For instance, Church Slavonic, with some orthographical and morphological adaptations to East Slavic traits, but with Church Slavonic syntax, was used for biblical and liturgical texts, whereas a variety of Church Slavonic, which can be called the hybrid register (cf. Section 4.1.3), is found in other texts, for example chronicles (Živov 1996: 15, 31–32). There were also several varieties of non-bookish Russian, of which chancellery language is the one that is most relevant in this thesis (cf. Uspenskij & Živov 1983: 150–157). Inherent in the notion of registers is that the same person could express himself in different registers depending on the type of text he was creating, and even within the borders of a single text (Uspenskij & Živov 1983: 162–166; Živov 1998: 223).

Speaking of bookish and non-bookish features, rather than Church Slavonic and Russian or East Slavic ones, stresses that what was important to the scribes was not the genetic, but the functional factor, i.e., not the Church Slavonic or Russian origin of a linguistic feature, but the status associated with it (Živov 1996: 19–20). An originally East Slavic phenomenon could for instance be adopted in the Russian redaction of Church Slavonic, and Church Slavonic and East Slavic elements could be seen as stylistically equivalent and equally acceptable in written texts. Also, what was seen as a marker of bookish language depended on the characteristics of the spoken language, and therefore these markers could vary over time (Živov 1996: 26–33).

4.1.2 Mechanisms for text production

Until the 16th century, the East Slavs did not possess any dictionaries or grammars of the Church Slavonic language. The usual way for a person in medieval Russia to learn Church Slavonic was not to study it, as one would study a foreign language. Rather, he would learn to read by spelling out syllables and later by reading and memorizing passages from the Psalter and other texts. In doing this, he would compare what he had read with his native language, and his mother tongue would serve as the basis for his written language as well. Professional scribes probably received additional education, but it seems to have concerned mainly orthography, not the lexical and syntactic levels of the text. Reading texts and imitating them still probably made up most of the scribes' education. Not everyone who learned to read also learned to write according to orthographical rules (Živov 1996: 20–23; 1998: 218–220; Uspenskij 2002: 119–121). The imitation of model texts expressed itself both in the contents of a literary work and in its linguistic traits (Živov 1998: 225).

Even in the 17th century, despite the fact that by this time there were guidelines such as Smotrickij's grammar (1st ed. 1619), it seems that many scribes still mainly used texts they had read as models for what they wrote.[50] Therefore, one may assume that such models played a role even for skilled scribes when determining how to construct the text lexically, morphologically and syntactically.

There were two main mechanisms at work when a new text was being written, two ways of relating to the model texts. One was the mechanism of *conversion* (*mechanizm peresčëta*), which meant that a relationship was established between the spoken language and the written text, so that a person with active knowledge of Church Slavonic could exchange, for instance, the perfect forms of his spoken language for simplex preterites. This was useful when a wholly new thought was to be expressed, and no set phrase had been learned that could express it. The second mechanism was *text orientation* (*mechanizm orientacii na teksty*). Since people learned the written language by learning large portions of text by heart, in many situations they would find that they already knew a suitable phrase and would not need to construct a wholly new one. This could concern the sentence level, but also syntagms and probably individual forms. Both mechanisms were put to work when a new text was being written (Živov 1996: 23–25). The principle of text orientation is essential to the reasoning in Chapter 7.

It must not be supposed that the intention of a scribe was always to write in correct Church Slavonic, and that all texts that contain Russian elements were badly written. The aim was usually to convey information and to do it in a manner that corresponded as closely as possible to existing texts of the same kind (Živov 1998: 225).

---

[50] Cf. also Kijanova (2010: 285), who explains that Remnëva's school is of the same opinion in this case.

4.1.3 The hybrid register

The term "hybrid Slavonic" was coined by R. Mathiesen (1984: 47–48) to describe a mixture of Church Slavonic and vernacular elements in different proportions, not as a random conglomerate, but as a "secondary linguistic system in its own right."

Živov (1996: 25–29) links the emergence of the hybrid register to the mechanism of conversion (cf. Section 4.1.2). A scribe who mainly used the mechanism of text orientation would produce a text very similar to the biblical texts, written in Church Slavonic. However, a scribe who mainly applied conversion would produce a text that differed in some ways from Church Slavonic texts, since the conversion might sometimes fail. This is the origin of the hybrid register. Situations arose when an element in the spoken language could, in different surroundings, correspond to different elements in the written norm. The scribe would then use the two elements alternately, and variation would arise. Because of this, variation became characteristic of hybrid texts.

It can be assumed that the scribe's own linguistic background, dialect, etc. had more influence on texts that were written with the help of conversion than those that were the result of text orientation. Hybrid texts can therefore be expected to differ greatly from each other.

Eventually, as the hybrid register became the basis of a new text tradition, we must no longer assume that scribes aimed at creating standard Church Slavonic texts, and that any deviation was considered a failure. A scribe could choose to apply only some markers of bookish language, namely the ones that were best suited and would most easily set the standard of the text. The important thing was that they were used at all, not that they were used consistently. This variation between bookish and non-bookish elements makes the label "hybrid" very suitable (Živov 1996: 32–33).

One may say that the hybrid register emerged in the chronicle genre. When the first chronicles were written in Rus', there were no models for them, which means that the mechanism of text orientation could not be used. Byzantine chronicles had been translated into Slavonic and could have served as models, but they were not written in the same way – they were not annalistic – and, moreover, they were not the kind of texts that were learned by heart. This meant that the scribes had to use the conversion mechanism, which led to deviations from the Church Slavonic norm (Živov 1998: 229–230, 242).

The chronicles were based on annual notes that were then compiled and elaborated. They often contained fragments of folk tales, treaties and hagiographic texts. Therefore, the chronicle genre can in itself be said to be a "conglomerate of different genres" (Kijanova 2010: 10). The very narrative was heterogeneous, and this was accompanied by linguistic variation (Petruchin 2003: 142). Later chronicles could use earlier ones as models, so that in later chronicles, the variation was a product both of conversion and of text orientation, where earlier chronicles served as model texts. Thus, the chronicles became the origin of the hybrid register, which then spread to other types of texts and became the main register into which translations were made in the 16th and 17th centuries, when the opposition between secular and religious literature was formed (Živov 1998: 230–232).

Since the chronicles were compiled over a long period, they may reflect language development with older parts written in a more archaic language (Živov 1995: 49–50; Petruchin 2003: 15–16). Still, it must be remembered that older parts were compiled and edited, so that more modern language can appear in a section of the text dealing with very early events, and formulaic expressions from earlier sources were used when describing certain later events, so that the language of these later events can contain archaic traces (Živov 1998: 237).

Contrary to this, Uspenskij (2002: 100–101) believed that Byzantine chronicles did in fact serve as models for Russian chronicles. In his diglossia paradigm, he placed chronicles firmly in the Church Slavonic tradition, noting, however, that they often contained a certain number of Russian traits. In his view, the dominating use of the simplex preterites and other syntactic constructions qualified chronicles as Church Slavonic.

Remnëva and the scholars who follow her theory (cf. Section 4.1) believe that even though Russian forms abound in the chronicles, the scribes still perceived their language as Church Slavonic. Because the different elements of the chronicle influenced the language, the result was not pure Church Slavonic, but Church Slavonic with a less strict norm (*snižennaja norma*) (Kijanova 2010: 15–20).

I adhere to the view that chronicles represent the hybrid register. As will be shown below, the translated text under discussion here shows many traits characteristic of the hybrid register.

4.2 Description of IV: 1–3: morphology

The chapters IV: 1–3 of the 1673–79 translation are the main object of this study. The reasons for this choice have been explained in Section 3.4. The linguistic features of this portion of the chronicle will be examined more closely against the background of the language situation explained above. Because orthography and phonology vary greatly between manuscripts and scribes, investigating them would have been too extensive a task. Instead, the description will concentrate on some aspects of the morphology and syntax of the text, even though some variation between manuscripts can be seen here as well.

The study describes the language of the main manuscript, ms. U (Slav 26–28), and exact figures for the occurrences of linguistic features only refer to the situation in this manuscript, but differences between manuscripts will be commented on when relevant, and features that vary to a particularly high degree will be especially stressed. All manuscripts included as variants in the edition have been used for reference and are referred to by their sigla (cf. Table 4).

4.2.1 Verbs

4.2.1.1 The aorist

In the 17th century, the aorist and imperfect were no longer actively used, and any knowledge of them was the result of some degree of education or at least imitation of model texts. The degree of correctness in the use of these tense forms can show something about the scribe's (or, in this case, transla-tor's) background and perhaps also about the model texts he used (Živov 1995: 45).

Most of the forms found in the text have the correct person and number form (cf. however *бяше* in Section 4.2.1.4). They are also for the most part found in the etymologically correct forms, spelled according to Church Sla-vonic of Russian redaction, e.g. 3rd person plural aorist forms ending in *-ша* instead of OCS *-шѧ*. They have been checked against Nandriş (1965) and the online OCS morphology website http://rhssl1.uni-regensburg.de:8080/OCS. Some verbs show parallel aorist forms and deserve comment.

The 3rd person singular aorist of *дати* in this text is *даде*, which was an innovative form based on the present stem of the verb and replaced OCS *дастъ* or *да* (Pennington 1980: 277). The 3rd person plural, however, is the original form *даша*. Of the related prefigated verbs, some have the old aorist forms and others have innovative ones: *здати* has the aorist *зда* and *создати* becomes *созда* (three times), but *вдати* is found in the form *вдаде* (four times), *отдати* in the form *отдаде* (twice), *воздати* in the form *воздаде* and *поддатися* in the form *поддадеся*. There is no variation be-tween manuscripts in this regard.

The verb *яти* belonged to a group of verbs that in the 3rd person singular aorist could take the ending *-тъ* (Borkovskij & Kuznecov 1963: 256). Such aorist forms can for example be found in the *Stepennaja kniga* (Otten 1973: 235). This form, however, was identical to the past passive participle *ятъ*. The form *ятъ* occurs twice in the edited chapters (in all manuscripts). In the following example, the verb form corresponds to the Polish *poimany*, and I therefore consider it to be a participle:

(42) y Asbaldus Hetman Rzymski **poimány** żywo iest spalon od Bulgarow ná ofiárę (Stryjkowski 1582: 99)

и Асвалдъ воевода римскїй **атъ** и живъ созжен *от* болгаровъ на жертвȣ (Slav 26, fol. 168v)

In another instance, the Polish finite form *zgwałcił* is translated as *ят ї насилова*. I have interpreted this instance of *ятъ* as an aorist with the ending *-тъ*:

(43)   Zonę Brátá zábitego Greczkę **zgwałćił** (Stryjkowski 1582: 131)

и женȣ брата своего гречанкȣ **я т ї** насилова (Slav 26, fol. 213v)

This is the only instance of this ending, and one may assume that it was motivated by the fact that the aorist would otherwise have consisted of only one letter. Aorist forms of corresponding prefigated verbs (*взяти, прияти, пояти, подяти*) do not have the ending *-тъ*.

The 3rd person singular aorist of the verb *жити* is *живе* rather than OCS *жи*, but the prefigated verb *прижити* is found in the form *прижи* (cf. Borkovskij & Kuznecov 1963: 255–256). This applies to all manuscripts.

4.2.1.2   The l-participle
This section deals with the form of the l-participle that forms part of the perfect tense (with or without an auxiliary verb), the pluperfect and conditional constructions. The distribution of elliptic and full forms of the perfect tense will be treated separately in Sections 4.3.1.2 and 4.3.1.3.

The forms found in this text for the most part correspond to those of today's Russian past tense. Verbs with consonant stems yield forms such as *отвелъ, отвели, унесъ, клалъ, могло, могли, достигли* and *изобрели*. The forms *реклъ, обыклъ, моглъ* and *перемоглъ* differ from the state in modern Russian. According to Pennington (1980: 277), such forms betray Polish or Ruthenian influence. There is no variation between manuscripts regarding these forms.

The Polish original has vowel alternations of the type *począł/poczęli*. This is reflected in one Russian plural form, which is found in all manuscripts: *зачелись* (Slav 26, fol. 198v). In other cases, ms. U uses forms with Russian vocalism: *почали* (Slav 26, fol. 150v) and *начали* (Slav 26, fol. 202v). There are, however, variant readings with the vowel *-e-* to both these instances in other manuscripts (most notably ms. B, which has *-e-* in both cases).

The form *пренебрехъ* has been classified as a perfect form in the masculine singular, where *-хъ* is the voiceless counterpart to a fricative pronunciation of *-гъ*. Mss. ERN show the spelling with *-гъ*.

The reflexive particle in perfect forms ending in a vowel mostly has the form *-сь*, sometimes *-ся*.

4.2.1.3 The infinitive

Until the 16th century, the original infinitive endings *-ти*, *-щи/-чи* and *-сти* dominated in texts from all registers, except in everyday texts (*bytovye teksty*), even though the final vowel had begun to disappear in the spoken language several centuries earlier. In the 17th century, however, the new endings *-ть*, *-чь* and *-сть* became more frequent, and the registers began to diverge more in their usage (Živov 2004: 131–137).

There are 274 infinitive forms in the text as found in ms. U. Two of them have a superscript final *-т*, and it can therefore not be determined if this stands for *-ти* or *-ть*. Four occurrences of the form *чаять*, originally an infinitive but by this time a particle (cf. Section 5.4.2.2), are also excluded from the table below, as well as four forms of *идти* and related prefigated verbs. The remaining 264 infinitive forms are distributed as seen in Table 7.

Table 7. Infinitive endings

	-ти/-ть	*-тися/-ться+-тца*	*-щи/-чь*	*-сти́/-сть*	Total
Old forms	172	25	6	10	213
New forms	42	2+1	2	4	51
% new forms	19.6	10.7	25	28.6	19.3

The total share of new forms is 19.3%, which stays within the limits of what is common for hybrid texts: 25% or less (Živov 2004: 158). It can be observed here, as in connection with certain other hybrid texts (Živov 2004: 141, 155), that forms of the type *сѣчи*, i.e. with East Slavic consonantism but with the Church Slavonic infinitive ending, do not occur. Another typical characteristic is that reflexive verbs show the lowest share of new forms. The spelling *-тца* may have been associated with chancellery language (Živov 2004: 148–150).

Eleven forms have variant readings in one or several manuscripts. The most common variation is the occurrence of the ending *-ть* where ms. U has *-ти*, six times all in all (twice in ms. R, three times in mss. ER and once in mss. BGN). There is also variation in the reflexive endings.

As a whole, the distribution of infinitive forms in this text is similar to that in the second half of the *Mazurinskij letopisec* (Živov 2004: 140–141).

4.2.1.4 The verb *быти*

The verb *быти* differed from other verbs in OCS and Old Russian texts in that it had three paradigms of simplex preterite forms, exemplified by the 3rd person singular forms *бяше, бѣ* and *бысть*. That *бяше* was imperfect and *бысть* aorist is well known, but the character of *бѣ* is disputed. C. H. van

Schooneveld (1959: 64–69) reports on different views on this, and comes to the conclusion that *бѣ* was an imperfective aorist.[51]

The use of these forms in chapters IV: 1–3 in ms. U is as follows. There are 42 forms from the *бысть* paradigm: 19 *бысть*, 2 *быхъ* (one of which is an auxiliary verb in a conditional construction) and 21 *быша* (one of which is an auxiliary verb in the pluperfect). There is also one instance of *пребысть* and one of *пребыша*. There are 47 occurrences of *бѣ* (four of which are auxiliary verbs in the pluperfect) and two of *бѣху*. There are four instances of the *бяше* paradigm: one *бяше* and three *бяху*. The form *бяше*, however, is incorrect, since it belongs to a plural subject. In ms. B, *бяше* has been corrected to *быша*, which is also found in ms. G. The only other variation between manuscripts, aside from scribal errors such as *бо* for *бѣ* or omissions, is that the form *бѣху* has been changed to *бяху* in both instances in ms. G and in one instance in mss. BN. Thus, the distinction between the *бѣ* and *бяше* paradigms is somewhat blurred in that several scribes changed *бѣху* to *бяху* at least once, and the only occurrence of the form *бяше* is incorrect.

It should also be mentioned that the forms from the *бысть* paradigm do not exclusively carry the meaning 'to become' in this text, as was often characteristic for them (cf. Uspenskij 2002: 238–247).

4.2.1.5 Adverbial participles

As explained in more detail in Section 7.3, by the 17th century, active participles in adverbial (or predicative) function had largely lost their inflection and were on their way to becoming the gerunds we find in present-day Russian. In the translation of the *Kronika*, adverbial participles take several different forms that have their origins in old inflectional endings.

The most common ending in the present tense is *-а/-я*, which was the masculine singular ending in certain conjugations. The ending *-ыи/-ии* occurs in e.g. *живыи* (Slav 26, fol. 157v), *сыи* (fols. 166r, 205r, 206v), *могіи* (fols. 181v, 199r) and *искіи* (fol. 210v). This is a remnant of the long (pronominal) form of the participle in the masculine singular of other conjugations. The ending *-учи*, which occurs for instance in *идучи* (fols. 152r, 153r), *будучи* (fols. 156r, 202v, 215r) and *бѣучи* (fol. 168r), has East Slavic consonantism, and the vowel *-u* has its origins in the feminine singular form (cf. below).[52] Forms ending in *-уще/-юще/-яще* have Church Slavonic consonantism, and *-e* originates in the masculine plural. Examples of this are *ведуще*

---

[51] Van Schooneveld uses the 1st person singular to symbolize the paradigms, i.e. *бяхъ*, *бѣхъ* and *быхъ*, which in my opinion is not quite appropriate, since the form *бяхъ* is a construct. I will therefore use the 3rd person singular.
[52] In the First Pskov Chronicle, Bjørnflaten (2010: 23) also found that participles with East Slavic consonantism all ended in *-u*, and Cocron's examples (Cocron 1962: 221–222) testify to the same thing.

(fol. 159v), *хотяще* (fols. 201v, 222r), *просяще* (fols. 212r, 218v) and *глюще* (fol. 224v). The only form with Church Slavonic consonantism ending in *-u* is the long form *хотящїи* (fol. 174v).

The form *зиждяи*, a long form of the participles in *-a/-я*, is remarkable because of the construction in which it occurs:

(44) Bo cáłe lat dwádzieśćia z sześć ty mury **budował** Anastasius Cesarz (Stryjkowski 1582: 98–99)

зане .к҃з. лѣтъ тѣ стѣны **бѣ зиждаи**. Анастасїи ц҃рь (Slav 26, fol. 168r)

Participle constructions with the verb *быти* were originally a calque from Greek and thus a sign of Church Slavonic syntax (Uspenskij 2002: 256). The use of this construction is a strong marker of bookishness, especially since the Polish original does not have anything similar.

The present tense adverbial participle of the verb *быти* is found in three different forms in the text: *сыи*, *суще* and *будучи*. The form *сыи* has masculine singular reference and *суще* masculine plural, but *будучи* is used without agreement in gender or number.

The past tense is dominated by forms ending in *-въ*, which was the masculine singular form in some conjugations. The forms *шедъ* (also found with the corresponding prefixed verbs), *зажегъ*, *рекъ/нарекъ* and *всѣдъ* have a zero ending, which was the masculine singular of other conjugations. There are also forms in *-вше*, which was the masculine plural form of the paradigm ending in *-въ*, and forms where *-ши* or *-ше* have been added directly to the verbal stem, which was the feminine singular or masculine plural, respectively, of the paradigm with a zero ending. Examples of the latter are *обрѣтши* (fol. 164r), *пришедше* (fol. 172r), *рекше* (fol. 209v) and *разбегшися* (fol. 217r). There are no examples of forms ending in *-вши*. There are also a few isolated forms that seem to be participles but have anomalous endings. They have not been taken into account here.

In both the present and the past tense, the ending *-u* originated in the feminine singular and *-e* in the masculine plural. In the 17th century, *-u* had spread to the plural, replacing the original ending *-e*. Once the feminine singular and the masculine plural began to be confused, the masculine singular could be used for feminine singular subjects as the only unambiguous singular form, and eventually all the forms were used interchangeably (Bjørnflaten 2010: 23–26).

The most common endings, i.e. *-a/-я* in the present tense and *-въ* and the zero ending in the past tense, are used here without agreement, but some of the other forms seem to be more strongly connected to their original gender and number category. Thus, *-ыи/-ии* is only used in the masculine singular and forms ending in *-уще/-юще/-яще*, *-вше* and *-ше* mainly in the plural.

There is quite a lot of variation between manuscripts regarding the forms of the adverbial participles. Of approximately 300 occurrences, 31 show some kind of variation. In most of these cases, some mss. have finite verb forms instead of participles, such as *обрѣтоша* in mss. ER instead of *обрѣтши* (fol. 164r) or *возбраняше* in ms. G instead of *возбраняще* (fol. 213r), although the latter case and a few others like it may be the result not of a substitution of forms, but of a general confusion of *ш* and *щ* in some forms of *skoropis'* (cf. Uspenskij & Živov 1983: 175–176). There are also a few instances of the opposite substitution: a finite form in ms. U corresponding to a participle in other mss. In some cases, all manuscripts have participles, but in different forms. Ms. G, for instance, has two instances of *пришедше* for *пришедъ* (fols. 198v, 199v), and in a few cases, one or more mss. have changed the particle *же* to the ending *-ше*, such as *утвердивше* in mss. ER for *утвердив же* (fol. 209v).

4.2.2 Nouns

4.2.2.1 The nominative plural

The original nominative plural forms of hard-stem masculine nouns ended in *-и*, and a few such forms are found in the texts, although the vast majority have the new ending *-ы*, originally the accusative plural form. The forms with the old ending are: *народи* (Slav 26, fols. 154r, 164v, 166r, 224v), *генети* (fol. 159r), *апостоли* (fol. 171r), *раби* (fol. 221v, 2x), *диакони* (fol. 224v). All these refer to humans, which is in accordance with the types of nouns that usually retained this ending in the 17th century (Cocron 1962: 65–67). Since *народъ* refers to a group of people, it is somewhat of a special case, and there are also numerous examples of the nominative plural *народы*. Other nouns with human referents (most of which are ethnonyms) are also found with the ending *-ы*, such as *болгары, сербы, долматы, карваты* (fol. 151r) or *готы, кимвры, и вандалиты* (fol. 165r), to name only a few. There are only two instances of variation between manuscripts: ms. N has *генеты* for *генети* (fol. 159r) and mss. BG have *идоли* for *идолы* (fol. 225v).

In Polish, this distinction remains to this day: masculine personal nouns take the old ending *-i*, whereas most other masculine nouns take the innovative ending *-y*. The use in the translation of the *Kronika* may therefore be influenced by the Polish system, even though the individual forms do not always correspond. The Polish *narod*, for instance, always has the nominative plural form *narody*, and the correspondence to *апостоли* is *Apostołowie*.

The form *наслѣдницы* (nine times) as a nominative plural of *наслѣдникъ*, *источницы* (once) of *источникъ* and *священницы* (twice) of *священникъ* show the effect of the second palatalization, which took place before the vowel -*i*, but instead of the original -*ци* we find -*цы*, since -*ц*- had become hard by this time. No variation is found between manuscripts. In Polish, masculine personal nouns ending in -*k* take the ending -*cy* in the nominative plural, which may have influenced the usage, although the individual forms in this text do not always correspond. The Russian *наследницы*, for instance, is often used to translate Polish *potomkowie*.

The nominative plural of nouns ending in -*анинъ*/-*янинъ* in ms. U takes the ending -*ане*/-*яне* in most cases: there are 75 such forms, compared with three ending in -*яня*, one in -*еня* (!), two in -*ани* and four in -*аны*. The form *срацыни* is an uncertain case and is not included in this group, since it is only found in the plural here, and the singular, according to SRJa, could be *срацинъ* or *срацининъ*. There is some variation between manuscripts regarding these endings, the most common being that one or several mss. may have -*яня* where ms. U has -*яне* (nine times). There are examples of this from all the other mss.

For these nouns, the ending in -*е* is the original one and has remained dominant throughout, although forms ending in -*и* and -*ы* can be found sporadically, cf. examples from the Hypatian Chronicle (Iordanidi & Krys'ko 2000: 108–112). The ending in -*я* was common in the 16th century and was still to be found in the 17th. It can perhaps be viewed as an influence from collective nouns in -*а* or -*ья*, since these plural forms of nouns designating people could be seen as collectives. Examples from the 17th century can be found for instance in Avvakum's and Kotošichin's writings (Cocron 1962: 73, 91–92).

4.2.2.2   The genitive singular masculine

As in other texts from the same period, the translation of the *Kronika* shows variation between the endings -*а*/-*я* and -*у*/-*ю* in the genitive singular of masculine nouns. The ending -*у*/-*ю* is not very frequent; there are only 26 instances of 21 different nouns (or 22, if the two meanings of *миръ* are counted separately) in the edited chapters according to ms. U.

The following list contains all genitive forms ending in -*у*/-*ю* with references to other studies and dictionaries where such forms are quoted from 17th-century sources. Former o-stems and u-stems will not be listed separately, since the old system was no longer intact in the 17th century.

бой (Sørensen 1958: 213; Cocron 1962: 37)

с вой до **бою** избранными (Slav 26, fol. 203r) (Pol. *bitwy*)

Олех же 8шед з **бою** (fol. 211v) (Pol. *pogromu*)

множества ради народа бежащих с тогож **бою** (fol. 211v) (Pol. –)[53]

---

[53] Cf. also Section 5.5.

воскъ (Sørensen 1958: 213; Cocron 1962: 37)

Олга же обеща ему ис Киева прислать **воску**, кож и людей работныⲭ (fol. 205v) (Pol. *Woskow*)

выборъ (SRJa)

ї з ближними без **выбор8** и стыда гдѣ кому полюбилось, сово-к8плялись (fol. 192r) (Pol. *rozności*)

выводъ

в начале **вывод8** народа полского (fol. 161r) (Pol. *wywodu*)

годъ (Sørensen 1958: 214; Cocron 1962: 37)

до Хр͡ста .рп.г͡ **год8** (fol. 185r) (Pol. *lat*)
до лѣта .ц͡кѳ. **году** (fol. 228r) (Pol. *roku*)

доводъ

из **доводу**[54] греческих, латинских, еврейских, хал͡дейскихъ писателей (fol. 149v) (Pol. *dowodu*)

долгъ (Sørensen 1958: 215; Cocron 1962: 37)

отздѣ слова яко л8тшаг͡, а не **долг8** или обещанїя 8поминаемсѧ (fol. 175v) (Pol. *rzeczy winney*)

домъ (Cocron 1962: 37)

не домовитъ от своего, своими р8ками зданного **дом8** (fol. 188v) (Pol. *Domu*)
Моисия с людми исраилтяны от фараона от **дом8** работы (fol. 206r) (Pol. *domu*)

Донъ (Sørensen 1958: 215; Cocron 1962: 37)

и вездѣ кр8гъ Кимерїя Босѳора, и черного морѧ, **Дон8**, Оки, Волги, Камы, Днеⲣра, Бога, Десны, Днестра, Д8ная (fol. 158v) (Pol. *Tanais*)

миръ (Sørensen 1958: 217; Cocron 1962: 38)

в лѣто от создания **мир8** (fol. 151v) (Pol. *Swiátá*)
советова Ярополк8 просити **мир8** и тишины (fol. 213r) (Pol. *poko-iu*)

---

[54] Mss. E and R have the genitive plural *довод*, but the genitive singular is probably the intended form.

мостъ

 с высокого **мост8** сверженъ (fol. 211v) (Pol. *mostu*)

народъ (Sørensen 1958: 217; Cocron 1962: 38)

 Изъ тогож славенского **народ8** (fol. 171r)

нарядъ (Sørensen 1958: 217)

 едва Игорь с третьею частию **наряду** в Киевъ 8бежа (fol. 200r)
(Pol. *Armaty*)

покой (Sørensen 1958: 219; Cocron 1962: 39)

 иже и **покою** не знали (fol. 180v) (Pol. *pokoiu*)

полъ (Sørensen 1958: 219; Cocron 1962: 39)

 с велиїм множеством кн︤з︥еи греческих и женска[55] и д︤в︥ча **полу**[56]
иде (fol. 223r) (Pol. *Fraucimeru*)

полонъ (Cocron 1962: 39)

 и множествѡ **полону** и добычи в печенѣжскомъ обоѕе набрали
(fols. 217v–218r) (Pol. *połony*)

поминокъ

 вмѣсто **поминк8** др8жбы том8же цесарю Авг8ст8 послали (fol.
180v) (Pol. *za upominek*)

счетъ (Cocron 1962: 41)

 с числом, лѣтъ вышеимянованныхъ греческого и латинского **счет8**
(fol. 152r) (Pol. *ráchunku*)

урядъ

 г︤о︥дрство и земля н︤ш︥а велика и обилна **8ряд8** ж в немъ нѣтъ (fol.
194r) (Pol. *správy*)

чинъ (Sørensen 1958: 224; Cocron 1962: 42)

 ток︤м︥о по меня противъ моего **чину** пришлите людеи честнѣйшихъ (fol. 202r) (Pol. *stanu*)

---

[55] Mss. E and R add. *и ѳранцы миром*, which is a distorted rendering of the Polish *fraucimeru*.
[56] Mss. B, G and N have *пола*, i.e. an a-genitive.

їбо межд8 ими много хр͠стїѧн тогож словенского **ѧзык8** быша (fol. 169v) (Pol. *iẹzyką*)

Most of these nouns are listed either by Sørensen (1958) or by Cocron (1962) as being found with the genitive ending *-y* in the 17th century. The word *выборъ* is found in this form in several examples in SRJa. Others (*выводъ, доводъ* and *мостъ*) correspond to genitive forms ending in *-u* of their Polish cognates, which could have evoked the choice of this form. The occurrences of *поминокъ, урядъ* and *языкъ* in this form are less easily explained, but such forms may be attested in other sources than the ones Sørensen and Cocron had access to. It should also be emphasized that many of the nouns mentioned above are also found in this text with the genitive ending *-a*. For instance, there are 39 occurrences of the form *народа* and 19 of *языка*.

There is little variation between manuscripts. Aside from the variant noted above – *пола* for *полу* in mss. B, G and N – there are four instances where mss. E and R have a form in *-у/-ю* where the others have one in *-а/-я*: *Ною, народу* (2x) and *уставу* instead of *Ноя, народа* and *устава*, respectively.

In Polish, far more nouns take the genitive ending *-u*. One might have expected a larger share of *-у/-ю* in the Russian translation than is the case, and the translator seems to have followed Russian norms rather than copying the Polish pattern.

4.2.2.3   The locative singular masculine

As in the genitive singular, there was variation in the ending of the locative singular masculine. Here, the alternatives were *-ѣ/-e* and *-у/-ю*. There are 14 occurrences of the locative ending *-у/-ю* in this part of the text in ms. U, but only six different nouns.

Just as in the previous section, references are made to studies and dictionaries where these forms are mentioned. Former o-stems and u-stems are listed together.

бродъ (Cocron 1962: 42)

сотвори ж Владиме*р* на том **броду**, идѣже бѣ побѣда др8гиї Переясловль (Slav 26, fol. 218r) (Pol. *ná tym brodzie*)

Донъ (Cocron 1962: 42)

8 че*р*ного моря, или на **Дон8** и по Волгѣ рекамъ посѣлились (fol. 190r) (Pol. *nád Tanais álbo Donem*)

Изборскъ

а Тр8вор8 на псковском въ **Изборѡку** (fol. 196v) (Pol. *w Zborsku/álbo Izborku*)

листъ (Cocron 1962: 43)

в глвѣ .а̄.*и* в книге .а̄.*и* же в **лист8** .а̄.м̄ же (fol. 160r) (Pol. *fol.*)

в книге .а̄.*и* в глвѣ .в̄.*и* в **лист8** .в̄.м (fol. 187v) (Pol. *fol.*)

в лѣтѡписи свое*и* в **лист8** .к̄е.м (fol. 189v) (Pol. *ná kárcie*)

в кнг̄ѣ .а̄. в главѣ .д̄. в **лист8** .ѕ̄. (fol. 192r) (Pol. *fol.*)

в книгѣ .в̄. в главѣ .г̄. в **листу** .к̄д.м (fol. 207r) (Pol. *fol.*)

во описанїи старо҇г лѣтописца московского на **лист8** .е̄.м (fol. 209v) (Pol. *fol.*)

в книгах своих о Москвѣ на **листу** .ѕ̄е.м (fol. 221r) (Pol. *fol.*)

Герберштеин на **лист8** .ѕ̄д.м (fol. 225v) (Pol. *folio*)

на .з̄.м **листу** во описанїи Москвы (fol. 226r) (Pol. *fol.*)

рядъ (SRJa)

во времена Иоан̄на третияго в **ряду** .ч҃ѳ.г̄ папы (fol. 153v) (Pol. *w rzędzie*)

холмъ

городокъ Либед или Любечь постави на высоком **холм8** (fol. 191v) (Pol. *ná korsi*)

The words *бродъ*, *Донъ* and *листъ* are attested in this form in Cocron's sources. In the case of *Изборскъ* and possibly *холмъ*, the Polish original may have served as an influence. The noun *рядъ*, which still has a u-locative in modern Russian, is found in this form in several of the examples in SRJa.

The noun *листъ* is never found in these chapters with any other locative ending. The words *рядъ, холмъ, бродъ* and *Донъ* are only found this one time each in the locative, so there is no material for comparison. *Изборскъ* is found once with the ending *-ѣ*.

There is no variation between manuscripts regarding the distribution of these locative endings.

As seen in the list above, the word *листъ* is constructed with the preposition *въ* up to and including fol. 207r, and with *на* beginning from fol. 209v. This distribution of prepositions is the same in all mss. that have been consulted. Two possible explanations have been found. Firstly, four of five constructions with *въ* are series of the type *въ книгѣ* [...] *въ главѣ* [...], which may favor the use of the preposition *въ* once again, whereas in the constructions with *на*, the immediately surrounding text is less formulaic. Secondly, in ms. B, there is a change of scribes between fols. 205v and 206r in volume

I (cf. Section 8.3.2), which corresponds to Slav 26, fol. 208r. The possible significance of this border is discussed in Section 6.10.

4.2.2.4   The a-expansion in oblique cases of the plural

The process known as the a-expansion concerned nouns of the o-, jo-, i- and consonant declensions in the dative, instrumental and locative plural and refers to the replacement of the original endings of the respective declensions by what was originally the endings of a- and ja-stem nouns. In other words, the endings *-амъ*, *-ами* and *-ахъ* spread at the expense of *-омъ/-емъ*, *-ы/-и/-ьми* and *-ѣхъ/-ехъ*, respectively.

The exact circumstances of this process and the internal chronology of the development of the cases in the spoken language have been debated, but in the written language, innovative forms spread in the dative and locative earlier than in the instrumental (Živov 2004: 270–271). Eventually, the use of new forms in the instrumental became more frequent, and in the second half of the 17th century, masculine o-stem nouns had the highest share of new forms in the locative, lower in the instrumental and even lower in the dative, i.e. L > I > D, which can be called the neutral distribution. There were differences between the registers in terms of both the share of new forms and their distribution between the cases. The neutral distribution was characteristic of non-bookish everyday texts (*bytovye teksty*) and of the hybrid register. Chancellery texts, on the other hand, showed the distribution I > L > D, which can be explained by a normalizing effort to avoid homonymy of the instrumental plural with the nominative and accusative plural. This distribution, but with much lower shares of new forms, can also be found in some standard Church Slavonic texts under the same normalizing influence. Thus, a high degree of orientation on model texts led to a low share of new forms, and a high degree of normalization led to the distibution I > L > D (Živov 2004: 314–319).

The a-expansion in the studied part of the *Kronika* is extensive, or *širokoe* (Živov 2004: 284), amounting to 34.3% (132 out of 385) if ambiguous cases are included (cf. below), or 40.2% (132 out of 328) if they are not.

The results for the instrumental plural of masculine o-stems, jo-stems, consonant stems and i-stems are partly uncertain due to the fact that the old o- and jo-stem ending *-ы/-и* was homonymous with the accusative and, later, nominative plural. An important theme in the text is explaining the names of the Slavic peoples, and constructions such as *нарицахуся* or *речени суть* are common. It seems that the normal way to construct these verbs was with the instrumental, but nevertheless, there are some cases where a nominative form, not homonymous with the instrumental, is used, as in example (45) (cf. also Slav 26 fols. 161v, 165r, 171v et al.), indicating that it was also possible to construct these verbs with the nominative.

(45)   славаки бо Д8най наричютъ **Вистеръ**, и латинники **Истеръ** (Slav 26, fol. 164v)

Forms ending in -*ы* or -*и* without attributes are therefore ambiguous in such contexts. Because of this ambiguity, two tables will be shown below, one where the ambiguous examples are included and one where they are excluded. The difference will be noticed in the cells containing instrumental endings for masculine o-stems, jo-stems, consonant stems and i-stems. The number of ambiguous cases amounts to 57, which means that they make up a large share. The greatest difference is seen in the masculine o-stems, where the exclusion of ambiguous cases reduces the number of old endings by more than half. In the tables below, the numbers in parentheses are the shares of new forms in percent.

Table 8. The a-expansion in oblique cases, ambiguous cases included

	Ending	m. o-st.		m. jo-st.		n. o-st.		n. jo-st.		m. cons.		m. i-st.		f. i-st.	
D	омъ/емъ	33		14		–		–		15		2		3	
	амъ/aмъ	3	(8.3)	5	(26.3)	2	(100)	1	(100)	–	(0)	–	(0)	1	(25)
L	ехъ/ѣхъ	15		–		10		–		6		–		2	
	ахъ/aхъ	27	(64.3)	7	(100)	8	(44.4)	15	(100)	–	(0)	–		6	(75)
I	ы/и	81		10		11		6		24		1		–	
	ами/aми	49	(37.4)	–	(0)	6	(31.6)	2	(25)	2	(7.7)	–	(0)	–	(0)
	ми	1		4		2		2		–		7		6	

Table 9. The a-expansion in oblique cases, ambiguous cases excluded

	Ending	m. o-st.		m. jo-st.		n. o-st.		n. jo-st.		m. cons.		m. i-st.		f. i-st.	
D	омъ/емъ	33		14		–		–		15		2		3	
	амъ/aмъ	3	(8.3)	5	(26.3)	2	(100)	1	(100)	–	(0)	–	(0)	1	(25)
L	ехъ/ѣхъ	15		–		10		–		6		–		2	
	ахъ/aхъ	27	(64.3)	7	(100)	8	(44.4)	15	(100)	–	(0)	–		6	(75)
I	ы/и	33		7		11		6		14		–		–	
	ами/aми	49	(59)	–	(0)	6	(31.6)	2	(25)	2	(12.5)	–	(0)	–	(0)
	ми	1		4		2		2		–		7		6	

As we can see from the tables above, new forms are almost completely absent from the consonant declension, represented by nouns ending in -*инъ*. They show only two instances of the new ending in the instrumental. This is in accordance with evidence from other texts, where this declension has also been seen to be resistent to innovations (cf. Živov 2004: 277). The masculine i-stems, represented by the two nouns *люди* and *дети*, also lack new endings, but are not very well represented to begin with. The instrumental forms *воеводы* and *добычи* of a-stem nouns are innovations not included in the tables above.

In masculine o-stem nouns, the locative is the most progressive in adopting new forms, followed by the instrumental and then the dative, i.e. the text follows the neutral distribution, as may be expected of a hybrid text. If the

104

masculine o- and jo-stem nouns are taken together, they are also in accordance with this distribution, whereas the jo-stem nouns by themselves show a larger share of new forms in the dative than in the instrumental.

The instrumental ending *-ми* is not uncommon even outside of the i-declension. This can be seen as a marker of bookishness (Živov 2004: 300–301), although the a-expansion as a whole (or absence of it) was not always a part of the system of markers of bookishness (Živov 2004: 318–319).

As for variation between manuscripts, it is mostly a question of isolated substitutions with no apparent tendency. The only exception is the dative plural, where ms. N has new forms instead of old forms in six instances. As opposed to these more modern forms, ms. N has the archaic instrumental plural *тѣлѣсы* instead of *тѣлами* (Slav 26, fol. 211v).

All in all, the distribution of innovative forms according to cases reminds of the one in the *Letopisec 1619–1691 gg.*, where, however, the share of new forms is only 19.17%, and of the distribution in Lyzlov's *Skifskaja istorija*, with 25.6% new forms (Živov 2004: 304–307). Thus, the share of new forms in the translation of Stryjkowski is higher than in these texts, although they can be said to belong to the same tradition, which testifies to a lower degree of connection to the tradition of the genre. However, the distribution of new forms according to declensions and cases is approximately the same. With its high share of new forms and the distribution L > I > D between the cases, this translation actually comes closest to the everyday register in its usage, although such extensive usage of new forms has been attested in other hybrid texts as well.

4.2.2.5 The vocative

Vocative forms are regularly used in the contexts where this is appropriate. It can be noted that the Polish original also has vocative forms, so the use of the vocative in the translation could be either a bookish element or a sign of influence from Polish. There are vocative forms of masculine as well as feminine nouns, some of the most frequent being *читателю любезныи* (six times), with the adjective always in a form identical with the nominative, and *царю* (four times). Other forms are *Риме* (Slav 26, fols. 178r, 178v), *великии княже* (fols. 198v, 216v), *Елено* (fol. 205v, 2x), *сыну* (fol. 208r), *Свадолте* (fol. 211v), *Владимиру* (fol. 216v) and *Владимере* (fol. 220v). The endings correspond to Church Slavonic norm, except in the case of the name *Владимиръ*, where two different endings are used. The ending *-е* is the etymologically correct one, and the ending *-у* may have been motivated by the Polish form *Włodimirzu*.

There are also a few instances of a nominative used in a vocative context, especially of feminine nouns, such as *госпожа княгини* (fol. 203r) and *княгини Ольга* (fol. 205r). The plural *господа сватове* (fol. 201v) – where the ending *-ове* is probably infuenced by the Polish *panowie swatowie* – and the former consonant stem *дцⷩи* did not have a separate vocative form.

The vocative forms do not differ between manuscripts.

4.2.3 Adjectives

4.2.3.1 The nominative and accusative plural of adjectives

The declination of long forms of adjectives, participles and ordinal numbers (for the sake of brevity, I will simply speak of adjectives below) in the nominative and accusative plural displays a combination of "old" (Church Slavonic of Russian redaction) and "new" (East Slavic) forms. The old forms were *-ии* in the nominative masculine, *-ыⷩ* (here usually spelled *-ыя*) in the accusative masculine and the nominative and accusative feminine, and *-аⷩ* (here usually spelled *-ая*) in the nominative and accusative neuter. The new ending *-ыⸯ* (here usually spelled *-ые*) originally belonged only to the accusative masculine and the nominative and accusative feminine, i.e. it was the East Slavic counterpart to *-ыⷩ*, but could by this time be used for all genders and both cases under consideration (cf. Živov 2004: 409–410).

In this part of the text according to ms. U, the new ending *-ые/-ие* is found in all gender and case combinations discussed here and is dominant in most of them, but all the old endings can also be found. It should be noted that in a few instances, the case and number of an adjective have been difficult to establish, especially in translations of Latin book titles that were not integrated into the syntax of the Polish text, or in other cases of obscure syntax. These instances do not affect the results to a great extent.

There are 141 adjectives in the nominative plural masculine. The most frequent ending is *-ые/-ие*, with 86 occurrences. The old ending *-ии* is found 52 times in the text. In twelve of these forms, adjectives of nationality with the suffix *-ск-* have the bookish ending *-стии*, due to the effects of the 2nd palatalization. This development was present in OCS and is also found in Church Slavonic texts of Russian redaction, but it was absent in East Slavic (Uspenskij 2002: 197). There is also one instance with the ending *-ыи* in a participle (Slav 26, fol. 188v), a form that had arisen in the language as a result of *-ы-* becoming a general plural marker (Živov 2004: 410). This form is included with the ending *-ии* in Table 10 below. The ending *-ыя/-ия* is found three times.

The accusative plural masculine shows five instances of the old ending *-ыя/-ия* and 24 instances of *-ые/-ие*.

In the nominative plural feminine, the ending *-ые/-ие* dominates (12 instances), but in one case the originally masculine ending *-ии* is used, perhaps because the adjective is separated from the corresponding noun by a few other words (Slav 26, fol. 171r). In the accusative, there are 45 instances of *-ые/-ие*, 12 of the old form *-ыя/-ия*, and one of the originally neutral ending

106

-ая, alongside an adjective ending in *-ыя*, which qualifies the same noun. Here, the adjective ending in *-ая* was probably influenced by the fixed expression *и протчая* 'and so forth':

(46) принесе же *с собꙋю* и мощи свꙗтаго Климонта, и їконы и книги и ризы и **протчая** 8твари ц҃рковныя (Slav 26, fol. 224r)

In both the nominative and the accusative plural neuter, three endings are found: *-ыя/-ия* (three in the nominative and six in the accusative), *-ая/-яя* (one in the nominative, 15 in the accusative, including the syntactically more independent occurrences of *и протчая*) and *-ые/-ие* (eight in the nominative, 25 in the accusative).

There are some cases, such as example (46), of adjectives with different endings modifying the same noun, a type of variation that was characteristic of the hybrid register (cf. Živov 2004: 421, 428).

As a whole, the new ending *-ые/-ие* constitutes 66.6% of all the nominative and accusative plural adjective endings, which exceeds that of all hybrid texts studied by Živov (2004: 418–437) except one. 41.4% of the instances of the ending *-ыя/-ия* (12 of 29) occur in positions where this ending was not originally used, but it is much less frequent than in some other hybrid texts, where *-ые/-ие* and *-ыя/-ия* are used for all gender-case combinations studied. 28.8% of the endings are correctly used old endings, which is approximately the same as in the later part of *Mazurinskij letopisec*.

Table 10 is patterned on the tables in Živov (2004) to facilitate comparison with the texts discussed there. The numbers for etymologically correct old endings have been set in boldface.

Table 10. Adjective endings in the nominative and accusative plural

	Npl masc.	Apl masc.	NApl fem.	NApl neutr.	Total
-ии/-ыи	**53**	–	1	–	54
-ыя/-ия	3	**5**	**12**	9	29
-ая/-яя	–	–	1	**16**	17
-ые/-ие	86	24	57	33	200
Total	142	29	71	58	300

Variation between manuscripts is quite frequent with respect to these adjective endings; approximately 45 of the 300 forms have another ending in one or more manuscripts. The variation goes in different directions and is difficult to describe in a general way, but the most common trend is that mss. E and R often have the ending *-ыя* where ms. U has *-ые*. This variation occurs in all gender-case combinations studied, so these manuscripts illustrate the above-mentioned tendency to use both *-ые/-ие* and *-ыя/-ия* without considering the etymology. There is also some variation regarding the old nominative masculine ending: on the one hand, ms. R often has what looks like a short form of the adjective (cf. Section 4.2.3.3), on the other hand, ms. N has a few instances of the ending *-ыи* where the others have *-ии*.

4.2.3.2   The genitive singular of masculine and neutral adjectives

In the genitive singular of adjectives referring to masculine or neutral nouns, the two endings *-ого* and *-аго* compete. The ending *-ого* prevails in ms. U with 204 against 74 *-аго*, or 73.4% and 26.6%, respectively, of the 278 instances. There is also one occurrence of the ending *-ово*.

The choice of form varies considerably between manuscripts: approximately half the instances show variation in at least one other manuscript. Moreover, there is variation between hands within the manuscripts. Ms. N, especially hand N1, uses *-аго* to a much greater extent than the others. To a lesser degree, ms. E also tends to use *-аго* where ms. U has *-ого*. In ms. R, hand R1 often uses *-ого* where ms. U has *-аго*, whereas hand R2 does the opposite. These differences between hands in a single manuscript, as well as between mss. E and R, which are usually very close to each other, probably show that it was acceptable for each scribe to apply the adjectival ending he preferred in these cases. The form ending in *-ово* has the ending *-ова* in mss. E and R, which have this ending in one other instance as well.

4.2.3.3   Short forms

There are a number of short forms of adjectives and participles in the text. Ordinal numbers, however, are always found in the long form when they are spelled out with letters. Possessive adjectives (except those with the suffix *-ск-*) form a category of their own (cf. Larsen 2005: 221) and are always used in the short form in this text. They will not be discussed further here, since variation is not possible (cf., however, Section 4.3.4).

The toponyms *Новгородъ*, *Новгородокъ* and *Бѣлоозеро* are also excluded here, even though the first elements are declined as short adjectives, because of the fixed form of these combinations and the absence of variation. The case forms of these toponyms attested are the nominative, the genitive, the dative, the accusative and the locative, i.e. all short forms that were possible at the time are found here.

With these excluded, there are 122 adjectives (of a total of nearly 2000) and 100 participles (of a total of approximately 225) in the short form. Of the total of 222 short forms, 124 are used predicatively, i.e. with verbs such as *быти*, *бывати* or *пребыти* or in a context where a verb of that type is implied or understood from the Polish original. 26 short forms are in a position that could be interpreted as either attributive or predicative. The ambiguity arises when the adjective or participle is modified in some way, which allows an interpretation of it as part of an elliptic relative clause. In example

(47), the adjective *медянъ* is clearly an attribute to *котлокъ*, whereas the participle *посвященъ* is ambiguous:

(47) В тож врема гепиды предки жмѡидскїя и литовскїе котлокъ **медднъ** по обычаю своемⷹ поганскомⷹ **посвященъ** вмѣсто поминкⷹ дрⷹжбы томⷹже цесарю Авгⷹстⷹ послали (Slav 26, fol. 180v)

Six of the forms are participles forming part of dative absolute constructions (always in the singular – as we will see below in Section 4.3.5.1, the two occurrences of dative absolutes with the plural have the participle in the long form). 62 forms are used as genuine attributes. Four forms are used independently of nouns, either because they are substantivized or because they are named simply as words, e.g. as explanations or translations of other words, such as in the following example:

(48) вмѣсто Сармата еже ѿ еврейского толкⷹется **высокъ** и **честен**, савроматы нарещи можахⷹ прѡтивнымъ обычае︥м ѿ савро*с* (Slav 26, fol. 184r)

Passive constructions with a predicative use of a past passive participle account for the large share of short forms in participles. Participles do not occur in an attributive position as often as adjectives do. Present passive participles are also used in the short form as part of passive constructions, but are more rare than the past passive participles. Present active participles are rarely used in the short form; this is the case only when they are part of dative absolute constructions.

Predicative short forms and the short forms in the ambiguous positions explained above are always in the nominative, which is inherent in the constructions themselves. The purely attributive short forms are found mainly in the nominative and accusative, both singular and plural, but there are also a few genitive singular forms and, in addition to the participles in dative absolute constructions, one more dative singular form. The instrumental and locative singular and the oblique cases in the plural are not attested. Adjectives in the short form follow the noun more often than they precede it (cf. Larsen 2005: 217), but prepositive short form adjectives are represented here in all existing case-number combinations except the dative singular.

In the nominative plural, the adjectives and participles can take either the ending *-и* (the old masculine nominative plural ending) or *-ы* (the old masculine accusative plural ending). To some extent, this follows the division between animate and inanimate nouns. For instance, the form *речени* (*суть*) is used frequently and always refers to people. The form *речены* (or *реченны*) can also refer to people, but once it refers to *руские земли*, which is not animate. This distribution of the endings *-и* and *-ы* also holds true in most cases for other adjectives and participles. There is also one instance of the neuter plural form *различна*.

In a few cases, ms. R has the short form *-u* in the masculine plural nominative where the other mss. have *-uu* (cf. Section 4.2.3.1). However, adjectives in the masculine singular nominative, which end in *-ыu/-uu* in other mss., also frequently have the ending *-ы/-u* in ms. R, such as in example (49).

(49) Прокопиї такожде **славны** и **дрѣвни** повѣстописецъ (RGADA 58, fol. 75r; cf. Slav 26, fol. 162r)

Since this is not the correct short form in the masculine singular, it is probable that this shortening of the ending was not an attempt to use the short form of adjectives and participles, but an idiosyncracy of the scribe's spelling, possibly reflecting his pronunciation.

4.2.3.4 Degrees of comparison

Comparative and superlative forms of adjectives and adverbs are discussed here together, since their forms do not differ from each other (cf. Pennington 1980: 256).

There are declinable as well as indeclinable forms of the comparative in ms. U. Among the declinable forms we find *меншии, лутчии, юншии* and *болшии*, although it can sometimes be discussed if this last form is positive or comparative. The context and comparison with the Polish original have served as determining factors.

Forms with the suffix *-еиш-*, such as *древнеишии*, or *-ш-* with a preceding palatalization of the stem, such as *крѣпльшии* or *твержшии*, can also be declined. This suffix originated in the feminine singular form of the comparative. In the 17th century, it was a slavonicism and, according to Cocron (1962: 129), used mainly in the titles of sovereigns. His observation does not, however, hold true for this text.

The most common ending in the undeclinable adjectives and adverbs is *-ѣе*. There are also many forms with the ending *-е*, such as *позже* and *выше*. Some indeclinable forms have the ending *-u*, such as *лутчи, болши, хужи* and *горши*, although several of these have variant readings ending in *-е* in other manuscripts, especially in ms. N.

The forms *крепчае* (fol. 150r), *смѣляе* (fol. 186r) and *скоряе* (fol. 217r) show an ending that had developed from *-ѣе* and that was often used with adjectives whose stem contained the letter *-е-*, in order to avoid having the same vowel in three consecutive syllables (Pennington 1980: 257–258). This, however, is not the case in the last of the three examples.

Aside from the above-mentioned variation between the endings *-u* and *-е* and various ways of spelling the consonant cluster in the word *лутче/ лутше/ лучше*, there is no variation between manuscripts.

110

4.2.4 Pronouns

4.2.4.1 Personal pronouns

The nominative of the first person singular in ms. U is either *азъ* (nine times) or *я* (three times). The accusative is *меня* (two times), *мя* (seven times) or *мене* (three times). The dative is expressed by *мнѣ* (ten times) or *ми* (six times). The genitive, the instrumental and the locative do not occur.

In the oblique cases of the second person singular, the forms found are: in the genitive *тебе* (two times), in the accusative *тебѣ* (one time) or *тя* (three times), in the dative *тебѣ* (two times) and in the locative *тебѣ* (one time). The instrumental does not occur.

The reflexive pronoun is usually used in its long forms *себя* (eleven times), *себе* (three times) and *себѣ* (30 times), but the accusative *ся* also occurs (once). The majority of these forms are in the dative case, which always has *себѣ*. The locative form is also always *себѣ*, whereas the genitive and accusative vary between *себѣ*, *себе* and *себя*. The enclitics of reflexive verbs are not included here.

There is little variation between manuscripts, except such that can be put down to scribal errors. One of the instances of *тебе* instead has the form *тебя* in mss. B, G and N, and one occurrence of *себѣ* is instead found as *себя* in mss. G and N.

The use of the short forms *мя*, *ми* and *тя* is a sign of bookishness (Cocron 1962: 136–137). Originally, the use of one form or another was connected with their status as full words or clitics. The long forms were used when they needed to be stressed, and the position of the short forms (which were enclitics) in the phrase was determined by certain rules. The earliest rules prescribed the use of the enclitics except in some very specific cases, but during the course of time, long forms became possible in all contexts (Zaliznjak 2008: 130–134). The choice of form in this text should also be viewed in relation to the Polish original, since the Polish system of personal pronouns included full and clitic forms, some of which (such as the enclitic *mię* in the accusative, which occurs frequently here) have since disappeared (Klemensiewicz et al. [1955] 1981: 321–322).

In the cases where the use in the Russian translation differs from that in the Polish original or from the old rules, it is nearly always a question of the long form appearing where a short form is to be expected. The only exception is the phrase *аз тя о Елено избрахъ* (Slav 26, fol. 205v), where a short form occurs instead of an expected long form. The position immediately before an appeal, such as *Елено*, was a situation where even according to the original rules the long form was preferred, although the short form was also possible (Zaliznjak 2008: 132). Moreover, the Polish original of this phrase has the long form *ciebie*. This makes the use of the short form in the translation all the more surprising. The general impression is that the short forms were markers of bookish language and not applied regularly, but also that the translator knew something about their proper use, since he used a short form incorrectly only once.

The forms of the personal pronouns in the third person singular and plural are largely identical to the ones used in modern Russian. In the nominative, the forms used are *онъ, она, оно* and *они*, and the oblique cases are also the modern ones.

In the accusative of masculine and feminine pronouns, however, there was still some competition at this time between the old accusative forms *и* and *ю*, respectively, and the forms that originally belonged to the genitive, i.e. *его* and *ея* or *еѣ*, respectively. In the masculine accusative, ms. U shows only the form *его*, originally the genitive form (sometimes spelled *ево*), and the original accusative *и* is not found. In the feminine accusative, on the other hand, the original accusative form *ю* prevails, and the genitive form *еѣ* or *ея* is never used in an accusative context. In the plural, the form *ихъ* is more frequent than *я*, which was the original accusative form.

Aside from one instance where *еѣ* in ms. U corresponds to *ея* in mss. B, G and N, the only variation between manuscripts concerns a few instances of confusion of *его* and *егоже* and similar cases.

The difference between the usage in the masculine and feminine may reflect the fact that *его* for the accusative was introduced earlier than *еѣ* or *ея* in the same contexts. However, this development took place several centuries earlier (Krys'ko 1994: 130–133), so that if it has any bearing on this text, it must be because of the usage in model texts, perhaps through different degrees of acceptability of the various forms.

4.2.4.2   Relative pronouns

In ms. U, there are 22 instances of the relative pronoun *которыи* in different forms. Far more common, however, are forms of *иже*, with approximately 200 occurrences.

In eleven instances, *которыи* is followed by a noun that echoes the word in the main clause to which the relative pronoun refers. All these occurrences correspond to an identical structure in the Polish original. Of these, only example (50) repeats the *same* noun in the main and subordinate clauses:

(50)   Tego dopiero wnuk Wasili wielki Xiądz Moskiewski/ Zamek Moskiewski począł **murem y wieżámi** obwodźić/ **ktore mury** potym przes lat trzydieśći cáłe potomkowie iego ledwo dokonáli (Stryjkowski 1582: 91)

того вн8къ Василїи, великїй кн͞зь московскїи, град Москв8 нача **стѣною каменною и башнями** обводити, **которые стѣны** въ .л͞. лѣтъ наслѣдницы его одва совершиша (Slav 26, fol. 156r)

In the other instances, the noun in the subordinate clause can be e.g. a synonym, a hyponym or a hypernym of the one in the main clause. The following example is typical:

(51) Drugą záś Columnę widziałem zá **Andrinopolim/ ná ktorym mieyscu**
      Bulgárowie niewdzięcznie oddáiąc dar pismá Hłaholskiego [...] prze-
      rzeconego Cesárzá Michálá Kuropłátá wzruszywszy mu przymierze
      porázili (Stryjkowski 1582: 88)

      дрȣгїи же столпъ видех за **Аⷩдрианополемъ на котором**
      мѣсте болⷢары неблⷢгодарно воздая даρ писмеⷩный [...] выше-
      реченного цⷬря Михайла Кȣрополата миρ разоρвавъ побиша (Slav
      26, fols. 152r–152v)

This construction was represented in different registers, but mainly in chancellery language and only sporadically in chronicles (Hüttl-Folter 1996: 54; Živov 2004: 111–112). S. C. Gardiner (1963: 124–125) remarks that it was found in the language of *Posol'skij prikaz*, but not in other Russian 17th-century sources, unless they were influenced by other languages. W. Witkowski (1978: 35) points to the fact that it became widely spread in Russian precisely during a time of Polish influence, and that Polish had used it for a long time, patterned on Latin constructions.

When the Polish relative pronoun was followed by a noun in this way, the translator seems to have preferred the translation *которыи*. In a few cases, *który* + noun was translated using *иже*, but always without a following noun; the construction *иже* + noun was probably impossible. The translation *которыи* + noun was closer to the original in these cases, which is probably the reason why it was preferred.

In some cases, forms of *иже* – most often its neutral singular form *еже* – are also used as a translation for Polish *co*, referring to a whole phrase. It may also be a translation for Polish relative *kto*.

An oddity is the form *оноже* (Slav 26, fol. 150r), which is used to translate a form of *który*.

The relative pronouns are as a rule declined according to their role in the subordinate clause. In a few cases, the relative pronoun does not agree formally with the noun, but rather semantically, such as on fol. 183r, where the Polish *Russacy* with a following plural relative pronoun is translated as the singular *Русь*, followed by a plural pronoun. The plural pronoun is probably motivated by the collective meaning of the word *Русь*, which also often takes plural verb forms. Another case is found on fol. 191v, where the Russian translation, like the Polish original, has a masculine relative pronoun referring to the toponym *Коревица* (*Korewica*). The Russian choice could be motivated by an underlying *градъ*, as well as, of course, by the Polish original, but the Polish use of the masculine is more difficult to explain.

4.2.4.3 Other pronouns

Forms of the pronoun *иnou* occur 82 times in ms. U, whereas the form *иnnыu* with *-нn-* only occurs twice. There are three occurrences of the short form *иnъ*. The form with *-нn-* can be seen as a polonism (Moser 2007: 235). There are a couple of more instances of the spelling with *-нn-* in other mss., and some additional variation that can probably be put down to scribal errors caused by the similarity of the letters *u* and *n* in some hands.

Forms of *momъ* and *mou* both occur frequently. Forms of *ceu* are also very frequent. The demonstrative *эmomъ*, however, does not occur at all.

The pronoun 'every' takes the form *кïuждo* (five instances), with no variation between manuscripts. It is mainly used independently, meaning 'everyone' (e.g. fol. 165r), but also together with a masculine noun (fol. 204r). The etymology of this word is *къ* + *жьдo* (Leskien 1886: 97), and originally, the first element was declined and the second was undeclinable, unlike today's *каждый*.

4.2.5 Numerals

Numerals (cardinal as well as ordinal) are often given as Cyrillic alphabetic numerals in ms. U, especially in the case of large numbers, such as years, but also in references to books, chapters and pages in Stryjkowski's sources. Ms. G (hand G2, cf. Section 8.3.3) uses alphabetic numerals in a few cases where the other mss. spell the numerals out in full. Ordinal numbers written as alphabetic numerals are often, but not always, followed by an indication of the case form as a superscript letter. This also varies between manuscripts, and will not be commented on below. The discussion below is based on the numerals that are spelled out in full in ms. U, and the variation that is mentioned also refers only to forms that are spelled out.

4.2.5.1 Cardinal numerals

Both *одинъ* and *единъ* are used approximately ten times each in different case forms. As in Kotošichin's text (Pennington 1980: 248–249), *единъ* shows long forms in oblique cases.

The forms of the number 'two' found in the text are *два* (accusative neuter, twice), *двѣ* (accusative feminine, three times: twice animate, once inanimate), *дву* (once genitive neuter, once accusative masculine animate, once genitive masculine animate), *двух* (once accusative masculine animate, and once genitive neuter as part of a compound numeral), *двемя* (instrumental masculine), *двѣма* (instrumental neuter, as part of a compound numeral). The only variation between manuscripts is that ms. R has the form *двемя* instead of *двѣма*.

These forms show that the distribution known from contemporary Russian, where *два* refers to the masculine and neuter and *две* to the feminine,

114

applies to this text, as to several other 17th-century texts. The variation between *дву* and *двух* is also known from other texts of the period (Cocron 1962: 189–190; Pennington 1980: 265), although it is unusual for *дву* to prevail as it does here. The instrumental form *двѣма* is the original one, and the form with the ending *-мя* is more recent, but there is no example here of the contemporary form *двумя*, where the vowel from the genitive form has spread across the paradigm. This is in agreement with Cocron's findings (Cocron 1962: 190–191).

The distribution of *оба* and *обѣ* corresponds to that of *два* and *двѣ*. There is also an occurrence of *обои* in the nominative neuter. This is originally a collective form, which later disappeared in Russian but remains in the oblique cases (Cocron 1962: 195–196). The other forms attested are *обоихъ* (accusative masculine animate and genitive feminine), *обоимъ* (dative masculine) and the unusual form *обою* (accusative feminine), which is probably also a heritage from the flection of *обои*. Mss. E and R have *оба* for *обои*, and ms. N has *обѣимъ* instead of *обоимъ*.

The forms of the numeral *три* that occur, aside from the nominative-accusative form, are the genitive *трех* (nine times), the dative *трем* (once) and the instrumental *трема* (once). Both the dative and the instrumental forms are the old ones (cf. Cocron 1962: 191). Mss. G, E and R have the newer form *тремя* instead of *трема*.

The number 'four' is only found spelled out in the instrumental *чатырма*, which, like *трема*, has an old ending that gradually fell out of use in the 17th century (Cocron 1962: 191). Mss. B and G have *четырма* here, and ms. N has *четырмя*, with the newer ending.

The genitive of the number 'six,' *шти* (in a compound numeral), is found once and was normal for this period (Cocron 1962: 192; Pennington 1980: 266).

The number 'ten' is found either with hard or soft final consonant, which varies between manuscripts.

The number 12 occurs once as *дванадесяти* (accusative), and the number 15 is found twice in the form *пятьнадесять*. In contrast to this, Cocron (1962: 193) and Pennington (1980: 266) list only the contracted forms known from contemporary Russian.

The number 20 is found both in its full and contracted form: *двадесять* and *дватцат*. *Пятьдесять* and *седмьдесять* are also found. More surprising is *четыредесять* (in a compound numeral) instead of the expected *сорокъ*, which may be explained by the fact that the Polish has *czteridzieśći*. There is variation between manuscripts as to whether the final consonant in these numerals is hard or soft, and mss. R and N have *сем-* instead of *седмь-*.

Higher numerals (hundreds and thousands) have the forms still found in today's Russian.

4.2.5.2   Ordinal numerals

Most of the ordinals have the same forms as in contemporary Russian. The following forms deserve to be mentioned.

According to Pennington (1980: 268), the normal word for 'second' at this time was *другои*, and it is also the only one attested in Cocron's sources (Cocron 1962: 202). In ms. U, however, the ordinal *вторыи* is found eight times in different cases. *Другои* is also used, but it can sometimes be hard to tell if it is intended as a numeral or as the pronoun 'other.'

The ordinal 'third' shows a variety of forms, which is in line with what is observed in other 17th-century texts, since it was influenced by other ordinals and shows endings belonging to the original flection of adjectives in -ьjь- as well as endings borrowed from ordinary adjectives in the long form (Cocron 1962: 202). The forms found here are the following: nominative-accusative masculine *третии* (seven times), genitive masculine and neuter *третияго* and *третьяго*, genitive feminine *третеи* (twice), dative masculine *третиему*, accusative feminine *третию*, instrumental masculine *третиим* and instrumental feminine *третьею*.

Other ordinals do not require comment, and there is no variation between manuscripts.

4.2.5.3   Other types of numerals

A few examples of numerals of multiplication or repetition can be found. These are: *единожды*, *дващи* (mss. E and R have *дважди*), *трижды* and *многажды* (once) or *многащи/многощи* (twice; ms. R has *многожды* in both instances). *Вдвое* also belongs here.

4.3   Description of IV: 1–3: syntax

4.3.1   Verbal tenses for past events

As explained in Section 1.3, chapters IV: 1–3 of the translation of Stryj-kowski's chronicle are part of a large segment of text (segment A) where mainly aorist and imperfect forms, i.e. simplex preterites, are used.

The perfect tense without auxiliary verb (elliptic perfect, cf. van Schoone-veld 1959; Matthews 1995) is also well represented in the text. For reasons explained in Section 4.3.1.3, it will be discussed apart from perfect forms with an auxiliary verb in the present tense, or "the Perfect tense proper, the full form" (Matthews 1995: 301). Not all scholars distinguish between full and elliptic perfect forms. When earlier studies are used as comparison below, it will be noted in each case if they treat these forms separately or jointly.

116

Full perfect forms are rare, as is the pluperfect (with an auxiliary verb in the aorist, imperfect or perfect). Table 11 shows the distribution of the tenses used for past events in IV: 1–3 according to ms. U.

Table 11. Distribution of tenses for the past in IV: 1–3

Tense or form	Amount	Percent	Comments
Aorist	711	66.3%	
Imperfect	163	15.2%	
Elliptic perfect	178	16.6%	Without auxiliary verb
Full perfect	9	0.8%	With auxiliary verb in the present tense
Pluperfect	11	1.0%	With auxiliary verb in aorist, imperfect or perfect
Total	1072	99.9%	

The simplex preterites – aorist and imperfect – dominate. Together they account for more than 80% of the verbal usage for past events. The elliptic perfect is more unusual, and the full perfect and the pluperfect rare exceptions. Some situations have been identified where they are especially liable to be used (cf. Sections 4.3.1.2 and 4.3.1.3).

4.3.1.1 The use of the aorist

Although approximately one tense form in six, referring to the past, is an elliptic perfect tense form, there are some verbs that occur more than six times, but always or almost always in the aorist. One may suspect that they are used formulaically. These verbs are listed below with details as to their occurrences. Only verbs that occur nine times or more in ms. U, and that have no more than one occurrence there in another form than the aorist, have been included.

Table 12. Verbs with a great majority of aorists in IV: 1–3

Verb	Total past forms	Aorists	Comments
взяти	22	21	1 elliptic perfect
возвратитися	9	9	
дати	12	12	
идти	26	25	1 imperfect
начати + начатися	23 + 2	22 + 2	1 elliptic perfect
повелѣти	25	25	
приити	27	27	
прияти	16	15	1 elliptic perfect
речи	17	17	
сотворити	10	10	
умерѣти	9	9	

4.3.1.2 The use of the elliptic perfect

Elliptic perfect forms amount to 16.6% of the verbs for past events in IV: 1–3. Some semantic, lexical and other patterns in the use of this tense can be discerned. Of the verbs that occur frequently enough to allow discussion, few have a large share of perfect forms. Therefore, unprefigated verbs are in some cases discussed together with their prefigated counterparts.

The verb поселитися

The verb *поселитися* is in ms. U (and most other mss.) almost evenly divided between the aorist (seven instances) and the elliptic perfect (five instances). In ms. G, the distribution is six aorists and six elliptic perfect forms. The verb also occurs once in the pluperfect. The earliest occurrences of this verb are from the 17th century (SRJa), so perhaps it seemed like an anomaly to use it in an archaic form. It is mainly used as a translation of Polish *osieść*, which in other cases is translated as *овладети*, usually in the aorist.

The verb сѣчь *with and without prefixes*

The verbs *сѣчь* (twice), *отсѣчь* (once) and *посѣчь* (once) only occur in the elliptic perfect (all in the plural). However, several of these occurrences are also found in the context of 'conquering the enemy' (cf. below) and may therefore be semantically motivated.

The verb мочь *with and without prefixes*

The verb *мочь* is almost evenly divided between the aorist (four instances) and the elliptic perfect (three instances). *Возмочь* is only found in the aorist (four instances) and *перемочь* in the elliptic perfect (once), so that this verbal root, with or without prefixes, occurs eight times in the aorist and four times in the elliptic perfect, which is quite a large share. No explanation for this has been found.

Verbs with the prefix вы-

In the analyzed chapters, as found in ms. U, 13 verbs with the prefix *вы-* occur one time each. Eleven of these are in the elliptic perfect and two in the aorist. This predominance of the elliptic perfect may be connected to the fact that the prefix *вы-*, which is of Russian origin, had stylistic connotations that could trigger the use of the perfect. Verbs with the prefix *из-*, which was the bookish counterpart of Church Slavonic origin, are mainly used in the aorist. There are only two minimal pairs, where the same verb occurs with both prefixes: *выбити/избити* (used in different senses) and *выити/изоити*. They follow the expected distribution of tenses, i.e. the verbs with the prefix *из-* are used in the aorist (cf. also Uspenskij 2002: 253).

Negated forms

Where the verb is negated, the share of elliptic perfect forms is unusually high, even though the simplex preterites, when added together, still dominate. Out of a total of 36 negated instances, 14 are in the aorist, 10 in the imperfect, 11 in the elliptic perfect, and one in the full perfect tense. Thus, in negated clauses, perfect forms (full or elliptic) make up 33.3%, clearly encroaching more on the aorist than on the imperfect.

The use of the perfect tense in negated clauses has been attested in the *Novgorodskaja pervaja letopis'*. There it has been explained by the fact that the perfect was often used to convey background information, in clauses with what P. V. Petruchin (2003: 119–121) calls lowered communicative status. As D. Matthews (1995: 303–304) phrases it, events expressed in the perfect tense (full or elliptic) are often "under absolute negation," negation not referring to any specific time, and they do not form a part of the narrative chain.

'Conquering the enemy'

There are three passages, similar in subject matter, where several (four to six) elliptic perfect forms are used together, which may mean that the use of the perfect tense is semantically motivated here. In the descriptions of how Olga massacred the Drevljans (example (52)), how Svjatoslav conquered the Greek (example (53)) and how Rus' conquered the Pečenegs (example (54)), the elliptic perfect is used for the actions:

(52) множество древлянъ **побили**, **посѣкли**, ї **потопили**, а иниї з женами и з дѣтми **погорѣли**, иныхъ ж зѣло много в Киевъ в неволю **отвели**, а иных яко скотъ **продавали** (Slav 26, fol. 204v)

(53) бежащихъ ж грекоⷡ **побивали**, **сѣкли** иныхъ поемше живых, потомъ Святославъ употребляя побѣды греческия страны, **разорял** и **п8стошилъ** (Slav 26, fol. 210r)

(54) Ру*с* же 8тѣкающих **били сѣкли**, **кололи**, **ловили**, иных в Трубеже рекѣ **потопили**, и множествѡ полону и добычи в печенѣжскомъ обосе **набрали** (Slav 26, fol. 217v–218r)

This can be labelled 'conquering the enemy' or, viewed more broadly, 'violent or dramatic action.' The use of the perfect tense here remains to be explained, but it seems to have been an active choice, especially in example (52), since the Polish parallel to this text passage does not have finite verb forms, but uses an impersonal passive construction.

4.3.1.3 The use of the full perfect

The full perfect (with the auxiliary verb *быти* in the present tense) will be treated separately, despite the fact that, as we will see below, the choice between it and the elliptic perfect (without auxiliary verb) is partly dictated by the subject, and their distribution is thus complementary. However, since the forms with auxiliary verbs were no longer in use in the spoken language of the 17th century (cf. Gorškova & Chaburgaev 1997: 330–331; Uspenskij 2002: 247–249), these forms can be seen as marked, which justifies treating them as a separate category.

There are only nine instances of the full perfect tense in these chapters, and all except one (Slav 26, fol. 174r) are found in direct speech. Since there is an obvious connection between direct speech and the full perfect tense, we will look more closely at the overall distribution of tenses referring to past events in direct speech. There are a total of 22 such verbs, and the distribution of tenses is as follows: 11 aorist forms, one imperfect form, two elliptic perfect forms and eight full perfect forms. In other words, 36.4% of the instances are in the full perfect, and the full and elliptic perfect forms together make up 45.5% of the instances. A similar proportion has been observed by Matthews (1995: 299) in direct speech in the Galician Chronicle, which relates events of the late 13th century.

All instances of the full perfect, including the one that is not found in direct speech, have the auxiliary verb in the first or second person (singular or plural). This is not surprising, since even in early texts, perfect forms in the third person singular or plural were sometimes used without an auxiliary verb, whereas the full perfect form remained in use much longer in the first and second persons (Zaliznjak 2008: 236, 239–240). Since it is natural for first and second person forms to appear in direct speech, rather than in narrative parts of the text, this explains the connection between the perfect and direct speech. In this way, one may argue that the distribution of elliptic and full perfect is complementary in this text.

As for the choice between the aorist and the full perfect in direct speech, it can be assumed that when rendering a person's speech, the translator might tend to use a form that was a little closer to his own spoken language. The full perfect, even if it was not in use in the late 17th century, probably seemed closer to the spoken language than did the simplex preterites. There are, however, instances of simplex preterites in the first person, both in direct speech and in the author's comments.

A connection between the perfect (full or elliptic) and direct speech in chronicles has been observed by other scholars as well, and it seems to have been a tradition of that genre (Matthews 1995: 299; Živov 1995: 73; cf. also Kijanova 2010: 57).

A typical occurrence of the full perfect is shown in example (55), where the narrative is written using only the aorist, whereas the full perfect is used in Jaropolk's speech to Svadolt (the elliptic perfect occurs in a marginal note not quoted here):

(55) в третїи день **обрѣтоша** его меж тѣлами чл҃вческими мертва, и **принесоша** тѣло его пред Ерополка. Ерополкъ ж **видѣ** тѣло брата своего **рече** к Свадолт8, Свадолте сего **пожелаѧ́ еси**, ї **погребоша** его в Овручи. (Slav 26, fol. 211v)

4.3.1.4 The use of the pluperfect

There are eleven instances of the pluperfect in these chapters. However, since all these forms except one correspond to pluperfect forms in Polish, it is more appropriate to speak of the *translation* of the Polish pluperfect than to discuss its use independently of the original. For this reason, the pluperfect will be dealt with in Section 6.8.2, where the translation of Polish pluperfects in the different segments will be compared.

4.3.2 The use of dual forms

Dual forms of verbs are not used in the sample chapters chosen from the chronicle. Some dual forms of nouns are found in chapters IV: 1–3, but only in the context of paired objects, such as eyes or hands, e.g. *от очию его* (Slav 26, fol. 223v), *впадох в руцѣ немилостивыи* (fol. 225v), *от руку их* (fol. 227v). This is in accordance with the usage noted by Kijanova (2010: 282) in many other late chronicles. However, the tendency found in her sources that instrumental forms were used in a higher degree than other cases cannot be confirmed here.

In most contexts of duality, plural forms are used, especially when they refer to two objects that are not inherently paired, such as two brothers or two rivers, cf. for instance *между Дравою, и Савою реками* (fol. 163r), *над [Д]непром и Доном реками* (fol. 177r), *Осколод и Дыръ [...] возвратишася* (fol. 197v), *кесари же гречестии Василии и Костянтинъ послаша* (fol. 209r), *з двемя сн҃ы* (fol. 212r), *х Костянтину и Василию сн҃ом* (fol. 222r). There are also examples of the plural with inherently paired objects, such as *по обоим*[57] *берегам* (fol. 166r), *своими руками* (fol. 188v, 2x), *в рукахъ* (fol. 214r).

If we look outside the chapters under consideration here, there is a part of the text that contains many dual forms. It is a short chronicle, quoted in its entirety by Stryjkowski, known as the *chroniċka* and discussed by several earlier scholars (cf. Section 2.3.1). It is quoted in chapter V: 4 of the *Kronika* (Stryjkowski 1582: 184–186) and found in Slav 26 on fols. 288v–291r. In this part of the text, the Russian translation contains a large number of dual forms, often used incorrectly, in singular or plural contexts. This incorrect use of dual forms is not limited to the quoted chronicle, but is also to be found in the text surrounding it, although it seems to be more frequent in the

---

[57] Ms. N has *обѣимъ*.

translation of the quoted text. Hypercorrect use of dual forms can be found in original Russian chronicles from the 17th century and has been explained as a way for the scribes to set the bookish standard of the text, i.e. they used them as markers of bookishness (cf. Živov 1995; Kijanova 2010: 50–51, 62). The beginning of the *chronička* may serve as an illustration.

> посемъ егда Ярославъ Владимеровичь великїи кн͠зь киевскїи умре, сынове же его трие **свободиста** дядю своего С8дислава ис пор8бья, сей абие бысть инокъ а Игорь в Смоленск8 8мре, и **разделиста** Смоленескъ на три доли, устрои Игорь в Переясловле цр͠квь ст͠аго Михайла каменн8ю. умре ж С8диславъ старецъ, а 8 Заслава киевского кн͠зѧ родися сынъ Стополкъ Михайло. родися Стаслав8 с͠нъ Олехъ. а по немъ вторый Дв͠дъ, посемъ третїи Глѣбъ, посемъ **прїидоста** половцы в р8ск8ю землю против8 ихъ **изыдоста** трие ярославовичи Заславъ, Стославъ, и Всеволодъ, и **бѣста** на Ѡл҃зе, **снїидостасѧ** рати. и гнѣвом Бж͠їимъ поражены с8ть хр͠стияне, и **бѣжаста** воеводы р8ския со множеством ратныхъ людей. (Slav 26, fol. 289r)

4.3.3 The category of animacy

The use of genetical genitive forms to express the accusative of animate nouns (hereafter A=G) in certain gender-number combinations in Russian has developed over time. The original accusative forms for the groups of nouns concerned were either identical with the nominative (hereafter A=N), as in the masculine singular, or coincided with them at an early stage, as in the masculine plural. Even though masculine nominative plural forms, distinct from the accusative plural, can be found in this text (cf. Section 4.2.2.1), the situation in the 17th century was such that it is possible to speak of variation between A=N and A=G.

The use of the A=G form for animate nouns began in the masculine singular and then spread to the masculine plural and later, because of the tendency towards unification of the genders in the plural, to the feminine and neutral plural (Krys'ko 1994: 126). Words for animals showed variation between A=G and A=N longer than words for humans, both in the masculine singular and in the plural (Krys'ko 1994: 200–201).

The distribution of A=N and A=G forms in this text, according to ms. U, is as follows.

In the masculine singular, humans, animals (a horse, fol. 198v) and gods (including the noun *идолъ*, fol. 224r, cf. Krys'ko 1994: 4) have A=G forms. This applies both when the noun is an accusative object and in positions after prepositions. This form is also used when the accusative object is the name of an author, used as a metonymy for his works, e.g. *чти Гербестеина* (fol. 209v). All in all, this fits in with Cocron's observations, although he found that the word *конь* varied between A=N and A=G in the singular (Cocron 1962: 98–99).

In the masculine plural, the use varies. The A=G forms dominate with personal nouns; there is no example of A=G for animals. There are some cases of A=N forms, that include ethnonyms such as *немцы* (fol. 187v) and *печенѣги* (fol. 208r), other humans such as *послы* (e.g. fols. 169v, 222r) and *жители* (fol. 174v), and the animals *кони* (fol. 207v). There is also an instance of A=G plural of a masculine a-stem, *воеводъ*. Constructions with the prepositions *въ* and *на*, especially formulas such as *иде на…* (cf. Section 7.4.2) and *послати въ…* (e.g. fols. 193v–194r, 194r, although this verb is usually constructed with *къ* + dative), seem to be a special case, and in these positions the A=N form is favored. Cocron (1962: 100–102) also noted a tendency towards the A=N form after prepositions, as opposed to uses without prepositions, where the form A=G prevailed in his sources.

There are not many instances of animate feminine plural objects, but in most cases where they do appear, they have A=N. This concerns humans, *жены* (fol. 222r), as well as animals, *рыбы* (fol. 180r) and *овцы* (fols. 201r, 203v). The A=G *овецъ* (fol. 177v) also occurs once. According to Cocron (1962: 101), it was unusual for feminine personal nouns to have A=N in the plural, but variation was common for feminine animals.

In Polish, the category of animacy developed at different times in the singular and the plural. For the accusative singular of animate masculine nouns, A=G forms are attested in early texts, in the 16th century it was a rule for persons and had also spread to animals, although that category was more conservative (Klemensiewicz et al. [1955] 1981: 271–272). Isolated instances of genitive forms for the accusative plural of masculine personal nouns are found in texts from the 16th century; they became more common in the 17th century, and by the 18th century the use of the old accusative forms had an archaic character (Klemensiewicz et al. [1955] 1981: 281–282). In Stryjkowski's Polish text we see variation between the two constructions, but A=G forms in the plural are by no means unusual or exceptions.

Sometimes the choice of form in the Russian translation is identical to the Polish original and can be considered to be modeled on it, but sometimes they are different, in which cases it is mostly Polish that has A=N and Russian A=G.

4.3.4 Possessive adjectives

In Old Russian as well as in Old Polish, possession could be expressed with a possessive genitive or a possessive adjective (in Old Russian, there was also a possessive dative, which, however, is not found in this text). The choice between them depended mainly on whether the possessor was expressed by a single word or several. Single-word possessors were typically expressed by a possessive adjective, and multiple-word possessors by a possessive genitive (Eckhoff 2006: 40–45). However, there were exceptions to this norm in Russian as well as in Polish (for Polish examples, cf. Pisarkowa 1984: 129).

Both the Polish original and the Russian translation of the examined chapters of the *Kronika* follow this principle quite faithfully, with no great differences between the manuscripts of the translation. An exception in the Polish text is the name *Noe* 'Noah,' which does not form a possessive adjective (but itself is declined as an adjective, since it ends in -*e*), whereas the Russian equivalent *Ной* regularly forms a possessive adjective, *Ноевъ*. In some instances, a possessive genitive in a Latin quote in the text is translated as a possessive adjective in Russian in accordance with the aforementioned norm. All in all, the translator seems to have been aware of the norm, applying it even when the Polish original diverged from it, when the original was in Latin, or when the text was altered in some way. When two single-word possessors were coordinated with a conjunction, they were treated as single-word possessors and translated with possessive adjectives (cf. example (59) below). H. M. Eckhoff (2006: 165–167, 212, 282) treats such examples as constructions with a complex possessor that should normally have been expressed with the genitive case.

The following examples illustrate cases where the original and the translation differ, although it is difficult to say if different norms applied in the two languages or if the Polish original diverged from the norm and the translator corrected this. It is a question of whether paratactic constructions are interpreted as one single (multiple-word) noun phrase or as (single-word) head nouns with (single- or multiple-word) appositions. The presence of the conjunction *albo* in example (56) seems to have put the translator in favor of treating it as a single-word possessor with an apposition, whereas in example (57), no conjunction is inserted between the elements, so the translator perceived them as a multiple-word possessor:

(56) co iesliby ták było/ tedyby ći Xiążętá potomkámi **Palemoná** álbo **Publiussa Liboná Rzymskiego Xiążęćiá**/ álbo towárzyszámi iego być musieli (Stryjkowski 1582: 118)

еже аще бы сице было, тогда тїи кн҃зи наслѣдницы **Палемоновы** или **П8влїа Ливона римского кн҃зя**, или товарыщи их бях8 (Slav 26, fol. 195v)

(57) A ieszcze zá żywotá **Olechowego opiekuná swego** poiął sobie w małżeński stan Olchę Práwnuczkę Gostomisselowę ze Pskową. (Stryjkowski 1582: 121)

а еще при животѣ **Охеха** [sic] **дядки своего** поя себѣ в с8пружство Олꙶ8 правн8чку Гостомилов8 изо Пскова (Slav 26, fol. 200r)

In the following example, the Polish original has a two-word possessor in the genitive, but in the Russian translation, one element has been removed and the construction has accordingly been altered to a possessive pronoun:

(58) A naprzod Swadolt nijaki przednieyszy Pan rádny **nieboszczyká Swento-sławá** przyiáchawszy ná Kijow do Jarozełká [sic] Xiążęciá Kijowskiego stárszego z brátow (Stryjkowski 1582: 129)

в началѣ первыꙗ дѵ҃мныꙗ **Свято с̑лаво в̑** бояринъ именем Свадолтъ, приѣха в̑ в Киевъ кь Ярополк8 кн҃зю киевском8 болшому о т братїи (Slav 26, fol. 211r)

In example (59), the Polish original names two authors joined by a conjunction and therefore expresses each single-word possessor as a possessive adjective. The conjunction has been omitted from the Russian translation, or else it has merged with the following name, which begins in the same letter, but the names are still given as possessive adjectives:

(59) Wywodzą też niektórzy Rusaki z Kolchis kráiny oney sławnej/ do ktorey Iason po złote runo álbo wełnę żeglował/ o czym sie iusz wyzszej z Historiey **Trogussowey y Iustinowey** powiedziáło. (Stryjkowski 1582: 113)

производятъ же нѣцыи р8сако в̑ о т страны колхиския славныꙗ, в ню же Иасо н по златое р8но ѣздил̑, о чем выше се г̑ в повести **Троговои И8стиновой** речеся (Slav 26, fol. 188v)

An interesting example is *вѣрующиꙗ в гс̑да н̑шего Иїсус Хрс̑та* (fol. 219v), where the first element is not declined at all, showing that this was perceived as a single name rather than as two. All other consulted manuscripts, however, have the first part in the form A=G as well.[58] There is a similar instance with a genuine genitive (not an A=G), namely *в произведении родословия Исс̑ъ Хрс̑това* (fol. 159r), where the first element is undeclined in all manuscripts. In the phrase *в познание истинного Бг̑а и Їсуса Хрс̑та сн̑а его единороднаго приведоша* (fol. 228r), which is also a genuine genitive form, both elements of the name are declined in all manuscripts.

There are no examples in the Polish text of a possessive adjective formed from a feminine noun, but in one case, the genitive of the name *Holha* is replaced in the Russian translation by the possessive pronoun *Олгинъ*.

The translation contains one possessive adjective formed from an i-stem noun, namely *по обычаю звѣрину* (fol. 192r). This corresponds to *obyczáiem źwierzęcym* in the Polish original. The Russian *гс̑дня* corresponds to Polish *Pańska*. Both languages have the suffix *-ьjь-* in *Boży/Божїи*.

---

[58] In mss. B and G: *Иїсса*, in mss. E and R: *Ии҃са*, in ms. N: *Иисуса*.

The flexional morphology differs between the two languages. The Polish text mainly uses pronominal forms of the possessive adjectives. In the Russian translation, mainly nominal forms are found, except in the oblique cases of the plural, which had always had pronominal forms, and in the genitive and locative singular feminine, where pronominal forms had begun to spread at this time. This text has only nominal forms in the locative singular masculine, where pronominal forms were also spreading (Cocron 1962: 121–123).

In Polish, the last remnants of the nominal flection of possessive adjectives with the suffixes *-ow-* and *-in-* gave way to pronominal forms in the late 16th century. The two sets of forms are found alongside each other in the nominative and accusative of the masculine and feminine during the last decades of the 16th century (Burzywoda et al. 2002: 127–129). The process of the disappearance of the possessive adjectives and their replacement by the genitive case of the corresponding nouns began, according to K. Długosz-Kurczabowa and S. Dubisz (2006: 468), in the 16th century. According to M. Siuciak, this process was practically finished in the 18th century (Burzywoda et al. 2002: 127–129). Among the examples listed by Siuciak, there are very few formed with the suffix *-in-*. Although nothing is said in the consulted grammars about the distribution between possessive adjectives and nouns in the genitive case, all their examples of constructions with possessive adjectives have a single-word possessor.

In the context of the Nikonian reforms, the Russian possessive genitive began to spread into the realm of the possessive adjectives and the possessive dative, patterned on the Greek genitive, which had a broad field of application. For this reason, the use of possessive adjectives in the 18th century became a non-bookish marker (Uspenskij 2002: 450–458). Since there are no traces of such corrections in the translation of the *Kronika*, we can conclude that it followed earlier Slavic tradition and was not influenced by the Nikonian reforms in this respect. This is to be expected, since the Nikonian corrections were mainly applied to translations from Greek.

4.3.5   The dative absolute

In Old Church Slavonic and in early stages of other Slavic languages, the dative absolute was used as an alternative to subordinate clauses of different kinds or to constructions containing adverbial participles, i.e. the equivalent of today's gerunds (cf. Section 7.3). It could express temporal, causal or other circumstances and had a backgrounding, subordinating function (cf. Corin 1995). In East Slavic it was frequently used in bookish texts, but never in non-bookish texts (Živov 2011: 148, cf. also Corin 1995: 269). In some late (18th-century) chronicles it was more or less the only Church Slavonic element, setting the level of bookishness in a surrounding of East Slavic verbal tenses and conjunctions (Kijanova 2010: 176–177, 203).

The dative absolute in its classical form, where the logical subject of the absolute construction is not identical to the subject of the main clause, was characteristic of bookish language in general, including chronicles. The tautosubjective dative absolute, with a subject identical to that of the main clause, is also frequently attested in East Slavic texts, including chronicles (Corin 1995: 276–277). No such constructions have been found in the translation of Stryjkowski's chronicle.

The dative absolute existed in Polish, but was, according to Długosz-Kurczabowa and Dubisz (2006: 475), due to Latin influence via Czech. The authors do not, however, give any Polish examples, only Church Slavonic ones from an earlier period (Długosz-Kurczabowa & Dubisz 2006: 439). Corin (1995: 270–272) believes that the dative absolute was inherited from Common Slavic, but that it was lost first in West Slavic. It is less well attested in Old Czech and Old Polish than in East Slavic.

As a rule, Stryjkowski does not use the dative absolute in Polish; Karplukówna (1985: 44) only found one instance (outside the sample chapters used here), probably with a Ruthenian chronicle as its source, where the noun is in the dative but the participle undeclined. The *ablativus absolutus* occurs in his Latin quotes. Since the choice of the dative absolute was independent of the Polish original and the construction was a bookish one, the examples cited below from the Russian translation are a sign of independence from the original and of the translator being acquainted with the bookish norm.

The four sets of sample chapters (cf. Section 1.3) have been searched for dative absolute constructions. The samples from segments B and D contain no such constructions, which is perhaps not surprising, since they, with their dominance of the elliptic perfect tense, have a less bookish character, and they are more influenced by the Polish original (this holds especially true for segment B, cf. Section 5.4.2.4). The occurrences from segments A and C are listed below.

4.3.5.1 Dative absolutes in chapters IV: 1–3

The translation of chapters IV: 1–3 contains seven examples of the dative absolute. In example (60), found in chapter IV: 1, it corresponds to a Latin *ablativus absolutus*:

(60) vbi asserit Sarmatas esse Slauos & Venedos, Ipsosque esse priscos Sarmatas, vel ut Graeci dicunt Sauromatas: **dispersisque** a turris Babilonicae edificatione, post diluuium uniuersae terrae **hominibus**, has oras occupasse opinentur (Stryjkowski 1582: 92_2)

идѣже глголетъ сарматомъ[59] быти словянъ и венедянъ, и тѣхъ быти древнихъ сарма*т*, или яко греки глголютъ саѵроматы и раз-сѣᴧннымъ по зданїи столпа вавилѡнска по потопе всеа земли людемъ, сия страны овладѣвшихъ непщ8ютъ (Slav 26, fols. 159r–159v)

The other instances all occur in chapter IV: 3. Four of them correspond to Polish temporal subordinate clauses:

(61) **Gdy tedy Rurik pánował** ná Wielkonowogrodskim Xięstwie w Ladodze/ á **Truwor** ná Pskowskim w Zborsku/ álbo Izborku/ Trzeći Brát ich Sinaus ná Białym Iezierze umárł bez potomstwá (Stryjkowski 1582: 118)

   Владств8ющ8 ж Рюрик8 на великоновгородскомъ княжстве в Ладоге, а **Тр8вор8** на псковском въ Избор͠ку, третїи братъ ихъ Сина8*с* на Бѣлѣозере 8мре *без* наслѣдия (Slav 26, fol. 196v)

(62) **á gdy to wyrzekł** wnet żmijá iádowita z onego łbá kuńskiego wyskoczyłá y uiádłá go w nogę (Stryjkowski 1582: 121)

   сия ж ему изрекш8, абие змїя їзо лба конского выскочила ї 8жалила его в ногу (Slav 26, fol. 199v)

(63) **á gdy** wielką mocą do Konstantinopolá **ćiągnął/ máiąc** s sobą po piętnaście kroć tysiąc okrętow/ y inszego naczynia wodnego/ zebrał sie przećiw im Romanus Cesarz Grecki z pomocą Rzymską/ y inszych Pánow Chrześćiáńskich (Stryjkowski 1582: 121)

   велиею *же* силою к Ц͠рюград8 ид8щ8 ему, **имѣющ8** ж пятьна-десять краты тыся*ч* караб*ле*и, и їныхъ с8довъ водяны*х*, собрався[60] противъ ево Рома*н* ц͠рь греческїи с помочью римскою, и їны*х* г͠сдре*и* хр͠стиянски*х* (Slav 26, fol. 200r)

(64) **A gdy sie** z woyskiem **Swentosław przybliżał** do Konstantinopolá/ Gre-kowie odkupuiąc sie wielką danią/ od gránic go Greckich odwroćili (Stryjkowski 1582: 129)

   Святослав8 ж с воинством х Костянтинополю **приближающ8-ся**, греки о*т* него иск8повах8ся данию велиею и о*т* греческихъ границъ его о*т*вратиша (Slav 26, fols. 210r–210v)

In example (65), the Polish original has a passive participle in the dative, which refers to the pronoun *mi* and is motivated by the modal *niegodzi*. The translation instead has an active participle, connected with *множествомъ* to

---

[59] Some mss. have *сарматов*, which is probably the correct translation, since the accusative with infinitive in the Latin original could be translated by an identical construction (cf. Section 5.4.2.3).
[60] Some mss. have *собрася*.

form a dative absolute. These forms could also be interpreted as instrumental singular, but I find this less probable.

(65) A **isz** mi sie **wielkością** nieprzyiáćoł **ogárnionemu** ućiekáć niegodzi/ y wymknąć sie prożno/ przeto ia mężnie á státecznie będę stał (Stryjkowski 1582: 128)

a **множествомъ** неприятел* и* мя **обшедшимъ** не подобаетъ мнѣ бѣжати и 8*и*ти невозможно, но м8жественно противъ ихъ б8д8 стояти (Slav 26, fol. 209v)

Example (66) has a conditional meaning. This is unusual, but nevertheless attested in early sources (Corin 1995: 278; Večerka et al. 1996: 187).

(66) ktory hárdo stoiąc [...] wołał ná Rusaki [...] **á iesliby niesmiał ieden/** tedy sam ná się trzech wyzywał. (Stryjkowski 1582: 134)

которой гордо стоя вопия на р8саковъ [...] **единомъ8 ж не смѣющъ8**, тре*х* на борб8 призываше (Slav 26, fol. 217r)

A fact that could be of some importance is that all these examples, except the first one, which has a correspondence in Latin, occur in the part of the text that relates information from original Russian chronicles, beginning with Rurik's reign, as we see in the first example. This could imply that the translator connected this syntactic feature with chronicle language, even though late chronicles, at least, differed greatly in this respect, as seen in Kijanova's study, where she found that some chronicles used this feature extensively and others lacked it altogether (Kijanova 2010).

4.3.5.2 Dative absolutes in chapters XII: 3–5

There are two instances of the dative absolute in chapters XII: 3–5. They correspond to subordinate clauses in the Polish original, which have a predominantly temporal meaning, although *gdy* had a wide range of uses.

(67) Czego **gdy Xiążę Constantin Koriatowic niechćiał** uczynić/ áni ná to pozwolić/ áby miał wiárę odmieniáć/ wzgárdził (powiádáią Látopiszcze) successią ná Krolestwo Polskie (Stryjkowski 1582: 427)

кн҃зю жъ Костянтин8 сотворити сего **не хотящ8**, ниже на то соизволити, дабы имѣлъ вѣр8 пременяти. пренебреже (гл҃голю*т* летописцы), наслѣдие королевства по*л*ского (Slav 27, fol. 193v)

(68) **Ale gdy omieszkał [Fiedor Koriatowic]** przydź ná odsiecz swoim Wołochom/ W tym czasie Olgerd z Litwą dobył Brásławia/ Skáły/ Sokolcá y Smotrycy zamkow pod Wołochy. (Stryjkowski 1582: 428)

омедливш8 же ем8 прїйти на выр8чк8 своимъ волошаномъ и в то время Оѧгердъ с Литвою взя Браславъ, Скал8, Соколецъ, и Смотриц8 городы 8 волошанъ (Slav 27, fols. 194r–194v)

4.4 Chapter summary

This chapter has been devoted to the language primarily in the chapters IV: 1–3 of ms. U, but also to some extent in other parts of the translation of Stryjkowski's chronicle, against the background of the language situation in 17th-century Russia. During this period, the language was not codified, at least not to any great extent. Studies of different text genres show that they can be arranged into four registers, two bookish and two non-bookish ones, and that the registers had different norms, which could probably be more or less pronounced and obligatory. The mechanism of text orientation led to continuity within each genre and influenced the language development.

The study shows that this text fits well into what has been called the hybrid register. It is dominated by simplex preterites, but has a 16.6% share of elliptic perfect forms, and other linguistic features display variation of a kind that has also been observed in other hybrid texts.

The linguistic features of the text can be placed along two scales. One concerns the use of bookish and non-bookish forms, or functionally Church Slavonic and Russian forms. It was apparently not always necessary to use bookish forms throughout; instead a few markers of bookishness could be used to signal the bookish character of the text. The other scale determines which forms tended to vary between manuscripts and which did not. If a feature varies, it may either vary freely – there may be substitution in both directions – or there may be conscious substitution in one direction. The norms concerning variation and conscious substitution could vary between scribes, and of course over time. Five of the manuscripts consulted for the edition were probably written within three decades, from 1679 to the first years of the 18th century. Ms. N is a century younger and therefore sometimes differs from the others.

The verbal system is quite typical of the hybrid register, dominated by simplex preterites and with frequent use of the bookish adverbial participles (the precursors of today's gerunds), which are found with a variety of endings. Polish influence can be suspected in some perfect forms. Variation between manuscripts is mainly found with regard to adverbial participle forms (approximately 10% of the participle forms have variant readings in one or more mss.), but also in the infinitive.

The nominal system shows some bookish traits, such as the use of old nominative plural forms of masculine nouns with the ending -u and vocative forms. Polish has both these features, and influence from the original can therefore not be ruled out, but in that case it would be influence from the system as a whole, not from individual forms, since they do not always match. The a-expansion in the oblique cases of the plural is more extensive here than in most hybrid texts, but the distribution of new endings according to cases and noun stems follows a pattern typical of this register. The presence of genitive and locative singular endings in *-у/-ю* is also quite consistent with what is found in other texts. The only studied nominal ending that varies to any considerable degree between manuscripts is the plural ending of nouns ending in *-анинъ/-янинъ*, which mainly varies between *-ане/-яне* and *-аня/-яня*.

The declension of adjectives shows variation similar to that in other hybrid texts. In the nominative and accusative plural, the "new" form *-ые* is dominant, but at the same time, there are such bookish traits as nominative plural masculine forms ending in *-стии*. In the genitive singular of masculine and neutral adjectives, *-ого* prevails over *-аго*. These two categories of adjectival endings show great variation between manuscripts and between scribal hands within manuscripts. Some scribes seem to have had conscious preferences, especially regarding the genitive singular forms, whereas others were inconsistent in their substitutions. Short forms of adjectives are found mostly in predicative position, but are also found attributively in several case forms.

The pronoun system shows signs of bookish language, such as the dominance of *азъ* over *я* and the use of the short (enclitic) forms *мя*, *ми* and *тя*. The latter are mostly used correctly, except in one case. The Polish original, which also has both long and short pronouns, may have influenced the use of these forms. Regarding third person pronouns in the accusative, a more archaic form prevails in the feminine and more modern forms in the masculine and the plural. The bookish relative pronoun *иже* is much more frequent than the non-bookish *которыи*. The pronoun system does not vary much between manuscripts.

The numerals show some archaic features, such as the instrumental forms *двѣма*, *трема* and *чатырма*. The forms *дванадесяти* and *пятьнадесять* are also archaic compared to other 17th-century texts, which show contracted forms. Among ordinals, *вторыи* is used rather than *другои*, and *третии* shows a variety of endings. There is occasional variation between manuscripts regarding numerals, but there are too few occurrences to tell if it is systematic.

As mentioned above, simplex preterites dominate the verbal system. The elliptic perfect is also quite frequent, and is especially liable to be used of certain verbs, under negation and in contexts involving violent or dramatic action. The full perfect is used almost exclusively in direct speech, and always in the first or second person.

Dual forms of nouns are used in some instances referring to inherently paired objects. The plural is, however, more common in these contexts. Dual forms of verbs are not used in this part of the text, although there are examples from other parts.

The accusative of animate nouns is A=G in the masculine singular, varies between A=G and A=N in the masculine plural and is mostly A=N in the feminine plural. The Polish original also shows variation, but is more inclined towards A=N.

Possessive adjectives are used with single-word possessors in accordance with tradition. Dative absolute constructions are used sporadically, which shows that the translator (at least of chapters IV: 1–3) commanded the Church Slavonic language quite well and consciously aimed at bookishness.

Syntactic features do as a rule not vary between manuscripts, which means that the text as found in ms. U is probably very close to what the translator intended in that respect. Morphological variation is much more frequent, which may have practical reasons – it is easier to replace a flectional ending than to rewrite a dative absolute construction – but probably also means that variation was accepted, especially in some categories.

In most of the studied cases, this text fits well in with what earlier scholars have found in hybrid texts from the same time period. It is not an archaic text through and through, but has some very obvious markers of bookishness.

5 Evaluating the translation

Aside from being set against the more general background of the language situation of the late 17th century, the *Kronika* should also be studied as a translation in relation to its source text and to other translations of the time. Therefore, this chapter will be devoted to translations in general and the strategies used in this translation in particular.

There are two main questions to be asked. The first is how accurate the translation is and was meant to be, as well as how to judge this. As an attempt at answering this question, some characteristics of the translation will be described, such as instances where the Russian translation differs in some way from the Polish original, or solutions to problems posed by particular Polish constructions. The second question is to what extent the language of the translation was influenced by the original or, possibly, by the translators' language. For this purpose, lexical and syntactic polonisms will be sought out and discussed.

5.1 *Posol'skij prikaz* and its translation activities

According to a note by Sparwenfeld in ms. U (cf. Section 3.6.2), the chronicle was translated in *Posol'skij prikaz* by several translators. Even without being aware of this note, some scholars have stated that the translation was rather precise and made in the tradition of *Posol'skij prikaz* (Lukičev 2004: 340).

It should be mentioned that Rogov (1966: 278–279) quotes a document connected with *Malorossijskij prikaz*, in which the binding of a Polish chronicle is mentioned, and believes that the chronicle in question may have been Stryjkowski's (cf. also Section 3.2.2). Both A. L. Ordin-Naščokin (head of *Posol'skij prikaz* in 1667–71) and A. S. Matveev (1671–76) were also responsible for *Malorossijskij prikaz* (Rogožin 2003: 77–78). Apparently, the two institutions also partly shared employees, since Stepan Čižinskij, in his aforementioned request for a raise (cf. Section 3.3.2), called himself a translator for *Posol'skij* and *Malorossijskij prikaz*. There was undoubtably a connection between the two, which makes it possible that the Polish chronicle was indeed Stryjkowski's, but *Posol'skij prikaz* is more probable as a candidate for the location of translating activities.

Posol'skij prikaz played a very important role in 17th-century Russia, being in charge of diplomatic relations with other countries. Because of its diplomatic duties, the need for translators and skilled scribes was great, and from the 1670s onwards, these translators and scribes were also employed in making books. Translating literature and poetry became a part of their duties. Poems and other literary works supplied information about other countries and were seen as sources of news (cf. for example Kudrjavcev 1963: 181; Moiseeva 1973: 438–439; Nikolaev 1989: 50–54; Lukičev 2004: 336).

Because of the intensive relations between Russia and Poland at the time (cf. Section 3.1.1), many documents and books were translated from Polish, and Russia was especially interested in anything that concerned Polish-Turkish relations. Pamphlets that slandered Russia were actively sought out (Rogov 1966: 260–262; Nikolaev 1989: 32–36). Russian ambassadors travelling to Poland were instructed to buy books in Polish and Latin – the two most common languages in the growing book collection of the *prikaz*, cf. Section 3.1.2 – such as historical works and dictionaries. This activity became especially intensive in the period 1667–71, under Ordin-Naščokin's leadership (Luppov 1970: 196–198).

Posol'skij prikaz employed not only translators and scribes, but also illustrators, bookbinders and gilders who had their part in completing the books (Belokurov 1906: 54; Luppov 1970: 42–43). Some books were kept in *Posol'skij prikaz* to serve as exemplars for later copies, and perhaps to be shown to foreign visitors (Kudrjavcev 1963: 186). They were often made alongside elaborate copies for the court. During the years 1671–76, when Matveev headed the *prikaz*, the writing and decoration of manuscripts for the court began to take place on a regular basis (Sazonova 2006: 372–375).

In the 1670s and 1680s, there were an average of 20 translators at a time in *Posol'skij prikaz*, of which three or four usually translated from Polish. Many of them were foreigners who in one way or another had entered Russian service, although there were also some Russians who had learned foreign languages. Some of the translators of foreign origin eventually became Russian subjects and converted to the Orthodox faith (Rogožin 2003: 46; Nikolaev 2004: 104–105). A. V. Beljakov, in his dissertation about the employees at *Posol'skij prikaz* in the late 17th century, has stated that in 1673–80, the number of translators from Polish usually varied between five and seven, except for the last year of the period, when there were only three. During this time, translators from Polish formed the third most numerous group, after Tatar and Latin (Beljakov 2002: 118, table 5). As was stated already by K. V. Charlampovič (1914: 430), Ruthenians (West-Russians, in his terminology) were often employed as translators in *Posol'skij prikaz*, since their knowledge of Polish and Latin usually surpassed that of the Muscovites. Thomson (1993: 194) claims that much of the translation activity in

Muscovy was due to Greek, Polish, Moldavian, Ukrainian and Belorussian immigrants.

If the anonymous 1673–79 translation of the *Kronika* was indeed made at *Posol'skij prikaz*, the translators may eventually be identified among those employed there in the 1670s, or at least they text may be characterized as Muscovite Russians, Ruthenians or Poles.

Stepan Čižinskij has already been mentioned and identified as having participated in translating Stryjkowski's chronicle (Section 3.3.2). A comparison of his known texts with the translation of the chronicle could perhaps lead to the identification of his contribution. Similarly, other identified translations could be compared to the Stryjkowski translation in an attempt to find similarities. This is not within the scope of this study, but may be a future project. As a basis for further study, the names of other possible translators will be listed here.

Known translators from Polish at *Posol'skij prikaz* in the 1670s–80s are: Semën Lavreckij, Grigorij Kul'čickij, Ivan Gudanskij, Gavrila Dorofeev, Ivan Vasjutinskij, Stachej Gadzalovskij, Stepan Čižinskij, Petr Dolgovo and Ivan Tjažkogorskij (Nikolaev 2004: 105). This list, which Nikolaev set up with the languages as a starting point, fits well in with the list made by Charlampovič (1914: 430–435) of translators with Ruthenian (West-Russian) names. The only one not mentioned by Charlampovič was Petr Dolgovo, which means that all the translators from Polish at that time except one had Ruthenian names. None of them, except Čižinskij, have been set in connection with the translation of Stryjkowski. The following is known about them.

Semën Lavreckij worked as a translator from Polish and Latin for *Posol'skij prikaz* from 1660 to the beginning of the 18th century. He was involved in the translation of *Velikoe zercalo* in 1675–77, cf. Section 6.2 (SKK 1993: 213–214).

Grigorij Kul'čickij translated from Belorussian and Polish starting in 1669 and was also involved in the above-mentioned translation of *Velikoe zercalo*, although by that time he was instead employed by *Malorossijskij prikaz* (Charlampovič 1914: 431; SKK 1992: 166).

Ivan Gudanskij worked as a translator from Polish and Latin for *Posol'skij prikaz* from 1666 to the 1680s. He was also involved in the translation of *Velikoe zercalo* (SKK 1992: 244–245), and in 1677, he made one of the two translations of the Melusina Saga (SKK 1993: 127–129).

Gavrila Dorofeev (or Dorofeevič) may, according to Charlampovič (1914: 432), be identical to Gavrilo Bolotinskij, who worked as a translator from Polish and Latin from 1674 to 1678.

Ivan Vasjutinskij worked for *Posol'skij prikaz* from 1675 to 1678. It is not known if he translated from other languages than Polish. He was also involved in the translation of *Velikoe zercalo* (Deržavina 1965: 27–28).

Stachej Gadzalovskij (or Godzalovskij) was a Pole from Vilnius who worked for *Posol'skij prikaz* from 1667 to at least 1689 and translated from Polish and Latin. Among his translations from Polish were *Alkoran Machmetów* (from an original printed in 1683), *Hippica albo nauka o koniach*, which he translated in 1685 (SKK 1992: 191) and a book about Polish heraldry, in 1682 (Sedov 2006: 477). According to Charlampovič (1914: 431), he translated a chronicle from Polish in 1671–73 while accompanying Muscovite troops in the Ukraine. He taught Sparwenfeld Russian and perhaps also Polish, and sold a Latin-Slavic dictionary to him (Birgegård 1985: 74–75).

Petr Dolgovo worked for *Posol'skij* and *Malorossijskij prikaz* until his death in 1678, with translation as one of his duties. He helped Nikolaj Spafarij translate a number of books, although his part in the work has not been determined (SKK 1992: 276).

Ivan Tjažkogorskij was a Catholic, possibly of Ukrainian origin, who worked in *Posol'skij prikaz* at least from 1668. He took part in the translation of numerous books from German, Latin and French, as well as from Polish. He died after 1704 (SKK 2004: 52–53).

Charlampovič (1914: 432) also mentions Christofor Silobratskij, who is never listed as an employee at *Posol'skij prikaz*, but who is mentioned in documents regarding a transfer from *Aptekarskij prikaz*.

5.2 Translation theory

The aim of this section is to provide the background and terminology for the remainder of the chapter, where the translation of Stryjkowski's chronicle will be characterized.

Many scholars who deal with translations try to determine their fidelity to the original, using categories such as literal, word-for-word or free. Such labels are mostly intuitive and only loosely defined. In our case, this can be illustrated by the contrast between M. P. Lukičev's (2004: 340) characterization of the 1673–79 translation of Stryjkowski's chronicle as rather precise (cf. Section 5.1) as opposed to the opinion expressed by C. Davidsson (1975: 74–75) that the sentence and clause structure of the translation often deviate considerably from the original. To some extent, this is a matter of which level of the text the observations are based on. For instance, major alterations and omissions are rare in the chronicle, and one would therefore be tempted to agree with Lukičev, but a more detailed study may yield different results. This should be attempted not only for the sake of placing the text in a category, but in order to be able to identify instances where the influence of the Polish original has been especially strong or weak.

G. Toury (1995: 53–69) has emphasized the role of norms in translation. Norms occupy the large space between rules and idiosyncrasies, and can bear more or less resemblance to either of these extremes. It is in the nature of norms that they vary across space and time, between different schools of translators, etc. There may be *extratextual* and *textual* sources for the reconstruction of translational norms, and Toury gives priority to the textual sources (the translations themselves) as primary products of the norms, whereas the extratextual sources (prescriptive theories and statements) are secondary and often do not agree with what can be observed from the actual texts.

The information gathered from extratextual sources can also be called *explicit translation theory*, i.e. translators' own statements about their work, their decisions and principles (Koller 2004: 34–35). Such statements about this period of Slavic translation exist only regarding Greek as a source language, and there are none about e.g. the norms at *Posol'skij prikaz*. Although we know that the translations made there were evaluated (Rogožin 2003: 264) and that translators had to prove their skills before they were accepted (Rogožin 2003: 41), we do not know the criteria by which they were judged, and no written instructions for their work have been preserved. Section 5.2.1 will be devoted to explicit translation theory regarding early Russian translations from Greek, even though we can be fairly certain that these norms only applied to a particular group of texts.

The textual sources provide us with *implicit translation theory*, i.e. the principles that can be deduced from studying the relationships between source texts and target texts (Koller 2004: 35). Section 5.2.2 describes some studies on early Russian translations where observations of this kind have been made.

A central concept in translation studies is that of *equivalence*, a term that refers to the relationship between the source text and the target text, which can be of different kinds. One pole on the equivalence scale is *formal equivalence*, which is oriented towards the original text, i.e. the source text. A formal-equivalence translation attempts to reproduce consistency in word usage and use the same grammatical forms as in the source text. Rather than rephrasing idioms, word play etc., marginal notes or footnotes are often used. The opposite pole can be called *dynamic equivalence*, which means that the translator focuses on the receptor response of the translation, which ideally should be the same as the response of the receptors of the original. No knowledge of the source culture should be necessary to understand the text (Nida 1964: 165–171).

A dichotomy of a similar kind is that of *adequacy* and *acceptability*. An adequacy-oriented translation aims at retaining the norms of the source language and source culture, whereas striving towards acceptability means adapting the translation to the target language and target culture (Toury

1995: 56–57). In this study I will use Toury's terminology, which I find convenient and suitable to my purposes.

In addition, I will use the term *domestication* or *domesticating transla-tion*, which, according to L. Venuti (2008: 13–20), is the adaptation of a translation to the target language and the target culture. In its mildest form, domestication is simply the effort to make the translation seem as fluent and natural as possible, to make the reader forget that it is a translation. The term can also be applied to the practice noted in Section 3.2.1 of not including the author's name, in order to disguise that it is not an original work, as well as to several other more serious interventions in the text (cf. Venuti 2008: 24–25; 43–46; 54–55). Venuti considers every act of translation to be an act of violence, but sees domesticating translations as more violent than their opposite, *foreignizing translations*. In this study, the term domestication will be reserved for the instances where information has been consciously adapted to Russian practice, such as the ones discussed in Section 5.3.3. The use of Venuti's term does not mean that I subscribe to his moral judgement on the translator's choice.

5.2.1 Explicit translation theory and early translations in Russia

Much of the literature on translations into Church Slavonic or Old Russian concentrates on translations from Greek, especially of religious texts, which is understandable, because their status as holy texts demanded that they be translated as faithfully as possible. This attitude towards holy texts was of course not unique to the Slavic context; it may suffice here to refer to St. Jerome, the translator of the Vulgata, whose famous claim that he translated not word by word, but sense by sense, was modified by "absque scripturis sanctis, ubi et verborum ordo mysterium est," 'except for the holy scriptures, where even the word order is a mystery' (cf. Ågren 1995).

Conflicts and reforms regarding religious texts reveal the explicit translation theory of translators and editors. For instance, the importance of being true to the Greek text and the awareness of the elements of language became apparent in the case of Maksim Grek. He systematically changed 2nd person aorist forms to perfect forms in order to avoid homonymy with the 3rd person aorist, since there was no corresponding homonymy in Greek, but was accused of heresy because of how others perceived these changes. Such changes were also made later during Nikon's reforms (Mathauserová 1976: 45–50; Uspenskij 2002: 230–238). Other examples from Nikon's reforms are the introduction of new forms in the masculine genitive plural in order to avoid homonymy with the nominative singular, and an increased use of the genitive case instead of the dative or possessive adjectives, again because of the situation in Greek (cf. Section 4.3.4). It is evident from editorial notes and polemic writings that the innovators actively oriented their work on Greek grammar (Uspenskij 2002: 450–467).

Another conflict related to translations took place in the 1680s between the Graecophile Evfimij Čudovskij and the Latinizer Simeon Polockij (cf. Section 3.1.2). The former had translated many religious texts from Greek and argued for literal translation. He preferred to use Slavic words with an etymology that corresponded to that of the Greek words, rather than the Slavic words that were actually in use. The latter, on the other hand, had published the controversial Rhymed Psalter, *Psaltir' rifmotvornaja*, in 1680, and in general had, one might say, a more acceptability-oriented view of translations (Mathauserová 1976: 42–44; Sazonova 2006: 92–93, 97–98). Evfimij Čudovskij famously expressed himself as follows:

> И подобает истинно и право преводити от слова до слова, ничто разума и рѣчений пременяя, и той есть преводитель вѣрный, иже и разум, и рѣчения преводит неложиво, ничто оставляя или пременяя (after Sazonova 2006: 93).

Interestingly enough, Simeon Polockij expressed himself in a very similar way, also attaching importance to the central concepts *rečenie* and *razum*, but stressing that neither should be *left out* rather than that they should not be *changed*. He also gave the word *rečenie* a broader meaning than Evfimij Čudovskij did (Mathauserová 1976: 53–55).

5.2.2   Implicit translation theory and early translations in Russia

As already mentioned, all explicit statements about translations made in Russia until the 17th century concern religious texts. Early secular translations were made according to other norms that allowed much greater liberties, but there does not seem to have been much discussion at the time on the nature of such translations, so that in these cases, we must rely on implicit translation theory (Mathauserová 1976: 37–38).

Although so many translations from Polish were made during this period, no comprehensive study of the translation techniques has been published. Observations on different approaches to translation have been made on the basis of single texts, text collections and genres, often in connection with editions. Besides the studies listed below, others that concentrate primarily on lexical aspects are mentioned in Section 5.4.1.

S. I. Nikolaev, whose bibliography of translations from Polish to Russian has already been frequently mentioned, has written a study of Russian translations of Polish poetry from 1650 to 1730, with a section on translation technique, although its pronounced main aim is to draw attention to the texts themselves and provide information about them (Nikolaev 1989).

E. M. Isserlin's study of the lexicon in six translations of *Dwór cesarza turećkiego* has already been mentioned in Sections 3.3.1 and 3.3.2. The translations that used a language she called *delovaja reč'* tended to prefer concrete words and terms, whereas those that were written in a language variety with archaic elements used abstract words and avoided terminology. She saw a connection between the type of words used and other linguistic features (Isserlin 1961: 16, 22).

G. Bergman's edition of the Melusina Saga, another translation from Polish, contains a commentary on translation technique (Bergman 1964: 166–183). She found instances of what she calls "censorship," i.e. omissions due to domestication. She also compared the clause structure of the original and the translation and found some tendencies, such as the use of the dative absolute in Russian for Polish subordinate clauses (cf. Section 4.3.5) or Russian active clauses for Polish impersonal passive constructions.

There are also studies on texts from the same time period translated from West European languages other than Polish. I. Maier (2008: 153–190) has commented on certain types of strategies in the *Vesti-Kuranty*, 17th-century translations of mainly German and Dutch newspapers into Russian. For instance, information deemed to be less important was often omitted, as were foreign names that were probably unknown to the translators. In other cases, changes were made in the translation compared to the original to make it more easily understandable: deictic expressions were replaced by more specific references to people or places, the location of cities was specified with additional information, and verbal forms could be changed to adjust to the time that had passed between the writing of the original news article and its translation (cf. the changed years in the *Kronika*, Sections 3.2.1 and 3.2.2). The transcription of toponyms and anthroponyms is also discussed there, as well as some words and constructions that might have presented difficulties for the translators.

Several texts from *Vesti-Kuranty* have also been studied separately. Perhaps the most relevant in relation to the present study is an article about a translation of a pamphlet from 1666, printed in Polish and German (Maier & Pilger 2003). Lexical and syntactic parallels show that the Russian translation was made from the Polish, not the German, text, which is illustrated with numerous examples. The scholars come to the conclusion that the translator was not a Pole.

A letter, translated from English to Russian in 1673, has been studied by S. C. Gardiner (1963), with a discussion of misunderstandings of the original, omitted words, calques and what Gardiner calls transformations, e.g. substitutions of a clause for a single word or one type of clause for another.

G. Hüttl-Folter's (1996) monograph on 18th-century translations from the French and their influence on Russian syntax concentrated on the translation of different types of clauses from French to Russian, providing tables of the amount of correspondences in three texts.

Studies such as these can, when taken together, give an impression of the implicit translation theory of a certain time period. They can also, of course, provide inspiration for work on translations that have not previously been studied.

5.3   Aspects of the translation technique

Aided by the terminology introduced in Section 5.2, we will now discuss different aspects of the translation. The study of the translation technique for verse sections is inspired by an earlier study, whereas the other aspects have been chosen because they strike the eye when comparing the source text and the target text. Depending on the point of view, the scope of the text studied will vary: sometimes only the chapters included in the edition will be treated, sometimes the four sets of sample chapters, sometimes text passages outside the sample chapters. The choice will in each case be justified by the approach taken (cf. Section 1.3).

5.3.1   Translation of verse

As mentioned in Section 5.1, translating Polish poetry was a part of the duties of the translators at *Posol'skij prikaz*. Some prose texts, among them Stryjkowski's chronicle, contained verse fragments, which meant that the translators were confronted with different tasks in the main text and in the verse sections.

In his monograph on Russian translations of Polish poetry in the 17th and 18th centuries, S. I. Nikolaev (1989: 113–116) examined the treatment of a verse from Ovid's *Epistulae ex Ponto* in five different translations into Russian, three from translations of Stryjkowski's *Kronika* (from 1668, 1673–79 and 1682) and two from translations of Guagnini. Here, as in several other places, Stryjkowski first quoted two lines of the poem in Latin, and then translated a larger part (eight lines) into Polish (cf. Section 3.2.1), including the two lines already quoted (Stryjkowski 1582: 105). In the 1673–79 translation, the Latin beginning was omitted and only the Polish text was translated, which shows that the translators preferred using Polish as their source language. The same tendency can be seen in translations of other poems as well (Nikolaev 1989: 58–60, 66–67). In the case of Stryjkowski, this probably only shows that the Polish text was given to translators whose preferred source language was Polish, and when confronted with Latin parts, they were capable of translating them (as can be seen by the many instances of

Latin text with no Polish counterpart that were nevertheless translated), but preferred working with Polish whenever possible.

Nikolaev (1989: 113–116) compared the three Russian translations of Stryjkowski's Polish version of the poem and commented on the number of syllables, word order and rhymes. In the translation from 1673–79, each line contains 13 syllables, like the original. The word order corresponds to that in the original, but in most cases, new rhymes are found. In contrast, the 1668 translation copies all the rhymes from the Polish verse and keeps very close to it in general, which results in a variation of syllables from 13 to 16 per line. Lyzlov's 1682 translation has not copied any rhymes and has 13 syllables per line.

Looking beyond this one poem, Nikolaev (1989: 62–63) also evaluated the general impression of the different translations of all verse sections in the *Kronika*, quotes as well as Stryjkowski's original verse descriptions of e.g. battles. In the 1673–79 translation, verse quotes, such as the ones mentioned above from Ovid, were translated as verse, but larger verse sections, written by Stryjkowski himself, were sometimes translated as verse, sometimes in prose. The latter is the case for example in chapter II: 7, as can be seen in Zoltán's (2006) edition of that chapter (cf. Section 1.2). In that case, even Stryjkowski's reference to the verses was abolished: "ále iusz czytay Rytmy násze" (Stryjkowski 1582: 49) was turned into the meaningless «но чти наши» (Slav 26, fol. 106r). Nikolaev says nothing about his general opinion of the 1668 translation, but comments on the fact that Lyzlov translated all Polish verse parts as isosyllabic verse in Russian. This was rather unusual for translated poetry at the time, even though it was becoming more wide spread in poetry originally composed in Russian (Nikolaev 1989: 67).

Since verse quotes make up only a small part of the chronicle, it is unlikely that the translators had a certain strategy for translating poetry; it was probably a result of their overall translating technique (Nikolaev 1989: 115). Neither can one detect a consistent way of translating poetry at *Posol'skij prikaz*: the choice of technique seems to have depended on the character of the poem and the purpose of the translation (Nikolaev 1989: 52, 113).

Whatever the attitude of the translators toward the verse sections may have been, it had practical implications for the linguistic properties of the result. Within segment A (books I–VI), where simplex preterites prevail (cf. Section 1.3), there are some chapters and parts of chapters that are written using almost exclusively the perfect tense, for example VI: 2, the second part of VI: 5, the first part of VI: 7 and the first part of VI: 8. All these parts are written in verse in the Polish original.

The choice of the perfect tense might have been a strategy on the part of the translator to keep as close as possible to the Polish source text. For instance, if a pair of line-final, rhyming Polish past tense forms did not refer to the same grammatical person, it would be difficult to replace them with

aorist or imperfect forms. However, perfect tense forms do not only dominate in line-final position.

For the sake of comparison, Nikolaev's criteria have been applied to a
few other portions that were originally written in verse. The Russian translation is given according to ms. U, and the syllable counts apply only to that
manuscript. The layout of the text has been checked in the best manuscripts
from each of the three groups (cf. Section 3.5), mss. B, U and N.

Chapter VI: 2 is written wholly in verse in the Polish original, and it is
also translated as verse. In mss. B, U and N, the text is even divided into
lines in the beginning, although this is not done throughout.

> Kazimirz Polskie Xiążę Siestrzeńcá Mśćisławá/
> Chcąc posádźic ná Xięstwo dźiedźicznego práwá/
> Przyciągnąwszy pod Halicz z woyskiem sie położył
> Pátrząc iákby y s ktorey strony Zamku pożył.
> (Stryjkowski 1582: 229)

> Племянника Казимер полской кнꙁь Мстислава,
> хотя всадит на княжство дѣдично права,
> пришед под Галичь с войском своимъ стал,
> смотря како бы и с коея стороны града досталъ.
> (Slav 26, fol. 347v)

The number of syllables in the Russian translation varies from 10 to 16. The
first two rhyming words correspond to the Polish original, but the next two
do not. The choice of the perfect tense in line three does not tell us much,
since it has to rhyme with the l-participle in the conditional construction in
line four, but the perfect tense is also used further on in the text.

In the Polish original, the first half of chapter VI: 5 is written in prose and
the second in verse. In the translation of the prose section, simplex preterites
dominate, but this changes when the Polish text switches to verse. Below,
the beginning of the verse part is given in the Polish original and the Russian
translation. In mss. B, U and N, the Russian text is not divided into lines, but
for the sake of clarity, such a division is made below.

> Roman Xiążę upháiąc hárdzie w swoiey mocy/
> Y w szczęściu ktore dźiwnie ludzkie spráwy toczy/
> Pod Zawichwostem leżąc bespecznie woiował/
> W Polszcze przez swe zagony lud siekł y mordował.
> (Stryjkowski 1582: 240)

> Романъ кнꙁь надѣяся гордо на своя силы
> и в счастье еже дивно чл҃вческие дела были,
> под Завихвостомъ безопасно стоя воевал,
> в Полше своими нагоны людей мꙋчилъ и посекалъ,
> (Slav 26, fols. 360r–360v)

The number of syllables varies from 14 to 17. The word order is chiefly retained, but three of four line-final words are new, only the pair *woiował – воевал* is left. Nevertheless, only the perfect tense is used, no simplex preterites. Aorist forms are, however, found further on in the text.

Chapter XIV: 5 contains several verse sections with short prose paragraphs between them. The Russian translation is not, in mss. B, U and N, divided into lines, and does not seem to be a conscious verse translation. Nevertheless, it will be divided into lines here, for the sake of comparison.

> Witołd chćiwy y sławy/ y páństwá wielkośći/
> Postánowiwszy Litwę/ y Ruś w bespieczności/
> Zebrał woyská/ á ciągnął polmi od Kijowá/
> Aż przyszedł przez Tanaim do Zamku Azowá:
> (Stryjkowski 1582: 506)

> Витолⷮъ желателныꙵ славы и гдⷭрьства величества
> оставивъ Литв8 и Росⷭию безбѣдн8
> собра воиска идꙗше полами до Киева
> дажъ чрезъ Донъ приде к твердыни Азова
> (Slav 27, fol. 363r)

The translator does apparently not aim at a verse translation. Simplex preterites are used, just as in the surrounding text. It can be noted that he translates *od Kijowá* erroneously as *до Киева*.

A large part of chapter XVII: 2 is written in verse in the original. The Russian translation is not divided into lines in mss. B, U and N, but to facilitate comparison this will be done here.

> Potym Swidrigieł z nowu w Witebsku mieszkáiąc/
> Zebrał wszystkę Ruską moc/ y sąsiad wzywáiąc/
> Z Kniáźiem Twierskim/ z Moskiewskim/ y z Mistrzem Liflandskim
> Ciągnął w Litwę y z Cárzem woiuiąc Kázáńskim.
> (Stryjkowski 1582: 582)

> Посемъ Свидригелъ паки в Витебску пребывая
> собралъ всю р8ск8ю сил8 и сосѣдъ взывая
> с кнⷩземъ тверскимъ с московскимъ и с мистромъ лифляндъскимъ
> шелъ в Литв8 и с црⷭемъ воюя казанскимъ
> (Slav 28, fol. 5r)

Here, the translation rhymes, and three of four line-final words correspond to the Polish original. It is difficult to judge if a conscious attempt has been made to render the verse form, or if the translator simply followed the Polish text very closely. Some instances further on in the text suggest that the latter is the case.

As we see, the translation technique differs, and one must agree with Nikolaev's conclusion that there was no general norm for translating verse.

It is often difficult to identify even the individual norms. As opposed to Nikolaev's findings from IV: 2, none of the examples above were translated with isosyllabic verse.

5.3.2 Omissions and additions

In this section, omissions from and additions to the text in the sample chapters, mainly in chapters IV: 1–3, will be discussed. Omissions of whole paragraphs will not be mentioned here, if it is probable that they result from mistakes rather than conscious choices. Such omissions are noted in the edition, however; cf. for instance Slav 26, fols. 154r, 199r and 227v.

To begin with, the dedication to chapter IV: 1 of the original has not been translated, or rather, it was translated and later crossed out in ms. B but is not found in the other manuscripts (cf. Section 3.6.1). However, the dedication to chapter XXIV: 4 was translated and not crossed out, and is therefore present in other mss. as well. The other sample chapters have no dedications in the original. Chapter headings, when present in the original, are always translated.

As was mentioned above (cf. Section 3.2.1), references to the author's experience were sometimes left out in the 1673–79 translation, just as in the one from 1668–70. The following examples are found in IV: 1–3:

(69)   á stąd też y nazwisko Sauromatow wywodźi/ iako ludźi gniewliwych/ y strászliwych/ ktorym popędliwość y iádowita srogość z oczu iáko Iászczorom okrutnym **(ktorychem sie ia w Turcech miedzy skáłámi nápátrzył)** pierszáłá (Stryjkowski 1582: 93)

и отт8д8 *на*реченїе саѵроматов̄ производитъ, яко людей гнѣвливыхъ и страшныхъ, имъже ярость и жестокость ядовита *из* очей, яко ящерица*м̄* свирѣпы*м̄* ѧвляшеся (Slav 26, fol. 161r)

(70)   własnymi dziedźicámi Paflagonskiey Ziemie z stárodawnych wiekow być sie powiádáią/ **o czymem ia też sam z niemi miał częste rozmowy/ Roku 1574. gdym tám był w tych kráinach.** (Stryjkowski 1582: 94)

но истиннїи дѣдичи паѳлягонские земли *из* древнихъ вѣко*в* быти сказываютсѧ (Slav 26, fol. 162r)

(71)   od Braiłowá/ Dźiurdźiewá y Urusciuká/ Zamkow podunaiskich/ **gdzieśmy sie my dwá kroć y tám y sám przewoźili.** (Stryjkowski 1582: 98)

от Браилова, Дюр*д*ѣева, и 8р8стюка городѡ*в* под8найскихъ (Slav 26, fol. 167r)

Outside the sample chapters, the following example from chapter II: 1 deserves to be mentioned. Had not the author's comment been omitted, it might have provided support for the dating of the translation:

(72)   Bo gdy długo nád tym Morzem/ ktore Prussy/ Duńska/ Swedska/
       Zmodźką/ Lotewską Ziemię zálewa/ mieszkáli/ **y ktorem ia też Morze
       swoią własną bytnością Roku przeszłego 1580. zwiedził**/ tráfiło sie […]
       (Stryjkowski 1582: 25)

       ибѡ внегда долго над тѣмъ моремъ, еже пр8сы датцк8ю шведскую
       жмоидскую лотовскую землю обливаетъ жиша сл8чися [...] (Slav
       26, fol. 55v)

There are also instances (although not ubiquitous) of 'us' and 'them' changing places or being left out, as there was in the 1668–70 translation (cf. Section 3.2.1):

(73)   á stolicę swoię záłożył w Sworcech álbo w Izborku/ á według Miechoui-
       ussá w Zborku/ ktory ono **nászy** zá správą Kniáziá Alexandra Połubiens-
       kiego byli wźięli/ Roku 1566. ále go odzierżeć nieumieli. (Stryjkowski
       1582: 117)

       градъ ж столныї сотвори в Сворце или въ Изборскѣ, а по Мѣховию:
       в Зборкѣ, егоже нѣкогда за промыслом кнзя Алеѯандра полу-
       бинског взяша **поляки** в лѣто .҂афѯs. но держать не 8мѣли (Slav
       26, fol. 195r)

(74)   Roku 6486. **według Rusi** od stworzenia Swiátá. (Stryjkowski 1582: 132)

       в лѣто от сотворения мира .҂sⷨпs.e (Slav 26, fol. 213v)

There are also other cases where the translator has omitted or modified
something. There may have been different reasons for this: in some cases the
translator may not have understood the source text completely, in other cases
he may have aimed at an acceptability-oriented translation.

In IV: 3, when speaking of the genealogy of the Russian princes, the
wording is changed to become more general, since, of course, when the
translation was made, Ivan IV was no longer tsar:

(75)   od ktorych też wielcy Kniáźiowie Moskiewscy/ **y dźisieyszy Iwan Wa-
       silewic** Ród swoy być z Rzymian twierdzą (Stryjkowski 1582: 118)

       от нихъж великие кнзи московские i н̄нешние великие гсⷣри
       род свои быти от римлянъ твердятъ (Slav 26, fols. 195r–195v)

In the following example, describing the struggle between the man from
Perejaslavl' and the Pečeneg, Stryjkowski compares them to Hercules and
Anteus (Heracles and Antaeus). The names of these heroes were left out in
the translation, but it cannot be determined if this was done by mistake or in
an attempt at acceptability – perhaps they were not well known to Russians.
The name Hercules occurs elsewhere in the chronicle as well, and there it is
not omitted from the translation, cf. example (151).

(76) zátym go zá gárdło uchwyćiwszy/ **nieináczey iáko Hercules Anteusá** ták długo duśił/ ász ná onym plácu duszę z niego wytłoczył. (Stryjkowski 1582: 135)

и за горло его 8хватї даже дшу на томъ мѣсте выломил (Slav 26, fol. 217v)

There are cases when the Polish original gives two synonyms and the Russian translation only gives one word, presumably the one that would be familiar to Russian readers (cf. also the treatment of parallel name forms, Section 6.6.2):

(77) Roku czwartego pánowánia Ninusa Krolá trzećiego Babilońskiego Twiskon **Gigas álbo Obrzym** Sarmaty Praw álbo ustaw uczy u Rhenu/ etć. (Stryjkowski 1582: 93)

в лѣто сего Нина четвертое, вавилонскогѡ третьяго пра Твисконъ **исполинъ** сарматов закона и устава поучает у Рена (Slav 26, fols. 160r–160v)

(78) Leoná trzeciego Cesárzá/ ktory był názwan **Ikonomachus/ to iest obrázow borzyćiel** (Stryjkowski 1582: 99)

Лв8 третїем8 црю, иже бѣ **образоборецъ** речен (Slav 26, fol. 168r)

(79) Bo Pausanias pisze/ isz sam widział Pancerz Sarmatski/ z rogow/ kopyt końskich/ ná xtałt **Karaceny/ álbo łuski Smokowey** uczyniony (Stryjkowski 1582: 108)

пишетъ бо Па8занїи, яко сам видѣ пансырь сармацкїй, из рога копытъ лошадиныхъ по подобию **чеш8и змииной** 8чиненъ (Slav 26, fol. 181r)

(80) Niktorzy też chcą ich miánować od **płći y barwy smladey álbo z rumiánoczarney**/ co iest pospolita płeć Ruskiego/ zwłaszczá Podolskiego y Wołyńskiego narodu (Stryjkowski 1582: 113)

инїи жъ хотятъ именовать от **цвѣта р8са**, иже есть ѻбще цвѣтъ р8ског и пѡдолского, ї волынскогѡ народа (Slav 26, fol. 188r)

(81) Wywodzą też niektorzy Rusaki z Kolchis kráiny oney sławney/ do ktorey Iason po złote **runo álbo wełnę** żeglował (Stryjkowski 1582: 113)

производятъ же нѣцыи р8саков от страны колхиския славныя, в нюже Иасон по златое **р8но** ѣздил (Slav 26, fol. 188v)

(82) á miásto dani y hołdu z kárzdego domu **bielczáne álbo wiewiorcze skorki** wybieráli (Stryjkowski 1582: 116)

и вмѣсто дани ї подданства со всякого двора **белечи кожицы** выбирали (Slav 26, fol. 192v)

147

(83) s którą Iaropełk tákże/ poki ieszcze **Mniszką álbo Czernicą** byłá/ przedtym niż ią zá żonę poiął/ miał Syná (Stryjkowski 1582: 131)

с неюже Ерополкъ пока еще **черницею** была прежде даже не пояти ем8 ю в жен8 имѣ с͠на (Slav 26, fol. 213v)

(84) Potym y drugie Záćmienie Słońcá było/ ták iż tego iednego Roku cztery się **Eclipses álbo Zaćmienia**/ Słońcá dwoie/ á Miesiącá dwoie przytráfiły. (Stryjkowski 1582: 760)

потомъ и др8гое затмѣние сл͠нца было такъ что тог͠ одного год8 четыри **затмѣния**, сл͠нца двое, а мс͠ца двое прил8чилися (Slav 28, fol. 319v)

The same strategy is applied when the Polish original uses two verbs that are more or less synonymous. This is quite frequent, and was perhaps a rhetorical device that Stryjkowski favored. These cases cannot, however, be explained by one of the words being foreign. Probably, the translator considered it redundant to give two synonyms, i.e. such phrases were not part of the norm. Another possible explanation could be that he could simply not think of two corresponding Russian synonyms. The following are only a few examples of this:

(85) Y od tych iusz porządek y successią pewną/ ták Rusacy wszyscy/ Wielcy Kniáziowie Moskiewscy **prowádzą y wywodzą** (Stryjkowski 1582: 89)

и от тѣх уже чинъ и наслѣдие извѣстное Р8сь вся великие к͠нзи мѡсковские **производят** (Slav 26, fol. 154r)

(86) tedy też ich potomkowie zá szczęśliwym winszowánim y własnością imion przodkow swoich/ y błogosłáwieństwem Noego Patriarchy/ osiádłośći swoie dáleko **rozszerzyli y rosciągnęli** (Stryjkowski 1582: 92₁)

тогда наслѣдницы ихъ по счасливом8 привѣтств8 и свойствомъ имянъ предковъ своихъ, и по бл͠гословенїю Нѡа патрїарха селения своя далече **распространиша** (Slav 26, fol. 158r)

(87) isz Moscus Mosoch álbo Moskwá/ Moskiewskie Krolestwá w Aziey wespołek y w Europie **záłożył y rozmnożył.** (Stryjkowski 1582: 93)

яко Мосхъ Мосохъ, или Москва московскїе ц͠рства во Асїи, к8лно и во Европе **8множи** (Slav 26, fol. 160r)

When the original text contains Latin quotes with Polish translations, usually only one of the two is translated into Russian. This is an understandable strategy, since the result would otherwise be a repetition of information. The translation is usually closer to the Polish wording, sometimes to the Latin, and sometimes it is difficult to determine which version was translated and which was left out. In example (88), the Polish text has probably served as

148

basis for the translation. The strongest argument for this assumption is that the words in bold typeface are absent from the Latin version:

(88) Máło záś potym pisze: *Num qui uero supra Roxanos habitent, ignotum est nobis, Roxani quidem aduersus Mitridatis Eupatoris Ductores belligerarunt.* A teras powiáda coby zá narody dáley po Roxanach mieszkáły/ niewiemy/ **etć. Iednák to pewna/** isz Roxani przećiw Hetmanom Mitridatessa Eupatora walczyli (Stryjkowski 1582: 111)

Мало ж ниже пишетъ, а н̄не какїе по рожанехъ народы жив8тъ не вѣмы **и проч, однакож тѡ извѣстно** якѡ рожане прѡтивъ воевѡд Миѳридата Еупатора били̂с (Slav 26, fol. 185v)

An exception is found in chapter IV: 2, where both versions are translated, even though the shorter Latin quote could easily have been left out:

(89) Támże też pisze ná końcu. *Omnibus ad occasum & meridiem paratis gentibus &c.* Gdy iuż ná zachod Słońcá y ná południe usmierzył Augustus woyną wszystki narody (Stryjkowski 1582: 108)

Тамъже пишетъ на концѣ, всѣм̂ на запад и полдень 8мирившимся народомъ, внегда на запад сл̄нца и на полдень умири Авг8стъ войною всѣ народы (Slav 26, fol. 180v)

There are isolated instances where the translator has added information that is not present in the Polish original:

(90) tám im opowiedział/ co z nim zá rozmowę miał około wiáry Chrześćiáńskiey Kirus Grecki Philosoph/ isz ktoby sie ochrzćił/ umárwszy ma wstáć z nowu/ y krolowáć ná wieki (Stryjkowski 1582: 136)

тамо возвести имъ бесѣд8 о вѣре хр̂стианскои Кирила ѳилосоѳа, аще кто кр̂стится **водою ї д̄хом во имя о̄тца и с̄на и св̄таго д̄ха**, умерыи имать востати, и ц̄рствовати во вѣки (Slav 26, fol. 220r)

The reason for this addition is unclear. Perhaps this was a fixed formula in the translator's mind, added out of pure habit, or from a sense of piety.

The following is an example of a minor change:

(91) według Ptolomeussá y inszych stárodawnieyszych: Roxolanow y Roxanow imię iásne było: Wszákże od tego ostátecznego do Missiey álbo Bulgariey wtárgnienia **Roxolanow** y od roku 72. do dzisieyszego 1580. iest iusz pułtorá tysiącá lat y ośm. (Stryjkowski 1582: 111)

по Птоломию, и їнымъ древнейшимъ рожоляновъ и рожанов̂, имѧ бѣ славно, а ѿ того нашествия послѣдняго **рожоляновъ и рожановъ** в Миссию, или Болгарїю, и ѿ лѣта .ѻв. до н̄нешняго .҂ах̂ог.г̄ есть .҂ах̂. с лишком̂ лѣтъ (Slav 26, fol. 186r)

The addition of the parallel ethnonym in the translation is probably explained by the fact that both variants were used in the preceding sentence.

5.3.3 Domestication

As explained above in Section 5.2, domestication is a term used for an adaptation of the translation to the target culture, sometimes involving quite substantial changes in the text. Below are some examples of changes that have been made in the Russian translation of Stryjkowski's chronicle. As opposed to the omissions in Section 5.3.2, which can at least theoretically be the result of the translators' limitations, these alterations are quite clearly due to a strategy of acceptability, and testify to the translators' knowledge of both the source and target cultures. The examples below are some of the most obvious changes made in the different sets of sample chapters.

Names
The transcription and adaptation of names into the Cyrillic alphabet is a separate question that will be discussed in Section 6.6.2, but in the tale about Olga's conversion to Christianity in chapter IV: 3, a more significant change has been made:

(92)   Ten cię sam wybáwić ma/ iakosz y zbáwił [...] trzech młodzieńcow **Sidrachá/ Misacha** y **Abdenago** z piecá ognistego (Stryjkowski 1582: 125)

той тя избавитъ, яко*же* избави [...] трехъ отрокъ **Ананию, Азариа, Мисаила** *от* пещи огненно*и* (Slav 26, fols. 205v–206r)

This refers to the Book of Daniel, chapter 3, where the Jews Shadrach, Meshach and Abednego refuse to bow down to Nebuchadnezzar's image of gold and are cast into a fiery furnace, but not burnt. In Daniel 1: 3–7, it is explained that the men's Hebrew names are Hananiah, Mishael and Azariah, but when they enter Nebuchadnezzar's service they are given new (heathen) names. They are then called by these names, but use the Hebrew names among themselves (as in Daniel 2: 17). Thus, there are two sets of names used in the Bible, of which Western tradition uses one set and the Russian tradition the other.[61]

The substitution here shows that the translator was well acquainted with the Bible and with the different traditions, i.e. he recognized the names used in Polish but assumed that his readers would be more familiar with the ones frequent in Russian tradition. In contrast to this, the 1668–70 translation transcribes the Polish set of names:

---

[61] Cf. in NPL (1950: 39): "въ имя святыхъ 3-и отрокъ: Анания, Азария и Мисаила".

триехъ отрокъ **Садраха Мисаха** и **Аведнаго** *от* пещи ѡгненыя
(RGADA 59, fol. 169v)

The subject of the fiery furnace was well known in Muscovy. It was the subject of a liturgical drama, the *Peščnoe dejstvie*, which was performed every year. Presumably, the Russian naming tradition was followed in the drama. The subject was taken up by Simeon Polockij in a play written around the year 1673[62] (*Istorija russkogo dramatičeskogo teatra* 1977: 58–62), but he used the Western names.

Measurements of distance

Different measurements of distance were used in Poland and Muscovy at this time. A Polish mile (before 1819) was 7146 m, whereas a Russian *versta* or *poprišče* was approximately 1077 m (Günther-Hielscher 1995: 240, 375). Thus, a Polish mile was approximately 6.6 Russian versts. There was also a Lithuanian mile, longer than the Polish mile, and a Lithuanian *versta*, longer than the Russian. One Lithuanian mile was equal to five Lithuanian versts (Brockhaus, Efron: *миля*). Pamva Berynda's dictionary probably refers to the Lithuanian measurements where it says: «Връста: пятая часть мили» (SRJa: *верста*).

The two Russian measurements *versta* or *poprišče* were identical in length and are used alternately in different sources, although *poprišče* prevails in religious texts and *versta* in secular sources, as can be deduced from the sources of the quotes under the two entries in SRJa. This division is not absolute, as the examples in the dictionary include parallel readings from different chronicles where one uses *versta* and the other *poprišče* (SRJa: *поприще*). In an example from a 17th-century text, *poprišče* is explained as «Поприще – верста, яже имать саженей 750» (SRJa: *верста, поприще*). Most of the chronicles listed in Section 7.2 seem to prefer *versta*.

In the translation of Stryjkowski's *Kronika*, Polish miles have usually been converted into Russian measurements, either *poprišče* or *versta*, by multiplying by five. There are eleven occurrences of the word *mila* in sample chapters A, and they are usually translated as *versta*, as in example (93). These chapters have only one occurrence of *poprišče*. The ten occurrences in sample chapters C are all translated as *poprišče*, as in example (94).

(93)   á Stolicę swoię ná wyspie Ieziorá Ladogi (ktorego iest wszerz **mil 60**. á wzdłuż **sto**/ iák Herberstein pisze) **trzydzieśći y siedm mil** od Nowogrodá wielkiego záłożył. (Stryjkowski 1582: 117)

---

[62] Published in Tichonravov (1874: 324–336).

151

столныи же град на островѣ озера ладожского (его*же* в ширину .т̄.
[300] **верстъ** а вдоль .ф̄. [500] **верстъ** пишетъ Герберсте*н*) .р̄п̄е.
[185] **ве*р*стъ** *от* великого Новагоро*да* постави (Slav 26, fol. 194v)

(94) Przeto im podobniey było z Olgerdem z Witebská do Moskwy przes puste
w on czás kráiny bez wieśći przyść/ y przez Twierskie przyiaćielskie
Xięstwo **mil 16.** od Moskwy grániczące/ nisz do Frankfortu z Wilná przez
100. mil (Stryjkowski 1582: 423)

того ради 8до6нѣе Литвѣ бысть с Олгердомъ, *из* Витепска под
Москв8 чрезъ п8стыя тогда страны *без* вести приѝти и чрезъ
тверское др8жеское княжство .п̄. [80] **поприщъ** *от* Москвы
им8щее нежели под Ѳранкоѳортъ из Вилна чрезъ .ф̄. [500]
поп*р*ишъ (Slav 27, fol. 183r)

The correspondence one Polish mile – five *versta* was the one usually used
at *Posol'skij prikaz* (Maier 2008: 190). Deržavina (1963: 329) observed in
the translation of *Velikoe zercalo* from 1677 that 12 plus five miles in the
Polish original were turned into 70 plus 30 *poprišče*. Thus, the correspondence in *Velikoe zercalo* was one Polish mile to six *versta* or slightly less.

In sample chapters D, the measurements have not been changed or recalculated. Instead, *milja* is used for all three occurrences of the Polish *mila*,
such as in the following example:

(95) A Owcyná Opiekun Wielkiego Kniáziá młodego Iwaná Wasilewicá z
wielkim woyskiem wtárgnął do Litwy tegoż Roku 1535. gdzie wielkie á
práwie Pogánskie okrucieństwo ogniem y szablą uczyniwszy/ dziatki nie-
winne y Białe głowy ná koły wtykáiąc/ y oboię płeć rozmáicie morduiąc/
áż się w **piąćinaście mil** od Wilná wroćił. (Stryjkowski 1582: 758)

а Ѡвцына дядя великого кн҃за молодого Ивана Васильевича с
великимъ во*и*скомъ пришо*л* в Литв8, тогож году .҂афле.г̄ гдѣ
великое паче*ж* пога*н*ское свирѣпство *ѡ*гне*м* и саблею, сотвори*в*ше,
дѣти неповин*н*ыꙗ, и же*н*скиѝ полъ на ко*л* взбива*ꙗ* и обоѝ полъ
м8ча немл*ст*во даже в **пятнатцати миляхъ** *ѡт* Ви*л*ни возврати*л*ся
(Slav 28, fol. 315v)

The different ways of treating the Polish *mila* in sample chapters A, C and D
speak in favor of the hypothesis that the segments were translated by different people (cf. Chapter 6), and show that the translators of segments A and C
aimed more at acceptability than did the translator of segment D. There are,
however, no examples from sample chapters B, and therefore this criterion
will not be used in Chapter 6.

Monetary units
In one place in sample chapters D, a Polish monetary unit is recalculated into
a Russian one:

(96) Zá czym był głod wielki w Wilnie/ iáko się to w on czás drogo zdáło/ pułbeczek żytá **po pułtory kopy** kupowano. (Stryjkowski 1582: 760)

и былъ голодъ великои в Вилне якоже в то время мнилося дорого полбочки ржи **по дватцати по пяти алтынъ** (Slav 28, fol. 319v)

The Polish *kopa* was associated with the number 60, and as a monetary unit it corresponded to 60 *groszy*. When the Ruthenian lands were incorporated into the Muscovite state, a *kopa* was considered equivalent to half a ruble (Brockhaus, Efron: *копа*). One ruble was equal to 200 *den'ga* (Günther-Hielscher 1995: 298) and an *altyn* to six *den'ga* (Günther-Hielscher 1995: 17), which means that one and a half *kopa* was indeed equal to 150/6=25 *altyn*. The situation in the Ruthenian lands probably made it necessary to master the conversion of these monetary units, and it is perhaps not surprising that a translator at *Posol'skij prikaz* had that ability.

Planet name
The name of the planet Saturn (Stryjkowski 1582: 87) was changed to *Кронъ* (Slav 26, fol. 150r), which was the usual name of that planet in Russian at the time (SRJa: *кронъ*).

5.4 Polish influence

An important criterion for characterizing the translation is identifying the influence of the Polish language, recognizable in the frequency of polonisms, i.e. words of Polish origin (lexical polonisms) or syntactic structures typical for Polish (syntactic polonisms). The influence of Polish on Russian was great during this period. Therefore, the occurrence of polonisms in the text may testify either to the character of this particular text or to the Russian language of the period in general. In the case of lexical polonisms, comparisons with historical dictionaries allow at least a tentative solution to that question.

From the point of view of the history of the Russian language, it is also important to take into account the influence of Ruthenian, which was geographically closer, and was spoken by many people even in Moscow. Many of the words characterized as polonisms may have been introduced into the Russian language not directly from Polish, but by way of Ruthenian (Kochman 1975: 22–27). Many of the translators employed in Moscow were of Ruthenian descent. Therefore it can be difficult to judge whether an apparent polonism is not in fact an influence from the dialect of the translator (cf. Isserlin 1961: 39). Either way, this influence characterizes the translation and the translator. In this study, I do not have the ambition to differentiate between Polish and Ruthenian influence, but it should be kept in mind that although I mostly speak only of polonisms, Ruthenian influence is equally probable.

In some cases, spoken Russian and Polish were similar to each other in usage, but opposed to Church Slavonic (e.g. Russian *которыи* and Polish *który* vs. Church Slavonic *иже*). In such cases, it is difficult to say if a certain feature in the text is a sign of Polish influence or of the influence of a non-bookish register in the Russian language. Other Polish features were instead similar to Church Slavonic grammar (e.g. the use of the vocative in Section 4.2.2.5), so the use of these features in the translation may be either a polonism or a marker of bookishness.

Lexical polonisms will be treated in Section 5.4.1 and syntactic polonisms in Section 5.4.2. Previous research on each of these topics will be presented in the respective sections.

5.4.1 Lexical polonisms

When speaking of the influence from Polish, most scholars have concentrated on lexical polonisms, either as their primary topic of investigation, such as Kochman (1975), Leeming (1968, 1973, 1976) and Ruposova (1982, 1985),[63] or in connection with studies of individual texts, such as Kosta (1982: 114–119). Three of these studies will be used for reference below, especially in Section 5.4.1.2, and will therefore be presented here.

S. Kochman's monograph *Polsko-rosyjskie stosunki językowe od XVI do XVIII w.* (Kochman 1975) is dedicated to Polish influence on the Russian lexicon from the 16th to the 18th centuries, including most of the latter, since he does not share the opinion of many other scholars that the Polish influence subsided in the 1730s. This monograph considers words of Slavic origin as well as international words borrowed into the Russian language by way of Polish, and determines the status of the words as polonisms by comparing the history of the cognates in the Slavic languages (Kochman 1975: 10–13). Kochman also points to semantic calques from Polish, i.e. Russian words whose meaning changed under the influence of the corresponding Polish word (Kochman 1975: 17–22). He examines approximately 100 words and gives examples from numerous Russian sources from the three centuries – mostly printed texts or later editions of manuscripts, but his sources also include some manuscripts. He also consults dictionaries contemporary to the texts, as well as historical dictionaries of all the languages involved (Kochman 1975: 147–154).

H. Leeming concentrates on so-called internationalisms and tries to emphasize the paths by which these international words have entered into the language – in this case, through Polish into the East Slavic languages. In his

---

[63] Cf. also references to her articles in Nikolaev (2008: passim).

monograph *Rola języka polskiego w rozwoju leksyki rosyjskiej do roku 1696. Wyrazy pochodzenia łacińskiego i romańskiego* (Leeming 1976), he studies the Russian vocabulary until 1696 (the beginning of the reign of Peter I) and lists more than 720 words that have their origins in Latin or the Romance languages. There are additional sections for words that were not morphologically adapted to the Russian language and for calques. His sources include printed texts and some manuscripts. The texts are of different kinds: translations from Polish and from other languages as well as original texts, e.g. ambassadorial reports, travel accounts, diplomatic correnspondence and other documents (Leeming 1976: 21–27).

In a study of polonisms in a Ruthenian text, Leeming (1968) constructed a scale on which he placed the polonisms he found, with the points Highly active – Very active – Active – Passive, according to the types of texts where the words appear. He used four groups of texts: dictionaries, Ruthenian legal texts, original writings in Ruthenian and translations (from Polish). The first three were called active contexts. A word that occurred in three active contexts was considered highly active, one that was found only in translations was considered passive, and the intermediate steps referred to words that occurred in one or two active contexts. A classification based on Leeming's article will be used here, but with only three categories, not four.

The term "polonism" is used here to cover several types of words, all of which had their origins in the Polish language. Some of them were introduced into Russian as a result of Polish influence, but soon became an integrated part of the language, without most speakers being aware of their foreign origin. Some words were used regularly, but mainly in interference texts, i.e. translations from Polish, texts written by Ruthenians or by Russians who had spent much time in Poland (cf. Moser 1998: 48–49). Some words were not incorporated into the Russian language, but are only found in isolated instances, probably as a result of misunderstandings or mistakes. All these types will be covered by the term "polonism," but inspired by Leeming (1968), they will be divided into *very active, active* and *passive* words.

These three types of words have to be defined anew for each time period: every polonism, even one that becomes a very active, fully integrated word, must at some stage have been passive and used only sporadically. It is therefore important to use the language of that time as a starting-point, and not compare only with the presence or absence of a word in modern-day Russian. There is a risk of seeing polonisms where there are none, since words that had developed independently in several Slavic languages may have been in use in 17th-century Russian and disappeared later. For instance, in the translation of Stryjkowski's chronicle, we find words such as *возрастъ* 'build, size' and *нагло* 'suddenly,' which would appear to be polonisms but which, according to N. Sablina (1982: 103), are not.

155

In Sections 5.4.1.1 and 5.4.1.2, words that can be suspected to be polonisms have been retrieved by methods that will be explained in the respective sections. These words have then been studied in the following way to determine their status in late 17th-century Russian.

To begin with, the sample chapters of the translated *Kronika* (cf. Section 1.3) have been searched for other occurrences of the Polish word corresponding to the suspected polonism, and alternative translations into Russian have been registered.

In addition to this, Russian historical dictionaries have been consulted, primarily SDJa, SRJa and Sreznevskij's dictionary, and in some cases also Vasmer's etymological dictionary. Sparwenfeld's *Lexicon Slavonicum*, which belongs to the time period under consideration, has also been used. The source material on which these dictionaries are based must be taken into account when evaluating their evidence. SRJa, in particular, has many interference texts among its sources, and Sparwenfeld's dictionary was largely based on Pamva Berynda's and Epifanij Slavineckij's dictionaries, both of which were Ruthenian rather than Russian, even though he used the second redaction of Slavineckij's Latin-Slavic dictionary, which was more oriented on Russian Church Slavonic than the first (Birgegård 1985: 31–32).

The Ukrainian historical dictionary SUM has been used to compare with the Ukrainian language from the 16th and early 17th centuries, and the Belorussian historical dictionary HSBM, with its main emphasis on the period from the end of the 15th to the middle of the 17th century, has provided information about the Belorussian language. As explained in Section 1.6, I prefer the term Ruthenian, but will not question the classification of texts as Ukrainian or Belorussian by the editors of these dictionaries. None of my conclusions depend on their distinctions.

Two Polish historical dictionaries, *Słownik staropolski* (SSP) and *Słownik polszczyzny XVI wieku* (SP XVI), have been consulted, as well as Linde's dictionary. References to them will not always be given explicitly in the text, only where it is deemed necessary.

Last but not least, the word index to the edition of *Vesti-Kuranty* (2009) from approximately the relevant time period (1656, 1660–62 and 1664–70) has been used as reference, since these texts, mainly translated from German and Dutch, are known to contain few polonisms, and an occurrence of a word in them would indicate that it was well incorporated into Russian. Below, references to *Vesti-Kuranty* are to this volume, unless otherwise stated. There is one identified translation from Polish in this volume, and one of the words discussed below (*взаимный*) occurs only in that text. Words that occur in that text and many other texts as well have not been commented on.

If a word is used consistently in the *Kronika*, if the historical dictionaries show examples not only from interference texts and if it is furthermore found in *Vesti-Kuranty*, it is considered to be *very active*. These are words of

Polish origin but in the late 17th century integrated into Russian to such a degree that they were a natural choice to many scribes and translators, even when the source language of the text was not Polish.

If a word is found in the chronicle, but not as the only alternative, if dictionaries mainly give examples from interference texts and if it is rarely used in *Vesti-Kuranty*, the word is *active*. This is seen as a sign that although the word was in use, it was not a part of everyone's vocabulary and was perhaps perceived as foreign.

If it is a rare exception in the chronicle, not registered in dictionaries as used at this time and not found in *Vesti-Kuranty*, a word is considered *passive*. Again one must remember that this label is only valid for this particular time period. A word that was passive in the 1670s may very well have been integrated into the language at a later stage.

The object of this study is not to list all the polonisms in the translation. Instead, a number of words that for some reason can be assumed to be polonisms are classified according to their degree of integration into the Russian language in the 1670s. In Section 6.9, the results of this classification will be discussed again with the aim to characterize the translation of the different segments of the *Kronika*.

5.4.1.1   Corrections and alterations

One way of determining if a word was perceived as foreign is to see if it is explained, or glossed, either in the text itself or in the margin. In this particular text, marginal glosses occur sporadically, but many of them are explanations of words of Greek origin, and the glosses have been left aside as not very relevant to the study of polonisms.

Other possible ways of detecting polonisms would have involved methodological difficulties. For instance, if a word was translated differently in different parts of the text, this might be a sign that it was a foreign element, but it would be extremely time-consuming and complicated to compare the translation of every Polish word, and therefore this is used as one of the defining factors in the classification of a word, not as a way of identifying words to study. To give another example, it could be interesting to look at words that were distorted by later scribes when copying the text, since this might mean that they did not recognize the word. This would have to involve comparing virtually every word in all manuscripts, and yet this method would not be quite reliable, since on the one hand there can be other reasons for such distortions, and on the other hand later scribes might have known Polish and recognized the polonisms, or else copied faithfully even words they did not know.

However, some of the lexical changes in ms. B (BAN 31.4.32, cf. Section 3.6.1) have already been mentioned as possible corrections of polonisms. These changes will now be examined more closely.

In the examples below, Russian cognates of Polish words have been crossed out and replaced by synonyms. This suggests that the crossed-out words were perceived as unacceptable, and the task here is to see whether this may have been due to their similarity with the Polish words. With this method, of course, only potential polonisms that were then removed from the text are identified. Those polonisms that remained and are found in the other manuscripts as well are not found by this method, even though it would perhaps be interesting to spot precisely these, since they were the ones that later scribes and readers came in contact with. Some of these are instead identified in Section 5.4.1.2.

Although the words discussed below did not remain in the text, most of them are attested in other Russian sources, which means that the discussion here of whether they are polonisms or not can still be relevant in relation to the language of the period as a whole.

In the examples below, bold typeface is used to mark the results of changes in the manuscript, and the words in square brackets, marked with "ante corr[ectionem]," are the ones that have been crossed out, and are thus under discussion as possible polonisms. In some cases, other changes have also been made, but this will not be indicated in the examples. Unless otherwise indicated, manuscript quotes in this section are from ms. B. References to this manuscript will therefore only indicate the volume and folio. The examples are given in the order in which they appear in the manuscript.

Прирождение

(97)   A Cain iż był s przyrodzenia zły (Stryjkowski 1582: 3)

Каинъ же сый **естеством** [ante corr. от прирождения] золъ (vol. I, fol. 11r)

SRJa has separate entries for *прирожение* and *прирождение*, but with similar meanings and examples. The meaning 'nature, character' of the word *прирожение* fits well here. One example of this meaning is taken from the 16th-century *Naziratel'*, which is a translation from Polish (there it is given as a synonym to *естество*: *Прирожение или естество содѣловаетъ на древесех листвие*), one is found in the 16th-century *Lucidarius*, which is probably a translation from German but has been said to contain polonisms (SKK 1989: 73) and one in a military instruction, translated[64] in the early 17th century.

In Sparwenfeld's dictionary, the word occurs several times, once as a synonym to *естество* (*Lexicon Slavonicum* I: 378), but this entry is taken

---

[64] The list of sources to SRJa does not provide information on the source language for the translation.

158

from Pamva Berynda's dictionary, which confirms the Ruthenian association of the word (cf. Birgegård 1985: 54–55). The word was, according to Leeming (1968: 296), highly active in Ruthenian, meaning that it occurred in several kinds of texts, not only in translations from Polish. It is found in HSBM in the form *прироженье*, with examples beginning from the 15th century.

The word *прироженье* occurs twice in *Vesti-Kuranty* (2009), once as a translation of the German 'Ursprung.' The noun *естество*, on the other hand, does not occur.

The Polish word *przyrodzenie* is found one more time in the examined chapters, but there it is translated with an adjective:

(98) á widząc isz trudno było mocą Miástá y Zamku dostáć/ dla twárdośći z **przyrodzenia** mieyscá/ udáłá sie do fortelu przemyslnego (Stryjkowski 1582: 124)

видя *же* яко неудобно бѣ силою града взяти крѣпости ради **есте́ственныя** мѣста пред восприя промыслъ творити (Slav 26, fol. 204r)

The word *прирождение* can thus be defined as a polonism that was well established in Ruthenian and had been in use in Russian for a long time by the late 17th century. It is so rarely used in the sample chapters that its status cannot be established from this text, but the historical dictionaries and *Vesti-Kuranty* suggest that it was very active.

Твердити

(99) Bo byli Heretikowie obrzydliwi/ ktorzy go zá Patriarchę swoiego wielbili/ á zwáli sie Caianámi/ y twierdzili to iż on słusznie Ablá zábił (Stryjkowski 1582: 3)

бях8 *бо* еретики скве*р*нїи *иже* па*т*риарха своего, величающиї его: нарицах8 же ся каиане, **г͠лющ͡е** [ante corr. твердях8] ж яко по истиннѣ Авеля 8би (vol. I, fol. 12r)

Sreznevskij lists the word *твьрдити* with four meanings, none of which, however, fits the Polish sense 'to claim.' SRJa, however, lists 'утверждать, констатировать' among other meanings, and has a few early examples of this use, as well as several from the late 17th century. SUM and HSBM have not reached the letter *T*. This verb does not occur in *Vesti-Kuranty* (2009).

In chapters IV: 1–3, the verb *twierdzić* occurs five times. Once it is translated as *г͠лолетъ* (Slav 26, fol. 156v), but the remaining four times the Russian cognate *твердити* is used (all in the present tense), which implies that the word was not perceived as foreign, at least not by that particular translator. Thus, the substitution in ms. B can probably not be explained only by the fact that it was similar to the Polish word, especially since two other words in the same sentence were also changed (*мерзостнии* to *сквернии* and *правдѣ* to *истиннѣ*).

Since the Polish word is only found in one set of sample chapters and there is little other information to go by, it is difficult to be certain, but the early examples in SRJa and the fact that *твердити* is used four of five times as a translation of the Polish cognate imply that it was very active, if it was a polonism at all.

Удѣльность

(100) Mścisław Chrobry Xiążę ruskie/ Mąż wielkiey dzielnośći (Stryjkowski 1582: 330)

Мстислав̄ храбрый кн҃зь р8скиї м8ж великои **храбрости** [ante corr. удѣлности] (vol. I, fol. 413v)

The word *удѣльность* is not listed by Sreznevskij, who only gives the word *удѣльный*, associated with *удѣлъ* 'lot.' The scribe probably meant to write *дѣльность*, which would be closer to the Polish word. SRJa has *дѣльный*, defined as 'fit for battle,'[65] but no corresponding abstract noun. SUM, however, gives 'courage' as one of the meanings of the noun in Ukrainian, and HSBM confirms this for Belorussian as well, with several quotes from what it defines as the Belorussian translation of Stryjkowski (the Ukrainian Chronograph, cf. Section 3.2.6). Neither *дѣльность* nor *дѣльный* is attested in *Vesti-Kuranty* (2009).

In the other examined chapters of the *Kronika*, the word *dzielność* 'courage' is usually translated as *мужество* or *храбрость*, and the word *дѣло* is used when the meaning is 'action.' This confirms the impression that the Russian translation in the example above was influenced by the Polish text, and it could be called a polonism, although one that apparently was not widely used since it is not recorded in dictionaries or by scholars. The word *дѣльность* should therefore be labeled passive.

Заведение

(101) Mendog Krol Litewski/ álbo żalem záwiedzienia/ y utrácenia ziem swoich/ Zmodzkiey/ Litewskiey/ Iatwieżskiey/ Weizeńskiey/ y Kurlandskiey poruszony (Stryjkowski 1582: 331)

Мендогъ король литов̄скиї или жалостию **отдачи** [ante corr. заведениꙗ] и пог8бления земель свꙩихъ жмоидцкой литовской, ꙗтвиской войженской ї к8рляндской движимъ (vol. I, fols. 415v–416r)

---

[65] «Пригодный для военных действий».

The Polish verb *zawieść* has several meanings, one of which, 'encumber with debt,' is illustrated with this very quote in Linde's Polish dictionary.[66] Neither SRJa nor Sreznevskij list *заведение*, and it does not occur in *Vesti-Kuranty* (2009). The verb *завести* does not seem to have this meaning in the dictionaries or in *Vesti-Kuranty*. The noun is found in SUM, but not in this sense. HSBM, however, gives an example of this meaning in Belorussian.

In Russian, the word *отдача* was clearly a better choice than the crossed-out word, which was almost certainly influenced by the Polish text. It was a passive word that did not gain a foothold in the Russian language.

Заложити, выворотити

> (102) Miástá wszystki nowo od Krzyżakow záłożone z gruntu wywrócił (Stryjkowski 1582: 332)
>
> городы всѣ ново *от* крыжаковъ **8строенные** [ante corr. заложеные] до основания **разори*лъ*** [ante corr. выворотыл] (vol. I, fol. 416v)

Both SDJa and SRJa list the verb *заложити* in the sense 'to found' (as do SUM and HSBM), and rather than being a polonism, this meaning seems to have developed independently in each of the languages concerned. The *Lexicon Slavonicum*, however, only gives the meaning 'pawning, mortgaging' for the noun and 'to put down' for the verb.

Vesti-Kuranty (2009) contains two instances of this verb, one of which has this meaning.

In chapters IV: 1–3, the noun *założenie* and the verb *założyć* are in most cases translated not by the Russian cognate, but by some other word, such as *устроити, поставити, сотворити* or the noun *основание*. Thus, the dictionaries and the evidence from the *Kronika* contradict each other. Perhaps the Polish and Russian words did not convey quite the same meaning, or perhaps there was some other reason for substituting them. This word is difficult to classify because of the contradictive information, but as a compromise it will be put into the middle group and called active.

As for *выворотити*, it is listed in SRJa as meaning 'to deduct, keep back (money or payment),' with an example from 1648, but this is not the meaning intended here. Nor is it found in *Lexicon Slavonicum*. In SUM, however, the verb is represented by four quotes, all from the same text: a chronograph from the mid-17th century. Three separate meanings are listed, but they are all related: 'to ruin,' 'to defeat' and 'to overturn.' HSBM shows a similar situation, with examples from different texts from the beginning and middle of the 17th century. It is not found in *Vesti-Kuranty* (2009).

---

[66] "[S]eine Gütter mit Schulden, mit Verschreibungen belasten, oneriren, beschweren".

This verb (or its aspectual partner, *wywracać*) is only found two more times in the sample chapters. In segment A, *wywracać* is translated as *искореняти*, and in segment C, *wywrócone* is translated as *развращенны*.

The situation in the dictionaries shows that the Russian verb *выворотити* in the sense under discussion here was not yet a part of the Russian language and that it was also quite new in Ruthenian at this time. This, together with the fact that it is absent from the sample chapters, shows that it was a polonism and a passive word.

Издавна, служити

> (103) tákże też Zamkow Litwie zdawná służących wiele pobrał. (Stryjkowski 1582: 658)
>
> також городы многие Ли*т*ве **исконно належащие** [ante corr. издавна служащихъ] побра*л* (vol. II, fol. 366v)[67]

According to SRJa, the word *издавна* is known in Russian since the 10th or 11th century. There is, however, no entry for *исконно*, although the corresponding adjective and the adverb *искони* are found in the earliest texts. SUM shows the same situation in Ukrainian. HSBM does not list the adjective or the adverb *исконно*, but has entries for *издавна* and *искони*. In *Vesti-Kuranty* (2009), *издавна* is attested, but not the other two words.

Throughout the sample chapters from segment A, *zdawna* is translated as *издавна*. In sample chapters B and C, *zdawna* occurs one time each and is translated both times as *древле*. Based on the evidence from dictionaries, however, there is no reason to believe that the substitution in the example above had any connection to polonisms.

As for *służyć*, the Polish verb meant 'to serve,' but sometimes, in connection with words for property, 'to belong to.' The Russian cognate does not seem to have had the latter meaning, according to SRJa, nor is it found in *Vesti-Kuranty* (2009). The dictionaries SUM and HSBM have not reached the letter *S* and could therefore not be consulted.

The reason for the substitution here was probably that the word *городъ* (ante corr. *градъ*) was interpreted not as a metonym representing the people in the city, which would have allowed the translation *служити*, but in a direct sense, making the verb *належати*, 'to belong to,' preferable. The use of *служити* with that interpretation would have been a polonism. As explained below in Section 5.4.1.2, *належати* was also a polonism, but at least one that was in use.

---

[67] This whole phrase is crossed out in the main text and the correction added in the margin. Aside from the words discussed here, the only difference is that *градовъ много* is changed to *городы многие*.

Опустити

(104) dla tego Husárze Węgierscy mnimáiąc by nászych było więcey/ nocą omylni uciekli opuśćiwszy Krolewicá Albrichtá (Stryjkowski 1582: 664)

того ради г҃сары венгерские разумѣя н҃ших быти болших нощию побл8дивъ бежаща **оставивъ** [ante corr. оп8стивъ] королевича Албрихта (vol. II, fol. 377r)

The Polish *opuścić* means 'to leave, desert,' and according to SRJa, *опустити* could have the same meaning, exemplified with a quote from the Gennadij Bible (1499). The verb *оставити* in this sense is also well attested, and as opposed to *опустити*, it is also found in SDJa. It was probably a more frequently used word, and *опустити* could be interpreted as a polonism here. HSBM shows that both verbs existed in this sense in Belorussian, whereas SUM has not reached the letter *O*. In *Vesti-Kuranty* (2009), *опустити* occurs twice, but one of these instances is a crossed-out occurrence in a draft, and in the fair copy it is replaced by *отставить*.

The Polish word is found in similar contexts twice in sample chapters A, where it is translated as *оставити*, once in sample chapters B, where the verb *отложити* is used, and twice in sample chapters D, also translated as *оставити*. This variation, in combination with the substitution in *Vesti-Kuranty*, speaks in favor of treating *опустити* as a polonism. It can be classified as active.

Скарбъ, лупъ

(105) y Miásto zburzyli/ gdzie wielkich skárbow y łupow dostáli (Stryjkowski 1582: 772)

и город зб8рилї гдѣ **много казни ї добычи** [ante corr. великих скарбов҄ и л8пов҄] достали (vol. II, fol. 553r)

The word *скарбъ* is well attested from Russian texts of different kinds, such as chronicles, meaning both 'riches' and 'treasury,' but Vasmer considers it to be a loan word from Polish. It is found once in *Vesti-Kuranty* (2009).

In sample chapters A, the Polish *skarb* is translated either as *сокровище* or as *казна*, depending on its meaning. The Russian cognate was apparently not seen as the most appropriate translation, and perhaps it was considered a polonism. The dictionaries SUM and HSBM have not reached the letter *S* and cannot contribute to our knowledge of this word. The fact that it is found in Russian texts but avoided in this translation allows us to characterize it as active.

The Polish *łup* means 'loot' (noun). The word *лупъ* is not listed in SRJa, but it has the words *лупежъ*, *лупитель* and *лупити* 'to undress; rob.' The noun is not found in *Vesti-Kuranty*, but the verb occurs once in the text identified as a translation from Polish. *Lexicon Slavonicum* mentions *лупъ* twice, as a synonym to *корысть* (II: 52) and *обряща* (II: 292), but in both cases it is taken from Pamva Berynda's dictionary, which points to its Ruthenian nature.

The word *lup* occurs twice in sample chapters A, where it is translated as *добыча*, and six times in sample chapters B, all translated as *здобычь*. Sample chapters C present one occurrence, translated as *корысть*, and sample chapters D have both *корысть* and *добыча*. All these words – *добыча*, *здобычь* and *корысть* – are found in SRJa and *Vesti-Kuranty* (2009) as well as SUM (which has, however, not reached *корысть*) and HSBM. Interestingly, the article for *здобычь* (*сдобычь*) in SRJa has the remark "cf. Old Polish *zdobycz*," which might mean that it should be regarded as a polonism. The word *здобычь* is also among the synonyms to *обряща* in *Lexicon Slavonicum*, which supports this assumption. In any case, the crossed-out *lup* would have been a polonism, and it should be characterized as passive.

5.4.1.2 Polonisms according to other scholars

This section is based on Kochman's (1975) and Leeming's (1976) monographs. The sample chapters of the translated chronicle were searched for words listed as polonisms by these two scholars. If a word is found at least once in the Russian version of the sample chapters, the translation of the Polish cognate in the rest of the sample chapters is studied. As above, the words are categorized as highly active, active or passive with the help of historical dictionaries, *Vesti-Kuranty* and the variation within the *Kronika*. These words will be discussed again in Section 6.9.

взаимный

Many Slavic languages have adjectives corresponding to *взаимный*, but in several of them, the word has been borrowed and not developed independently. In Russian, this is shown by the fact that the Polish phrase *w zajem* went through a semantic development that formed the base for the adjective *wzajemny*, whereas the Russian cognate did not. The word entered the Russian language through Ruthenian, and Ukrainian and Belorussian still retain the vowel -*e*-. It is first attested in interference texts, often in the form *взаемный* (Kochman 1975: 133–138). According to SRJa, it is attested since the late 17th century. It is found only once in *Vesti-Kuranty* (2009), and this is in a translation from Polish. Ukrainian mainly showed the form *взаємный* (SUM) and Belorussian *взаемный* (HSBM).

In the sample chapters of the *Kronika*, it is found once in sample chapters A as a translation of Polish *wzajem* and twice in sample chapters C, translating *wet za wet* and *wzajemny*. The adverb *взаемъ* is found once in sample chapters D as a translation of *wzajem*. No other translations are found for these Polish words, which shows that although *взаимный* may have been of

Polish origin, it was at this time integrated into the Russian language. It can therefore be called very active.

граница

According to Kochman (1975: 62–68), Common Slavic *granь* originally meant 'pole, post,' and the meaning 'border' was a West Slavic innovation. He also claims that the derivate *granica* was originally West Slavic, which is shown by its occurrence first in Polish, then in Ruthenian and from the end of the 15th century in Russian diplomatic acts, often concerning the western borders of Muscovy. Therefore it is to be considered a polonism in Russian.

In SRJa, the only occurrence listed in the meaning 'border' is from 1685, and there it is glossed: *границу, то есть рубеж*. The word is frequent in *Vesti-Kuranty* (2009), although *рубежъ* is even more common there. It seems to have been well attested in 16th- and 17th-century Ukrainian (SUM) and Belorussian (HSBM). There is, however, an occurrence of the word *граница* in a birch-bark letter dated to the 1430s–1450s, which complicates the picture (Zaliznjak 2004: 680–681).

It is found several times in the sample chapters as a translation of Polish *granica*: once in segment A, four times in segment B and once in segment D. Sample chapters A mainly use *рубежъ* and sample chapters C use *пределъ* to translate *granica* (cf. Section 6.7.3). The variation in the ways of translating the Polish word implies that *граница* was perceived as foreign, at least by some translators, and that it was an active word.

доводъ

The noun *доводъ* is derived from the verb pair *доводить/довести*, which originally meant 'to investigate' and then 'to prove,' a shift in meaning that occurred earlier in Polish and Ruthenian than in Russian. However, the noun *доводъ* in the sense 'argument,' connected to the latter meaning of the verb, occurred first in Ruthenian. In any case, this speaks of influence of the western neighbors on Russian (Kochman 1975: 55–56). The first example in SRJa in that sense is from 1532, but it does not occur at all in *Vesti-Kuranty* (2009). 16th-century Ukrainian shows this meaning (SUM), and the first examples in HSBM are from the middle of the 15th century.

It is found four times in sample chapters A. The adverb *доводно*, not mentioned by Kochman, also occurs four times in those chapters. These words are used to translate Polish *dowod* and *dowodnie*, respectively. There are, however, several other ways of translating the two Polish words, of which *свидетельство* and *свидетельствованъ* occur three times in sample chapters A and *приводъ* three times in sample chapters C. The variety of translations indicates that this was a polonism and not fully integrated into the language, i.e. an active word.

доказати

The original meaning of the verb *доказати* in all Slavic languages was 'to finish speaking.' The modern meaning 'to prove,' which is represented in most Slavic languages, developed in Polish in the 15th century, probably under the influence of Latin *docere*. According to Kochman's sources, the first occurrences in Russian are from the beginning of the 18th century (Kochman 1975: 51–53). In other words, the example in the translation of Stryjkowski's *Kronika* is two decades earlier than the occurrences previously known. SRJa does not list this word, and neither does Sreznevskij. It does not occur in *Vesti-Kuranty* (2009). SUM gives Ukrainian examples in this sense from the early 17th century and the earliest Belorussian examples in HSBM are from the late 16th century.

It occurs once in sample chapters A as a translation of Polish *dokazować*. The Polish verb appears three more times in the sample chapters, although sometimes it is difficult to determine the exact meaning of the verb. It is translated differently every time: *творити* in segment A, *учинити* in segment B and *получити* in segment C. This variation, together with its absence from the dictionaries and from *Vesti-Kuranty*, shows that *доказати* was a polonism and very rare in the language of the time. It is therefore classified as passive.

знакъ

The noun *znak* is well attested in 16th-century Polish texts, but in Russian texts from that time, other derivatives of the same root are used, such as *знамя* and *знамение*. *Знакъ* did not appear in Russian until the 17th century, and then primarily in interference texts. The word appeared in Ruthenian in the second half of the 16th century (Kochman 1975: 138–140). According to SRJa, it is first attested in a translation from Polish, made in 1628. It is found several times in *Vesti-Kuranty* (2009), which also has *знамение*, but never *знамя* in this sense. Both SUM and HSBM contain numerous examples from the 16th and 17th centuries.

It is found twice in sample chapters A, once in sample chapters B and once in sample chapters D as a translation of Polish *znak*. In addition to these occurrences, *znak* is translated three times as *знамение* and once as *знамя* in sample chapters A, which shows that although *знакъ* was rather well integrated, it nevertheless competed with the older Russian words. It can be characterized as active.

костелъ

The word *костелъ* is, according to Leeming (1976: 72), a polonism, which is not surprising, since it refers to a Catholic church. He gives numerous examples from the 17th century, and SRJa also has some from the 16th century. HSBM has examples from as early as the 14th century.

166

It is found twice in sample chapters A, five times in sample chapters B, once in sample chapters C and seven times in sample chapters D as a translation of *kościół*. In some cases, *kościół* is translated as *церковь*, and in sample chapters C, the most frequent translation is *храмъ*. The word *костелъ* usually refers to Catholic churches, but given the variety of translations in the different segments, the consistency of this has not been verified. Since this word refers specifically to a West European concept, it has not been placed in a category.

лежати

The geographical meaning of the verb *leżeć* 'to be situated' appeared in Polish in the 15th century, probably under Latin influence. Examples of the Russian *лежати* in the same sense can be found in interference texts from the 16th and 17th centuries (Kochman 1975: 83–84). The earliest example in SRJa in this sense dates from the 14th century, which does not fit this picture, but the other two examples cited there are taken from 17th-century texts. The earliest examples in HSBM are from the 15th century. The verb is found in this sense in *Vesti-Kuranty* (2009), although it is rare.

This meaning of the verb is found ten times in IV: 1–3, where the geography of the Slavic world is described. The Polish original has *leżeć*. The Polish verb is used in this sense only twice in the other sample chapters, but neither of these occurrences is translated as *лежати*: once (in segment B) the Polish phrase *na południe leżącej* is translated as *полуденнои*, once (in segment D) the verb is translated as *стояти*. Despite this, due to the consistency in the translation in segment A and the fact that it is used in *Vesti-Kuranty*, it can be labeled a very active word.

музыка

Музыка and its derivatives, originally from Greek but borrowed via Latin *musica*, was adopted from Polish *muzyka*, as can be seen by the choice of the vowel *-ы-* (Leeming 1976: 82–83). In SRJa, it is listed as an alternative spelling to *мусика*, and the earliest occurrences for both spellings are from the 17th century. HSBM gives the spellings *музыка* and *музика* in examples beginning from the early 16th century. *Vesti-Kuranty* (2009) shows one instance each of *музыка* and *музика*.

The Polish-influenced spelling is found once in segment D, whereas elsewhere in the text, we find *мусикия* (segment C) and *мусикиискии* (segment D). Both these words are attested earlier than *музыка*, according to SRJa. In the Polish original, the word is sometimes spelled in the Polish way, sometimes in the Latin way, but the variation between these forms does not coincide with the Russian variation in spelling. The variation justifies calling this an active word.

мша

Мша comes from a Latin word (*missa*) that was borrowed into Russian by way of Polish *msza*. It is found in Russian texts since the 16th century (cf. Leeming 1976: 81). Since it refers to the Catholic mass, it is not surprising that a word from the closest Catholic neighboring country was borrowed. According to HSBM, it is found in Belorussian since the late 15th century.

Here (in sample chapters D) it occurs once as a translation of *msza*, in the immediate vicinity of such polonisms as *музыка* and *костел* (cf. Section 5.4.1.3). Because it refers to a foreign concept, it has not been placed on the scale.

належати

The verb *належати* could have many meanings in the early stages of the Slavic languages, some of which are found for instance in OCS, such as 'to advance,' 'to take by force' and 'to threaten.' However, the meanings 'to rely,' 'to depend' and 'to be appropriate,' which developed in Polish in the 16th century, were probably not derived from the earlier meanings, but rather from the construction *leżeć na* + locative, the existence of which makes it probable that this is a Polish innovation. In this case, however, chronology does not support this claim, since Russian diplomatic documents from the 16th century show examples of the meanings 'to depend,' 'to be appropriate' and 'to belong' (Kochman 1975: 95–98). SRJa lists 13 meanings for this verb, but 'to depend' is not among them. The earliest example of 'to be appropriate' is from the 15th century, and two more are from the late 17th century. All the examples for 'to belong' are from the late 17th century (cf. also Section 5.4.1.1). All the meanings discussed here are attested in Belorussian since the 16th century, according to HSBM. *Vesti-Kuranty* (2009) has several instances of the verb, and although it is sometimes difficult to determine the exact meaning, it can at least be established that it is found in the sense 'to be appropriate' a few times. The meaning 'to belong' is, however, much more frequent.

J. Besters-Dilger (1997: 21) sees the impersonal modal *надлежит* or *належит* 'it is appropriate' as a borrowing from Polish or Ruthenian, independent of the development of the verb *надлежать*. She does not comment on the status of other meanings of this verb as independent developments or polonisms.

Here, the verb is used in the senses 'to belong' (once in segment A, once in segment B, twice in segment C) and 'to depend' (once in segment B). The Polish original has *należeć* or *przypadać*. The Polish verb *należeć* is never translated in any other way in the sample chapters. All in all, the history of this verb is complicated, but the lack of variation in the translation shows that even the more recent meanings were not perceived as foreign, and it can therefore be labeled very active.

панцырь

Панцырь and *пансырь* were two alternative spellings, of which the first shows influence from Polish, the second, according to Leeming (1976: 85), from German. SRJa gives examples of both spellings, but *пансырь* is attested already in Gennadij's Bible from 1499, whereas the earliest occurrence listed in the dictionary of *панцырь* is from the 17th century. Both spellings, as well as *панцеръ*, *панцирь* and several more, are found in HSBM, but their chronology in Belorussian can not be established. *Vesti-Kuranty* (2009) has one instance of the noun, spelled *пансырь*, as well as the adjectives *пансерный* and *панцерный*.

Both spellings occur close to each other in the translation of the *Kronika* (segment A):

(106) пишетъ бо Па8занïи, яко са$\widehat{м}$ видѣ **пансырь** сармацкïй, из рога копытъ лошадиныхъ по подобию чеш8и змииной 8чиненъ, которо$\widehat{и}$ крѣпостию и легкостию не х8жи бы$\widehat{л}$ греческого (каковы $\overline{нн}$е 8 на$\widehat{с}$) **панцыр$\mathcal{A}$** (Slav 26, fol. 181r) (cf. also example (79))

The Polish word in both cases (Stryjkowski 1582: 108) is *pancerz*. Mss. E and R use the spelling *пансырь* in both cases. These are the only occurrences of the Polish word in the sample chapters, so that there is no variation in translations that could shed further light on the status of the Russian word as a polonism. Judging by the evidence from dictionaries and *Vesti-Kuranty*, it should probably be called active.

папежъ

Папежъ is attested already in the Ostromir Gospel from 1056/1057, but despite this occurrence in a Church Slavonic text, Leeming (1976: 86) considers the word to be a polonism when found in 17th-century texts. According to Uspenskij (2002: 74), however, the presence of this word is a sign of West Slavic influence even in the case of early texts. HSBM shows several 16th-century examples. In *Vesti-Kuranty* (2009), *nana* is much more frequent than *папежъ*.

In all sample chapters of the *Kronika*, the translation *nana* prevails, but in sample chapters B, the translation *папежъ* occurs once, next to *nana*.

(107) выправи$\widehat{л}$ таже Болесла$\widehat{в}$ П8дикъ у Але$\mathcal{z}$андра **папежа** четвертаго привилия [...] обаче то к дѣл8 не пришло, аще **папа** писа$\widehat{л}$ к арцыбископ8 гнѣзнинском8 [...] (Slav 27, fol. 35r)

The Polish word in both cases is *papież* (Stryjkowski 1582: 340). Curiously enough, a 17th-century example of this word in SRJa also is a quote that contains the words *nana* and *папежъ* alongside each other. Due to its foreign reference, this word has not been categorized.

порядокъ

Kochman (1975: 110–111) claims that Polish *porządek* is attested since the mid-16th century, Ruthenian borrowed the word in the late 16th century, and Russian *порядокъ* is attested since the late 17th century. SRJa confirms the date for Russian, but according to HSBM, there is one occurrence of this word in Belorussian from as early as 1499. The word occurs twice in *Vesti-Kuranty* (2009).

It is found only once in sample chapters B as a translation of Polish *porządek*. In another instance, in sample chapters A, *porządek* is translated as *чинъ*. The material from these chapters is too small to contribute to a characterization of the word *порядокъ*, but the fact that there is an alternative translation, together with the information from SRJa, motivates characterizing it as active.

предокъ

According to Kochman (1975: 114–115), *предокъ* is found in diplomatic correspondence, under influence from Ruthenian, from the 15th century, and in Russian literary texts from the 18th century. SRJa gives an example from a 15th-century interference text, but also several from the 17th century. HSBM has many examples from the late 15th century. The word occurs twice in *Vesti-Kuranty* (2009).

In the translation of the *Kronika*, this word is of course especially frequent when the ancestry of different peoples is discussed, and hence it is used 20 times in the sample chapters from segment A, but only once each in the other sets of sample chapters. It is used as a translation of Polish *przodek*, which is never translated in any other way. This gives the impression that the word was not perceived as foreign, but was fully integrated by this time, and thus very active. This does not quite agree with the picture conjured up by Kochman that it was only used in specific contexts before the 18th century.

склонный, склонение

The adjective *склонный* and the nouns *склонность* (not found here) and *склонение* are borrowed from Polish. They appear in interference texts from the middle of the 16th century and more frequently in 17th-century translations (Kochman 1975: 21, 125–126). Most of the examples of *склонный* in SRJa are from the 1690s, and only one, taken from *Vesti-Kuranty*, is earlier, from 1646. In the sense found here, *склонение* is first attested in the *Naziratel'* from the 16th century, which, as has already been mentioned, is a translation from Polish. These words are quite frequent in *Vesti-Kuranty* (2009).

Склонный occurs once in sample chapters A as a translation of the comparative *skłonniejsze*. The noun *склонение* is found once, also in sample chapters A, as a translation of *nachylenie* 'inclination.' There are no other occurrences of the Polish words, and there is too little material here to characterize the Russian words further, although the evidence from *Vesti-Kuranty* indicates that the words were fully integrated into the Russian language at this time and should be labeled very active.

5.4.1.3 Polonisms in context

The following example is intended to show a larger context with several polonisms. Some of them have been discussed above, whereas some have not been mentioned and will be commented on below.

Stryjkowski 1582: 748	Slav 28, fols. 294r–294v
Mikołay też Rádziwił/ y Stánisław Gastołt z wielkim kosztem z Polski w **Musice** ćwiczonych mieli przez sto/ **po Moskiewsku**/ y po Tátarsku/ y **Kozácku** przybránych młodzieńcow/ ktorzy z Instrumentámi rozmáitymi musices z Száblámi y z Saydakámi ná krzywych botách przed **Cesárzem** w **Kościele** figurą záwżdy **Msze** y Nieszpory spiewáli	Миколаи такожъ Радивилъ и Станиславъ Гаштолдъ с великимъ накладомъ ис Полши в **м8зыке** совершенныхъ имѣли болеи ста **помосковску** и потатарски и **показацку** устроеныхъ молодцовъ которые с розными инъстр8менты и наряды м8сикиискими с саблями и з саадаками в кривых сапогахъ пред **цесаремъ** в **костеле** всегда **мшу** и вечерню пѣли

Besides the polonisms *музыка, костелъ* and *мша*, that were mentioned above, it is fair to suppose that the adverbs *помосковску* and *показацку* were influenced by the Polish original, where such adverbs have the ending -*и*. Ms. N also has *потатарску* instead of *потатарски*. *Цесарь* was not a polonism as such, but the use of this word rather than *царь* may have been influenced by the Polish *cesarz*.

5.4.1.4 Summary of lexical polonisms

The study of the alterations in ms. B showed that some polonisms were removed from the text in connection with editorial work. Their status as polonisms is attested by dictionaries and by the treatment of the corresponding Polish words in other places in the text. In some cases, the substitutions were apparently made for other reasons, even though the removed word was a cognate of the word used in the Polish original. This is the case with the replacement of *издавна* by *исконно*.

To identify polonisms that remained in the text, earlier works on the Polish influence on the Russian lexicon were taken as help. Some of the words listed in them were found in the text, and their status as polonisms was investigated with the help of alternating spellings or translations, historical dictionaries and other texts from the same period.

Words referring to Western concepts, such as *папежъ*, *мша* and *костелъ*, form a separate category, and their status as polonisms is not disputed. A number of other words of Polish origin were grouped into very active, active and passive words. Among the very active words is *предокъ*, which is so frequent in the Russian text that it does not seem to have been a foreign element at all. Possibly, Kochman's sources led him to draw a mistaken conclusion about its status as a polonism.

At the other end of the scale we find *доказати*, which has not previously been attested in 17th-century texts, and was probably still quite foreign to the Russian language at this time.

The following table shows the classification of the polonisms studied in Section 5.4.1.2. Their distribution among the sample chapters will be discussed again in Section 6.9. The words in question are marked in boldface, and other translations of the Polish cognates are also included. Empty cells signify that the Polish cognate does not occur in the original of those chapters and that the Russian word does not occur in the translation. The word "other" means that there is no single word in the Russian translation that corresponds to the word in the Polish original. The number of times a word occurs is not given in this table.

Table 13. Lexical polonisms in the sample chapters

	A	B	C	D
Very active	**взаимный**		**взаимный**	**взаемъ**
	лежати	(other)		стояти
	належати	**належати**	**належати**	
	предокъ	**предокъ**	**предокъ**	**предокъ**
	склонный **склонение**			
Active	**граница** рубежъ	**граница**	пределъ	**граница** рубежъ
	доводъ **доводно** свидетельство		приводъ	
	знакъ знамение знамя	**знакъ**		**знакъ**
			мусикия	**музыка** мусикиискии
	панцырь пансырь			
	чинъ	**порядокъ**		
Passive	**доказати** творити	учинити	получити	

172

5.4.2 Syntactic polonisms

The syntactic influence from Polish on Russian has been less frequently studied. The main scholar on that area is Michael Moser who, in his 1998 monograph, examined some syntactic structures that can be assumed to originate in Polish or Ruthenian influence on 16th- and 17th-century Russian (Moser 1998: 73–76). In a later article, he studied some types of subordinate clauses that were rare before the days of Peter I, but that are not necessarily polonisms (Moser 2000).

W. Witkowski (1978) also concentrated on Polish influence on Russian hypotax, but stressed that this mostly took place through the mediation of Ruthenian.

In the following, all four sets of sample chapters have been examined for some of the constructions that were classified as syntactic polonisms in Moser's 1998 monograph. The choice of these particular constructions was quite subjective and motivated mainly by the fact that they were relatively easy to identify.

5.4.2.1   The spread of *do* + genitive

In OCS as well as in Old East Slavic, the construction *do* + genitive with a local meaning could only be used in limitative contexts, expressing movement to a limit but not beyond. From the late 15th century, this construction had gained ground in Polish and occurred in many cases where *w* or *k* had earlier been used. From Polish, the usage spread to Ruthenian texts, as well as to Russian interference texts. The use of *do* + genitive to express finality is also a sign of interference. Such constructions were common in Russian until the 18th century, but then they disappeared (Moser 1998: 260–273). In the *Kronika*, this use of *do* + genitive is found, but not with equal frequency everywhere.

In the sample chapters from segment A, the construction *даже до* + genitive is frequently used with the names of rivers, seas and cities in a limitative sense. Aside from that, there are only two occurrences of *do* + genitive, compared with approximately 140 instances where the construction is translated by other means. In the first case, the Polish original has two constructions with *do* next to each other, one of which is translated using *къ* + dative and the other *do* + genitive:

(108) Ci gdy przypłynęli **do vyścia** Dunayskiego/ ciągnęli wzwodę swoie nawy/ áż przyżeglowáli **do uścia** Sawu y Drawu rzek/ potym Sawem rzeką pod gory Włoskie Alpes przyszli (Stryjkowski 1582: 96)

тїи пришед **к 8стью** дȢнаискому влекоша вверхъ воды карабли свои, таж прїидоша **до устьѧ** рѣкъ Савы и Дравы, потом рекою Савою под горы волоскїе алпїискїе прїидоша (Slav 26, fol. 164r)

The other occurrence has final meaning, and the local construction in the same sentence is translated using *въ* + accusative:

(109) Holha też iáko obiecáłá/ z Kijowską Sláchtą/ mężámi **do bitwy** przebránymi/ ná czás náznáczony/ **do Choroscienia** przyiácháłá (Stryjkowski 1582: 123)

О*л̃*га же яко обеща с киевскою шляхтою, с вой **до бою** избранными на время назначенное **в Хоростинъ** пр̈иде (Slav 26, fol. 203r)

In the translation of sample chapters B, as a contrast, the construction occurs frequently, 21 times, but the Polish counterpart is also translated by other means 33 times. The following is a typical example, where the great dependence of the translation on the original is also shown by the large share of lexical cognates:

(110) wyiechał z Monasteru Pinskiego/ **do Nowogrodká**/ á potym zebrawszy się z Nowogrodczány w Xiążęcym potćie ruszył się **do Kiernowá**/ gdzie go wszyscy Pánowie/ Boiáre/ y Pospolstwo [...] przyięli (Stryjkowski 1582: 338)

выѣха*л̃* їз мн*с̃*тря пинско*г̃* **до Но*в̃*городка**, а посемъ собравши*с* но*в̃*городчаны в княжо*и* почтѣ, двигн8*л̃*ся **до Ке*р*нова** гдѣ ево всѣ господа бояря ї поспо*л̃*ство [...] прияша (Slav 27, fol. 32r)

In example (111), the construction of the Polish verb is transferred into Russian. *Nawiedzać do* + genitive was acceptable in 16th-century Polish, but historical dictionaries do not give any examples of *посещати до* in Russian:

(111) iż ktobykolwiek wtorego dniá Miesiącá Czerwcá náwiedzał **do Kośćiołá** Sendomirskiego Pánny Mariey (Stryjkowski 1582: 333)

что*б* хто ни есть втораго дня м*с̃*ца їюня посѣща*л̃* **до костела** сендомирского пр*с̃*втые дѣвы Мар̈и (Slav 27, fol. 20v)

The sample chapters from segment C offer only seven examples of *до* used in this manner in the Russian translation, as opposed to nearly 60 cases where the construction is translated by other means. The following is one of the seven occurrences:

(112) Przeto skoro Olgerd **do Wilná** przyiáchał z Moskiewskiey wypráwy/ ná przełożenie słuszney skárgi Gástoltowey dał sciąć pięć set Wilnowcow (Stryjkowski 1582: 424)

того ради кой часъ О*л̃*гердъ **до Ви*л̃*ни** с москов*с̃*ского походу пр̈иде, на предложение праведныя жалобы Госто*л̃*дово*и* повелѣ .*ф̃*. виленцовъ 8сѣкн8ти (Slav 27, fol. 185r)

The translation of sample chapters D contains 12 instances of this use of *do*, whereas the corresponding Polish construction is translated in other ways approximately 100 times. In example (113), two different translations are used close to each other, one in the main text and one in a marginal note (marked by asterisks). In another similar case, however, on fol. 307v, *do* is used both in the main text and in the margin.

(113) Przeto Pánowie Koronni w niebytnośći Krolewskiey posłali **do Węgier** Janá Laskiego Arcibiskupá Gniezniénskiego/ y Krystophá Szydłowieckie-go woiewodę Krákowskiego *Posłowie Polszcy **do Węgier*** (Stryjkowski 1582: 749)

того ради кор8нные в небытиї королевскомъ послали **к венграм** Ӕна Ляского арцыбиск8па гнезнинскогѡ и Криштоѳа Шидло-вицкоѓ воеводу краковскогѡ *послы полские **до венъгров*** (Slav 28, fol. 298v)

The following is another example of two different translations in close vicinity to each other:

(114) A potym tegoż Roku odiáchał Krol Sigmunt z Litwy **do Polski** ná Siem Piotrkowski/ ktory odpráwiwszy/ iáchał **do Krákowá** (Stryjkowski 1582: 756)

а потомъ тогож году отѣхаѓ король Жигм8нтъ с Литвы **до Полши** на сеимъ петрковскиї которои совершиѓ поѣхал **в Краков** (Slav 28, fol. 311v)

To sum up, all sets of sample chapters contain instances of this syntactic polonism, and it is especially frequent in segment B. It is difficult to say if the occurrences of the construction are due to the influence of the Polish original or the translators' own usage, or both. A tentative guess would be that in the chapters where it occurs only sporadically, these instances are due to carelessness in translation, whereas in segment B, where it occurs frequently, it may have been part of the translator's language.

5.4.2.2 Necessity expressed by *имѣти* + infinitive

The modality of necessity in the Slavic languages has some qualities that have made it a subject of study in several articles (e.g. Besters-Dilger 1997, 2005; Hansen 2000). The earliest stages of the Slavic languages did probably not have an auxiliarized expression of necessity. In OCS, for instance, all words that conveyed a sense of necessity or obligation – aside from the most common way of expressing necessity, the construction *dative + infinitive* – also had a lexical meaning and were restricted syntactically, which disqualifies them from being fully-fledged modal auxiliaries (Hansen 2000: 86–90).

Many of the Slavic languages filled this gap in the system of modals, so to speak, by borrowing the German *müssen*, among them (before the 14th century) Polish, where it took the form *musieć* (Hansen 2000: 80–82). Through Polish influence on Ruthenian, the verb was adopted by the *prosta mova* (Besters-Dilger 2005: 239–240, 247), and eventually by Ukrainian and Belorussian, which still use the verbs *мусити* and *мусіць*, respectively (Hansen 2000: 82–83).

The spread of the Polish construction *mieć* + infinitive, which expresses a weaker necessity than *musieć*, is less obvious. In OCS, the verb *имѣти* had three functions: it expressed possession, modality (of necessity or possibility) and future. By the 17th century, the use of this future-tense construction in Russian texts was a clear sign of Church Slavonic influence (Moser 1998: 330–331).

In Polish, the modal meaning seems to have been present even in the earliest preserved texts, which can be illustrated with a very well-known example from the *Kazania gnieźnieńskie* (late 14th century), where it is found as a gloss for *musieć* (Besters-Dilger 1997: 23–24). There are also plenty of Ruthenian examples from the 16th century where this construction expresses deontic necessity. Russian interference texts from the 16th and 17th centuries often contain this construction, which points to it being a syntactic polonism, although it cannot be excluded that the influence came from Ruthenian rather than from Polish (Moser 1998: 331–335).

The examples below will be divided into three types: future (or future preterite) meaning, counterfactual meaning (cancelled future preterite) and modal meaning (deontic or epistemic). Epistemic meanings have not been widely discussed in previous literature. It is often hard to distinguish the modal use from the future meaning that was influenced by Church Slavonic, and classification can sometimes be difficult. The meaning of the verb is often determined and emphasized by words in the context. To enable the reader to verify the classification, page and folio references to all examples, even those that are not quoted, are given below in the form (118 – 26: 195v), which should be read as (Stryjkowski 1582: 118 vs. Slav 26, fol. 195v).

Only *имѣти* is studied in Moser's monograph, but below, the different ways of translating both *musieć* and *mieć* in all sample chapters will be listed, since both constructions open possibilities for polonisms.

Constructions with musieć
The Polish original of the sample chapters from segment A contains six occurrences of *musieć*. In the translation, the modal is omitted and a finite form of the main verb used five times (118 – 26: 195v; 118 – 26: 196v; 134 – 26: 216v; 137 – 26: 220v; 137 – 26: 221r), whereas *имѣти* is used once:

(115) A tu Czytelniku miły rzecz y porządek spraw Włodimirzowych trochę **przerwać muszę** (Stryjkowski 1582: 143)

176

Читателю любезный описание дѣйствъ Владимировыхъ немного **оставити їмам** (Slav 26, fol. 228r)

The sample chapters from segment B have only one occurrence of Polish *musieć*, which is translated with a modal construction using the verb *долженствовати*:

(116) A gdy Litwá most ná Preglu zbudowáłá/ s ktorego do Zamku sturmowáli/ wiele ich zbitych strzelbą od Krzyżakow poległo/ ták iż **musieli** od oblężęnia odciągnąć (Stryjkowski 1582: 332)

а егда Литва мостъ на Прегле устроила с которого к городу прист8пали много их збитых стрелбою от крыжаков полегло, такъ что **долⷤжнъствовали** от осады отити (Slav 27, fols. 17v–18r)

In sample chapters C, the Polish construction with *musieć* occurs once and is translated with *принужденъ*:

(117) Teodricus z Aldemburgu Mistrz Pruski […] wćiągnął do Litwy Zimie […] ále gdy się Litwá i Zmodź stale broniłá/ obaczywszy prożną pracą/ y uśiłowánie swoie dáremne/ tákże utrátę w ludziach pod często przegrány-mi szturmámi/ **musiał** się do Prus wrocić (Stryjkowski 1582: 426–427)

Ѳеодоритъ с Алⷣденъб68рга магистрѣ пр8скиї [...] вниде в Литв8 зимою [...] но егда Литва и Жмоид м8жественнѡ защишах8ся, ураз8мѣвъ тщетный тр8д и 8сердствование свое праздное, такожъ гибель людемъ в частых прист8пех, **прин8жденъ** возвратитися в Пр8сы (Slav 27, fol. 191r)

Sample chapters D have seven occurrences of *musieć* in the Polish original. In the translation, the construction is replaced with a finite form of the main verb five times (752 – 28: 305v; 753 – 28: 307r; 755 – 28: 311r; 756 – 28: 311v; 758 – 28: 316v) and translated with *долженъ* once (762 – 28: 323v). Once, it is slightly altered in that the modal is removed and a finite verb used instead, but it is not a direct translation of the verb in the Polish original:

(118) Mikołay Fierley z Dąbrowice Hetman wielki Koronny z Pány y z Sláchtą Ruską/ y Podolską gonił ich áż do Wisniowcá/ ále iż nie rowną widział/ **musiał** dáć pokoy. (Stryjkowski 1582: 750)

Миколаи Ѳирлеи з Долⷣбровицы гетⷨман великиї кор8нныї съ гⷭдами и з шляхтою р8скою и подолскою гналъ ихъ дажъ к Вишневц8 но понеже неравную себе ихъ сил8 видѣлъ **отст8пилъ** от нихъ (Slav 28, fols. 300r–300v)

The Polish construction *musieć* is thus sometimes translated with a finite form of another verb, sometimes with a modal construction, but never with the cognate in the sample chapters. A search of the entire online text of the

Kronika in the 1846 edition (cf. Section 1.2) and comparison with ms. U reveals that of the 190 hits for forms of *musieć*, only one is translated by the cognate мусити. This example does not belong to the sample chapters, but is nevertheless given below. It is, however, found in a verse section, which might mean that the translator felt bound by the rhyme:

(119) Przeto Litwinie bracie niezayrzy też Rusi/
      Gdyż też są niemniey sławni zeznáć káżdy **muśi**/ (Stryjkowski 1582: 247)

      сего ради литвине брате не зазри же Р8си
      понеже неменши славы с8ть истинн8 всякъ рещи **м8си**
      (Slav 26, fol. 368r)

Thus, modal words of different kinds sometimes occur as translations of *musieć*, but it is more common to use a finite form of the main verb.

Constructions with future mieć

As mentioned, *mieć* or имѣти as an auxiliary verb to form the future tense (or the future preterite, if the auxiliary verb is in a past tense) is an old construction that is also found in OCS, but here it occurs as a translation of the Polish cognate, which probably motivated its use. It is often difficult to draw a clear line between temporal and modal uses, but I have chosen to interpret examples as temporal if they describe something positive, intended or done voluntarily, so that obligation and necessity are less probable.

There are four cases in sample chapters A where *mieć* is used as a part of a future or future preterite construction, and these are all translated using имѣти. Besides the one given below, they are found on 125 – 26: 205v (close to the counterfactual example (125)), 130 – 26: 212r and 136 – 26: 220r.

(120) Drzewlánie będąc temu rádzi/ isz iusz wszystkie Xięstwá Ruskie ich
      Xiążęciu/ z ták wielką Małżonką będą podáne/ zá ktorym powodem nád
      Russaki wzaiem/ będąc pirwey poddánymi/ Pány **być mieli** (Stryjkowski
      1582: 123)

      древляне ж том8 обрадовавшеся, яко всѣ княжства р8ские кнѕю их
      с толь великою женою подданы б8д8тъ, и тѣмъ над р8саками
      взаимно б8д8чи перво подданными, гс̃дами **быти имѣяху** (Slav
      26, fol. 202v)

There is one example in sample chapters B of a future preterite (future in the past), translated using the same construction. The phrase "co się y sstało" prevents a counterfactual interpretation:

(121) Bo ták rozumiał/ co się y sstało/ iż Iatwieżowie iáko do zwyćięstwá/ ták
      do mężney smierći uporni/ **mieli** mu **dáć** bitwę/ choćby też y przegráli
      (Stryjkowski 1582: 339)

їбо такъ чаялъ что ї быть, что ятвѣзы яко к побѣде такъ к мⷶжественно*и* смерти упрямые їмѣли с нимъ **дать** бой хотя бы таже ї проигра*лї* (Slav 27, fol. 33v)

There are no examples in sample chapters C of this use of *mieć*.

The following instance from sample chapters D is an example of the future preterite, translated with the same construction:

(122) Tegoż czássu Mendlikierey Carz Prekopski gdy był wziął żołd od Krolá Sigmuntá/ y **miał ciągnąć** záraz z Litwą na tę woynę przećiw Moskiewskiemu/ tedy w tym chytrze postępuiąc/ położył się nie dáleko od woyská Krolewskiego (Stryjkowski 1582: 747)

в то*ж* время Мендликереи царь перекопскї взявъ казну *от* короля Жигимⷶнта и **имѣлъ итти** в то*т* же часъ с Ли*т*вою на ту войну прот*и*в моско*в*ского тогда в томъ хитро чиня сталъ недалече *от* воиска королевского (Slav 28, fol. 292v)

Thus, *имѣти* is always used in the translation when the construction carries a future meaning. This was to be expected, since this use was not entirely alien to Russian.

Constructions with counterfactual mieć

If the verb *mieć* is part of a conditional construction with the particle *by*, it often has a counterfactual meaning, i.e. it points at something that was going to happen, or was supposed to happen, but did not. Events assumed to be true but that prove not to be, i.e. hearsay, are also included here. It is to some extent an additional meaning that adds to a meaning of future or obligation. Sometimes, the fact that the event did not come to pass is expressed very clearly, sometimes it can only be deduced from a wider context.

This meaning is found three times in the Polish original of sample chapters A. One of these is translated with a modal construction using *имѣти*:

(123) A iżby Miásto Moskwá inszym kráinom przezwisko od siebie **dáć miáłá/** to nie pewna (Stryjkowski 1582: 91)

Ѧко дабы градъ Москва иным странамъ прозванїе *от* себе **дати имѣло**[68], сїе не подлинно (Slav 26, fols. 156r–156v)

In one case, the modal verb is removed and a finite form of the main verb – which happens to be *имѣти* – is used:

(124) Wszákże y to swoie mniemánie/ y ono żeby od Twiskoná/ **mieli** początek **mieć** Sarmatowie samże Bielski kassuie (Stryjkowski 1582: 93)

---

[68] Some mss. have *имѣла*.

однакож и то свое мнѣнїе, и яко от [Т]вискона им8тъ начало сарматы, самъ же Белскїи отставляетъ (Slav 26, fol. 161r)

One occurrence is translated with a *dative + infinitive* construction. This example also contains an instance (*имаши* [...] *пояти*) that expresses intention and has been labeled as future (cf. above):

> (125) y iákosz mię masz poiąć ochrzćiwszy mię sam iáko Oćiec/ y názwawszy mię sobie corką/ gdyż w zakonie Chrzesćiáńskim/ y u Pogánow to iest rzecz obrzydliwa y niesłychána/ áby **miał oćiec** corkę **poymowáć.** (Stryjkowski 1582: 125)
>
> како имаши мя пояти крестивъ самъ яко о͞цъ, и нарекъ мя дщерь себѣ, понеже в законѣ хр͞стианскомъ, и въ языцех вещъ есть скверна, и неслыхана о͞ц8 дще*р* **поимати** (Slav 26, fol. 205v)

In the sample chapters from segment B, there are two examples of this counterfactual construction in Polish, where the verb *имѣти* is used in the translation:

> (126) Bo Koronę otrzymawszy/ Krolem sie wszystkiey Ruśi tytułował/ á w Greckiey wierze (Rzymskiey zániechawszy) po stáremu trwał/ y co **miał** Chrześćian od Tatar **bronić**/ to ich sam przez Hetmany swoie/ y Litwę z Swarnem Siestrzeńcem swoim/ á z Mendagiem Krolem Litewskim do Polski násyłał. (Stryjkowski 1582: 331)
>
> ибо об͞держа͞в венецъ королемъ всеа Росиї їмяновася. а в греческо*и* вѣре (римск8ю отложа) по прежнем8 пребыва͞л, ї что **їмѣлъ** хр͞стиянъ от татаръ **боронить**, то их самъ чрез гетманы свои и Литв8 с Сварном племянником своимъ ї с Мендогомъ королем литовским на Полш8 насыла͞л (Slav 27, fol. 14v)

> (127) á danią się małą okupili/ niżby márnie wszyscy od száble okrutney pogáńskiey/ y z zamkiem **zginąć mieli** (Stryjkowski 1582: 333)
>
> а данию малою ок8пились нежели бы вотще всѣ от сабли м8чи-те͞лской поганско*и* и з городом **погибн8ти** їмѣли (Slav 27, fol. 19r)

Sample chapters C show three instances of the construction, two of which are translated with *имѣти* and one with a *dative + infinitive*. They all express hearsay:

> (128) A iesliby się tu komu rzecz niepodobna zdáłá/ áby Olgerd z Litwą/ **miał** ták bez wieści pod Miásto Moskwę **przyćiągnąć** z Witebska/ Tedy o tym wiedz Czytelniku miły (Stryjkowski 1582: 423)
>
> аще ли бы ком8 здѣ не8добна являлася вещъ, дабы О͞лгердъ с Литвою **имѣлъ** толь безвѣстно. из Вите*л*ска под Москв8 **прїити**, вездѣ 8бо о любимый читателю (Slav 27, fol. 182r)

180

(129) Látopiszce Litewskie swiádczą/ iżby y **Alexander Koriatowic** záraz po Constantinie y Jurgim Brátach **miał umrzeć**/ á iżby Fiedor czwarty Brát po ich smierći **miał** Podole **osieść**/ ále Cromer swiádczy z Długoszá/ y z pewnych dowodow/ iż był żyw potym Roku 1366. (Stryjkowski 1582: 428)

лѣтопи҃сцы литовские свидѣте́лств8ютъ, акибы и **Алеꙁандр8 Кориатовичю**; абие после Костянтина, и Георгия братияхъ **8мрети**, и аки Ѳеодо҃р братъ четвертый Подолие **имѣлъ засѣсти**. но Кромеръ свидѣте́лств8етъ из Дл8гоша и из подлинных приводовъ, яко посемъ живъ бысть лѣта .҂ат꙼ѕ. (Slav 27, fol. 195r)

The sample chapters from segment D contain no examples of the counterfactual construction. All in all, the translations are varied, but often contain a modal element, either *имѣти* or a dative construction.

Constructions with modal mieć
There are several constructions with the verb *mieć* (often in the present tense) where the main meaning is a modal one. Several of these describe the conditions of an agreement or a promise, and although they also have a temporal aspect, the element of obligation involved in such agreements calls for a modal interpretation. There are also a few examples of epistemic necessity, i.e. something supposed.

The translation *имѣти* is used three times in sample chapters A, two of which are identical contexts close to each other:

(130) Bo Sławacy **máią być** własnie y prawdźiwie zwáni według zdánia mądrych ludźi Sławakámi od sławy (Stryjkowski 1582: 102)

понеже славаки **имѣютъ быти** свои́ственно и ї́стинно реченнїи по разс8ждению раз8мныхъ людей словаки о҃т славы (Slav 26, fol. 172v)

(131) iáko gdy **máią mowić** *digna*, mowią *dina uel dinia* [...] Tákże też gdy **máią mowić** *Slauo Slauonia uel Slauones*, mowią *Siauo, Siauonia, y Siaui* (Stryjkowski 1582: 103)

внегда бо **им8тъ гл҃голати**, дигна, говорятъ дина, или диния [...] сице же егда **им8тъ гл҃голати**, славо, славонїя, или славонескъ, гл҃голютъ сиявонїѧ, сиявѡ, и сияви (Slav 26, fols. 174r–174v)

Once, the Polish construction *mieć* + infinitive is translated with the particle *чаять* 'probably,' etymologically an infinitive (cf. Pennington 1980: 264), that expresses epistemic modality:

(132) y Powiát Radimicki Polskiego Xięstwá (**ma być** podobno Radomski) podbił pod swoię moc (Stryjkowski 1582: 132)

ї 8ѣздъ радимицкіи полского княжства (**чаять** радомскіи[69] под свою держав8 покори (Slav 26, fol. 214v)

In the Polish original of sample chapters B, there are two instances of the construction with *mieć* in a modal sense. One of them is found in close vicinity of the counterfactual example (126). In both cases, the same construction is used in Russian:

(133) Tegoż Daniela znowu w Drohiczynie ná Krolestwo Ruskie koronowáli/ á wzięli od niego przysięgę/ iż opuściwszy Ceremonie Greckie/ tak on sam/ iako wszystek narod Ruski/ **miał** Kosciołá Rzymskiego wiernie á szczerze **násladowáć** (Stryjkowski 1582: 331)

тогож Даниїла паки в Дрогичине на короле͡вство р8ское помазали, ї взяли у него клятв8, что о*т*ложи*в͡* дѣства греческие тако о*н* самъ яко ї весь народъ р8скиї **їмѣлъ** костел8 римском8 вѣрно ї истинно **наслѣдить** (Slav 27, fols. 14v–15r)

(134) W czym Sabinom/ Samnitow/ Weientom/ Equom/ Campanom/ Kartaginenczykom/ Spartenom *ad Termopillas*, y inszym rozmáitym narodom [...] przyrownáni á snáść y sowito w Rycerskich dzielnościach nád nich przełożeni **być máią.** (Stryjkowski 1582: 340)

в чемъ сабино*м* самнитомъ веентомъ эквамъ кампаномъ каρθагиненчикомъ, спартяномъ у термопи͡ллямъ и протчимъ разнымъ народамъ, [...] привровнены а знать и с8г8бо в рыцерскихъ дѣлехъ паче ихъ старѣишины **быти имѣютъ** (Slav 27, fols. 34r–34v)

There are six occurrences in the Polish text of sample chapters C of *mieć* expressing modality. One is in a marginal note that has been omitted in the translation. Three are translated into Russian using *имѣти*:

(135) Suriwił (podobno **ma być** Swidrigel) (Stryjkowski 1582: 425)

С8р8вилъ, чаю **имать быти** Свидригиле*и* (Slav 27, fol. 188r)

(136) Czego gdy Xiążę Constantin Koriatowic niechćiał uczynić/ áni ná to pozwolić/ áby **miał** wiárę **odmieniáć**/ wzgárdził (powiádáią Látopiszcze) successią ná Krolestwo Polskie (Stryjkowski 1582: 427)

кн͡зю жъ Костянтин8 сотворити сего не хотящ8, ниже на то соизволити, дабы **имѣлъ** вѣр8 **пременяти**. пренебреже (гл͡голю*т* летописцы), наслѣдие королевства по͡лского (Slav 27, fol. 193v)

(137) zgodził się/ iż Iurgi Narimuntowic **miał** do pewnego czássu ná Krzemieńcu **pánowáć** (Stryjkowski 1582: 429)

---

[69] The other half of the parenthesis is missing in Slav 26, but is present in, for instance, mss. B and N.

помири́лся, что Юрьи Нарим8нтовичь до подлинногѡ времени на Кременцѣ **имѣлъ кн҃жити** (Slav 27, fol. 197r)

In one case, the translation omits the modal verb and uses a finite form of the main verb:

(138) postępuiąc nakłádow woiennych nagrodę/ záchowánie státecznego pokoiu raz potwierdzonego/ y gránice z Litwą takie iákieby słuszne **być miáły/** y ná ktorych Olgerd z rycerstwem swoim przestánie. (Stryjkowski 1582: 421)

обещая 8бы́тко́в воинскихъ воздаяние сохранение постояннаго мир8, единожды по́дтверженнаго, и предѣлы с Литвою, таковы каковы истинные **были**, на которые О́лѳерд8 с воинствомъ его 8годны б8д8тъ (Slav 27, fol. 179v)

In another instance, the verb *mieć* with its implication of obligation has been replaced by *обещати*, which conveys a similar meaning:

(139) támże przydano/ iż Krol Kázimierz y Lubárt/ **mieli** sobie zobopolną y wzaiemną pomoc ná káżdego nieprzyiacielá **dawáć** (Stryjkowski 1582: 429)

тамже приложено, что король Казимеръ и Любартъ **обещаша** себѣ о́бщ8ю и взаимн8ю на всякого неприятеля **давати** помощъ (Slav 27, fol. 197v)

The following examples of *mieć* in a modal sense occur in the Polish original of sample chapters D. They all describe agreements, and the translation always uses *имѣти*:

(140) A tá byłá Summá rzeczy postánowionych/ y społnie uchwalonych ná tym sławnym ziezdzie [...] Przymierze też z Moskiewskim przećiw Litwie postánowione **miał wypowiedzieć** (Stryjkowski 1582: 748)

а то было овершени́ вещеи постано́леныхъ и единомышленно ухваленыхъ на то́м славном сьѣздѣ [...] примирие то́ж и с москов-скимъ противъ Литвы учиненное **имѣл о́тказать** (Slav 28, fols. 294v–295r)

(141) Mistrzá tákże Pruskiego do uczynienia y wypełnienia powinnośći y do posłuszeństwá/ y áby Koronie Polskiey/ y Krolowi przysięgał/ **przywieść/ álbo go odstąpić miał** iáko spolnego nieprzyiacielá (Stryjkowski 1582: 748)

мистра тако́ж пр8ского ко 8чинению и исполⷩнению долъжности и к подданству и что короне полскои и королю прсягнулъ **привести или о́тступити имѣлъ** аки ѡт о́бщагѡ неприятеля (Slav 28, fol. 295r)

(142) iedná częśc Rzeczypospolitey Koronney/ ku obronie przećiw Tátarom/ druga ná wystáwienie Kośćiołá Arcibiskupiego Gnieznienskiego **miáłá być** oddána. (Stryjkowski 1582: 751)

едина часть рѣчи посполитои кор8ннои на защищение против татар др8гая на строение костела арцыбискуⷠского гнезнинского отдана **їмѣла быти** (Slav 28, fol. 303v)

In one instance, a Polish construction with *mieć* is translated using *долженъ*. The modal meaning is made clear by the words *według postánowienia y powinnośći*:

(143) Potym Carz Prekopski ná Nowie Czerwcá Miesiącá/ ktory **miał** według postánowienia y powinnośći do Moskwy **wtárgnąć** (Stryjkowski 1582: 749)

Потом царь перекопскиї в началѣ мⷭца июня которои **долженъ былъ** противъ постановления и долⷤности Москвѣ нашествие **учинити** (Slav 28, fol. 299r)

The modal construction with *имѣти* is thus represented in all the sample chapters, and there are also a few cases where other modal words are used.

Whereas *mieć* was regularly translated by modal words and often simply by its cognate *имѣти*, Polish *musieć* was usually replaced, sometimes with modal constructions, sometimes with indicative forms. The Russian cognate *мусити* occurs only once, outside the sample chapters. The expression of necessity with *имѣти* was a polonism that, as seen in these chapters, was quite frequently used in the Russian language during a certain period. The fact that *имѣти* was used as a translation not only of *mieć*, but also in one case of *musieć*, shows that it was in active use.

The reason why *musieć* was replaced but *mieć* often translated by its cognate may be that *musieć* was perceived as more foreign – *имѣти* existed with another meaning, but *мусити* did not. There might also be a semantic explanation. Since *musieć* expresses strong obligation, it implies that the main action referred to did indeed take place, and it can therefore be expressed without a modal construction in the translation. Weak obligation, as expressed with *mieć*, may tend towards a counterfactual meaning, or does at least not imply as strongly that the action took place, and therefore a modal is needed in the translation as well.

5.4.2.3 The accusative with infinitive

The accusative with infinitive (*accusativus cum infinitivo*, abbreviated *aci*) is a syntactic construction well known from Latin and Greek, in which the subject of a subordinate clause is in the accusative case and the verb in the infinitive. The construction arose in Polish as a calque from Latin. According to K. Długosz-Kurczabowa and S. Dubisz (2006: 474), this construction was rare in 15th-century Polish, because translations from Latin were often made with Czech texts as support in that period, but from the 16th century, as more translations were made without the help of Czech texts, the frequency of *aci* constructions grew. It declined in the 18th century, as the influence of Latin became weaker (Klemensiewicz et al. [1955] 1981: 436).

K. Pisarkowa (1984: 152–154) emphasizes the frequency of examples with the verb *być* in contexts where it is actually redundant. In such cases, the accusative in the construction is usually a reflexive *się*. This use of the *aci* is not found in classical Latin, but was a Polish innovation. In some cases, the infinitive *być* is not overtly expressed, but D. Ostaszewska still counts these as an "incomplete" (*niepełne*) variety of the construction (Burzywoda et al. 2002: 270–271). Such examples have not been counted below, only occurrences where the infinitive is expressed.

In Church Slavonic, the *aci* could occur as a calque from Greek (Uspenskij 2002: 256–257). It could also originate in supine constructions, which expressed finality. In later East Slavic texts, however, it was rarely used in such contexts, and was instead the result of Polish influence. This can be seen by the fact that it spread earlier in Ruthenian than in Russian, and that it was typical of interference texts (Moser 1998: 182–202).

The original text of sample chapters A contains 31 instances of the *aci*, either in Polish or in Latin. 23 of these are translated using the same construction. In the majority of cases, the infinitive is *быти*, as in example (144), but there are a few exceptions, such as example (145):

(144) Albertus záś Crantius Niemiecki Historyk **mieni być** názwánych **Słowakow** od wielamownośći słow (Stryjkowski 1582: 102)

Албер̃тъ же Крантїи немецкїи повѣстникъ гл҃голетъ быти реченныx славаков̃ от многорѣчїя словъ (Slav 26, fol. 172v)

(145) á potym według swego rachunku roku od stworzenia Swiátá 6370. **Xiążąt Wareckich trzech Bratow rodzonych/ Rurika/ Truwora y Sinaussa** w Xięstwach swoich […] **pánowáć piszą.** (Stryjkowski 1582: 89)

потоm же по своему щету в лѣто оt создания мира .҂ѕто, кн҃зеи варяговъ трех братоɞ Рюрика, Тривора, и Синавса, в княжстваx своихъ [...] гс̃дрствовати пиш8т (Slav 26, fol. 153v)

However, there are also a few examples of some other construction being used in the translation instead: a gerund, a prepositional phrase or a subordinate clause.

Sample chapters B have only one instance of a Polish *aci*. The same construction is used in the translation.

In sample chapters C, the Polish original contains two instances of the *aci*. In both cases, the translation has the same construction. There is also one instance of a subordinate clause in the Polish original that corresponds to an *aci* in the Russian translation, which shows that this construcion could be used independently of the Polish original:

> (146) Witołtowi Synowcowi iego przypissuią niebácznie/ niepátrząc w tey mierze rożnośći czássow/ y prawdziwego doswiádczenia istotney rzeczy y porządku lat/ Bo **mnimáią by** tylko **ieden Witołd** w Litwie **był sławny** (Stryjkowski 1582: 423)

> Витоллд8 племяннику его безразс8днω припис8ютъ, невзирая в томъ разности времяни, истинного испытания самого дѣла, и лѣторазположения, **мнят** бо **единого** точию **Витоллда** в Литвѣ **быти славно и** (Slav 27, fols. 181r–181v)

Sample chapters D have only one instance of a Polish *aci*. It is translated using the same construction.

This polonism is thus represented in all sets of sample chapters, and the corresponding Polish or Latin construction is translated by other means only in a few instances.

5.4.2.4 Summary of syntactic polonisms

These three syntactic polonisms are all to be found in the translation of Stryjkowski, and what is more, they are present in all four segments of the text. Table 14 shows the data for these types of polonisms in the sample chapters. The figures for *mieć* show first the counterfactual examples, then the purely modal ones, i.e. "1+2" means that one counterfactual example and two modal ones have been translated as indicated. The figure "2+1" for *aci* in sample chapters C means that the construction is used twice as a translation of *aci* and once of another construction.

Table 14. Syntactic polonisms in the sample chapters

	A	B	C	D
do → до	2	21	7	12
do → other	ca. 140	33	ca. 60	ca. 100
mieć → имѣти	1+2	2+2	2+3	0+3
mieć → other	2+1	0	1+2	0+1
aci → aci	23	1	2+1	1
aci → other	8	0	0	0

With the reservation that some of the constructions are much more frequent than others in the Polish original, the table indicates that the use of the construction *до* + genitive in Russian was avoided to a higher degree than the other syntactic polonisms. Possible explanations for this could be either that it was perceived as more foreign, and therefore generally avoided even in the segments that otherwise use a large share of polonisms, or that it was easier to avoid than the other constructions, in the sense that substitution of a preposition is easier than changing the other constructions.

The sample chapters from segment A avoid syntactic polonisms to a higher degree than the others. Although the *aci* is frequent in these chapters, there are other ways of translating the construction as well. The three remaining sets of sample chapters do not present other solutions for the *aci*. B and D tend to translate modal *mieć* with *имѣти*. Segment B has a far larger share of Russian *do* + genitive than the others, and must therefore be said to be the richest in syntactic polonisms. As will be discussed in Section 6.9, segment B is also characterized by lexical polonisms of the active category.

5.5 Comparison of text passages

To catch elements of the translation technique that have not been covered in the sections above, parallel passages will be shown and discussed. I have chosen passages where the translation differs more than usual from the original.

Stryjkowski 1582: 129–130	Slav 26, fol. 211v
Ták tedy Iaropołk Swadoltową rádą poduszczony/ podniosł woynę ná Bráta/ y poráźił woysko iego Drewlanskie/ á Olech sámo Xiążę ućiekáiąc z pogromu ná Zamek swoy Waraż (według Miechouiussa) niemogł sie wćisnąć przed wielkim tumultem Ludu uciekáiącego.	Сице ж Ерополкъ по совѣтѸ СвадолтовѸ поѸщенъ подя войнѸ на брата, и вой его древлянские поби, Олех же Ѹшед з бою (по Меховию) множества ради народа бежащих с тогож бою, не возможе вгнестиᷱ во град свой Варяж.

The translation of *Swadoltową rádą poduszczony* is not quite correct. The translator evidently began by changing this construction into *по совѣтѸ СвадолтовѸ*, but then added *поѸщенъ* as a translation of the Polish participle.

The word order in the translation of *poráźił woysko iego Drewlanskie* has been changed in that the verb has been moved to the end. Also, the noun has been transferred to the plural (the spelling with *ŭ* is only an orthographical trait and does not indicate a singular ending), perhaps because the Polish adjective has an identical form for the neuter singular and the plural.

The attribute *sámo Xiążę* has not been translated.

The constituents from *á Olech* onwards have changed places in the Russian translation. The relation between finite verbs and participle forms has been preserved, but the information about the crowds is given before the information of where Oleg was going. Also, the information *с тогож бою* has been added by way of explanation.

Stryjkowski 1582: 130	Slav 26, fol. 211v
A Iaropełk ubieżawszy Zamek Waraż y opánowawszy go/ kazał Brátá Olechá szukáć/ ktorego pod mostem miedzy trupámi ledwo trzeciego dniá náleziono umárłego/ zá ukazánim iednego Drew-laniná/ á kazawszy go przed siebie przynieść/ rzekł do Swadołta pátrząc ná trup Braterski: Swadołcie/ otoś tego pożadał. Potym go pochowano w Ow-ruczey.	Ерополкъ ж во град Варяж вниде и повелѣ брата своего Олеха искати, и по взятїи града в третїи день обрѣтоша его меж тѣлами чл҃вческими мертва, и принесоша тѣло его пред Ерополка. Ерополкъ ж видѣ тѣло брата своего рече к Свадолт8, Свадолте сего пожелаⷧ еси, ї погребоша его в Овручи.

Here, the two participles *ubieżawszy* and *opánowawszy* have been replaced by the finite verb *вниде*, which does not express the process of conquering. This is instead expressed in the temporal *по взятїи града*.

The location *pod mostem* is left out of the translation, as is the explanation *zá ukazánim iednego Drewlaniná*. The Polish relative clause in which these elements occur is transformed into a main clause, coordinated with the preceding one with the conjunction *u*.

The Polish original continues with the participle construction *kazawszy* [...] *przynieść*, whereas in the Russian version, the finite form *принесоша* is used instead.

Then the Russian translation calls Jaropolk by name again. The Polish gerund *pátrząc* is turned into the aorist *видѣ*, which might have been a scribal error but for the fact that all consulted manuscripts show this reading. The constituents *rzekł do Swadołta* and *pátrząc ná trup Braterski* have changed places in the translation.

The Polish impersonal construction *go pochowano* is changed to *погребоша его*.

Stryjkowski 1582: 130–131	Slav 26, fol. 212v
Potym záraz swieżym zwycięstwem y przybáwienim Pskowskiego Xięstwá posi-lony do Kijowá przeciw Brátu Iaropołkowi ciągnął/ á gdy mu Iaropełk niesmiał polá stáwić/ záwárł sie w Kijowie/ Włodimirz też Kijowá usilnie dobywał/ ále isz go wyrozumiał trudno mocą dostáć/ wypráwił táiemnego Posłáńcá do Bludá naywiernie-yszego Páná rádnego Iaropołkowego/ ktorego zowiąc Oycem y obiecuiąc wielkie dáry/ prosił áby mu dodał rády/ ktorymby sposobem Iaropełká brátá mogł zábić.	Потомъ Владимеръ тою побѣ-дою и присовок8плением себѣ княжства псковскаго 8крепився, иде х Киев8 противо Ярополка, Ярополкъ сяде в Киеве, а Влади-меръ осадⷣ его, и разумѣ яко силою не взяти его, посла таино кь Ярополков8 вѣрном8 д8мно-м8 боярину к Бл8д8 нарицая его оⷮцомъ, и посла к нему дары доволны, моля дабы подаⷧ ем8 совѣтъ Ярополка 8бити

Here, the Polish participle *pośilony* in the first clause is replaced by the gerund *укрепився* in Russian. The word order in the main clause has been altered by bringing the verb to the front.

The clause *á gdy mu Iaropełk niesmiał polá stáwić* has not been translated, but it is difficult to say if this is because the translator was inattentive or because he did not know the expression *pole stawić* 'to give battle.'

The phrase *Włodimirz też Kijową uśilnie dobywał* has been slightly simplified. In the following phrase, an accusative with infinitive has been altered to an infinitive construction.

The word order in the presentation of Blud has been changed, so that instead of his name coming first and then the explanation of who he is, as in Polish, it is the other way around in Russian.

The relation between main and subordinate clauses has been changed, so that instead of the verb sequence *zowiąc* [...] *obiecuiąc* [...] *prosił*, the Russian translation has *нарицая* [...] *посла* [...] *моля*. The end of the sentence has been simplified.

5.6 Chapter summary

This chapter has been devoted to the translation of the *Kronika* as a target text in relation to its source text. Against the background of explicit and implicit translation theory in connection with early Russian texts, some aspects of the translation were highlighted.

As a parallel to an earlier study by S. I. Nikolaev, the translation of a number of verse sections was studied. They differed as to their adherence to rhyme and syllable count.

Obvious departures from the source text were discussed, such as omissions, additions, the numerous instances where two Polish near-synonyms were expressed by only one Russian word and cases where Polish names or measurements were adapted to Russian practice. The latter procedure (domestication) shows that the translators were capable of identifying information that would not be understood by a Russian reader and adapting it, i.e. their strategy was acceptability-oriented.

The influence of Polish on Russian – possibly mediated by Ruthenian – was quite significant at the time when this translation was made. Therefore, the occurrence of polonisms (lexical or syntactic) may characterize either this text or the language of the time in general. Historical dictionaries, editions of other texts and the works of earlier scholars were used as material to try to solve this question.

The lexical influence was discussed on the basis of words that have been crossed out in ms. B, probably because they were cognates to the words in the Polish original. Two monographs on this subject were also used to identify polonisms. The studied words were characterized as very active, active or passive in relation to the Russian language of the time. The very active words can be said to reveal Polish influence on the language in general, since these words were already integrated into Russian, whereas the active words are more indicative of the influence on this particular text, since words from this group were used by some translators and not by others and otherwise occurred mainly in interference texts.

The results regarding some individual words were contrary to expectation. For instance, in ms. B an instance of the word *издавна*, found many times in the translated *Kronika* and attested in dictionaries and sources, has been changed to *исконно*, a word that is not found anywhere else. The occurrence here of *доказати* is two decades earlier than those previously documented. The word *предокъ* is used here so regularly that it was categorised as very active, contrary to the statement by S. Kochman that it was not in general use before the 18th century.

Three syntactic structures, identified by previous scholars as polonisms, were also studied. The use of *до* + genitive with a local but not limitative meaning is found in all sets of sample chapters, but the corresponding Polish construction is more often translated with the expected *въ* + accusative or *къ* + dative. The translation of modal *mieć* as *имѣти* also occurs in all sets of sample chapters and is either dominant or occurs in equal proportions with alternative translations. In connection with this, the translation of Polish *musieć* was discussed. The accusative with infinitive, or *aci*, is also found in all sets of sample chapters, although some have very few occurrences. Only in one segment are other solutions to translate this construction sometimes found.

The sample chapters from segment B have the highest frequency of (active) lexical and syntactic polonisms. The differences between the segments in this regard will be discussed more closely in Chapter 6.

190

6 Variation between different segments

As mentioned in Section 1.3, the text of the translated *Kronika* can be divided into segments according to the distribution of verbal tenses referring to past events. Table 1 from that section is repeated here as Table 15.

Table 15. Division of the chronicle into segments according to dominant tenses

Books	Dominant tenses	Segment label
I–VI	Aorist/imperfect	A
VII–X	Perfect	B
XI–XIV	Aorist/imperfect	C
XV–XXV	Perfect	D

This chapter will be devoted to these segments and ways of distinguishing between them. The indications that the translation was divided are strong, but based on the verbal tenses alone, it cannot be determined if there were two, three or four translators. Answering this question is one of the aims of this chapter. The other aim is to evaluate the criteria used for distinguishing between translators and discussing their usefulness for this and other similar studies.

6.1 Previous studies on authorship attribution

The field of authorship attribution – establishing the authorship of a given text, mostly with the help of identified texts by possible authors as comparison – is well developed. Less work has been done on what could be called translation attribution, which poses slightly different problems. Many of the parameters used in authorship attribution must be ruled out when the object of study is a translation, especially if the translation is close to the original, since they are properties of the original text rather than of the translation. If they are to be used, they cannot be computed without comparing the results with the original.

According to B. M. Kloss (1980: 105–106), moreover, early Russian texts are more difficult to study in this way than modern ones, since many traits of the text were determined by the genre and theme, which led to less pronounced stylistic differences between authors. The compilative character of many texts also adds to the difficulties.

In the following, I will avoid the term 'style' (*стиль*), since I consider it to be ambiguous. Kloss uses it for the sum total of an author's individual preferences,[70] but it also echoes Lomonosov's three styles of language, and to avoid that association I will speak of authors' preferences rather than their style, and use the term 'register,' introduced in Section 4.1.1, for 'style' in Lomonosov's sense.

Despite the difficulties connected with early Russian texts, Kloss (1980: 106) gives examples of studies that have been made on chronicles, where scholars have been interested in identifying sources and learning when one scribe took over after another. He has investigated the authorship of the *Nikonovskaja letopis'* (16th century), comparing it with the works of some authors of the period. His methods include comparing the frequency (or existence) of certain lexemes, identifying biblical quotes preferred by the different authors, as well as observing rhetorical strategies (Kloss 1980: 112–130). The particular lexemes used in his study cannot be applied to Stryjkowski's text, despite the fact that both are chronicles, because Kloss has chosen words from the religious sphere that are not as widely represented in the *Kronika*. Also, the *Nikonovskaja letopis'* is more than a century older than the translation of Stryjkowski's chronicle.

A. A. Gippius (2006) has performed a detailed study of the *Novgorodskaja pervaja letopis'*, using the distribution of 76 parameters on different linguistic levels to determine the borders between the scribes of the manuscript from which the extant copy of this chronicle was made. The parameters were grouped into features of codicology and palaeography, graphics, orthography and phonetics, morphology, syntax, lexicon, structure and style (Gippius 2006: 129). In his work he also lists other attempts to segment chronicle language (Gippius 2006: 119–120).

When the object of the study is a translated text, some of the difficulties mentioned by Kloss are avoided. For instance, a translation is not a compilation in the sense of e.g. chronicles. Also, the presence of the original provides something with which to compare the variation. Nevertheless, I have not been able to find many such studies, at least not on early Russian texts.

E. M. Isserlin's comparison of the six translations of *Dwór cesarza tureckiego* (Isserlin 1961) has already been mentioned several times (cf. especially Section 5.2.2). Its aim is slightly different, since the material consists of several translations of the same text and the author does not need to prove that there were different translators, but the methods may perhaps be applied to other texts as well.

---

[70] «Мы бы сказали, что стиль – это определяемая задачей исследования совокупность характерных для данного писателя особенностей его творчества» (Kloss 1980: 103).

Regardless of whether one is working with an original text or a translation, one can choose criteria from different levels of the text. When working with a manuscript, the graphical and orthographical levels could be useful, but mainly when dealing with an autograph, since spelling, punctuation etc. can vary greatly between scribes. There are exceptions, such as Gippius' above-mentioned study, in which he found that the scribe probably copied the graphics and orthography of the exemplar faithfully, so that such criteria could be used (Gippius 2006: 130–139). Many computerized methods of authorship attribution that have otherwise proved successful are problematic because they would merely show the variation between scribes, not between authors or translators. This is true of for instance the distribution of letter bigrams or trigrams, i.e. the distribution of two- or three-letter combinations (Graham, Hirst & Marthi 2005: 409–412).

Lexical markers have often been applied. In some cases, synonym pairs can be used, or the presence or absence of certain words, but it can be difficult to find enough such pairs or characteristic words to reach certainty (Mosteller & Wallace 1964: 10–14). Some factors that Isserlin (1961) noted in the aforementioned study, such as the distribution of general and specific words or the use of terminology, could probably also be used to distinguish between translators within the same text. Good results have been reached by looking at the frequency of so-called function words (Mosteller & Wallace 1964).

Morphological and syntactical factors have been less frequently applied, since they are more difficult to search for automatically, and authorship attribution is a computer-dominated field. Word bigrams and trigrams, i.e. the distribution of two- or three-word combinations, combine elements of lexicon and syntax (Juola 2006: 265–266).

6.2 The practice of dividing translations

As seen in Section 3.6.2, Sparwenfeld wrote in his copy of the chronicle that it was the work of several translators. Sobolevskij (1903: 42) mentioned, when discussing the role of *Posol'skij prikaz* in the translation activities of the period, that it was not unusual for larger texts to be divided between several people. There are also 17th-century documents – from *Posol'skij prikaz*, no less – that tell about instances of books being divided between translators.

For instance, the French text *L'instruction du Roy en l'exercice de montes à cheval* by A. de Pluvinell was divided into six parts of 50 folios each, which were distributed between six translators, although not all of them fulfilled their duties (SKK 1992: 242–243). Another example was the compilation *Wielkie zwierciadło przykładów*, originally written in Latin (*Speculum magnum exemplorum*) but translated into Polish and from Polish into Russian in 1675–77 (*Velikoe zercalo*). Documents reveal that it was divided into five parts, which were given to different translators (Deržavina 1965: 27–28; SKK 1992: 165–171). The manner of translation is, according to scholars, similar throughout the text and executed in a way typical of translations from *Posol'skij prikaz*, and it is therefore difficult to identify the translators. The text has probably been the object of later editorial work. The parts translated by different individuals can perhaps be determined mechanically: many "examples," or chapters, were not translated into Russian, which may be explained by assuming that each translator only managed to translate part of his task before the work was interrupted for some reason. The gaps would in that case correspond to the breaks between translators (Deržavina 1965: 29; Walczak-Sroczyńska 1976: 504–506; SKK 1992: 244–245).

In some cases, later scholars have believed certain texts to be the works of several translators, judging not by documents, but by the character of the texts themselves. Sometimes their reasons for believing this are not stated explicitly. For instance, O. A. Djačok, who has written about translations of Guagnini's *Sarmatiae Europeae descriptio*, claimed such a division in connection with two of the translations (one of which may be connected with *Posol'skij prikaz*). In neither case, however, can we be absolutely certain that the evidence speaks of different translators, rather than simply different scribes (Djačok 1990: 22, 29).[71]

Since this practice is documented, there is no reason to doubt that Sparwenfeld's note is true, although it still remains to find a way to determine the borders between translators and characterize their different individual preferences.

6.3 The segments

The segments mentioned above are not completely homogeneous within themselves, even with regard to verbal tenses. There are variations that can be explained thematically, lexically, syntactically or by other factors (cf. for example Sections 4.3.1.2 and 5.3.1). However, since the dominance of the different tenses in the respective segments is so great, such factors can probably explain the variation between simplex preterites and the perfect tense only *within* the segments, not *between* them.

The variation between the segments could be a sign that several translators have been at work. The possibility that a single translator chose different linguistic means for the translation in different parts should, however, also be taken into consideration. Two well-known examples of authors switching

---

[71] One of the translations is a Ukrainian translation of Guagnini that, according to Djačok (1990), was the joint work of 47 translators!

registers within their texts are Kotošichin, who used genetic Slavonicisms mainly in the historical account of the tsars in the first chapter of his text (Pennington 1980: 382–385) and when writing about icons (cf. Uspenskij 2002: 95), and Avvakum, in whose autobiography, dominated by the perfect tense, some parts with mainly doctrinal content show a higher share of aorists (Timberlake 1995: 37–38). In these texts, however, the variation is usually thematically motivated.

Even assuming that the differences between segments point to several translators, we cannot distinguish between segments A and C, and between B and D, respectively, without using additional criteria (cf. Section 1.3). To determine whether one person worked with several parts of the text, or whether all four segments were translated by different people, we need to find other factors that can express the individual preferences of the translator, and that are not too easy for a scribe to alter. If they coincide with the borders between the segments, we may assume that we have identified the borders between translators.[72]

Finally, it is possible that there were more than four translators, and that there are segments in the text that happen to coincide in their use of verbal tenses and therefore have not been detected in the initial examination. This risk was inevitable when dealing with a manuscript text of this size, since it could not be searched digitally. One such possible border within the sample chapters will be discussed in Section 6.10.

6.4 The sample chapters

The *Kronika* is a large text, too large to be examined in its entirety in search of differences between translators. Therefore, sample chapters from each of the four segments have been chosen and compared. One set of sample chapters is IV: 1–3, which are the object of the edition. For comparison, three consecutive chapters from each of the other segments have been chosen. The only criterion was that they had to be written in prose in the Polish original, since the translation of verse seems to differ from the translation of prose, at least as far as verbal tenses for past events are concerned (cf. Section 5.3.1). Table 16 shows the selected sample chapters, the approximate number of

---

[72] It is not entirely certain that the borders between the segments lie precisely along chapter boundaries. For instance, one would assume that the easiest place to divide a book would be along the quires, if the book itself was taken apart and distributed to the translators. The borders mentioned here do not coincide with quire boundaries, book VII beginning on the third leaf in a quire and books XI and XV on the fourth leaves of their respective quires, all in quires that contain six leaves. Books VII, XI and XV all begin on a right-hand page, however, so that division could still have been made at these boundaries. The consulted copies of the *Kronika* all have the same quire boundaries.

words they contain (in the translation) and the headings of the chapters or –
for chapters that do not have a heading – a short characterization of what
they are about.

Table 16. The sample chapters

Seg-ment	Sample chapters	No. of words	Headings
A	IV: 1–3	18,160	IV: 1 The writing systems of the Slavic peoples. The origins of the name *Moskwa*.
			IV: 2 О производѣ славногѡ народа рȣского, словенского, сармацкого, и для чего речени сȣть славѧне
			IV: 3 О бѣлой ї черной Росиї, Восточных, полȣношных, и о полȣденныхъ народѣхъ древнихъ, и їхъ князяхъ великоновгородцкихъ, изборских псковскихъ белоѡзерскихъ киевских лȣцкихъ володимерских волынских галицкихъ подгорскихъ, подоꙁских и їныхъ
B	VIII: 3–5	5,390	VIII: 3 Ѡ короновани̇ сȣгȣбом на королевство рȣское Данїила Романовича литовского, галицкогѡ, владимерского дрогицкого, ї протчаꙗ, кнꙁꙗ лѣта от Хрⷭ҇та ҂асмs.ѓ [1246] а посем .҂аснг.ѓ [1253]
			VIII: 4 О разоренїи сȣгȣбом Мазовша чрез Литвȣ и Рȣсь лѣта .҂асꙁв.ѓ [1262] и о ȣсечени̇ Семовита кнꙁꙗ
			VIII: 5 Воисиелкъ или Волстиникъ снъ Мендога короля бȣдȣчи первои̇ їнокомъ закона рȣского из мнⷭ҇тря яко Казимеръ первыи полски̇ на великое княжство литовⷡ҇ское и жмоидцкое избранныи̇ ї возвышенныи лѣта .҂асꙁд. [1264]
C	XII: 3–5	5,120	XII: 3 О гордомⷩ҇ ѡтвѣте Дмитрея Смечⷱ҇ка великого кнꙁꙗ московⷡ҇ского Ѻлгердȣ и великомȣ княжствȣ литовⷡ҇скомȣ посланомъ и о ѡтдани̇ великоденнаго ейца лѣта .҂атꙁв. [1332]
			XII: 4 Ѡ разоренїи Мазовⷲ҇ши ѡт Литвы и преславной храбрости литовⷡ҇ской внегда ополчахȣся крыжакомъ в городе Пȣлене лѣта .҂атꙁs. [1336]
			XII: 5 Ѡ завладѣни̇ рȣскихъ стран великимъ Казимеромъ королем полским, и о умирени̇ его с кнꙁи литовскими лѣта .҂атм. [1340]
D	XXIV: 3–5	7,380	XXIV: 3 The Congress of Vienna in 1515.
			XXIV: 4 Ѡ разоренїи земель рȣскихъ чрез татары и о войне прȣскои̇
			XXIV: 5 Ѡ кѡронацыи̇ Жигмȣнта Авⷢ҇ȣста великого кнꙁꙗ литовского на королевⷡ҇ство полское лѣта .҂афл.е [1530]

6.5 Parameters for comparison

Based on what was said in the beginning of this chapter, the parameters with
which to compare the segments may be chosen from different linguistic levels, and the choice depends in part on the type of text. In this case, the deci-

sive properties of the material are that it is a 17th-century Russian text, preserved in manuscripts and translated from another language.

The first property forms the basis for the primary division of the text into segments, since during this time there were different registers that could be used in written language (cf. Section 4.1.1). The choice of verbal tenses for past events can be said to be determinative of the register chosen by the author or translator. In 17th-century texts, other morphological variables tended to follow this distribution, according to the so-called principle of register harmony (Timberlake 1995: 26; Živov 2004: 155). Even when they did not coincide fully, there was often a tendency towards a certain distribution of different variables. Thus, for example, the use of *-mu* and *-mь* in the infinitive of verbs followed much the same pattern as the distribution of verbal tenses and would say little about individual preferences (cf. Živov 2004: 181–182). Such register-dependent variations are therefore not suitable parameters for this study.

Because of the second property, that it exists only in manuscripts, it is important not to use criteria that vary between scribes. By comparing the different manuscripts, a number of criteria can easily be ruled out. For instance, orthographic variation does not help in identifying the translators. Some morphological factors, such as the plural adjective endings discussed in Section 4.2.3.1, can also be seen to vary between manuscripts, and are unsuitable for this reason. An exception to the rule about orthographic variants may be the spelling of foreign names. One could imagine that foreign toponyms and anthroponyms, not well known in Russian, may be transcribed differently by different translators and not changed deliberately by later scribes who were not acquainted with the names. Therefore, the transcription of names will be studied in Section 6.6.

The third characteristic of the text, the fact that it is a translation, might prove more helpful. This makes it possible not only to count the occurrences of certain words, a method which in itself has been seen to yield good results when applied to other languages (Mosteller & Wallace 1964: 10–14), but to compare the ways of translating words from the original. Here, pairs of synonyms or near-synonyms can be useful. If a Polish word had two translations into Russian, which were more or less synonymous, the use of one or the other of these could tell something about the preferences of the translator. In connection with the work on the edition, it was established that variation between manuscripts in this regard is very rare, which means that the choice of words is that of the translators, not of the scribes. It is of course important to bear in mind that some lexical pairs may have been dependent on register harmony, as some were associated with Russian and some with Church Slavonic. This must be judged from case to case. Sections 6.7.1, 6.7.2, 6.7.3 and 6.7.4 deal with sets of synonyms.

Usually, it is said that the less meaning a word carries, the more suitable it is for studies such as this one, since it will be more topic-independent (Mosteller & Wallace 1964: 17; Juola 2006: 242, 265). This means that conjunctions and prepositions would be preferable. However, there were in many cases parallel sets of conjunctions, some of which were used as markers of bookishness (cf. Kijanova 2010), and this group of words has therefore not been used to a great extent. The occurrence of the preposition *do* in contexts not typical for Russian, which has been dealt with in Section 5.4.2.1, rather belongs to the syntax.

Syntactic criteria can be difficult to apply, partly because they may be dependent on the register rather than on individual preferences, partly because it can be difficult to find a significant number of them in a reasonable amount of text. The translation of Polish pluperfect is treated below, but certain other syntactic features that have been discussed elsewhere in this study and seen to vary between segments, such as the dative absolute (Section 4.3.5), are probably connected to register harmony and therefore not suitable for this purpose.

In the following sections, tables with the numbers of occurrences of different words or forms will be shown. It should be noted that they represent the distribution in those parts of the original that were actually translated. That is to say, an occurrence in a marginal note or paragraph that was left out of the Russian translation is not listed at all in the table, whereas the notification "translation: none" means that that particular word or construction was left out, even though the surrounding text was translated. The entry "translation: other" may mean that the whole context was rewritten so that no single word can be said to correspond to the one under discussion, or that the word used in the translation is so isolated that it has not been necessary or possible to include it. In some cases, such translations are commented on in the text.

6.6 Anthroponyms, toponyms and ethnonyms

Whereas the study of lexical or syntactic variation is a question of finding different target-language correspondences to one source-language element, studying the transcription of names in the translation of the *Kronika* involves an element of generalizing. Since the sample chapters deal with such different periods of time and different places, it is natural that the same names do not occur in all sample chapters. Instead, one must search for patterns, and therefore, before turning to the sample chapters, a categorization of the names must be made according to the questions we wish to answer.

6.6.1 Categories of names

The text contains names of different origin. Presumably, Russian names would be more easily recognized by the Russian translator than foreign names and therefore easier to transcribe correctly. Greek and Latin names – and other foreign names as well – may not have been well known to a Russian scribe. Therefore, looking at the way the names were transcribed might provide some information about the translators, their different strategies and possible mistakes.

Maria Karplukówna, in her monograph on Stryjkowski's language, has devoted a chapter to Ruthenian influence on his language, which is noticed primarily in his treatment of Russian and Ruthenian words and names (Karplukówna 1977: 43–70). Her results have been taken into account when examining how these names were then transcribed back into Russian.

Polish or other Slavic names that have a Russian equivalent could either be transcribed or "translated," i.e. the corresponding Russian name could be used. They do not always refer to Polish people; what matters here is the form of the name. A person who translated from Polish would probably be familiar with both the Polish and the Russian form of the name, and individual choices could become apparent in this category.

Latin forms abound, since the (mainly) Polish text of the *Kronika* is interspersed with Latin elements, longer quotes as well as the names of Stryjkowski's sources (authors and their books). Latin names and Latin forms of other foreign names were declined either with Latin endings, and in such cases usually additionally marked by being printed in an antiqua typeface, or with Polish endings, in which case they were printed in blackletter together with the rest of the text. Polish names occur either in their Polish form or Latinized. This is connected to the fact that Polish authors often wrote in Latin and were probably well known in Poland by the Latin forms of their names. The important feature here is again not the nationality of the bearer of the name, but the Latin ending. Greek endings are treated in the same way as Latin ones.

In Polish, as in most Western European languages, Latinized forms of Greek names were and are used. Russian, on the other hand, had borrowed these names directly from the Greek, which meant that the Russian transcription reflected a later Greek pronunciation. Therefore, the Russian and the Polish ways of transcribing the names differed (cf. Uspenskij 2002: 449). Sobolevskij (1903: 79–80) mentioned Greek names as a criterion for describing the translation of the *Kronika*. He stated that the translator of 1673–79 knew Greek, because he sometimes used Greek versions of names, whereas there were no Grecisms in the 1688 translation. It may be interesting to see if this applies to the different segments in equal degree.

In the Polish original, the spelling of many Russian (and other) names varies. This is probably due to the fact that Stryjkowski used sources in different languages, primarily Polish, Latin and Russian. Variation in the original does not always coincide with variation in the translation.

To sum up, four questions can be posed: How are Russian names transcribed? Are other Slavic names transcribed, or have the translators chosen the corresponding Russian names? How are Latin and Greek endings treated? How are Greek names transcribed?

6.6.2 The transcription of names in the sample chapters

The types of names included in this part of the study are anthroponyms, toponyms and ethnonyms, including adjectives derived from these. They are divided into groups according to the questions posed above. Other frequent names or names worthy of comment are also discussed, as well as the treatment of parallel name forms.

Ms. U has been used as material for all sample chapters, but in segment A, other manuscripts have been consulted for comparison. For the other segments, this has only been done in isolated instances.

6.6.2.1 Transcription in segment A

Russian names

In chapter IV: 3, tales from early Russian chronicle tradition are told, such as the arrival of the Varangians and the reigns of Rurik, Igor, Olga, Svjatoslav and Vladimir. Therefore, numerous names associated with Russian tradition (although partly of Scandinavian origin) occur in segment A, many of them several times. Some names have unexpected forms in Polish, but the translator has transcribed many of them according to Russian tradition. The names, in normalized forms, are listed below in alphabetical order according to the Latin alphabet. The conclusions from this section will be repeated and discussed in Section 7.5, with an emphasis on the possible influence from chronicle language. Here, the primary goals are to see if the translator has been consistent even when the original is not, and if so, which form he has chosen.

Dir (the brother of Askold) is spelled in several different ways in the Polish original: usually *Dzir*, with two instances each of *Dyr* and *Dir*. The spelling in the Russian translation varies between Диръ (two times, once for *Dir* and once for *Dzir*) and Дыръ (eight times, once for *Dir*, mostly for *Dyr* and *Dzir*). This shows that in the case of this name, the translator did not use one form consistently, but neither does the translation reflect the Polish spelling.

Igor is usually called *Ihor* in the Polish text, but sometimes *Ikor* or *Igor*. One instance of *Ikor* is mentioned as a misprint in the errata list after the end of the chronicle, but there are other occurrences that have not been corrected, and in some instances, variation in spelling is intended, as is shown by such cases as *Ihor álbo Igor* and *Ikorus álbo Igorus* (Stryjkowski 1582: 121).

Karplukówna (1977: 58) believes that variants with *k* may have their origins in the Ruthenian habit of writing *кг* instead of *г* to indicate a non-fricative pronunciation, although she does not give any examples of this particular name with that spelling. The familiar form *Игорь* is always used in the Russian translation.

Jaropolk is sometimes called *Iaropołk*, sometimes *Iaropełk* in Polish, where *Iaropełk* is a polonized form, showing a Polish development of **ḷ*, i.e. syllabic *l* (Karplukówna 1977: 47; cf. Klemensiewicz et al. [1955] 1981: 121). There is variation in the Russian translation as well, but of a different kind: sometimes *Ярополкъ*, sometimes *Ерополкъ*. The spelling varies between manuscripts.

Oleg can refer to two persons: Rurik's successor or Oleg Svjatoslavič. Both of them are usually called *Olech* in Polish and *Олехъ* in the Russian translation. This spelling might be the result of a fricative pronunciation of *г*, i.e. [ɣ], which became voiceless [x] in word-final position. Pronouncing the letter *г* as a fricative was at this time characteristic of Ruthenia and of bookish pronunciation all over Russia (Uspenskij 2002: 155–159) and is still known from southern Russian dialects, Ukrainian and Belorussian. When referring to the former of the two men, this spelling occurs not only when the consonant is word-final, but also in inflected forms, e.g. *Олеха*. Here, as opposed to the case of *Игорь*, the translator seems to have followed either the Polish original or a Ruthenian norm. In the case of the latter Oleg, however, there is some variation in the Polish text, which is partly mirrored in the translation. Some Polish inflected forms seem to be forms of the feminine *Olga*: the first dative form in the phrase *Oldze álbo Olhowi* (Styjkowski 1582: 127), the accusative forms *Olhę* and *Holhę* (Stryjkowski 1582: 129, 130) and the genitive *Olhy* and *Holhy* (Stryjkowski 1582: 132). In the translation, these forms are sometimes treated just as *Olech*, e.g. *Олеха*. In some cases, however, they are rendered as *Олгу* (dative) and *Олга* (accusative and genitive). In ms. N, two instances of the genitive are altered to *Олега*.

In the Polish text, *Olga* is sometimes called *Olha* and sometimes *Holha*. There are also a few instances of the spelling *Olcha*. The initial *H-* in *Holha* occurs in other names and words of Ruthenian origin as well (often before the letter *-o-*), as well as in some words of other origin. It may be either a feature of Stryjkowski's dialect, or an influence from Ruthenian (Karplukówna 1977: 34–35, 55–56). The second *-h-* or *-ch-* may reflect the pronunciation, just like the *-ch* in *Olech*. Despite this variation, the name is always recognized in the Russian translation as *Ольга*. The spelling of this name thus differs from that of *Oleg* in being more consistent with Russian tradition.

In the name *Svjatoslav*, the *-ja-* has its origin in an old nasal vowel, which is rendered in different ways by Stryjkowski, although rarely with a Polish nasal *ę* or *ą*. The forms *Swatosław* and *Swetosław* probably originate in

Stryjkowski's chronicle sources, and *Swentosław* and *Swantosław* in Polish historical works using the Latin alphabet (Karplukówna 1977: 49–50). In the Polish text of these chapters, *Swentosław* is the most common spelling. It is always transcribed *Святославъ* in Russian. The translator seems to have followed Russian tradition rather than the Polish original.

The name forms *Wołodimierz*, with pleophony, and *Włodimirz*, without pleophony, were used alternately by Stryjkowski, although *Włodimirz* is more frequent (cf. Karplukówna 1977: 44). The Russian translator wrote the name without pleophony, but with variation in the second part of the name: *Владимиръ* or *Владимеръ*. There is great variation between scribes (within and between manuscripts) in this regard.

The relative adjective derived from the name *Moskwa* has the Polish form *Moskiewskie*, but is always *московское* in the translation (cf. Karplukówna 1977: 47).

Karplukówna (1977: 49–50) notes the unusual spelling *Pereasław*, which can be found in Russian chronicles, albeit rarely. The Russian translation has *Переяславль* or *Переясловль*. The spelling varies both within manuscripts and between them.

The Pechenegs are usually called *Piecynigowie* in the Polish text. Karplukówna (1977: 51) takes the spelling *-nig-* as an example of the Ukrainian development *ě > i. This does not, however, explain the spelling with *-су-*. In ms. U, this word is always spelled *печенѣги*, and although this spelling dominates in other manuscripts as well, some of them also have forms such as *печинеги*, *печиниги* or *печениги*.

Polish and other Slavic names
When Polish name forms occurred that had a corresponding Russian form, that Russian equivalent was normally used in the translation. For instance, the name of the author himself, *Maciey*, was turned into *Матвеи* or *Матфеи*, *Michał* became *Михаилъ*, *Mikołay* became *Николаи*. It may be noted that *Ian* (i.e. *Jan*) usually became *Иоаннъ*, the canonical, Church Slavonic form of the name, rather than *Иванъ* (Uspenskij 1969: 5–7; cf. also Sections 6.6.2.3 and 6.6.2.4). In one instance, however, it is transcribed as *Янъ*.

Latin and Greek endings
When dealing with Latin and Greek names or foreign names in Latin forms, the translator usually replaced the Latin and Greek endings with Russian (or Church Slavonic) ones, just as is done in modern Russian. For instance, *Livius* became *Ливии*, *Iosephus Flavius* became *Иосифъ Флавии*, *Eneas Sylvius* became *Енеи Силвии* and so on. This also holds true for the inflected forms of the names, including possessive adjectives formed with the suffix *-ов-*, such as in the following example:

(147) **Blondus** záś ktory przed lat stem y dwudziestą o náchyleniu ku zgubie Rzymskiego Cesárstwá/ Historią pisał/ gdzie **Arkadiussowego** y **Honoriussowego** pánowánia/ ktorzy byli Cesarzámi/ Roku od Christusá Páná 298. wzmiankę dawnieyszą czyni (Stryjkowski 1582: 95)

Блондъ же, иже за сто и за дватцать лѣтъ о склоненїи к погибели римского цр̃ства повѣсть писа, идѣже **Аркадїева** и **Онорїева** властвованїа, иже бѫх8 цр̃ьми, в лѣто от Хр̃ста .счи. поминовенїе древнѣйшее творитъ (Slav 26, fol. 163v)

The result of this replacement of the endings is that although the Polish original used the forms *Kuroplates* and *Kuroplat* alternately, the Russian form was always *Курополатъ*, and the form *Кромеръ* was used for both *Cromerus* and *Cromer*.

According to the same principle, *Moises, Moizesz* and *Moses* were all rendered as *Mouceu* and *Karolus* as *Карлъ*.

Transcription of Greek names
Greek names were usually given in Russian, not Latinized, transcription, but there is some variation. As mentioned above, Greek endings were replaced by Slavic ones. The Polish *Berosus* (from Greek Βήρωσσος) was always given as *Виросъ*, and *Mitridates* (Greek Μιθριδάτης) became *Миѳридатъ*. *Strabo* (Greek Στράβων), however, was alternately called *Страбонъ* (twice), *Стравонъ* (twice), and even *Страѳонъ* (once), and *Herodotus* (Greek Ἡρόδοτος) was written *Иродотъ* (twice) or *Геродотъ* (once).

This Grecized way of transcribing names was sometimes even applied to names that were not Greek, such as the Latin *Publius Libo*, transcribed as *Пувлии Ливонъ*, with -*в*- instead of -*б*-, although this was supposed to be the Roman nobleman from whom the Lithuanians descended (cf. Section 2.5). Examples of such "purism," in the words of H. Leeming (1976: 12–13), or hypercorrection, can be found in other texts as well, where words of non-Greek origin have been changed in this way. Such examples as these led Sobolevskij to believe that the translator knew Greek, although I would rather say that he knew how Greek names were to be transcribed into Russian.

Parallel name forms
Other patterns, not directly connected with the categories discussed above, can also be discerned in the translation. For instance, in many cases Stryjkowski used two parallel forms of a name, either from different languages, such as one Slavic and one Latin, Greek or German form, or two forms found with different spellings in different sources, where both forms could be Slavic or the origin difficult to determine. The translator could then either transcribe both names or choose one that was familiar to him.

A typical example of this is the river Don. In the Polish text, it is often called *Tanais albo Don*, the first being the Latin name form and the second Slavic. Sometimes only the Latin form was used. The translator, however, always used the form *Донъ*, even when the Polish text only had *Tanais*, such as in the following example:

(148) ciągneło dáley potomstwo iego w pułnocne kráiny zá **pontskie álbo czarne morze**/ gdzie nád **Tanais álbo Donem** y Wołgą rzekámi/ y nád Ieźiorem/ álbo odnogą morzą Meotis/ w ktore **Tanais** wpada w polach szeroko osiedli (Stryjkowski 1582: 92₁)

иде далѣе наслѣдие его в пол8нощныѧ страны за **пѡнтское или черное море**, идѣже над **Дономˊ** и Волгою реками, и над озером меотїйскимъ в которое **Донъ** впадаетъ, в степѧхъ пространно поселишася (Slav 26, fol. 158r)

Example (148) also shows that the Black Sea was called by both its Latin and Polish name, and both names were expressed in the translation. Usually, however, only the Russian name was used, even when the Polish text had the Latin form *Pontus Euxinus*.

In cases where two Slavic name forms or different – sometimes distorted – versions of a name were used, the translator could also choose between transcribing both names or only one. One may assume that the translator was more disposed to transcribing both names if they were unusual and unknown to him, or if they were so distorted that he could not judge which one was correct. In the following example, both names have been translated in all cases:

(149) Trzecie Xiążę Warackie **Truwor álbo Trubor** wziął Xięstwo **Pleskowskie**[73] **álbo Pskowskie** w udział trzydzieści y sześć mil od Wielkiego Nowogrodá/ á stolicę swoię záłożył **w Sworcech álbo w Izborku**/ á według Miechouiussá w **Zborku** (Stryjkowski 1582: 117)

Третїи кн͠зь варяжскїи **Тр8воръ или Тр8боръ** прия кн͠жство плесковское или псковское 8дѣлное .р͞п. верстъ от великого Новагорода градъ ж столныи сотвори **в Сворце или въ Изборскѣ**, а по Мѣховию: в **Зборкѣ**[74] (Slav 26, fol. 195r)

Only a little further on, however, *w Zborsku/ álbo Izborku* was translated as *въ Изборску*, and *w Pleskowie álbo we Pskowie* as *во Пскове*.

---

[73] The *-l-* is an original part of this name, and the form *Плесковъ* is found for instance in the Primary Chronicle. In the 17th century, however, *Pleskow* might have been associated with the German form Pleskau. It is difficult to say if Stryjkowski found the name in an early Russian source or in a German one. The translators at *Posol'skij prikaz* had probably seen the German form in texts.

[74] Some mss. have *Зборске*.

Generally speaking, the practice of transcribing or translating only one name was used mainly for familiar places, such as the Black Sea and the Don, although there are exceptions, as shown above. In approximately 35 out of 60 cases where the Polish original has two names, there are also two names in the translation. Instances where two names are cited for the express purpose of comparing them are excepted from this count, and the difficulties of drawing that border is the reason for the approximate numbers.

Another pattern is the variation between names and their adjectival forms, such as the Sea of Azov in example (148). In the Polish text, it is called by its Latin name, Meotis (for Maeotis), but the translator transformed this into an adjectival construction. The same relationship between nominal forms in Polish and adjectival forms in Russian occurs in several places in the text, although it seems to be limited to a few names. The Sea of Azov is treated in this way two more times, and we also find *Iezioro Ladoga* vs. *озеро ладожское* (117 – 26: 194v),[75] *Babel Wieża* vs. *столпъ вавилонскии* (94 – 26: 162v; 109 – 26: 183r) and *gory Włoskie Alpes* vs. *горы волоскїе алпïискїе* (96 – 26: 164r). There are two examples of the opposite: *Dźwinnych y Niemnowych* vs. *Двины и Немна* (92₁ – 26: 158v) and *Bramy Korssunskiey* vs. *града Корсуня врата мѣдные* (137 – 26: 221r).

Variation in the Polish original is found with respect to the city of Constantinople. It is usually called *Konstantinopol* or *Constantinopol*, with only four instances of *Czarygrod*. Two of these occur in the tale about Oleg and his horse, one in the report of Igor's campaign on Constantinople and one in the tale about Olga's christening, which suggests that the name may have been taken from Russian sources. Regardless of the Polish form, it is usually translated as *Царьградъ* (28 times, including derivations), but 14 times it is transcribed as *Константинополь* (most of these are instances of the derived adjective). The Greek name is especially common in some contexts, associated with the emperor and the church. For instance, the emperor of Constantinople is called *царь константинополскии* five times, compared to only one instance of *царя цареградцкого* (Slav 26, fol. 153r). The translator may have wished to avoid the repetition of the root *царь*. It is also used when speaking of the patriarch of Constantinople (three occurrences vs. one with *цареградскии*) and in the phrase *римскии и константинополскии* (twice). A typical example of the treatment of this name is the following:

(150) gdy z wielką Armatą ciągnał do **Konstantinopolá** wodną bitwą był poráżon od Romaná Cesárzá **Konstantinopolskiego**/ y wielką poraszką był odbity y odpędzony od **Czárygrodá**. (Stryjkowski 1582: 121)

---

[75] The same system for references is used here as in Section 5.4.2.2.

внегда иде с великимъ нарядомъ к **Цр҃юграду**, водянымъ боемъ от
Романа цр҃я **константинополско͡г** ізбиен бысть і с великимъ
8рономъ отогнанъ бысть от **Цр҃яграда** (Slav 26, fol. 200v)

The treatment of names in IV: 1–3 can be summarized as following Russian
tradition in most cases. Most Russian names are given in their familiar form
even when the Polish original shows variation (although there are exceptions), Russian equivalents are usually given of other Slavic names, and
Latin and Greek endings are always replaced by Slavic ones. The treatment
of parallel name forms varies, possibly according to the degree to which the
names were familiar to the translator.

6.6.2.2   Transcription in segment B

Russian names
Chapters VIII: 3–5 relate the actions of the Russian prince Daniil Roma-
novič, who in the Polish original is usually called *Daniło*, but also (twice)
Daniel, whereas the form *Даниилъ* is always used in Russian. His brother is
called *Wasiłko* in Polish, but in the translation, he is called *Василко* the first
two times he is mentioned and *Василии* the third time. In other words, variation in Polish corresponds to invariation in Russian and vice versa.

Name forms ending in *-o* and *-ko* were typical of Polish dialects under
Ruthenian influence, and Karplukówna (1985: 39) believes that Stryjkowski
had found them in chronicles.

Polish and other Slavic names
Here, as in segment A, Russian equivalents of Polish name forms were used:
Michał, which occurs twice, was turned into *Михаилъ*, *Matheusz*, which
occurs once, into *Матфеи*, *Ian* (once) into *Иоаннъ*, *Ierzy* (once) into
Георгии, *Hrehor* (twice) into *Григории*, and *Andrzey* (five times) into
Андреи. Not all Polish names have Russian correspondences, of course, so
that for instance *Agnieska* (sic) is transcribed as *Агнишка*.

Latin and Greek endings
Latin and Greek endings in names were usually replaced. *Miechovius* was
usually rendered as *Меховеи*, sometimes as *Меховии*. The name forms *Cromer* and *Cromerus* were both turned into *Кромеръ*, except for one instance
(Slav 27, fol. 14r) where we find the spelling *Кромерии*, which actually
would be the equivalent of the non-existent form *Cromerius*. *Petrus* was
given as *Петръ* and *Paleologus* as *Палеологъ*. In one instance, however, the
name *Bolesław Pius* was given as *Болеславль Пиюсъ* (335 – 27: 24v).

Other names and parallel name forms
When two forms of a name or two parallel names were used in Polish, both
of them were usually given also in the Russian translation. An approximate
206

14 cases of 17 were treated in that way, whereas in the remaining three cases, only one of the name forms was transcribed. It may be observed that most of the names featured in these chapters were not Russian, so that a Russian translator might not be able to judge which of two forms was preferable.

There are many names in these chapters that do not fall within the categories dealt with above, such as *Mendog*, *Konrad*, *Dowmant* and *Woisiełk*. They were probably unfamiliar to the translator and were transcribed fairly accurately, except that *Dowmant* was usually changed to *Довмонтъ*. *Woisiełk* was transcribed as *Воисиелкъ* or *Воиселкъ*, although there is occasional variation between manuscripts. In ms. B, for instance, *Воисиелкъ* has in a few instances been altered to *Воиселкъ* in connection with the changes made in that manuscript (cf. Section 3.6.1).

6.6.2.3   Transcription in segment C

Russian names
The most frequently occurring Russian name in these chapters is Dimitrij, which in Polish is spelled *Dimitr*, but in Russian usually *Димитрии* (once *Димитреи*, once *Дмитреи*).

As in segment A, the Polish name form *Włodimirz* (pleophony occurs only once, in the derived adjective *Wołodimirski*) can be rendered as either *Владимеръ* or *Владимиръ*. There is some variation between manuscripts in this regard: in ms. N, for instance, only the spelling *Владимеръ* is found in these chapters (in segment A, however, there is variation between the two forms in ms. N, just as in the other mss.). There are no instances of a spelling with pleophony in the translation.

There is also one occurrence of the name *Swatosław*, transcribed as *Святославъ*, and one of *Wassil*, given as *Василии*. The name *Iurij* occurs twice, and it is given as *Юрии*. It may be noted that the Polish version of the name is declined as an adjective (genitive: *Iuriego*).

The name *Siemion Iwanowic* (which refers to a prince) is translated as *Симеонъ Иоанновичь*. Despite the fact that both the name and the patronymic in the Polish original seem to be adapted from Russian *Семен Ивановичь*, the canonical name forms *Симеонъ* and *Иоанн-* have been chosen in the translation (cf. Uspenskij 1969: 5–7). See also Sections 6.6.2.1 and 6.6.2.4 for the names *Иванъ* and *Иоаннъ*.

Polish and other Slavic names
The name form *Иоаннъ* is also used once in correspondence to the Polish name *Ian*.

The most frequent Polish name is *Kazimierz*, which is mostly transcribed as *Казимеръ*. The spelling *Казимиръ* occurs once in ms. U, but mss. B and N have *Казимеръ* in all instances. The first part of the name seems to be transcribed according to the spelling rather than the pronunciation of the Polish name.

Piotr is transcribed, as expected, as *Петръ*.

Gregorz – a Polish name form, although it refers to a saint – is rendered as *Григории*.

Iurgi occurs five times, and the Russian translation varies: twice it is *Георгии*, three times *Юрии*.

Latin and Greek endings

Throughout most of the sample chapters from segment C, the translator has attempted to replace Latin and Greek endings in names. We find, for instance, the usual *Меховии* for *Miechovius* and *Кромеръ* for *Cromerus*, as well as *Белскии* for the unusual name form *Bielscius*.

This treatment of the names is, however, less consistent than in the other sample chapters. The following passage from chapter XII: 3 about the absence of heroes in Polish, Russian and Lithuanian history shows several deviating forms:

> (151) Nálázłoby się wiele w Polszcze/ w Litwie y w Ruśi **Herculessow/** Hectorow/ **Achilessow/ Ewripilussow/ Diomedessow/ Pandarussow/ Patroclessow/** Nestorow/ Aiaxow/ Antenorow y **Eneassow/** kiedyby byli **Homerussowie/** álbo Maronowie/ a ku temu hoyni **Mecaenassowie/** Polionowie/ Augustowie, etc. (Stryjkowski 1582: 423)
>
> мнози обрелися бы в Полше, и в Литвѣ, и в Росиї **Герк8лесы**, Гекторы, **Ахиле̂ссы, Еврипил8̂ссы, Диомеде̂ссы Пандар8̂ссы, Патрокле̂ссы**, Несторы Аяксы, Антеноры, и **Енеа̂ссы**, когда быша **Гомиры** или Мароны, и к том8 щедрые **Меценассы**, Полионы, Авг8сты, и иные (Slav 27, fols. 181v–182r)

As we see, in most of the cases, the Latin and Greek endings were not replaced; instead the Russian endings were simply added to them. Perhaps the translator did not recognize the names, and only in the case of Homer, whom he may have known better than the others, did he use a Russian form.

There are other examples of Latin or Greek endings being included in the Russian translation. In chapter XII: 3, contrary to the usual translation of *Miechovius* as *Меховии*, the words *u Miechouiuszá/ Cureussá* are translated *у Меховиуса у Кореусса*. The form *Herkulessowego* is translated as *Геркулессова*. In chapter XII: 4, *Metellus* is turned into *Метулусъ*.

In contrast with segment A, where the name *Karolus* was translated as *Карлъ*, the endings of three inflected forms of this name in chapter XII: 4 are included in the translation: *Karolussa* vs. *Карлуса*, *Karolussowego* vs. *Каралусова* and *Karolussa* vs. *Корлуса*. The variety of spellings indicates that this name was not familiar to the translator.

Other names and parallel name forms

There are two occurrences of parallel name forms in the Polish original of these chapters. *Twierskie álbo Tuwierskie* is given as *Тверское* (although in most cases the Polish text also has only one form: *Twierskie*). In the other instance, both forms are transcribed: *Ugrę álbo Iuhrę Rzekę* is transcribed as *Угру или Югру реку*. Since these are the only two instances in these chapters, no certain conclusions can be drawn. The river Ugra, which, as the chronicle explains, originates close to Smolensk and joins the river Oka near Kaluga, could have been familiar to a translator in Moscow. There is thus no reason to believe that the translation of both name forms is due to the tendency found in other chapters, that only one name was translated in the case of familiar (Russian) names, whereas both forms were transcribed when they were less familiar.

Polish or Lithuanian names with no Russian equivalent are frequent in these chapters. Examples are *Kieystut*, which is consistently transcribed as *Кеистутъ*, *Gedimin* vs. *Гедиминъ*, *Olgerd* vs. *Олгердъ*, *Witołd/Witołt* vs. *Витолдъ* and *Gastołt*, which is alternately spelled *Гастолдъ*, *Гастолтъ* or *Гостолдъ*. The alternation between *-дъ* and *-тъ* can be explained by devoicing in word-final position.

6.6.2.4 Transcription in segment D

Russian names

There are few Russian names in the sample chapters from segment D. The most frequent name is Vasilij, in Polish somewhat inconsistently written as *Wasił*, *Wasil* or *Wasiley*, of which the last form testifies to Ruthenian influence (Karplukówna 1985: 37). It was usually rendered as *Василеи*, but once as *Василии*, which amounts to a difference between Russian and Church Slavonic endings.

Iwan and *Iwanowic* are given in the Russian forms *Иванъ* and *Ивановичь*, respectively.

Siemion is treated in different ways: we find *Семенъ*, *Симеонъ* and the unusual *Семионъ*.

Polish and other Slavic names

In these chapters, the correspondence of Russian equivalents to Polish names varies. Some names are given predominantly in their Polish form, other in the Russian variant. The ones listed below are the most frequently occurring.

Andrzey is given as *Андреи* (four times).

Ian is transcribed eight times as *Янъ*, 18 times the equivalent *Иванъ* is chosen and once *Иоаннъ*. We see, then, that in these sample chapters, as opposed to those from segments A and C, the Russian form of the name is preferred to the Church Slavonic one (cf. Sections 6.6.2.1 and 6.6.2.3), although the Polish name form also occurs.

Iurgi (nine instances) and *Ierzy* (one instance) are mostly translated as *Юрьи*. Only once is *Iurgi* transcribed as *Юрьгии*.

Maciey is turned into *Матвеи* (five times), but the name *Maciejewski* is transcribed as *Мацевскии*.

Mikolay/Mikolaiewic is rendered as *Миколаи/Миколаевичь* 14 times and as *Николаевичь* only twice.

Piotr/Piotrowic is, as expected, given as *Петръ/Петровичь* (three times).

The frequently occurring names *Wladislaw* or *Stanislaw* do not seem to have presented a problem to the translator, and were transcribed as *Владиславъ* and *Станиславъ*, respectively.

Latin and Greek endings
Latin and Greek endings in names were mostly replaced by Russian ones, such as *Iodocus Decius* vs. *Иодокъ Декии*, but there are a few exceptions: *Piotr Mraxius* is rendered as *Петръ Мраксиусъ*, *Woyciech Fontinus* as *Воитехъ Фолтинусъ* (sic) and *Pirrus* as *Пиррусъ*.

The name *Carolus/Karolus* occurs three times in these chapters in the forms *Karolussowe* vs. *Карлусовы*, *Carolus* vs. *Карлусъ* and *Carolus cesarz* vs. *Король* (*король*?) *кесарь*.

Other names
One name that occurs very frequently is *Sigmunt* or *Sigismund*. The Russian form is either *Жигимунтъ* or *Жигмунтъ*, approximately 15 times each, with one single instance of *Жигмонтъ*. The spelling with *Жиг-* was not oriented on the Polish spelling or pronunciation, but rather on Russian tradition, as it occurs in *Vesti-Kuranty* (2009) and in various chronicles.

The name *Helżbieta* is rendered twice as *Елисавефа* and four times as *Елисавета* or *Елисаветь*. *Isabella* is given as *Есавелъ*.

There are no instances in these chapters of two name forms being used together.

6.6.2.5   Summary of the transcription of names
The four segments are fairly similar in their intention to use Russian versions of Latin names, but this is executed less consistently in the chapters from segments C and D than in the other sections. When it comes to giving the Russian equivalents of other Slavic names, the chapters from segment D frequently use the Polish forms of *Mikolay* and to some extent of *Ian*.

Since the sample chapters deal with different historical events and therefore mention different persons and places, it is difficult to find material that is useful for comparison. Still, the two differences mentioned above are not without importance.

210

6.7 Lexical variation

Some Polish lexemes can have two or more Russian translations that are more or less synonymous. The distribution of these near-synonyms can give a clue to the translators' individual preferences. Since the choice between them may have been influenced by the register of the text, some comments on their history have been included to help evaluate the findings and increase the validity of the results.

The Polish words discussed below have been chosen because they occur in all sample chapters and, more importantly, can be translated in several ways into Russian. On account of the difficulty of finding lexemes that fit both demands, it has been necessary to use lexemes that are not equally frequent in all parts of the text. This makes the results difficult to rely on in some cases, but some tendencies may nevertheless be discerned.

As was explained in Section 6.6.2, the sample chapters have been examined as found in ms. U. In some cases, mss. B and N, as the best representatives of their groups (cf. Section 3.5), have been used for comparison, and variation has sometimes been discovered, but for the sake of consistency, the numbers given in the tables always apply to ms. U. Variation between the manuscripts will be commented on, however.

6.7.1 The translation of *różny* and *rozmaity*

The Polish words for 'different' and 'difference' occur rather frequently in the text. Two adjectives are used: *rozmaity* and *różny*. The corresponding noun is *różność*. Adverbs formed from these adjectives also occur sporadically. They are counted together with the adjectives, since they are too few to justify separate treatment.

The two Polish adjectives (and adverbs) are represented in Russian by *розныи* and *различныи* (usually with this distribution of the spellings with *раз-* and *роз-*, although there is some variation between manuscripts) and the two nouns *разность* and *различие*.

Розныи and *различныи* seem to be more or less synonymous, although this is not entirely certain. The distribution of the spellings *раз-* and *роз-* could possibly point to a connection with register harmony, since *ro-* was the result of an East Slavic development of Common Slavic **or-*, whereas *ra-* was the corresponding Church Slavonic result (Uspenskij 2002: 192).

These words occur very frequently in the sample chapters from segment A, whereas they are less frequent in segments B, C and D.

6.7.1.1 Translations in segment A

In IV: 1–3, the word *różny* occurs 13 times, *rozmaity* 29 times and *różność* nine times. The translation *различныи* is preferred for both adjectives, but there are also examples of *розныи* for both adjectives. They are also sometimes left out in the translation. The treatment of the noun is inconsistent: it is translated as *разность* twice and as *различие* five times. Once a different construction is used, involving the adjective *различныи*, and once the noun *выборъ* is used in the translation.

The dominance of the translation *различныи* can be seen in the following example:

(152) insze **rozmáitych** Narodow ięzyki początki rozmnożenia/ własnośći/ y **rozne** dla **rozności** gránic wymowy swoie máią (Stryjkowski 1582: 95)

иные **различныхъ** народовъ языки начала умнѡжения свойства, и **различны различныхъ** ради р8бежей рѣчи свои имѣюⷮ (Slav 26, fol. 162v)

Table 17 shows the distribution of translations in ms. U. Differences between manuscripts amount to a few omissions and two instances of the spelling *разлучие* for *различие* in mss. E and R.

Table 17. Translations of różny, rozmaity and różność in IV: 1–3

	розныи	разныи	различныи	разность	различие	other/none
różny	2		10			1
rozmaity	2		22			5
różność			1	2	5	1

6.7.1.2   Translations in segment B

In VIII: 3–5, the Polish word *rozmaity* occurs four times, *różny* once and *różność* twice. The adjectives are always translated as *розныи* or *разныи*. The spelling varies between manuscripts, and in fact ms. U seems to be an exception here, since both mss. B and N have only *разныи*. The noun *różność* is translated as *разность*.

Table 18. Translations of różny, rozmaity and różność in VIII: 3–5

	розныи	разныи	различныи	разность	различие	other/none
różny	1					
rozmaity	1	3				
różność				2		

6.7.1.3   Translations in segment C

In XII: 3–5, the adjective *rozmaity* occurs four times and the noun *różność* once. The preferred translation for *rozmaity* is *различныи*, which is used three times of four. *Разныи* occurs once (mss. B and N also have this spelling).

Table 19. Translations of różny, rozmaity and różność in XII: 3–5

	розныи	разныи	различныи	разность	различие	other/none
różny						
rozmaity		1	3			
różność				1		

6.7.1.4 Translations in segment D

In XXIV: 3–5, the adjective *rozmaity* and the adverb *rozmaicie* are used 15 times, whereas *różny* is used only once and the noun *różność* does not occur at all. The Russian adjectives *розныи* and *различныи* occur with nearly equal frequency. The spelling varies between manuscripts: mss. U and B both have only *розныи*, but ms. N has three instances of *разныи/разно*. Once, the adjective *всякии* is used, and once the adjective is omitted in a slightly obscure translation.

Table 20. Translations of różny, rozmaity and różność in XXIV: 3–5

	розныи	разныи	различныи	разность	различие	other/none
różny	1					
rozmaity	6		7			2
różność						

6.7.1.5 Summary of *różny* and *rozmaity*

It is difficult to compare the segments, since these words are more common in some sample chapters than in others. The sample chapters from segments B and C contain so few examples that only a tendency towards a certain distribution can be seen. Still, it seems that segments A and C prefer the translation *различныи*, segment B prefers *розныи* and D has even shares of *различныи* and *розныи*. In segment B, *разныи* is used alongside *розныи* in ms. U, and it is the only spelling used in these chapters in mss. B and N. In segment D, ms. N shows variation between *разныи* and *розныи*.

6.7.2 The translation of *zamek* and *miasto*

As we will see below, the Polish word *zamek* 'castle, fortress' was usually not translated in this text by its cognate *замокъ*, but by *городъ* or *градъ*. This indicates that at the time of translation, the distinction between modern Russian *город* and *замок* had not yet been established. Therefore, there is some variation in the translation of the Polish words *zamek* and *miasto* 'city, town,' with the diminutive *miasteczko*. The distribution of the translations of these Polish words may reveal the practice of different translators.

Variation in the translation of the Polish words *zamek* and *miasto* has also been observed in a study (Bergman 1964) of the two Russian translations of the Melusina Saga, one from 1676, one from 1677 (SKK 1993: 127–129). In the major part of the manuscripts belonging to the first translation, *miasto* was translated as *градъ* and *zamek* as *городъ*. In the latter part of one manuscript, *zamek* was instead translated as *крепость*. The manuscripts of the second translation use mainly *градъ* or *мѣсто*, and sometimes *замокъ* (Bergman 1964: 22–26). This shows that these words presented a challenge to translators, and confirms that they may be subject to individual choices and therefore useful for our purpose.

In the tables below, occurrences of two words together have been listed separately, since some unusual translations can be found in these contexts. Thus, an occurrence of *zamek y miasto* does not add to the count under *zamek* and *miasto*, but is only counted under its own heading. Occurrences of *zamek* or *miasto* in combination with the Polish word *twierdza* 'fortress' have also been included. The expressions *stolica*, *stołeczne miasto* and *główne miasto* 'capital' have been noted, since they have a lot in common with the studied words and appear in the same contexts. Since they do not occur in all sets of sample chapters, they are only discussed in the text and do not appear in the tables.

6.7.2.1 Translations in segment A

In IV: 1–3, *zamek* and *miasto* occur frequently, *miasteczko* four times on its own and once in combination with *zamek*, and *twierdza* occurs only once together with *zamek*.

In most cases where they stand alone, *zamek* and *miasto* are translated as *градъ*. *Zamek* seems to have presented a challenge to the translator, since it is translated in a variety of ways, although *градъ* is predominant. *Miasteczko* is translated as *городокъ* three times, once as *городъ* and once, in combination with *zamek*, as *местечко*. It also occurs once in a marginal note that was not translated.

Zamek and *miasto* seem to have been perceived as synonymous, because even when they occur close to each other in the text, they are usually translated with the same Russian word, so that in Polish, there is an opposition – in example (153), the *city* was surrounded, and Olga barricaded herself in the *castle* – whereas in the Russian translation, this distinction is ignored:

(153) Piecinigowie [...] przyciągnęli do Kijowá/ y oblegli **Miásto**/ á ná **Zamku** Kijowskim záwárłá sie byłá Hołha (Stryjkowski 1582: 127)

печенѣги [...] прїидоша под Киевъ, и осадиша **град**, во **градѣ** же киевскомъ заперлась была Олга (Slav 26, fols. 207v–208r)

214

When the two words occur together in the Polish text as *zamek y miasto*, this combination is most often translated only as *градъ* (seven times). Only once has the translator chosen two different Russian words. In the two cases when *zamek* is combined with other words than *miasto*, both words are translated.

Table 21. Translations of zamek, miasto etc. in IV: 1–3

	градъ	городъ	замокъ	крепость	городокъ	none	others
miasto	23	2				4	
zamek	22	2	2	1	1	3	
miasteczko		1			3		
zamek y miasto, miasto y zamek	7					2	1 (городы и замки)
zamek y miasteczko							1 (грады и местечка)
zamek y twierdza							1 (городы и крепости)

Polish expressions for 'capital,' such as *stolica, stołeczne miasto, miasto y zamek stołeczny, główne miasto* and *główny zamek*, are usually translated as *столныи градъ*. Since *stolica* could at this time also carry the meaning 'throne' (cf. SSP), it is sometimes translated as *престолъ*, including instances when either reading was possible.

The general picture in these chapters is that *zamek* and *miasto* are seen as practically synonymous, and *замокъ* occurs rarely. When *zamek* and *miasto* occur together, they are usually translated with one word. *Градъ* is used rather than *городъ*, which is probably due to register harmony (simplex preterites dominate in these chapters).

6.7.2.2 Translations in segment B

In VIII: 3–5, *zamek* and *miasto* are frequent, and *miasteczko* occurs once. *Twierdza* is used twice, but always in combination with another word. The Latin word *urbs* also occurs once, in the name of a church.

The dominating translation for both *zamek* and *miasto* is *городъ*, and *городокъ* is used for *miasteczko*. The two words *zamek* and *miasto* were probably perceived as synonymous, since they were both translated as *городъ*, even when they occured next to each other and referred to different things:

(154) Sendomirskie **Miásto** spalili/ Potym **Zamku** na ktorym się byłá wszystka Sláchtá Sendomirska [...] záwárli [...] dobywáli (Stryjkowski 1582: 333)

сендомирскои **город** сожгли, посем **города** в которомъ была вся шляхта сендомирская [...] заперлись [...] доставали (Slav 27, fol. 18v)

In example (155), it seems that the translator did not even understand that the words *zamek* and *miasto*, used next to each other in the original, refer to the fortress and the town around it, and translated the passage as though there were two different fortresses or towns:

(155) **Zamek** Lubelski/ ktory był ná ten czas drzewiány/ y **Miasto** spalił (Stryj-kowski 1582: 331)

городъ любелскиї который былⷶ в то время деревяный ї дрⷹгой город сожже (Slav 27, fol. 16r)

In these chapters, the translator has apparently tried to find two words in Russian where two words occur together in Polish. As shown in Table 22, this is solved in different ways. The following translation is perhaps not very adequate:

(156) Helzberk/ Krutzbork/ Konigsberg álbo Krolewiec/ Bartenstein **Zamki y Miástá** pod Krzyżaki wzięli. (Stryjkowski 1582: 334)

Гелзберкъ, Крⷹжборкъ, Конисбергъ їли Королевецъ, Бартен-штеиⷩ, **городки и городы** под крыжаки взяли (Slav 27, fol. 23v)

The translation of the Latin *urbs* is also curious:

(157) tákie iákie w Rzymie ma Kościoł ktory zową *Sanctae Mariae de **urbe***. (Stryjkowski 1582: 333)

сицевые каковы в Риме їмѣетъ костелъ которыи зовⷹтъ свⷮтыя Марїи с **мѣста** (Slav 27, fol. 20v)

Even though the original here is in Latin, not Polish, where *miasto* could have motivated the choice of *мѣсто*, this unusual translation is chosen.

Table 22. Translations of zamek, miasto etc. in VIII: 3–5

	градъ	городъ	замокъ	городокъ	others
miasto		6			
zamek		17	1		
miasteczko				1	
zamek y miasto, miasto y zamek					2 (городки и городы, город и замокъ)
miasto y twierdza					1 (грады и твердыни)
zamek y twierdza					1 (городов и башенъ)
urbs					1 (мѣсто)

The word *stolica* occurs four times and is translated three times as *престолъ*, once as *столица*. The combination *stolicę zamek* is translated as *столныи городъ*.

The translator of these chapters probably considered *zamek* and *miasto* to be more or less synonymous and preferred the translation *городъ* for both, but did not think it appropriate to use only one word for them when they occurred together. Instead he tried to find ways to express both in Russian, and he was consistent in using two Russian words to translate two Polish ones. The word *твердыня* was a part of the translator's vocabulary, but he apparently did not think it was the most suitable translation of *zamek*. *Городъ* was used rather than *градъ*, which is probably due to register harmony.

6.7.2.3 Translations in segment C

In chapters XII: 3–5, the Polish words *zamek* and *miasto* are used frequently. *Twierdza* occurs twice in combination with *zamek*. The Latin *arx* is found once. Adjectives formed from these nouns are also used, mainly *zamkowy*.

In these chapters, *городъ* or *градъ* are often used for both *miasto* and *zamek*, but the translator also introduces *твердыня* as a translation for Polish *zamek*, which is chosen almost half the times when *zamek* occurs. It should be noted that the translation *замокъ* does not appear at all.

The word *крепость* also occurs as a translation for *zamek*, alone or together with *twierdza*, as in the following examples:

(158) tákże insze wszystkie **zamki/ y twierdze** Podolskie […] posiadł y opánował (Stryjkowski 1582: 428)

також. **крѣпости** подоⷧские […] осѣлъ и облада (Slav 27, fol. 194v)

(159) wziął **Miasto z obeimá Zamkami** przez podánie (Stryjkowski 1582: 429)

взялъ **град** с обѣма **крепостьми** здачею (Slav 27, fol. 196v)

Often when two words are used in Polish, they are translated with two words in Russian as well:

(160) (Bo sámo **Miásto y Zamek** Tuwer tylko 36. mil od Miásta Moskwy) (Stryjkowski 1582: 423)

(самый **град и твердыня**. Тверь .рп. поприщъ[76] оⷮ Москвы града) (Slav 27, fols. 182r–182v)

---

[76] Cf. Section 5.3.3 regarding the recalculation of the measurement.

(161) więcey niż pięćdziesiąd [sic] **twierdzy y zameczkow** wziął y spalił. (Stryjkowski 1582: 424–425)

вящи пятидесяти **крепостеи и городовъ** побра и позже (Slav 27, fol. 186r)

In one instance, one Polish word is translated by two Russian words, although in the corresponding marginal note, *zamki* is translated only by *твердыни*:

(162) á **zamki** iż były drzewiáne spalił (Stryjkowski 1582: 429)

твердыни ж или **грады**, понеже быша древяны, созже (Slav 27, fol. 196v)

Table 23. Translations of zamek, miasto etc. in XII: 3–5

	градъ	городъ	замокъ	крепость	твердыня	none	others
miasto	7	1				1	1 (столныи град)
zamek, zamkowy	14	4	2		17		1 (твердыни или грады)
zamek y miasto, miasto y zamek, zamkowy y miescky	1						2 (град и твердыня, твердыни и грады)
zamek y twierdza, twierdza y zameczek				1			1 (крепостеи и городов)
arx					1		

Miasto stołeczne is translated as *столныи градъ* and *stolica* as *столица*.

In these chapters, then, there is an attempt to distinguish *miasto* and *zamek*, but it is not carried out consistently. The occurrences of the translations *твердыня* and *крепость* for *zamek* (but never for *miasto*) may suggest that the translator did not see the Polish words as being entirely synonymous. *Градъ* is used more often than *городъ*, which is in accordance with the register of these chapters.

6.7.2.4 Translations in segment D

In chapters XXIV: 3–5, the Polish words *zamek*, *miasto* and *miasteczko* are used. *Городъ* is the most common translation for both *zamek* and *miasto*, and it is also used once for *miasteczko*, which is, however, usually translated as *городокъ*. *Zamek* can also be translated as *замокъ* and *крепость*, and in example (163), where it means 'prison' rather than 'fortress,' it is translated more freely into Russian:

218

(163) inszych do **Zamkow** ná więzienie rozesłał/ á drudzy ná morze uciekli. (Stryjkowski 1582: 754)

а иных в **ссылⷦку и в тюрмы** poсоⷩлал а иные ушли на море (Slav 28, fol. 308r)

Two of the three times when *zamek* and *miasto* occur together, they are translated as one word. One instance is more unusual:

(164) Soliman potym wziął Budzyń y insze **Zamki y Miástá** (Stryjkowski 1582: 754)

Солимаⷩ потоⷨ взяⷧ Будзынь ї иныя **городы и мѣста** (Slav 28, fol. 308v)

Here it seems that the translator first chose his usual translation, *городы*, for *zamki*, and when he then wanted a separate translation for *miasta*, he wrote the similar-sounding *мѣста*.

Table 24. Translations of zamek, miasto etc. in XXIV: 3–5

	градъ	городъ	замокъ	крепость	городокъ	others
miasto		8				
zamek, zamkowy		13	3	1		2 (в ссылку и в тюрмы, королевскихъ)
miasteczko		1		5		
zamek i miasto		2				1 (городы и мѣста)

The word *stolica* occurs only once and is translated as *столица*.

The translator seems to have regarded *zamek* and *miasto* as more or less synonymous and preferred the translation *городъ* for both of them, but *zamek* also gives rise to some rather free translations. The occurrences of *замокъ* are all found within a small part of the text. The use of *городъ* rather than *градъ* is in line with the register of these chapters.

6.7.2.5   Summary of the translation of *zamek* and *miasto*

Judging by the sample chapters, there are similarities between the four segments in that *zamek* and *miasto* are treated more or less as synonyms in all of them, but there are some differences as well. The most obvious difference is the frequent use of *твердыня* in segment C. The segments also differ in how they handle combinations of Polish words: whether they translate them as one word or two, and which translations they choose. Segment B is the most consistent in using two Russian words for two Polish ones, although such occurrences are rare in all the sample chapters. These differences, taken together, are large enough to point towards different translators.

Градъ and *городъ* are found in very early Russian texts, and they both originally designated a fortification as well as – later – the towns that emerged around them. This translation is from the period when the words *градъ* and *городъ* were going from this more general meaning to the later, more specific one, and a part of their sphere of usage was taken over by new words (Isserlin 1961: 36–37).

The earliest attestation of the word *замокъ* in this sense in SRJa is from 1549, found in a document concerning Polish and Lithuanian lands. Vasmer defines it as a loan from Polish, and Leeming (1973: 346) considers it to be a loan word in Ukrainian by virtue of its semantics and prosody, although the vowel shows the expected East Slavic development of Common Slavic *zamъkъ*. It can be noted that it has the stress on the penultimate syllable, as all Polish words do. The use of *замокъ* in the translation, although rare, could therefore possibly be informative as to the origins of the translators.

The word *крепость* was originally an abstract noun, connected with the adjective *крепкий*, i.e. meaning 'strength' (it is found in this sense in Slav 26, fol. 204r). In the 16th–17th centuries, it took on more concrete properties, referring, on the one hand, to a document that confirmed ("strengthened") an agreement and, on the other hand, to a stronghold, a fortress (Isserlin 1961: 35–37). In SRJa, the earliest example of *крепость* in the sense of 'fortress' is from 1613. At the time the translation was made, this word had not been in use for very long, which could be the reason why it was not used throughout the text. However, it probably does not speak of any Polish influence.

The modern Russian *столица* did not occur in texts until the early 17th century and was evidently not common. The earliest example in SRJa is from 1610, and Kochman (1975: 130), who lists it in his monograph over polonisms in Russian, quotes an example from 1607–08, found in a document regarding diplomatic relations between Muscovy and the Polish-Lithuanian Commonwealth. Before this word entered the language, there were several other expressions, one of which was the noun phrase *стольныи градъ* (or *городъ*), found in the translation of the *Kronika* and attested from very early texts (Kochman 1975: 129–130).

6.7.3   The translation of *granica*

As mentioned in Section 5.4.1.2, there is some variation in the translation of the Polish word *granica* 'border.' It occurs a handful of times each in sample chapters A, B and C, but unfortunately only twice in the sample chapters from segment D. Within each of the first three segments, the translation is rather homogeneous.

6.7.3.1 Translations in segment A

In chapters IV: 1–3, two words are used as translations of *granica*: *рубежъ* is used nine times and *граница* once. The use of *граница* may be a lapse by the translator, since Kochman (1975: 62–68) considers it to be a polonism, as discussed above.

6.7.3.2 Translations in segment B

All four occurrences of *granica* in chapters VIII: 3–5 are translated as *граница*.

6.7.3.3 Translations in segment C

All six occurrences of *granica* in chapters XII: 3–5 are translated as *предѣлъ*.

6.7.3.4 Translations in segment D

There are two occurrences of *granica* in chapters XXIV: 3–5. It is translated once as *рубежъ* and once as *граница*. The word *предѣлъ* occurs only as a translation of *kaplica*, meaning 'chapel.'

6.7.3.5 Summary of the translation of *granica*

Only sample chapters A, B and C contain enough occurrences of the word *granica* to allow a conclusion. They all prefer different Russian words, but there is little variation within each set of sample chapters, which is a sign that these were the preferences of different translators. The use of *граница* in the translation is probably influenced by the Polish cognate, although, as explained in Section 5.4.1.2, it is not entirely certain that the word is a polonism. It is more difficult to draw any conclusions about what motivated the choice between *рубежъ* and *предѣлъ*.

6.7.4 The translation of *roku*

Throughout the chronicle, annalistic formulas are frequent. They can be divided into introductory formulas, such as *roku 454*, *roku od Christusa Pana 713*, *roku od stworzenia świata 4074*, and the connecting formula *tegoż roku*. They are so frequent in all the sample chapters that variation in the translation will show clearly. Such expressions are well known from Russian chronicles as well, and variation may say something about to what degree the translators were acquainted with chronicle tradition. Therefore, the results from this section will also be commented on in Section 7.4.1.

Not all expressions occur in all sample chapters, which makes comparison difficult in some cases. The most obvious example of this is that the use of *od stworzenia świata* and *od Christusa* depends on the sources Stryjkowski was referring to. In the tables below, complex expressions have been divided, so that *roku od stworzenia świata 4074* appears both as an instance of *roku* and of *od stworzenia świata*. For practical reasons they are separated into different tables. Occurrences of the word *rok* outside of the formulas are not included in the tables, but are in some cases discussed in the text.

6.7.4.1 Translations in segment A

This section relates the ancient history of the Slavs according to writers of the Antiquity as well as Russian chronicles. Therefore, the dates here refer to diverging views as to when something happened and form part of the narrative, rather than occurring as chronicle formulas. In several places, there are chains of references, including dates according to old Russian and European chronology, sometimes also from the foundation of Rome.

The Polish introductory formula *roku* is nearly always translated with a prepositional phrase: *въ лѣто*. Twice it is translated with a bare genitive: *лѣта*. The word *годъ* is sometimes used, but never in this formula. Evidently, both words were part of the translator's vocabulary, but the norm seems to have required the use of *лѣто* in the annalistic formula. The connecting formula *tegoż roku* does not occur in these chapters.

Table 25. Translations of roku... *etc. in IV: 1–3*

	в лѣто...	лѣта...	году...	тогоже лѣта	тогоже году	в томже году	none	others
roku...	45	2						
tegoż roku								

The expressions *od Christusa* and *od Christusa Pana* are usually translated as *от Христа*, with two instances of *от Христа господа*.

The translation of the expression *od stworzenia świata* varies in an interesting way. In the beginning of these chapters, it is translated as *от создания мира* (the last time is Slav 26, fol. 204v), but in one instance as *от сотворения свѣта* (Slav 26, fol. 211v), using cognates of the Polish words. The remaining five times, the expression is translated as *от сотворения мира*. This gives the impression that something changed in the translator's work (cf. Section 6.10).

Table 26. Translations of od Christusa *etc. in IV: 1–3*

	от Христа	от Христа господа	от создания мира/миру	от сотворения мира/миру	none	others
od Christusa	13					
od Christusa Pana	10	2				1
od stworzenia świata			8	5	1	1 (от сотворения свѣта)

6.7.4.2 Translations in segment B

In these chapters, the Polish introductory formula *roku* is usually translated using a bare genitive: *лѣта*. Outside of the introductory formula, i.e. in the connecting formula *tegoż roku* or in less formulaic constructions such as *na drugi rok*, the translation involves the word *годъ*, such as *тогоже году, въ томже году* or *на другои годъ* (three times, not included in the table). Just as in the sample chapters from segment A, *годъ* was a part of the translator's vocabulary, but the annalistic formula triggered the use of the word *лѣто*.

Table 27. Translations of roku... etc. in VIII: 3–5

	в лѣто...	лѣта...	году...	тогоже лѣта	тогоже году	в томже году	none	others
roku...		25						
tegoż roku					2	3		

There are only two instances of *od Christusa* and one of *od Christusa Pana*. They are translated as *отъ Христа* and *отъ Христа Бога*, respectively.

Table 28. Translations of od Christusa etc. in VIII: 3–5

	от Христа	от Христа господа	от создания мира/миру	от сотворения мира/миру	none	others
od Christusa	2					
od Christusa Pana						1 (от Христа Бога)
od stworzenia świata						

6.7.4.3 Translations in segment C

Here, the Polish *roku* is usually translated with the bare genitive *лѣта*. The word *лѣто* is also used outside of the introductory formula, i.e. in the connecting formula *тогоже лѣта* or in non-formulaic expressions such as *въ будущее лѣто* or *во второе лѣто* (these are not included in the table). The word *годъ* is also used in such contexts, but less frequently than in other segments.

Table 29. Translations of roku... etc. in XII: 3–5

	в лѣто...	лѣта...	году...	тогоже лѣта	тогоже году	в томже году	none	others
roku...		15					1	
tegoż roku				5	1			1 (того лѣто)

The expression *od stworzenia świata* is translated as *отъ создания мира*, and the only occurence of *od Christusa Pana* is translated as *отъ рождества Христова*.

Table 30. Translations of od Christusa etc. in XII: 3–5

	от Христа	от Христа господа	от создания мира/миру	от сотворения мира/миру	none	others
od Christusa						
od Christusa Pana						1 (от рождества Христова)
od stworzenia świata			3			

6.7.4.4 Translations in segment D

In these chapters, the Polish *roku* is most frequently translated as the bare genitive *году*, and the word *годъ* is also used outside of the fixed formula. Only seven times do we find the translation *лѣта* in formulas, compared with a total of 63 instances of *году*.

Table 31. Translations of roku... etc. in XXIV: 3–5

	в лѣто...	лѣта...	году...	тогоже лѣта	тогоже году	в томже году	none	others
roku...		7	23	1			4	1 (в... году)
tegoż roku					38			

The formulas *od Christusa* and *od stworzenia świata* do not occur in these chapters.

6.7.4.5 Summary of the translation of *roku*

The sample chapters differ clearly with regard to the translation of the annalistic formulas. Segments A, B and C all prefer the lexeme *лѣто* in the translation of the introductory formula *roku*, although in segment A, it is usually *въ лѣто*, and in segments B and C a bare genitive, *лѣта*. Segment D prefers the translation *году* (genitive). In the connecting formula, as a translation of *tegoż roku*, only segment C uses *лѣто*, whereas segments B and D have *годъ*, and the formula does not occur at all in segment A. Segments A, B and D use the word *годъ* in other contexts, outside the formulas, but segment C prefers *лѣто* in those contexts as well.

Since the expressions *od stworzenia świata* and *od Christusa Pana* do not occur in all sample chapters, it is not possible to draw any conclusions based on them.

6.8 Syntactic variation: the pluperfect

Although syntactic structures can be difficult to use as a criterion for identifying translators because of their possible connection with the opposition between Russian and Church Slavonic, or between non-bookish and bookish language, an attempt has nevertheless been made to study the translation of the Polish pluperfect.

6.8.1 The pluperfect in Russian texts

There are two types of pluperfect found in early Russian texts. Both kinds consisted of an auxiliary verb and an l-participle, but differed with regard to the tense form of the auxiliary verb. The Church Slavonic pluperfect, often simply called the pluperfect, had the auxiliary verb *быти* in the imperfect or imperfective aorist. The other, often called the Russian pluperfect, had the auxiliary verb in the perfect tense, full or elliptic (Uspenskij 2002: 251–252; Petruchin 2003: 56–58). In this text, there are no instances of the full perfect form as an auxiliary verb, only elliptic perfect forms.

The pluperfect is traditionally said to refer to an event preceding another event, expressed in a past tense form, typically the aorist. It could also be used to signify absolute remoteness in time, i.e. that an event happened very long ago (Živov 1995: 48). Some scholars consider the Church Slavonic and Russian pluperfect to be identical in meaning, but in early non-bookish texts, the Russian pluperfect may also signify an interrupted event or an event that happened but was later cancelled (Gorškova & Chaburgaev 1997: 361–364; Petruchin 2003: 56–58).[77] The modern Russian construction with *было*, that has a similar meaning, is usually said to be a continuation of this usage (Petruchin 2003: 89). The bookish pluperfect could also carry this meaning, but probably under influence of the Russian pluperfect (Petruchin 2003: 190).

Until the 17th century, the auxiliary verb of the Russian pluperfect was conjugated, but in the 16th and 17th centuries there are also occurrences of a pluperfect with the auxiliary in the neuter singular, but with the main verb agreeing with the subject. This construction achieved the modern sense of an interrupted event. Gorškova and Chaburgaev (1997: 361–364) seem to consider the shift between agreement and non-agreement to have taken place in the 17th century, as they cite examples like *пошли были* and *дошли было* from the 1620s. Pennington (1980: 283) speaks of "isolated instances" of agreeing forms in the 1640s. Cocron (1962: 236–238) lists only occurrences with the auxiliary in the neuter singular (*было*) from the 17th century, but among these there are examples of the original, temporal meaning, as well as the meaning of an interrupted event.

---

[77] Cf. also Petruchin (2003: 91–92) for examples from chronicles.

6.8.2 The pluperfect in the sample chapters

For the sake of brevity, the two types – Church Slavonic and Russian pluperfect – will both simply be called the pluperfect below, but this does not mean that the form of the auxiliary verb is without importance. In fact, when the translations of Polish pluperfect forms are listed, the tense of the auxiliary verb will be the main criterion by which they are categorized. The results will be summed up in Section 6.8.2.5, Table 32.

In the Polish pluperfect, both the main verb and the auxiliary verb were always in agreement with the subject. This tense could be used both for an event preceding another event, expressed in the past tense, and for an event that was unrelated to other events but had occurred long ago. It was common in the 16th and 17th centuries, but is almost out of use in modern Polish (Burzywoda et al. 2002: 171–173).

There are a few occurrences in the Polish text (as a matter of fact, one in each set of sample chapters) of the combination *by* + auxiliary verb + l-participle, which conveys a conditional meaning, and which Długosz-Kurczabowa and Dubisz (2006: 316) call "more complex forms of the conditional mood" ("bardziej złożonych form trybu przypuszczającego"), common in 17th-century Polish. Three of these constructions are translated as *бы* + l-participle. Although the conditional is a mood and not a tense, these constructions will nevertheless be referred to as "conditional pluperfect" and "conditional perfect," respectively, to capture the distinction between them.

6.8.2.1   The pluperfect in segment A

In the Polish original of chapters IV: 1–3, the pluperfect occurs 30 times, one of which is a conditional pluperfect. Three of these occur in text sections that were not translated, which leaves 27 pluperfects to study.

Ten of the Polish pluperfect forms are translated as pluperfects. The auxiliary verb is the aorist *быша* once, the imperfective aorist *бѣ* four times, a perfect form with agreement once and a perfect form in the neuter singular four times.

17 times, other tenses or constructions are used in the translation: the aorist 12 times, the imperfect once, the elliptic perfect once, participles twice and an infinitive once (the conditional example).

The following example can be interpreted in two ways. As I see it, there are two pluperfect forms with a single auxiliary, *byli zábili y pogrzebli*, since both these events precede the main narrative. The translator, however, probably interpreted only the first of the two as a pluperfect, since he translated the second one as an aorist:

(165) Wyzwoliłá potym sobie u nich isz poszłá ná mieysce/ gdzie iey mąż pierwszy Ihor Rurikowic Xiążę był pogrzebiony/ bo go támże w Chorostinie Drewlánie **byli zábili** y **pogrzebli** (Stryjkowski 1582: 123)

8проси потомъ 8 них поити на мѣстω идѣже м8ж ея первыї Їгорь Рюриковичь кн҃зь погребенъ бысть, тамо бо в Хоростинѣ **8били быша** его древляне и **погребоша** (Slav 26, fol. 203r)

In one case, the Russian translation uses a pluperfect construction (with the auxiliary verb *бь*) when the Polish original does not:

(166) Ale Rochmidá [...] niechiáłá ná to pozwolić/ ále zá Iaropełká Brátá iego y nieprzyiacielá w małżeństwo sie bráłá/ od ktorego też dziewosłębow **oczekiwáłá**. (Stryjkowski 1582: 130)

Рохмида ж [...] не восхотѣ за него итти но за брата его и неприятеля Ярополка от негож и сватов̑ **ожидала бѣ** (Slav 26, fol. 212r)

There is great variation in these chapters, with the aorist and the pluperfect as the most common choices and a variety of tenses for the auxiliary verb of the pluperfect.

6.8.2.2 The pluperfect in segment B

In the chapters VIII: 3–5, the pluperfect occurs 15 times, one of which is conditional. This conditional pluperfect is translated with a conditional perfect construction. The remaining 14 pluperfects are all translated using a pluperfect, always with the auxiliary verb in the perfect tense. In 12 of these cases, the auxiliary verb is in agreement with the subject, and twice it is in the neuter singular. The following example is typical for these chapters:

(167) Bowiem Bolesław Xiążę usłyszawszy iż Sendomierzá dobyli Tatarowie/ **ućiekł był** z żoną do Węgier. (Stryjkowski 1582: 333)

но убо Болесла̑в кн҃зь услыша̑в, что Сендомиръ взяли татары, **ушоЛ бъıЛ** з женою до венгеръ (Slav 27, fol. 20r)

This is the conditional example:

(168) Iuż bárdzo duszno y cięszko [...] nietylko Mázowszu/ ále y Bolesławá Wstydliwego Xiążęciá Krákowskiego y Sendomirskiego Monarchy ná ten czás Polskiego kráinom od Litwy było/ **by był** Pan Bog sam pomocy y rátunku z niebá zesłáć nie **raczył**. (Stryjkowski 1582: 335)

уж сѣло д8шно ї тяжко [...] не токмо Мазовшѣ но и Болеслава стыдливого кн҃зя краковскогω и сендоми𝑟ского манарха в то времα полского странам, ї от Литвы было, егда **бъı** гс҃дь Бг҃ъ помощи с нбс҃и сослати не **соизволилъ** (Slav 27, fols. 25r–25v)

One example shows disagreement between the auxiliary verb and the main verb both in the Polish original and the Russian translation. This is probably motivated by the incongruency of the feminine singular *szlachta* and its plural meaning:

(169) Potym Zamku na ktorym się **bylá** wszystka Sláchtá Sendomirska/ Paniętá y pospólstwo z żonami/ z dziatkámi/ y maiętnośćiámi **záwárli** przez cáłą noc y dzień uśilnym sturmowánim dobywáli (Stryjkowski 1582: 333)

посем города в которомъ **была** вся шляхта сендомирская, гс͠да ї поспо́лство з женами и з детми ї с ыменниемъ **заперлисъ** через всю ночь и д͠нь силным прист8пом доставали (Slav 27, fol. 18v)

The preservation of almost all the Polish pluperfects in these chapters indicates that the translation keeps very close to the original, an observation that is confirmed by the fact that the grammatically dubious construction in example (169) was copied so closely.

In ms. N, both instances that here have the auxiliary verb in the neuter singular instead have an auxiliary verb that agrees with the subject. Unfortunately, it was not possible to consult ms. B in this respect, since this was discovered at a late stage in the work. However, as will be seen in Section 6.8.2.4, mss. B and U have identical readings in segment D, whereas ms. N shows a trend towards agreement in the auxiliary verb. Therefore, it will be assumed that this is the case here also, and that the results from ms. U represent the original readings.

6.8.2.3   The pluperfect in segment C

In the Polish original of chapters XII: 3–5, the pluperfect occurs ten times, one of which is conditional. One instance is in a marginal note that is not translated into Russian at all. In correspondence to the Polish pluperfect, the translator has chosen the aorist seven times, a conditional perfect construction once (for the conditional pluperfect example) and a participle construction once. In other words, the pluperfect is never used in the Russian translation of these chapters.

6.8.2.4   The pluperfect in segment D

In the Polish original of chapters XXIV: 3–5, the pluperfect occurs 20 times, one of which is conditional. 14 of these instances are translated into Russian using the pluperfect. In nine of these 14 instances, the Russian auxiliary verb agrees with the subject; in four instances, it is in the neuter singular and does not agree with the subject; and in one instance the subject is in the neuter singular so that it can not be determined if the auxiliary verb is meant to be in agreement or not. The pluperfect is translated with perfect forms five times (one of which is a conditional perfect as a translation of the conditional pluperfect) and a participle once. In the following example, the pluperfect is used in the translation, although there are some other changes in the syntax:

(170) Potym ná schodzie Novembrá/ Tátarowie ktorzy z Moskwy wyciągnąws-
zy/ **położyli się byli** u czarnego lássu/ rozdzielili zagony ná cztery wo-
yská/ z ktorymi do Ruśi y ná Podole wtárgnęli. (Stryjkowski 1582: 752)

потом в ысходе ноября татаровя которые с Москвы вышли **стали
было** под Чорным лѣсом и раздѣлилис̃ на четыре ча̃сти воиска с
которыми в ру̃ские стороны и в Подолье вступили (Slav 28, fols.
304r–304v)

In ms. N, two more auxiliary verbs, that are in the neuter in ms. U, are in
agreement with the subject, i.e. the proportions are 11 in agreement, two not
in agreement and one in agreement with a neuter singular subject. The usage
in ms. B coincides with that in ms. U. Since two of the three manuscripts
deemed to be the best in their respective groups show the same readings, and
moreover, since these two are 17th-century manuscripts, whereas ms. N is
from the 18th century, the readings in mss. U and B probably convey the
original intention of the translator.

6.8.2.5 Summary of the pluperfect

Table 32 shows the translation of the pluperfect in all sample chapters.
"4+1" in segment A refers to the occurrence in IV: 1–3 of a pluperfect with
imperfect auxiliary without Polish counterpart, whereas "9+1" in segment D
refers to the form with a neuter singular subject, where it cannot be determined if the auxiliary is meant to be in agreement.

Table 32. Translation of the pluperfect in all sample chapters

	Segment A	Segment B	Segment C	Segment D
pluperf. with aux. *быша*	1			
pluperf. with aux. *бѣ*	4+1			
pluperf. with agreeing l-aux.	1	12		9+1
pluperf. with neut. sg. l-aux.	4	2		4
aorist	12		7	
imperfect	1			
perfect	1	1 (cond.)	1 (cond.)	5 (1 cond.)
other	1 inf. (cond.) 2 part.		1 part.	1 part.

In other words, the four segments behave rather differently with regard to the
pluperfect. In segment A, it is translated with the pluperfect approximately
one third of the times it occurs in Polish, using a variety of tenses for the
auxiliary verb. In segment B, it is translated in close keeping with the Polish
original, usually keeping the verb agreement in the auxiliary verb. In segment C, the pluperfect is absent from the translation altogether. In segment
D, it is usually translated as pluperfect, but less consistently than in segment

B. Verb agreement of the auxiliary verb is also less common than in segment B. The Church Slavonic pluperfect is only used in segment A, and then only in half of the cases.

The form with the auxiliary verb *бъша* stands out from what other scholars have observed about the pluperfect. Gorškova and Chaburgaev (1997: 325–326), for instance, discuss only forms with auxiliary verbs from the *бяше* and the *бъ* paradigms (cf. Section 4.2.1.4), and van Schooneveld (1959: 122) says outright that a form with *бъша*, found in the Primary Chronicle, "stands alone and is obviously a corruption."

The share of pluperfect forms in chronicles decreased with time. In the Primary Chronicle and the First Novgorod Chronicle, it was 1%, whereas in the *Mazurinskaja letopis'* from the 17th century, it was only 0.1%. This probably means that the pluperfect was no longer recognized as a part of the tense system by later scribes and was replaced by other tenses (Živov 1995: 60–61, 73). The *Stepennaja kniga* contains only 53 examples, all forms of the Church Slavonic pluperfect (Otten 1973: 333). No percentage is given in Otten's study, but since there are 12 000 instances of the aorist alone, the share of pluperfect forms is considerably less than 0.01% (Otten 1973: 62).

In the sample chapters studied from the translation of the *Kronika*, the pluperfect is used with varying frequency: 1% in the chapters from segment A (cf. Section 4.3.1), 3% in segment B, 0% in segment C and 2.5% in segment D. These numbers, except of course for the one in segment C, might be said to be quite high. What they reveal, however, is the degree of dependence of the translation on the original, rather than any independent use.

In this light, one might say that the translator of segment A probably knew the most about the bookish language, since he was able to transfer Polish pluperfect with auxiliary verbs in the perfect tense to Church Slavonic pluperfects, but he was perhaps not entirely sure of their use, since he also chose other tenses. The translators of segments B and D were the most dependent on the Polish original, and the translator of segment C was the most independent, but probably not well versed in the use of the pluperfect tense.

6.9   Polonisms in the sample chapters

In Section 5.4 above, lexical and syntactic polonisms in the sample chapters were studied. Some differences between the sets of sample chapters could be seen, but as this was not the primary goal of that section, the results reached there will now be discussed again with focus on this aspect.

In Section 5.4.1.2, 15 words that have been pointed out as polonisms by earlier scholars were studied, and 12 of these were categorized as being either very active, active or passive. It was mentioned that this classification may reveal something about the translators of the different sample chapters.

For this purpose, only the active words are used. This is based on the assumption that very active words, which were already integrated into the language, would have been used by most people, perhaps without their realizing that the words were of Polish origin. Passive words, on the other hand, were so rare at the time that they may simply have been mistakes, due to misunderstandings or inattentiveness rather than the translator's language usage.

Table 33, which is a section of Table 13, shows the distribution of the six active words (in boldface) in the sample chapters, along with other translations of their Polish cognates. In this table, the number of times each word occurs as a translation of the respective Polish cognates is included in parentheses.

Table 33. Lexical polonisms in the sample chapters

	A	B	C	D
Active	**граница** (1) рубежъ (9)	**граница** (4)	пределъ (6)	**граница** (1) рубежъ (1)
	доводъ (4) **доводно** (4) свидетельство (3)		приводъ (3)	
	знакъ (2) знамение (3) знамя (1)	**знакъ** (1)		**знакъ** (1)
			мусикия (1)	**музыка** (1) мусикиискии (1)
	панцырь (1) пансырь (1)			
	чинъ (1)	**порядокъ** (1)		

Of the six words that were categorized as active, only one can be compared in all four segments, since the only Polish cognate that occurs in all sets of sample chapters is *granica*. Nevertheless, the table shows that when sample chapters A contain a polonism categorized as active, the corresponding Polish word is also translated in other ways in the same chapters. Sample chapters B contain three active words and no alternative translations. Segment C, on the other hand, never chooses a polonism as a translation for these Polish words. Segment D shows parallel translations in two cases and one polonism without a parallel translation.

Judging from the active category of words, segment B is the most prone to use lexical polonisms, segment C the least, and segments A and D vary in their use.

Section 5.4.2.4 shows that sample chapters B also have a larger share of syntactic polonisms, although the only syntactic polonism that occurs in numbers large enough to judge is the construction with *do + genitive*.

Both these criteria also point to the segments having been translated by different people.

6.10 Other possible borders in the text

The division into segments is based on a linguistic feature that is easy to detect: the choice of tense for past events. During the work with the text, however, other variations have been revealed that are not as obvious, but that bring into focus the question of the history of the text.

The importance of ms. B was established in Chapter 3. As was explained in the summary of that chapter, the alterations in the text would make it probable that this was a working draft of the text and the exemplar for later copies, were it not for the fact that there is a lacuna in the text where other mss. do not have one. This makes the early history of the text somewhat unclear.

Nevertheless, in at least one place, a change of hands in ms. B coincides with variation in certain features. It concerns the border between hand B3 and B4, between fols. 205v and 206r of volume I (cf. Section 8.3.2), which corresponds to Slav 26, fol. 208r in ms. U. Several differences have been noticed between the text written by hand B3 and that written by hand B4.

In the part of the text that was written by hand B3, marginal notes from the Polish original are not translated. The first six pages of text written by hand B4 have marginal notes, but then they cease.

As noted in Section 4.2.2.3, hand B3 writes *въ листу* whereas hand B4 writes *на листу*.

When translating the phrase *od stworzenia świata*, discussed in Section 6.7.4.1, hand B3 writes *отъ создания мира* and hand B4 writes *отъ сотворения свѣта* or *отъ сотворения мира*.

Despite these differences, I do not believe that this particular border points to different translators. Firstly, it seems more plausible to shift between translators at the beginning of a chapter than in the middle of a paragraph. Secondly, as mentioned, this is probably not the original translation, although it is an early copy. Thirdly, compared to other features of the text that are consistent throughout sample chapters A, these differences are rather small. They are probably the result of editorial work rather than a shift in translators.

6.11 Chapter summary

The point of departure for this chapter was the assumption that the 1673–79 translation of Stryjkowski's chronicle was the joint work of several translators. This was suggested by Sparwenfeld's note in ms. U, by the use of different verbal tenses in different parts of the text and by the fact that although the date 1673 occurs in the text, the one translator known by name who participated was not employed until 1678, and could therefore not have been the only one. It was not unusual for larger texts to be divided among translators.

Since it seems quite certain that several people were involved, one aim with this chapter was to use the text as material to identify criteria that can distinguish between translators. The other aim was to apply these criteria to four sets of sample chapters (A, B, C and D) to find out if they had all been translated by different people, or if the same person had translated A and C or B and D, respectively. The parameters for comparison were chosen with regard to the facts that this is a 17th-century text, preserved in manuscripts and translated from a known source text.

A division of proper names according to origin or type of name proved to be a useful method, but the treatment of names was to a large extent similar in all segments, and the characteristics of the segments often consisted of isolated deviations from a norm that all translators seemingly had in common. For instance, sample chapters C and D stood out by not consistently replacing Latin endings by Russian ones, but there were few examples of this.

The distribution of the synonyms *розныи*, *разныи* and *различныи* as translations of Polish *różny* and *rozmaity* was seen to coincide with the distribution of tenses, and without further knowledge about these two words, it cannot be excluded that this difference is a matter of register harmony, rather than of individual preferences. The translations of Polish *zamek* and *miasto* were more varied, which made this criterion very interesting, but complex. The results would have been difficult to judge without support from the other criteria. The translations of the word *granica* were helpful, since there was a clear distinction between the sample chapters, but little variation within each set. Annalistic formulas were frequent and therefore useful. The sample chapters were quite consistent in this regard as well.

The only syntactic criterion applied was the translation of the Polish pluperfect. The sample chapters treated it rather differently, although the distinction was not as clear-cut as with some of the lexical criteria.

The active polonisms from Section 5.4.1 were difficult to use, since most of them did not occur or have correspondences in all sets of sample chapters. When treated as a group, they showed a certain tendency, which would probably be strengthened if a larger number of polonisms were studied.

The chapters from segment A were characterized by the following: they consistently adapted names to Russian practice, translated *zamek* and *miasto* mostly as *градъ* and *granica* as *рубежъ*, used the annalistic formula *въ лѣто*, a variety of translations for the pluperfect, and there was also variation in the use of lexical polonisms.

The chapters from segment B had the following properties: names were mostly treated according to Russian norm; *zamek* and *miasto* were mostly translated as *городъ* and rendered with two words when they occurred together; *granica* was translated as *граница*; the introductory annalistic formula was *лѣта* and connecting formulas were formed with the word *годъ*;

the pluperfect was strongly influenced by the Polish original; and lexical and syntactic polonisms were frequent. Some of these facts point to a translator with Polish or Ruthenian as his native language (cf. also Section 5.4.2.1).

In the chapters from segment C, Latin and Greek endings of names were not as consistently replaced by Slavic ones as in other segments; the word *твердыня* was introduced as a translation for *zamek* and used more than half the time, with *градъ* as the other alternative; *granica* was translated as *пределъ*; the annalistic formulas were similar to those in segment B; the pluperfect was never used in the translation; and lexical polonisms were rare. The latter two characteristics suggest that the translator actively tried to avoid words and constructions similar to the Polish original.

The chapters from segment D had the following characteristics: Slavic names were not consistently given in their Russian form; *городъ* was the most frequent translation for *zamek* and *miasto*, but with a few occurrences of *замокъ*; *granica* was translated as *рубежъ* or *граница* (although only once each); the annalistic formulas were mainly formed with the word *годъ*; the pluperfect was strongly influenced by the Polish original; and there was variation regarding the lexical polonisms.

It seems fairly certain, then, that the four segments were all translated by different people, but there are examples of variation within segments that still remain to be explained. A study devoted exclusively to ms. B would probably reveal more about the history of the text and help identify the results of later editorial work.

7 Comparison with original chronicles

The chronicle is a very old and important text genre in East Slavic tradition. The best-known chronicles are the earliest ones, but compilations and continuations of chronicles were still being made in the 17th century. The Russian translation of Stryjkowski differed from early East Slavic chronicles because it was not annalistically structured. It was, however, similar to new types of chronicles that had begun to emerge at this time. Therefore it may be said to belong to the chronicle genre, and if the translators made this association, it may have activated the mechanism of text orientation (cf. Section 4.1.2).

It has been proposed, however, that the translators who in the 17th century began to translate secular texts perceived their task as to some extent separate from previous written tradition, and translated texts differ in some ways from original ones, such as chronicles (Živov 2004: 147). Despite the subject matter, the translation of the *Kronika* may have had more in common with translated texts on other topics than with original chronicles. Therefore, this chapter – which is based on the article Watson (2010) – will be devoted to a comparison between the translation of Stryjkowski's *Kronika*, on the one hand, and a selection of original Russian chronicles, on the other, to find out if the language of the translation shows any signs of being connected with chronicle tradition. The comparison is made on the basis of a syntactic construction, a few formulaic expressions and the transcription of names known from chronicles.

7.1 The chronicle genre in the 17th century

The task of the chronicles differed very much over time, and with it their form. As a rule, the earliest chronicles were kept in monasteries and to some extent at princely courts. Most chronicles from this period take a local view of events, depending on which town they were kept in, and there were such chronicle centers in many different Russian towns. In the late 15th century, however, Moscow assumed a leading role in Russia and consequently took over chronicle writing, making its interpretation of history the official one. Local chronicles were more or less replaced by chronicles kept for the benefit of the Grand Princes and, later, the tsars. State officials took over the task of chronicle writing from clerics, and state documents began to be incorporated into the chronicles (Kijanova 2010: 10–12).

Early Russian chronicles have received much attention, but chronicles written from the end of the 16th century onwards have been less thoroughly studied. At this time, the old kind of annalistic chronicle, beginning from the creation of the world, had given way to new kinds of texts. On the one hand, there were chronicles with a traditional, annalistic structure, but with a lesser scope, covering perhaps the reign of one or a few tsars. On the other hand, historical narratives that were not annalistically organized appeared and partly replaced the chronicles. Instead of continuing older chronicles, they were based on other sources (Lichačëv 1947: 376; Vovina-Lebedeva 2004: 376–377; Kijanova 2010: 11–12). This form of narrative, in Russian called *chronograf* (as opposed to *letopis'*), had become dominant on Eastern Slavic territory in the 17th century, influenced by Polish and Western European sources (Myl'nikov 1996: 16). A well-known example of this tradition is the *Novyj letopisec*. Instead of the annalistic form it has short chapters that deal with such subjects as a battle, the coronation or death of a tsar, the building of a town or monastery (Lichačëv 1947: 384; Vovina-Lebedeva 2004; cf. PSRL XIV: 23–154). Another innovation was the appearance of short chronicles, a form that probably indicates that they were accessible to more people. Noble families also began keeping their own chronicles (Kijanova 2010: 13–14).

At the same time, from the middle of the 16th century onwards, official Moscow chronicle writing decreased. One reason for this may have been that the chronicles could no longer satisfy the state's needs for documentation. Diplomats and state officials needed more information than chronicles could supply, and that role was taken over by archives. Thus, the official Moscow chronicles were replaced by documents on the one hand and historical narratives on the other hand (Lichačëv 1947: 375–376, 423). In the 17th century, the centers for chronicle writing were instead to be found in the provinces. Regional chronicles were kept in a traditional manner, primarily in Novgorod and Pskov (Lichačëv 1947: 375, 386; cf. also Kijanova 2010: 156–157). In 1657, there was an attempt to centralize official chronicle writing to *Zapisnoj prikaz*, headed first by Timofej Kudrjavcev and then by Grigorij Kunakov, but its work was not successful, and it was closed a few years later (Lukičev 2004: 362–375).

In short, early and late chronicles differed greatly from each other, and the variation between different types of late chronicles was great. A comparison of the three chronicles from the last quarter of the 17th century that have been published in volume XXXI of PSRL gives an example of the varieties of chronicles at that time. The *Mazurinskij letopisec* (PSRL XXXI: 11–179) continues the tradition of beginning the tale from Noah and his sons (cf. Section 2.4). It also retains, to some extent, the annalistic form, arranging the information according to years rather than under any other sort of headings, but it does not count empty years, as the earliest chronicles did. The *Letopisec 1619–1691 gg.* (PSRL XXXI: 180–205), as the heading tells us, begins in 1619 and consists of additions to other historical texts in a compilation (PSRL XXXI: 6). It is also written in an annalistic form, but with many long accounts. The *Letopisnoe skazanie Petra Zolotareva* (PSRL XXXI: 206–233), on the other hand, does not attempt to give any early history, but has a set theme: the invasion of Astrachan by Stenka Razin's troops in 1670. Some paragraphs open with references to years, but it is mainly arranged under thematic headings. The list could be made much longer, but these three will suffice to give a picture of the diversity of the texts that fit under the name of late Russian chronicles.

The heritage from the chronicles continued to be present for some time, even in historical works of the new kind. For instance, the traditional appeal of the chronicler to his readers to correct any mistakes they might find in the text can be found also in later, non-anonymous texts (Robinson 1963: 46–47; cf. also Kijanova 2010: 168). On the one hand, the authors had made a conscious choice to write a new type of historical text and not to continue the tradition of chronicle writing, which was seen as insufficient (Robinson 1963: 53), but, on the other hand, they knew that genre so well and used such sources that the result was often a compromise between chronicle and chronograph (Robinson 1963: 57).

7.2 Method of comparison

Because of the long time span of Russian chronicle writing, and because of the hybrid nature of chronicles and their language (cf. Section 4.1.3), it is not easy to determine what is typical of chronicle language. Early and late chronicles differ, and many chronicles reflect the development of the language from their earliest parts to the latest (cf. Gippius 2006). The development of new types of chronicles probably also introduced new characteristics of chronicle language.

To capture at least some aspects of chronicle language, the comparison in this chapter has been conducted with two different starting points. The first is to make use of earlier studies of chronicle language, especially the language of late chronicles, and study the translation of Stryjkowski's *Kronika* to see if similar patterns can be found there.

However, most earlier studies (some of which were presented in Section 1.7) do not aim to single out what separates chronicle language from other types of texts, but either use chronicles as material to study some linguistic feature, such as Petruchin (2003), or show the variation between individual chronicles, such as Kijanova (2010). In other words, it is impossible to say if the results achieved in those studies characterize a genre – chronicles – or a certain time period, geographical area, etc., and their results are not easily compared with the translation of Stryjkowski.

For instance, the parameters used by Kijanova (2010) – simplex preterites, the dative absolute and the dual number – are indeed interesting when determining how archaic or bookish a 17th-century text is, but the fact that she has not quantified her results in any way makes it difficult to relate the translation of the *Kronika* to them. Also, when she reports her findings of dual forms in late chronicles, this does not necessarily mean that the use of dual forms is typical of chronicle language; it only means that the chronicles were written in a bookish register. Another problem is that constructions such as the dative absolute may not be very frequent even in a bookish text, which makes any statistics very uncertain. Nevertheless, considering the great number of chronicles included in her study and the different types of chronicles represented, it provides an interesting point of comparison.

The second starting point is to single out formulas in the translated text that strike the eye as reminding one of chronicle language – a very subjective choice, but reminiscent of the process of text orientation, and therefore suitable nevertheless – and then comparing them with the Polish original, on the one hand, and Russian chronicles, on the other hand. If one of these expressions in the Russian translation corresponds to several different expressions in the Polish original, this has been seen as evidence that the expression is formulaic. If the same expression is frequent in original chronicles, it shows that chronicle language may have been the inspiration for using that particular expression. This does not exclude the possibility that the same expressions may have been frequent in other text genres as well. A further study on formulaic expressions could include comparisons with several genres.

Even though we know to some extent which chronicles Stryjkowski had access to (cf. Section 2.3.1), this does not mean that precisely these chronicles are the most probable models for the Russian translation, since the translators may have been acquainted with wholly different chronicles. They may have come in contact not only with 17th-century chronicles, but also with considerably older texts. Therefore, parallels have been sought in various types of chronicles, listed below, that represent possible types of model texts, but it can naturally not be assumed that these very chronicles were role models used by the translator. In some cases this would not even be possible: the *Mazurinskij letopisec* used Stryjkowski's *Kronika* as a source (Živov 1995: 53) and the first edition of the *Synopsis* was printed when the translation work had already begun. Instead, these texts should be seen as other representatives of the tradition of history writing, and similarities with these chronicles do not mean that they influenced the translator, but that they and the translation of Stryjkowski's *Kronika* belonged to the same branch of that tradition. The chronicles listed below have been chosen for different reasons, but share the trait that they contain a relation of the events described in IV: 1–3 of the *Kronika*, so as to facilitate the comparison of phrases and formulas. The following chronicles were chosen:

1) The Primary Chronicle (*Povest' vremennych let*, PVL) according to the Laurentian manuscript, because of its central position among chronicles and its great accessibility. The first 60 pages of the 123-page edition have been studied (PVL 2007: 7–66), up to and including the year 6544 (1035/36). An online word index, covering the whole chronicle, has been consulted.[78] The Hypatian copy, in the digitalized version in the Regensburg Diachronic corpus of Russian,[79] has also been used to some extent.

2) The First Novgorod Chronicle (*Novgorodskaja pervaja letopis' staršego izvoda*, NPL), as another representative of the earliest chronicles (NPL 1950: 15–100). It has been thoroughly studied by Gippius (2006), which facilitates comparison. An online version has also been consulted.[80]

3) The *Piskarëvskij letopisec*, a chronicle from the first half of the 17th century, as a representative of late chronicles (PSRL XXXIV: 31–220). Some aspects of the text have been studied by Petruchin (2003). An online version has also been consulted.[81]

4) The *Mazurinskij letopisec*, another late chronicle, approximately contemporary to the translation of the *Kronika*. The first 50 pages of the 170-page edition, up to and including the year 6662 (1153/54), have been used (PSRL XXXI: 11–60). It has been studied by Živov (1995).

5) Belorussian-Lithuanian chronicles (cf. Section 2.3.1), because they are similar to Stryjkowski's sources and because if the translators were of Ruthenian descent, they may have been acquainted with chronicles of this kind. The main emphasis is on the *Suprasl'skaja letopis'* from the 16th century (PSRL XXXV: 36–67), since few of the other Belorussian-Lithuanian chronicles accessible in print contain accounts of early Kievan history. The 15th-century *Nikiforovskaja letopis'* (PSRL XXXV: 19–35), which is very similar to it, but slightly shorter, has also been used to some extent. Online versions of these chronicles have been consulted.[82]

6) The Kievan *Synopsis* in the 1681 edition, by virtue of its being a widely spread printed book, approximately contemporary to the translation of the *Kronika*. It has a different character than the annal-

---

[78] www.lrc-lib.ru/rus_letopisi/Laurence/lavrfrm.htm
[79] www-korpus.uni-r.de/diakorp
[80] www.litopys.org.ua/novglet/novg.htm
[81] www.krotov.info/acts/17/azaryin/b61.htm
[82] www.litopys.org.ua/psrl3235/lytov16.htm, www.litopys.org.ua/psrl3235/lytov15.htm

istic chronicles and represents another branch of the tradition of history writing. The first 88 pages of the 254-page text in a facsimile edition have been chosen for comparison, since they correspond to the subject matter in the relevant chapters of Stryjkowski's *Kronika* (Rothe 1983: 143–231).

In the cases where a chronicle is available online or where there is a concordance, these resources have been used alongside the printed editions. It will not be specified in each case which of these sources has been used. Page references and quotations given below apply to the printed editions.

7.3   Coordination of finite verbs and participles

In modern Russian, the relationship between a gerund and a main clause is a hypotactic one, which means that they are asyndetically linked: no conjunction is used to express the relationship between them.[83] The same rule applied to participial constructions in Greek and, under Greek influence, in Old Church Slavonic. This rule was sometimes broken in OCS, so that the participle and the main clause were syndetically linked, usually with the help of the conjunction *u* (Večerka et al. 1996: 204–205). In Old Russian, syndetic linking was even more common, such as in the following example, found in an early entry in the Primary Chronicle:

(171) И заутра **въставъ и рече** к сущимъ с нимъ ученикомъ: "Видите ли горы сия? [...]" (PVL 2007: 9)

Several scholars have pointed out that this construction was quite common in chronicles (Alekseev 1987: 188; Živov 1995: 56–57; 2011: 143–144). Therefore, the translation of the *Kronika* has been searched for such constructions. Before proceeding to the study, however, a matter of terminology should be cleared up, and the history of what we know as the gerund should be outlined.

In OCS and early Old Russian texts, participles – active and passive, long and short forms – were as a rule declined, regardless of their function, according to the gender, number and case of the word to which they referred. The active participles in some positions later lost their inflection and developed into today's gerunds, namely when they were used adverbially, i.e. as secondary predicates,[84] or copredicates (cf. Haspelmath 1995: 17–20).

---

[83] Cf., however, Weiss (1995: 268–270) on some constructions that border on syndetic linking.
[84] This is not to be confused with the Russian term *vtorostepennoe skazuemoe*, which has been used to describe precisely the contexts with syndetic linking and other constructions that

The modern term 'gerund' cannot be applied to the Old Russian situation, but using the term 'participle' without further specification would also be incorrect, and therefore a term is needed that covers all the stages of development of this construction. There have been numerous suggestions for such terms, cross-linguistically speaking. One term widely used in Slavic linguistics is 'adverbial participle,' since these forms are verbal adverbs (Haspelmath 1995: 45–46), or "a nonfinite verb form whose main function is to mark adverbial subordination" (Haspelmath 1995: 3). Because of their status as predicates in a subordinate construction, they have sometimes been called 'predicative participles' (Bjørnflaten 2010: 19–20). Haspelmath (1995: 45–46) prefers the term 'converb.' Here, 'adverbial participle' has been chosen to describe the form during the whole of its development, since the construction studied below originates in a time when the form in question was still a participle, but in the 17th century probably should be seen as containing a gerund. In this way, the origins of the form as a participle is emphasized, and the choice is also in keeping with Slavic scholarly tradition. In unambiguous contexts, for the sake of brevity and to avoid repetition, 'participle' will also be used.

The loss of declension of adverbial participles seems to have begun before the 14th century, and in texts from the 17th century, uninflected forms are widely used. The change began with adverbial participles with a plural reference (in both the present and past tense) adopting the ending -*u* instead of -*e*. This resulted in ambiguous forms and the deterioration of the declension system. Several endings competed for dominance, and in the 17th century, the endings -*а/-я* and -*учи* in the present tense, and -*въ* and -*вши* in the past tense, respectively, were not distinguished (Bjørnflaten 2010: 21–27). The distribution of the endings represented in the *Kronika* can be found in Section 4.2.1.5.

According to A. A. Alekseev (1987: 192–193), syndetic linking was especially common when the adverbial participle construction preceded the finite verb, and especially after a past adverbial participle, where his material, *Skazanie o Mamaevom poboišče* in a redaction from 1526–1530, shows a share of 41% syndetic constructions (cf. Alekseev 1987: 188–189). In the Hypatian copy of the Primary Chronicle, the share is 24%, and in the Kievan chronicle 40% (Živov 2011: 144). It is frequent in other later texts as well (Živov 1995: 56–57). Examples abound in Kijanova's material (late chronicles), and she states that the construction is common in chronicles, even though she does not specify if it characterizes them as opposed to other genres.[85]

---

bear witness to an intermediate stage in the development from participles to gerunds (Alekseev 1987: 187).

[85] Cf. for example Kijanova (2010: 57, 133, 186, 241).

There are examples with postpositive adverbial participles as well, and Živov (1995: 56–57) considers the independent predicative status to be especially emphasized in such cases.

The syndetic construction shows the tendency in chronicles towards paratax and the "stringing" (*nanizyvanie*) of clauses (Alekseev 1987: 195). If we look beyond participle constructions, the high frequency of the conjunction *u* between main clauses and in the beginning of sentences testifies to this tendency (Alekseev 1987: 195–196; Gippius 2006: 170–171). Dative absolute constructions, that were also subordinate constructions with a participle form as one of their constituents, could also be syndetically linked to the main clause (Corin 1995: 262–264). Several other constructions also attest to the independence of participles in OCS and the early stages of other Slavic languages (Večerka et al. 1996: 199–214; cf. also Weiss 1995: 274–275). Corin (1995: 272) mentions the common Slavic character of the syndetic construction and sees its origins in Czech.

Syndetic linking of adverbial participle constructions existed in Polish throughout the 17th century, but disappeared towards the end of the 18th century (Grybosiowa 1973: 91–92; Sokołowska 1976: 73–77; Pisarkowa 1984: 224–225, 245). T. Sokołowska (1976: 73–77) specifies that different conjunctions were generally used with prepositive and postpositive participles: *a* when the participle was postpositive, *i* when it was prepositive. She gives examples of both positions, but it can be noted that there are very few examples of postpositive past participles. D. Ostaszewska lists a few examples with postpositive adverbial participles, mainly in the present tense, but the distribution of conjunctions proposed by Sokołowska cannot be observed here (Burzywoda et al. 2002: 274).

With this in mind, we turn to the translation of the *Kronika*. Participles with no apparent link to a preceding or following main clause have been excluded from the counts below. This applies to a few instances of participles in parentheses, and also to the adverbial participles *идучи* and *едучи*, which seem to function differently than other verbs. *Идучи* in Slav 26, fol. 152r appears in parentheses, making the link to preceding clauses less strong, and where it appears on fol. 153r, the subject in the preceding main clause is inanimate and cannot in any way be the subject of the adverbial participle. This also applies to the form *едучи* on fol. 168r. Therefore, these forms are not connected to a main clause. Hüttl-Folter (1996: 270, 286–287) gives similar examples of what she calls absolute gerund constructions, where the adverbial participle does not refer to the subject of the main clause, but has a more general meaning. Several of her examples also contain verbs of motion. This independent use of adverbial participles is attested in Old Polish as well as in Old Russian (Sokołowska 1976: 111–112).

The study is based on the text found in ms. U, and it may be noted that there are some differences between manuscripts in this regard: not primarily in the presence or absence of conjunctions, but in verb forms that are finite forms (e.g. aorists) in some mss. and participles in others. For instance, in Slav 26, fol. 212v, there is a whole chain of participles that are not connected with a finite verb form, since the finite verb form in the Polish original has been altered to a participle in ms. U. This form is an aorist in some other mss., so that if the study had been based on ms. B, one prepositive past participle and one postpositive present participle would have been added to the material. This means that the percentages of syndetic constructions in the table below may be slightly different if calculated on other manuscripts, but the general picture would probably be the same. Variation between manuscripts will be commented on in connection with the examples below.

The share of syndetically linked participle constructions in the Russian translation of the *Kronika* is not as large as in the original chronicles studied by other scholars. There are 18 examples of the construction in IV: 1–3. The conjunctions used are *u*, *a* and *но*. *Ho* is not traditionally found in this role and is not mentioned by Večerka et al. (1996: 204–208), but is found here twice.

The 18 occurrences are distributed as follows according to the tense of the adverbial participle and its position in relation to the main clause.

Table 34. Constructions with adverbial participles

	prepos. synd.	prepos. asynd.	postpos. synd.	postpos. asynd.
present participle	7 (9.7%)	65 (90.3%)	5 (6.9%)	67 (93.1%)
past participle	6 (5.2%)	109 (94.8%)	0 (0.0%)	13 (100.0%)

As we see, the hierarchy of frequency of the syndetic construction established by Alekseev (1987: 192–193), *prepositive past participle > prepositive present participle > postpositive participle*, does not show here, but instead we see *prepositive present participle > postpositive present participle > prepositive past participle*. Since there are rather few examples, they will all be listed below. The primary division will be according to how the construction relates to the Polish original, but within those groups, a subdivision will be made according to the tense of the adverbial participle and its position. As for the primary division, the relation between the original and the translation can be one of the following:

a) there is an identical construction in the Polish original,

b) the Russian translation uses the same verb forms as the original but has inserted a conjunction, i.e. *participle + finite verb* becomes *participle + conjunction + finite verb* or *finite verb + participle* becomes *finite verb + conjunction + participle*,

c) a finite verb has been changed to an adverbial participle, i.e. *finite verb + conjunction + finite verb* becomes *finite verb + conjunction + participle* or *participle + conjunction + finite verb*,

d) an adverbial participle has been changed to a finite verb, i.e. *participle + conjunction + participle* becomes *participle + conjunction + finite verb* or *finite verb + conjunction + participle*.

There are three examples of case a), where the Polish original has an identical construction. In all cases the adverbial participle is prepositive. One example contains a past participle:

(172) zebrał sie przećiw im Romanus Cesarz Grecki z pomocą Rzymską/ y inszych Pánow Chrześćiáńskich/ á **stoczywszy** srogą bitwę z Ruską Armatą ná Morzu czarnym/ **y poráźił** wielkie woyská Ruskie ná głowę (Stryjkowski 1582: 121)

собрався[86] противъ ево Рома*н* ц҃рь греческїи с помочью римскою, и ї́ных г҃дре*и* хр҃стиянских, **сотворивъ** ж ополчение с рускимъ нарядомъ на чо*р*номъ мори, **и поби** великие воиска руские (Slav 26, fol. 200r)

The other examples contain present participles:

(173) A iżbych tu krotkośći y teskliwemu czytelnikowi **folguiąc/ y** inszych Cesárzow Greckich/ Rzymskich/ tákże tysiąc dowodow o Sarmatskiey Rycerskiey dzielnośći **opuśćił/** tedy to sámá rzecz pokázuie (Stryjkowski 1582: 108)

и дабы здѣ кроткости, и тоскливом8 читателю **норова, и** ї́ныхъ[87] цесарей греческихъ римскихъ, такоже ҂а. свидѣтелствъ о сармацко*и* воинской храбрости **оставил** (Slav 26, fol. 182r)

(174) Ktorego wielkiego gwałtu Cesarz Constantinopolski nie **mogąc** wytrzymáć/ **á** pomocy ná odsiec zniskąd sie nie **spodziewał/** przeiednał Olechá wielkimi dárámi/ odkupuiąc pokoy (Stryjkowski 1582: 120)

и то*г* насилия ц҃рь константинополскїи не **могїи** выде*р*жать, і помочи на выр8чку ниотк8д8 не **чаялъ,** 8толи Олеха великими дары поко*и* пок8пая (Slav 26, fol. 199r)

The following examples illustrate case b), where the Russian translation uses the same verb forms as the original but has inserted a conjunction. The majority of these contain prepositive past participles:

(175) ktorey potym kośći Włodimirz wnuk **ochrzśćiwszy** sie/ zá swięte **podniosł** y iest miedzy swięte policzona (Stryjkowski 1582: 127)

кости ж ея вн8къ Владимеръ **крестився, и** в мѣста с҃тыя **подя, и** межд8 с҃тыя причтена (Slav 26, fol. 208v)

---

[86] Mss. B and G have *собрася*.
[87] Ms. N has *инныхъ* instead of *и ї́ныхъ*, i.e. an asyndetic construction.

(176) Nátychmiast tedy pośiliwszy Ricerstwo/ z wielkim pędem rzućili sie y gwałtownie uderzyli ná przećiw stoiące woysko Greckie/ á **przerwawszy** y **przebiwszy** uprzeymą nawáłnośćią ich uffy szykowáne/ zwycięstwo **otrzymáli** (Stryjkowski 1582: 128)

8твердив же тогда воинствω иде с великою скоростию и 8дари жестоко напротивъ стоящее воинство греческое, **разорвав** же и **розбивъ** великимъ нашествием полки 8строенные ихъ, **и** тако побѣд8 **возприяша** (Slav 26, fols. 209v–210r)

(177) Potym Włodimirz będąc iusz zupełnym Iedynowłaycą wszystkiey Ruśi/ zebrał wielkie woysko/ s ktorym **przepráwiwszy** sie przez Dunay/ **opáno-wał** Ziemie Bulgarską [...] (Stryjkowski 1582: 133)

и б8д8чи совершенным самодержцем всеа Росїи, Владимер **шед** с велиїмъ войскомъ чрез Д8наи **и овладѣ** земли болгарскую [...] (Slav 26, fol. 215r)

(178) á Peresławiánin przyskoczywszy nie dał mu się powtore popráwowáć/ ále go záraz **osiodławszy począł** tłuc w sczeki áż mu zęby wespołek ze krwią pádáły (Stryjkowski 1582: 135)

р8синъ ж не даде ем8 встати **всѣд** на него **и нача** бити по щекам, что з8бы 8 него с кровию выпадали (Slav 26, fol. 217v)

Two examples contain prepositive present participles:

(179) á Popowie **dawáiąc** káżdey gromádzie z ossobná imię/ Timochwiey/ Wasil/ Piotr/ álbo Siemion/ polewáli ich wodą/ á modlitwy nád niemi zwykłe odpráwuiąc/ **chrzćili** wszystkich męsczyznę y niewiásty/ w Imię Oycá y Syná y Duchá swiętego. (Stryjkowski 1582: 140)

сщенницы ж **крестяще** их во имя отца и сна ї свтаг дха, **и даваху** имъ имяна, Василїи. Петръ, Иоан, Тимоθеи Симеон. и проч (Slav 26, fols. 224v–225r)

(180) co **ráchuiąc** z dzisieyszym Rokiem Páńskim kiedy to piszą 1579. **uczyni** 599. Lat. (Stryjkowski 1582: 423)

и **считая** с ннешнимъ лѣтомъ гднимъ ., афθθ.и и тогω б8детъ, .фчθ. лѣтъ (Slav 26, fol. 226v)

Yet another example has a postpositive present participle:

(181) woyská z obudwu stron **stały** spokoynie **pátrząc** ná onę biesiádę chłopká máłego z obrzymem (Stryjkowski 1582: 134)

войска ж с обоих странъ **стоях8** тихо, **и зряще** на борбу малого мужичка со исполином (Slav 26, fol. 217v)

In the following cases, examples of c), Polish finite verbs have been changed to adverbial participles in the Russian translation. In example (182), two finite forms have been turned into prepositive past participles:

(182) ále skoro sie **wywiedzieli** liczby Zołnierzow iego/ wnet też woyská swoie Greckie **spissáli/ y wiedli** przećiw Swentosławowi (Stryjkowski 1582: 128)

егда же **увѣдавше** число войнства егѡ, вскоре воя свои греческие **собравше, и** противо Святослава **ведоша** (Slav 26, fol. 209r)

Two examples have prepositive present participles. Both of these use the conjunction *но*:

(183) **Widząc** to Piecinigowie/ isz sie im potężnie Włodimirz stáwił/ nie **smieli** náćieráć wstępnym boiem/ **ále posłáli** do Włodimirzá z táką kondićią [...] (Stryjkowski 1582: 133)

видя же печенѣги яко Владимиръ противо их стоитъ во множестве силы, не **смѣя** на него боемъ наст8пати, **но просиша** 8 него [...] (Slav 26, fol. 216r)

(184) gdy ich tákże słudzy […] puśćić nie **chieli/** iáko nieprzyiacioł y przychodniow/ ász ich tákże […] rozgámi y puhami **rospłoszyli** etć. (Stryjkowski 1582: 138)

тако*ж* сл8ги и плѣнники [...] хозяевъ своих [...] яко неприятел*еи* в домы п8стити не **хотяще, но** по многих бране*х* хозяева **изгнаша** и*х* такожде и про*ч*: (Slav 26, fol. 222r)

The majority, however, contain postpositive present participles:

(185) A gdy go insze Xiążętá dárámi błágáły/ odkupuiąc pokoy/ á Swentosław Złotá y Panadokmi Kleinotow (iako ich Ruskie Kroniki miánuią) nie **chciał** bráć **y gárdził** nimi/ A tyłko száty y broni/ Zbroie/ Tarcze/ Miecze od Grekow przysłáne **przyymował.** (Stryjkowski 1582: 128)

и егда Святослава инїй кн͠зи 8молях8 дары, прося покоя, злато*м* и панадокми бисере*в* (яко р8ские лѣтописцы имян8ютъ,) не **вос-хотѣ** приїмати, **и гн8шаясь** ими, токмѡ *от* грековъ одежды, ор8жия збр8и щиты. мечи присланные **приемля** (Slav 26, fol. 210r)

(186) Y **począł rádzic** Blud Iaropołkowi znowu/ áby pokoiu u Brátá nád się dáleko mocnieyszego prośił do Włodimirzá też potáiemnie **wskazáł/** isz mu iusz wnet chcę brátá wydáć/ y przedeń przywieść. (Stryjkowski 1582: 131)

видя *ж* изн8ждение ихъ Бл8д, **совѣтова** Ярополк8 просити мир8 и тишины 8 брата своего Владимера. **а** Владимер8 **предвозвѣщая,** что 8же Ярополка хощет выдать, и пред него привести (Slav 26, fol. 213r)

(187) á naprzód Báłwan bárdzo wysoki **postáwił** Piorunowi álbo Porkunowi/ Bogowi gromow/ chmur/ y łyskáwic. Ktorego nabożniey z wielką ucżćiwośćią **chwalił** (Stryjkowski 1582: 132)

и по̂строи́л началнои болванъ зѣло высокъ Пер8н8 или Перк8ну бог8 громовъ темныхъ о̂блако̂в̄ и молнїи и бл҃гочинно его **почитая** (Slav 26, fol. 214r)

(188) Drugie Báłwany były miánowáne/ Uslad/ Korssa/ Dassubá/ Stribá/ Symaergla/ Makosz/ etc. Ktorych Russacy Kumerami iednostáynie **názywáli/ y** tym ofiáry **czynili/** y modlitwy Boskie wyrządzáli (Stryjkowski 1582: 132)

иныя ж болваны нарече 8слад, Корсса, Дасс8ба, Стриба, Сима, ерѓла [sic], Макошь, и протчая, ихже Р8̂с̂ к8мирами **нарицах8, и** жертвы имъ **творяще**[88] (Slav 26, fol. 214r)

There is one example of case d), where a Polish adverbial participle has been changed to a finite verb in Russian. This example contains past participle forms in Polish, but the participle that remains in the Russian translation is in the present tense.

(189) Ták tedy Syny **opátrzywszy** Swantosław **y rozdzieliwszy** im Xięstwá porządnie/ niemogł gnusnieć w pokoiu (Stryjkowski 1582: 127)

И тако Святославъ сн҃ы 8строя и раздели имъ княжства, самъ ж в покое не возможе пребывати́ (Slav 26, fol. 209r) (cf. also example (197))

In some of these examples, the translation also differs from the Polish original in choice of words, word order or syntax. These are perhaps the most interesting examples, since they show a conscious choice by the translator.

All the examples listed above, except no. (173), which corresponds to an identical construction in the Polish original, are found in IV: 3, the chapter that relates events from Russian chronicles. This fact may imply that the construction was perceived as inherent to chronicle language. Still, the share of such constructions in this translation does not come close to the numbers mentioned for original chronicles. Also, Alekseev's information about the conditions under which this construction is most common does not hold true for the translated *Kronika*. The reason for this difference in distribution is unknown.

When compared to the Polish original, different alterations (or absence of alteration) seem to be connected to different tenses and placements of the

---

[88] Ms. R has *творях8*, making this an ordinary coordination of finite verbs in that manuscript.

Russian adverbial participle. This is illustrated by Table 35. The reason for these differences has not been investigated.

Table 35. Types of translations in relation to the position and tense of the participle

	a: no alteration	b: conj. added	c: finite → part.	d: part. → finite
past prepositive	1	4	1	
pres. prepositive	2	2	2	1
pres. postpositive		1	4	

The sample chapters from segment B contain one instance of case b), where a conjunction has been added in the Russian translation:

(190) á Dowmant też iáko Hołdownik z nimi był poszedł ná tę woynę według powinnośći/ upatrzywszy czás pogodny **wróćił** się názad z ludem swoim/ **wymowiwszy** się u Hetmáná Mendogowego wiełką á gwałtowną potrzebą. (Stryjkowski 1582: 336)

а Довмонтъ таж якѡ гол̑довникъ с ними бы́л̑, пошел̑ на тое войн8 против8 дол̑жности, а 8смотря время согласное **возвратил̑сѧ** назад с людми своими, ї **спросившис** у геѳмана Мендогова великою ї н8жною потребою (Slav 27, fol. 27v)

The sample chapters from segment C do not contain any examples of the construction.

The sample chapters from segment D contain six occurrences. Five of these are concentrated to chapter XXIV: 5. There are three instances of case b), where a conjunction has been added:

(191) A w tym Prokop y Alexander Sieniawscy z Herbu Leliwy rodzoni Brácia/ **przypadwszy** z Rotámi swieżymi w bok Wołochom/ **rozerwáli** ich (Stryjkowski 1582: 757)

а в томъ Прокоѳиї и Алеӡандръ Синав̑ския з геρб8 леливы. родныя братья **присⷦкоча** с ротами свѣжими в бокъ волоховъ **и розоρвали** ихъ (Slav 28, fol. 313v)

(192) skoczyli wszyscy zápalczywie do Wołochow/ ktorzy zárázem tył **podáli/** rożno po polách **uciekáiąc** (Stryjkowski 1582: 757)

скочили всѣ с храбросⷮтию к волохомъ которые тоⷮчасъ **возвратилисѧ и** розно по поламъ **утекая** (Slav 28, fol. 314r)

(193) A ták **złączywszy** się z Polaki **ciągnęli** zá Moskwą/ wzięli Zamek Homel w Siewierskiey ziemi nád Rzeką Sos. (Stryjkowski 1582: 758)

и тако **соединившесѧ** с полѧками **и шли** на Москвою и вӡяли город Гомелъ, в северскоⷯ землѣ над рекою Сожъ (Slav 28, fol. 316r)

There is one instance of case c), where a Polish finite verb has been changed into a participle:

(194) Tegoż cżássu Mendlikierey Carz Prekopski gdy **był wziął** żołd od Krolá Sigmuntá/ **y miał** ciągnąć záraz z Litwą na tę woynę przećiw Moskiewskiemu (Stryjkowski 1582: 747)

в тож время Мендликереи царь перекопскиї **взявъ** казну от короля Жигим8нта **и имѣлъ** ити в тот же часъ с Литвою на ту войну против московского (Slav 28, fol. 292v)

In these chapters, we also find two instances where a finite verb has been changed to a participle and a conjunction has been added, i.e. a combination of b) and c):

(195) Tegoż roku Piotr Opalenski **poszedł** do Turek/ **ziednał** przymierze z obiemá Krolámi dożywotne/ od Turkow/ Tátarow y Wołochów. (Stryjkowski 1582: 757)

тогож году Пеⷮръ Ѡпаленскиї, **пошоⷧ** до т8роⷦ **и примириⷡ** со ѡбема королѧми до живота, ѡⷮ т8рковъ, татароⷡ и волоховъ (Slav 28, fol. 314v)

(196) Tám też skárbow y inszych rozmáitych wzdobycy Litwá y Polacy bárdzo wiele **dostáli**/ wszákże ogień nie máło **popsowáł.** (Stryjkowski 1582: 758)

тамже богатства и иных различных здобычи Литва и поляки зело **побрали, а** ѡбаче немало и огонь **попалиⷡ** (Slav 28, fol. 316r)

These two examples may have another explanation, however. In both cases, the participle is in the past tense with the ending -в. In this part of the text, there are several more cases of Polish past tense forms in -*l* being translated as Russian forms in -в (cf. also example (194)). This raises the question of whether these forms are really meant as participles, or if they might rather bear witness to the translator's Ruthenian origin, since the corresponding ending in modern Ukrainian is -в and in Belorussian -ў.

Because of this uncertainty in how to define the forms in -в, the proportions of syndetic and asyndetic participle constructions in sample chapters D have not been calculated, but as we see, all four possible combinations of tenses and positions are found: present and past participles, prepositive and postpositive.

7.4 Formulas

It has been observed that chronicles used fixed formulas and clichés to a great extent, especially when reporting recurring events: births, deaths, natural phenomena or battles. Some of these formulas could vary over time.[89] In late chronicles, some such expressions still remained as a reminder of chronicle tradition even when most other traditional elements had been abandoned (Kijanova 2010: 154–155). If these formulas were familiar to the translators of the *Kronika*, one might expect that they would insert them in appropriate places of the translation, according to the principle of text orientation.

Due to the fact that little has been written about formulaic expressions, there is no easily applicable method with which to compare the texts. Those that have been mentioned by earlier scholars have been sought out, with the addition of others that, on reading the translated *Kronika*, strike the eye as frequent.

As explained in Section 7.2, occurrences of the selected constructions in the translation of the *Kronika* have been compared to the corresponding places in the Polish text. If a construction in the translation differs from the one used in the Polish original, or if it corresponds to several Polish expressions, this has been seen as an indication that it presented itself as a formula to the translator and was an active choice on his part. Similar contexts have then been sought out in the original chronicles used as material for comparison to determine whether chronicle language may have been the source of the formula in question. This procedure has not been applied to the annalistic expressions, since they are undeniably formulaic.

7.4.1 Annalistic formulas

As seen in Section 6.7.4, the translation of annalistic formulas differs between segments. In segments A and B, the word *лѣто* is used in the introductory formula, whereas the word *годъ* occurs in other contexts, and their distribution is rather consistent. The fact that both words were part of the translators' vocabulary makes the choice of *лѣто* seem formulaic. In segments C and D, *лѣто* and *годъ*, respectively, are dominant throughout, so that it is more difficult to judge to what degree they are formulaic. The most relevant results from that section are summarized in Table 36.

Table 36. Summary of the annalistic formulas

	в лѣто...	лѣта...	году...	тогоже лѣта	тогоже году	в томже году	non-formulaic use
A	45	2					годъ
B		25			2	3	годъ
C		15		5	1		лѣто/годъ
D		7	23		39		годъ

---

[89] Cf. Čiževskij (1960: 57–58, 102, 205, 259–260) for examples from different periods.

Original Russian chronicles differ in their way of expressing this. According to V. N. Ščepkin (1967: 157–158), *в лѣто* dominated in early texts, but *лѣта* took over in official documents in the late 15th century and in ecclesiastic and literary texts in the course of the 17th century. The use in Ruthenia varied, but *лѣта* dominated in the 16th century. The expression *року* spread there in the 17th century.

The consulted chronicles point in the same direction. The Primary Chronicle mainly uses the introductory formula *в лѣто* (*от сотворения мира*), and connecting formulas include *в сеже лѣто*, *в тоже лѣто*, *тогоже лѣта* and *в таже лѣта*. The word *лѣто* is used outside the formulas as well, whereas the word *годъ* is rare. Segment C of the translated *Kronika* comes close to this use, in that it also has *лѣто* in both formulas, but the introductory formula in the Primary Chronicle is the one found in segment A.

Similarly, the First Novgorod Chronicle uses *в лѣто* as the introductory formula and several different versions of the connecting formula: *в тоже лѣто* or *томже лѣтѣ* and, in the later part of the chronicle, *тогоже лѣта* (Gippius 2006: 181–183). The construction *томже лѣтѣ* is not found in the translation of the *Kronika*. Again, there are similarities with segment C and segment A.

The *Piskarëvskij letopisec* has almost exclusively the word *лѣто*. The introductory formula is *въ лѣто* or *въ лѣта*, the connecting formula *тогоже лѣта*. The word *годъ* is found only sporadically. This is also reminiscent of segment C.

The *Mazurinskij letopisec* uses *лѣта* (*от сотворения миру*) and the phrase *тогоже году* very frequently, although other expressions are used as well. There are also instances of *от рожества Христова*. This reminds of the expressions in segment B.

Not all Belorussian-Lithuanian chronicles are annalistically organized, but the annalistic formulas still occur. The *Suprasl'skaja letopis'* and the *Nikiforovskaja letopis'* mainly use *въ лѣто* as the introductory formula and *тогоже лѣта* as the connecting formula, although the *Suprasl'skaja letopis'* also contains other connecting formulas, such as *въ тоже лѣто*. The word *годъ* is not very frequent. This is similar to what is found in segment C, and the introductory formula is identical to that in segment A.

The *Synopsis* is slightly differently organized, and although there are annalistic formulas in the text, they do not introduce every year's entry, as they do in more traditional chronicles. There are some occurrences of expressions containing the word *рокъ*, such as *року от создания мира* (Rothe 1983: 178, 182, 187, 190), *року от сотворения свѣта* (Rothe 1983: 214, 236) and *року от рождества Х͞в͞а* (Rothe 1983: 270, 272, 351, 357–360), i.e. containing the Ruthenian word for 'year,' which is not found in the translation of Stryjkowski's *Kronika*, but also of expressions with *лѣто*, for instance *лѣта* (or *въ лѣто*) *от создания мира* or *от рожества Хѣа* (Rothe 1983: 234, 275, 362, 381). The *Synopsis*, then, is rather heterogeneous and it is difficult to draw parallels with the *Kronika*, in particular because of the frequent use of *рокъ* in the *Synopsis*.

Judging by this criterion only, segment A is closest to the Primary Chronicle and the Belorussian-Lithuanian chronicles, segment B to later chronicles, in particular the *Mazurinskij letopisec*, and segment C to the First Novgorod Chronicle, the *Piskarëvskij letopisec* and Belorussian-Lithuanian chronicles. Segment D seems to be less connected to chronicle tradition.

As we see, it is not easy to generalize about the use of annalistic formulas in original chronicles, since for example the two late chronicles differ in their treatment of the connecting formula – the *Piskarëvskij letopisec* seems to follow earlier tradition, and the *Mazurinskij letopisec* is more innovative. Later chronicles of course relied on earlier ones, and the variation may depend either on their different sources or on their differing degree of faithfulness towards them. This, in turn, demonstrates the difficulties in determining the influence of these chronicles on the translation of the *Kronika*.

7.4.2 The verb *идти* referring to military campaigns

In Old Russian from the 11th and 12th centuries, the verb *идти* and its prefigated forms had a broader meaning, to be compared with the English verb 'to go,' whereas *ѣхати* and its prefigated forms was marked with respect to the manner of motion. By the 14th century, their roles had been reversed, so that *ѣхати* was unmarked and *идти* could only mean 'to walk' (Gippius 2006: 176–177).

The early stage is found in for instance the Primary Chronicle, where reports of military campaigns and diplomatic undertakings often begin with *иде на* + ethnonym or toponym in the accusative (cf. Section 4.3.3), such as *иде Игорь на Греки* (PVL 2007: 22), *иде Володимеръ съ вои на Корсунь* (PVL 2007: 49) and many more. Prefigated forms of the verb *идти* were also used in such contexts, such as *Михаилъ царь изиде с вои брегомъ и моремъ на болгары* (PVL 2007: 12), where the word *моремъ* indicates that it is not a matter of walking.

In sample chapters A of the Russian translation of Stryjkowski's *Kronika*, this use of the verb occurs 20 times, most often as a translation of the Polish verb *ciągnąć* (12 times), but also for *wyprawić się* (four times) and other verbs (*przypuścić, przybliżać, wrócić się, pospieszać się*, one time each). The translation *идти* for *ciągnąć* is also the usual one in contexts other than military or diplomatic, but the verb *wyprawić się* can be translated in other ways, even in a military or diplomatic sense. The frequent use of *идти*, especially in the aorist, which gives a very formulaic impression, may reveal that this was a fixed formula in the translator's mind, especially since it is used to translate so many Polish verbs. The following is a typical example:

(197) Ták tedy Syny opátrzywszy Swantosław y rozdzieliwszy im Xięstwá porządnie/ niemogł gnusnieć w pokoiu/ znowu **sie wypráwił do Bulgári-ey** (Stryjkowski 1582: 127)

И тако Святославъ с҃ны 8строя и раздели им княжства, самъ ж в покое не возможе пребыва҃тї паки **иде на болгары** (Slav 26, fol. 209r) (cf. also example (189))

Here, the aim of the campaign is changed from *do* + toponym to *на* + eth-nonym, which is reminiscent of the use in Russian chronicles.

The Primary Chronicle has already been mentioned, and it is very consistent in this regard: *ѣхати* is only used three times in the whole chronicle, whereas *идти* occurs more than 200 times.

The First Novgorod Chronicle uses this construction in its earlier part, whereas *ѣхати* is first found under the year 6754 (1245/46) (Gippius 2006: 177).

The *Piskarëvskij letopisec* uses *идти* in a formulaic way, both the unprefigated and prefigated forms. It is also to be found in the *Mazurinskij letopisec*, even if this chronicle seems to prefer prefigated forms to the unprefigated verb.

In *Suprasl'skaja letopis'*, prefigated forms of *идти*, such as *поиде*, are common, but the unprefigated verb is less frequent. Forms of *ѣхати* are used, almost always prefigated. The situation is the same in the very similar *Nikiforovskaja letopis'*.

The *Synopsis* sometimes uses *идти* or its prefigated forms in this way, but it does not give the same formulaic impression as other chronicles. The following example illustrates this:

(198) Събравши же Владимїръ велик8ю сил8 вѡинск8у, пойде къ Таврикїи, юже н҃нѣ Перекопом нарицаютъ (Rothe 1983: 212)

The fact that this use of the verb is found even in late chronicles shows that the language in them was influenced by their sources. However, this meaning of the verb *идти* in earlier times was of course not unique to chronicles, so that for the translated *Kronika* we cannot exclude the possibility that other text genres served as models. Still, it seems certain that the translator perceived it as a fixed formula, and the inspiration probably came from early texts, whatever their genre.

If this can be seen as the opening formula for campaigns, the closing formula known from the Primary Chronicle and other chronicles – *возъвратишася въ свояси* (cf. PVL 2007: 13, 21–23, 57; PSRL XXXV: 29, 47, 48) or similar constructions – is not found in the Russian translation of Stryjkowski. Instead, forms of the verb are used on their own, without the addition of *въ свояси*.

7.4.3 Deaths

Deaths and births are often considered to be formulaically expressed in chronicles, usually in the aorist (cf. Kijanova 2010: 42–43). There is only one reference to a birth (the birth of Christ) in sample chapters A of the *Kronika*, so that no conclusions regarding its status as a formula can be drawn.

When reporting deaths in the past with the help of a finite verb, the translation of the *Kronika* mainly uses *умре*. There is one occurrence of (*от жития*) *преставилисъ*, i.e. in the perfect tense, as opposed to the nine aorist instances of *умерети*. The prevalence of this verb is not surprising. The Polish correspondences of these occurrences are mainly *umrzeć* for human beings and *zdechnąć* for animals (more specifically, Oleg's horse). One of the instances of *умре* (Slav 26, fol. 211v) is a free translation of the Polish passive phrase *był zátłoczony y záduszony* (Stryjkowski 1582: 130), and the occurrence of *от жития преставилисъ* (Slav 26, fol. 192r) corresponds to *żywot z smiercią przemienili* (Stryjkowski 1582: 115).

It can also be noted that throughout the *Kronika*, even in the segments that use mainly the perfect tense, the verb *умерети* almost always occurs in the aorist, which confirms observations by other scholars that this was a very widely spread formula. Uspenskij (2002: 110–111), for instance, points to the fact that *умре* was still used alongside *умер* as late as in the 18th century.

The three verbs that dominate in original chronicles are *умерети, преставитися* and *скончатися*. They are partly used in different contexts.

The Primary Chronicle mainly uses *умре* for both human beings and animals (cf. for instance PVL 2007: 41–44, 58–65). There are also instances of *сконча животъ* or *скончася* (e.g. PVL 2007: 10, 58, 60), and quite many examples of *преставися*, concentrated in parts of the text (e.g. PVL 2007: 57–58).

The First Novgorod Chronicle has a handful of occurrences of *умре*, (e.g. NPL 1950: 22, 27), but *преставися* prevails in most parts (especially NPL 1950: 28–44, 79– 98). There are only a few instances of *сконча животъ* or *скончася* (NPL 1950: 76).

In the *Piskarёvskij letopisec* there are numerous occurrences of *умре*, especially in some parts of the text (e.g. PSRL XXXIV: 49–70). However, in most parts *преставися* is prevalent (e.g. PSRL XXXIV: 69–84, 97–119, 139–144). The form *сконча(ся)* is only used about a dozen times, mostly towards the end of the chronicle.

In the *Mazurinskij letopisec*, the verbs have different spheres of usage in that *сконча(ся)* is used mainly for saints and martyrs (cf. especially PSRL

XXXI: 15–25 and 32–35), *умре* (PSRL XXXI: 26, 28, 36, 38) or *преставися* (PSRL XXXI: 53, 54, 56, 59, 60) for princes and *умре* for Oleg's horse (PSRL XXXI: 37).

Nikiforovskaja and *Suprasl'skaja letopis'* are not quite as consistent in this division. *Умре* is widely used (PSRL XXXV: 19, 20, 23, 27, 29, 32 for *Nikiforovskaja letopis'* and 37, 38, 45–47, 49, 54, 61 for *Suprasl'skaja letopis'*). They also use *преставися* (PSRL XXXV: 23, 28–33, and 41, 45, 46, 49–57, 61, respectively), often for church officials but also for princes. The following example from *Suprasl'skaja letopis'* shows two verbs with different subjects:

(199) В лѣто 6885. **Приставися Алексеи митрополит** февраля 12. Того жь лѣта **умре князь великы литовскыи Олгирдь**, и сяде по немь сынь его менши Ягаило. (PSRL XXXI: 49)

The *Synopsis* has *издше* (from *издохнути*) for Oleg's horse (Rothe 1983: 171), otherwise *умре* (e.g. Rothe 1983: 172) and *погибе* (e.g. Rothe 1983: 176), but often avoids this formula altogether, instead referring to a person's death with *по смерти* or similar expressions.

The form *преставися* is common in many other late chronicles as well (Kijanova 2010: passim); *умре* is less frequent in these, but it does occur (Kijanova 2010: 214–215).

Here, then, the usage in the translation of the *Kronika* is formulaic compared to the Polish original, but does not quite reflect the more diverse pattern from original chronicles.

7.5 Names

Section 6.6.2.1 discussed the Russian renderings of the anthroponyms, toponyms and ethnonyms used by Stryjkowski in chapters that related to Russian chronicles, with the purpose of finding patterns that could distinguish between translators. Here, some of the Russian names discussed in that section will be compared with occurrences of the same names in Russian chronicles. Of course, many anthroponyms were common in the 17th century and known not only from chronicles, and toponyms and ethnonyms could also be known from other sources or from experience. Therefore, the most interesting points here will be names that occur in an unexpected form.

As we have seen, the translation of the *Kronika* knows two spellings of the name *Dir*: Диръ and Дыръ, of which the second is more common. However, the Primary Chronicle, the *Piskarëvskij letopisec*, the *Suprasl'skaja letopis'*, the *Nikiforovskaja letopis'* and the *Synopsis* all use only the form Диръ. The First Novgorod Chronicle of the older redaction does not contain this tale, since the beginning is missing, but the younger redaction only has the form *Диръ*. In this case, then, all chronicles agree, and the translator uses a different form than they do. There is only one person by that name in the chronicles, and the name occurs only a handful of times in each chronicle, so that tradition was probably not strong here.

In the translation of the *Kronika*, corresponding to Polish *Iaropołk* and *Iaropełk*, we see a variation of the spellings *Ярополкъ* and *Ерополкъ*, within and between manuscripts. The Primary Chronicle, the First Novgorod Chronicle and the *Synopsis* have only *Ярополкъ* (or *Яропълкъ*), and other names with the same first element are also spelled *Яро-*. The *Piskarëvskij letopisec* and the *Mazurinskij letopisec* show mainly the form *Ярополкъ*, but also isolated instances of *Ерополкъ*. The *Suprasl'skaja letopis'* and the *Nikiforovskaja letopis'* only have *Ярополкъ*, but the index of names in PSRL XXXV (288) shows that the spelling *Ерославъ* for *Ярославъ* can be found in one of the Lithuanian-Belorussian chronicles. This variation in spelling is thus probably typical of late texts.

The Polish original of Stryjkowski's chronicle has the spelling *Olech* for *Oleg*, and the Russian translation spells the name *Олехъ*. In a few cases, the Polish original has what seem to be forms of the feminine name *Olha* or *Holha* instead, but the translation uses masculine forms beginning in *Олг-*. The Primary Chronicle, the First Novgorod Chronicle, the *Mazurinskij letopisec*, the *Suprasl'skaja letopis'*, the *Nikiforovskaja letopis'* and the *Synopsis* all know only *Олегъ* (or *Ольгъ*), usually with the stem *Олг-* in inflected forms. In the *Piskarëvskij letopisec*, the spelling *Олегъ* also dominates, but there is one single occurrence of *Олехъ*. Inflected forms vary between the stems *Олг-* and *Олег-*. However, as seen from the index of PSRL XXXV (291), Belorussian-Lithuanian chronicles using the Latin alphabet have forms such as *Oleh* and *Olh*. The spelling *Олехъ* in the Russian translation of the *Kronika* is probably dependant on the Polish original rather than on chronicles, but it is not without interest that there are chronicles where a similar form can be found. The forms in *Олг-* agree with what is found in chronicles.

The name *Olga* has the forms *Olha*, *Holha* or *Olcha* in the Polish original, but is always *Ольга* in the translation. *Ольга* is the common spelling in all chronicles (and probably other texts). The Primary Chronicle also occasionally has *Вольга*. Belorussian-Lithuanian chronicles written in the Latin alphabet use the form *Olha* (PSRL XXXII: 222). As opposed to the treatment of the name *Oleg*, this name follows Russian tradition.

Although the Polish original of the *Kronika* uses the spellings *Swatosław*, *Swetosław*, *Swantosław* and *Swentosław* alternately, this name is spelled *Святославъ* throughout the studied chapters of the translation. This is also the usual form in for instance the Primary Chronicle, the First Novgorod Chronicle, the *Mazurinskij letopisec*, the *Piskarëvskij letopisec* and the *Nikiforovskaja letopis'*. It dominates in the *Suprasl'skaja letopis'*, which, however, also has two instances of *Свѣтославъ*. In the *Synopsis*, the form *Святославъ* is used in the first (1674) edition and *Свѣтославъ* in the third (1681) (Moser 2007: 259). In the Russian translation of the *Kronika*, the translator has used what is apparently the original form of the name and not the alternative form, which may be Ruthenian, since it occurs in a Belorussian-Lithuanian chronicle and in the Kievan *Synopsis*.

As for the variation between *Владимиръ* and *Владимеръ* in the translation of the *Kronika*, it relates in the following way to original chronicles: the Primary Chronicle uses forms with pleophony, mostly *Володимеръ*, with some instances of *Володимиръ*. The First Novgorod Chronicle also usually has pleophony, with many instances of both *Володимеръ* and *Володимиръ*, but the latter dominates. The *Mazurinskij letopisec* does not have pleophony; the usual form here is *Владимеръ*. The *Piskarëvskij letopisec* has approximately equal shares of *Володимеръ* and *Владимеръ*. The *Suprasl'skaja letopis'* and the *Nikiforovskaja letopis'* are dominated by *Володимеръ*, with slightly fewer instances of *Владимеръ* and isolated cases of forms ending in *-миръ*, with or without pleophony. The *Synopsis* has *Владимиръ*. Forms of this name without pleophony appeared in the 14th century in connection with the so-called Second South Slavic influence (Uspenskij 2002: 42). It seems, then, as if variation in the second part of the name, as in the translation of Stryjkowski, was common in chronicles, and that a consistent spelling without pleophony in the first part was typical of late texts. All possible spellings of the name are attested from chronicles.

7.6 Chapter summary

In this chapter, the history of the chronicle genre was briefly summarized, with the emphasis on late chronicles, with which the translation of Stryjkowski's *Kronika* might perhaps best be compared. By the 17th century, the original annalistic way of writing chronicles had partly given way to thematically organized historical narratives, some of the roles of chronicles were instead filled by archival documents, and new text types such as short chronicles had appeared. This means that there were several types of chronicles that differed greatly from each other, something that must be considered when discussing the validity of the conclusions. If we suppose that the translators oriented their work on chronicles and other historical texts of which they had experience, the result may turn out very different depending on if they associated it with annalistic early chronicles, later chronographs, short chronicles, etc. A diverse selection of chronicles was chosen as material for comparison, in order to represent different types of history writing, early and late, from various regions.

The language of the translated *Kronika* was compared with that of these original chronicles by searching the translation for traits mentioned by other scholars as being typical for chronicles. The syntactic construction *participle + conjunction + finite verb* was found to be present in the translation, but to a lower degree than in original chronicles. In the sample chapters from segment A, this construction is mainly concentrated in chapter IV: 3, which presents events from the Primary Chronicle. It also occurs several times in the sample chapters from segment D.

Formulaic expressions have also been mentioned as a typical feature. The annalistic formula varies between segments of the *Kronika*, but most segments have something in common with the formulas used in chronicles of different kinds. The exception is segment D, which seems to be less oriented on chronicle language in this regard. The use of the phrase *иде на* + ethnonym in connection with military campaigns and the aorist *умре* to report deaths both seem to have a formulaic character, but it is difficult to determine if chronicles have served as model texts for them. In the former case, the influence may have come from other early texts, and in the latter case, chronicles use a more complex array of verbs.

The spelling of names partly coincides with that in chronicles, and in some cases, influence from Belorussian-Lithuanian chronicles can be suspected. These names may of course have been familiar to the translators for other reasons.

Thus, the translation of the *Kronika* seems to follow chronicle tradition to some extent, since there are instances where it is more similar to Russian chronicles than to the Polish original text, but there is a limit to the influence from chronicles. Due to the variety of chronicles and their different features, it has been difficult even to say what characterizes chronicle language.

8   Editorial principles

The editor of a manuscript faces the decision of how closely the edition should follow the manuscript text. To begin with, there is a choice between a diplomatic and a critical edition.

A diplomatic edition is as exact a copy as possible of a single manuscript, often without variant readings (Lichačëv 2001: 484). A critical edition, on the other hand, aims to establish the readings of the protograph and involves emendations that are not found in any of the manuscripts (Öberg 1992: 60).

A so-called modified diplomatic edition unites features from both these types. Which features are taken from which type of edition may vary, but the main principle is that the text of one manuscript is followed faithfully. Reading may be facilitated by insertion of capital letters, word division and punctuation. Errors in the text can either be corrected, which is marked somehow, or left as they are, but commented on in the critical apparatus (cf. Öberg 1992: 85–90). This edition is a modified diplomatic edition, and its characteristics are explained in Section 8.2.1. The readings of the Polish original have been given in the apparatus where deemed necessary.

Lichačëv (2001: 483) claims that a diplomatic edition of a single, early, well-preserved manuscript without variants from other copies may be suitable for linguists who are not interested in the changes that the text underwent. I wish to argue, on the contrary, that a very interesting aspect for linguists is to see which linguistic features vary between manuscripts and which do not.

The aim of this chapter is to explain the choice of manuscripts for the edition, clarify the principles according to which they are reproduced and explain the abbreviations and symbols used. It also contains a description of the scribal hands found in the relevant chapters in all the manuscripts included in the edition.

8.1   Choosing the manuscripts for the edition

Since the Polish original is available for comparison, choosing the main manuscript has been a matter of finding the one with the least omissions and mistakes compared with the original. A comparison of the manuscripts with each other and with the Polish original has shown that there are three groups of manuscripts (cf. Section 3.5) that together give a good picture of how the first draft of the translation may have looked.

Manuscripts from all three groups have been included in the edition. Besides the best one from each group (U, B and N), manuscripts derived from these (G, E and R) have also been included to illustrate how the text developed. The remaining five copies of the text (in six mss.) have been excluded because they are more recent or more corrupt representatives of their groups.

The relationship between the manuscripts has been established with the help of lacunae and other major differences that would have been difficult for a scribe to correct. Such differences might, of course, be eliminated by a scribe using two exemplars, i.e., contamination is possible. Since the readings in the various manuscripts are so similar, it is difficult to determine if contamination has taken place, but this does not seem to be the case.

The possibility of a scribe correcting his copy with the help of the Polish original cannot be ruled out (cf. Lichačëv 2001: 394). For example, Sparwenfeld evidently had access to the Polish original, since he copied its title page etc. (cf. Section 3.6.2), and if he did, so might the scribes who originally copied the manuscript. It is perhaps not so likely that a scribe would look up the errors he found in the manuscript he was copying and correct them according to the Polish original, but it is not impossible. There are occasional signs that later scribes had access to the Polish original, such as the addition of *и франџы миром* in mss. E and R, corresponding to the Polish *fraucimeru* (cf. Slav 26, fol. 223r), but this is only an isolated instance, and there does not seem to have been any systematic correction.

8.2 The reproduction of manuscripts in the edition

There are different opinions as to the edition principles for early Russian texts. Editions aimed at linguists differ from those published for the benefit of historians and scholars of literature (Lichačëv 2001: 470–474). This is a linguistic edition, and the principles for the reproduction of the main manuscript, as well as the variants in the critical apparatus, have been chosen accordingly.

8.2.1 The main manuscript

The edition principles for the main manuscript are based on the ones used by Anne Pennington in her edition of Kotošichin (Pennington 1980: 13), as well as the ones used in the editions of *Vesti-Kuranty* (2009: 62), since these are two highly regarded editions of texts from the same century as the *Kronika*. Since they are diplomatic editions, the question of variants from other manuscripts is not discussed there. The handbook *Pravila lingvističeskogo izdanija pamjatnikov drevnerusskoj pis'mennosti* (*Pravila* 1961) has also been consulted.

According to the principles of the abovementioned editions, I distinguish between *e* and *ѣ*, *u* and *ï*, *y* and *ȣ*, *з* and *ѕ*, *я* and *ѧ*, *o* and *ѡ*. The letters *ï*, *i* and *j* are all represented by *ï* (which is here, unlike in the two other editions, preferred to *i* because it is the more common variety), and *e* and *є* are represented by *e* (cf. Pennington 1980: 191). I have chosen not to distinguish between *я* and iotized *a*, as the edition of *Vesti-Kuranty* does. Several Greek letters occur in the text, some only as numerals, some in words, and they are also rendered in the edition: *ѵ*, *ѳ*, *ѯ*, *ѱ*.

The text contains two letters that were not entirely typical for the 17th century. There is one instance of the letter *э*, which at this time was a sign of chancellery usage, influenced by Ruthenian practice (Pennington 1980: 191). The letter *й*, which occurs sporadically in the manuscript, was not regularly used in Russian before the 18th century, but could be found under Ruthenian influence in the 17th century (Pennington 1980: 193). It is sometimes difficult to distinguish from the letter *u* with a spiritus, which could be written over a vowel following another vowel (cf. below).

Superscript letters are printed in the line in italics. Abbreviations have not been expanded. Capital letters are introduced in the beginning of paragraphs and for proper names, including possessive adjectives derived from proper names by way of the suffixes -*ов*- and -*ин*-, but not adjectives formed with the suffix -*ск*-, since they have a more adjectival character. As for words that can be either toponyms or ethnonyms, such as *Москва*, *Литва*, *Лотва*, *Жмоидь* and *Русь*, they have been capitalized throughout.

Word division in the text has been normalized. The scribes often did not leave spaces between words or were inconsistent in word division. For instance, compound nouns and adjectives were often written as two words but have here been written as one word. Prepositions have been separated from the following word, although they were at the time often joined into one.

Some words consisting of two parts are almost always separated in the manuscripts, although we would write them as one word today (most notably *Царъ градъ* and *Новъ городъ* and related words). These have been joined into one word, except where they are divided by e.g. a punctuation mark.

The particle *же* deserves to be mentioned separately, since it can have different meanings. Etymologically, what we in Russian see as one *же* are two different words, of which one, derived from *-dje*, had the form *жде* in OCS, whereas the other was *же* in OCS as well as in Old Russian (Vaillant 1951: 288; cf. Gippius 2001: 158, 175). The former was a particle with an identifying function that formed demonstrative and relative pronouns and adverbs. Such words are here written jointly, because their meaning is formed by both elements together, and *же* does not carry a meaning of its own. This applies to forms of the relative pronouns *иже* and *оноже*, the demonstrative pronouns *тоже* and *сеже* 'the same' and adverbs such as *идѣже*, *егдаже* and *тамже*, among others. The other *же* was a conjunction and carried a meaning of its own, for which reason it is written here as a separate word. To determine which meaning of *же* is meant, and thus if it should be written jointly or separately, the Polish original has been used for reference. If the Polish text has *a* or *też*, the Russian *же* has been seen as a translation of this and separated from the preceding word. In this way, *tenże* = *тотже* and *a ten* = *тотъ же* can be kept apart. There are some cases that are on the border between the two meanings, and where the Polish original does not provide help. In these cases, individual solutions have been found, which may be questioned, of course.

The punctuation of the main manuscript is followed. This includes commas, a comma followed by a period, and parentheses. The square brackets used in the manuscript have been changed to regular parentheses, and square brackets are reserved for the editor's comments. Asterisks mark text that was written in the margins. Unlike in the editions mentioned above, line breaks are not marked here, but page breaks are marked by two vertical lines.

In a few instances, the last letter of one word is also the first letter of another, such as in *наднепром*. If the latter word, in this case *Днепр*, also occurs outside of this combination, so that one may assume that the scribe knew the proper form, this has been rendered by *над* [*Д*]*непром*. In other cases, I have hesitated to make such corrections, since there are no signs to show what the scribe perceived to be the correct form. It is for instance difficult to know if *иустин* (for Latin & *Iustinus*) is meant to be *Иустин, и Устин* or *и* [*И*]*устин*. In this particular case, I have opted for *Иустин*.

As mentioned above, abbreviations are not expanded. Such abbreviations are usually covered by a *titlo*, which is rendered in the edition. A *pokrytie* over superscript letters is also reproduced. Sometimes, a *titlo*-like sign appears next to superscript letters. This sign, which seems to fill the same function as a *pokrytie*, is not reproduced.

The acute accent *oxia* (Steensland 1997: 15–19) and the grave accent *varia* (Steensland 1997: 19–26) are reproduced, as well as *paerok* (Steensland 1997: 68–70), which originally stood for an omitted ъ or ь, but can here be written between any two adjoining consonants. The *spiritus* (Steensland 1997: 48–49), often written over initial vowels and vowels following another vowel, is omitted. The placement of diacritical marks in the manuscript is very inconsistent. It is often difficult to determine the placement of accents, as well as to distinguish the oxia and the paerok.

In general, the goal has been to produce a text that gives a faithful impression of the main manuscript but is nevertheless clear and legible. It is not within the scope of this thesis to comment on all the graphical variants used by the different scribes, but they will hopefully not disturb the reading of the text, and possibly arouse curiosity in some readers.

8.2.2 The critical apparatus

In the critical apparatus, I give variant readings from five further manuscripts. One aim of these variants is to come as close as possible to the protograph, i.e. the translation as it was first recorded in a manuscript, as we can suppose that if the correct reading (when compared to the Polish original) is found in one or several manuscripts, it is probably taken over from the protograph.

Furthermore, the variants show the different forms in which the text lived on. This may be of interest when studying the development of language norms, determining what difficulties the scribes had in copying the text and what liberties they took with it.

Variants include errors, corrections and omitted, added or substituted words. The placement of words or phrases in the margin or above the line is also commented on. Orthographical as well as morphological variants are included.

The variations between *e* and *ѣ*, *и* and *ï* etc. are not included, nor the purely graphical alternations between Cyrillic and Greek letters, such as *ѳ* and *ф*, *ѯ* and *кс*. A special case is *v*, which can alternate with both *y* and *в*. Such variants are therefore included. The alternation between abbreviated and non-abbreviated forms is as a rule left out, unless the abbreviation is very unusual. In general, it can be said that ms N, which is a late manuscript, has nearly no Greek letters (except when used as numerals) and fewer abbreviations. The variation between numerals spelled out in full and Cyrillic alphabetical numerals is not included. Ms. G has alphabetical numerals more often than the others.

In most manuscripts, voicing assimilation of prepositions to the following word is reflected in the spelling, e.g. *из Володимеря* but *ис корабля*. In ms. N, the prepositions have in most cases achieved their modern form. The preposition *къ* before words beginning with *к*- is regularly dissimilated in all manuscripts except ms. N, e.g. *х королю* vs. *к королю*. These alternations are not reproduced in the apparatus, except for the few cases where such alternations occur in other manuscripts than ms. N. I do, however, include variation between voiced and voiceless prefixes (*безчестие/бесчестие*) and between forms of prepositions such as *въ/во*.

Variations in paragraph breaks and punctuation are not shown in the apparatus, with an exception for the placement of parentheses. Neither is variation in spacing between words included, except in isolated cases when it affects the meaning or implies that the scribe did not understand the text he was copying. Line breaks are usually not marked in the variants, but if an unusual reading can be explained by a line break, it has been marked with a vertical line. Diacritical marks are not reproduced in the apparatus.

Alterations and corrections in ms. B are always included in the apparatus. As for the other manuscripts, alterations are mentioned when they seem to be the result of conscious work on the part of the scribe, e.g. when a word in the exemplar can be read in different ways and the scribe has first written one and then corrected it to the other. Corrections of apparent slips of the pen, unrelated to other mss., are not included in the apparatus. When alterations have been made by writing the new letter on top of the old one, it can sometimes be difficult to determine what the original reading was, in which case the uncertain letter or letters are enclosed in curled brackets: {}.

In some of the cases when text has been lost in one of the manuscripts, due to e.g. trimming of the pages, it has been supplied from other manuscripts and enclosed in square brackets.

The manuscripts are quoted in the order BGERN. When several of the manuscripts in the critical apparatus have similar readings, but differ among themselves in details, such as the use of superscript letters or variations between *e* and *ъ*, *u* and *ï*, etc., the form given in the critical apparatus is the one found in the first of the mentioned manuscripts. Additional marginal notes, mainly found in ms. G, are separated from the other variants and designated by letters instead of numbers.

8.3 Properties of individual manuscripts

Six manuscripts are involved in the edition, and each manuscript is the joint work of several scribes. Therefore, many elements in the manuscripts are characteristic of one scribe only – this is particularly true of the graphic variants and superscript marks used, but orthography and morphology are also affected. Many factors, such as spelling, spacing and the use of certain graphemes and diacritical marks, vary greatly not only between manuscripts, but also between different scribes within a single manuscript. It is, of course, important to separate the traits of the text and of the scribe when examining the text. Below, the division of the text between different hands in the relevant chapters is given for each of the manuscripts in the edition, and some characteristics of each hand are listed.

References to the tables of letter shapes in L. V. Čerepnin's *Russkaja paleografija* (1956) are given when possible, so that the reader will not have to rely only on verbal descriptions. Unless otherwise indicated, references are made to the table of 17th-century *skoropis'* (Čerepnin 1956: 365–366), with the variants of each letter numbered from left to right.

8.3.1 Ms. U

The edited text is found in Slav 26, fols. 148v–228v. The distribution of hands in the selected chapters is as follows:

U1, fol. 148v (and before) to fol. 154v (cf. Illustration 4). A very ligatured hand that adds flourishes to many letters. The letter ж is quite flat (cf. же, line 4 from the bottom). The letter м in word-final position is often superscript as an almost vertical wavy line (cf. том, line 5). At the end of a paragraph, this hand sometimes uses a period and a comma after each other, and once (fol. 150v) above each other in the shape of a semicolon.

U2, fols. 155r–188v (cf. Illustration 5). This is a clear and distinct hand that uses the letters й and є and sometimes hyphenates words. The letter щ is occasionally written with the "tail" in the middle, in the old way, like Čerepnin's variant no. 2 of that letter (cf. дщерь, line 4). The letter ꙗ is used frequently. Several varieties of в are used, of which one is tall with two rounded parts that do not meet in the middle (cf. великого, line 4). The letter 8 is sometimes written not in one stroke, but the top and the bottom part seem to be written separately (cf. 68д8чи, line 7). The letter ҙ is often written carefully, with the "tail" traced rather than scribbled. The letter ж is found mainly in two designs, one with a connected bow to the right, like Čerepnin's no. 3, and one where the stroke from the upper left to the lower right is very pronounced. Superscript м has the same shape as the ordinary letter. There are very few examples of superscript х.

U3, fols. 189r–228v and after (cf. Illustration 6). A more ligatured hand. The letter ж is often small and round, у (rather than 8) is more common than in the other hands. Superscript з and м are very similar and wavy. Superscript х is frequent and looks like a horizontal 8. In punctuation, this hand uses a big round dot, comma or semicolon, and also dashes.

8.3.2 Ms. B

The relevant chapters are found in vol. I, fols. 146v–221v. The distribution of hands is as follows:

B1, fol. 146v (and before) to 168v and fols. 180r–192v (cf. Illustration 7). An upright hand with many ligatures and superscript letters. The letter и is often quite large and similar to Čerepnin's no. 9. The letter 8 often has a sweeping left stroke. The letter п in the beginning of words is often large. The word же is often written in full in superscript. Whether in the line or as superscript, these letters are ligatured so that the lower right stroke of the ж curves around and connects to the top of the е (cf. line 8 and 8множения, line 9). The letter в is often written with a box on the left and then a bow, like Čerepnin's no. 10. In superscript м, the left arch is more pronounced than the right. Marginal notes from the Polish original are absent.

B2, fols. 169r–179v. This hand is very similar to B1, but does not have the characteristic ligature of же. Also, it has two variants of the letter д, one similar to the printed one and one with a downward tail, whereas B1 prefers the former kind. Marginal notes from the Polish original are absent.

B3, fols. 193r–205v. A hand that is similar to the other two and that has the ligature же found in B1, but without the superscript м so typical for that hand. The letter ж is often connected on the left side, and both sides droop a little. The printed-style д prevails. Marginal notes from the Polish original are absent.

B4, fol. 206r (foliated as 201) to 221v (and after). A small hand with low letters and the rows close together. There are many superscript letters. Marginal notes from the Polish original are translated.

8.3.3 Ms. G

The relevant chapters are found on fols. 106v–165v. The distribution of hands is as follows:

G1, fol. 106v (and before) to 110v. An upright hand with rather low and regular letters. Dots are sometimes used to separate words. The letter к is one of the more pronounced letters, reminiscent of Čerepnin's no. 9, and its tail is often written with the broad side of the pen, which makes it even more prominent. The letter я is sometimes written as an iotized a, similar to Čerepnin's no. 13.

G2, fols. 111r–121v. This is a slightly inclined hand with few ligatures. Superscript м is often simply a stroke or a bow, like Čerepnin's no. 7, but more bent. Superscript p is very similar to Čerepnin's no. 5, but with a downward hook on the right end. The letter ж, when written in the line, consists of three separate strokes, but as a superscript it is written in one stroke and is rather flat.

G3, fols. 122r–140v. This hand, which uses a broad pen that makes some lines very pronounced, has many letter shapes in common with hand G2, such as the superscript p and the difference between in-line and superscript ж. The bow-shaped superscript м, however, is not found at all. The letter ꙃ is also written in a different way, with a more pronounced upper part. This hand uses the letter s (*dzelo*). The shift between G2 and G3 takes place in the middle of a quire.

G4, fols. 141r–148v and 157r–165v (but not after). A very upright and narrow hand with relatively few superscript letters, but with many tall letters and pronounced strokes in for instance к, с and ж. The latter has an unusual shape, where the top-left to bottom-right stroke is made separately and the other two form a diagonally flattened loop. The letter ω is frequent.

G5, fols. 149r–156v. A small hand with many flourishes and round shapes. Superscript м is wavy. Superscript в forms a pretzel and then continues to form a titlo for itself, rather like Čerepnin's no. 12, but horizontal.

G6, marginal notes and occasional corrections in the text. A hand with narrow, angular letters.

8.3.4 Ms. E

The relevant chapters are found on fols. 70r–119v. The distribution of hands is as follows:

E1, fol. 70r (and before) to 79v. A rather irregular hand with many superscript letters, sometimes low but sometimes sprawling. The letters с, и and ï are often very high. The letter ѣ is often connected to the preceding letter and written in one stroke that starts with the vertical line, then traces the bow, crosses the vertical line to the left and then to the right. This is the most characteristic trait of this hand. It can also begin with a top stroke and not really have a crossing line, so it is shaped rather like a high and large ъ. The letter у is sometimes large and curved to the left so that it resembles the letter э. This is another very characteristic trait.

E2, fols. 80r–119v. An irregular hand, similar to E1 but lacking its characteristic traits. The letter ѣ instead often is similar to Čerepnin's no. 10, where the crossbow is written first and the line is then looped down to cross it. In the letter ж, the three strokes are sometimes not connected at all, like in Čerepnin's no. 1. The letter у can have the leaning shape in this hand as well. The letter ѧ occurs frequently in a shape like Čerepnin's no. 5. In the preposition от, the letter т is often superscript and shaped like a bow or a horseshoe with the opening facing downwards. The letters де are often superscript, but in a form not mentioned by Čerepnin.

In this manuscript, prepositions are sometimes omitted. This is also typical for ms. R.

8.3.5 Ms. R

The relevant chapters are found on fols. 70r–113v. The distribution of hands is as follows:

R1, fols. 70r–77v. This is an even and regular hand where most of the letters are low, but there are also flourishes and superscript letters. The letter п in the beginning of words is often very large. The letter ѕ (*dzelo*) is used rather frequently and in many different words. The letter ж is often written elaborately in one stroke, rather like Čerepnin's no. 1 in the table of 16th-century *skoropis'*, but larger and more sweeping (Čerepnin 1956: 362).

R2, fols. 78r–113v (and after). This is also an even and regular hand with letters that are just as low as the ones of hand R1, but with fewer flourishes. This hand also uses the letter ѕ (*dzelo*) in many words. It is sometimes written not smoothly, but with a point before it curves to the right, in a way not shown by Čerepnin. The letter е is often shaped as a mirrored 3 with the upper bow larger than the lower, like Čerepnin's no. 2 in the 17th-century table. The letter к is sometimes tall with a part in the middle where the two strokes overlap, so that they look like a single line. The letter ѡ is frequent. The vertical lines in the letters ш and ц are sometimes slightly wavy.

In this manuscript, the adjective ending *-ыи* is often written *-ы* (cf. Section 4.2.3.3).

8.3.6 Ms. N

The relevant chapters are found on fols. 108v–168v. The distribution of hands is as follows:

N1, fol. 108v (and before) to 158v. This is a small hand with rounded letters and practically no superscripts or flourishes. The letter д is usually like no. 11 in Čerepnin's table of late 18th-century *skoropis'* (Čerepnin 1956: 481), but can also have its upwardly stretched tail shaped differently, have a tail that points straight downward or be shaped almost like a modern printed д. The letter к often consists of two parallel lines. The letter в is sometimes box-shaped. The letter б is similar to the modern handwritten letter, like no. 3 in Čerepnin's table of early 18th-century *skoropis'* (Čerepnin 1956: 478). The letter г is shaped like the modern handwritten letter.

N2, fols. 159r–168v (and after). This hand is very similar to hand N1 but the tips of some flourishes are more tightly curled. The letter д is often similar to the modern printed letter but can also have a tail that points downward and to the left or, sometimes, upward, but more curled than the similar variant in hand N1. The letter б is similar to the modern printed letter, like Čerepnin's no. 5 from the early 18th century (Čerepnin 1956: 478). The letter г is similar to the modern printed letter, but with an upward curl at the end.

This is the latest manuscript, and some unique features of the language set it apart from the other manuscripts. Firstly, as mentioned above, prepositions are not assimilated to the voicing of the following word. Secondly, hand N1 regularly writes the genitive singular ending of masculine or neuter adjectives as *-аго*, not *-ого* (cf. Section 4.2.3.2). Thirdly, while the other manuscripts regularly have the form *вси*, this manuscript often has *всѣ* instead.

8.4 Abbreviations and symbols used in the edition

ad., add.	Added
ante corr.	Before correction
in marg.	Written in the margin
in ras.	Erased or crossed out
in textu	Written in the text, as opposed to in marg. or suprascr.
om., omm.	Omitted
suprascr.	Written above the line
{}	Uncertain readings
[]	Text supplied by the editor; editor's comments
**	Text written in the margin of the main ms.

9 Summary and conclusions

A tu niechay będzie Czytelniku miły Xiąg dokończenie.

Stryjkowski 1582: 462

In the wave of translations from Polish into Russian in the 17th century, Maciej Stryjkowski's *Kronika Polska* was one of the few historical works to be translated. It was translated several times, however, in part or in whole, and there are 28 known manuscripts preserved of the Russian translations added together, as well as two manuscripts belonging to a Ukrainian translation. It was thus an influential text, and the 1673–79 translation, which is preserved in more copies than the others, is especially interesting for several reasons.

This thesis had as its aim to describe as many aspects as possible of the 1673–79 translation, its history and language. Three chapters, approximately 80 folios in the main manuscript, were in focus. They were edited with the aim to be of use to linguists.

There are twelve manuscripts belonging to this translation, but two manuscripts, kept in different libraries, are two halves of a single copy of the text, so there are eleven copies. The manuscripts can be divided into three groups according to the relationships between them. The best manuscripts of each group are ms. B (BAN 31.4.32), ms. U (UUB Slav 26–28) and ms. N (RNB Ėrmitažnoe sobranie, no. 551).

According to my observations, ms. B is the earliest extant manuscript, probably from the end of the 1670s. Corrections and changes in the manuscript, previously believed to be part of preparations for printing, were shown to be editorial corrections at an early stage of the history of the text. The changes are numerous and diverse, and although some of them may have been made in order to avoid polonisms, others remain to be explained.

Ms. U is the main manuscript of the edition. It is also an early manuscript – written before 1685 – and contains copies of a number of pages from the Polish original, a translation of the title page and a note, written by its owner, Johan Gabriel Sparwenfeld, that reveals that it was translated in *Posol'skij prikaz* by several translators at the behest of tsar Aleksej Michajlovič.

Ms. N is a late manuscript, made in the 1780s for Catherine II, but according to its title page, it was copied from a manuscript from 1679.

There was no standardized written language in 17th-century Russia. Instead, the situation can be described as an interplay of four registers, two bookish and two non-bookish. In the translation of the *Kronika*, some parts have many features typical of the bookish hybrid register, whereas other parts have some non-bookish characteristics and may perhaps have been influenced by chancellery language.

The language of the edited chapters, as found in ms. U, was subject to particular study. These chapters are typical of the hybrid register. The simplex preterites, by that time purely a feature of bookish written language, dominate over the elliptic perfect tense, used in speech and in non-bookish texts. There are numerous examples of morphological variation, often following patterns that can be found in other hybrid texts as well, although sometimes more reminiscent of chancellery texts. Several syntactic structures that were markers of bookishness can be found in the text, such as the dative absolute and occasional dual forms of nouns.

Besides this variation of bookish and non-bookish forms within the chapters as recorded in one manuscript, the variation between manuscripts was also studied. It was found that some linguistic features, such as adjectival endings and the forms of participles, tended to vary between manuscripts to a higher degree than for instance pronouns, the choice of verbal tense or the syntactic structure of the text. Where there was variation, it could be seen that some scribes had consciously replaced, for instance, the adjective ending *-ozo* with *-azo*, whereas others had made substitutions in both directions. This implies that some scribes accepted variation where others followed a norm that prescribed one ending.

The relation between the Polish source text and the Russian target text was studied and described in terms of adequacy and acceptability. In many cases, it was seen that the person who translated chapters IV: 1–3 identified information that may have been unfamiliar to a Russian reader and adapted it, e.g. recalculated measurements of distance from Polish to Russian standards. However, the text contains both lexical and syntactic polonisms, i.e. words and syntactic structures influenced by the Polish language. It could not be established with any certainty if this is due to the influence of the Polish original or of the translators' own usage – many translators employed in Moscow were Ruthenians, and the Ruthenian language had long been under Polish influence for geographical and political reasons.

There is reason to believe that the translation was the joint work of several people, and a preliminary division of the text into segments was made on the basis of the verbal tenses used to relate past events: simplex preterites or the perfect tense. These segments were used throughout the thesis, but the number of translators and the exact division of the text between them was not known. Therefore, one chapter was devoted especially to this question, and to identifying criteria that may be helpful in future attempts of a similar kind, such as comparing the distribution of a number of synonyms and near-synonyms in different text segments. The study confirmed that there were

270

quite obvious differences between the four sets of sample chapters chosen for comparison, but further study is needed to establish if there are still more segments that have not been identified. If the same parameters were used to compare the segments of this text with identified works by translators known to have been active in the 1670s, it would perhaps be possible to attribute parts of the *Kronika* to specific translators.

Since it is a historical text and genre tradition was strong in this period, the *Kronika* was compared to a variety of original chronicles in order to see if they influenced the language of the translation. It was stated that the translation contains some formulaic expressions that may have been inspired by chronicles, but on the one hand, influence from other text genres cannnot be ruled out without further study, and on the other hand, the chronicle genre is very diversified and difficult to characterize.

The 1673–79 translation of Stryjkowski's *Kronika* can be described in terms of tradition – chronicle tradition and the chancellery tradition of *Posol'skij prikaz* – and translation – the influence of the Polish source text and the translators' strategies when they chose to deviate from it. The tradition of the hybrid register was strong in the chapters that were in focus, but a comparison between manuscripts shows clearly that this tradition allowed a certain amount of variation, at least with regard to some linguistic features.

Although a number of lexical and syntactic polonisms were found in the translation, there are also numerous instances where the translator could have chosen a cognate of the Polish word but did not, used a syntactic structure that did not exist in Polish or followed Russian norms and traditions in some way. It is therefore quite informative as to the norms of the written language in late 17th-century Russia.

This thesis treats many aspects of the text, some of them in a cursory way. I therefore have many suggestions for further study. Ms. B and its numerous changes deserves more attention, not only because this may answer some questions about the history of the translation, but also because a systematic study of the changes may reveal more about the norms of *Posol'skij prikaz*. I have already mentioned an extension of the comparison between text segments to involve translations made by people employed at the *prikaz* in the 1670s, in order to attribute text segments to individual translators and to characterize their language.

A comparison of the Russian translations with each other would say something about the translation norms during the last decades of the 17th century. The Ukrainian translation could also be used for comparison. Last but not least, an edition of the whole chronicle would be desirable.

Contact has been established with the Regensburg Diachronic Corpus of Russian to make the edited text searchable within that project.

Appendix: Edition

IV:1

Матѳе́я[1] Стрико́вского[2] Осостѣ́вича[3]
Кро́ника[4] по́лская р8ска́ѧ киевская моско́вская, ||

И[5] ḯзвѣстный[6] вы́во́ды[7] всѣхъ наро́до̄в слове́н'скихъ с вели́кимъ
радѣ́нием и тр8долю́бнымъ т'ща́нием собраны.
Кни́га .д̃. ѧ
Глава́ .а̃. ѧ
Бг҃ъ срдцъ чл҃вческихъ извѣстнѣйшïй[8] свидѣтель у́нѣе вѣ́сть ко́ль
вели́къ преизящ'ный и неудо́бный тр8д[9] и крѣпльшïй паче
гор'диско[10] *каѳамского̄гѡ[11]* у́зла Алез̆а́ндромъ[12] разсѣченого̄гѡ[13]
[14](поне́же бѣ[15] невозможно[16] розвяза́ти[17] 8зо̄л)[9],[14] подя́х чита́телю
любе́зный, радѣ́я с прилѣ́жанием, дабы́х тïй[18] и́стин'ный и[19]
свидѣтелствова̄н[20] вы́вод наро́дов на́ших[21] сарма́т'цских[22]
славе̄нских[23] р8ских, а притом литовских изяви́л̄. ка́ко отк8д8
каковы́м обычаем от наслѣ́дия Ноева поидо́ша, ка́ко ж и каки́мъ
прил8чаем в сих страна́х посели́шася, и от малых нача́л̄, в толь

вели́кие наро́ды и простра́нство владѣ́ния || произрасто́ша сего
намѣ́рения ча́сть, я́ко в нача́ле сей кро́ники мое́и при вы́воде наро́да
лито́в'скаго[24] простра́н'но и дово́дно, из[25] и́стинны̄х[26] и разли́чных
повѣстописцо̄в̄[27] [28]изя́вих[29]; та́же наро́дов всѣх под н̄бомъ на сей
вселе́н'ней[30] жив8щих[28], от Нѡевых же сыно́в[31] и наслѣ́дникомъ[31]
изря́дным родосло́вием ид8щихъ, нача́ла и умноже́ния[32], я́ко ис[33]
кора́бля[34] изведо́х. тогда па́ки егда прïидо́х к дѣя́ним[35] р8ского[36]
наро́да изста́ри[37] сла́внаго[38], а ча́ять предревне́ишаго, исто́чника

---

[1] В Матѳеа GER Матвѣя | [2] EN Стриковскаго R Стрии́вского | [3] N Осостовича |
[4] R кроника | [5] ER omm. | [6] BN ïзвѣстны G ïзвѣстнымъ | [7] U ante corr. воеводы
ER воеводы | [8] N извѣстнѣйшей | [9–9] BGN in marg. | [10] В гор̄дïиско ER гордискои |
[11] B in marg. на поле каѳимско̄г G каѳимска ER omm. N кафимскаго | [12] G Алез̆а́ндра |
[13] G раченого ER разсѣченнаго | [14–14] N om. parentheses signs | [15] G бо | [16] ER незможно |
[17] G развязати | [18] BGN ти | [19] ER omm. | [20] G свидѣтелствованый ER свидѣте̄л̄ствова̄л̄ |
[21] G в̄шихъ | [22] BGERN сармацких | [23] BGRN словенских | [24] GR литовского̄ | [25] ER ï |
[26] G ыстинныхъ | [27] GN повѣстописцев | [28–28] B in marg. | [29] G изяви | [30] R селеннеи |
[31–31] B suprascr. | [32] Е умн̄ожишения | [33] R и | [34] R карабля | [35] BN дѣяниям G
деяниномъ R дѣяниемъ | [36] ERN р8скаго | [37] R изтарïӣ | [38] R сла́вного

словенских всѣхъ земе́ль и наро́дов, яви ми ся вещъ[1] бы́ти потребна, на семъ пе́рвомъ нача́ле кро́ники[2] р8ской, паче ж родословием наро́дов слове́нскихъ р8ских изря́дным по возмо́жству ра́зума и си́л на́ших, из дово́ду[3] греческих, латинских, еврейских, ха́лдейскихъ писа́телей положи́ти, дабы́, на ѡснова́нїй ‖ [4]гораздо укрепле́н'номъ удо́бнѣе и крепчае[4] могли́ слича́ть дѣяния р8ских и лито́вских наро́дов.

Мно́гия бо по́вести я́же безсме́ртием[5] дѣла чл҃вческая[6] украша́ютъ, полские. лито́вские. р8ские, и иных наро́дов ск8дости ра́ди люде́и разумных погибоша сего ра́ди зача́л наро́дов своих дѣтелства и владѣ́ния[7] кн҃зе́и, и[8] ї́звѣстнаго[9] времени[10], [a] во ѡ́ноже что бысть вѣдати не мог8т, народы бо на́ши словенские сарма́тцкие[11] в ст8деных страна́х[12] полу8но́щных[13] положены склон'ны бях8 всегда к ссо́рамъ[14], к м8чителствам и ко владѣ́нию чюжих земе́ль, не́жели ко уче́нию сие же за поведением и со́бством[15] неприятнаго[16] н҃ба и бра́нливаго[17], ем8же сия страны подлежа́т, Крона и ско́рпия ‖ ядови́таго[18]. и́же р8ских земе́ль болш8ю ча́сть заслони. сего ра́ди мно́зі на́ши предки дѣяні́и темномра́чною[19] но́чью уд8шен'ных[20] в вѣчном'ра́чныхъ вертепа́х[21] и пропасте́х[22] *слепых*[23] погибоша, от нихже бы ӥ҃не наслѣдницы зраки прило́ги, и поуче́ния[24] добро́дѣтеле́и и дѣяне́й[25] воин́ских избира́ти, и посторо́н'ным наро́домъ доброе разумѣ́ние, и вѣдомость[26] о славных предка́х свои́хъ, и са́ми о себѣ к великом8 и сла́вному розглаше́нию, и́мени[27] своего учини́ти могли́;

Ѡднако́ж, Р8сь, Москва́, и бо́лгары, или во́лгары от Во́лги реки́ (по кото́рои простра́н'но издавна живях8) речени[28], такожде ины́е славяне[29] пе́рвее, неже́ли мы́ поляки писать почали[30]. Михаилъ бо, К8рополатъ[31] ц҃рь конста́нтино‖по́лскїй[32, b] рат8я[33] з бо́лгары[34], с славяны[35] народа р8ского[36], иже в то вре́мя греческия[37] г҃дрства разоря́х8, и Ѳраки́и, такожде Да́лма́ции[38] часть велик8ю овладѣ́ли, по до́лгих боях примирися с ни́ми в лѣто от рж҃ства[39] Хр҃ства .ѱч. и на

[1] BGN вещь | [2] Е кройники | [3] ER довод | [4-4] E written twice, the first time circled | [5] R бе́змертиемъ | [6] N человѣче́скїя | [7] Е владѣ́яния | [8] ER omm. | [9] R извѣстного | [10] N времяни | [11] BGERN сармацкие | [12] B ante corr. страных | [13] ER пол8ношнихъ N полуношныхъ | [14] Е сорамъ R соромъ | [15] ER событвомъ | [16] BR неприя́тного | [17] R бранливогѡ | [18] R ядовитогѡ | [19] B ante corr. темномрачныхъ | [20] G 8д8шенно | [21] BGN вертепехъ ER ввертепа́х | [22] Е пропо̂стехъ | [23] B suprascr. GERN in textu | [24] ER по8чение | [25] N дѣянїй | [26] Е вѣдома̂сть | [27] ER имяни | [28] ER реченї | [29] BG славяня N словяня | [30] BR почели | [31] ER К8рополатъ | [32] G костентинопо́лскїй ER костянтинополскїй N константинипольской | [33] E ante corr. р8тая R р8тая | [34] R болгоры | [35] Е сля́вяны | [36] ERN р8скаго | [37] ER греческая | [38] G да́лмацкїй | [39] R ржества

[a] G in marg. хара́ктеръ севѣрныхъ наро́довъ | [b] G in marg. константинопо́лскїй ц҃рь К8рополатъ присла славя́ном̃ письмена

знакъ[1] др8жбы и[2] о́бщаго примире́ния рече́нный ц͠рь К8рополат, всѣмъ бо́лгаром и словяном[3] посла в'мѣсто дара слова. [4]а. б. в.[4] и прочая, яже тогда из гре́ческих новоизобрѣ́тены бы́ша славя͠н ра́ди., Тѣх сло́в я́ко всегда́ быва́етъ новая вѣщъ[5], всяка прия́тнѣ́йшая, а́бие ухвати́лись бо́лгары, сербы, до́лматы, карва́ты[6], и Р8сь, и тѣми слова́ми дела́ свои́ и кро́ники писа́ти нача́ша не то́к'мѡ тѣх ǁ дѣ́л чи́нъ в кни́ги снося́, яже 8 них и от них творѝми[7] бя́х8, но и[8] яже до́лгою па́мятью в ра́зумѣ[9] своемъ[10] от дре́вних предков свои́х слы́шан'на имя́х8 писмом на вѣчн8ю сла́в8, в кни́ги свои́[11] собира́ли и сокрови́щствова́ли, вырazумѣ́въ[12] я́ко по́вести сокро́вище безсме́ртныя[13] сла́вы с8ть.,

Поля́ки[14] ж на́ши едва́ нача́ша писа́ти от Хр͠ста в лѣ́то .ц͠зв.е во́ время Мечисла́ва[15] пе́рваго[16] хр͠стия́нского[17] кн͠зя по́лскаго, и Болесла́ва храбраго[18] пе́рваго[19] короля́ корено́ванного[20] Ѡттоном[21] це́сарем в Гнѣ́зне в лѣ́то .ц͠чθ. їхже однако Р8сь .с͠ѳ. лѣ́т в дре́вности по́вести и писма́ своего́ предвари́ли[a], [22]р8с͠сіане[23] бо[22],[24] нача́ша писа́ти, в лѣ́то от созда́ния мир8 ǁ яко грѣ́ки и Р8сь, счита́ют, .͵s͠ys.[25] се есть[25] от Хр͠ста .ф͠ч, или́ ма́ло что по́зже, а по ри́мскому щету[26] в лѣ́то от созда́ния мира .͵дф͠ме. от заложе́ния Ри́ма в лѣ́то .͵афна, от Хр͠ста[27] ж[28] .ѿ͠а,[29] ї[30] о том всѣ́ латин'ские, и гре́ческие[31] пѡвѣстопи́с'цы сѡглас8ются и[32] в лѣ́то .͵афод. в Ц͠риградѣ[33] са́мъ иск8сих, идѣже истяз8я прилѣ́жно, о дре́вностях[34] гре́ческих и визан'ти́йских видѣхъ сто́лп мра́мор'ный с написа́нием ц͠ря Михаи́ла К8рополата[35], и с число́м, лѣ́т вы́шеимяно́ван'ных[36] гре́ческого[37] и лати́н'ского[38] счет8. егоже рече́н'ный ц͠рь поста́ви [39]*вь Едику́л[40] иду́чи старои́ замо́к вели́ко͠г[41] Констянти́на[42]*[39] в зна́мение побѣ́ды на бо́лгарех и срацы́нех пол8че́н'ныя[43]. др8гіи же сто́лп видех за Ан͠дрианопо́лемъ[44] на котором мѣ́сте бо́лгары небл͠года́рно[45] воздая́ дар писме́͠нный[46] ǁ и́мъ в' зна́мение др8жбы прислан͠ного[47],

---

[1] G з|нокъ | [2] ER omm. | [3] GER славяном | [4-4] B ante corr. .а̄. .б̄. .в̄. ER .а̄. .б̄. .в̄. | [5] BGRN вещь | [6] U ante corr. кр{о}аты G к8рваты Е кавр아ты R киврать | [7] N творимы | [8] ER omm. | [9] ER р8з8мѣ | [10] Е своимъ | [11] ER своеи́ | [12] Е выр8зумѣвъ | [13] G безсмертные | [14] R поляни | [15] R Мѣчислова | [16] R первого | [17] G хр͠стианско͠г EN хр͠стиянскаго | [18] GR храброго | [19] R первого | [20] BEN коронованна͠г R коронованского | [21] B ante corr. Охтоном | [22-22] R р8сси анебо | [23] B р8с͠сиана G р8ссияне N руссіяня | [24] G om. | [25-25] N счесть | [26] G счет8 | [27] R р͠жества | [28] G om. | [29] Е .ѿ͠а. | [30] ER omm. | [31] R греческиꙗ | [32] ER omm. | [33] GER Ц͠риградъ | [34] G древностиꙗх | [35] R К8рополита | [36] GER вышеименованныхъ | [37] BERN греческа͠г | [38] EN латинскаго | [39-39] BG in parentheses N in parentheses, in textu | [40] ER Единоку́л | [41] EN великаго | [42] G Костен́тина BER Костя́нтина | [43] N полученные | [44] BG Адрианополемъ ER Он͠дрианополе́м | [45] ER бл͠года́рно | [46] G писмены́ | [47] GN присланнаго

[a] G in marg. начало писменъ полскихъ

274

вы́шереченного[1] ц҃ря Михайла К8рополáта[2] мир разорвáвъ[3] побиша, ꙗко с погро́ма едва сам убежа, потомъ ѿ[4] отчаяния монах бысть, однáкожъ от тѣхже болгаров убиен бысть.,

Кто́ бывáл во Андрианóполїй[5] или б8детъ у́зритъ знамения[6] тѣхъ дре́вних боев болгарскихъ[7] з‘ гре́ки б8лавы ко́жаны и древя́ны ди́внымъ образом сотворенны[8, a], я́дра[9] на чепях рогаты желѣзны, ослопы[10] с великими гвоздми[11], с8лицы з желѣзом острым накрстъ обостренным, и́хъже пехо́та ри́мская ‖ ꙗко Ливїй[12] пишет, на[13]встрѣче первои[13] употреблях8 обломки сабель старых, и тѣ всѣ ди́в'ные воинские[14] ор8дия, повѣшены с8ть на стенѣ, ид8чи чрез лáв'ки ис[15] т8рского[16] города во Андрианополь[17] кáменный хрстиянскїи[18] у великих врат, кото́рымь я гораздо присмотрілсꙗ.,

Ѿт того тогдá Михаила К8рополата[19] ц҃ря преградцкогѡ[20], болгары, Р8сь, и всѣ славяня[21] кромѣ поляков, и чехов писмена прияв дѣла свои писáти начаша, по убиенїй[22, b] ж К8рополатове гдрствова[23] на црствѣ греческом Левъ ормꙗнской, иже Хрна болгарского[24] кнꙗзя уби, во время Карла[25] великого[26] цéсаря, в лѣто ‖ от Хрста .ѿа. и во времена Иоанна третияго в ряду .чѳ.г꙼[27] пáпы.

Сице ж россиáне[28] áще от[29] .фп. лѣт, се есть от Хрста .ѿа. писмо имѣютъ[30], однáко вси[31] лѣтописи[32] р8ские, то́кмо тѣх бы́ти[33] пе́рвых[c] кнꙁеи в гдрствах своих сказываю[т], Кїя, от негож[34] Киев Стѣка, от негож Стекавица Корéва и сестр8 ихъ Лебед8, Оскольда ж и Ди́ра наслѣдников их, потом же по своему щéту в лѣто от создания[d] ми́ра .҂ѕто, кнꙁеи варягов трех братов Рюрика, Тривора, и Синавса[35], в княжствах[36] своихъ новгородцких[37], псковских, изборских и бѣлоозерских[38] гдрствовати пиш8т ‖ и от тѣх уже чи́нъ и наслѣдие извѣстное Р8сь вся вели́кие кнꙁи мѡсковские[39] производꙗт, далнеиших[40] же и древнейших начал народа своего произвести не мог8т ск8дости ради повестей. и повестописцев꙼[41, 42].,

[1] BEN вышереченнаг꙼ | [2] R К8рополита | [3] G розорвавъ | [4] B ante corr. со | [5] BN Андрианополи G Адрианополїй | [6] G знамение | [7] R болгорскихъ | [8] R сотворены | [9] N ядрa | [10] B ante corr. ослобы G ословы | [11] N гвоздями | [12] N Хивїй | [13–13] BGN первои встрѣче | [14] ER воиски | [15] ERN из | [16] ERN т8рскаго | [17] BG Адриянополь N Андрїянополь | [18] N христїанскїй | [19] R К8раполатои | [20] BN преградцкаго G преградцкого E преградцкаго | [21] ER словяне | [22] G 8биение R 8биени | [23] GER гдрства | [24] BN болгарского | [25] G Корла | [26] EN великаго | [27] ER ег꙼.ѕ. | [28] B россианя G росияня N россїяня | [29] N om. | [30] G имѣет | [31] N всѣ | [32] N лѣтописцы | [33] ER бытии | [34] ER него | [35] B Синауса ante corr. Синавса G Синав8са E Синеуса ante corr. Синавса R Синев8са | [36] N княжествахъ | [37] R новгороцкихъ N новгородскихъ | [38] E бѣлозерьскихъ | [39] ER мѡсковския | [40] G долнѣишихъ | [41] N повѣстописцовъ | [42] [Paragraph untranslated]

[a] G in marg. ѡр8жїе древних꙼ | [b] G in marg. црь гречески Левъ | [c] G in marg. Кїй, Щекъ, Коревъ, и Лебеда кнꙗзя росстїй, наслник꙼ их Диръ (in ras.) | [d] G in marg. Рюрикъ, Тр8воръ и Синевъ кнꙁи з варꙗговъ призваны на црство новогородцкое (in ras.)

Ѻднакож то есть крѣпльшее и тве*р*жшее[1] основа́ние, что[2] якѡ о*т* иных сынов Но́я[3] и наслѣдников его[4]. инїи умно́жишася разли́чни[5] народи, та́ко и о*т* Мосоха колѣноначалника на́шего шеста͡г сына Иаѳетова, и о*т* наслѣдников его Р8с͡са[6], [7]Лѣха, и Чѣха[8] вся Р8сь[7,9] поля́ки, Москва, бо*л*гары чехи, и колико [10]*йхъ под н͡бом*[10] словѣ́нского[11] языка[12] употреб*л*яю*т*[13], истинное начало, и произвожде́ние им8*т*, с которы*м* простра́н'нейшим доводом н8жных ради вин͡ до иного[14] времяни[15] о*т*ложихися[16] ‖ здѣ то́к'мо о Мосо́хе колѣноначальнице словѣн'ском*ъ*[17] вкра́тце мѣста[18] положю[19], у л8т'чих повѣстопи́с'цовъ[20] иже то и́мя Мосо*х*. Мо́скъ, Мо́ска, Моски, Мо́сковь[21], Мо*с*ховит[22] Модока*р*[23] и прочее изда́в'на воспомина́ю*т*., В нача́ле Моисей пр͡оркъ, и[24] Б͡жия закона[a] давецъ в' бытиях в главѣ ҃.і.и Вирос͡ с͡вщенникъ и повѣстопи́сецъ[25] ха*л*дейскїи дре́внїи в книгах ҃.д.*х* и ҃.е.и в лѣто по потопе ҃.р*л*а.е сице пи́ше*т* Мо́сх же. Мо́с'хи[26]. некупно[27] во Азїи и вь Еврⷪпе[28] насели. о чем ї на иных мѣстех, еже здѣ нарочно оставляю вспоминае*т*[29].,
Потом[30,b] Зенеѳон[31] в по́вести возврата грекоⷡ[32], Апполо́нїи[32] в стихѣ[33] аргонаутическом, Иродот[34] и к ней[35] Юлїи Солин, в главѣ ҃.К.и и ҃.М.и Птоломїи в книгѣ ҃.е. в главах ҃.s.и ҃.ѳ.и и ҃.Гі.и. Пли́нїи[36] естестве͡нныя повести в книге ҃.е.и в главѣ ҃.кз.и и в кни́ге ‖ ҃.s.и. в'[37] Гл͡вѣ[38] ҃.ѳ.и и[39] ҃.і.и. Тро́гъ, Помпей[40], Иустин Пом'пей͡с Мел'ля, в повести о селе́нїи в'селе́н'ныⷶ, в' Гл͡вѣ ҃.Б.и Иосиф[41] Ѻла́вїи[42]. дре́в'нос'тей ев'рейскихъ в' кни́ге ҃.а.и. Фило́нъ[43] Иудеа́нинъ, д'рев'ностей вив'лїиских*ъ*[44], Кор'ни́лїи, Та́цитъ Страбо́нъ, и п'рочие в'си д'рев'нїи[45] ев'рейстїи, ха*л*'дѣйстїи[46], г'речес'тїи[47], латин'скїи, и лѣтопис'цы д'ревнїи, а

---

[1] BG тверждьшее R тве*р*жшъе N твердшее | [2] B suprascr. | [3] ER Ною | [4] ER add. и | [5] G различнїи | [6] ER Р8са | [7-7] E in marg. | [8] EN add. ї | [9] R ad. ихъ под н͡бом | [10-10] B suprascr. GN in textu R om. | [11] EN словѣнскаго | [12] B ad. под н͡бом suprascr. in ras. | [13] G употребляе*т* | [14] N инаго | [15] BGRN времени | [16] N отложится | [17] R словенскиⷨ | [18] G мѣсто | [19] N положу | [20] ER повѣстописⷰцевъ | [21] GE Московъ | [22] BG Моховитъ | [23] G Модакаръ | [24] BN из ER omm. | [25] ER повѣстописⷰцевъ | [26] UB ante corr. Мосхы | [27] GN нок8пно | [28] B Еvрⷪпѣ | [29] ER восⷪпоминае*т* | [30] B ante corr. пом | [31] ER Зеноѳонъ | [32] ER Апполомїи | [33] ER стихь | [34] N Иродомъ | [35] G не | [36] ER Плини | [37] ER omm. | [38] N книгѣ | [39] G om. | [40] R Помпе | [41] R Иосивъ | [42] R Ѻлаѳиї | [43] N Филозъ и | [44] G дивлиⷶских | [45] R древни | [46] ER халдѣⷶисти | [47] R греческїи

[a] G in marg. свⷶщенникъ Виросъ лѣтописецъ халдейски | [b] G in marg. Ксеноѳонтъ греческїи Тацитъ Апполониї Светониї Иродотъ Прокопиї Иродотъ, Птоломиї Еутропиї Плиниї Ѻлоръ Поузаниї, Зонориї грекъ | [c] G in marg. Трогъ Помпей Ї8стинъ Помпей Меля Иосиѳъ Ѻлавиї Ѳилонъ Ї8деаⷶнинъ Корнилиї Тацитъ Страбонъ Несторъ преподобни Викентиї кадл8бскиї анонимъ Дл8гошъ ѳранц8з Мѣховиї Декиї Ваповский, пола[к] Кромеръ эпископъ Бѣльскиї Тилеманъ Стелла Гесариї Карионъ, немцъ Ѳилиппъ Меланктонъ Есей Силвиї Волатеранъ Датравиї Ѳеодоръ Герберъстеинъ Їо*р*нандъ Ироникъ немецъ

154v

155r

276

нестарого[1], инїи же нⷩшего вѣка лѣтѡписцы, Мѧрецкиⷯ, Викен'тиї[2], Кадꙋл8бскїй[3], аноним ѳранц8зъ, Дꙋл8гошъ, Меховїи, Їостъ, Декїи в древностяхъ пол'скихъ и родѣ Ѧгелоновѣ, Вапо́в'скїи Кро́меръ в' книгѣ .а҃.и в[4] гла̃вѣ .е҃.и и .и҃.и и .ві҃. Бѣлски[5] полскїе, Тилеманъ[6] Стелля Гесарїи, Карїо́нъ Ѳили́пъ Мелянктонъ К8рей немецкїе, Еней[7] Си́лвїи, Волѧтера*н* Датра́вїи, италїискїе[8], и ческїе[9] повѣстописцы, Мосо́ха и Москвы́, *началоводца*[10] и странъ того и́мени[11] вос'поминове́нїе[12] на мно́гихъ мѣстехъ изрѧд'но т'воря́тъ, Ѳео́доръ, також'де Библиа́ндръ, о из'рѧдномъ ро́дѣ толкова́нїѧ еврейскаѧ си́це гл҃гле*т*, || Мосохъ, или Месохъ ча́сть Асїи[13] к' По́н'т8 в'зѧ̀, идѣже мос'хи́ты или мос'хови́ты, и москитскїе го́ры, и с'меж'наѧ Кападдокїи[14] мѣс'та.

И аще б з'дѣ к'то̀ рек'лъ, а҆ко н҃нешняѧ[15] Москва бѣлой[16] Ро́сїи наро*д* недавныхъ вѣкѡв, нача̀ з'ватися Москвою о*т* реки и града сто́лногѡ[17] Мос'квы́ тогда̀ си́це есть. Москва̀[a] бѡ за́мокъ из' давныхъ в'ременъ, то́кмѡ о*т* древа с'р8б'ленъ и нез'на́тенъ[b] бѣ а҆ко о томъже Гер'беръс'те́инъ в' лѣтописи[18] в[19] княжства московского[20] пи́шетъ, даже вели́кїи кн҃зь Ива́нъ Даниловичь до .сл҃. лѣтъ из' Володи́мерѧ[21] пр͠столъ с'вой п'ренесе[22], по совѣт8 Петра̀ мит'рополи́та кїев'скогѡ[23, c] и р8с'когѡ[24], мит'рополитъ бо то́й Пе́т'ръ та́мо пр͠столъ с'вой мит'рополїи избрал бѣ, д'лѧ ст҃ваго нѣкоторого[25] Алеѯ́а, у егоже гроба[26] на Мос'квѣ[26] чудеса̀[27] ав'ля́х8ся, тѣмъ же Москва̀ г'ра*д*[28] прос'ла́вис*ѧ*[29] чудесы тѣми и вели́кихъ кн҃зей пр͠столом, по смер*т*и бо || Ива́на Дани́ловича, тогож и́мени[30, d] їⷩнъ Ива́нъ Ива́новичь та́мо пр͠столъ дер'жа́ше, по не*м*[e] Дими́т'рїи[31], по Димитрїи Васи́лїи[32], и́же поѧ́въ д'щерь[33] у Ви́тол'та[34] великого[35] кн҃зѧ литовского[36] [37] А*н*натазию или[38] Со́фию[37], Васи́лиа[39] с'лѣпо́го по себѣ нас'лѣдника ос'та́ви, о*т* негоже потом Їва́нъ б8д8чи великим кн҃земъ мос'ко́в'скимъ в'сещас'лив'шимъ[40], испод си́лы и подда́н'ства

---

[1] ER add. и N нестараго | [2] B ante corr. Вякентиї | [3] В Кадл8бски N Калдубски | [4] R om. | [5] ERN Бѣлский | [6] ER Тилїма*н* | [7] R Ене | [8] Е италинские R италианские | [9] ER греческие | [10] B suprascr. GRN in textu | [11] ERN їмяни | [12] GR воспоминание | [13] ER Осиї | [14] G Каподдокиї R Кападдоский | [15] G н҃нешня R ннешняя | [16] G бѣло | [17] Е столнаго | [18] G лѣтописиї | [19] B in ras. GN omm. | [20] EN московскаго | [21] ER Володимера | [22] ER принесе | [23] EN киевскаго | [24] Е к8*р*скаго R к8рского N рускаго | [25] Е нѣкотораго | [26-26] U in marg. B suprascr. | [27] N чудеса | [28] B suprascr. | [29] B ad. град in ras. | [30] ER имяни | [31] ER Дмитриї | [32] Е Васили | [33] ER дше*р* | [34] N Витонта | [35] EN великаго | [36] N литовскаго | [37-37] B ante corr. Анастасию Софию ли | [38] ER из | [39] R Василья | [40] ER всещас͠тливши*м* N всесщасливши*м*

[a] G in marg. Москва Блондъ, С8идъ, Албертъ Крантиї, нем: Л8и Ѳранцъ, нем: а Зонаръ, греч: | [b] G in marg. великий кн҃зь Їванъ Даниловичь до 230 л: престолъ свой пренесе *из* Владимира въ Москв8 | [c] G in marg. Петръ митрополитъ московский | [d] G in marg. Їоаннъ Їоанновичь | [e] G in marg. Димитриї Василиї Василиї темный Їоаннъ грозный

277

тата́р'ского[1] выбился. каза́нск8ю орд8, Пе́р'мь, Сиби́рь, Лопянъ, Юго́рїю[2] отнюд8же[3] пред'ки вен'гровъ[4], Болга́рїю[5] асїиск8ю и їны́ѧ с'тра́ны си́лѣ с'вое́й покори́, и порабо́ти, от лито́в'ского[6] гсдрства .ѯ. гра́дов в'зѧ, с[7] шве́ды и с' лиѳла́н'ты вели́кїе вои́ны веде́[8], и той[9] нача́ писа́тися[10] цр҃ь и гсдрь в'сеа́[a] Росі́и[11] того́ в'н8къ Васи́лїи, вели́кїй кн҃зь мос'ков'скїи[b], град Москв8[12] нача́ стѣ́ною ка́мен'ною и баш'нями обводи́ти, кото́рые с'тѣ́ны в'ъ .л. лѣтъ нас'лѣ́дницы его́ од'ва совер'ши́ша, оба́че и са́мъ Гер'берсте́н[13] Жигм8н'тъ[14] вы́ше во[15] описа́нїи[16] гра́да Мос'квы́ си́це гл҃голетъ, я́ко дабы́ гра́дъ Москва́ ‖ ины́м страна́мъ п'роз'ва́нїе от себе́ да́ти имѣ́ло[17], сїе́ не по́д'лин'но[18], но вои́с'тин'н8 вѣщ'[19] возмож'на[20], я́ко от реки́ гра́дъ и́мѧ прїѧ́, и́бо а́ще сам гра́дъ Москва́ пре́ж'де сего́ не бы́с'ть с'то́лный и гл҃ва того́ наро́да[21], одна́кѡ из'вѣ́с'тна вѣщ'[22] ес'ть, я́ко и́мѧ московскаго[23] наро́да[24] бѣ з'на́т'но повѣ́с'тописц'ом[c] д'ре́внимъ от Мосо́ха, тож'де[25] и К'роме́р в' гл҃вѣ .й.и[26] в' кни́гѣ .а.и к'ро́никъ по́лских, по до́лгих произвож'де́нїахъ[27] сарма́ц'ких наро́довъ, о Москвѣ́ гл҃голетъ, си́це же гл҃в8[28] .й.[29] в кни́гѣ[28] .а.и зак'люча́етъ, ни же́ есть невѣ́рно и́мъ, (се есть Москвѣ́) Мос'хом Модоко́м, и́ли Ама҃зови́том дре́в'лере́чен'ным[30] нѣ́когда во́ и́мѧ сосѣ́довъ, и бли́ж'нихъ р8с'с'овъ, и́ли рожоля́новъ п'рейти *или́ премени́тис[31]*, пото́мъ же с'та́рое[32][33] (се ес'ть и́мѧ москов'ское)[33] вос'прїѧ́ти,

Мосо́хъ у́бо сн҃ъ Иаѳето́въ шесты́и, в'н8къ Нѡе́въ за Сарма́том бли́ж'нимъ свои́мъ, его́же[34]Мойсей въ[34] .л҃. гл҃вѣ, Їосифъ ‖ д'ре́в'нос'тей еврейс'кихъ в кни́гѣ .а.и в гл҃вѣ .д҃і. Истро́ва, или́ Ек'та́нова сн҃а, вн8ка Си́мова, п'равн8ка ж[35] Нѡе́ва бы́ти свидѣ́телств8ютъ, шед от Вавило́на по с'мѣше́нїи[36] язы́к с' наро́дом свои́мъ все́мъ и з' сн҃ы[37] И́стровыми, се есть[38] с'лавѧ́ны[39] кото́рые к ни́мъ прис'та́ли, я́ко Ви́рос пи́шетъ, идо́ша о́ба ч'ре́з ар'ме́нскїе[40] горы, и ски́ѳскїе, или тата́рскїе[41] полѧ, от восто́ч'ныхъ стра́н[42], к' пол8но́щным̑ часте́м в'селе́н'ны́ѧ, в' нача́ле же на брега́х пон'тскагѡ[43] или чернаго[44] мо́рѧ поселиша́сѧ, в' лѣ́то .рла. по пото́пѣ,[45] от владѣ́нїѧ[45] же Нимвро́това в' Вавилонѣ в' лѣ́то .к҃е., а

---

[1] N татарскаго | [2] G Ю̑горию | [3] G отнудуж N онюдужъ | [4] G венгеро̑в | [5] G Болгорию | [6] EN литовскаго | [7] R с8 | [8] ER omm. | [9] N то | [10] N ad. и | [11] N Россїи | [12] N Москвы | [13] ER Гербѣстен | [14] BGN Жигим8нтъ ER Жигл8нтъ | [15] R ево | [16] R писании | [17] BGN имѣла | [18] R подлиннои | [19] BRN вещь | [20] G возможно | [21] ER народу | [22] BGERN вещь | [23] GR московского | [24] ER народу | [25] ER omm. | [26] ER .й. | [27] BGRN произвожденияхъ | [28–28] R om. | [29] E .й. | [30] N древле реченымъ | [31] ER премянитис̑ | [32] G старая | [33–33] R om. parentheses signs | [34–34] ER Моисѣевъ | [35] N om. | [36] Е сⷨѣшенися R сⷨѣшения | [37] ER сн҃омъ | [38] B ad. с | [39] ER словяны | [40] R армянские | [41] N татарскїя | [42] UB add. {и} in ras. | [43] G понⷮгиискаг̑ ER понтискаго | [44] BGR черног̑ | [45–45] ER овладени

[a] G in marg. Василий | [b] G in marg. строенїе Москвы | [c] G in marg. Мосохъ родоначальникъ максоватянъ р8ссовъ, славянъ, роксолѧновъ и московитанъ N повѣстописцемъ

противъ иныхъ повѣстопис'цовъ[1] и землемѣровъ *от* потопа .ҁое. [2]*от*
Адама,[2, 3] ж҃ .҂а҃ѿл. народы р8с'кие начашасѧ[4] їз словенскогѡ[5] ѧзы'ка,
и́хъже из'давна[6] сѷтое писанїе в библїи, и всѧ древния повѣстопис'цы
[7]не ро҃ссїаны,[7, 8] нарицах8сѧ, но мо́с'хы,[9] мосохи,[10] месехи[11] модѡ́ки,
мос'сены,[12] мос'хойкойки, *от* тог҇ ихъ колѣноначалника[13] Мосо́ха
Иаѳетовича, не *от* н҃нешней новой Москвы, їже || а́ще с8ть одногож
народа р8ского,[14] илѝ роӡолянского,[15] *от* тогож Мосоха, оба́че
пренебрегли было того имени[16] употребляти во многия вѣки, ток'мо
рос'с'ияны,[17] *от* трехъ братовъ кнѧзей варя́ж'скихъ и *от* Ол'гѝ, илѝ
Еле́ны и В'ладимера[18] монарха, и др8гагѡ Мономана́ха,[19] и ѝныхъ
кн҃зей нарицах8сѧ, ни же знатно бѣ в то время то ѝмѧ Москвы́,
в'негда то́к'мо кѝев'ские, владимерскїе, великонов'город'цкїе,[20]
черниговскїе, галицкїе, с'молен'скїе кн҃зи в р8ских землѧ́хъ
живях8,[21] ѧ́ко выше[22] сегѡ дос'та́точ'но нач'теш'сѧ,
Таже потомъ до дв8х со́тъ и[23] нѣскол'ко[24] десѧ лѣтъ, тò древнее и́мѧ
колѣноначалника[25] р8с'кого[26] и сармацкого[27] Мосоха воскресили,[28]
в'негда Москва́ *от* Москвы́ града, и *от* рекѝ по пренесенїи пр҇стола из'
Володимерѧ[29] зваⷮ начаша, но к' дѣл8 п'рис'т8паю,
То́тъже Мосохъ сн҃ъ Иаѳетовъ живы́и || у чорного[30] мо́рѧ[a] в'[31] великъ
народъ 8м'ножисѧ, потом в тѣхъ поляхъ колховъ,[32] к'ралев'ство
з'латым[33] р8номъ с'лавное 8строихъ, и п'рѡс'транно населивъ, и
народ с'лавенскїи,[34] р8скїи в' нем ум'ноживъ и́де далѣе нас'лѣдие его
в' полѹнощныѧ страны за пѡнтское илѝ черное мо́ре, идѣже над
Дономⷩ и Волгою реками, и над озером меотїйскимъ[35] [36]в' которое,[36]
До́нъ впада́етъ, в степахъ п'ространно посели'шасѧ, и во м'но́гия[37]
народы в'кра́т'це времѧни[38] 8м'ножишасѧ[39] тако, а́ко в' нас'лѣдїи
Иаѳетове и Мосохове с'войств8 имѧнъ ихъ испѡлнитисѧ, Иаѳетъ бо
от хал'дейскагѡ[40] и ев'рейскаго[41] ѧзыка п'ространно илѝ
п'рос'транѧющїисѧ,[42] Мосохъ же ростягиваяйсѧ,[43] и да́л'нїи
толк8етца[44] тогда́ наслѣдницы и́хъ по счас'ливом8[45] привѣ́тств8 и

---

[1] R повѣстописцевъ | [2–2] R отдано | [3] G Адма | [4] R начаша | [5] N словенскаго |
[6] R їсадавна | [7–7] N нерсоиланы | [8] ER ро҃ссианы [sic] | [9] G мсхы | [10] BGN мосохы | [11] ER
месихи | [12] ER мо҃ссень | [13] G колѣнаначаⷧника | [14] ERN р8скаго | [15] N роксолянского |
[16] B имяни ante corr. им{енне} GERN имяни | [17] BERN россианы G росꙗны |
[18] B Владимира | [19] B Мономаха ante corr. Мономонаха E Мономонаха N Мономаха |
[20] GR великоновгороцкие N великоновгородскїе | [21] N живаху | [22] ER ниже | [23] G или |
[24] ER нетолко | [25] B колѣнѡчаⷧника G колѣнѡнасалника | [26] ERN р8скаго |
[27] N самарцкаго | [28] R воскресили | [29] ER Володимера | [30] GR черноⷢ EN черⷩнаго |
[31] ER omm. | [32] B колⷯоръ а corr. колховъ G колхор N колгоръ | [33] R злотымъ |
[34] ER словенскиⷯ | [35] R меотискимъ | [36–36] R второе | [37] R многие | [38] BN времени |
[39] G умножися | [40] BR халⷣейскоⷢ | [41] B еврейскоⷢ | [42] ER пространꙗющися |
[43] G растягиваяйсѧ E ро҃стягиваися R ро҃стягивалися | [44] B suprascr. G толкуется in
textu RN in textu | [45] E с҃частливомꙋ N щасливому

[a] G in marg. ѿ Мосоха Колхида и златое р8но

свойством[1] имянъ предковъ сʼвойхъ, и по блгосʼловенїю Ноѧ патрїарха селения своя далече[2] расʼпространиша[3], яко вʼсѧ

полꙋнощныя[4] сʼтраны ‖ и[5] межвостоʼчʼныя часʼти вʼселенʼныѧ народамі сʼловенского[6] ѧзыка исʼполнити, начавъ же ѿ капʼпадокїйскихъ[7][8] и колхінʼскихъ[8,9] кралевствъ и вездѣ крꙋгъ Кимерїя[10] Босʼѳора, и черного[11] морѧ, Донꙋ, Окѝ, Волги, Камы, Днепра, Бога[12], Десны, Дʼнестра[13], Дꙋная[14], дажъ до Двины и Немʼнà долʼгимъ разстоянїем͡ъ[15] источниковъ вʼсѣ береги овладѣша, тàже даже до ледяного и валʼтїискогѡ[16] илѝ венедїиского[17] помосковски[18] варѧжского[19] морѧ ѥже ннѣ лиѳлянты Лиѳляндїа[20] и Свѣю[21] обливаетъ, и до Норвегїи достигаетъ имя силꙋ и власть сʼловенско͡г[22] ѧзыка распространѝли[23].

Сармотъ[24,а] же илѝ Сарматъ[25] снъ Иекʼтанѡв внꙋкъ Симовъ, правнꙋкъ Ноѧ патрїарха, по Иосиѳꙋ[26] в книгѣ .а҃. и вʼ глвѣ .д҃ї. древностей[27] еврейскихъ и по Моисею бытїе л҃.е йже такожʼде бѣ в сихъ странах полꙋнощныхъ с Мосохом͡ дѣдом двоюроднымъ[28],

поселился[29] бѣ сарматом͡, даде имѧ ‖ и пʼрозʼваʼнїе яко насъ вʼсѣхъ сарʼматами се ѥсть высокими народами ѿ него зовꙋт[30]. Тилеманъ вʼ произʼведенїи родосʼловиѧ[31] Исс͡ъ Хрс͡това, сѝце сармата реченїе изʼлагаетъ, сего ради ѿ Риѳата сн͡а Гомерова, риѳиане йже сꙋть[32] сарʼматы и генеты, имя ж генети[33] зʼнаменꙋетъ[34] у евреѵ, пришелствꙋющїи греки имяноваша[35] номады, се есть вездѣ[36] иной паʼжити[37], иныхъ мѣстъ ищꙋщїи[38]. сарʼматъ же толкꙋется вожʼдь высоты, илѝ вожʼдь выʼшʼнїя[39] страны.

Кʼромер еп͡скпъ варменскїи, такожде вʼ лѣтописи своей, еюже дѣяния полская изо тʼмы и їзʼ мрачноглꙋбокихъ[40] пропастей изʼгребены, освѣти[41] сице разʼсꙋжденїе[42] блгоразꙋмное о пʼрозʼванїи ї выводе сарʼматъ, вʼ начале книгъ первых в глвѣ .в҃ї. пишетъ под имянованиемъ[43], идѣже глголетъ сарʼматом[44] быти сʼловянъ и венедянъ, и тѣхъ быʼти дрѣвʼнихъ сарʼмат[45], или ꙗко греки глголютъ

саѵроматы[46] ‖ и разсѣѧнным по зʼданїи столʼпа вавилѡнска по

---

[1] R воⁱинством | [2] ER далеча | [3] R росⁱпрастраниша | [4] B полꙋнощные | [5] R om. | [6] GEN словенска͡г | [7] G кападокиⁱских ER кападокиских | [8–8] G om. | [9] ER колкинⁱских | [10] N Кирлерїя | [11] EN черⁱнаго | [12] ER Бга | [13] N Днепра | [14] G suprascr. | [15] ERN расⁱтоянием | [16] GN валтиⁱнскаго ER валтиского | [17] GN венедїⁱнскаго ER венедискогѡ | [18] R помосковⁱскийⁱ | [19] N варяжⁱскаго | [20] BGERN Лиѳляндия | [21] GN всею | [22] N словенⁱскаго | [23] ER росⁱпространили | [24] ER Сарматъ | [25] ER Сарⁱмакъ N Самартъ | [26] N Исифу | [27] ER древноⁱсти N древⁱстей | [28] ER роднымъ | [29] R поселися | [30] ER зовѣт | [31] E родасловия R родасловоня | [32] G есть | [33] N генеты | [34] BGN знаменает | [35] BGERN именоваша | [36] UB ante corr. {на} G ad. на | [37] BGN add. и | [38] R идꙋщиⁱ | [39] BN вышⁱние | [40] G мраⁱчноⁱглꙋбокихⁱ | [41] N освяти | [42] R расⁱсꙋждение | [43] BGN именованием | [44] BGN сарматоⁱв | [45] ER omm. | [46] G сауроматы N саврⁱаматы

а G in marg. сарматы ѿ Сармата сына Їектанова, внꙋка Симова и правнꙋка Ноева Мосохъ же бе емꙋ дѣдъ двоюродным

потопе всеа́ зем‛ли людемъ, сия страны́ ов‛ладѣвшихъ неп‛щ8ютъ, а
не от [Т]виско́на но от Сармо́та[1] илѝ Сармата, егоже Моисїи[2] Иосифъ
ев‛рейстїи[3] писатели, Истрова илѝ[4] Иектанова[5] сна Симова вн8ка,
Но́ева пра́в‛н8ка бывша[6] поминаютъ и́мя и[7] начало вед8ще[8] и п‛рочее
З‛дѣ и́маши читателю любе́зный, паче иныхъ моихъ в‛ сличенїи
раз8мо*в*[9] раз‛личныхъ повѣстописатѣй[10] [sic] доводы, и паче моего
из‛вѣс‛тными[11] свидѣтелствы укреп‛ленное раз8мѣнїе великого[12] и
честного[13] м8жа разсуж‛денїемъ о сарматѣхъ, ꙗко от Сармата[14] или
от[15] Сармата сна Иек‛та́нова[16] вн8ка Симова правн8ка Ноева речени
с8ть, а не от [Т]вискона илѝ Аскины[17] Гомерова[18] сна, яко нѣцыи
лѣтопис‛цы немецкїе, а чаять и Дл8гошъ писали, ни от Ꙗвана и
Елѝс‛сы[19], ‖ ꙗко Мехо́вїи в‛ гла́вѣ .а̃. и в кни́ге .а̃. и же в‛ лис‛т8 .а̃.м̃ же,
в‛ произ‛веденїи пе́р‛ваго[20] начала полского[21] положѝ мимо дѣла:
Ꙗван‛ бо и Елисъ[22] сн̃ъ его греческия[23] наро́ды умно́жиша, и
латѝн‛скїе, а не сарматъ, ѝже ꙗзыком и н‛ра́вами дре́в‛ними, далече
с8ть от грековъ латѝнников, такожде и от нѣмцо*в* разлѝч‛ни[24].
А[25] ꙗ́ко Виро́съ халдеянинъ[26] пи́ше*т* в книге .д̃. и Т‛вискона[27] бы́ти
крале*м* сар‛мацким от Дона даже до Рена рекѝ, також‛де в кни́ге .й̃. и
вос‛поминаетъ, яко в лѣто .рла̃. от потопа Твиско*н* сар‛маты великїе
народы ум‛но́жи, тогда та*м* а́бие полагаетъ, ꙗ́ко Мос‛хъ Мосохъ, илѝ
Москва моско́в‛скїе ца̃рства во[28] Асїи, к8пно и во Евро́пе[29] 8мно́жи.
Та́мъже в тойже к‛ни́ге пишетъ, [30]в лѣто[30] сего Нѝна четвертое,
вавило́н‛скогѡ[31] третьꙗго ца̃ра Т‛виско́нъ ис‛полинъ ‖ сар‛мато*в*
зако́на и устава[32] поучае*т* у Ре́на.
Тогда́ Кроме*р*[33] гл̃ꙗ из‛ра́д‛ными с‛казанми ꙗ́ко с‛лавяне и сар‛маты
не с8ть нѣм‛цы в‛ гла́вѣ .ѕ̃. и в книге .а̃. и сие разделѝ, ꙗко и Вирос‛са
при п‛равдѣ его повѣсти ос‛та́ви[34], и сар‛матовъ илѝ с‛лавяновъ не от
[Т]вискона но от Ассармота[35], илѝ Сармата умно́жены бы́ти изьꙗвѝ.
а Кранцїя Иоранда[36], и Ѳранци́ш‛ка, Ироника повѣс‛тописцо*в*[37]
немецкихъ, силною[38] мочью п‛рав‛ды побѣж‛денныхъ сꙗза, и
раз8мѣниꙗ ѝхъ с‛вѣтлыми их же выводами[39] [40]отвел, о[41] сем и
Плинїи из‛ра́д‛но учен, земле[40]мѣ*р* и повѣстописатель вь
естественнѣ*и*[42] повѣсти в книге .д̃. и в‛ главѣ .в̃і.[43] с‛видѣтелств8етъ
си́ми[44] с‛ловесы гл̃ꙗ, са*р*маты ж пойс‛тиннѣ не с8ть нѣмцы, но от

---

[1] В Ассармота ante corr. Сармата G Сармото R Са*р*мата N Ассармата | [2] ERN Моисѣ*и* |
[3] R евреисти | [4] N om. | [5] R Нектанова | [6] R быша | [7] ER omm. | [8] ER вед8щу | [9] ER
разумомъ | [10] BGERN повѣстописателе*и* | [11] G извѣстным | [12] N великаго | [13] ERN
честнаго | [14] BN Ассармота G Са*р*мота | [15] BGN omm. | [16] G Иктанова | [17] N Аксины |
[18] R Гемерова | [19] R Елѝ*с*вы | [20] GR пе*р*вого | [21] ERN пол͠скаго | [22] Е Елѝ*с*ъ R Елѝ*с*лъ |
[23] N греческїе | [24] G различн{ы}*х* ER различнїи | [25] R Т [sic] | [26] N холдеянинъ |
[27] N Твикона | [28] R ва | [29] В Еѵро́пе G У́ропе | [30–30] N вмѣсто | [31] GEN вавилонска͠г |
[32] Е у͠ставу R 8ставу | [33] В ante corr. Краме*р* | [34] Е о͠стави | [35] GE Са*р*мота R Са*р*мата |
[36] BGN Иорнанда | [37] R повѣстописцевъ | [38] ER силою | [39] ER выводамъ | [40–40] ER omm.
| [41] B in ras. GN om. | [42] ER естественϊе | [43] ER .д̃і. | [44] N сим ante corr. сими

нихъ Вислою рекою прекⷧлонⷨсѧ [1]к востокꙋ[1] сл҃нца ѿделéни,
Тож разꙋмѣ́ние Плинїево[2] о сармáтѣх ‖ подкрепляютъ[3] извѣⷭтными
свидѣтелствы Корнилїи, Тацитъ, Страбонъ, Пⷮталомїи[4], и[5] їнїи
сⷧлавнїи[6] повѣстωписⷱцы и земⷧлемѣры.
Инїи пáче же Белскїи, вⷪ начале выводꙋ народа полского[7] пишꙋтъ,
савроматїю[8] быти реченнꙋ[9] ѿ людей с очⷨми[10] ящеричьи[11], савроⷭ[12]
бо греческїи[13] ѧ̀щерица, омма, глаз, и ѿтꙋдꙋ нареченїе савроматовⷠ[14]
пⷬроизⷡводитъ, ꙗ́ко людей гнѣвливыхъ и страшныхъ, и́мъже ярость и
жéстокость ядовита из очей, ꙗ́ко ящерицам̅ сⷡвирѣпым̅ ѧвляшеся[15],
однакож и то свое мⷩнѣнїе, и ꙗ́ко ѿ [Т]вискона имꙋтъ начало
сармáты, сáмъ же Белскїи[16] ѿтставляетъ[17] и на разсꙋжⷣденїи
бл҃горазꙋмномꙋ[18], доктора Кромера, ꙗ́ко ѿ Ассармота[19] сн҃а
Иекⷮтанова[20], вⷩнꙋка Симова, произидоша[21] сармáты полагается,
понеже и Тилеман Сⷮтелⷧля[22] докторⷬ[23] ученый, на декѣ родосⷧловиѧ
Хрⷭтова саврома́та[24], не ѿ савроⷭ[25], ‖ и омнїа[26] греческихъ сⷧлов, но
ѿ халдейскогⷲ[27] ѧзыка изⷬрѧдным разꙋмом̅, вожⷣа[28] высоты, илй
вожⷨда вышния страны толкꙋетъ[29],

IV:2

Матⷡвѣ́ѧ[30] Осо́стовича Сⷮтрикóвⷭского[31], о произⷡводѣ сⷧла́вⷩногⷲ[32]
наро́да рꙋского[33], сⷧловенского[34], сармацкого[35], и для чего речéни
сꙋть сⷧлавáне.
Главà .б҃.ѧ.
О сⷧловéнахъ и сⷧлавéнⷭскихъ[36] земⷧлях, наро́да рꙋского[37] илй
сармáцⷵкого[38], ѿкꙋдꙋ сїе ихъ прозвáнїе произⷬрасⷮтѐ, разлиⷱчⷩны сꙋть
мнѣнїя различныхъ повѣстописⷱцовъ читателю любезⷩный[39], обаче тò
ѧ́вѣ покажꙋтⷭся, яко сⷧлавяне, или сⷧлавáки[40] предки наши бы́ша
сⷧлавнїи[41] воинⷭскою храбростию[42], во вⷬремѧ еще войны
траѧнской[43], но понеже селенїя свои имѧхꙋ ‖ вⷪ Паѳлягонїи, и в
странѣ Асїи менⷨшои у чорного[44] мóрѧ, идѣже н҃не тꙋрки и греки

[1–1] G ко свⷮѣтꙋ | [2] В Плиниев а corr. Плиниево N Тинїе | [3] R подкрѣпляетⷮ | [4] BGN
Птоломїи | [5] R om. | [6] R славни | [7] ERN полскаго | [8] В савроматию G сауроматию | [9] В
реченⷩ G реченⷩо N реченъ | [10] В ante corr. очиⷤ N очиⷤ | [11] R ящерниⷩ | [12] GR саурⷭо
N саврос | [13] В гречески ante corr. греческий GN гречески | [14] В ante corr. савроматы
G сауроматовⷠ EN савроматовъ R савраматовⷡ | [15] R являшася | [16] G Бѣлкїⷭ | [17] R
оставляетⷮ | [18] BGN бл҃горазумномⷮ | [19] U ante corr. Ассармата Е Ссⷡармота R Сармотова |
[20] R Нектанова | [21] ERN произыдоша | [22] G Стеля | [23] N досторъ | [24] BG савромата ER
саврамата | [25] BG саврⷭо | [26] R омнина N омина | [27] GERN халдеⷩскаⷢ | [28] ER пожда |
[29] ER толкꙋетъсѧ | [30] BG Матѳеа N Матфея | [31] EN Стриковскаго | [32] BGEN славнаⷢ |
[33] ERN рꙋскаго | [34] GEN словенскаⷢ | [35] N сармацкаго | [36] ER словенⷭскихъ ї |
[37] EN рꙋскаго | [38] N сармацкаго | [39] R любезны | [40] Е славяки R словяки | [41] R славни |
[42] R храброⷭтью | [43] N троянской | [44] EN чоⷬрнаго

жив8тъ, меж'д8 и́ми ж с'лавѧн, сербовъ[1], болгаровъ, болшая часть, и́же не пришелцы[2], а́ко т8р'ки жив8тъ но и́с'тиннїи[3] дѣдичи паѳлягонские зем'ли из древнихъ вѣков быти сказывают'сѧ.[4]
П'рокопїи[a] та́кож'де с'лав'ный[5] и д'ревнїи[6] повѣстописецъ п'реже[7] .ҁа҃з. лѣтъ о войнѣ готской пишѧ[8]во времена[8] Иустиниана[9] ц҃рѧ константинополского[10], в лѣто от Хр҃с̃та .ф҃ки. и папы .мѳ.ꙉ Иларїо́на поминаетъ о славака[11],
Иорнан'дъ[b], Алянъ такожде дрѣв'нїи повѣстописецъ пишетъ, яко [12]т̀ѡ и́мя[12] илѝ прозванїе с'лавянъ[13], во времена его ново бѣ в лѣто от Хр҃с̃та .у҃чв. но рѣчь с'лавенск8ю, еяже н҃не ‖ в'сѝ[14] употребляютъ, дре́в'нюю[15] быти с'видѣтелств8ютъ,
Бы́вшее[16] ꙗ́ко та́ко есть, по с'мѣшенїи бо ѧзыков у столпа вавилонска, первыи бѣ[17] языкъ хал'дейскїи и ев'рейскїи, илѝ жидовскїи, потом скиѳскїи[18] или татарскїи, та́же египе'тцкїи[19, c], еѳио́п'скїи и ин'дѣйскїи, потом греческїи[20], латинскїи[21], и нашъ с'ловенскїи[22], шестыи от Мосоха шестаго[23] с҃на Иаѳетова, по нем̃ немецкой от [Т]виско́на[24], тѣ язы́ки с8тъ по всей вселенней лѣт'чїе, от нихъже ꙗ́ко от источниковъ живыхъ, иные различныхъ[25] [26]народовъ языки начала умножения свойства, и различ'ны раз'личныхъ[26] ра́ди р8бежей рѣчи свои имѣют е́же всяком8 покаж8[27], аще к'то вопроситъ, а́ще и .о҃в. ѧзыка против вож'довъ и к҃нзей переменилос̃[28] у стол'па вавилонского[29] от одного, но бл҃гораз8мный бывалой[30] и[31] иск8сенъ ѧзыком̃ ‖ сам собо́ю т̀ѡ разс8ди́ти мо́жетъ, си́це же е́же Иорнан'дъ[32] и́же п'реж'де .ꙉа҃р. лѣтъ писѧ лѣтопись с'вою, с'видѣтел'ств8ет ѧзы́къ с'ловен'скїй бы́ти д'рев'нїи[33], и т̀ѡ из'рѧд'но пи́шетъ, по потопѣ бо то́тчас̃ в' лѣто .ꙉра. по Вирос̃с8.
То́тъже Иорна́н'дъ їже в лѣто от Хр҃с̃та .фпд.[d] п'ри Ма8рикїи[34] ц҃рѣ, .н҃е.м̃[35] пишет, а́ко с'лавѧ́ки над Ис'тромъ, илѝ[36] Д8наемъ к' пол8нощнымъ с'трана́мъ жи́ша, потом же п'реше́дъ Д8на́й, Мис'сїи[37] о́бѣ, Пан'но́нїю[38], вен'гры[39], и рак8шень, Македо́нїю, Ѳракїю, Ис'трїю разори́ша и п'лени́ша, сотворивъ же мечемъ безопас'ное[40] себѣ жили́ще в тѣхъ с'транахъ, инїи[41] в' тѣхъ тамъ зем'ля́хъ[42], инїи же

---

[1] R серпов̃ | [2] G пришлецы | [3] ER истинныї | [4] [Phrase untranslated, cf. example (70)] | [5] R славны | [6] R дрѣвни | [7] Е прежде R om. N прежъ | [8–8] R om. | [9] R Ї8с̃тина | [10] GE кос̃тян̃тинополского̃ RN кос̃тянтинопол̃скаго | [11] BGN словаках Е славака R славка | [12–12] R тития | [13] N словянъ | [14] N всѣ | [15] R древнею | [16] B ante corr. еже имѣло быти | [17] N om. | [18] ER греческиї | [19] ER египецкий N египецкїй | [20] BGN греческо̃и | [21] BGN латинско̃и | [22] BG словенско̃и | [23] Е шестого | [24] N востока | [25] G различны | [26–26] R om. | [27] B покажю | [28] Е перемянилос̃ | [29] N вавилонскаго | [30] ER бывало | [31] R om. | [32] G Їорнад̃ | [33] R древни | [34] R Ма8рике | [35] Е нем̃ъ RN немъ | [36] ER add. над | [37] N Мисїи | [38] G Панконию | [39] G венгеры | [40] R бѣзопасеное | [41] R и їни | [42] N ad. и

[a] G in marg. Прокопиї | [b] G in marg. Їѡрнандъ | [c] G in marg. первые ѧзыки | [d] G in marg. причина рекомых̃ славѧнъ

меж'д8[1] Д'ра́вою, и Савою река́ми во Иллирикѣ и в' Дал'ма́тїи
посели́шасѧ, и в'си[2] к8п'но са́ми собо́ю тѣ зе́м'ли славен'скими от
слав'ныхъ свои́хъ дѣл нареко́ша п'рос'транѧѧ[3] ж р8бѣжи с'вои,
безпреста́н'ным̃ войнами, покой себѣ и нас'лѣд'никомъ ‖ с'воимъ в'
ни́хъ 8креп'лѧѧ, ри́м'скїе[4] и констан̃тинопо́л'скїе[5] ц̃рства в' конецъ
ослаби́ша[6], и пол'ки[7] и́хъ с'лабы сот'вори́, о сем прⷱⷭ'траннѣе
обрѧ́щеши у речен'ныхъ повѣстописа́телей, Иѵрнан'да[8] и П'рокопїѧ.
Б'ло́н'дъ же, и́же[9] за́ с'то и за д'ват'цать лѣтъ о с'клонѣ́нїи к'
погибели ри́м'ского[10] ц̃рства повѣсть писа́, идѣже Ар'ка́дїева[11] и
Онорїева[12] в'лас'твованїа[13], и́же ба́х8 ц̃рьми, в лѣто от Хрⷭ҃та .ѿчи.
поминовѣ́нїе д'ревнѣйшее т'вори́тъ[14], помина́етъ же и с'ловен'скїи[15]
народ, ѩ́ко в' то в'рѣмѧ у́же бѣ с'лавен.
Т'ро́гъ же Пом'пей, тѣхъ в'сѣхъ повѣс'тописателей[16], д'ревнѣйшїи
повѣстописец ри́м'скїй, и́же до ржⷭ҃тва еще̃ Хрⷭ҃това разли́чныхъ
наро́довъ дѣѧнїа писа́, Ї8стинъ из него̃ в к̃нге .лв.и о наро́дѣ[17]
словѣ́нскомъ, и́хъже истрими[18] зов8тъ сице пи́ш8тъ[a], ѩ́ко Оетъ или́
Аетъ ‖ ц̃рь колхїискїе[19] зем'ли́, над чорным мо́рем̃ лежащїѧ, недале́че
от рекй До́на с Москвы тек8щеи, внегда ем8 Иас'со́нъ[20] со
ар'гана8ты[21] Мидїю дщерь[22] сок'ро́вищи[23] (еже[24] сокровище р8но̃
з'латое творцы наричютъ) унесъ, пос'ла[25] за ним в пого́ню .҃и.
людей[26] на с8дахъ черным мо́рем[27] тїи пришед к 8стью д8наискому[28]
влекоша вверхъ воды̃ карабли[29] свои, таж прїидоша до устьѧ рѣкъ
Са́вы и Д'равы, потом рекою Савою под горы волоскїе алпїискїе
прїидоша, а чрѣзъ горы на п'лечахъ к брегамъ[30] мо́рѧ
адриатицкого[31], корабли с'вои п'ринесо́ша, гонѧ и ищѧ аргонаутов'[32]
Иас'сона з'лодѣевъ и і́з'мѣнниковъ и хищников, кралѧ[33] с'воего Оеты,
но их та́мо не обрѣт'ши[34], ѩ́ко чаѧх8 ос'та́вивъ корабли с'воѧ̃[35]
п'рїидоша на полѧ италїискїе, идѣже н̃не Аквилеѧ градъ с'лавный, и
та́мо улюби́в'ше положенїе доброй[36] зем'ли обилныѧ посели́шасѧ,
не[37] вⷪⷭ'хотѣвъ назад в' дом кра́ла колхїиского[38] воз'врати́тисѧ, или́
боѧ́сь королѧ своег̃ ‖ Оеты, ѩ́ко не догониша воровъ с'воихъ, или
ѩко ск8чило и́мъ п'лаванїе по мѡрю и волоки́та,

---

[1] ER землю | [2] N всѐ | [3] R проⷭтранная | [4] ER римская | [5] BEN кѡнстянтинополскіе
G костѧн̃тинополскіе R костѧнтинопоⷧское | [6] R оⷭлаен̃иша | [7] R полскій |
[8] G Иорнан̃да R Иѵрналⷣа | [9] ER omm. | [10] ERN римскагѡ | [11] B ante corr. Арнадиева |
[12] ER Анориева | [13] GN властования | [14] G дворитъ | [15] N славенскій | [16] B ante corr.
вовѣстописателей | [17] ER add. в | [18] N истримъ | [19] BG колⷯийскій N конхійскій |
[20] R Наⷭсонъ | [21] ER архана8ты | [22] ER дщерь | [23] N сокровище | [24] R om. | [25] N пославъ |
[26] R om. | [27] G ad. и | [28] ER д8наіском̃ | [29] BGN корабли | [30] G брегом̃ | [31] R адриацкогѡ
N адрїатицкаго | [32] ER арганаутоⷡ | [33] R коробля | [34] ER обрѣтоша | [35] BGN свои |
[36] B добро Е добра R добраи | [37] U ante corr. но ER но | [38] GERN колхиискаг̃

[a] G in marg. колхида

Си́це[1] 8бо посел́ив'шеся[2] на́ши с'лова́ки в поля́хъ италíйскихъ п'ри
брега́хъ мо́рѧ адриа́тского[3], е́же н҃не Виницею[4], и страны́ еѧ
обливае́тъ, реко́ша ѧ и́стры[5] от І́стры илѝ Д8на́я рекѝ, еюже из'
мо́рѧ от своеѧ́ страны́ кол'хи́ды прип'лы́ша, а́ки бы ре́клъ
ис'три́ичики[6], [7-7]илѝ д8на́йчики, с'лава́ки бо Д8на́й[7] наричю́тъ[8]
Ви́с'теръ, и латинники[9] Истеръ, я́ко Ови́дíи о Понтѣ́[10] и Ма́зи́м8[11] и
инíи наро́ди, идеже от моро́зовъ с'та истеръ,
Ин'дѣ же в' кни́ге .з҃.и[12]
З'ри́ши[13] [14]у́же а́ко[14] пос'реде́ Истро́выхъ водъ тѧш́кíе[15] во́зы, паст8хъ
жесто́къ ѧтви́жскíи[16] прово́дитъ, ‖
То́йже д'воименна́го[17] Ис'тра[18], та́кожде[19] инíи повестописа́тели[20] и
землеме́рцы Д8на́й Ис'тръ наричю́тъ, с'лова́ковъ[21] же надъ мо́рем
адриа́т'ским[22] простра́нно жив8щиѧ, истри́чики или и́стры зов8́тъ, и
от зде́ дово́дно и я́в'но кíиж'до зре́ти мо́жетъ, а́ко с'лава́ки во Асíи і
во Евро́пѣ[23] из'да́вна[24] 8м'но́жишасѧ, италíйскихъ[25] и еллинскихъ[26]
стран м'но́го ов'ладѣ́ша [27]но в'си[27] от нас'ле́дíя Иаѳето́ва, и Мосо́ха
с҃на его́, нача́ла с'вои имѣ́ѧ в'сегда́, ї́с тѣ́х с'транъ я́же н҃не Москва́
держи́тъ, и от о́зера меотíйского[29] и черного[30] мо́рѧ в' сия с'траны́
евро́п'скíе[31], в нихъже прос'тра́нно и н҃не жив8́тъ, п'риходи́ли от
стран с'т8де́ныхъ и́ща неба л8тчаго[32], и с'тра́нъ обилне́йшихъ, в'
нача́ле сарма́ты, рожо́ляны, и р8са́ки[33], с' Мидрида́томъ[34, a] короле́м
понт'ски́мъ[35] вели́кíе войны́ и дол'ги[36] воева́вшíи[37], по нихъ пото́м
го́ты, кимвры, ї ван'дали́ты, и́хъже ча́с'ть в тѣ́х с'трана́хъ, идеже н҃не
‖ Лит'ва, Лотва, и Ж'мо́йдь[38] поселиса[39], я́ко с'ве́йские и да́тцкíе[40]
де́ѧнíя, и Кили́кíи, Кимвръ в нача́ле войны́ дитма́рскиа[41] Карíо́нъ
[42]в' кни́гахъ[42] вторы́хъ, мона́р'хíи третей ве́ка вто́раго[43], Иоаким
К8рей, ѳрейс'тадíйскíи[44] в по́вести ш'лен'ской, поро́дою не́м'цы
с'виде́телств8ю́т,
Д'р8га́ѧ же ча́с'ть тѣ́х ван'дали́товъ, гото́в[45], и ким'вро́в всю
Ев'роп8[46], ели́кѡ есть вен'герск8ю[47], греческ8ю[48], їталíйск8ю[49],

---

[1] ER сие | [2] R поселишася | [3] N адрíатскаго | [4] B Виницыю ante corr. Виницыею GN Виницыю | [5] G om. | [6] GRN истричики | [7-7] N om. | [8] G нарич8тъ | [9] R латинский | [10] B ante corr. монтѣ | [11] ER Ма́зам8 | [12] ER omm. | [13] B ante corr. зриш{н} G зриж R зришиï | [14-14] N яко ужъ with numbers above: 2 1 | [15] ER тяжские | [16] ER ятвиж́ский | [17] R двоимен́скогѡ | [18] B ante corr. Истры | [19] ER add. и | [20] R пове́сто . писателеи | [21] N славаков | [22] R адриацким | [23] BG Еvропѣ | [24] R исадавна | [25] R италискихъ | [26] R елинскихъ | [27-27] R нови | [28] ER начало | [29] GN меотиискаго E меотинского | [30] EN че́рнаго | [31] B еvропские G еvропския | [32] N лучшаго | [33] B ante corr. р8сакиï | [34] U ante corr. Мидридат{а}мъ E Мидритам R Митритамъ | [35] R полским N понтйіским | [36] B ante corr. долгиï | [37] N воеваша | [38] G Жмод R Жмодьи N Жмоидъ | [39] G посели|лися | [40] ER дацкия | [41] N дитмарскïе | [42-42] R om. | [43] N второго | [44] ER ѳрѣйстадискиï | [45] R om. N готовъ | [46] BG Еvроп8 | [47] ER венгръскую | [48] R om. | [49] ER їталискую; R ad. и

[a] G in marg. Митридатъ и дѣла славѧнъ

ѳранц8жск8ю, ¹и гишпа́н'ск8ю¹ зе́м'лю, с'ловéн'скими² ³и немецкими, також'де с' литовскими³ наро́ды, си́лы о́бщіе совок8пив повоева́ша⁴.

Тѣж ван'далиты. и Аѳ'ри́кѣ т'ретей части в'селéн'ныѧ, и Рим8 не с'п8стили⁵ иже⁶ жестоко разориша, и во Аѳрикѣ двѣсти лѣтъ жиша, о чем понеже⁷ ꙗ́в'ная свидѣтелства и́мамы, не хощ8 долго мешкать, ‖ По ван'далитѣхъ⁸, сар'матѣх, гот'тѣхъ, и роꙁолянехъ, от тѣхъже по́ль и с'тра́нъ пол8нощныхъ и вос'точныхъ моско́в'скихъ⁹, инїи народи тогож с'ловéн'ского¹⁰ ѧзыка произыдоша¹¹, и́же волгары¹², или́ бол'гары¹³, от Волги¹⁴ реки имѧновашеся¹⁵, Болгарїя же илй Во̅л̅гария éсть вели́каѧ страна́ по обоим̅¹⁶ берегам̅ реки¹⁷ Волги меж Ев'ропою¹⁸ и Асїею, та река начася во р'жовской¹⁹ землицы²⁰ московской, или́ езера²¹ Волго, набравъ же в себя много рѣкъ великихъ течетъ чреꙁ моско̅вские страны́ далече, потом чреꙁ казанск8ю²², заволск8ю, нага́йск8ю, астараханск8ю²³, и иные татарскїе орды прешед за Астараханью²⁴ в кастїиское²⁵, или гирканскѡе и порское²⁶ мѡ́ре, éже Москва хвалы́н'ским морем̅ наричетъ седмьдесѧтъ²⁷ двѣма²⁸ устьи впадаетъ, помосковски²⁹ Волга, а потатарски³⁰ Еделс8, Птоломїи и греки Уго³¹ и́мѧ ей даша, Белскїи же н̅ш̅ заод'но имя к'лал̅ вмѣсте з Доном̅ невѣдомъ³² сыи³³ московскихъ с'тран, ‖

От той³⁴ тог'да реки³⁴ Волги и с' тѣхъ поль³⁵ (ихъже и н̅н̅е кн̅ѕь московскїй г̅с̅дрь болгарскїй³⁶ пишетсѧ, пошед с' вели́кою ордою и м'ножеством̅³⁷ людеи предки н̅ш̅и с'ловенскїе болгары илй во̅л̅гары прїидоша в начале к черном8 мо́рю, ища л8тчихъ³⁸ странъ, аще нѣцыи³⁹ пиш8тъ якw и́хъ ис' тѣхъ поль татары согнаша, и тw не к' дѣл8, ꙗ́ко ни́же л8тчи⁴⁰ обꙗвимъ, и там̅ у черного⁴¹ мо́ря меж Доном̅ и Днеп'ром̅ рѣками, идеже н̅н̅е киркелскїе⁴² крымскїе⁴³ и ман'кѡпские татары многое времѧ спокоино жи́ша В'негда же в тѣхъ полах умножишасѧ ов'ладѣша ⁴⁴по в'ремени⁴⁴ ⁴⁵ и Таурик8⁴⁶, ю́же⁴⁷ н̅н̅е перекопскїи царь столным̅ градом̅ ов'ладѣ, потом услышавъ о раздорѣх̅⁴⁸ римскихъ цесарей, а понеже и Атила в

---

¹⁻¹ R om. | ² ER своинскими | ³⁻³ N om. | ⁴ R повоѣваше | ⁵ N пустили | ⁶ G и | ⁷ B ante corr. якw | ⁸ ER вондалитех | ⁹ GERN add. и | ¹⁰ GRN словенска̅г̅ | ¹¹ ER про⎪зыдоша | ¹² ER полгары | ¹³ R болгоры | ¹⁴ R Воги | ¹⁵ BGN именовашася ER їменовашеся | ¹⁶ N объимъ | ¹⁷ G om. | ¹⁸ BG Европою R Ероповъю | ¹⁹ GR ржевскои | ²⁰ B ante corr. землиц{и} ER землице | ²¹ G osepa E езерра | ²² G om. | ²³ RN а̅страханскую | ²⁴ RN Астараханью | ²⁵ ER кастинское | ²⁶ R поморское | ²⁷ B седмъдесѧтъ RN семдесятъ | ²⁸ R двемя | ²⁹ ER помосковскии | ³⁰ ER потатарскии | ³¹ U ante corr. Рro B Рro ante corr. Лго N Рro ante corr. {е}го [Pol. Rho] | ³² R невѣдомомъ | ³³ R сы | ³⁴⁻³⁴ ER рѣки тогда | ³⁵ N полъ | ³⁶ R болгорскии | ³⁷ R множествѡ | ³⁸ N лучшихъ | ³⁹ R недыи | ⁴⁰ G л8тче | ⁴¹ EN чернаго | ⁴² B ante corr. кирпелские N кирсеельскїе | ⁴³ BGN кримские | ⁴⁴⁻⁴⁴ G suprascr. | ⁴⁵ GER времяни | ⁴⁶ BG Таурик8 N Таврику | ⁴⁷ N еже | ⁴⁸ R sрадорехъ

то врѣ́мѧ с҄ г8ннами, илѝ юграми [1]от реки́[1] Югры, ис҄[2] тѣхъже странъ
московскихъ прешед[3] бол҄ш8ю ча́с҄ть Ев҄ропы[4], овладѣ́в венгерск8ю
зе́м҄лю, разорил бѣ подвигн8шася и болгары с8хи́м и вода́ным́[5] ||
п8тем с҄ кн҃зем[a] свои́мъ Дер҄балωм[6], в Дакїю в҄ то врѣмѧ римск8ю
стран8, идѣже н҃не волоши м8тѧнѧ меж Д8ная и Д҄нестра[7] жив8тъ, и
тѣ страны из҄гнавъ дак ωв сами силою ов҄ладѣша в лѣто ѿ Хр҃ста .ӱк.
потом в лѣто .ӱнд. услышав[8] о смерти Ѳеодосїа ц҃рѧ преидоша в
Мисїю[9] чрезъ Д8най, сице же обою Миссїю ма́л8 и велик8 удо́б под
греческими ц҃рьми, видѧ ихъ раздоры вн8трен҄нїа овладѣша, и ѿ
своего нареченїа тѣ страны Болгарїею нарекоша, а́же и днесь тако
наричем[10], а́ко и сами бол҃гары[11] н҃нешнїи а́вѣ то[12] ис҄повѣд8ю т,
а́кω предки и́хъ из҄ московскихъ странъ изыдоша. жив8тъ ж
болгары с҄лавѧне[13] меж высокими каменными гора́мі за Д8наем
выѣхавъ из҄ м8лтѧнской земли, ѿ Брайлова[14], Дюрдѣева[15], и
8р8стюка[16] город ωв[17] под8найскихъ,[18] тїи же потом́ болгары,
с҄лавѧне, Ѳракїи[19] болш8ю[20] часть ов҄ладѣша. Зинона || ц҃рѧ
констан҄тинопо́л҄скогω[21], в҄ лѣто ѿ Хр҃ста .ӱо́s. порази́ша, и Ц҃рьградъ
побѣдительств8ѧ в҄зѧ́ша и сож҄гоша. сего ради в҄ лѣто .ӱчв. ц҃рь
Анастасїи пятьдесѧты́й ви́дѧ велик8ю сил8 и наѣз҄ды[22] болгарскїе,
устрои долг8ю стѣн8 ѿ Силиврїи[23], а́же над самимъ Галеспонтωм́
лежитъ даже[24] до черного[25] мо́рѧ, хотѧ имѣти покой с[26] своими
ц҃реграж́аны[27] за тою с҄тѣ́ною ѿ болгаровъ, Ѳракїю же с
Адрианополем́ остави без҄ крѣпости, ю́же в҄сю овладѣша болгары, и
с҄тѣны тѣ роз҄мета́въ[28]. па́ки в волости ц҃реградцкїе[29] наѣз҄жали, о
чем К҄ромеръ во имѧнова́нїи[30] сармати́скихъ[31] наро́довъ в҄ главѣ .й҃.и
пиша́ в҄[32] свидѣтел҄ство приводитъ Помпо́нїа Лета, но[33] а́зъ бытїемъ[34]
свои́мъ из҄вѣ́с҄тнѣйшїи, и очеви́д҄ной[35] с҄видѣтель, и́же бы́хъ дважди[36]
в҄ Силиврїи[37], который городъ над мо́рем́ Гелес҄по́н҄том[38] с҄[39]
т8рскимъ город̄кωм́ с ка́мени виситъ, .м҃. верстъ ѿ Ц҃рѧграда, а стѣн
тѣхъ нѣ́с҄колько десѧтъ[40] верстъ || за Силиб҄рїею, и н҃не а́вные[41] з҄на́ки
со р҄ва́ми и вала́ми[42], и кїиждо и́же т8ды́ поѣдетъ уз҄рѣ́ти
воз҄можетъ. па́че же[43] к҄ чернωм8 мо́рю ѿ Ц҃рѧграда в҄ Бѣлъгородъ

[1–1] R om. | [2] N и съ | [3] R пришед | [4] BG Еѵропы | [5] Е вадяны́м̄ | [6] ER Дербилом |
[7] ER Нестра | [8] B ante corr. услышовъ | [9] G ante corr. Месию N Месїю | [10] N наричюм |
[11] Е бол҃горы | [12] B suprascr. | [13] N словяне | [14] B ante corr. Брандѣева | [15] B ante corr.
Дюрдѣва ER Дюрдеѣва [sic] | [16] G 8р8стюска | [17] ER градо̄в | [18] [Phrase untranslated, cf.
example (71)] | [19] G Ѳраки | [20] R болшуую [sic] | [21] В кωнстянтинополско̄г GERN
констянтинополскаго | [22] N наѣзд | [23] R Силаврїи | [24] N дажъ | [25] ERN чернаго |
[26] ER omm. | [27] В ц҃реграж̄яны GER ц҃реграж́ены N царягражаны | [28] ERN разметавъ |
[29] BRN ц҃реградские | [30] ER именовании | [31] R самартиіских | [32] ER omm. | [33] B ad. (яко
г҃летъ аутор сеа книги) in ras. | [34] Е бытимъ R бытем | [35] GER очевидно | [36] ER дважди |
[37] R Силаврїи | [38] B ante corr. Гелестон̄том ER Гелеспо̄н̄тотом | [39] ER omm. | [40] BRN
десять | [41] ER явныꙗ | [42] N волами | [43] ER add. и

[a] G in marg. кн҃зь Дербалъ

волóскои ѣд8чи, занѐ .к҃ѕ. лѣтъ[1] тѣ с'тѣны бѣ[2] зиж'дѧи[3]. Анас'тáсïи
ц҃рь в числѐ пѧтьдесятый, во в'сѐ врéмѧ г҃дрствовáнïѧ с'воегѡ.
совер'шивъ же ц҃рства с'воегѡ .к҃ѕ. лѣтъ громо́мъ 8биенъ бы́с'ть,
болгáры ж с кн҃зе́мъ с'воѝмъ Х'р8нóмъ т'ретïимъ[4] по с'мерти[a] его
грéческïе г҃дрства п'лениша и овладѣ́8 безоⷮпóрнѡ,
Потóмъ в' лѣто ѿ Хрⷭ҇тá .ѱ҃иï. Л'в8 т'ретïем8 ц҃рю, и́же бѣ
образоборецъ речéн вышеимѧновáн'нïи[5] бóлгáры[6] помощствовах8,
в'негдá с'рацы́ни Цр҃ѧграда дѡбывáх8 .и҃. лѣтъ, и́хъже болгáры
с'лавя́не[7] в конéцъ из'бѝша, занѐ и́хъ мѡⷬ и глáд одолѣвáше[8] зѣлò,
с'вер'хъ того с'рацы́нскïе корáб'ли[9] и катор'ги[10], тѣжъ болгáры на
Елес'пóн'тѣ и Пропóн'тидѣ[11] || из'рáдным 8хитрéнïемъ, под водóю
óгнь под'ложи́въ[12] воз'жегóша[13], о семⷨ и Карïѡ́н нем'чи́нъ[14] в'
лѣтопи́си[15] своéй в[17] кни́гѣ .г҃.и[17] монáр'хïи[18] .д҃.и вѣка .г҃.г҃
воⷭ҇'помина́етъ,
Потóмъ в' лѣто .ѱ҃ѕ. а ѿ соз'дáнïѧ ми́ра по ри́м'ском8 с'чот8[19] .҂дод. а
ѿ основáнïѧ ми́ра[20] .҂афна. Никиѳо́ра ц҃рѧ кон'стан'тинополскогѡ[21],
тѣжъ бóл'гáры со всѣⷨ вóйском греческимъ и ри́мскимъ из'бѝша и
самогò[22] убѝша, потóмъ Михáйла К8рополáта[23] у Адрианополя[24], я́ко
в тѡⷨ в' начáлѣ п'рос'трáннѣе речéсѧ в конéцъ побѝша, а́ко и[25] самъ
едвà 8бѣжè[26] а с ѿчáѧнïѧ[27] ж не совершивъ на ц҃рствѣ дв8 лѣтъ в
мнⷭ҇трь пос'три́жесѧ, и тáмъ в'сѐ вóйска ри́м'скïе в помочь[28] грекѡ́мъ
п'ришéд'шïѧ падóша, [29]и Ас'вáлдъ[29] воевóда ри́мскїй ѧ́тъ и жи́въ
созжéн[30] ѿ болгáровъ на жéртв8, ||
Ѿ того́ж Михáйла К8рополáта[31] речéннïй[32] болгáры аз'б8чные
словà, и́хъже н҃не в'сѧ Р8сь упот'реб'лѧетъ[33], вмѣсто дáра п'рия́ша, по
той побѣ́де[34] Бос'н8, Далмáтïю[35], Иллирикъ, и в'сѐ стрáны ри́мскïе
над морéмъ егéйскимъ лежáще[36], дáже дò мóрѧ адриáтского[37]
ов'лáдѣша, и наро́дами с'ловéн'скими дáже до н҃нешнихъ времéн
напóлниша, Истринопóль[38] грáд на р8бежáхъ италíйскихъ[39], его́же[40]
н҃не виницы́ане[41] дер'жáⷮ, сѝлою в'зѧ́ша, идѣ́же .҂е҃.і. людéй

[1] B suprascr. | [2] G om. ER б | [3] B ante corr. зиждѧ ad. и in ras. | [4] ER третим | [5] Е
вышеименован̅ныі R вышеïменнованныи | [6] ER бол̅горы | [7] GE славяня R словяня |
[8] Е одолѣвше R одѡлѣвые | [9] N карабли | [10] BGERN катарги | [11] ER Пропон̅дите |
[12] N положивъ | [13] B suprascr. | [14] N немеинъ | [15] G лѣтописиі | [16] G своемⷨ | [17–17] ER .г҃.
кн̅ге | [18] ER манархиі | [19] BGN щот8 ER сщот8 | [20] GN Рима [Pol. Rzymá] |
[21] B кѡн̅стянтинополского G костянтинополскоⷢ Е костянтинополⸯскаго
RN констя́н̅тинополскаго | [22] N самаго | [23] G Кураполата N Куропотолата |
[24] GR Адрианаполя Е Ан̅дрианаполѧ | [25] ER omm. | [26] BGN убѣжа | [27] ER очтания |
[28] ER помощъ | [29–29] ER Насвал̅дъ | [30] BGN сожженъ | [31] G Кураполата Е К8ратополота
R Коратополота | [32] ERN речениі | [33] G употреблѧютъ ER 8потребляетсѧ |
[34] ER побѣже | [35] R Долматию | [36] RN лежащиѧ | [37] ER адриацкаго N адрïатскаго |
[38] ER Истранополь N Итринополь | [39] ER итталийскихъ | [40] ER add. и | [41] Е виницеане
R виницеане

[a] G in marg. кн҃зь Хр8нъ

л8тчихъ[1] в' неволю взѧша. внегда́ же Ал'гим8ндъ кро́ль
лен'гобардскїи с воискѡм на нихъ собрасѧ[2] хотя и́хъ от т8д8 выгнать,
на голов8 его побиша, ꙗко в тѣх странах и ннѣ с'лавяне[3] великїе[4]
осады им8т,

Ов'ладѣша потом Епиром и Албанїею идѣже Абланечь[5],
С'вятыград[6], Яи́ца, Лы́с'с8[7], Мо́кр8[8], Бѣлгород, Добр8ю[9], К'ро́ю,
Нов'город, с'лавен'скими[10] имяны[11] ‖ реченные городы и за́м'ки
сос'тро́иша.

Па́па римскїй[12] Николаи .а̃. а по́с'ле Їоанна[13] жены т'ретїй[13, 14] в лѣто
от Хрс́та .ѿн҃. писа́ к ни́мъ с'ловесы млс́тивыми, да крщ҃енїе с'в̃тое, и
вѣр8 Хрс́тов8 восприим8тъ, на ч'то они охотно соблг҃оволиша, и́бо
меж'д8 и́ми много хрс́тїѧн[15] тогож с'ловенского[16] ѧзык8 быша[a], паче
же греческїѧ вѣры, пос'ла́ тогда к' ни́м Николай па́па пос'лы свои́[17] и
людеи[18] дх҃ѡвныхъ[19] м'ного, и́же бол'гаровъ, и і́ных с'лавян[20] во
Ѳракїи и в Мисїи крс́тиша, и научиша хрс́тїанской[21] вѣре по
рим'ском8[22] чин8, ѳор'тиниа́ны[23] ж с'вщ҃енники греческїе, и́же
п'режде сего закон8 с'воему изучиша, от нихъ из'гнаша[24], называѧ
ихъ отс'т8п'никами.

Си́це внегда̀ в'си[25] болгары единомыш'ленно[26] п'рїѧша с'в̃тое
к'рещенїе, услышавъ яко с'рацыни Гиш'панїю и і́талїанскїе[27] ‖
зем'ли. и Ѳра́нцїю с'вирѣпо повоеваша, и частїю Гиш'панїи[28]
овладѣша, и Гарганау́м[29] гор8 с'лавн8ю во Ап8лїи[30] в'зѧша, зане
цесари хрс́тїан'скїе[31] не можах8 с8противитисѧ, собрашася
доброволнѡ бол'гары[32], с'ловяне[33], идо́ша же моремъ и землею во
Ап8лїю, идѣже с'рацынов[34] .л̅. из'биша, потом же у прис'таница
ан'конского[35], и неаполитанского[36] да́въ с' прот'чими[37] во́йски
с'рацын'скими[38] бо́и, корабли[39] и ка́торги[40] дивнымъ вымыслом
сож'гоша, и в'сѣх махметан[41] разсыпаша, бысть сїе от Хрс́та в' лѣто
.ѿн҃.[42] при цесаре Лодвикѣ втором сн҃е Лотарїеве, от Махмета ж
проро́ка с'рацынского[43] в лѣтѡ .мг҃. по щет8 Карїа́нов8. кня́зь же
бол'гарскїй[44] по той с'л8ж'бе хрс́тїанской[45], приѧ[46] закон п8стынный,

[1] Е л8тших N лучшихъ | [2] R собрался | [3] ER славянѧ | [4] B suprascr. | [5] ER Обланечь
N Ялбланечь | [6] R Сѣ̃тыиград | [7] B ante corr. Лысса | [8] B suprascr., ante corr. Мокр{а}
G ante corr. Мо{то}р8 | [9] B ante corr. Добр{о}ю | [10] ER словенскими | [11] BGN имены |
[12] ER римски | [13–13] B in marg. | [14] B ad. .г̃.и in ras. Е трети | [15] GN хрс́тианъ | [16] EN
словенскаго R славенскаго | [17] N своя | [18] ER людем | [19] ER духовным | [20] BGN словян |
[21] BE хрс́тиянской | [22] ER мирском8 | [23] ER ѳортинианы | [24] G ad. и | [25] N всѣ | [26] Е
единомышлено | [27] B италиянские | [28] ER Гишпани | [29] R Горгана8мъ | [30] ER Аполи |
[31] BEN хрс́тиянские | [32] Е болгоры | [33] GN славяне ER славянѧ | [34] B ante corr.
срацын{а}в | [35] N анконскаго | [36] Е неапалитанскаго R неапалитан'ского
N неаполитанскаго | [37] GN прочими | [38] B ante corr. неаполитан'скими | [39] ER карабли |
[40] GER катарги N картоги | [41] R махметянъ | [42] ER .ѡн҃ѳ. | [43] EN срацынскаго |
[44] ER болгарски | [45] B хрс́тиянскои suprascr. ER християнскои | [46] G приѧл

[a] G in marg. болгары римское исповѣдание приемлютъ

сн҃8 с'воем8 зда̀ в'ласть, иже занеже недоб'рѣ вла́с'твова, к' том8
вѣрою[1, a] θорт8ниꙗн[2] п̃реградцкихъ[3] бѣ напаа҆н, повелѣ о̃ц҃ъ ем8 о́чи
вылⷹпить вышеⷣ из мн̃стрⷶ || сн҃а[b] же ю́н'шаго бол'гаромъ[4] даде́
кн҃за, са́мъ же в мн̃стрь воз'вративсꙗ[5], тамѡ житїе совеⷬ'ши, однакоⷤ
потѡмъ болгары и едва не всѝ[6] с'лавꙗне дла сосѣдственногѡ[7]
с'мѣⷤ'ства во греческїи[8] законъ п'ревратилисꙗ, в немъже и н҃не с8ть,
Си́це тоⷢ'да̀ изⸯ тѣхъ р8ского[9] колѣна бол'гаровъ и҆лѝ волгаровъ[10], иже
от Во́лъги рекѝ из московскихъ странъ изидоша[11] [12] тѣ народы[12]
с'лавѣн'скїе[13] от мо́рꙗ θракїйского[14], даже до венедїйского[15]
прострⷶⷩ'но[16] доⷧблиствїеⷨ[17] войн'скимъ 8м'ножишасꙗ, ꙗко серъбы
и́же тою землею овладѣша, и́дѣже бѣ преⷤ'де сего Мис'сиꙗ ма́лаꙗ
н҃не Серъбїею зов8тъ, и҆лѝ Сéрвїею. болгары[18] и́дѣже преⷤ'де сего
Мис'сиꙗ великаꙗ Босна, идѣже прежде[19] сего[20] бѣ[21]Ливⷹрнїꙗ[20, 22],
н҃не босенскаꙗ зеⷨ'лꙗ, а гдѣ преⷤ[23] сего бы́лъ[21] Иллирикъ и
Доⷧматїꙗ, н҃не раг8зы, каⷬ'ваты раскїи || и҆лѝ ра́чеве, карниолꙗне,
алба́ны, ис'трїане, и п'ро́т'чїи[24] меⷤ горъ жив8щїи[25], и[26] над моремъ
адриатицким, в'си[27] тѣхъже боⷧгареⷷ и҆лѝ волгарей[28] моско́в'скихъ
от Волги рекѝ нас'лѣдницы с8ть и́с'тиннїи и[29] с'лавѣн'ским[30] ꙗзыкоⷨ
да́же до н҃нешнихъ в'ремеⷩ о҆бще говоряⷮ, и с'лавꙗны наричюⷮ'сꙗ[31],
па́че же с8щїи во Иллирикѣ в Даⷧматїи[32] и в' Ливⷹр'нїи[33],
Иⷥ тогоⷤ славенского[34] народ8 бѣ с'вⷮы҃и[35] Іероним[36, c] даⷧ'мацкїй
учитель и с'толпъ кос'тела повсемственного[37], и́же бл̃годатїю житїꙗ
ц'вѣтꙗше в лѣто от Хрⷭта[d] .т҃зи. такоⷤ Кирилъ и Меѳодїи первїи
с'ловенстїи[38] апо́с'толи от тогоⷤъ народа бол'гарскѡ[39] быша в лѣто
.т҃ѯе. во в'рема Юлиана отс'т8п'ника противъ егоⷤ[40] Кирил писа
книги из'ря́дныꙗ[41] с'лавенскимъ[42] ꙗзыкѡⷨ и латинскимъ поборяꙗ
вѣре хрⷭтїа́н'скои[43], а тѣ к'ниги а́ко Карїѡн свидѣтелств8еⷮ в книгахъ
.г҃. с8ть, и н҃не с'лавенскїи[44] в книгохранителнице А́на Реуⷦ'лина
славноⷢ[45] || бг̃ос'лова во г'раде п'θоренскоⷨ.

---

[1] G вѣ*ру* | [2] G θ8рт8нииꙗⷩ | [3] G п̃реграцких Е п̃реградкихъ N цареградских |
[4] N болгарамъ | [5] G возвратисꙗ | [6] Е всиⷯ N всѣ | [7] ERN соседственⷩаго | [8] ER греческо*и*
| [9] ERN р8скаго | [10] R волгороⷡ | [11] ERN изыдоша | [12–12] N народы тѣ | [13] G словенские
ER словенскиꙗ | [14] ERN θракискаго | [15] ER венедицкаго N венедїйскаго |
[16] Е простаⷩно R простолно | [17] N доблиствїеⷨ | [18] Е боⷧгоры | [19] BGN преⷤ | [20–20] ER
были в8рниꙗ | [21–21] B suprascr. | [22] B ante corr. Люв8рниꙗ, ad. и in ras. N Лтвурнїꙗ | [23] ER
прежде | [24] Е протчи N протⷱїе | [25] Е жив8щи | [26] ER omm. | [27] N всѣ | [28] R валгаре*и* |
[29] ER omm. | [30] ER словеⷩским | [31] BGN наричⷮ8сꙗ | [32] RN Доⷧматїⷯ | [33] R Ливурⷮи |
[34] Е словеⷩскаго R словеⷩского N славенскаго | [35] Е сⷮвы | [36] ER Неронимъ | [37] ERN
повсемственⷩаго | [38] ER словеⷩтїи N славенстїи | [39] N болгарскаго | [40] ER его |
[41] R ї҆зрядные | [42] ERN словеⷩским | [43] BGE хрстияⷩскои | [44] GEN словенскїи
R словенски | [45] RN славнаго

[a] G in marg. болгары приемлютъ законъ греческиⷯ | [b] G in marg. премѣна князей иⷯ̑ |
[c] G in marg. сⷮвы҃и Иеронимъ даⷧмацкиⷯ | [d] G in marg. Кирилъ и Меѳодиⷯ

А чего́ ради, и каковы́ ра́ди вины́ и п'рил8ча҄, болгары[1], Р8сь, карваты, далматы[2], се҄рбы, босны[3], илирики[4], и інїи[5] [6]тогож народа предки на́ши[6], с'лавяне с8ть речени[7], различных[8] с8ть повѣстопис'ц̄ωв разꙋмѣнї҄, ꙗ́ко выше сего написахъ.

С8йдъ[9,а] в' книгахъ с'воихъ, славен'скїй[10] народ быти с'лавный[11] за Ис'тро́м̄ или Д8наем полагаетъ, идѣже н̄н҄е болгары и сербы реченнїи[12] ж от шлꙗхетства[13] и с'лавных дѣ҄л̄ войн'скихъ с'лавоны, или славаки[14], а не склавоны, яко италїане[15] г̄л̄голютъ которым̄ проз'ванїемъ хотꙗху различны быти от скиѳовъ и тата҄р, понеже гре́ки меж генеты или сар'маты[16] народами словенскими, [17]и меж[17] татары никакова различї҄ не творꙗх8[18], о сем̄ Їоаким̄[19] К8реи во исторїи шленской немчи҄н породою воспоминаетъ, генеты и ван'далиты ‖ с'ловꙗны бы́ти от Мосоха рожденными пиша́, и́же готовъ с тѣхъ поль, идѣже[20] н̄н҄е Ли҄тва и Р8сь бѣла҄ из'гнаша, инїи же с тѣми готами в западные[21] с'траны прїидоша, також с кимвꙗ҄ны, ꙗко н̄ши предки с'лавяне из'давна в немецкихъ землꙗх осады прос'транные[22] имѣша даже до лѣта . ҂а҃р҃м҃ѳ҃.г̄[23] внегда на них вси[24] к̄нꙗ҄зи немецкїе восташа при цесаре Кон'раде[25], и[26] из'гнаша и́хъ изо[27] Ми́снїи[28] и[29] їз р8бежей королевств8 датцком8[30] смѣжныхъ и́бо .ф҃. лѣтъ пребыша во идолос'л8женїи, то́тъже[31] К8реи немчи҄н пишетъ, а́ко егда по смерти Аттилы королꙗ вен'герского[32] жестокагω[33], народы сармацкїе с'лавенского[34] ꙗзыка от моря леденаго[35] и от озера меотїйско҄г[36] из' р8скихъ с'тран московскихъ великою силою пришедше из'гнаша, ис' тѣхъ по́ль а́же н̄н҄е Полша в' себѣ содержи҄т нѣмцо҄в сенонов, генм8н'д8ро҄в и боѥ҄в[37], о чем̄ и Ваповской[38] кан'торъ крако́вско҄и ‖ полꙗкъ в лѣтописи с'воей, юже не соверша и не выда҄в 8м'ре, пише[39] сице, яко с'лаваки, или с'лавꙗне наши предки от озера с'ловеного[40] е́же есть в москω҄вскихъ с'трана́хъ речени[41] с8ть, и того длꙗ полꙗки, чехи[42] болгары, и[43] інїи вси́[44] славяне и Р8сь и́мꙋтъ произвожденїе с'вое от Мосоха, или[45] Москвы с̄на Иаѳетова, понеже из странъ московскихъ произидоша[46], [47]о сем̄[47]

---

[1] ER бол̄горы | [2] ER до҄лматы | [3] R боины | [4] BG илирика | [5] G іннии | [6–6] N предки наши тогожъ народа with numbers above: 3 4 1 2 | [7] R реченїи | [8] Е разчныхъ | [9] E ante corr. С8итъ R С8дъ N Сиудъ | [10] ER словен̄ски | [11] Е славны | [12] ER реченїи | [13] B ante corr. шлꙗгетства G шлꙗхле҄тства Е шлꙗхо́ства R шлꙗхо́тства | [14] G словаки | [15] BGN италияне | [16] ER со҄рматы | [17–17] N имже | [18] B ad. и in ras. N ad. и | [19] Е Їокимъ | [20] B ante corr. иже | [21] R саподные | [22] ER простра҄н̄ныꙗ | [23] R ad. а | [24] N всѣ | [25] R Кондрате | [26] ER omm. | [27] B ante corr. {о}з G из | [28] R Мисїи | [29] ER omm. | [30] Е дацкому | [31] ERN т8тже | [32] Е венгрьскаго RN венге҄рскаго | [33] G жестакагω | [34] ER словенскаго N славенскаго | [35] BGR леденогω | [36] ER меотискаго N меотїйскаго | [37] G обоиꙋ҄в ER боиꙋ҄в | [38] ER Вапавскои | [39] R пише҄т | [40] ER славеного N словенаго | [41] R реченїи | [42] ER add. и | [43] E om. | [44] Е всиї N всѣ | [45] ER add. от | [46] ER произыдоша | [47–47] B ante corr. сиеи

[а] B in marg. о҄тстав

та́ко Ваповской пишетъ.

Алъбертъ[1] же Кра́н'тïи немецкïи повѣстникъ глаголетъ бы́ти реченных с'лавако́в[2] от многорѣ́чïя с'ло́въ е́же есть явное без'дѣлïе неразс8дного[3] разꙋмѣнïя его, понеже с'лаваки имѣютъ быти своиственно и ïстинно реченнïи[4] по разс8ждению разꙋм'ныхъ людей с'ловаки[5] от славы, и́бо сами с'лаваки[6] и болгары от природно́г[7] ѧзыка р8ского[8] то и́мя единомышленно даша от славы, и от свои́хъ славных воинских || дѣл, сице же а́ко онꙋ сами с'ла́в'ными и с'лаваками себѣ нарицах8, тогда и лати́н'ники[9] с нимиж долго ратовах8 в гсдрствах ради греческихъ и[10] ïталïйскихъ[11], начаша ихъ нарицати с'лави́ны и с'лавы, страны ж ихъ С'лавонïа а не с'ловины[12], или словы[13], и не от[14] С'ловонïа[15] от словъ но от славы[16], того ради р8са́ки, поляки, и[17] чехи древнïе[18] на́ши предки, а́ко в'сегда л8ч'ши[19] с'лав8 нежелꙗ сокровища люблах8, тогда кнꙗземъ и снꙋомъ своим, и ïнымъ своего наро́да людемъ о́бче[20] имена давах8 союзны и сложены с[21] славою, а́ко С'вятос'лавъ, П'рꙑмыславъ С'тос'лавъ, Борис'лавъ, П'рес'лавъ, Выробос'лавъ, се есть и́же свои́мъ м8жеством̂ слав8 себѣ выроботал, Имис'лавъ емлясꙗ за слав8, С'танислав[22] с'тановляй[23] себѣ с'ла́в8, Дивис'лавъ[22], Мечис'лавъ от меча славны́и[24], Залиславъ, В'ладис'лавъ, Ꙗрослав, Бретис'лавъ, Мирос'лавъ[25], Доброславъ, Прибыс'лавъ, Заславъ, Болес'лавъ || Венцеславъ,

Вѣщъ[26] у́бо пра́в'де подоб'на, о чем̂ и К'ромер в повестяхъ и во в'сѣхъ ученïахъ свободныхъ бжественныхъ с'видѣтелств8ет в[27] главѣ .гꙏ. в книге .а҃. о дѣлехъ полских, а́ко тïи болгары, и́же над Д8наемъ и над греческим морем̂ жи́ша, в'негда велïя и п'реславная делеса воинскаꙗ противъ ри́м'ского[28] и кос'тян'тинополского[29] цртва а́ко выше рекохомъ творях8, и частые[30] побѣдителства над римляны и над греки пол8чах8, чести ради и х'валы п'рослав'льших'сꙗ дѣл̂ своихъ особое имꙗ сами себѣ даша, и нарицах8сꙗ с'лаваки[31], или славнïи, или имъ то[32] и́мя иные[32] и́хъ народа люди, Р8сь Москва, и поляки даша, желая земяномъ[33] свои́мъ добро́и с'лавы, тогда от их щас'ливыхъ и славных дѣл нарекоша ихъ с'лавиа́ны, илй слава́ки, а нас̂ бы свои́хъ нас'лѣдникꙑв || нарѣкли слабаки от с'лабости, занѐ зѣло́ ослабѣли ес'мꙑ[34],

В' тꙑм же зѣло пог'рѣшаютъ италïа́не[35], и ïхъ лѣтописцы, и́же на́съ и

[1] ER Албѣрдъ | [2] BGN словаковъ | [3] RN неразсуднаго | [4] ER реченïï | [5] ER славаки | [6] G словаки | [7] G прероднаго ERN природнаго | [8] ERN р8скаго | [9] ER лати́нски | [10] ER omm. | [11] ER итали́нскихъ | [12] ER славины | [13] ER славы | [14] BGN omm. | [15] ER Славониꙗ | [16] B ad. но от славы in ras. | [17] ER omm. | [18] N древнïи | [19] E л8тши R лучшиï | [20] G о́бча ER обще | [21] ER omm. | [22–22] G suprascr. | [23] ER становляꙗи | [24] R славꙏны | [25] N in marg. | [26] N вещь | [27] ER во | [28] RN римскаго | [29] BN констꙗнтинополꙏскаго G констꙗнтинополского ER костꙗнтинополꙏскаго | [30] ER частыꙗ | [31] N словаки | [32–32] N имянные | [33] G ante corr. семляномъ RN семляном | [34] R естмы | [35] BG италияне R ïтталиане

їны*х* бол'гаровъ народа р8ского[1] с'клавоны, и склавы, в латинскомъ ѧзыкѣ пиш8*т* и зов8*т*, во италїискомъ[2] же скѧвоны[3], и скѧвы[4] вмѣсто с'лаваковъ[5], илй славонωв[6] которое[7] погрешéніе о*т* неумѣнїя нашего ѧзы́ка вор'вало*с* и вкралось, в повести Прокопїевы Иорнан'довы[8], и Блóн'довы з'натнω о*т* писцωв италїйскихъ[9], иже хотѧ по малод8шїю юнош'ск8[10] младен'чески молвить многощи[11] .і҃. слово вмѣ*ст*ω .л҃.[12] г҃лолютъ. [13, 14]а г҃лолѧ[13, 15] с'лóво[14] чаще и*з* словъ їталїйскихъ и латин'ских рѣче*и*[16] выметываютъ, в'негда бо и́м8тъ г҃лолати, дигна, говорѧтъ дина, или динія, и́гнисъ, инисъ, ин*с*игне, инсине, плѧцетъ, пѧцетъ, илй ‖ италїанскїй[17] пиáце, или пиязе[18], флѧт8*с*, фѧт8*с* и прочая, сице[19] же егда и́м8тъ г҃лолати, с'лаво[20], с'лавонїя[21], или славонескъ[22], г҃лолютъ сиѧвонїѧ, сиѧвω, и сиѧви, сиѧвони вмѣсто славоны, а понеже у нихъ нѣтъ никакова различия[23], аще бы к'то молвил сиѧвω[24], илй сцїаво, и славо ц слово[25], илй .л҃.[26] меж [27].с. и .і҃.[27] вмѣшаютъ[28], тогда о*т*здѣ знатно не8мѣющїи писцы ихъ, хотѧщїи г҃лолати, илй писати нѣчто о нашихъ предкахъ славакахъ[29], не писаша насъ славы, илй славоны[30], но[31] склавоны, илй склавы[32], которы*м* именем[33] н҃не италїаны[34] в'си[35] паче же виницейскихъ стра*н* жители неволника и всякого[36] раба к8пленого[37] склавы и скѧвы[38] нарицаютъ, сїе же того длѧ яко внегда италїане[39] 8 моря Адрїатицкого[40] жившїи[41], венеты, лонгобарды[42] безпрестанные[43] во*и*ны о р8бежахъ з' болгары и со инѣми ‖ с'лавóки[44] предками нашими имѣша, тогда на войнѣ, или загонами в неволю поиманыхъ славоко*в* имене*м* и́хъ неволничьи*м* нарицах8 склявоны[45], и скѧвы, ѧ́ко бѣ обычай древле у грековъ, и у ри*м*лянъ неволниковъ своихъ сы́ры и геты, ѧко и*з* Сирїи и і*з* Гетїи, идѣже н҃не волоская землѧ̀ и перекопская ор'да бывах8 поиманы, яко н҃не т8рки древнихъ вещей не во*с*поминая италїан[46], кааvразовъ, раг8зовъ[47], и кандикикωв[48], також н҃шихъ р8саковъ Москв8 ихъже множеств ω на каторгахъ[49] поиманы*х*[50], фре*н*гауръ[51], и ур8*ст*ауръ неволниками наричютъ[52]

[1] ERN р8скаго | [2] Е италискомъ R и*т*талиа*н*скомъ | [3] Е склѧвоны R склавоны | [4] R склавы | [5] B ante corr. славековъ | [6] N ad. (или славоновъ) | [7] ER которые | [8] N Иронандовы | [9] ER италиских | [10] Е юншску R юношеску | [11] BN многащи G многащиї R многожды | [12] N люди | [13–13] G ангелъ | [14–14] B ante corr. .г҃. же | [15] N глаголь | [16] B ante corr. в рѣчи G рѣчеим | [17] BGN италиянскиї | [18] ER пиазе | [19] B ante corr. ще | [20] ER слово | [21] ER славаниѧ | [22] R словенескъ N славонекъ | [23] ER разлучиѧ | [24] ER сиѧва | [25] ER сиово | [26] ER люди | [27–27] R сиї | [28] N вмещаютъ | [29] N словакахъ | [30] N слованы | [31] R на | [32] ER скавы | [33] N имянемъ | [34] BGN италияны | [35] N всѣ | [36] EN всякаго | [37] N купленаго | [38] R склявы | [39] BG италияне | [40] N Адрїатицкаго | [41] BG живщиї R живши | [42] B ante corr. лонгобардыї ER лонгабарды | [43] G беспрестанные ER безпрестанныя | [44] ER славоками N словаки | [45] N скѧвоны | [46] BG италиян | [47] ER рагозо*в* | [48] R калдикиковъ N кандикиновъ | [49] BGN катаргах | [50] ER поима*н*ныхъ | [51] R денгау*р* | [52] BGN нарич8*т*

Си́це тогда читателю любезный[1], славаки речени с8ть от славы, и славныхъ дѣл своихъ, понеже ихъ и латинскіе всѣ[2] лѣтописцы славоны и славяны пиш8т, или потом яко н̃не сами себѣ наричютъ[3] словакωв[4] возмогоша то и́мѧ[5] себѣ ‖ да́ть, а́ки бы ре́клъ истиннїи ис'вѣс'тнїи[6], пос'тоя́н'нїи[7] неложнїи в словѣ от слова учтивогω[8], и їстинныхъ[9] обещаней[10], и[11] їзвѣстного[12] речения своегω, понеже то ещё до н̃нешняго дни 8 чехов карватовъ[13], и у насъ поляковъ хранимо есть, я́ко добрым̂ и чесным̂[14] словом обещаютца[15] зап'латить, исполнить[16] и доставить отздѣ слова[17] яко л8тшаг̂[18], а не долг8 или обещанїя 8поминаем'сѧ егоже не исполнить 8 людеи[19] истинно бл̃городныхъ доброт8 и слав8 любящихъ бываетъ великое безчестие[20], яко и́нъ л8т'чи бы ран8 принял[21] нежели слову своем8 не быть г̃диномъ, но н̃не нѣцыи[22] говорить обык'ли[22] или[23] ѧ чех слова[24] держатца[25], отздѣ является[26] яко н̃ши[27] предки слав8 и чес'ть и прав'дивые слова в'сегда любили, того для и толь славное, от славы и от правды ст̃ыѧ имя пол8чиша, яко[28] ихъ н̃не инїи[28] с'лавныхъ славак8, славо́ны[29], ‖ инїи[30] ж словаки[31] наричютъ[32],

Аще тогда от с'лавы, или честных и їс'тинныхъ словъ реченни[33] с8ть славаки и словаки[34], в'се то добро и одна рѣч, понеже мало различїе[35] в первом̂ слогѣ, с'ла́, или с'ло́, ибо и болгары вмѣсто слово[36], гл̃голютъ с'лаво[37], також сербы внегда ком8 что обещают, тако ми Бг̃а на мою вѣр8, на мое с'лаво[38] витежское,

Такожде Иорна́н'дъ п'реж[39] ҂ар̃. лѣт поминая о народѣхъ на́шихъ в повѣсти с'воеи однако ихъ с'ловаками[40], славинами, и славаками нарицаетъ сими словесы, ѧко слава́ки[41] с лѣвой с'тороны сарма́ц'кихъ горъ, которые Бе̑зскидъ, или Татры нарицаем̂ жиша во времена его, а иные над Вис'лою рекою прос'транные осады имѣли, еже раз8мѣет'сѧ о р8саках галицкихъ, острожскихъ, подолских бѣлских, хелмскихъ[42], ‖ л'вовскихъ п'ремыслскихъ[43], которые страны, и н̃не подгорскими[44] наричем̂, для того понеже починаются от го́ръ венгерскихъ, а что пи́шетъ тотъже Иорнандъ а́ко[45] инїи славаки над Вислою во время его в лѣтω ҂дчв. осады имѣли, то раз8мѣется[46] о нашихъ поляках (и́же от широких по́ль и от ловов

---

[1] R любезны | [2] BG вси | [3] BN нарич8т | [4] E славоков̂ R славанов | [5] ER add. в |
[6] ER исвестнїй | [7] E постоѧнїй | [8] BGERN учтиваго | [9] R їистинныхъ | [10] GER обещание |
[11] ER omm. | [12] ERN известнаго | [13] R їарватовъ | [14] ER честным | [15] RN обещаютсѧ |
[16] R їсполнить | [17] ER слава | [18] В лутчшаго G л8тчаго N лучшаго | [19] E люде | [20] G
бесчестие N бещестїе | [21] G принелъ | [22–22] B suprascr. | [23] GN илий̂ | [24] E ad. дер in ras. |
[25] N держатся | [26] ER ѧвлѧетца | [27] G suprascr. | [28–28] N нынѣ ихъ инїи with numbers
above: 2 1 3 | [29] R славаны | [30] ER и ини | [31] ERN славаки | [32] N наричутъ | [33] GE речени
R реченїи | [34] ER славаки | [35] ER разлучиѧ | [36] R слова | [37] ER слово | [38] ER слово |
[39] ER прежде | [40] ER славаками | [41] G словаки | [42] B ante corr. холмских N холмскихъ |
[43] N перемысльскихъ | [44] N подгорским | [45] ER add. и | [46] B раз8мѣетца

которое[1] полеваньем[2] зов8тъ рече́ни с8ть) о помо́рчикахъ, кас8бахъ,
маз8рахъ, чехах, и́же також'де из' р8ского[3] болгарскогѡ[4]
словенского[5] народа и странъ начаша произ'вож'денїя с'вои имѣя с
розными[6] воеводы и с[7] кнѕи ро́з'ню в тѣх землахъ перед тысячью[8] и
нѣсколкѡ сотъ лѣт выбивъ нѣмцовъ поселилис̂, ис тѣхъже болгаров
или волгаровъ[9], от Волги рекѝ московскои, и́нъ народ р8ской
отл8чилсѧ иже[10] в тѣх странахъ, А́же н̅н̅е Волынью нарицаем̂
поселились, а[11] от Волги реки, и от волгаровъ волгинцы[12] з землею ||

7r

своею Волгинем̂ речени с8ть,
Которой[13] народ и н̅н̅е в вои́н'скихъ[14] дѣлехъ яко и п'редковъ их
видим быти славных[15], А́ко[16] с8ть, л8чане, володимерцы,
кремен'чане, грод'ляне, овр8чане, житомиряне, корчане, збара́жане,
и́же потомъ киевскїе подлѧскїе[17], подолскїе, и їные с'мѣж'ные р8скїе
страны народом своимъ напол̅ниша, инїи[18] же в тѣхъ полях (идѣже
н̅н̅е низовые[19] казаки жив8тъ) також[20] над [Д]непром[20] и Доном
реками и в Таврикѣ, идѣже н̅н̅е татары перекоп'скїе остались, а с
ними готты, А́твижи, половцы, печенѣги[21], и їные сарматы[22] др8жб8
яко с побратымами из одного народа ид8чими жили, н̅н̅е остатки
их с8ть над черным̂ морем, меж перекопскою ордою и меж волохъ,
которые наричются бе́зсаравы[23], словенским А́зыком̂ гл̅голющїи, ||

7v

О тѣхъ написа́ Ови́дїи[24] Насон т'ворецъ из'ра́дный, вмѣстѡ
велико̅г[25] дива к римляном̂ егда[26] бѣ в сылке, в Таврике, идѣже н̅н̅е
Кара̀, Крим, и Бѣл̅городъ[27] волоской, и їдѣже очаковъ, каневъ,
черкасы и Киев[28],
Пи́шетъ же си́це о Понтѣ к' Маѯим8[a]

Посредѝ неприѧтель жив8 аѕ увѣчный[29], [30]аки ми[30] с отечествѡм̂
от́атъ есть[31] ми́ръ вѣ́чный[32], їже ядом[33] А́щеричьим[34] маж8тъ
стрѣлы свои[35], дабы к смерти п'ридали, ви́нъ великихъ вдвое, з'дѣ
во́инъ ор8женныи стѣны в'сѣ осади́л̅, б8дто[36] овецъ в' хлевине волкъ
стра́ш'ный[37] оградил, кро́в'ли от с'трѣлъ ежатсѧ, с сторонъ
напе́ренныхъ, и одва здеру́житъ крѣпость воротъ затворе́нныхъ, ||

---

[1] ERN которые | [2] B ante corr. полев{е}ньем | [3] ERN р8скаго | [4] EN бол̅гарскаго | [5] BG
словенского ER словен̅скаго N славенскаго | [6] N разными | [7] ER omm. | [8] BG тысечью
N тысечею | [9] Е волгоро̂в | [10] B ad. в тѣх in ras. | [11] R om. | [12] В волгынцы ante corr.
волынцы GN вол̅гын̅цы Е воглин̅цы R воглицы | [13] R второ́и | [14] Е во̂нискиіхъ | [15] B
славны ante corr. славных N славны | [16] E suprascr. | [17] Е подляш̂скіе R подлямские |
[18] G и инни ER и їниї | [19] BGN низовы | [20-20] N над Днепромъ | [21] BG печинеги | [22] G
со́рматы N серматы | [23] BGN бессаравы | [24] G Овиди | [25] EN великаго | [26] B ante corr.
по{л}егда N гда | [27] B ante corr. Бѣл̅город | [28] ER Киевы | [29] ER увѣчны | [30-30] R акимъ |
[31] B естъ ante corr. есмъ N есмъ ante corr. есвъ | [32] ER вѣчны | [33] G ядам |
[34] В А́щечимъ ante corr. А́зще{з}чимъ G А́зщеρчимъ N язъсчесчимъ ante corr.
язъчесчимъ | [35] B ante corr. сво{е} | [36] R бу́тто | [37] B ante corr. страш{но} R страшны
N страшнїй

[a] G in marg. творение Овидї{и}я Hasona

295

К' том8ж Ма҃зим8,

Или҆ ч҆тѡ савроматы, ѧтвизи свирѣпи[1], творѧтъ и ѿ Таврики[2] люди мно҃г лѣпїи, гдѣ Д8най становится там пове҃рх8 воды, бѣгаютъ скоры҃м конемъ ч҆ре҃з[3] рек8 в заводы, болшая[4] часть людей Риме, тебе[5] не боятсѧ, ни же ор8жїѧ воевъ аузонских страшатся, устремляю҃т ихъ л8ки, и полны саадаки[6], и в далнїе[7] привычны[8] п8ти аргамаки, к том8 привычны[8] тер҆пѣть жаж҆ды и голоды, а неприятель гонѧ ихъ не найде҃т воды,

Тойже[9] в книге .д҃.и

Зриши что ѧтвиженин тол тяжкїе[10] возы, гони҃т с҆ред Д8найских вод надѣа҃с в морозы, зриши ѿтрав8[11] с остры҃м смѣше҆н҆8 желѣском, дабы однимъ смерти[12] вин8 здѣлал[12, 13] потиском[14],

Иная м҆ногаѧ со удивленїемъ писа҆ Овидїи[15] ‖ о сарматѣх, и ди҆в҆ной[16] храбрости готтѡв и гетовъ, и с҆лавакѡв в[17] своих элегїахъ[18] о Пон҆тѣ, и а҆вѣ то показ8е҃т, ѧко н҃ши сарматы, Р8сь, ят҆вижане, волгынцы[19], Лит҆ва, Ж҆мойди, и Москва не были подданны си҆лѣ и владѣнїю римском8 егда глаголетъ,

Болшая[20] часть люде҃и Риме тебе не боятся, и прочаѧ, яко мало что выше сегѡ написас҆,

Писа такожде Ови҆[21] с҆лавенским[22] ѧзыкѡ҃м или҆ р8скимъ стихи, к том8 бо его бл҃гоѧзычїе рѣчи приведе якѡ научишася ея совершенно внегда глаголетъ,

Сие вы҆ зна҆йте геты и вы҆ савроматы[23], изучих҆ся сармацки[24] и[25] гетски[26] глаголати, ‖

О сем҃и Їродо҆тъ[27] в҆ кни҆гѣ .д҃.и с҆видѣтелств8е҃т, а҆ко сарматы наро҆да р8ского[28] и҆же па҆че ми҃сковъ[29] се есть волгаровъ, и паче скиѳовъ татары в то҃ вре́мѧ краснѣйш8ю[30] рѣчь имѣли, в҆ начале вмѣ҆сто дебелые[31] рѣчи красот8 с҆ловъ изобрели ѿздѣ являетсѧ, яко сарма́ты н҃ши различ҆ни были н҆ра́вами[32] и народо҃м и язы́комъ ѿ скиѳов, или҆ тата҃р, аще древнїи повѣстописцы греческїе латинские, всѣ народы пол8ночные[33] и меж҆довосточ҆ные ски҆ѳами и сар҆матами заодно нарицах8, полѧковъ р8сакѡвъ, Литв8 и Москв8 и тата́ръ одинъ наро҃д быти ложно, раз8мѣѧ в к8ю лож приводѧ и҆хъ равное свирѣпїе в воин҆скихъ дѣлехъ, ихъже ѧ҆ко природнаго[34] ремесла воин҆ского[35] безпрестанно[36] училисъ[37], того длѧ и П҆роко́пїи[38] солга҃в си҆це пишетъ

[1] ER свирѣпїи | [2] R Таврикиї | [3] G чере҃з | [4] BGN бо́лша | [5] BGN тебя | [6] B саидаки ante corr. саадаки GN саидаки | [7] ER далине N дальные | [8-8] ER om. | [9] N тоже |
[10] ER тяжкия | [11] BGN ѿраву | [12-12] B ante corr. двѣ вины | [13] ER здѣлати | [14] B ante corr. потаском | [15] ER Овдїи | [16] ER ди҃вно | [17] N om. | [18] E улегиахъ R улегнахъ | [19] B ante corr. волынцы N волгинцы | [20] R олша҆ [space left for initial] | [21] G Овидꙗ ante corr. Ови҆ |
[22] ER словенским | [23] R сав҃рѣматы | [24] BGN са́рмацкий | [25] B in ras. N om. | [26] GN гетскиї | [27] B ad. то҃т in ras. | [28] ERN р8скаго | [29] R ми҃ковъ | [30] N краснѣйшему | [31] ER дѣблые | [32] ER нравом҃ | [33] ER полуношные | [34] G природного | [35] ERN воинскаго |
[36] G беспрестанно | [37] N улилось ante corr. улились | [38] ER Прокопи

о словакахъ[1], склявóны народъ скиѳской во времѧ Иустинïáна[2] нападоша[3] на Иллирикъ[4], и велïѧ беды сотвориша, о чемъ обрѧщеши[5] про͡страннѣе ‖ у Волѧтерана[6] в҆ книге .й.и во Иллѝрикѣ потомъ нескоро осмотрелись во л҆жи своеи повѣстопи͡с҆цы греческïе, яко тоиже Волятера͡н[7] в книге .з҃.и в Сармацыѝ[8] во͡споминаетъ, токмо ж потомъ на[9] тѣ народы с҆лавéн҆скïе[10] сарматами нарицаху, и҆же меж Вис҆лою, Дóномъ, и меж мóре͡м немецким и горами венгерскими[11] жѝша, я҆кѡ поляки, маз8ры, пр҃сы старые, Литв8, Жмойдь[12], Р8сь и Мос҆кв8, тïи же вси[13] [14]о силѣ[14,15] римской нимало ч҆то радѣша, аще Светонïи и[16] Еутропïи пиш8тъ, еже и[17] Меховïи в кни҆ге .а҃.и в главѣ .s҃ı. и Волятера͡н в книзѣ[18] .з҃. вос҆поминае͡т[19], я҆кѡ Домитиáнъ[20] в начале противо[21] им воевà, но[22] к҆равав8[23] побѣд8[24] пол8чѝ, понеже дв8 воевод, Аурелïя[25] Ѳ8ска, и О͡лпия Савина[26] с҆ полками и[27] с҆ воиски великими сар҆мáты нáши 8бѝли, Ан҆тонïи Пïи також, и Антонïи Веръ цесари со инѣми[28] сарматы и с р8сáки у рекѝ Дóна, частые бои имѣх8[29], но с малою ‖ корыс҆тïю[30], с҆ тѣмиж сарматы Вален҆тинïанъ[31], Гален, Маӡиминиян[32], Галïéнъ, Диок҆литïанъ[33], Провъ, Каръ, Др8съ, и[34] инïи цесари[35], и м҆нози воеводы римстïи[36] долго, но[37] во т҆ще воевах8,
П҆рок8л҃а[a] же х҆валится[38], о с҆воем м8жес҆твѣ, ѧко из[39] Сарматïи с҆то девѝцъ поимал, от нихъже в одн8 ночь[40] десять[41] с҆воевалъ, а в҆ пѧтнатцать[42] дней (сколко моглъ гл҃гетъ[43]) всѣ перемоглъ, Помпонïи[44] ж Мелла[45] в кни҆гѣ .г҃.и в главѣ .д҃.и пише͡т, ѧко сармацкïе народы с҆лавенскïе в҆сегда быша с҆вободны и не8кротимы[46], того д҆лѧ и Ав҆г8стъ кесарь обладавый[47] в҆сею в҆селенною[b] вь егож времѧ Хр͡стосъ родисѧ[48] внегда совѣтоваша[49] ему воевать противъ сармáтъ сѝце гл҃голя, ѧ҆ко м҆нѣ не лѣть éс҆ть златою удою рыбы ловѝть, áки бы рé҆лъ не хочю болши потерять нежели сыскáть, ‖ о сем ч҆ти п҆ространнѣе у С҆ветóнïа[50], тоꙗже Ав҆г8стъ кесарь писа к Лент8лю воевоꙁе с҆воем8, да не дерзаетъ дразнить воиною сарматовъ, и҆же и покою не з҆нали, и в силѣ воин҆ской мóч҆ни быша, о семъ Ѳлóръ в книгах .д҃.х

[1] G славаках | [2] BGN Иустинияна | [3] G наподоша | [4] R Идлирикъ | [5] BG обращеши | [6] G Волятерена ER Волятероана | [7] Е Волятера͡н R Волятеряль | [8] N Сармаціи | [9] BGN omm. | [10] ER словен҃ские | [11] Е венгрьскими | [12] R Жмѡд N Жмоидъ | [13] N всѣ | [14–14] N осѣли | [15] R стѣ | [16] G om. R н | [17] ER omm. | [18] RN кнгѣ | [19] BGN воспоминаю͡т | [20] BGERN Домитиян | [21] ER противу | [22] N на | [23] BGN кроваву Е какаву ante corr. кравару R каков8 | [24] R ad. (побѣд8) | [25] N Аумрелïя | [26] B ante corr. Санина | [27] R из | [28] Е иними R иными N йнѣмъ | [29] N имяху | [30] R корыстью | [31] BGN Валентиниян | [32] ER Маӡимиян | [33] B Диоклитиян ante corr. Диоклитиниян GN Диоклитинъ | [34] E om. | [35] G цесариï | [36] R римскиï | [37] N на | [38] R увалится | [39] ER и | [40] R нощь | [41] G десятъ | [42] R пятнцать | [43] G om. | [44] ER Помпиï | [45] N Мельня | [46] G не8кротимыї | [47] ER овладавыї | [48] G ante corr. родиша | [49] ER советоваше | [50] BGN Светония

[a] G in marg. м8жество Прок8л҃а | [b] G in marg. Авг8стъ кесарь

Тамъже пишетъ на концѣ, всѣм̄ на запад и полдень 8мирӣвшим‛ся[1] наро́домъ, в‛негда[2] на запад сл҃нца и на[3] полдень умирӣ Авг8с‛тъ войно́ю в‛сѣ народы пос‛лали к нем8 послѡв ски́ѳы и сар‛маты др8жбы сосѣдственной[4] проса, я́ко свободнїи люди,

В‛ тож в‛рема гепиды п‛рѣд‛ки жмѡидскїя[5] и литовскїе[6] котлокъ медан̄ по обычаю с‛воем8 поганском8 посвященъ вмѣсто поминк8 др8жбы том8же цесарю Авг8с‛т8[7] пос‛лали, о чем Килики́й[8] Кимвръ[9], в произ‛водѣ кимврѡв и С‛ветонїи[10]. ||

А у Ж‛мойди[11] Лот‛вы̀ и 8 к8р‛сѡвъ па́че же у людей поселскихъ[12] и н҃не видим̄ л8чшее[13] быти сокро́вище, котликъ[14] или горшекъ[15] мѣдан̄[a]

Си́це тогда Авг8стъ кесарь силнѣ́ишїй разс8ж‛даше себѣ др8жб8 наших сар҄матовъ, с‛лавⱶн̄[16], то́жде Троⱶн̄ сотворѝ, а́ко внегда да́ковъ и ятвижо̀в[17] побѣдѝ, сарматовъ в др8жб8 себѣ прия, да[18] безопаснѣ́йшїи[18] от их наѣздѡв б8дет, о чем Дион Каси́и в трояне,

Ор8жїе[b] и́хъ бѣ, л8ки, самострѣлы, рогатины долгїе, мечей[19], сабель[20] ск8дос‛ти ра́ди желѣза и р8жа долгѡ не з‛нали, пишетъ бо Па8занїи[21], яко сам̄ видѣ[22] па́н‛сырь сар‛ма́цкїй[23], из рога копытъ лошади́ныхъ по подобию чеш8и змиино̀й 8чиненъ, которо̀и крѣпостию и легкостию[24] не х8жи[25] был̄ греческого[26] (каковы н҃не 8 нас[27]) пан‛цыра[28], ||

Иус‛тинїанъ[29] же .н҃в. цесарь[30] не могѝ ни войною ни др8жбою сарматов с‛мирӣти[31], городы и к‛рѣпости противъ ихъ з‛даше, хотя[32] и́мъ проход до Д8ная заборонить[33] но ихъ и тѡ не 8страши, о сем чти П‛рокопїя о з‛данїахъ И8стиниана[34],

Тѣж сар‛ма́ты на́ши, Аттилю с‛лавногѡ[35] короля̀, и́же стра́хъ[36] в‛селенныя писася на поляхъ каталоницких[37] пѡбиша, в па́мⱶть же толь с‛лавные[38] побѣды, на щитахъ с‛воихъ дв8хъ воиновъ верховыхъ[39] з голыми мечми[40] обыкли было писати, дабы тѣмъ явили м8жество[41] с‛вое воинское, е́же в‛ толикой цѣнѣ 8 нихъ бы́с‛тъ[42], яко Гипократъ в‛ кни́гахъ о возд8сѣ i водѣ[43] пишетъ, а́ко не ток‛мо м8жїе[c] нѡ и жены упражнⱶх8ся[44] войною[45], а ка́ꙗ бы трехъ

[1] N умилившимся | [2] B ante corr. всегда | [3] ER omm. | [4] R сосѣдственнѡ | [5] R жмодския | [6] ERN литовския | [7] N Августа | [8] ER Килики | [9] E Кимвръ | [10] BN add. от | [11] GR Жмоди | [12] U ante corr. посолскихъ ER посо̄лскихъ | [13] ER лутшее | [14] B ante corr. котлитъ | [15] BGERN горшокъ | [16] G словⱶн | [17] R ятвижѡк̄ | [18-18] E дабы зопаснѣишиї R дабы заѡпастнѣйшиї | [19] B ante corr. мечи | [20] B ante corr. сабли | [21] ERN Поузаниї | [22] G видел | [23] N сармоцкїй ante corr. сармацкїй | [24] B ante corr. {го}гостию ER легостию | [25] GRN хуже | [26] ERN грѣческаго | [27] B ante corr. нахъ | [28] ER пансырⱶ | [29] BGN Иустиниян | [30] E цеса́ръ | [31] R смирить | [32] ER хотяху | [33] B ante corr. запоронит | [34] BGERN И8стинияна | [35] ERN славнаго | [36] R сирах | [37] G каталоницкихъ | [38] BGN славныя | [39] ER верховых | [40] ER мечи | [41] G множество | [42] G быть | [43] BGN водах | [44] B ante corr. 8правляхуся | [45] B ante corr. на воинѣ GN воинѣ

[a] B in marg. отстав | [b] G in marg. ор8жие сарматов | [c] G in marg. законъ женамъ

м8жей на войнѣ не 8била, ‖ таковыхъ недос'тойныхъ к с8п'р8жеств8
раз8мѣвах8, и дабы здѣ кроткости, и тоскливом8[1] читателю норовᲛ[2],
[3]и їныхъ[3] цесарей греческихъ римскихъ, такоже[4] .а҃. свидѣтельствъ[5]
о[6] сармацкои войн'ской храбрости ос'тавил, тогда то̀ само дѣло
Მвляетъ, яко подлинно не лѣнью, ни с'панїемъ, то́ль великого[7] и
широкого[8] владѣнїя достигли, от моря ледяного[9] далече за
моско́в'скими с'транами такъже[10] от моря балтїиског[11] еже пр8сы,
лиῴлянты и Свѣю обливаетъ, даже до[12] адриацкого[13] мᲝрᲛ
виницѣйского[14], и даже до Гелеспонта[15] и черного[16] морᲛ, в которой
ок'р8ге н҃не вез'дѣ народ сармᲛц'кїй и словенскїй осады с'вои
[и]мѣютъ[17], подачам Алеѯандра вели́кого̄[18] подтверженные[19] с'
ни́мъже, и с[20] отцомъ[21] его[22] Ѳилипом[23] до р҃жтва Хр҃стова в[24] лѣто

.т҃і. по Иосиῴ8 древнос̄теи еврейских ‖ во[25] владѣнїи вселенныя
работах8, твердятъ же то̀ чехи под'линнω, Მкѡ при Алеѯандре
великомъ предки ихъ бы́ша с'лавнїи, и для с'лавныхъ[26] дѣл̄ от славы
с'лаваки речени[27] с8ть, я́ко и п'ривилїи Алеѯандров в дере́в'неи[28]
с'воей лѣтописи словенским Მзыком̄ писанной[29] 8казываютъ,
карваты ж и бол'гары т'вердятъ, Მкѡ привилїи подлинный[30] на
хартїи Алеѯандровъ с'ловакомъ[31] данъ[32], и з'латы́ми[33] с'лова́ми во
Алеѯандрїи писан, и н҃не в казнѣ т8рскои, его́же[34] в'зᲛ Магметь[35]
ца́рь в'мѣсте с Ц҃ремъградомъ[36], понеже и т8рки не иным̄ народом̄
толь м'ного стра́нъ в'селе́н'ныᲛ[37] овладѣша, ток'мо с'ловéн'ским, из
негоже Მнычан[38] [39]и аджамагланы[39] творᲛт.
Но[40] понéже тѣ наро́ды сармᲛц'кїе[41], болгарскїе, р8скїе, готскїе,
по́лскїе, волы́нскїе, ван'далскїе[42], чéс'кїе от Аѳетова сына Мосоха
8м'ноженные, толь зѣлω ‖ х'ра́б'ры бы́ша, я́ко в'сю Ев'ро́п8, Асїи обѣ
и Аѳрик8 повоева́ша[43], тогда̀ Მзык с'вои природный[44] с'лавéн'скїй[45]
длᲛ раз'нос'ти р8бежей, и чáс'того[46] меж чюжими наро́ды общенїᲛ
помѣшали, Მкѡ еди́нъ народ 8[47] др8гово[48] н҃не едва̀ рѣчь языка
общего[49] выраз8мѣти мо́жетъ, а́ще и от тогож[50] народа сармацкого[51],
и от тогож Მзыка с'ловенского̄[52] от с'мешенїᲛ Მзыков 8 столпа

[1] R тоскловом8 | [2] N наровя | [3-3] N инныхъ | [4] ER такождѣ | [5] N свидѣтельствомъ | [6] ER
а | [7] ERN великаго | [8] ERN широкаго | [9] N ледянаго | [10] N такожъ | [11] BG ба́лтиского
ERN балтїискаго | [12] GER да | [13] G одриацкого ERN адриацкаго | [14] ERN виницеискаго
| [15] B ante corr. Геспонта R Гелесполта | [16] ERN чернаго | [17] BGERN свои имѣют | [18] EN великаго | [19] ER подтверⷤение | [20] BGN со | [21] BGN оⷮцем | [22] GER ево | [23] BGN
Ѳилиппом | [24] ER omm. | [25] R по | [26] B ante corr. славы | [27] R речении | [28] U ante corr.
дъревнеи BGERN древнеи | [29] ER писано | [30] ER подлинниⷩ | [31] ER словаков | [32] G дань
| [33] G ꙁлотыми | [34] ER его | [35] ERN Магметъ | [36] ER Цесаремградомъ | [37] G вселенные |
[38] G янычеⷩ | [39-39] ER наджамаглаⷩы | [40] N om. | [41] Е сармаⷣские R сармадские |
[42] ER вондалские | [43] ER повоева | [44] Е природны | [45] G словенски ER словенскиⷨ
N славанскїй | [46] GERN чаⷭтаго | [47] ER а | [48] ER др8гова | [49] ER обшаго | [50] N того |
[51] EN сармацкаго | [52] BG славенского ERN словеⷩскаго

Вавило́н‘ского¹·ᵃ зачато҇², и о҃т тогожъ колѣноначáл‘ника³ Иаѳета и
Мосоха сына его произ‘вожéнïе⁴ полное имѣю҃т. сего рáди
собственный⁵ языкъ словеⷩскïй с‘тародревнïй является⁶ быти р8скïи
москов‘скïй⁷, понéже та Р8сь ихъже Москвою зовéшⷯ⁸ из‘давна в тѣх
странáхъ пол8нощных⁹ и воꙅточныхъ гдѣ и¹⁰ н҃не поселилиꙅ далѣ не
волочились, того для н‘равовъ и обы́чьⷶ¹¹ и языка древнего¹² не
могли́ из‘менить, ꙗко то инымъ народⷩⷨ иже иꙅ‘¹³ тѣхъ с‘трáнъ
¹⁴московскихъ ‖ вы́ш‘ли п‘рил8чи́лоꙅ̃¹⁴, понеже в‘ различныхъ
с‘транахъ в‘селенныя в¹⁵ воинѣ упраж‘нялися¹⁶, тогó рáди сéр‘бы,
карваты, рáчи, болгары¹⁷, з греки, с веⷩгры, и с‘ т8рки, дол‘маты ж,
карниоляне с‘тириꙗне¹⁸, иꙅ‘трiане¹⁹, иллирики, с вꙩлохи, ш‘ленскïе,
моравяне²⁰, чехи, миꙅ‘сiане²¹, поморяне, каꙅ‘с8вïане²², с нѣм‘цы, Р8сь
бѣлая с‘ Москвою, и с‘ татары, подгоряне, маз8ры подляшане, Р8сь
черная, волынцы, и Литвы часть ²³с‘ поляки²³, а поляки со всѣми
народы н‘равы п‘латье²⁴ и ꙗзыкъ отчастиᵇ природной²⁵ помѣшали,
ꙗко по доꙅ‘тоинꙅ‘тв8 наꙅ обеꙅянами, хамалеóнами в‘сѧ̃къ нарещи
мóжетъ,

Си́це тогда и́маши читателю любезный²⁶ произ‘ведéнïе²⁷ народа
литꙩвского²⁸, ж‘мойдского²⁹, сарматовъ, славѧнъ, Р8сïи³⁰, и³¹ ïных, и
ꙗко сарматы речени с8ть от Асармата³², или́ ‖ Сар‘маты, о неⷤже ч‘ти
бытïя л҃і. гл҃в8, у Иосиѳа древностей ев‘рейскихъ книги а҃. гл҃в8 д҃і. или́
речени с8ть сар‘маты ꙗко скиѳовъ народ татарскїй из‘гнали, и
выбили³³ иꙅ‘ Сар‘мáцыи³⁴, ихъже потꙩⷨ грѣки ꙗко выше сего речесѧ
сил8 ихъ поз‘нáв‘ше вмѣстоꙅ Сармата³⁵ éже от еврейского³⁶
толк8ет‘сѧ высокъ и чéс‘тен, савроматы³⁷ нарещи можах8
прꙩтивнымъ обычаеⷨ от саврос éже от греческаго³⁸ раз8мѣет‘сѧ
ѧщерица и оⷨма, око, се есть народ сь ѧщеричьи очмѝ с‘вирѣпïя
рáди воин‘ского³⁹, славаки ж наричютъ⁴⁰ от славы, и от с‘лавнꙩ̃г⁴¹
воин‘ского⁴² дѣла, или́ с‘лаваки от с‘лóва, ꙗко во иꙅ‘полненïи⁴³ с‘лóва
обещанïѧ усердно постоя́н‘ни⁴⁴ были, н҃не же к самой повести
р8ской⁴⁵ вó имя всѣх вещеⷯ и начала Б҃га п‘рист8паеⷨ̃⁴⁶, ‖

183v

184r

---

¹ ERN Вавилоⷩскаго | ² N зачатаго | ³ ERN колѣнаначаⷧника | ⁴ RN произвождение |
⁵ BG сопственный́ Е собственны N собственной | ⁶ G являⷮтся | ⁷ G московски |
⁸ В зовеⷨ ante corr. зову GN зовемъ | ⁹ BGN полунюшных | ¹⁰ ER omm. | ¹¹ R ꙩбычая |
¹² BGERN древняго | ¹³ ER с | ¹⁴⁻¹⁴ R suprascr. | ¹⁵ B въ ante corr. во | ¹⁶ B ante corr.
8пражнялила | ¹⁷ ER боⷧгоры | ¹⁸ Е стрияне | ¹⁹ G истрияне | ²⁰ GR
моровяне | ²¹ BGER миссияне N мискїяне | ²² G каскувиане ER карсувияане | ²³⁻²³ ER
omm. | ²⁴ ER платья | ²⁵ N приходно | ²⁶ ER любѣзны | ²⁷ G произведения | ²⁸ ERN
литꙩвскаго | ²⁹ ER жмоидьцкаго N жмоидскаго | ³⁰ ER Р8си N Руссїи | ³¹ R om. |
³² N Ассармата | ³³ U ante corr. выбыли | ³⁴ N Сармацïи | ³⁵ ER Сармати | ³⁶ BERN
евреⷩскаго | ³⁷ G совромоты R саврꙩмоты | ³⁸ BG греческого | ³⁹ ERN воиⷩскаго |
⁴⁰ N наричютъ | ⁴¹ ERN славнаго | ⁴² ERN воинскаго | ⁴³ Е иꙅполⷩени | ⁴⁴ Е постоянинѣ
R постояннѣ | ⁴⁵ B suprascr. | ⁴⁶ N приступаеⷮ

ᵃ G in marg. древность языка московскаго | ᵇ E in marg. о платье | ꙅ E in marg. сарматы
толⷧ[...] высокꙩ̃ и честе[...] R in marg. сарматы толкуеⷮся высокъ ж и честенъ

34v Мат'ѳеа[1] С'трїковского[2] Ѳсостóвїча; о бѣлой ї чéр'ной Росиї,
Востóчных, пол8ношных[3], и о[4] пол8денныхъ нарóдѣхъ дрéвнихъ, [5]и
їхъ[5,6] князяхъ велѝконовгородцкихъ[7], изборских пскóвскихъ
белоѡзéрскихъ киев'ских л8цкихъ[8] володимерскихъ[9] волы́нских[10]
гáлиц'кихъ подгор'ских, подолских и їныхъ,
Глава .г҃.

Дрéв'нїй всѣх славенскихъ[11] народовъ источницы[12,a] и отрас'ли
р8ской земли, и їхъ с'лáв'ные родос'лóвия[13] отк8д8 бы, и коея рáди
вины или собства[14], Р8сь имянованы[15] были, различныхъ с8ть
8ченыхъ людей о том мнѣния[16] и произвождения, ибо такожде быша
5r Р8сь греческимъ и латинским повѣсто‖пис'цомъ незнáеми[17], яко и[18]
иные пол8ношные[19] нарóды ихъже в'сѣхъ заодно скиѳами, или
сарматами нарицах8, áще рожоляновъ, и рожановъ имя, еже с' р8сáны
или росаны и Росиею сличает'ся, не бѣ таино древ'нимъ
землепис'цом ибо и П'толомїи всю вселенн8ю опис8я, також
[20]*Стревон повѣстописец ї Плинїй*[20] полагаютъ[21] селения, и
дер'жáвы рожоля́нские в' сармацы́и недалеке от моря или озера
меотийского[22] в' котóрое Дóнъ впадаетъ, идѣже москов'ские, и
белор8ские народы жив8т, и кáневцы белоцерквяне, потивляне[23]
резанцы, чер'ниговцы[24], тиї, рожоляне[25], или рожáне, яко Волѧтеранъ
воспоминает[26]по Стравон8[26], великие[27] воины имѣх8 с
Миѳридатомъ[28] Евпаторомъ силнымъ королемъ Таскою воевóдою
своимъ до Хрста .рп.г҃ гóд8 С'траѳонъ же самъ в' к'нигах землемѣрия
5v с'воегѡ ‖ сед'мыхъ[29] пишетъ си́це[29], о древнихъ р8ских осадахъ,
рожани ж илѝ р8бани[30] 8к'лонѧс к[31] межвосточнымъ и
пол8нощнымъ[32] странам меж Донѡмъ[33] и Д'непромъ реками [34]в поля́х[34]
жив8т.

Мало ж ни́же пишетъ, а н҃не какїе по рожанехъ[35] нарóды жив8тъ не
вѣмы и п'роч, однакож тѡ из'вѣстно я́кѡ рожане[36] пр҃тивъ воевѡд
Миѳридата Еупатора билис҃, сия с8ть с8щїя[37] с'лова̀ Стравоновы.

---

[1] BGRN Матѳѣя Е Матвѣѧ | [2] ERN Стриковскаго, ER add. s | [3] ER полунощныхъ | [4] ER omm. | [5-5] Е ииихъ [sic] | [6] R їных | [7] Е великоновгороцкихъ RN великонов̄городскихъ | [8] N in marg. | [9] N володимирскихъ | [10] B ante corr. волынскои | [11] ER словен̄ских | [12] N истокницы | [13] ERN родославиѧ | [14] ER событва | [15] BGN именованы | [16] GER нѣния | [17] N незнаемы | [18] ER omm. | [19] R полунощные | [20-20] BGN in textu | [21] G пологаютъ | [22] G меотиского ER меотискаго N меотийскаго | [23] BGERN п8тивляне | [24] G черниговъцыи | [25] BG рожоляня | [26-26] ER пестранову | [27] ER великия | [28] Е Миѳридатам | [29-29] BGN сице пишет | [30] N русани | [31] R и N ко | [32] BGN пол8ночным ER полуношным | [33] B ante corr. Домом | [34-34] N suprascr. | [35] R ражанехъ | [36] ER ражане | [37] BGN с8щие

[a] G in marg. о произведенїй р8совъ, или россиянъ

Корнилїи Тацитъ[1] потомъ в҃ лѣтописи[2] с҃вꙏей в книге .з҃і. також древнїи повѣстꙏписецъ идеже опис8етъ временà в҃ладѣнїѧ Оттона[a] Силвїѧ, ѝже ос҃мыи бѣ по Иулїи[3] кесаре сѝце пѝшетъ о роӡолѧнехъ[4], в҃негда гл҃голетъ кн҃зи рим҃стїи по с҃мерти Нероновой Галба, и Оттонъ[5] Силвїи и Вителлїи, ко вн8т҃реннимъ[6] войнамъ мыс҃ли обратиша, Оттои[7] же поставлен кесарь Галб8[8] убѝ, и Вителлїѧ т҃риж҃ды побѝ, тогда роӡолѧне нарόдъ ‖ сармацкїй из҃бивъ два войска[9] рим҃скїе, тѣмъ с҃мѣлѧе с великою надеж҃дою[10] в Мис҃сию[11] идеже н҃не болгары вст8пиша, сие же бысть в лѣтꙏ[12] от созданїѧ мира .ꙁд҃і. по Карионов8 с҃чот8[13] в книге .г҃.и монархїи[14] .д҃.и вѣка .г҃.г҃, а от ос҃нования Рима .ꙏке.г҃[15] от Хрс҃та ж .ꙏв.г҃ однакож еще до рж҃ства Хрс҃това за нѣсколко сотъ лѣтъ по[16] Птоломию, и їнымъ древнейшимъ роӡолѧновъ[17] и роӡановъ, ѝма бѣ[18] с҃лавно, а от того нашествия пос҃лѣднѧго роӡолѧновъ[19] и роӡановъ в Миссию[20], или Болгарїю, и от лѣта .ꙏв. до н҃нешнѧго .ꙁахог.г҃ есть .ꙁах. с҃ лишкомъ лѣтъ,

Но[21] отк8д8 бы роӡолѧне, [22]россанами, и р8саками[22], или Р8сью имѧновани[23] былі тр8дно догадат҃сѧ,

В҃ начале обретаемъ у Езекилѧ пр҃орка в главѣ .л҃и. и .л҃ѳ. поминовенїѧ ‖ кн҃зѧ Росска, Мосоха, Ѳовелѧ, и Тогормы о семъ соглас8ютъ, Евсевїи кесарїйскїи[24], Ѳеодотиόнъ Симмахъ[25], и .б҃. преводниковъ[26] библїи, о чем Иеронимъ ст҃ый[27] помышлѧетъ, аще ли собственное какова народа сие слово рόс҃съ[28] 8 Езехїила[29] являетъ, или нѝ[30], но ꙗко Мосохъ 8 Моисеѧ московскихъ народов колѣноначалника авлѧетъ, також у Иосиѳа древностей в книге[31] .а҃. в главѣ .а҃і. Асар҃мότъ[32] или Сарматъ, являетъ сарматовъ, Асханиꙁ[33] илѝ Твискон[34], нѣмцов, Гомер҃ же ким҃врꙏв, Тогорми, готтꙏв[35], Аванъ еллиновъ[36], и волошан, и проч[37], ꙗко [38]уже о том вы́ше сего[38] достаточно рекохом, тогда то ѝмѧ Рос҃съ[39] 8 Еsекïилѧ[40] пр҃орока близъ с҃личается[41] с прозванїемъ Р8си и [42]розсовъ[43] или[42] р8ссовъ аще то ѝмѧ Рос҃съ[44] не обрѣтается нигдѣ кромѣ библїи 8 Езекïилѧ но ни 8 Виросса ни же у Иѡсиѳа, ‖

[1] BG Тацыт | [2] ER лѣтописиї | [3] BG Июлиї | [4] ER роӡолѧнехъ N роӡолѧнахъ | [5] R Оттонь | [6] G вн8треннымъ | [7] ER Отои N Оттонъ | [8] R Голб8 | [9] ER воина | [10] ER надеждью | [11] BG Мисию Е Мисклю R Мисилю | [12] BGN лѣта | [13] BGN щоту ER сщоту | [14] ER манархиї | [15] Е .ꙏке.г҃ | [16] G о | [17] ER роӡалѧном | [18] G себѣ | [19] ER роӡалѧнов | [20] G Мисию ante corr. Миссию | [21] R ио | [22–22] BG россами | [23] BGN именовани | [24] Е кесарински R кесарїнскии | [25] BGN Сыммах | [26] ER проводников | [27] Е ст҃ы | [28] ER рос | [29] BG Есехïлѧ ERN Езекиïлѧ | [30] BG omm. | [31] B ante corr. книг{и} | [32] ER Асармат | [33] BG Асханисъ | [34] R Твиксонъ | [35] BG тотꙏв R голтꙏв | [36] ER еллиномъ | [37] R прочих | [38–38] N выше уже о томъ сего with numbers above: 3 1 2 4 | [39] BG Р8ссъ ER Россь | [40] Е Езекилиïа R Еsекилия | [41] BG сл8чаетсѧ | [42–42] BG omm. | [43] N россовъ | [44] ER Россь

[a] G in marg. Оттонъ, Га{л}ба, Силвиï и Вителлиï

Ев҆сивїи[1] жъ тѣмъ с҆ло́вѡмъ рос҆съ[2], римлянъ раз8мѣти хо́щетъ, но свѓтый Еронимъ что б тѣмъ ᲊв҆лалосъ не обрѣте, а ри́м҆ляне жꙋ от Рѡм8ла реченныхъ быти[3], и ос҆нованныхъ крѣпко вменᲊ́ютъ, о чемъ пространнее ч҆ти у Волятярена[4] в҆ книгахъ[5] .ᵴ.[6] тажъ Мирсилиᲀ, По́ртиᲀ, Катона[7] и їныхъ, и́же нигдѣже творятъ поминъ п҆роизведенїᲀ Рима от Рос҆са, хотя ихъ тысяча, о томъ различными производы гранятся, производя Римъ от различныхъ ктиторовъ различнѡ быти, и от различныхъ винъ реченный то[8] токмѡ извѣстно ᲀкѡ греки древнїи и нн҃ешнїи, Р8с не Р8сью, но Рос҆сїею зов8тъ и пиш8т, чаять[9] для того ꙗко Р8сь от тогѡ с҆лова[10] рос҆съ[11] у Езекїиля реченн8[12] быть чаютъ[13], еже азъ раз8мныхᲊ людеⷤ разᲊмномᲊ разсᲊж҆денїю[14] в҆рᲊчаю, ||

Д҆лᲊгошъ же и Меховїи в книге .а҃.и в гла҃вѣ .в҃.и в҆ лис҆т8 .в҃.мꙋ лѣтѡпис҆цы нш҃и полскїе пиш8тъ, б8дтѡ[15] р8скїе[16] зем҆ли реченны[17], и 8м҆ножителны[18] быша от Р8с҆са, вн8ка, или ᲀко нѣцыи гл҃голютъ от роднагѡ[19] бра́та Лехова и Чехова, сице Лех, лехицк8ю[20], илѝ лацк8ю, юже нн҃е зовемꙸ полск8ю[21] (от пространныхъ пол, и полеваньа[22], илѝ поленевъ сармацкихъ народовъ реченн8[23]) землю ов҆ладѣлъ и 8множилъ, Чехъ же вторый братъ ческие страны выгнавъ боемъ нѣмцы[24] с҆лавенскимъ[25] народомъ осадилъ, ихъже чехи от тогож Чеха и нн҃е нарицаемъ, потомъ Р8съ[26], илѝ Р8с҆са (егожъ имᲀ однимъ словомъ .у. не согласᲊется со Езекїилемъ[27])[28] Рос҆съ[29] третїи братъ, Леховъ и Чеховъ свойственный[30] нас҆лѣдникъ

Мосоха[a] от Аѳета великїе и про҆страⷩные || народы р8ские в полᲊнощ҆ныхъ[31] и меⷤвосточныхъ с҆транахъ[32], и на полдеⷩ умножи, осади, и от своего имᲀни[33] тѣ земли Рос҆сиею (ᲀко и їные братья евѡ лехи и чехи) именова, Инїи жꙸ от роѕоляновъ[34] народоⷡ сар҆мацкихъ московскихъ, иже с Миѳридатѡ́м[35] королемꙸ поⷩт҆скимъ[36] ратовах8, р8саки роѕоляны[37], и р8ссаны вменяютъ быти речены[38], инїи[39] жъ хотятъ[40] именовать от цвѣта р8са, иже ес҆тъ[41] ѻбще цвѣтъ р8ско́г[42] и[43] пѡдолского[44], ї волынскогѡ[45] народа, тоѓ для нш҃и[46] ихъ нн҃е называюⷮ р8саками[47],

---

[1] В Е8вꙸсѣвиⷮ G Е8всꙸеи N Евсевїⷤ | [2] ER россь | [3] G бытиⷮ | [4] N Волятерана | [5] Е кнг҃их | [6] ER .ᲂ. | [7] ER и Отона | [8] BG omm. | [9] G чаетъ | [10] R слава | [11] В р8сꙸь G р8сꙸъ ERN россь | [12] G реченно | [13] BG чаю | [14] ER разсужденิᲀ | [15] BR б8тто | [16] G р8зские | [17] G реченныⷮ ER речены | [18] GN 8множителныⷮ | [19] N родного | [20] R лехидкую | [21] BG полꙸскою | [22] BG полеваяⷧ ER полеваныᲀ N полеваля | [23] R реченин8 | [24] N немцовъ | [25] ER словеⷩскимъ | [26] GRN Р8сь | [27] BGN Есекиⷤлевымꙸ ER Езекилемꙸ | [28] BGN omm. right parenthesis sign | [29] BG Р8сꙸ N Россъ) | [30] R своиствеⷩны | [31] GEN полᲊношныхъ | [32] BG страⷩ | [33] BGN имени | [34] BGER роѕоляноⷡ | [35] BG Миѳрадатомꙸ | [36] BG полꙸскимъ ER понтискимꙸ | [37] ER роѕоляны | [38] BG речеⷩныⷮ | [39] BG иⷮни | [40] ER хотях8 | [41] В с8ⷮ in ras. G с8ть suprascr. | [42] RN р8скаго | [43] BGN omm. | [44] N подольскаго | [45] N волынскаго | [46] BG нш҃их | [47] Е р8сакаⷨ

[a] G in marg. народы р8ские

се есть р8сы волосы им8щими,

С8ть нѣцыи иже р8ск8ю землю и р8саки от Р8сы города[1] зѣло
предревнягѡ от Новагорода великогѡ[2] на полнок[3] [sic] .з̄. верстъ

лежащаго быти реченных || чаютъ[4], но то йхъ чаание зѣло
неподобнѡ[5], само дѣло являетъ, понеже не домовитъ от своего,
своими р8ками зданного[6] дом8, но домⷮ от домовитого[7] имени бывает
ся речеⷩ, такожъ не городокъ Р8са, хотя и предревнїи, р8скимъ
народоⷨ и́мя дадѐ, но[8] р8саки, городокъ своими р8ками состроили, ї
своимъ именемъ нарекоша, яко же не от реки, ни же от града
Москвы, Москва, но река и граⷣ от народа московскогⷪ[9] имянованы[10]
с8ть, я́ко Кракоⷡ от Крока[11], Римъ от Ром8ла, Антиохия от Антиоха,
Нинивїи от Нина и проⷱ[12] реченныи[13] с8ть от своих здателей, а не
з'датели от тѣх вещеⷨ яже сами создаша, произ'водятъ же нѣцыи
р8сакоⷡ от страны колхиския[14] с'лавныя, [15]в нюже[15] Иасон[16] по
златое р8но ѣздиⷧ, о чем выше сеⷢ в повести Т'рогова̀и И8стиновой
речеся, латинники[17] ж ихъ зов8тъ р8с'сы, р8тены и розоляны[18].
[19]Но Москва ї вси[20] белор8с'цы не п'риемлют тѣх вышепѡмян8тых)[21]

|| народа своего р8ского[22] или росїиского[23] произведеней[24] и
нареченеⷨ, яко правдѣ несоглаⷭных, а твеⷬдятъ то̀, яко Р8с̄ или
р8ские наро́ды издав'на Россиею[25], се есть люди по простран'ным
частеⷨ вселенныя разсияниї речени с8ть, и в тоⷨ произведѐнїи[26]
Москва соглас8ется з греческими древними повѣстописцы, иже
всѣхъ сарматовъ нома́дами[27], сѐ есть с мѣста на мѣсто
преселяющимися[28], и спо́рами се есть разсѣяными[29] наричюⷮ, еже
киⷤждо прилѣ́жно чита́я сⷮтая[30] писания у пр⷟роковъ о́брящетъ, їже
часто словесѐ разсѣянїя [31]8потребляютъ, егда о́ разсѣянїи[31] наро́довъ
гл⷟ютъ;
А р8ские или росїиские[32] наро́ды з'[33] своими словен'скаго[34] язы́ка
жи́телми боⷧш8ю[35] часть Евро́пы и Asїю[36] нѣкоторые[37] страны̀
поча́въ от моря ледено́го[38], даже до моря межзем'ского[39] и
адрїати́цкого[40], идѣже виницейские деⷬжавы, такожде от

лифля́нского[41] пр8ского[42], или || балтиⷭкого[43] и венедїиского[44] мо́ря

---

[1] N гораздо | [2] EN великаго | [3] BGRN полⷩночь | [4] В чаю | [5] ER неподобны |
[6] EN зданнаго | [7] N домовитаго | [8] G на | [9] ERN московⷭкаго | [10] BN именованы G
именовани | [11] BG Крова | [12] R прочиї | [13] BN реченны | [14] BGN колхииⷵкиꙗ | [15–15] BG
вновь ж | [16] BG Иассонъ N Ияссонъ | [17] E латинински R латинский | [18] BG розоляня
R рожаляны | [19] R ad. left parenthesis sign | [20] E всиⷨ N всѣ | [21] BGN omm. right parenthesis
sign | [22] ERN р8скаго | [23] E росискаго RN росⷭсїйскаго | [24] BG произведение |
[25] ER Росиею | [26] ER произведени | [27] R номодами | [28] GER преселяющимъсꙗ |
[29] BGER разсѣянныиⷨ E ante corr. разсѣянныꙗ | [30] ER сⷮтыꙗ | [31–31] N in marg. | [32] ER
росиⷵкⷠ N росⷵсїйскїе | [33] G om. | [34] BG словенского | [35] B ante corr. б{8}лⷨш8ю |
[36] BG Азия | [37] N нѣкоторыꙗ | [38] N леденаго | [39] N межьземскаго | [40] N адрїатицкаго |
[41] E лиⷣлянскаго N лифлянтскаго | [42] N прускаго | [43] E боⷧтиского R бонтиского
N балтⷪйскаго | [44] E венедицкаго R венедицкого N венедⷵйскаго

304

даже до каспїиского[1], поⷩтского[2], егеїскогѡ[3], елеспоⷩтскаго[4] мо́ря насѣяли и наполнилѝ, аще въ иныⷯ[5] мѣстехъ иные наро́ды яко Литва, Лотва ї тата́ры греки ита́лиане[6], и не́мцы меⷤ славянъ[7] по смѣжств8 и различию[8] страⷩ смѣшалиⷭ. но́, отк8д8 ни есть р8ссаки[9], и їные р8ские наро́ды имя и прозвание им8т, о́днако всѝ[10] словеⷩ'ского[11] язы́ка употребляютъ, и всѝ[12] с8ть уⷤ хрⷭтиане[13], о́вїи по чин8 ихъже есть бол'ша́я часть, греческом8 яко Москва́ бѣлая Р8сь болгары бо́сны[14] сербы. о́вїи по риⷨ'ском8 8чению[15], яко поля́ки маз8ры, чехи[16] моравяне, карваты далⷨаты[17], поморчики, шлеⷩ'заки[18], каринты, стириане, раг8шане, и їнныⷯ[19] мно́го наро́довъ славенского[20] р8скогѡ[21] язы́ка употребляющиⷯ; пишеⷮ такожде Дл8гошъ в лѣтѡписи своеⷨ в лист8 .к҃е.м в книгаⷯ ‖ .а҃.ⷯ яко Одона́кръ[a] кн҃зь р8скиⷯ Римъ взя и владѣ имъ, еже и я обрѣⷧ у Волятера́на, в кни́гѣ .в҃.и но[22] того́ кн҃зя нарица́етъ Одоа́къ, малѡ что отⷨѣнивъ, оба́че его не р8скагѡ[23] нарица́етъ, то[24] италиа́нина[25]. и како за по́мочию[26] готовъ[27] Римъ в'зя, и владѣ[28] имъ .д҃і. лѣтъ, в то́мъ Дл8го́шъ с Волятера́номъ п8сть споⷬ чиня́тъ, я[29] в томъ[29, 30] не вда́юсь;

Тѣхъ ж р8саковъ часть перво[31], 8 чеⷬного[32] моря, илѝ на Доⷩ8 и по Волгѣ река́мъ посѣлились, инїи же о чемъ к8пно всѝ[33] лѣтописⷰы р8ские соглас8ютца[34], наⷣ д8на́искими берегами страны овладѣли їдѣже н҃не венгерские и болгаⷬ'ские[35] земли, ихъже тогда норцы или нори́цы нарица́ху потомъ ж иные́ наро́ды р8ские славеⷩ'ские по различнымъ страна́мъ роспростеⷬлись и разсѣялись, иже различными имена́ми оⷮ рѣкъ с'траⷩ ‖ и кн҃зей[36] своихъ разли́чно именовани суть яко волгары или болгары, и волыⷩцы оⷮ Волги, моравяне[37] оⷮ Моравы рекѝ, илѝ оⷮ Мора́та[38] кн҃зя, полочане оⷮ Полоты рекѝ, чехи оⷮ Чеха, поляки оⷮ поⷧь или[39] поля́новъ наро́доⷡ иныⷯ р8скихъ иже в тѣⷯ страна́хъ идѣже н҃не Киевъ, селе́нїя своѝ[40] имѣх8[41], потомъ внегда наⷣ Д8наемъ поселились, изгнали ихъ воло́ши ис тѣⷯ странъ, а инїи ис тогож наро́да наⷣ Вислою реко́ю 8 нѣмцовъ и наⷣ Одрою у сасовъ страны позавлаживали[42] с кн҃земъ

---

[1] ER каспиского N каспїйскаго | [2] N понтскаго | [3] G егескогѡ N егейскаго | [4] BG елеспоⷩдского ER елѣспоⷩтского | [5] BGER ыныⷯ | [6] BG італияне | [7] G словянъ | [8] G различаю E различною R различию | [9] ER р8саки | [10] N всѣ | [11] N словенскаго | [12] N всѣ | [13] BG хрⷭтияне | [14] ER босныї | [15] B ante corr. у{о}ению | [16] BGN чехы | [17] BGRN долⷨаты | [18] R шлеⷧзаки | [19] BGER їныⷯ N ante corr. иныхъ | [20] ER словенского N славенскаго | [21] ERN р8скаго | [22] G на | [23] G руского | [24] BGRN но | [25] BG италиянина | [26] R помощию | [27] BG гоⷮворов R готоⷡ | [28] BG владѣⷧ | [29–29] BG omm. | [30] N то | [31] ER пеⷬвоⷨ | [32] RN чернаго | [33] N всѣ | [34] BGN соглас8ютⷭя | [35] E боⷧгорские | [36] E кн҃зе | [37] BG моровяня | [38] R Морота | [39] ER add. оⷮ | [40] R своя | [41] N имяху | [42] B повлаживалѝ ante corr. пожавлаживалѝ G повлаживали

[a] G in marg. Одонакръ кн҃зь р8скиⷯ

своимъ Лехомъ от негож дѡ ннѣ насъ ляхами а тѹрки лехтами[1]
венгры ленгевами, Литва и Жмоидь[2] лынками Лотва лейсами
наричютъ[3]. а иныхъ нарицахѹ дровканы от дровъ занѣ в лѣсахъ в
гѹстыхъ и порослыхъ рощахъ живяхѹ, ||

Дреговичи[a] же над Двиною быша[4], иніи же над Десною и Сѹлою
рѣками северскими, иніи гдѣ Днепръ и Волга начинается кривичане[b]
речени быша, ихъже бѣ столный[5] град Смоленескъ[6]. такожде сербы
карваты[7] беляне поморчики, и[8] інные[9] славенского[10] языка народы
рѹские, различными прозванми[11] от различныхъ стран и кнзей
речени сѹть, но подлинныхъ повѣстописцовъ имѣти не можемъ даже
до Кия Стѣка, и[12] Корева[13] кнзеи. тотъ Кіи илй Кигъ Стѣкъ и
Коревъ[14] кнзи рѹские братья[15] были родные четвертая ж сестра[c] их
Лебеда илй Лебедь от народа и наслѣдиа[16] Іаѳетова и Мосоха сна
егѡ, и тіи властовати начаша. Кіи или Кигъ старѣйшіи, град Киевъ
от своего имени[17] на рекѣ Днепрѣ постави, идѣже потомъ бѣ
столный град и глава самодержавства[18] рѹского[19]; || вторый братъ
Стѣкъ недалече[d] Киева сострои град на горѣ Стекавицѹ от своего
имени[20]. такожде[e] Коревъ трети брат их Коревицѹ в ѹдѣлномъ
своемъ княжстве[21] ѹстрои егоже потомъ Вышгород[22] звали сестра ж
их Либеда[23,f] на рекѣ Либедѣ[24] селения свои положивъ тамъж
городокъ Либед или Любечь[25] постави на высоком холмѹ,
Тіи кнзи верховнѣйшіи братья[26] родные[27] имѣху иныхъ кнзеи под
своею властию много иже часто ѹ нихъ воеводы быша из[g] нихъ бѣ
первый Радзимъ от негож речени сѹть радимчане, над рекою
Саскою[28] Вяткою[29] от[h] негож вятчане над рекою Волгою и Вяткою,
Дѹлеба от[i] негож дѹлебяне над Бѹгомъ ихъж[j] ннѣ лѹчанами зовемъ,
но тѣ народы рѹские, иже от Родима от Дѹлебы и Вятка
произвождение имѣли || по обычаю звѣринѹ в лѣсах жили, і з
ближними без выборѹ и стыда гдѣ кому полюбилось, совокѹплялись,
о чёмъ кроники руские Длѹгошъ и Мѣховіи в кнгѣ[30] .а. в главѣ .д. в
листѹ .ѕ. пространнѣе свидѣтелствѹют,
Потомъ внегда три брата реченные[31] кнзи рѹские Кіи Стѣкъ[32] и

---

[1] G леттами | [2] N Жмоидъ | [3] N наричутъ | [4] G ad. и | [5] G стольны | [6] N Смоленскъ |
[7] BG калваты | [8] ER omm. | [9] BGER іные | [10] B славенскаго E сьловенскаго ante corr.
соловенскаго R словенского N словенскаго | [11] ER прозванными | [12] G om. |
[13] ER Кореза | [14] BG Коренев | [15] BG братия | [16] BGERN наслѣдия | [17] ER імяни |
[18] ERN самодержства | [19] N рускаго | [20] ER имяни | [21] ER княжествѣ | [22] ER Вышград |
[23] BGN Лебеда | [24] BG Либеди | [25] BG Лебечь | [26] BG братия | [27] GER родныя |
[28] R Сансою | [29] U ante corr. Вятко BGN Вятко | [30] BGN кнгах | [31] ER реченный |
[32] B Скѣк G Щѣкъ

[a] G in marg. дряговичи | [b] G in marg. кривичи | [c] G in marg. Кії | [d] G in marg. Щѣкъ |
[e] G in marg. Хоревъ | [f] G in marg. Лебеда | [g] G in marg. Радзимъ и радзимичи | [h] G in
marg. вятчане | [i] G in marg. Дѹлеба | [j] G in marg. дѹленчяне

306

Коре́въ от жития преста́вились[1], с͠нове и наслѣ́дницы ихъ после ихъ долго кі́иждо на своем 8дѣле с миром властвовал͠і, даже пото́мъ вь ихъ мѣсто Оскалдъ Аскол͠тъ[2] или Осколод, и Дыръ кн͠зи[a] от ихъ же народа наст8пи́ли[3]. инїи[4] ж р8сїане в пол8ношныхъ[5] стра́нахъ простра́н'но над о́зеромъ Илменемъ или И͠лмеръ, егож в ширин8[6] .м̄. вѣ́рстъ а в длин8 .ӟ. вѣ́рстъ, сидѣ́ли, тїи же Новъград вели́кіи[b] на Волхо́вѣ рекѣ, яже н̄не среди́ гра́да идетъ поставили, и Гостомила[7] из[8] посреди́ себя ‖ в кн͠зя избра́ша. толи́ка ж тогда бѣ мо́чь вели́коновгородцковъ[9] и в толи́кои чести и разумѣ́нїи[10] у иностра́н'ныхъ тотъ град вели́кіи Но́въгород[11] бѣ, яко Кран'тїи немец'кіи[12] повѣстописецъ в книгѣ .а̄. в главѣ .а̄. так8ю при́тчю о нихъ воспомина́етъ, хто[13] мо́жетъ или смѣетъ что́ против Б͠га и вели́кого[14] Новаго́рода[15],

Ѡбрѣта́етъ же ся в лѣтописяхъ р8скихъ древ'нихъ яко коссеры (иже каковъ народ бѣ вѣдати не мо́жемъ) нѣкоторыми частьми р8скихъ стран издавна владѣ́ша, и вмѣсто дани і поддан'ства со всякого[16] двора́ белечи кожи́цы выбира́ли, такожде вареги или варяги владѣ́ли ими м'ного, о тѣхъ варегахъ отк8д8[17] бы они бы́ли различна с8ть раз8мѣния, понеже і р8ские лѣтописи кромѣ само͡г ‖ ихъ прозва́ния, далняго[18] о[19] них[20] произведения не творя́т, но понеже Москва, вели́коновгорожане[21]. пско́вичи[22], бал'тїиское[23] мо́ре, еже пр8сы, Свѣю да́т'чанъ, лиѳлянты, Финля́ндию, и часть моско́вскихъ стран обливаетъ варяжское мо́ре нарица́ютъ, тогда видится вѣ́щъ[24] бы́ти явлен'на, яко или свѣиские или дат'цкие[25] и пр8ские кн͠зи для смежства о́бщих р8бежей ими обладах8,

Есть ж Вагриа[26] град издав'на зело славен от вандалит[27] поста́вленъ недалече Лю́бка, на р8бежа́хъ голштѣн'ских[28], от негож балтиіское[29] море, варяжское именованно нѣцыі быти разумѣ́ютъ,

Но[c] понеже вандалиты тогож словѣн'ского[30] язы́ка по разс8ждению нѣкоторых повѣстопи́с'цовъ 8потребляли в тѣ[31] ж времена́ зѣло силни[32] в[33] г͠сдрствах своихъ ‖ воин'скою[34] храбростию бы́ша видная вѣ́щъ[35] бы́ти извѣ́ста[36] яко р8са́ки в то время ис тѣхъ вагровъ, или[37]

---

[1] В прес͡лавилис G прес͡лавились ante corr. преславились | [2] BG Аско͠лдъ | [3] В настопили | [4] ER ини | [5] BGR пол8нощныхъ | [6] N широту | [7] ER Гостоми͡сла | [8] BG и | [9] BGERN великоновгородцов | [10] ER раз8мѣни | [11] ER Новъград | [12] N немецкой | [13] N кто | [14] N великаго | [15] ERN Новаграда | [16] ER всякова N всякаго | [17] В откод8 G отк8ды | [18] ER долняго N дальняго | [19] BG от ER omm. | [20] ER их | [21] BGN add. и Е великоновогорожане | [22] Е псковичиі | [23] BG балтинское | [24] N вещь | [25] ER дацкие | [26] BGER Вагрия | [27] G вадалит | [28] R гонштенскихъ | [29] BG балтинское R болтиіское | [30] EN словенскаго | [31] ER тѣх | [32] BG силны | [33] ER omm. | [34] В ante corr. воинскую | [35] N вещь | [36] G извѣсна ER извѣстно | [37] ER ыли

[a] G in marg. Осколдъ и Диръ | [b] G in marg. Новъградъ и Гостомыслъ | [c] G in marg. варяги или вандалиты

варяго̂в[1] и вандалитовъ от наро́да словен'ска[2] кн҃зей себѣ избїраша[3] и власть имъ над р8скими г҃дрствы вр8чи́ша. внегда бо на Р8си́ на полѣдень лежащей Оскал'дъ и Ды́ръ наслѣдницы Киевы на[4] киевскомъ кн҃жствѣ кн҃жи́ша, наро́ды р8ские простра́н'но в полв8ношных[5] восточныхъ странах розмно́жили̂с[6]. долго ж без стареишихъ владѣтеле́и общими́[7] ненави́стьми возжени вреди́телные[8] задо́ры и[9] войны домовые власти ра́ди и старѣйшин'ства на кн҃зе́и и меж себя всчинал̃і, и то ви́дя Гостомил̃ъ[10] м8ж че́стенъ, бл҃горазуменъ, и вели́кого[11] почте́ниа у новгородцовъ нача и́мъ совѣтовати понеж согласи́тись не могли́ в вы́борѣ кн҃зя из посреди себя для разности чино́въ, дабы̀ посла̃ли || в ва́ряги, и[12] тре́хъ

194r

бра́товъ кн҃зей варяжскихъ ижѐ тогда воин'скою храбро́стию сла́в'ни бы́ша на г҃дрство р8ское вы́брали[13], и призвали,
Сей бл҃горазумный[14] совѣтъ Гос'томило̂в похваля Р8сь послаша тотъча̂с пословъ в варяги и хъ кн҃земъ их, г҃ля просто̀ си́це, г҃дрство и земля н҃ша велика и[15] обилна 8ряд8 ж в немъ нѣтъ, прїиди́те вы̀ г҃дрств8йте и владѣйте на́ми,
То посолство приня́въ три бра́та родны́е[16] кн҃зи[17, a] варяжские[18], Рюрикъ Синаусъ илѝ Сине́въ, и Тривор или Тр8бор идо́ша в Р8сь[19] абие с[20] послами в лѣто от создания ми́ра по р8ском8 счет8[21] .ѕ҃то. еже кажет'ся быти Кромер8, от Хр̃с҃та .ѿ҃за. внегда ж прїидоша к р8скимъ р8бежамъ, с вели́кою охотою от всѣхъ чино́въ *росїиских*[22]

194v

приняны[23] бы́ша || абие же г҃дрство р8ское доброволнѡ волными людми подданое[24] на три части три бра́та кн҃зи меж собою раздѣли́ли[25], Рюрикъ стареишїи кн҃жство вели́кого[26] Новагорода[27] взя в[28] 8дѣлъ столныи же град на островѣ озера ладожского[29] (егоже в ширину .т҃. верстъ[30] а вдоль .ф҃. верстъ пишетъ Герберсте́н[31]) .р҃пе. ве́рстъ от вели́кого[32] Новагорода[33] постави[34],
Сина8съ ж или Сине́въ облада̀ страна́ми р8скими над бѣлымъ озеро́м, егож вдоль и поперѐгъ[35] .ѯ҃. верстъ от Новàгоро́да вели́кого[36], а от Москвы .ф҃. верстъ,
Над тѣмъж озеро́мъ, в негож яко славя́т рѣкъ .т҃ѯ. впа́даетъ, а то́лко одна река Сосна[b] из него выхо́дитъ рече́нныи[37] кн҃зь Синаусъ

---

[1] ER говоря̂в | [2] E слове́нскаго R славе́нскаго | [3] U ante corr. избраша | [4] G над | [5] BG полв8нощных | [6] R розомножоли̂с | [7] N suprascr. | [8] E вредите́лныа | [9] BG omm. | [10] E Гостоѻми̂л R Гостоѻми̂л | [11] EN вели́каго | [12] R из | [13] E выбрани | [14] N благоразумной | [15] ER omm. | [16] B ante corr. р{8}дные | [17] BGN кн҃зя | [18] E воряжские | [19] BG Роѻ | [20] ER omm. | [21] BGN щету | [22] N россїйскихъ | [23] B приня́т̃ї G приняли E прияны R прияты N приняты | [24] BGRN подда́нное | [25] ER розделили | [26] EN вели́каго | [27] ER Новаграда | [28] BGN во | [29] N ладожскаго | [30] R suprascr. | [31] ER Гербесте́н | [32] N вели́каго | [33] ER Новаграда | [34] G поставить ER поставили | [35] E попе́рьхъ | [36] N вели́каго | [37] BG чере́нныи

[a] G in marg. Рюрикъ, Сине8съ и Тр8воръ | [b] BG in marg. Шексна

крѣпос҃ть и град ‖ стол҇ныи постави, идѣже н҃не кн҃зь вели́кїи
моско́в҇скїи н҃нешнїи казны свое҆и болш8ю часть для безопаства[1]
мѣ́ста хра́нити обы́к҇лъ,

Тре́тїи кн҃зь варяжскїи[2] Тр8воръ или Тр8боръ прия кн҃жство
плесковское или҆ пско́в҇ское 8дѣ́лное .р҃п. верстъ от вели́кого[3]
Новагорода[4] градъ ж столныи сотвори в Сворце или҆ въ Избо́рскѣ[5], а
по Мѣ́ховию: в Збо́ркѣ[6], его́же нѣ́когда за промыслом кн҃зя
Алеѯа́ндра полу́бинског[7] взя́ша поля́ки в лѣ́то .҂афѯ҃ѕ. но де́ржать не
8мѣ́ли,

Свидѣ́телств8ют лѣтописи р8ские якѡ тѣ три́[a] бра́та Рюрикъ
Сина́всъ[8] и Тр8во́р[9] кн҃зи преждеречѐннїи[10] произведе́ние наро́да
[11]своего подлинным родосло́вием[11] имѣ́ях8 и҆з велмо́жъ ри́мскихъ
кеса́рскогѡ[12] ро́да, от ни́хъж вели́кие кн҃зи моско́в҇ские і н҃неш҇ние
вели́кие гс҃дри род свои҆ бы́ти ‖ от ри́млянъ тверд́ятъ, еже аще бы

5v

си́це было, тогда тӥи кн҃зи наслѣ́дницы Палемо́новы или҆ П8влїа[13]
Ливо́на ри́мского[14] кн҃зя, или товары́щи[15] и́х бях8, [16]иже в сїя страны̀
полꙋнош҇ные[16, 17], идѣже н҃не Жмоидь[18] лиѳля́нты, илѝ Лотва и
Лит҇ва .с҃.ф. [19] бл҃городных ри́м҇ских и с чатырма[20] ро́ды[21] л8ч҇шими[22]
8рсино́в[23], колю́мновъ кесари́новъ[24] і кита́вров[25], в кораблях[26] чрез
аглинскїи[27] и балтїискїи[28] окиа́нъ[29] тѣснота́ми з8ндскими[30]
земнымъ ди́вным жребием[31] бж҃їмъ приплы[32]

Есть к том8 земли́ца Вара́гия[33] или҆ Верагїа[34] в гс҃дрствѣ[35] саѳо́йского[36]
кн҃зя меж италиа́нскою[37] и ѳранц8зскою[38] землею недале́че
лятобро́нтговъ, и воконте́в, яже тогда бѣ[39] страно́ю римскою і з[40] тои҆
аще тӥи кн҃зи с Палемо́номъ[41] в сия страны̀ пол8нош҇ныя прїидо́ша, ‖

r

тогда вераги́ские[42] или҆ варагские кн҃зи от италиан҇скои[43] отчины
варагїи[44] нарица́х8ся, страну ж лотовскою[45] в то вре́мя Варагїю[46]
именова́ша в неиже (47егда Палемо́нъ[48] в Жмо́йди и в Лит҇вѣ47 со
ины́ми ри́м҇ляны поселися[49]) обла́даша, и с тѣхъже[50] враговъ или҆
вараговъ р8са́ки тѣх тре́хъ кн҃зеи брат́ью помян8тых Рюрика Сина́вса
и Тр8вора[51] на гс҃дрства р8ские прия́ща[52];

---

[1] R безопас҃ства | [2] Е варяжски | [3] N великаго | [4] ER Новаграда | [5] BG Ы҆зборске | [6] BGN Зборске | [7] N полубинскаго | [8] ER Синав | [9] G Тривор | [10] BG преждереченїй | [11–11] BG omm. | [12] N кесарскаго | [13] BGER П8влия | [14] EN римского | [15] EN товарищи | [16–16] N in marg. | [17] BGERN полуношныя | [18] GER Жмодь N Жмоидъ | [19] UG ante corr. .с҃ф. BERN .с҃ф. | [20] BG четырма N четырьмя | [21] B ante corr. род{а} | [22] ER лутчшими | [23] ER 8рсанов | [24] ER кесаранов | [25] B ante corr. китавром | [26] G короблях | [27] BG аглинские | [28] BG балтинский ER болтийский | [29] BG окиян | [30] ER зуискими | [31] G жребиим | [32] BG плиты | [33] ER Варягиа N Варагїа | [34] BGN Верагия | [35] ER гс҃дртво | [36] BGE саѳонского R соѳонского N сафойскаго | [37] BG италиянскою Е италиянскую R їталиа́н҃ского | [38] BGN ѳранц8зскою Е ѳранц8зскою ante corr. ѳранц8зскую R ѳранц8зскую | [39] ER бы | [40] G с | [41] ER Полемономъ | [42] BG верагиские | [43] BG италиянскои | [44] ER вараги | [45] BGERN лотовскую | [46] R Варагиею | [47–47] ER in marg. | [48] ER Полем[онъ] | [49] BG поселяся ER поселилися | [50] Е техъжа | [51] BGN Тр8вара | [52] BGERN прияша

[a] G in marg. отк8да произошли кн҃зьа варѧжские

309

Аще р8саки и лѣтописцы их кто óнй и каковы́ люди бы́ли, варяги
сказать не умѣютъ. поне*же* совершен҅но просто лѣтопись свою
начинаютъ си́це[1] послала *де* Р8̂с к҅ варягомъ[2], *гля* иди́те вы
гсдрств8ите, и владѣйте на́ми, и про*ч*: а винъ и произведенеи[3]
никакихъ не творя*т*, того бо в то время разумъ ихъ не *дюстигъ*,
повѣсть бо вели́кого[4] иск8ства, и различных кни*г* чте́ния и совѣта
употребляе*т*, иже аще хощетъ[5] ю ‖ доводно[6] и изя́щно на свѣтъ[7]
произнесть яко*же* и мы в томъ произведенïи р8ских и литóвских
нарóдовъ долго мы́слили и мозгомъ[8] вертѣли, радѣя истин҅но в
совершéнство вéщъ[9] предприятую[10] привестѝ,
Владств8ющ8[11] ж Рюрик8 на вели́коновгородскомъ[12] княжстве[13] в
Ла́доге, а[14] Тр8вóр8 на п҅сков҅ском въ Избóр*с*ку[15], трéтïи бра́тъ ихъ[a]
Сина8*с*[16] на Бѣлѣозере 8м҅ре бе*з* наслѣдия[17], на *гсдрстве* р8скомъ
бѣлоозе*р*скомъ соверша̀ тóкмо два лѣта, то*г* княжства[18] власть по
нéмъ Тр8во*р* брат *кнзь* псков҅скïи прïя но и[19] той недолго на п8стом
мѣстѣ сѣде, понеже в год по бра́те Синаусе[20] 8мре во П҅скове и та́мъ
по обы́чаю поган҅ском8 на превысóко*и* моги́ле погрéбен.
Рюрикъ ж старѣйшии[21] бра́тъ *кнзь* вели́коновгородскïи[22] после их оба
княжства[23] бѣлоозерское[24] ї пскóвское[25] прïя[b], потомъ *ж* ‖
дворяномъ своимъ и др8зямъ заслуженымъ гра́ды в р8ских земляхъ
роздалъ. одном8 Смолéнескъ[26] инóм8 Пóлоцкъ[27], М8ромъ Бѣлоозеро,
Ростó*в*̂ и пра́чая[28];

Осколод й Ды́ръ наслѣднїцы Кí́евы, *кнзи*[29] р8скихъ земель на
полꙋ*д*нь лежащихъ, и ка́ко Грéкию воеваша[30], и Ц*ря*града добыва́х8,
На Р8сѝ на пол*д*нь лежа́щей на княжствѣ[31] киев҅скомъ Осколод и
Ды́ръ наслѣдницы Киевы, в то время велича́во[c] обладаху тïи собравъ
вели́кое войско р8ское, яко лѣтописцы их свидѣтелств8ютъ[32], в
с8днахъ водяных на кара́блях[33], и на ката*р*гах[34] и в[35] стругах идóша в
Грекию чéрнымъ мóремъ, и обидоша[36] Ц*рь*град греки[d] *ж*, ины́я
пóмочи и надежды ‖ кромѣ *гсда* *Бга* не имѣя, молях8ся непрестан҅но

---

[1] ER omm. | [2] N варягамъ | [3] B ante corr. произведени G произведениï | [4] N великаго |
[5] N хочетъ | [6] ER довол*н*о | [7] ER add. и | [8] ER мозго*в*̂ | [9] N вещь | [10] B ante corr.
предприяти | [11] G владычеств8ющ8 R властьств8ющу | [12] G великоновог*ю*роц*к*юмъ |
[13] ER княжестве | [14] G о | [15] GER Ызборск8 N Исборску | [16] N Синяусъ | [17] B наслѣдïа |
[18] ER княжества | [19] ER omm. | [20] B ante corr. Сива8се N Синяусе | [21] B старѣйшый
G старѣ*и*ши | [22] G великоновогороцкий Е великоновогодцкий R великоно*в*̂городцкиï
N великоновогородской | [23] ER княжества | [24] GER бѣлозе*р*ское | [25] Е пскопское ante
corr. псковское | [26] EN Смоле*н*̂скъ | [27] Е Полоцскъ R Подлонскъ | [28] Е прочьѧ |
[29] ER *кнзеи* | [30] N воевоша | [31] ER княжестве | [32] G свидѣ*л*̂ств8ю*т* | [33] N корабляхъ |
[34] N каторгахъ | [35] N om. | [36] GERN обыдоша

[a] G in marg. смерть Сине8са и Тр8вора | [b] G in marg. раздѣление Р8си боѧрамъ | [c] G in
marg. Осколдъ и Диръ въ Киевѣ | [d] G in marg. ихъ осада на Ц*рь*г*р*дъ

дабы̀ ихъ *от тои* свирѣпои осады р8саковъ свободи́лъ таж[1] патриархъ
Сергíи взявъ *ризу* дѣвы Марíи, яже[2] тамо[3] бѣ, меж про́чими мощ'мѝ
честно блюдо́ма (яко лѣтопись р8ская воспоминаетъ) омочи ю̀ в
мо́ре[4] и абие море восколебася[5, a], яко кораблямъ[6] р8скимъ
разбива́ти*с*, толи́ко, яко Осколод и Дыръ кн͠зи кíев'ские с ма́лыми
людми едва[7] в Киев̄ возврати́шася,
Пото́мъ[b] 8мрѐ Рюри́къ кн͠зь вели́коновг̄ородскíи[8] пско́в'скíи[9] ї
бѣло̀ѡзе*р*скíи[10] с͠на ж Игоря оста́ви, егоже[c] со всѣмъ г͠сдрством
р8скимъ вдаде в соблюдение[11] Олех8[12] нѣкоем8 ближнем8 своем8
иже слы́шав̄[13, d], яко Осколод и Ды́ръ возвратишася в Киев̄ 8терявъ
наряд под Ц꙽̄ремъгородомъ[14], абие[e] в с8днѐ взявъ с собою Игоря
Рюриковича прíи́де в Киевъ Днепромъ рекою || и призва[15] ихъ[16] на
розговоръ прия́тел'скíи[17] Осколо́да[18] и Ди́ра[19] кн͠зеи кíевскихъ їже
ничесогоже[20] неприятелского[21] *от* своихъ не надѣ́ясь, с малыми
людми прíидо́ша в[22] обо*з* Олеховъ и Игоревъ[23] на Днепръ. тамъ
Олехъ показà имъ Игоря г͠ля[d], сей[24] есть наслѣдникъ всѣ*х* княжствъ[25]
р8ских с͠нъ Рюриковъ, а мнѣ ближнíи, и та́ко обоихъ кн͠зеи и[26]
бра́товъ Осколо́да[27] и Ды́ра перед собою повелѐ уби́ти, ї[28] овладѐ
Ки́евомъ, ї всѣми р8скими княжствы[29] к нем8 належащими, и
простра́н'но на восто́къ на по́лночь, и на полдень, г͠сдрство ї
еди́нообладател'ство свое разширѝ многие страны̀ смежные си́лою и
вы́мысломъ к посл8ша́нию своем8 и Їгоревъ8 прин8дивъ,
Сице ж наслѣдие с8щих кн͠зеи р8скихъ кíев'скихъ, ї коре́вичевъ[30] в
Осколодѣ[31] и Дырѣ, внегда их Олехъ об͠ма́номъ изби, || соверши́лось,
а из кн͠зеи варяжскихъ иные кн͠зи *от* Игоря[32] даже до н͠нешняго
вели́кого[33] кн͠зя моско́в'ского[34] но́вы́мъ родос'ло́виемъ зачѐлись,
Идѐ[e] пото́мъ с во́искомъ[35] Олех на древляны со Игоремъ иже бы́ша
такожде народа р8ского[36], и покоривъ их под власть[37] свою̀[38] да́нь на
них положѝ по побѣде ж ра́д8яся[39] в Ки́евѣ повелѐ к себѣ привесть
коня егоже бо́лши[40] всѣ*х* любля́ше[41], призвавъ ж волхво́въ вопросѝ
ихъ, что о то́мъ конѣ чаяли бы, иже[42] пришед[43] реко́ша, якѡ ты

[1] N такъже | [2] ER юже | [3] ER тамъ | [4] BGN мори | [5] ER восколыбася | [6] BGN кара*б*лямъ | [7] N о*т*꙼до́ша | [8] Е великоновгородкии R великоновг̄ороцкии N великоновгородцкой | [9] N псковской | [10] N бѣлоозерской | [11] G соблюдении | [12] ER Ольгу | [13] BGN услыша*в̄* | [14] BGRN Ц꙽̄ремъградомъ | [15] ER призвавъ | [16] ER omm. | [17] R прия́те*л*ски | [18] R Осколда N Осколада | [19] Е Дыра ante corr. Дира R Дыра | [20] G ничесоже | [21] N непрїятельскаго | [22] GER во | [23] BGN Игаревъ | [24] ERN се | [25] EN княжествъ R княжесть | [26] BGN omm. | [27] R Осколда | [28] ER omm. | [29] Е княжа́твы R княжествы | [30] ER коре́вичавъ | [31] R Осколдѣ | [32] G Ыгоря | [33] N великаго | [34] N московскаго | [35] R во*и*скимъ | [36] ERN р8скаго | [37] ER властию | [38] ER своею | [39] Е радуса̀ | [40] N больше | [41] ER любляше N любляши | [42] R они же | [43] G пришедше

[a] G in marg. побѣгъ | [b] G in marg. смерть Рюрика | [c] G in marg. Игорь | [d] G in marg. Олегъ | [e] G in marg. походъ его въ Киевъ | [d] G in marg. Осколдъ и Диръ убиени | [e] G in marg. побѣда надъ древляны

вели́кїи княже о҃т сего конѧ 8мре́ши, того для повелѣ егѡ о҃т себя
отвесть, и особъ[1] храни́ти, ї собравъ болши[2] воі́скъ из р8скихъ земе́ль
иде водяны́м нарядомъ чрез чорное[3] мо́ре в Цр҃ьград, егоже силою
вели́кою достава́ше[a], безпреста́нно мо́ремъ и землею к ба́шням и к‘
стѣнам ‖ приступая и то҃г насилия ц҃рь константинополскі́и[4] не могіи
выде́ржа́ть[5], ї по́мочи на вы́р8чку ниот҃к8д8 не чаялъ[6], 8толи Олеха
вели́кими дары поко́и пок8пая, ї прося дабы о҃т осады[7] о҃тст8пи́лъ.
Олехъ ж8[8] видя́[9] я́ко не можаше града добы́ть, дарми утоле́н сотвори́
помирясь[10] ж с ц҃ремъ гре́ческим, и посовѣтовавъ с ни́мъ, остави там
(яко Р8сь пи́шетъ) скит҃ъ[11] свой, илѝ ге́рбъ с щито́мъ на вѣ́чную
па́мять, ї тот гербъ или́ скит҃ъ[12] меж иными дре́вностьми сим
о́бразомъ, каковъ н҃не г҃дрь моско́вскои употре́бляеть на вратах
галатских[13] противъ Цр҃яграда по дре́внему пи́сан҃[14] зна́те҃н есть;
Потомъ возврати́ся[15] из[16] Царягра́да[17] в Киевъ[17, b] Олех в‘ осе́нь, ї
помяну о конѣ своемъ, о҃т негож҃[18] сме́рть ему волхвы́ принять
предвѣща́ли, повелѣ же его привести́ к‘ себѣ, внегда ж возвѣсти́ша
ем8, яко 8ж 8мре ‖ без него, повелѣ проводи́ти себе х ко́стем его,
ви́дети ихъ, прише́д[19] же на мѣсто идеже лежа́х8 ко́сти, сяде на ни́хъ
а ины́е лѣтописи пи́ш8тъ и Гербестеи́н[20] яко ногою в ло́б 8да́ри г҃ля,
се провеща́ли есте смерть прияти о҃т сего коня[21], онъ ж яко ви́дите
8мре, я[22] бы не хотѣ́л чтоб тож и во҃лхвомъ[23] прил8чи́лос҃, сия ж ему
изре́к‘ш8, а́бие змїя[24] і́зо лба ко́нского[25] вы́скочила ї 8жа́лила его в
ногу и о҃т[26] то҃г 8мре. соверша́с҃ на г҃дрстве киевском, новгоро́дцком[27]
псковском, изборскомъ, ї бѣлоозе́р‘скомъ .лг҃. лѣта, погребе́н на горѣ
Стекавицы[28] по ѡ́бычаю поганско́му,

Игорь[29] Рюри́ковичь вели́кїи кн҃зь и самоде́ржецъ земель ру́ских,
По сме́рти Олехово́и Игор҃[30] Рюрикови́чь нача владѣти в Киевѣ в
вели́комъ Новѣго́роде, во́ Пскове в Бѣлѣозере, и на всѣх кня́жствах и
земляхъ ‖ р8скихъ на западе по́лночь и на по́лдень лежащих, а ещё
при животѣ Охеха[31] [sic] дядки своего поя себѣ в с8пружство[32] Ол҃т8
правн8чку Гостоми́лов8[33] изо П‘скова, на древля́н дань[34] вели́кую ї

196 [199r] (marked as 199r at left)

---

[1] B ante corr. особ8 | [2] N больше | [3] GERN черн҃ое | [4] E косте҃нтинополскиı̈ R
костѧ҃нтинополски N констянтинопольскıй | [5] G возде́ржат | [6] R чаяль | [7] B ante corr.
осад{а} | [8] E жа | [9] G видѣвъ | [10] ER помиряся | [11] G щит҃ ante corr. скит҃ | [12] G сщіт҃ ante
corr. скит҃ | [13] GN галацкихъ | [14] [Phrases untranslated] | [15] E возвратисъ | [16] G ис | [17–17] R
om. | [18] G него | [19] G прише́д‖ше | [20] BG Герберстеинъ | [21] ER add. и | [22] G яко |
[23] R волхвамъ | [24] BGN змїи | [25] RN конскаго | [26] G о | [27] B новгоро́дцком
E новгоро́дцкомъ | [28] N Щекавице | [29] R Игор҃ъ | [30] N Игор҃ъ | [31] BGN Олеха E Олега
ante corr. Охеха R Олега | [32] N супружство | [33] B ante corr. Гостомилова
GE Гостоми҃слов8 | [34] ER omm.

[a] G in marg. ослежание Цар҃яграда | [b] G in marg. вознратъ къ Киев8 | [c] G in marg.
смерть Олега

нестерпимую положи́[a], болши[1] нежели дядка[2] его Олехъ[3], собравъ ж вели́кие во́йска иде мо́ремъ в гре́ческую землю, идѣже Никоми́дию, и Їраклию грады славны[4] осади́, и попали́ и много странъ греческого[5] цр҃я Романа плѣни в Вифинїи[6], и в Понтѣ. велиею же силою к Цр҃юград8[7] ид8щ8 ему[7], имѣющ8 ж пятьнадесять краты тысяч[8] карабле[9] и, і ны́хъ с8довъ водяны х, собрався[10] противъ ево[11] Роман цр҃ь греческі́и с помочью ри́м'скою, и ны́х[12] г҃дре и хр҃стиянских[13], сотворивъ ж ополчение с рускимъ наря́домъ на[b] чо рномъ[14] мо́ри[15], и поби́ вели́кие[16] во́иска ру́ские, яко едва Игорь с тре́тьею частию наряду[17] в Киевъ 8бежа, і потомъ примирися[18] с цр҃ем гре́ческимъ; о томъ побо́ищи Игоровѣ[19], ‖ лѣтопис'цы р8ские не воспомина́ют. но Л8итпрандъ изрядный лѣтописецъ вещей во Евро́пѣ сотвореных[20] пи́шетъ[21] в кн҃гѣ .е. в главѣ .ѕ. пи́ше т[22], яко Ингеръ р8ско и коро́ль сице онъ его называ́етъ хотя рещи Игорь, внегда иде с вели́кимъ наря́домъ к Цр҃юграду, водянымъ боемъ от Романа цр҃я конста́нтинополско г[23] і́збие н бысть і с вели́кимъ 8ро́номъ отогна́нъ бысть от Цря́града,

А Зонаръ[24] греческой повѣстописа́тель, не имяну я кн҃зя Игоря пи́шетъ, яко Р8сь[25] имѣя с собо́ю пятьнадесять краты корабле и[26] Цр҃ьград хотя́х8 взя́ти идѣ ж от грѣкъ зѣло избиени бы́ша яко от толико г[27] числа карабле и[28] мало что их 8бежа̀, тѣм Р8сь от наѣздовъ в греческую землю 8де ржались. Игорь[29] же вели́кіи кн҃зь возврати́в ся из Цр҃яграда в Киевъ, иде противо[30] дре в лян в маломъ числѣ люде и, хотя с них па́ки ‖ побо́ры бра́ть, тог'да дре́в'ляне[31] с кн҃зе м своимъ Нискиниемъ, а по нѣкоторы́мъ[32] Ма́лди том[33] речен'нымъ нача́ша д8мати о тѣхъ побора х, и какъ бы ис[34] толь[35] тяш'ко и нево́ли вы́бится[36], реко́ша же меж себя, внегда волкъ пова́дится[37] во ѡвцы, тогда[c] все ста́до разори т сего ра́ди ви́дя Игоря в маломъ числѣ, 8дариша силно на 8ро́чищи 8 города Корес'те́ня[38], ї уби́ его кн҃зь древлянскі́и[39] Ма́лди тъ[40] или Нискини́я[41]. идѣже и погребенъ в Корестенѣ[42] [43]в могилѣ зѣло высо́кой в лѣто[43] от созда́ния ми́ра .ѕ.у҃ни. по щёт8,

---

[1] N больше | [2] ER дятька | [3] R Ѡлегъ | [4] ER славни | [5] ERN греческаго | [6] RN Виѳанїи | [7–7] G ид8щему | [8] N тысящь | [9] N кораблей | [10] BG собрася | [11] BGN его | [12] В инныхъ | [13] BGRN хр҃стианскихъ | [14] ERN черномъ | [15] N море | [16] ER великия | [17] N ante corr. наряда | [18] R помирися | [19] ERN Їгоревь | [20] BGERN сотворенныхъ | [21] BGN omm. | [22] R om. | [23] ER костянтинополскаго N констянтинопольскаго | [24] N Зокаль | [25] ER р8сы | [26] ER карабле и | [27] BGN толикаго E таликого | [28] G корабле и | [29] R Игоръ | [30] ERN против | [31] N древляны | [32] N нѣкоторомъ | [33] G Мандитѡмъ | [34] BGN из | [35] N столь | [36] GER выбитьца | [37] G повадитца | [38] R Кѡростеня | [39] ER древленскиї | [40] G Мандит | [41] G Ниспиния R Нискния | [42] R Коросте́нѣ N Корестени | [43–43] ER omm.

[a] G in marg. походъ Игоря въ Грецию | [b] G in marg. потеря Игоря | [c] G in marg. бой древлянскаго кн҃за Мандита со Игоремъ и смерть послѣдн҃аго

Како Олга о́том'стѝ на древля́нех сме́рть м8жа своего Игоря,
По[a] 8биенїи от дре́влян, м8жа своего Игоря Рюри́ковича княгиня[1]
Олга с си̅номъ единоро́дным[2] Святославомъ р8ские
вели́конов̅городские[3] и ки́евские гс̅дрства ‖ прия в свое прав'ле́ние,
яже не якѡ жен'скїи по́л слаба̄ы[4], но яко преизряднѣишїи[5] мона́рхъ
8правляше, и со всѣх странъ от наездовъ неприятелских Асадм8[6] и
Кѣлт8 воево́дамъ сродником 8биен'наго м8жа своего 8краин'ные[7]
оборо́ны вручи́въ 8крепи́ла,
Пото́мъ дре́вляне возгорде́вся в' свобо́дѣ пор8гаясь кие́в'ляномъ[8],
яко гс̅дря ихъ убившїи[9], послаша[10] к Олгѣ двадесять[11] чл̅вкъ честных
люде́и наговаривая ю̀ бл̅гоиску́сно, пото́мъ ж грозяще и хотя́ще ю к
тому принудити, да кн̅зю их Нис'ки́нию и по нѣким Ма́лдит8
с8пружств8ет, ихъж она вы́слушавъ повелѣ яму вели́ку во дворѣ
выкопати[12], и всѣхъ тѣхъ пословъ в ню живых вмета́ть. потом[b] же
сама̀ наклони́в'ся над ямою, вопроша́ше их, ка́ко ли тамо
пребыва́ете гс̅да сва́тове, и повелѣ их землею ‖ живых завали́ть, то
сотворивъ, абие гон'ца к дрѣв'ляном посла бл̅года́ря их[13] яко о нѐи[14],
яко о вдовѣ осиротѣв'шеи[15] попече́ние им8тъ, гл̅я яко[16] аз 8же м8жа
моего от ме́ртвых воскреси́ти не мог8, а понеж еще млада кн̅зю
бы̅шем8 в с8пружство не отрица́юся, то́кмо по меня проти́въ моего
чину приш'ли́те люде́и честнѣйшихъ, и в бол'ши́хъ числѣх[17], а не яко
первых, древляне то 8слышавъ с вели́кою радостию посла́ша к Олгѣ
пятьдесять[18] старѣиших бояръ їзбранных, инїи[19] же полагаютъ
четы́редесять[20] ш'тѝ со множеством люде́и,
Иже в Ки́евъ внегда приидо́ша в ладиахъ[21] и в с8дѣхъ различных
рекою Днепром повелѣ княгини[22] Олга им8[23] баню велию
изгото́вити и посла к ни́мъ прося дабы в бане от того тр8да и далне́и
доро́ги попо́тилис̄, ї очистилис̄, пото́мъ же ‖ дабы с посолством к неи
приш'лѝ.
Тїи же том8 бл̅гоприят'ств8[24] ра́ди с8ще идоша в баню, внегда ж
мы́тись и вѣниками, аее ее ох́ъ о́хъ хвостатис̄[25] на́чали[26], повелѣ
баню[27] соломою[28] и хворо̄стом вкру́г о́бвесть, и зажечь, яко всѣм
им, и с рабы своими з'горѣ́тѝ[29]. а Ол̅га абие пословъ своих к
древляном посла с[30] об'вѣ́щением, яко едетъ 8же к ни́мъ хотя бы́ти
с8пр8жницею кн̅зю их, им же же гс̅дрни[31], ток'мѡ дабы̀ 8гото́вали

---

[1] B ante corr. княгини | [2] N единородномъ | [3] ER великоновгородцкие | [4] E слаб{и}и
R слабяй | [5] B преизряднѣйшый | [6] GER Осадму | [7] E 8краиные | [8] ER киявляном |
[9] GN убивши | [10] R пѡ̄ллаша | [11] N двадесятъ | [12] BGN выкопать | [13] BGN имъ | [14] R нѣ |
[15] E осиротѣвшиї | [16] E яка | [17] N чинех | [18] BN пятьдесятъ | [19] G и ї̈ни | [20] B четыресят |
[21] N ладіяхъ | [22] RN кн̅гиня | [23] R ad. (имъ) | [24] E бл̅гоприястсву́и | [25] BGN хвостатца
E хвоста́лис̄ | [26] BGN начели | [27] E банею | [28] E саломою | [29] ER згорѣть N съгорѣти |
[30] ER со | [31] R гс̅дрнею

[a] G in marg. Ѡлга | [b] G in marg. месть Ѡлги

медо́въ доволство[1] к прїѣзд8, еже по обещанию своем8 первом8 м8ж8 Игорю поминовение сот'вори́ти. древляне ж том8 ѡбрадовавшеся[2], яко всѣ княжства р8ские кн҃зю их с толь вели́кою женою подданы[3] б8д8тъ, и тѣмъ над р8саками взаим'но б8д8чи пер'во поддан'ными, гс҃дами бы́ти имѣяху тотчасъ в Хоростинѣ столномъ граде своем мѣды и всякое[4] доволствѡ ‖ на бракъ преслав'ный[5] угото́ваша, Ол҃га же яко обеща́ с киевскою шляхтою, [6]с вой[6] до бо́ю избран'ными[7] на время назначен'ное в Хоростинъ прїиде древляне[8] ж в свѣтлыхъ 8крашенияхъ к неи выѣхавъ, прияша ю с велиею радостию, потомъ ж начаша вопрошати гдѣ первїи[9] и вторїи[10] их послы: она́ же ѡтвеща, якѡ за нею инымъ п8тѣмъ по мал8 ей сокро́вищи ѣд8тъ, мѣстами вѣдомыми яко ѡтчен'ники[11]. 8п'роси́ потомъ 8 них поити[12] на мѣстѡ идѣже м8ж ея первыї Ігорь[13] Рю́рикович кн҃зь погребе́нъ бысть, тамо бо в Хоростинѣ 8били бы́ша его древ'ляне и погребоша.,

Пришед же на могилу нача ѕѣлнѣ пла́кати, [14]сотворивъ же[14] м8ж8 своему поминовение повелѣ на том мѣсте высоком[15] могилу осы́пать, реко́ша же дрѣвляне[16] гс҃жа княги́ни[17] м8жа твоег҃ 8били[18] ес҃мы, бѣ[19] бо немлс҃тивъ, яко волкъ ‖ дираше ов'цы. Ол҃га же закрыв'ся[20] 8таивъ гнѣвъ в срдцы[21] умол'ча́, одѣяв[22] же ся в ри́зы свѣтлы, яко на бракъ нача́ 8гощати дрѣвлянъ, своимъ же всѣмъ бояромъ запрети́ пи́ти мед, внегда ж дрѣвляне упишася абие безвѣстно пѡвелѣ[23] их киев'ляномъ своимъ р8би́ти, м8чити, колоти[24] би́ть. сѣчь, ї[25] 8бивати, убиша ж[26] их тогда .,е҃. сотворивъ же то, и ѡтмстивъ[27] смерть м8жа своего печалну свадбу древляном оста́ви сама ж в Ки́евъ возврати́ся[28], Пото́мъ собра́въ[29] вели́кое во́йско в Ки́евѣ на др8го́е лѣто, подвигн8ся[30] с сн҃омъ своим Святосла́вомъ Игоровичемъ[31] проти́въ дрѣвлян, на8ча́я его дабы и ѡн убиение ѡтца своего ѡтм'сти́лъ[32], побивъ ж ра́ти древлянские, оста́н'ки[33] бѣжа́щих с побоища[34] гоняше даже до Хоростина гра́да[35] столного[36] идѣже множество древлян заперлос҃ бѣ, и то́ю оса́дою целый ‖ год м8ча́ше в Хорос'тинѣ[37] гра́де, ви́дя же яко неудобно[38] бѣ си́лою гра́да в'зяти крѣпости ра́ди есте́ственныя мѣста пред восприя промыслъ твори́ти, и посла к жи́телемъ и ко гражданомъ[39], гл҃я 8же ѡтмстихъ смерть м8жа своег҃, однаков[40] ѡт вас не ѡтст8плю, аще каковы ни есть да́ни не дади́те

---

[1] U ante corr. доволно | [2] ER ѡбрадовавшися | [3] BGN поданы | [4] N всякїе | [5] N преславной | [6-6] ER своим | [7] ER избран҃ними | [8] E древляня | [9] N первыи | [10] N вторыи | [11] ER ѡтченникиї | [12] GR поитти | [13] N om. | [14-14] N сотворивше | [15] E высокам R высоко | [16] N древлено | [17] G кн҃игини ERN княгиня | [18] G убил | [19] N се | [20] BGN add. и | [21] N серцы | [22] G одѣевъ | [23] E повѣли | [24] ER колоть | [25] ER omm. | [26] E жи | [27] R ѡтмстив҃ | [28] G возратися | [29] G собра | [30] BGN подвин8ся R подвигнувся | [31] GERN Ігоревичемъ | [32] N отмстивъ | [33] ER остатки | [34] G бобоища | [35] E города | [36] ERN столнаго | [37] E Горостине | [38] BGN неудѡб | [39] N гражданам | [40] G еднаковъ ante corr. ед{и}наков

ми[1]: не хощ8 же бол'шия[2] да́ни, токмо дади́те[3] ми ннѣ вмѣсто да́ни по три гол8бя, и по три воро́бя, древляне ж бѣднїи[4] с охотою сотвори́ша то. Ол҃га ж гол8бямъ[5] и воробямъ[5] повелѣ в хвосты вплѣта́ть фетиль, с сѣрою и з голо҃вiею[6] зажегъ же головен'ки п8сти ихъ при вѣ́чере, сице ж кïиждо[7] гол8бь и гол8би́ца[8] в домъ свой, а воробеи[9] под застрех8, илѝ под[10] кровли, обы́клые с огнемъ назад из воиска р8ского[11] прилетѣвъ[12] во мно́гих мѣстех град зажглѝ то́тъчасъ, а Ол҃га в то в'ремя к прист8п8 со всѣх странъ с вели́ким окрикомъ[13] и ш8момъ иде, ïдѣже || из зажженнаго[14] гра́да бежащихъ мно́жество дре́влянъ поби́ли, посѣкли, ï потопи́ли, а инїи з' жена́ми и з дѣт'ми погорѣли[15], ины́хъ[16] ж зѣло много в Ки́евъ в нево́лю отвелѝ, а иных[17] яко ско́тъ продавали[18]; сице ж Олга отм'сти҃в смѣрть м8жа своего зна́тно, и добы҃в всѣ иные гра́ды древлян'ские яже того ра́ди стра́ха и промысла неслы́шан'наго[19] и необыклого[20] добровол'нω поддавалис̑[21] возвратися в Киевъ с вели́кою ра́достию с сномъ своимъ Святославомъ црвчемъ[22],

Потомъ[a] в лѣто от создания мира, ҂sу҃з҃г.г҃ иде с вели́кою честию в корабляхъ в Цр҃ьград, ï пришед з двором своимъ р8скихъ[23] бояръ[24] к' греческом8 цр҃ю, Їоан'ну Цимис҃хию, отдаде ему вели́кие дары, иже ю вели́мъ[25] обил'ствомъ в Цр҃ѣградѣ угоща́ше, во время ж доброй[26]

мысли по8ще́нъ || бл҃голѣпиемъ и сла́вою побѣди́телствъ ея, к' том8 простран'ствомъ[27] гс̑дрства р8ского[28], рече еѝ, достойна есѝ княги́ни[29] Олга бы́ть[30] на цр҃ствѣ гре́ческомъ с на́ми в семъ гра́де нн҃емъ[31] Цриг҃ра́дѣ, и наговарива́лъ ю в с8пружство[32], вдовец[33] бо сый[33] жены́ не имя́ше[34], Ол҃га же отвѣща ем8, о цр҃ю, аз есмь[35] язычен'ка, семо ж прïидохъ, да вѣры вашей на8чю́ся[36] хр҃стиян'ской[37], аще же хо́щеши мя взя́ти[b], крестѝ менѐ, тогда наста́ви ю патриархъ[38] цр҃еградской[39] в вѣре[40] хр҃стиан'скои[41], потомъ ж ю со множеством бояръ р8скихъ крести, самъ ж цр҃ь Иоан[42] по проше́нию ея бѣ отц҃ъ крестны́и[43] со ины́ми кн҃зи гре́ческими, даде же имя ей Елена, яко и первои цр҃це своей и бл҃гослови ю патриархъ гл҃гля бл҃гословен'на ты в жена́хъ р8скихъ, ибо [44]8блажа҃т тя[44] снове р8стïи[45] в послѣднемъ родѣ вн8ковъ твои҃х; ||

---

[1] ER omm. | [2] G болшие | [3] ER даите | [4] N бѣдныи | [5-5] B suprascr. | [6] BGEN головнею | [7] GER киждо | [8] GE г8л8бица | [9] ER вороби | [10] G пот | [11] ERN р8скаго | [12] B ante corr. прилетѣвъ | [13] BGN крикомъ | [14] B ante corr. зажженны G саженою ERN зажженнаго | [15] GN add. ï | [16] B иннⷪыхъ | [17] BN инныхъ | [18] N подавили | [19] ER неслыⷳнаго N неслышаннаго | [20] BGN необыклаго | [21] BGN подавалис̑ | [22] E цр҃евнямъ | [23] E р8ским R р8скими | [24] R бояры | [25] ER великим | [26] G добрые | [27] E пространсвомъ | [28] EN р8скаго | [29] N княгиня | [30] E бысть | [31] N нашимъ | [32] R супр8жество | [33-33] R болшиї | [34] R имяше | [35] N есмъ | [36] G на8ч8ся | [37] BGRN хр҃стианской | [38] E патриах | [39] ER цр҃еградцкои | [40] G горе | [41] E християнскои | [42] GER Їоаннъ | [43] E крестны | [44-44] E 8блажатⷶ | [45] E р8сктиї

[a] G in marg. Ѡлга въ Цр҃ѣгрⷣѣ | [b] G in marg. крѣщение Олги съ болⷶры

Потомъ *же* призва ю́ к себѣ ц҃рь по крещенїи к стол8, и речѐ ей, 8бо
аз тя о[1] Еле́но избра́хъ, яко[2] и сама̀ мнѣ обеща́лася еси в жен8 бы́ти
на ц҃рство гре́ческое, Елена ж о*т*вѣща̀ ем8 како имаши мя пояти
крестивъ самъ яко о҃тцъ, и наре́къ[3] мя дще́рь себѣ, понеже в законѣ
хр҃стиа́нском[4], и въ языце*х* вещ[5] есть скверна, и неслы́хана о҃тц8
дще*р* поимати, и рече ц҃рь. прехи́трила мя еси о[6] Еле́но, потом *ж*
даде дары зла́ты, сре*б*ряны, серязи, и ри́зы, шолковы ї златот҄ка*н*ны,
Олга же обеща̀ ему ис Киева прислать воску, кож и людей работных,
иде же к па*т*риарх8 моля бл҃гословения в до́мъ сво́й, г҃ля, с҃нъ мо*и*
Святосла́въ язы́ческъ, да избавитъ мя г҃дь от всякаго[7] зла.
патриа*р*хъ[8] ж речѐ к не*и*, дщи[9] моя вѣрная во Христѣ[10], яко
крести́лася еси и во Хр҃ста облек҄лася еси, той тя изба́витъ, яко*же*
избави пе*р*выї ‖ род Но́евъ в ковчегѣ,[11] Лота *о*т содомлянъ, Моисия[12]
с людми исраил҄тяны от фараона *о*т дом8 работы, Дв҃да от Са8ла,
Данила[13] из челюстей[14] льво́выхъ, трёхъ отрокъ Ана́нию, [15]Аза́риа[16],
Ми́саила[15] *о*т пещи о́гненно*и*, сице ї тебѣ изба́витъ. сия ж рекъ, даде
ей бл҃гослове́ние, и свещён҄ника[17]. Олга же со всѣмъ дворо*м* своимъ
всѣдъ в кораблі̀ возврати́ся[a] бл҃женно в Ки́евъ, о семъ Зонара̀[18]
повѣстописецъ простра́ннω пи́шетъ[19], та Олга или Еле́на пе́р҄вая
бы́сть хр҃стиянкою[20] в҆ Р8си́[21], и мно́гих росиа*н* ко Христ8 обратѝ,
сего ра́ди ю Р8сь 8подобля́етъ сл҃нц8. яко сл҃нце бо мир осия, си́це и
она св҃тымъ креще́ниемъ р8ския наро́ды просвѣтѝ[22]. но с҃на
Святослава никоимъ обы́чаемъ ко креще́нию и к позна́нию
истин҄ного[23] Б҃га привести не можаше, бѣ бо sѣло храбръ и всего себѣ
воинском8 житию вдаде. ‖ сего ради и ма́тери о*т*товаривался, яко
повнегда крести́тися мнѣ, с кѣ*м* ра́товати б8д8[24], и отечество
храни́ти. сице ж велия храбрости, и[25] искуства[b] воинскаго[26] бѣ
преждеречён҄ный Святославъ, яко внегда лѣтъ свои*х* достигн8ти ем8
всегда в по́ле с воинствомъ своимъ жи́ти никакихъ помѣшекъ[27], и
напрасных снаря́довъ в во́йске своемъ не поп8сти во́зити, такъ*ж*[28] ни
котловъ никакова с8дна повареннаго[29] единъ от[30] воевъ[31] его[30] не[32]
ймяше[33] мясо токмо[34] вя́лое и хлѣ*б* с8хо́й[35] самъ во[36] всѣми всегда
яда́лъ, шатровъ и самъ не зна́л, кромѣ шалаша̀ и епанчі̀ на голо*и*

[1] ER omm. | [2] Е яка | [3] ER нареклъ | [4] Е хр҃стиянском | [5] GN вещь | [6] ER omm. | [7] BGR
всякого | [8] Е патриах | [9] G дши | [10] ER Хр҃ста | [11] [Phrase untranslated] | [12] GER Моисея |
[13] R Даниїла | [14] Е чюлюсте*и* | [15–15] ER Мисаилу Азария | [16] B ante corr. Азарию |
[17] N священника | [18] G Зонора Е ad. д{и}*чер* R ad. чедаръ | [19] N in marg. | [20] GRN
хр҃стиянкою Е християнском | [21] G Р8сиї | [22] N посвѣти | [23] GERN истиннаго | [24] U ante
corr. б8д8тъ G бѣд8 | [25] R om. | [26] Е воинискаго R воинского | [27] ER помѣшакъ |
[28] BGN та*же* | [29] N повареннаго | [30–30] G своего | [31] Е евоевъ N во*и*его | [32] ER omm. |
[33] G имяше | [34] N только | [35] N сухъ | [36] BGERN со

[a] G in marg. возвращение Олги въ Киевъ | [b] G in marg. карахтеръ Свѧтослава с҃на
Игореви и Олги

землѣ[1] под небомъ сиживалъ, такъж[2] сѣдло или а*р*чакъ[3] в головы положа, сы́палъ[4], сы́и мона*р*хъ[5] всѣхъ зе́мель р8скихъ сего ради *сластолюби́вых*[6] гре́ковъ удо́бно одолѣва*л* и г*с̃*дрства их би́ралъ; ||

Святославъ Игоровичь[7] вели́кïи к*н̃*зь илѝ *ц̃*рь кïев'скïи переяславскïи[8] и[9] ïныхъ. самодержецъ всеа Р8сïи в лѣто[10] .҂sу҃з̃г.г̃
Свято*с*лавъ Игоровичь[11] вн8къ Рюри́ковъ внегда́[a] ем8 ма́ти О*л*га во креще́нïи Елена всѣ княжства[12] р8ские кïев'ские вели́коновгородцкие[13] псков'ские[14] белоозерские, и ïные[15] во владѣнïе[16] соверше*н*но даде, собравъ[17] вели́кие ра́ти с[18] своих земель в начале жъ на козары, илѝ[19] кос'серы люди наро́да р8ского[20] иже испод владѣния его выбивались[21], ѝде и добылъ град ихъ[22] столный Белавесь[23] речен'ный, а[24] сама́хъ козаровъ[b] с к*н̃*зем их побѣди́въ к посл8ша́нию приведе, и дань на нихъ положѝ, о семъ Дл8гош и Мѣхо́вïи в книге .в̃. в главѣ .г̃. в листу .к҃д.*м* свидѣтелствую*т*[25], ||

потомъ по лѣтописямъ р8ским и по*л*ским, собравъ вели́кие ра́ти иде на бо*л*гары даже за Д8на́и, ихъж многащи[26] побѣди́въ взя о*т* нихъ .п̃. градовъ над Д8наемъ, и[27] с'воими р8саками осади́въ в Переяславлѣ[28] столный град г*с̃*дрствъ своих постави, *м̃*три ж своей О*л*гѣ и ве*л*мо́жамъ своимъ д8мнымъ кïе*в*ским возвести г*л̃*я, яко в Переясла*в*ли[29] возлюблен'ныи мой стол'ный град, посредѣ[30] *ц̃*рствъ моихъ, понеже сюды мнѣ *и*з греческо*и* земли приво́зятъ зла́то, сребро драгие вѣщи, ви́на и[31] различные ово́щи, *и*з венгеръ[32] такожде зла́то сребро́[ω] и кони добрые, с Р8си ко́жи[33] меды[34] во́скъ и людей работныхъ,
И*с*[35]в' то[35] вре́мя печенѣги ис тѣхъ стра*н*, идѣже Литва, *о*т го́товъ[36], ятвижовъ половцовъ, и алянов[37] смѣшена[38] прïи||до́ша под Кïевъ, и

осади́ша град, во граде же кïев'ском запер'лась была[39] Олга сь Ярополком[40] Оле́хомъ[41] и со Влади́меромъ[42] трема[43] вн8ками[44], с*н̃*ами Святославовыми[45], к нем8жъ Олга посла скор8ю по́мочь г*л̃*гля, ты чюжихъ земе*л* взыскиваешь, а меня матерь твою и с[46] с*н̃*ами твоими печенеги[47] мало не взялѝ, понеже отошли было[48] яко

---

[1] BGN земли | [2] E такжа | [3] G о*р*чакъ | [4] ER спалъ | [5] R ad. ï | [6] GN in textu ER сластолюбимыхъ in textu | [7] ERN Игоревичь | [8] E перьясло́вскïй N om. | [9] E om. | [10] R лѣта | [11] ER Игоревичь | [12] ER княжества | [13] BGN великонов*г*ородскïе E великоновогородцкие | [14] B suprascr. | [15] BN инные | [16] N владѣнïи | [17] BGN собра | [18] ER omm. | [19] ER add. на | [20] ERN р8скаго | [21] E выбивались | [22] G om. | [23] ER Белавесъ | [24] E о | [25] G свидѣтелств8етъ | [26] E многощи R многожды | [27] R из | [28] GE Переясловле | [29] G Переясловли | [30] ER посреди | [31] ER omm. | [32] E венгръ | [33] E кожа | [34] G миды | [35–35] ER во | [36] ER готтовъ | [37] N ялянов | [38] BGN смѣшенна | [39] R было | [40] G Ярапо*л*комъ | [41] ER Олеховымъ | [42] ER Владимиром | [43] GER тремя | [44] R ad. с | [45] E Святославивыми | [46] G з E om. | [47] BG печиниги N печениги | [48] G бы

[a] G in marg. Свꙗтославъ владѣетъ | [b] G in marg. Свꙗтославъ воюетъ | [c] G in marg. ѡсада Кïева *о*т печенегъ

Мѣхо́виї[1] пи́шет, 8слышевъ[2] вѣсти от руских язы́ковъ будто[3] на них Святосла́въ[4] с[5] великимъ во́йском идетъ, но лѣтопись[6] р8ская свидѣтелств8ет, яко Святосла́въ скóрω прїиде ис Переясловля[7] с воин'ствомъ сво́имъ разгна[8] и поби пе ченѣги, обаче же мати его з боляры[9] прилѣжно жела́ше, чтоб жилъ в Ки́евѣ он же не восхотѣ в Ки́еве жити. и егдаже Святославъ в Переясловль[10] возвращашеся, глагола[11] ем8 мати его Ол'га, сн8 мой[a] любезный[12], аз 8же 8мру гдѣже мене вос'хощеши да погребеши[13] (аки вѣдая смерть свою)[13] в третїи || день умре и погребена в Ки́еве, кости ж ея вн8къ Владимеръ[14] крестив'ся, и в мѣста[15] стыя подя, и межд8 стыя причтена от костянтинопол̄ского[16] патриа рха, день ж ея празнуем[17] мсца июля .аї.г̄ дня,

розд̄лъ[18] снов̄ъ Святославовыхъ[19] Святославъ же по смерти м̄тре[20] своея Олги или Елены раздели княжения р8ския трем сном своимъ[21] Ерополку Киевъ, Олг8 или Олеху древляны з грады Хоростином, и Переясловлемъ[22], Владимир8[23] великїи Новъгород, понеже новгородцы по совѣт8 нѣкия жены Добрыни, Владимера в князя[24] себѣ умолиша, бѣ же в Новѣграде[25] гость нѣкто великїи, прозваниемъ Калюща Малецъ[26] имѣя[b] же 8 себѣ[27] двѣ дщери имя единой[28] Доброня и другои Малюска, Малюска ж бѣ 8 княгини Олги ключницею[29], от нея же[30] Святославъ имѣ Владимера[31], || И тако Святославъ сны 8строя и раздели[32] им княжства,

Святос'лавъ па́ки на болгары[33], сам ж в покое не возможе пребыва тї паки иде на болгары[34], и шед над чермным[35] морем чрез Даки́ю, или волоскую[36] зем'лю, чрез Д8наи преиде[37], и град славный болгарскїи Переясловль[38] речен'ныи[39] велїимъ[40] прист8помъ взя и овладѣ, потомъ Василию и Костян'тину[41] кесарем гречес'кимъ воин8 предвозвести[42], в лѣто от Хрста гсда .цов. по счет8[43] Меховиову и Дл8гошев8[44]. *Святослав в[45] грецкую[46] землю,* ї прииде во греки[47] с войскомъ р8скимъ. кесари же гречестїи Василїи и Костян'тинъ послаша к нем8 послы моля примирения и ти́шины, и колико[48] во иска имяше[49], вѣдати от него желаше, обещевая дань дати на

---

[1] ER Мехови | [2] BGERN услышав̄ | [3] GER б8тто | [4] G Свято̄славъ | [5] R om. | [6] R лѣтописецъ | [7] GRN Переяс̄лавля | [8] R разогна | [9] E баляры | [10] GN Переяславль ER Переясло̄в | [11] N глаголя | [12] N любезной | [13–13] G om. parentheses signs | [14] R Владие р | [15] UB ante corr. мѣсто | [16] E костянтинапол̄скаго N константинопольскаго | [17] R празднуемъ | [18] E розделил̄ R раздели | [19] BN add. їли Олех8 E Святослов[о]выхъ | [20] GERN м̄три | [21] G своему ante corr. своим | [22] RN Переяс̄лавлемъ | [23] E Владимер8 | [24] R кн̄зи | [25] BGN Новѣгороде | [26] R Маледъ | [27] GN себя | [28] N единою | [29] B ante corr. клюцницею | [30] G неиже | [31] R Владимира | [32] G роздели | [33] E болгоры | [34] E бо̄лгоры | [35] ERN чер̄нымъ | [36] ER воложскую | [37] E преïдеи | [38] ER Переясло̄в N Переяславль | [39] E реченны | [40] G великимъ | [41] RN Кон̄стян̄тин8 | [42] E предвосвести | [43] ERN щету | [44] N Длугошову | [45] ER omm. | [46] G греческую | [47] E грекиї | [48] N колика | [49] BGN имяше

[a] G in marg. смерть Олги | [b] G in marg. гость Калюща

всякого[1] р8ского[2] чл҃вка, егда же увѣдав'ше число войнства егѡ[3], [4]*вымыслъ[5] грече скїи противо росиян[6] лукав[7]*[4] вскоре воя свои греческие[8] собравше, и противо Святослава ведоша, ї внегда обои[9] воиска прот҃ив себя сташа, Р8сь же видя множес'тво греков пристраш'ни бы҃ша, Святослав же видѣ[10] войско свое в боязни, рѐче, *рѣчь[11] Святославова к воинству* не виж8 мѣста, кое бы нас здѣ безопас'но от неприятелеи скрыти мог ло[12], || земли ж и с'лавы р8ские в р8ки неприя́тел'ские пода́ти никогда сего в мысли своеи не имѣлъ ес'мь[13], но противо неприятелеи м8жествен'но воюя[14] или смерть славн8ю приѝмемъ, илй безсмертныя[15] славы себѣ докажемъ[16], аще преслав'нѡ и м8жествен'но воюя 8мр8[17], имени своем8 [18]вѣчныя славы[18] засл8ж8[19], егда ж побѣж8[20] вѣчн8ю срамот8 и понос восприм8[21], а м'ножествомъ неприятелеи мя о бшедшимъ не подобаетъ мнѣ бѣжати и 8ити невозможно, но м8жес'т'вен'но про́тивъ[22] ихъ б8д8 стояти, и глав8 за отечество свое напред всѣмъ[23] на страхование полож8. *о семъ чтй Гербестейна[24]* сию Святославов8 рѣчь Гербестеин[25] во описанїи старог[26] лѣтописца москов'ского[27] на лист8 .е҃.м описует воини ж и все воинство р8ское, [28](перво испужав ся)[28] глаголаниемъ кн҃зя своего яко прибытием[29]

новые помощи опо л чени[30], тотчас единогласно возопиша, *охо́та русаков* рекше гдѣ глава твоя ц҃рская тамо и н҃ши да б8д8тъ[31], [32]8твер див же[32] тогда воинствѡ || иде с вели́кою[33] ско́ростию и 8дари жестоко напротивъ стоящее воин'ство греческое, [34]разо рвав же[34] и розбивъ вели́кимъ нашествием полки 8строенные[35] ихъ, и тако побѣд8 во зприяша[36], *побѣда росиян[37] над[38] греки* бежащихъ ж греков побивали, сѣкли иныхъ[39] поем'ше живых, потомъ Святославъ употребляя побѣды греческия[40] стра́ны, разорял[41] и п8стошилъ, и егда Святослава инїи кн҃зи 8молях8 дары, прося покоя, златом и пана́докми[42] бисерев[43] [44](яко р8ские лѣтописцы имян8ютъ,)[44] не восхотѣ приѝмати, и гн8шаясь ими, токмѡ от грековъ одежды, ор8жия[45] збр8и щиты, мечи присланные[46] прием'ля;

[1] N всякаго | [2] N рускаго | [3] E ad. вскоре in marg. R ad. вскѡре | [4–4] ER in textu |
[5] ER вымыслих | [6] BG россиян ER росиан | [7] ER лука | [8] G греческия | [9] ER оба |
[10] GER видя | [11] ER русь | [12] ER мочно | [13] B есмъ GR есть | [14] B ante corr. вою{емъ} |
[15] GE бесмертныя N безсмертные | [16] E да окажемъ R дакажемъ | [17] E 8мрем R 8мре |
[18–18] BGN славы вѣчныя | [19] R засл҃ѣж8 | [20] E побѣг8 ante corr. побѣж8 | [21] BN восприм8
| [22] ER против8 | [23] N свѣмъ | [24] BGN Гербер стеина ER Гербъстеина | [25] BN
Гербер стеинъ E Гербъстеинъ R Гербостеин҃ъ | [26] ERN стараго | [27] ERN москов҃скаго |
[28–28] G om. parentheses signs | [29] G пребытием | [30] G ѡпо л чении N ополчены | [31] E б8тут |
[32–32] ER 8твер дивше | [33] BG велиею | [34–34] N разорвавше | [35] R устроенныя |
[36] GR восприяша | [37] B россиян G россианъ E рисс[...] R росиан | [38] G на | [39] N in marg. |
[40] G греческие | [41] ER разорил | [42] GER понадокми | [43] BGN висеров | [44–44] G om.
parentheses signs | [45] N орижїя | [46] G прис ланые ER присланныя

симъ[1] Святославъ греки себѣ приклони, Сицевою[2] храбростию велиею и мꙋжествомъ его греческие народы возбꙋждены[3] пришедше ко кесаремъ своимъ и ко кнꙗземъ глаголаша[4], и мы желаемъ и хощемъ быти под[5] такимъ цремъ иже не злато но орꙋжия взяти любитъ. Святославꙋ ж с воин'ствомъ[6] ‖ х Костянтинополю[7] приближающꙋся, *Святослав на Црегороде велие дани взявъ отиде,* [8]греки от него искꙋповахꙋся данию[8] велиею и от греческихъ границъ его отвратиша[9], яко болши[10] ихъ не воевати емꙋ, ї возвратися с вѣликими стадами велбꙋдовъ отяхченныхъ[11] златомъ ї с велики́ми сокровищи в болгары. сего Святослава Занаꙗрь древнїи лѣтописатель[12] в книгах ҃г.х Святослаба[13] нарица́етъ. возвращая[14] же ся с велики́ми добычи к Переясловлю[15] рꙋскомꙋ, и х Ки́евꙋ; зашедше емꙋ в пꙋть печенѣги на зломъ мѣсте, и к бою непристоиномъ, Святослав̄ же бися с ними и пораженъ, взятъ бѣ[16] печенежским кнꙗземъ Кꙋромъ или Кꙋресом речен'нымъ, *Святослава побили и главу ему отсѣкли печенѣги[17]* кнꙗз же[18] повелѣ[19] емꙋ главꙋ[19] отсещи, и їз черепа главы его повелѣ чаши сотвори́ти[20] ї златомъ обложи́ти, ї сотвори на нем надписание[21] таково, чꙋжаго[22] искꙋи[23] свое погꙋбляетъ, и всегда бл҃гия мы́сли[24] Кꙋрес̄ ис тои чаши пияше, обновляя слав̄ꙋ своея побѣды и памяти, ‖

О тѣхъ печенегахъ ихъже Занаръ грекъ зоветъ пацы́н'никами[25], Вапонїи[26] ж пев̄цы́нами[27] каковы люди были обрящеши[28] об них в произведенїи половцов̄, ї ятвигов̄ побратимовъ литов'ских, ихъж во оные времена всякими прозванїи нарицаху. а той князь Кꙋрес̄ бѣ литвинъ, яко имя его являет,

О убие́них[29] [30]дрꙋг̄ дрꙋга[30] бра́тїи[31], сновъ С'вꙗтосла́вовыхъ; По смер'ти С'вꙗтосла́ва Рюриковича[32], самоде́ржца рꙋского[33], снове[34] его̀, трѝ, хотя гора́здо[35] и їзрядно[36, a] при живо́тѣ отꙐцове, к'няженïи рꙋскими раздѣлены[37] бѣхꙋ[38]. но не возмогоша междꙋ собою в ти́шинѣ жи́ти. в нача́лѣ первыи дꙋмныи[39] Свято̄славов̄ боѧринъ

---

[1] N самъ | [2] Е сицовою | [3] ER возбꙋжденны | [4] GN гл҃голаше R глаша | [5] G пот |
[6] G воиском | [7] ER Костянтинꙋполю N Константинополю | [8-8] N suprascr. | [9] E ante corr. отвратися | [10] N больше | [11] BGERN отягченныхъ | [12] G лѣтописецъ | [13] GR Святославаъ |
[14] R воздращая | [15] B ante corr. Преясловлю GN Переяславлю | [16] G ad. c |
[17] G печенегскии кн҃зь Кꙋромъ | [18] G om. | [19–19] BG главу ему | [20] N оттворити |
[21] R подписание N надписанные | [22] EN чюжаго R чюжажого | [23] N ищаи | [24] B ante corr. мосли G могли | [25] N пацыинниками | [26] G Вопонїи Е Вапоини R Вапонни N въ апонїи | [27] U ante corr. п{о}в̄цынами ER пов̄цынами | [28] BG обращеши | [29] ER убиенїи |
[30–30] B suprascr. ER дрꙋгаго | [31] ER брата | [32] G Игоревича ante corr. Рюриковича [correction made in hand G6] | [33] ERN рꙋскаго | [34] G сыновеи | [35] N in marg. | [36] Е їзрадно |
[37] ER раздѣлѣнныхъ | [38] G бяхꙋ | [39] Е дꙋмны ante corr. дꙋрны

[a] G in marg. Ярополкъ

именем[1] Свадолтъ[2], *Свадолтъ вторыї[3] Ахитоѳел[4],* приѣха$\widehat{в}$ в Кі́евъ
кь Ярополк8 к$\overline{н}$зю кі́ев'ском8 болшом$у$ о$т$ бра́тіи, нача ем8
совѣто́вати да изгонитъ о$т$ княжения древлян'ско$г$[5] и
переясло$в$||ского[6] бра́та с'воего Олеха, рняся ем8 яко $\overline{с}$на его[a]
речен'наго Лют8[7] Оле$х$ 8би[8] на лова$х$,
Сице ж Еропо́лкъ по со́вѣт8 Сва́дол'тов8[9] по8щенъ подя войн8 на
бра́та, и[10] вой его дре́в'лян'ские побй, Оле$х$ же 8ше$д$ з бою [11](по
Мѣ́ховию)[11] множес'тва ради народа бежащи$х$ с того$ж$ бою, *сего
града Ге$р$бестеин[12] и кроника кі́евская не означили ток'мо Дл8го$ш$
и Мехо́вїи и кроники нѣ́которые руские,* не возможе вгнести$\widehat{с}$ во[13]
град[14] свой Варяж. но о$т$ войскъ Яропол'ковы$х$[15] прис'т8па́ющих ко
граду с высо́кого[16] мо́ст8 свер'женъ и межд8 м'ножества[17] людей
н8жно 8мрѐ в лѣ́то[18] о$т$ сотворения свѣта ҂$\widetilde{sупе}$. Еро́полкъ[19] ж во
град[20] Варяж в'ниде и[21] повелѣ бра́та с'воего Олеха искати[22], и по
взятіи[23] града в третїи день обрѣто́ша его[24] ме$ж$ тѣлами[25] ч$\overline{л}$вческими
мер'тва, и принесо́ша тѣло́ его́ пред Еро́полка. Еро́полкъ ж ви́дѐ тѣ́ло
брата[26] своего рече к' Свадолт8[27], С'вадо́лте[28] сего пожела$\widehat{л}$[29] еси, ї
погребо́ша его в Овру́чи[30]. *Овр8$\widehat{ч}$[31] град,*
Влади́ме$р$[32] в[33] варяги[34] побѣжа 8слышавъ сие Владимеръ[35], яко
Яро́полкъ[36] брата своего Олга[37] 8би, бежа и$з$ вели́кого[38]
Нова́||города[39] за́ море к варя́гом[40], а на вели́ком княженіи
новгородцко$м$[41] Яро́полкъ посади намѣ́сника[42] своего, и себе сотвори
самоде́ржца всеа Р8сиї[43], Владимеръ[44] же взя себѣ варяговъ на
помощ, иде на свое княжение, и намѣ́сника[45] Яро́полкова[46] ї$з$
вели́кого[47] Новагорода[48] ї$з$гна, [49]*Владиме$р$[50] [51]Но$в$город паки[51]
оты́ска[52]*[49] вь его$ж$ мѣсто постави своего имене$м$[53] Добры́ню, са́мъ ж
собра войско р8ское, и соединя[54] с варяги[b] противо Яропол'ка во́ева
8прежда́я его[55] в то́мъ, вѣдѐ[56] бо[57] яко имя́ше Яро́полкъ во́йн8
подяти проти́в8 его,

---

[1] G їмянем | [2] ER Свадалтъ | [3] В вторы | [4] G Ахитовелъ | [5] N древлянскаго |
[6] R переясла$в$ского N переяславскаго | [7] R om. | [8] ER 8бий | [9] R Свадалтов8
N Свадонтову | [10] N om. | [11–11] G om. parenthesis signs | [12] BGN Гербе$р$штеинъ | [13] ER в |
[14] ER город | [15] G Еропо́лковыхъ | [16] N высокаго | [17] N множествомъ | [18] ER лѣта | [19] BG
Ера́полкъ | [20] G граде | [21] ER omm. | [22] ER искать | [23] E взяти | [24] N егож | [25] N тѣльсы |
[26] G suprascr. | [27] G Свандоту ER Свалдот8 | [28] GER Свалдоте | [29] G ad. ли | [30] G Овр8чиї
N ad. градѣ | [31] G Авр8чь | [32] N Владимиръ | [33] ER ва | [34] ER вряги | [35] N Владимиръ |
[36] ER Еро́полкъ | [37] N Олега | [38] G великова N великаго | [39] ER Новаграда | [40] ER
варяхомъ | [41] G но$в$городцким N новгородском | [42] GRN намѣ́сника | [43] N Россїи |
[44] RN Владими$р$ | [45] RN намѣ́сника | [46] G Яропо́лка | [47] N великаго | [48] E Новаграда ad.
и R Новагра | [49–49] ER omm. | [50] N Владимиръ | [51–51] N паки Новгородъ | [52] G отиска |
[53] GN їмянемъ | [54] ER соединя$\widehat{с}$ | [55] ER ево | [56] G вѣдя ER виде | [57] N om.

[a] G in marg. ωлегъ убитъ | [b] G in marg. достоино замѣчанїя

В то ж вре́мя посла́[1]. и[2] ко[3] Рехво́льду[4] кн҃зю п'ско҃вскому[5] (иже из
варя҃г прїиде)[5] просяще[6] 8 него в' жен8 дщери Рохмиды[7] [8](Рохмида[9]
ж про Владимера вѣдяще[10] бы́ти неистова ло́жа)[8,11] Святосла҃в же с
наложницею[12] Малюскою его прижи)[13] не восхотѣ за него итти но за
брата его и неприятеля Яропол'ка[14] от негож и с'вато҃в ожидала[15] бѣ.
Владимеръ, разгнѣвася[16] на Рехво́льда[17] об'ра́ти на него войс'ка
готовые свои, и Пско҃в взя, самого[18] ж Рехъво́льда[19,a] з двема сн҃ы его
8би́, а дщерь || Рохмид8[20] в' жен8 себѣ в'зя си́лою

Потомъ Влади́меръ[21] тою побѣдою и присовок8плением[b] себѣ
княжства[22] псков'скаго 8крепив'ся, иде х Ки́ев8 противо[23] Яропол'ка,
Яропо́лкъ[24] сяде[25] в Ки́еве, а Владимеръ[26] осадї его, и разумѣ яко
силою не в'зяти его, посла таино кь[27] Ярополков8 вѣрном8 д8мном8
боярину к Бл8д8 нарицая его от҃цомъ[28], и посла к не́му дары
доволны[29], моля дабы пода҃л ем8 совѣтъ Яропол'ка 8би́ти
Вы'раз8мѣвъ Владимерово[30] послание Бл8д обѣща́я[31] Ярополка
убити, [32]точию б с прилежанием Ки́ева доставалъ[32,33] Влади́меръ, а[34]
Яропо́лк8 совѣтъ дая, дабы в Ки́еве не жил повѣдая яко множество
ки́евля҃н[35] рабо҃в его на здравие 8мышляютъ, ї яко ко Владими́ру[36]
пристаю҃т;

Си́мъ Бл8довымъ лес'ны́мъ[37] совѣтомъ, Ярополкъ ис Ки́ева уиде во[38]
градъ Роденъ иже стоитъ на 8стье[39] рѣки Юрсы, идѣже чаяше
з'дра́вие свое сохра́нити[c]. ||

Влади́миръ[40] же Ки́евъ в'зя, и осадивъ своими войски
велико̀новгородскими[41] и варяжскими, иде с воинствомъ за
Еропол'комъ[42] и во граде Родене[43] осади его. и повелѣ ко граду и
баш'нямъ прист8пати тяшко[44] по м'ногое в'ремя. воиска[45] ж
Яропол'ковы во граде б8д8чие[46] изн8ждены бя́ше[47], видя ж
изн8ждение ихъ Бл8д, совѣтова Яропол'к8 проси́ти ми́р8 и ти́шины 8
брата своего Владимера[48]. а Вла́димер8[49] предвозвѣщая, что 8же

---

[1] ER omm. | [2] N послы | [3] N къ | [4] U ante corr. Рехволоду B ante corr. Всеволоду
N Росвольду | [5-5] G om. parentheses signs | [6] ER просящ8 | [7] N Ротмиды | [8-8] G om.
parentheses signs | [9] R Рохмѣда N Ротмида | [10] ER вѣдяща N вѣдаше | [11] N om. right
parenthesis sign | [12] E наложницею | [13] G om. right parenthesis sign | [14] E Ерополка | [15] E
ожадала | [16] E развгнѣвася | [17] U ante corr. Рехволода B ante corr. Всеволода G Рохва҃лда
R Рехвалда | [18] N самаго | [19] U ante corr. Рехъволода B ante corr. Всеволода G Рохва҃лда |
[20] N Ротмиду | [21] BR Владимиръ | [22] ER княжества N княжъ | [23] E противъ8 N противо
ante corr. против{у} | [24] ER add. же | [25] N сядь | [26] R Владими́р | [27] ERN къ |
[28] BGN от҃ием | [29] G доволи | [30] R Владимирово | [31] BGN обѣща | [32-32] ER in marg. |
[33] G достави҃л | [34] ER omm. | [35] GER киявлянъ | [36] BGEN Владимер8 | [37] BGN лестным |
[38] ER в | [39] E 8сье | [40] GEN Владиме́р | [41] ER великоновогороцкими | [42] N Ярополкомъ |
[43] ER Родине | [44] BGN тяжко | [45] G воиско | [46] GER б8д8чи | [47] B ad. ыша suprascr.
G быша | [48] R Владимира | [49] B Владиме́ду R Владимир8

[a] G in marg. Владимиръ иде на Псковъ | [b] G in marg. потомъ къ Киеву | [c] G in marg.
Киевъ взя҃тъ

Ярополка хоще‌т выдать[1], и пред него приве‌сти, Ярополкъ ж‌
пос‛л8ша сове‌та Бл8дова лс‌ти́ва[2] поддадеся в силе на мл‌сть, [3]брат8
своем‌у[3,4] Владимер8[5] желая о‌т него еже дасть ем8 на пропитание, да
тѣмъ бл‌годаренъ б8детъ. Владимер8[6] ж сие бысть годе, потомъ Бл8д
советова Ярополʼк8, да идетъ ко брат8 и поддасʼтся[7] ем8,
возбраняще[8] же Ярополʼк8 др8гïи д8мной[9] бояринъ, именем Вераско,
Ярополкъ[10] ж Вераскова[11] сове‌та пренебрехъ[12], посл8ша[a] Бл8да, и[13] ï‌з
града изиде[14] ко[15] брат8, ‖ егда же исхождаше и‌з врать, абие о‌т дву
варяговъ 8биен бы‌сть, еже самъ Владимиръ[16], о‌т нѣкия башʼни
зряше[17] видѣвʼ же Ярополʼка[18] брата 8биенна, то‌т‌час‌ посла во град
варяговъ войно‌в своих, и жен8 брата своего гречанʼк8 я‌т‌ï насилова, с
неюже Ерополкъ[19] пока еще черʼницею[20] была прежде даже не пояти
ем8 [21]ю в жен8[21] имѣ с‌на тѣмъ о‌бразомъ вожделения[22] ради еже
г‌с‌дрствовати[23], Ерополкъ[24] 8би[25] Олеха брата, Ярополка же[26]
Влади́миръ[27] 8би́,

В‛лади́меръ вели́кий С‛вя‌тослави‌ч[28] самодерʼжецъ р8скïи, перʼвыï‌
христианинъ[29] бысть в лѣто о‌т со‌творения ми́ра ҂s‌у‌п‌s.е,
Влади́меръ[30] С‛вятосла́вичь, внук Игоре‌в правн8к Рю́риковъ овладѣ
княжениями р8скими бра́тïи своих, Олга[31] ï Ерополка[32] ‖ и всю Р8сь
пол8но‌ш‌ню8[33], восточню8 и на[34] по‌лдень лежащю8, бѣлю8, и
черню8. под свою держав8 приведе, сего ради писася ц‌ремъ или
королемъ, самодержцемъ и вели́ким кн‌земъ всеа[35] Роси́и, престолъ ж‌
свой и‌з великого[36] Новагорода[37,c] в‛ Ки́евъ пренесе[38], а за 8биенных
бра́тïи своихъ Олга[39] и Еропо́лʼка[40], б‌гомъ своимъ жерʼтвы при́нося,
мʼножество бо‌лвановъ и капищъ[41] поганʼских в Ки́еве и на иных
горах и полях ки́евских наставил, и по‌строи‌л началнои болванъ[d]
зѣло вы́сокъ Пер8н8 или Перк8ну[42] бог8 громовъ[43] темных о‌блако‌в и
молнïи и бл‌гочинʼно его почитая, тѣло ж его изрядно и‌з древа
выреза, глав8 же сре‌бряну 8ши златыя, ноги желѣзныя со‌дѣла, в
р8кахъ ж камень держа, подобием грома палящаго, яхонʼты и

---

[1] G вѣдать | [2] GR лстиво | [3–3] B ante corr. брата своего | [4] N своеполу | [5] R Владимир8 |
[6] E Владиме‌р R Владимир8 | [7] N поддася | [8] B возбранеще G во‌збраняше | [9] GER
д8мныї | [10] B Ерополкъ | [11] N Верашкова | [12] ERN пренебрѣ‌г | [13] G om. | [14] BGN изыде |
[15] BGN к | [16] BGEN Владимеръ | [17] GER зряще | [18] G Ерополка | [19] GRN Ярополкъ |
[20] ER черницою | [21–21] N om. | [22] G во‌зждѣлеѣия ER вождения | [23] Е г‌с‌дрьствати |
[24] GRN Ярополкъ | [25] ER у | [26] N om. | [27] BGEN Владимеръ | [28] G Свѣтославичь |
[29] BGER хрстиянинъ | [30] GR Владимиръ | [31] N Олега ante corr. Олга | [32] N Ярополка |
[33] N полунощную | [34] B но | [35] N всея | [36] N великаго | [37] ER Новаграда | [38] GN принесе |
[39] N Олега ante corr. Ольга | [40] N Ярополка | [41] G капищь | [42] N om. | [43] ER боговъ

[a] G in marg. Ярополкъ убиенъ | [b] G in marg. Владимиръ | [c] G in marg. пренесение
престола и‌зъ Новагорода въ Киевъ | [d] G in marg. к8миръ Пер8нъ

сапѳирами[a] 8крашен'ныї[1]. иныя ж бол'ваны нарече 8слад, Корсса[2], Дасс8ба, Стри́ба, [3]Сима, ергла[3, 4] [sic], Макошь[5], и прот'чая, ихже Р8с̑ к8мирами нарица́х8, и жертвы имъ творя́ще[6], ||

Созда же Владимеръ[7] и град вели́кїи меж Волгою и Окою рѣками[b] во свое имя Владими́р[8] зѣло во странѣ изобилно́й от Москвы .рп. поприщъ[9] на востокъ сл҃нца и тамо ис Киева престо́л пренесе, и быть[10] до кн҃зя Ивана Даниловича белор8ского[11], кн҃зь ж Иванъ Даниловичь из Владимера[12] пр́стл к Москве пренесе[13], обрати[14] потомъ Владимеръ мысль свою к воин́ской[15] бодрости[16, c], воева ж в начале Мечислава кн҃зя полского[17], ї в̑зя грады Премышль[18], и Цы́рвень ї 8ѣздъ радимицкїи полского[19] княжства[20] ([21]чаять радомскїи[22] под свою держав8 покори, и дань возложи каков8[23] поляком дава́лӣ[24] о томъ Длугошъ и Меховїи кни̑г[25] .в̑. глав̑[26] .а̑. и .г̑. страница .к̑д. и проч:[27] пиш8т,

Дѣте́и[28] Владимиръ[29] от приоб́щенных ем8 же́н имяше от Родмиды[30] дщери[31] князя Рехволда[32] псков̑скаго[33], трех сыновъ Изяслава Ярослава Всеволода и двѣ дщери. з грекинею Святополка || с ческою[34] княгинею Святослава, Станислава, з бо̑л̑га́ркою[35] Бориса и Глѣба[36], свер́хъ тѣх женъ имяше 8 себя нало́жниц в Вы́шграде[37] .т̑. в Берестове, и в се́брах[38] .с̑. в Белѣграде .т̑. всѣхъ было число́м .ѿ. и 68д8чи совершенны́м[d] самодер́жцем всеа Росїи, Владимер шед с велиїмъ[39] войском чрез Д8на́и и овладѣ земли болгарскую. сербскую, карвацк8ю, седмиградцкую[40], виятицкую, ятвишскую[41] д8лепскую и страны идѣже н҃не волохи м8лтяне[42], и татары бобру́цкие, и всѣхъ к посл8шанию своем8 единым подемомъ пригна и дань[43] велию на них возложи, яже греческим ке́сарем давали[44]; во время ж сея[45] ево войны в р8ския кн҃жния прии́доша печенѣги, и осадиша Бѣлгород, в немъж пребывах8 Владимеровых .т̑. наложниц, печенѣги ж под градомъ стоя[46] многое время, не возмогоша ем8 ничего[e] 8чинити, но[47] совѣщаша под нимъ стоя́т̑и,

[1] ER 8крашен́ны | [2] N Корса | [3–3] [Pol. Symaergla] | [4] R Еругла | [5] GRN Макошъ | [6] R творях8 | [7] GR Владимиръ | [8] GERN Владимер | [9] G поприщь | [10] BGERN бысть | [11] N бѣлорускаго | [12] GR Владимира | [13] N принесе | [14] EN обратиї | [15] G воиско́и | [16] ER бодрасти | [17] N польскаго | [18] ER Перьмы́шль | [19] ER по́лскаго | [20] ER княжества | [21] GER omm. parenthesis sign | [22] R радомски BN add. right parenthesis sign | [23] N каковъ | [24] ER давати | [25] N книги | [26] GER глава | [27] ER прочиї | [28] R дѣде́и | [29] BGERN Владимер | [30] R Рохмиды | [31] N дщеры | [32] B ante corr. Всеволода G Севолода N Рогволода | [33] Е псков̑ского | [34] Е че́сною R че́стною | [35] G бо́лгарскою | [36] Е Хлѣба | [37] ER Вышеграде | [38] GRN се́рбах | [39] GERN великимъ | [40] GER седмиграцкую N седмиградскую | [41] ERN я́твижскую | [42] G м8нтяне | [43] G данъ | [44] ER давати | [45] G сеа | [46] N стояху | [47] N не

[a] G in marg. Усладъ Ко́рсса Да́сс8ба Стриба Сима Е́ргла Макошъ | [b] G in marg. градъ Владими́р и пренесение во оный престоли из Киева | [c] G in marg. война съ Полшею | [d] G in marg. военныя дѣйствия Владимира | [e] G in marg. вымыслъ вѣлгородцевъ противъ печенегъ

дондеже грацких[1] жителеи гладом изморятъ, граждане ж видя печенѣговъ долгое около || града облежение, помышляше имъ здатися глада ради, и бѣ из них муж в возрасте престарѣлом возбрани[2] печенѣгом града здати, и повелѣ двѣ кади киселя развести[3], третию ж 8готовати сыты медвяные, и вывести печенѣгом [4]в' табор, [5](печенѣгомъ[4] скучно без дѣла стоятѝ)[5, 6] глаголя печенѣгомъ, стоя в поле снѣдиа[7] не имате і се белогородцы[8] по любви своеи к вам прислали; дондеже со Владимером[9] гсдремъ своим для вас приготовятся[10] л8тче, печенѣги ж видя се разумѣша яко гладом их[11] не ізморѝти, града же силою не взя́ти, и того для отидоша от осады; белогородцы ж малым вымыслом отш8тилис̑,

Потом печенѣги собрався с велиімъ[12] воинством идоша х Киев8, Владимир[13] же слыша[14] про поход их иде противо[15] их, и ста обозом

8 реки Трубежи сь[16] единои страны || печенѣги[17], з др8гие[18] ж Владимер видя же печенѣги яко Владимиръ[19] противо их стоитъ во множестве силы, не смѣя на него боемъ наст8пати, но просиша 8 него единаго[20] от воин братися со[21] единым[22] же их страны борцом печенѣгом, и аще р8ской воинъ преодолѣетъ печенѣга тогда печенѣги Владимеру сл8жити б8д8тъ, аще ж печенѣг преодолѣетъ р8ского[23] воина, тогда печенѣгомъ Р8сь подлежати и сл8жити б8д8тъ, а буде такои борецъ не обрететца[24] межд8 вами тогда мы рускую землю три годы[25] воевать[26] б8дем, сего ради лутче вам без[27] кровопролития одного борца за всѣх поставить,

Владимер высл8шавъ от печенѣгов послания печален бысть зѣло, помышляя в себѣ глаголя, аще не поставлю борца печенѣги помыслятъ, что во княжениях моих ни един воин к бою достоинъ

|| обрестися[28] можетъ, того́ ради на моеи державе р8скои вѣчная[29] 8коризна б8детъ, егда ж поставлю с печенѣгомъ и борца от р8скихъ вой[30], печенѣг его преодолѣетъ, тогда бесчестие[31] и подданство[32] печенѣгом приобрящ8; во время ж тои ево мысли приіде пред Владимера переяславлянин[33] м8ж старъ глгля[34]. прю велѝкіи княже Владимир8[35] снъ мои можетъ братись с печенѣгомъ, о сем блгодарств8й[36]. радостенъ бысть Владимер, и повелѣ ем8 сна своего пред ся привести, егда ж приіде юноша пред Владимера[37], вопроси

---

[1] В градскихъ ERN градцкихъ | [2] N возобрани | [3] GR розвести | [4-4] N suprascr. | [5-5] G om. parentheses signs | [6] N om. right parenthesis sign | [7] GE снѣдна RN снѣдия | [8] E бѣлогородци | [9] R Владимиромъ | [10] G приготоватца N приготовятца | [11] B ante corr. имъ | [12] BGERN великимъ | [13] BGERN Владимер | [14] ER omm. | [15] N противу | [16] G со N съ | [17] ER add. ж | [18] E др8гуя R другую | [19] GERN Владимер | [20] RN единого | [21] ER сь | [22] В единын | [23] ER р8скаго | [24] B ante corr. оберетца ER оберетца | [25] R года | [26] G воевати | [27] BG бес | [28] N обретися | [29] N вѣчна | [30] G воин | [31] BER безчестие | [32] ER подданством | [33] E переясловлянин | [34] B а corr. глг{а}я | [35] GERN Владимер8 | [36] N бладарствуй | [37] В Владимира

его Владиме*р*[1],[2] смѣеш[3] ли братися з багатыре*м*[4] печенѣжским, рече[5]

юноша ц͠рю преславныї[6] [7]аз ра*б*[7] тво*и* н͠не 8зриши како печенѣги з багатыре*м*[8] своим пре*т*[9] твоею де*р*жавою посрамлени б8д8*т*. видя[10] Владими*р*[11] велию[12] храбрость юноши в мало*м* возрасте, [13]се*и* бо переясловлянин[14], яко о не*м* Длугошъ и Меховїи в книгах, ‖ .в͠. глава .і͡. свидѣтелств8ю*т*, бысть средняго возраста[13], с8мняшеся[15] о побѣде, [16]однако*ж*[17] посла к печенѣгом, дабы[16] з багатыре*м* своимъ, к бою выходилї, а о*н* их с воиномъ[18] своим ожидае*т*. во8трїи *ж* печенѣги сташа во стройствѣ, и го*р*до понося, борца на уготованное[19] мѣсто послали, ч͠лвка[a] толста и плечи́ста возрастом подо*б*на Голиад8[20], которой[21]го*р*до стоя[21] вопия на р8саковъ поношая и х8ля их, скоряе[22] *ж* равнаго себѣ, единомъ *ж* не смѣющ, трех на борб8 призываше, изыде из[23] р8скаго[24] войска переясла*в*лянинъ[25], ч͠лвкъ ма́лъ но кренастъ. видя *ж* его печенѣгъ посмѣя[26] ем8 и назва его желваком, егда *ж* межд8 собою сошлися, снялися оба крѣпко за поясы, поистин͠нѣ яко Даре*с* с Енътелюссом Енеасовы[27] бо*р*цы[28], печенѣгъ то*л*стотою тѣла[29], р8сакъ[30] *ж* крѣпостию управляше, печенѣгъ высокъ[31] ч͠лвкъ, р8сакъ[32] *ж* ни́зокъ, ма́ло накланя́шеся[33], [34]разбѣгши *ж* ся[34] 8дари ‖ печенѣга главою в толстое брюхо близ лона[35] под[36] п8пом даже 8паде. войска[37] *ж* с[38] обоих странъ стоях8 тихо, и зряще на борбу малого мужичка со исполином, потомъ вставъ печенѣгъ с великим стыдо*м* хотѣ*л* переяславлянина[39] 8дари*т* крѣпко кулаком, о*н* же скоро о*б*ращся *от* печенѣга отбѣже, печенѣ*г* же ч͠лвкъ тяжелой[40] *от* крѣпкаго[41] 8дарения кулакова еже мин8ло[42] р8сина[43] по*т*кн8в͠ся[44] 8паде на землю, р8синъ *ж* не даде ем8 встати всѣд на него и нача бити по щекам, что з8бы 8 него с кровию[45] выпадали, и за го*р*ло его 8хвати́[46] даже д͠шу на томъ мѣстѣ выломи*л*, видѣв *ж* сие Владимеръ с войскомъ вскоре на печенѣги наступи. печенѣги *ж* видя[47] безсилие и бесчастие[48] свое разбѣгошася по полямъ. Ру*с* же 8тѣкающи*х*[49] били сѣкли, кололи, ловили, иных в Трубеже рекѣ потопили, и множеств<ω полону и добычи в

[1] В Владимиръ | [2] [Phrase untranslated] | [3] BGN смѣеши | [4] GRN богатыре*м* | [5] Е рюче | [6] Е преславны | [7-7] G ω*б*разъ | [8] GRN богатыре*м* | [9] GER пред N пре | [10] G видѣ | [11] BGERN Владиме*р* | [12] N великую | [13-13] G ad. parentheses signs | [14] BRN переяславлянин G переясла*в*линъ | [15] ER сомняшеся | [16-16] ER in marg. | [17] Е однокож | [18] N воискомъ | [19] G 8готование | [20] BN Голияд8 R Галиаду | [21-21] ER го*р*достию | [22] R скоряа | [23] В и | [24] N руского | [25] ER переясловлянин | [26] ER посмѣяса | [27] R Енвасовы | [28] ER бу*р*цы | [29] B suprascr. G om. | [30] Е р8синъ ante corr. р8сакъ R р8синъ | [31] R высосъ | [32] Е р8син ante corr. р8сак R р8синъ | [33] GER наклоняшеся | [34-34] ER разбѣгшиса | [35] ER луна | [36] G по*т* | [37] G ва*и*ска R во*и*ско | [38] G со | [39] В переяславленина Е переясло*в*лянина | [40] ER тяжоло*и* | [41] ER крепкова | [42] ER минула | [43] G р8сини на | [44] N подкнувся | [45] ER кровью | [46] [Phrase untranslated, cf. example (76)] [47] ER видѣ | [48] GERN безчастие | [49] N утекаущихъ

печенѣжскомъ обозе || набрали, славнѹю побѣдѹ единымъ переяславляниномъ[1] [2](не йнако яко евреяня[3] от Давида[4] на т[5] ѳилистимы[6])[2] воспрїяша. сотвори[7] ж Владимер на том броду, идѣже[a] бѣ побѣда дрѹгїй Переясловль[8], на память семѹ яко пересловленинъ[9] над богатырем[10] печенѣжским [11]побѣду одержа[11, 12] переясловлянина[13] ж славным богатырем[14], а отца ево[15] чстным члвком ѹчини[16];

Бысть Владимиръ[17] велиїмъ[18] и славным во всем свѣте монархомъ, илй самодержцем всѣхъ земель росіиских[19], живе беззаконно кѹмиры хваля, прїидоша ж к нему от розных королеи[20] и князеи и народов ѹчителї различных [21]вѣръ и законовъ, в началѣ[21] махметяне[22] татары египтяне[23] и арапленя[24], с протчими[25] цари аргавенскими, ѹвещевая его да их вѣру и законъ приїметъ егож Владимер

пренебреже, || являше бо ся емѹ быти скареденъ и мерзокъ, потом прїидоша послы от папы кесареи и кнзеи римских илй латынских[26] и немецких, просяще[27] его дабы вѣру и законъ хрстиянскїи[28] прїял[29], Владимер[30] ж и на сие не изволи, яко дѣиствие латинское[31] мало блгочстно, и костелы их недобрѣ ѹкрашены являхуся посем же ї от евреев[32] ѹвещеван[33], да приїмет законъ Моисеов[34], он же и того не восхотѣ, понеж Моисеовы[35] законы[36] тяжки суть, и не имяше у него никоторой вѣры и закона послы мѣста токмо греческихъ[37] кѣсареи и патриарховъ[38] послы нѣкое мѣсто имяше, обаче видя различие[39] различных вѣръ и законовъ не восхотѣ никоея прияти;

Посла же Владимир[40] в розные гсдрства послов[b] своих увѣдати о чинѣх вѣры ї о дѣиствах всяких народовъ прилѣжно, в началѣ ж

повеле ѣхать в болгарскую землю, ї свидѣ||телствовати[41] вѣры их иных посла в Рим иных в нѣмцы, во Аѳрику, во Египет, и в Скиѳию[42], иже присмотрився[43] в различных народѣх[44] различным вѣрамъ и дѣиствам, прїидоша же потом во[45] Црьгород[46] возвестиша ж сие кесарем Констянтину[47] и Василию, яко от Владимера монарха

---

[1] В переясловлениномъ GE переясловляниномъ N переяславлениномъ | [2-2] G om. parentheses signs | [3] BGN евреяне | [4] G Давыда | [5] G ї от N над | [6] RN ѳилистины | [7] G сотворивъ | [8] ERN Переяславль | [9] BGE переясловлянинъ RN переяславлянин̂ | [10] G болгарем R бгатырем | [11-11] B suprascr. | [12] GN ѡбдержа | [13] GRN переяславлянина | [14] R бгатыремъ | [15] N его | [16] G учинили | [17] BGERN Владимеръ | [18] G великимъ | [19] ER рѹсіискихъ N росискихъ | [20] Е коралеи | [21-21] BG in marg. N om. | [22] G махмотяне | [23] В египтеня N египтяня | [24] BGRN арапляне Е арапляня | [25] ER прочими | [26] ER илатинских | [27] GN просяше | [28] GRN хрстиянский | [29] G приалъ | [30] В Владимир | [31] G латынское | [32] G евреѡв N евреехъ | [33] B suprascr. | [34] BERN Моисѣевъ | [35] ER Моисѣевы N Моисеовъ | [36] N закон | [37] G греческим | [38] Е потриарховъ | [39] N om. | [40] BGERN Владимер | [41] R свидѣтелствовать | [42] N Кифїю | [43] G приосмотрився R присматрива | [44] N народахъ | [45] ER в | [46] GER Црьград | [47] GER Костянтинѹ

[a] G in marg. градъ Переяславль во знамение побѣды | [b] G in marg. посольство для разѹмѣниа вѣръ

російског҃ проведа́тї вѣры приідоша по́слы. кесари ж слыша҃в сие радостны бѣх8[2], повелѣша ж ихъ прияти чстно, пока́заша[3] ж послом[4] и чинъ црꙑковныи по устав8 греческом8, ї одари҃в ихъ о͡тп8сти́ша ко Владимер8 в Ки́евъ, и да гсдрю своем8 о греческо́и вѣре, л8тчи[5] возвестя́т, посла[a] с ними ко Владимеру[6] патриа́рхъ и кесарь Констянти́н[7] грека Кирила[8,b] ѳилосоѳа м8жа учена, сей Кирилъ[9] пришед ко Владимиру[10], о вѣре хрстиянско́и[11] много бесѣдова с ним, вдаде же[12] ем8 о͡т патриарха[13] и о͡т кесарей вмѣсто поминко҃в запону[14] златую на неи́же вырезано[c] изрядно страшный суд Бжіи к семуж присмотряся Владимир[15], моли́[16] ѳилосоѳа, да повѣдае͡т ему написанна́я ‖ на запонѣ, кі́и одесн8ю с8дїи[17] и кі́и ош8юю[18] стоятъ, повѣда же ем8 ѳилосоѳъ[19] яко одесную стояти б8де͡т вѣр8ющия[20] в гсда н҃шего Иїс8с[21] Хрс҃та, и творящіи[22] дѣла блгая, за сиеж по смерти вѣчный[23] живо͡т и црство нбс҃ное восприі́мут, ош8юю[24] ж[25] стоятъ[26] в жива Бга не вѣрующіи[27] без закона[27] и без вѣры живъше[28], дела слые[29] творящіи[30], тіи во огни адскомъ вѣчно ос8жденї[31] б8де͡т. Владимиръ[32] ж слыша҃в[33] сия воздохну и рече́, блгословенíи[34] сíи[35] иже одесную станутъ, горе же тѣмъ иже ош8юю[36], ѳилосо҃в[37] [sic] же о͡твѣща, аще крестишися, и ты будеши одесную, аще ж[38] во идолопоклоненíи[38] жити б8деши, мѣсто твое со всѣми людми земель твоих ош8юю, а потом в[39] вѣчном ос8жденïи[d], Владимир[40] же обеща крс҃титися, и одаря[41] ѳилосо́ѳа о͡тпусти.

Призва Владимиръ[42] ближнихъ[43] своих боя́р ї д8мных люде́и во град Владимер иже над Клязмою. ‖ к нем8ж и престолъ свой ис Киева пренесе. тамо возвести имъ бесѣд8 о вѣре хрстиянско́и[44] Кири́ла[45] ѳилосоѳа, аще кто крс҃титися[46] водою ї д҃хом во имя[47] о͡т҃ца и с҃на и свꙗтаго д҃ха, умеры́и имать востати, и црствовати во вѣки, неверным же и некрещым[48] по смерти м8ка и ос8ждение вѣчное, тако Владимеру[49] о͡т изображения послѣдняго[50] суда Бжия на запоне, вѣра[e] хрстиянская[51] в срдцы утвердися, но не имѣ блгочестивыхъ

---

[1] В росс҃ійскаго GER росїйскаго | [2] BGN бях8 | [3] R показа N показавша | [4] N посламъ | [5] N лутче | [6] В Владимиру | [7] BGER Костянтинъ | [8] R Кирилла | [9] ER Кири́лъ | [10] GERN В҃ладимер8 | [11] R хрстиꙗн҃скои | [12] Е жа | [13] R по͡триарха | [14] G sапан8 | [15] GER Владимер | [16] G моля | [17] ER судї | [18] GERN ѡшую | [19] BN ѳилосо҃в | [20] ER вѣр8ющії | [21] BG Иї́сса ER И҃іса N Иисуса | [22] Е творящи | [23] Е вѣчны | [24] ERN ошую | [25] N om. | [26] G стоѧть | [27–27] Е беззаконна R беззако́н҃но | [28] G жив8ще ER живꙗше | [29] R слыя | [30] ER творящи | [31] BG ос8ждениї | [32] GER Владимеръ | [33] R услыша҃в | [34] R блг҃ослове́н҃нїи | [35] G сие | [36] ER ошую | [37] GE ѳилосо҃ѡ | [38–38] N не крестишися и тако | [39] ER omm. | [40] RN Владимер | [41] ER одари | [42] BER Владимер | [43] N ближнахъ | [44] BEN хрстиꙗнской | [45] В Кирили R Кирилла | [46] GR крестит҃ца | [47] Е има | [48] BGER некрещенымъ N некрещеннымъ | [49] G Владимир8 ER Владимерь | [50] G послѣднего | [51] GR хрстиꙗнская |

[a] G in marg. возвращение посло҃в изъ Грецїї съ ѳилосоѳомъ Кириломъ | [b] U in marg. Cyrill{os} Meth{ios} | [c] G in marg. бесѣда егѡ | [d] G in marg. ѡтп8скъ | [e] G in marg. забвение

людей намѣрения его к совершению вскорѣ привести, сего ради в забвенїе положи;

Собра[1] же великое войско от великого[2] Новагорода[3, a] новгородцовъ[4] и киевлян, пойде в Таврику южн пне Перекопью зовем, взя Каѳ8 или Ѳеодосїю град славныи[5] у грековъ, потом и столныи[6] всеа[b] Таврикїи град Корсунь. (егож[7] Савелїи в книгах вторых Херсоном а Меховїи Корсхимъ нарицають) у преславногѡ[8] пристанища моря понтїискаго[9], особое сокровище кесареи греческих осади и всѣми ‖ силами многое время добываше его бѣ бо труден к нем8 прист8пъ к том8 ж и гречестїи воини[10] добре храняху егѡ[11], Владимеръ[12] ж с осадными[13] людми нача договариватис̃ здатися[14] им, гл̃голя аще доброволно[15] не поддад8тся[16] стоятӣ б8дет еще до трех лѣтъ, и доколе их достанетъ, чего потом себя жалѣтӣ б8дут, греки ж гроз его не слушах8, и стоя под[17] Корсунем[18] еще .ѕ. мсцовъ градцких[19] сидѣлцовъ хотя принудит[20], и нужда[21], однако[22] в своемъ упорствѣ пребываху[c], но единъ из них протопоп Анастасїи[23] написа на стрелѣ словеса своя сице, ц̃рю Владимере, б8де хощеши град вскорѣ добыти, вѣ́ждь яко[24] трубы есть подземные к востоку сл̃нца имиж идетъ в Корсунь прѣсная вода, ты ж прекопавъ оныа[25] трубы, вод8 отимешъ[26] корсуняном[27], и здад8тся[28] тебѣ, с тѣмъ писмомъ стрелу выстрели прямо шатра[29], Владимеръ[30] ж ‖ повелѣ стрел8 принести пред себя и писмо чрез[31] преводника[32] прочте скоро трубы под землѣю повелѣ прекопати. корсуняне[33] видя отятие воды на мл̃срдие его з градом и нарядом морским и градским[34] и с[35] сокровищи кесарскими[d] здались,

В н̃шихъ[36] древних росїиских[37] лѣтописцах напи́сано, и Жигимонтъ[38, e], и Гербештеин[39] в книгах своих о Москвѣ на листу .ѯ.м свидѣтелств8ю т[40], новгородцы[41] егда чрез[42] .ӟ. лѣтъ были со Владимером[43] под Корсунем, жены ж их истосковався[44] природною сверботою от многаго жда́ния мужеи своих, с8мневахуся о их возвращенїи, мняще яко на войнах м8жи их погибоша[45] рабовъ своих и плѣнниковъ в м8жеи мѣсто себѣ прия́ша, по взятїи ж

---

[1] G собрав | [2] N великаго | [3] ER Новаграда | [4] ERN новогородцов̃ | [5] ER славны | [6] Е столны | [7] ERN сегоже | [8] G преславнаго N преславъ | [9] GN понтїиского Е понтискаго R понтискогѡ | [10] R воинӣ | [11] BN ево | [12] BGN Владимир | [13] Е осадними | [14] R здати ея | [15] BGN доброволне | [16] G поддадутца | [17] G пот | [18] N Курсунемъ | [19] BN градскихъ | [20] В принд8и ante corr. прин8дитӣ G прин8ди N принудити | [21] N ad. бѣ | [22] Е однака | [23] Е Анас̃таси | [24] B suprascr. | [25] N оные | [26] N отымешъ | [27] N корсунямъ | [28] G здад8тца | [29] N шетра | [30] G Владимир | [31] G черезъ | [32] R переводника | [33] ER корсуняны | [34] G градцким | [35] ER omm. | [36] G н̃нешнихъ | [37] N россїйскихъ suprascr. | [38] N Жигимонтъ | [39] BGE Герберштеинъ | [40] G свидѣтелств8етъ | [41] ER новогородцы | [42] G черезъ | [43] В Владимиром | [44] N истосткcovався | [45] ER побиша

[a] G in marg. воюетъ на Грецию | [b] G in marg. ѡблежание Корс8нѧ | [c] G in marg. измѣна протопопа Анастасїи | [d] G in marg. здача Корс8ня | [e] ER in marg. зри о ново[го]родцахъ

Корсуня новгородцы[1], возвратишася в великїи Новъгород[2], града Корсуня врата мѣдные, и колоколъ зѣло великъ (яже и до днесь 8 соборные[3] цркви в Новѣгороде[4] есть) с собою привезоша на знамя побѣды[5]; ‖ раби ж и плѣнники которые жены за себя побралї господ своих во град пустить не хотях8, и воставъ противъ[6] господ своих со оружием отбити их хотяху. внегда ж с ними господа воинским оружием бой сотвориша, 8лучиша над ними побѣд8 плен'ники, по совѣту ж нѣкоего[7] старѣйшаго войсковое[8] оружие сабли мечи отложше, и вземше дреколиї ї плѣти тѣмъ их наказаху, ихже раби 8страшишася помянувъ яко прежде господие такими палками[9] и плетми их наказывах8[10] а не саблями, ї тако из града бежаша[11] вонъ, и прїидоша на мѣсто болотное прилежащее[12] над рѣкою Мологою[13] от Углеча .ї. верстъ, и тамо сѣдоша в[14] осаде и крѣпость построиша хотя от господ[15] своих оборонитися[16] но господа их иныхъ повѣсиша иных четвертоваша ї достоиными казньми противъ их дѣл казниша,

Симъ лѣтописям на подобие описуютъ[17] [18].ї. 8стин у Строга и у Помпия[18] книг .в. ‖ и Геродот у Мелпомена, о татарех илї скиѳех також сл8ги и плѣнники поем'ше жены хозяевъ своих [19]возвращающихся же[19, 20] от воины[21] по .з. лѣтех яко неприятелеи в домы п8стити[22] не хотяще, но по м'ногих бранех хозяева изгнаша их такожде и проч:

По взятїи Корсуня Владимер[23] протчие[24] грады и местечка, и вес таврискїи[25] островъ под свою державу покори, и посла х Костянтину[26] и Василию сном[27] Иоанна Земиски[28] х кесарем греческим послы своя. лѣта от сотворения мира .6утs. возвѣщая им яко Корсунь славныи[29] ихъ[30] град пристаничныи[31] со всею Таврикою взя, ї слышахъ яко им8т сестру, и да[32] дад8т ему в жену, аще не дад8т[33] сотворю такожде, и Констянтинополю[34], и протчим[35] греческим градом[36] якож и Корсуню[37]. кесари ж отвѣщаша не достоит нам хрстиянским монархом за иновѣрного князя родныя сестры дати, а егда отст8пня болвановъ, ко истинному Хрсту Бгу ншему приступиши, [38]и в нш8 хрстиянскую[39] ‖ вѣру пристỳпиши[38] и крести́шися, тогда сестры ншея тебѣ во святыи бракъ возбраняти не будем, слышавъ же сие рече[40] прежде послах к вам послы їже

[1] ER новогородцы | [2] ER Новъград N ad. из | [3] BN соборныя | [4] R Новеграде | [5] B ante corr. побѣдомъ | [6] G ad. ихъ in ras. | [7] G никоего | [8] R воинское | [9] E полками | [10] E наказаваху R накаsоваху | [11] BGN бежаше | [12] G предлежащее | [13] B ante corr. Молохою | [14] ER во | [15] B госпов G господов | [16] N оборонитись | [17] N отписуютъ | [18–18] [Pol. Iustinus ex Trogo Pompeio] | [19–19] G возвращающих же ся | [20] N om. | [21] ER воинъ | [22] G п8сти|тити | [23] G Владимиръ | [24] ER прочие | [25] GE таврискиї R тевриский | [26] N Констянтину | [27] G suprascr. | [28] R Земискиї | [29] E славны | [30] R om. | [31] E пристаничны | [32] GR omm. | [33] BGN дадят | [34] GER Костянтинополю | [35] ERN прочим | [36] B ante corr. врадомъ N градамъ | [37] E Курсуню | [38–38] N in marg. | [39] GRN хрстианск8ю | [40] N suprascr.

возвестиша ми изрядно подробну вся о в҃шем законе, егож возлюбих, вѣра ж и дѣиства в҃ши угодни мнѣ суть, и тако пришлите[1] еп҃скпа иже мя[2] кр҃стит, сами ж с сестрою своею вскоре ко мнѣ приѣзжаите или пришлите ко мнѣ в супру́жество, аз же Корсунь[3] ї всю тавриц'кую[4] и по́нтскую[5] страну вам возвращу. слышавъ Ко́нстянти́н[6] ї Василïи кесари бл҃года́рно́и[7] Владимеро́в о́твѣтъ возрадовася[8] велиею[9] радостию и начаша молити Анну сестру свою, да иде́т за Владиме́ра в супружство[10], она ж о́трицашеся ѕѣло. братия ж е́и рекоша, аще не пойдешъ что ко́рсуняном и тавриком Владиме́р[11] со́дѣла, то сотвори́т и греком, к тому ж и го́рши безчестие[12] на на́с мстити б8де́т, аще[13] ж Бг҃ъ россïйскую[14] землю. ‖ св҃тым крещением просвѣти́т, а[15] греческую землю браком твоим о́т пленения свободит вѣчная слава и безсме́ртное[16] бл҃гословение о́тселѣ возрасте́т на тебѣ, Ан'на це́саревна, бра́тïи со слеза́ми[a] о́твеща да буди воля г҃сдня, и всѣдши в кора́бли пои́де х Корсуню, бра́тïи[17] ж ея кесари провождаху[18], яко[19] Длугош[20] и Меховïи пишу́т, с велиѝм[21] множеством кн҃зеи греческих и жен'ска[22] и дв҃ча полу[23] иде, ихже бл҃гоприятно[24] Владиме́р прия, и како скоро кесаревну во град и в полаты ко́рсунския[b] введоша, абие внезапу наиде на не́г слепота по изволению Бж҃ию. нача же Владиме́р с8мнѣватися креститися л҃[25] ему[26] илѝ ни[27] мняше[26,28] бо яко бози[29] его для его намѣрения что похотѣ́л[30] креститися наказаша. кесаре́вна ж посла ко Владимеру, аще не крестишися не избудеши слѣпоты, слышав҃[31] сия Владиме́р Святославичь внукъ Игоре́в и О́лги́нъ правнукъ Рюрико́в[c], крестися в Корсунѣ ‖ в вѣру греческую хр҃стиянскую[32] во имя о́т҃ца и с҃на и св҃таго д҃ха в лѣто о́т сотворения мира .ѕ҃уѯ҃s. а о́т Хр҃ста по Длугош8 и Меховию .ц҃ч.[33][34] а Кроме́р полагае́т[d] в книгах[35] .г҃.х .ѕ҃уѯз.[34] а о́т Хр҃ста .ц҃п.[36] егда ж архиеп҃скпъ[37] корсунскïи возложи руку на Владимира[38] и бл҃гослови его да прïѐметъ д҃хъ св҃тыи тогда[39] о́т[e] очию е́г о́тпаде яко чеш8я. тогда абие прозрѣ́въ[40] хвалу г҃сд8 Бг҃8[40] воздаде г҃ля, н҃не познахъ исти́нна́г[41] Бг҃а, кр҃стиша же ся[42] с нимъ вси[43]

---

[1] N пришлете | [2] N имя | [3] Е Курсунь | [4] R тавридскую | [5] ER по́нтцкую | [6] BGER Костянтинъ | [7] Е благоро́дно́и R бл҃городно | [8] N возрадовашася | [9] ER велию | [10] BGN супружество | [11] BG Владими́р | [12] GN бесчестие | [13] B ante corr. {е}ще | [14] ERN росïйскую | [15] ER omm. | [16] G бесме́рное | [17] B брати GN братия | [18] G провозждаху | [19] G ad. до in ras. | [20] BN Длугож | [21] N великимъ | [22] ER add. и ѳранцы миро́м | [23] BGN пола | [24] B бл҃гопря́тно | [25] ERN omm. | [26–26] Е и мняше ante corr. или нинямъше | [27] R и | [28] N мняше | [29] Е болезнь ante corr. бози R болѣзн | [30] BGN похотѣ ER хотѣ́л | [31] Е ad. же | [32] GR хр҃стианск8ю | [33] ER .ц҃ѣ. | [34–34] N om. | [35] BG книг | [36] ER .ц҃в. | [37] Е архиепи҃скуп8 | [38] BERN Владимера | [39] ER add. ж | [40–40] BGN г҃сд8 Бг҃у хвалу | [41] B истинного | [42–42] B ante corr. кр҃сти|ся же с ER крестишася | [43] Е всѝи

---

[a] G in marg. прибытие царевны Анны греческой въ Корс8нь | [b] G in marg. слѣпота Владимирова | [c] G in marg. крещение Владимира | [d] G in marg. по рож{д} 988 год | [e] G in marg. Владимиръ prospe

332

бояря[1] его, и воинство[2] росїиское, Владимеру[3] жъ во сѣтом крещеннїй[4] имя дано новое греческое Василїи,

Венчася[5] же и сѣтым браком со[6, a] Анною кесаревною греческою, в велиеи радости всег народа, в Корсуни[7, b] ж на горѣ созда[8] храм во имя сѣтаго Василия тезоименника[9] своег[10] на память сѣтаг крещения[c] своег[11] Корсунь[12] ж [13]и Каѳу и всю Таврику[14] отдаде ‖ греческимъ кесаремъ[13, 15], самъ ж всѣд[16] в корабли[17] с новобрачною кесаревною, и получа с ними прощение возвратися[18] ко 8стию Днѐпра потом же с8хим п8тем, приѝде в Киев с велиею радостию[d] всего народа, принесе же с собою[19] и мощи сѣтаго[19] Климонта[20], и їконы и к'ниги и рѝзы и протчая[21] 8твари цѣрковныя[22], и протопопа Анастàсия ис Корс8ня иже[23] совѣтова чрез стрелу о трубах подземных, и прочих[24] попов дьяконов пѣвцовъ, монахов, и мастеровыхъ[25] людеи из грековъ з доволным платежем нанятых строенѝя рàди цѣрквеи,

Егда[e] ж приѝде в Киевъ вскоре повелѣ разрушати и їскореняті[26] из основанїи[27] кумѝры, Харса[28], Стриба, Мокосса, и Волосса, балвава[29] [sic], иже бѣ почитаем богъ скотїи[30] и лѣсныи, (якож бѣ у аркадовъ Пан Ѳавнус и проч[31]) во изпразнителное[32] всенародное мѣсто вовреши[33], и в нечистотѣ 8топѝти, Перуна началног[34] идола[35] х коневому хвосту привязати и влещи[36] ‖ чрез град к Днепру, и навязавъ[37] каменья 8топити в Днепрѣ,

Народи[38] ж невѣрнїи плакахуся по богах своих слезнымъ негодованием,

Повелѣ Владѝмир[39] в гсдрстве своем росиском учинити заказ, да вси крестятца[40], и нарече крѣщению всенародному день, аще ж кто не креститца[41], наказание да восприѝметъ[42] сия слышавъ[43] народ с радостию идях8 крѣститис в Киевъ, инии[44] ж на 8реченные[45] мѣста (по нихже[46] гречестїи свѣщенницы для сѣтаго крещения поставлены быша) глѣюще друг друг8 аще бы сие дѣло не было добро не крѣстилися[47] бѣ великиѝ кнѣзь и бояре ево[48], облекше же с и ереи и

---

[1] BGERN бояре | [2] Е воинствои | [3] В Владимиру | [4] BGERN крѣщенїй | [5] ER венчаша |
[6] ER с | [7] N Корсуне | [8] B ad. и in ras. | [9] B ante corr. тезоименинника N тезоименитства |
[10] B ad. а in ras. GN add. а | [11] B suprascr. | [12] ER Корсуни | [13–13] N кесаремъ отдадь |
[14] G Таврин8 | [15] Е кесерам | [16] В вс{в}дъ | [17] В карабли | [18] G вовратися | [19–19] N in marg.
| [20] N Климента | [21] R протчия | [22] G цѣрковные | [23] B ante corr. яже GN аже |
[24] ERN протчихъ | [25] ER мастеров | [26] N изкореняти | [27] ER основаниа | [28] ER Хорса |
[29] N балвана | [30] ER скоти | [31] G прочїи | [32] G испразнителное | [33] Е воврещїи |
[34] BGE началнаго N начелное | [35] Е идала | [36] ER врещи | [37] Е навезав | [38] G народиї |
[39] BERN Владимер | [40] BG крѣстятся | [41] BGN крѣстится | [42] N возприѝметъ | [43] Е слывав |
[44] ER ини | [45] ER уреченныя | [46] B ante corr. нимже | [47] ER крѣстился | [48] G его

---

[a] G in marg. Владимиръ вѣнчанъ со Анною | [b] G in marg. храмъ с Василиа | [c] G in marg. возвратъ Корс8ни, Каѳы и Тавриды грѣком | [d] G in marg. приѝде въ Киевъ и принесе мощи стаго Климента | [e] G in marg. разр8шение к8миров

диакони[1] в ризы стоях8 на скамях к тому 8строенных на рекѣ Днепрѣ, ї вхождаху людие во Днепръ толпамї овїи по пояс инїи ж по шею свⷺщенницы ж крестяще[2] их во имя оⷭца и сⷩа ї свⷮаⷢ дⷯа, ‖ и даваху имъ имяна[3], Василїи. Пеⷦтръ, Иоаⷩ[4], Тимоѳеи Симеоⷩ[5]. и проⷱ[6],

В тоⷤ[7] время дванадесяти[8] сⷩоⷡ Владимеровых имѣⷡшихъ[9] от женъ и наложницъ, Вышеслава, Изаслава[10], Святополⷦка, Ярослава, Всеволода, Святослава, Мстислава[11], Бориса[12]. Глѣба, Станислава, Посвизда, С8дислава, особо крⷭти[13] епⷭкпъ[14] корсунскїи, и вдаде их по крещенїи, и с нимⷥ[15] колико сотъ детеи боярскихъ[16] в на8чение граⷨмоты, греческои и словенскои[17], (которую[18] мы и[19] нⷩе[18] россиане[20] 8потребляем,) приставя к нимъ 8чителеи добрыхъ и їскусных во всяком учении, созда же в Киеве и[21] цⷬрковь во имя вседержителя сⷫса из великаго[22] камения[23], ᵃ на мѣсте идѣж стояⷧ идоⷧ Перунъ да цⷬрковь[24] во имя свⷮаго Василия тезоименника[25] своеⷢ и їных множество цⷬрквей на различныхъ мѣстехъ идѣже прежде различные к8миры стоях8, от многих сокровищ

кирпичныя[26] ‖ каменⸯныя[27], и от древа, взя[28] же у патриарха костяⷩтинополского[29], ᵇ Киев8 пеⷬрваго[30] митрополита Ѳотия, Нов8городⷦк8[31] архиепⷭкупа[32] Леонтия, Иоакима[33] корсунскогѡ[34] преведе[35], ᶜ на архиепⷭкпство в великїи Новъгород, [36]пришед же[36] в Новъграⷣ[37] Иоаким вся[38] к8миры и їдолы[39] сокруши, Перуна ж вве[р]же в реку Волⷯховъ яже течетъ посⷬредѣ[40] града из озера Илⷨеня, а егда Перуна тащили, [41]в Волⷯховъ[41] и били паⷧлками по д8тому т8ловищ8, в то время в нем кричаⷧ[42] бѣсъ, ѡ беда[43] мнѣ впадоⷯ в руцѣ немлⷭтивыⷯ[44] и плыⷯ противо[45] воды под велиⷦкїи мостъ, (яко о том лѣтописцы нⷲи руские и Гербеⷬштеин[46] на лист8 .ѿд.м во[47] описанїи Москвы согласно свидѣтелств8ютъ) сице Перунъ рече яко всѣмъ слышащим, се вам новгородцы[48] на память мою, сим веселится воспоминая[49] мене, абие ж рекъ сия выкинуⷧ на мостъ меж народа

---

[1] BGN диякони | [2] N крестяше | [3] BGN имена | [4] GRN Їоаннъ | [5] Е Семеоⷩ | [6] R прочїи | [7] BN то | [8] ER дванадесяⷮ | [9] B ante corr. имущихъ | [10] GN Їзяслава ER Изослава | [11] ER Миктислава | [12] G ad. ї | [13] B in ras. GN omm. | [14] BGN add. крⷭти | [15] ER ним | [16] Е баяⷬскихъ | [17] BERN славенскои | [18–18] BG и нⷩе мы N нынѣ мы | [19] ER omm. | [20] ER росиане N россїяне | [21] ER omm. | [22] GERN великого | [23] ER каменя | [24] N церковъ | [25] B ante corr. тезоименинника R тесомеⷩника | [26] N кирпичные | [27] N каменные | [28] N взят | [29] Е костяⷩтинаполскаго N константинополского | [30] G пеⷬвого | [31] ER вовугородку | [32] N архїепископа | [33] ER Иоанна | [34] Е корсунⷭкаго | [35] GN приведе | [36–36] N пришедше | [37] G Новъград | [38] ER взя | [39] BG їдоли | [40] ER посреди | [41–41] B ante corr. до Волⷯхова | [42] BGN крича | [43] B бѣда ante corr. беда | [44] B ante corr. немлⷭтивые G немлⷭтивыя ER немлⷭтивы | [45] N протиⷡ | [46] N Гербештеинъ | [47] BG в | [48] ER новогородцы | [49] B возпоминая

ᵃ G in marg. храмъ во имⷶ сⷫса | ᵇ G in marg. первый митрополит Ѳотиⷤ, архиепⷭкпы Леѡнтиⷤ и Їоакимⷤ | ᶜ G in marg. сокр8шение кумироⷡ въ Новѣградѣ

из воды па~лку, и сказывае~т Москва ‖ что и н~не единожды в год
сл8чае~тся в Новѣгороде великом, и сеи[1] глас[a] слыша~н бывает, егож
услышавъ абие с великимъ ш8мом стекаютца[2] и па~лками[3] дру~г з
другом бьютца, и от того то~л жестокии ш8мъ возрастае~т[4] что едва
ихъ началные с вели́кимъ трудом смирити мог8тъ; сице ж от то~г
времени[5] ве~с рускиі бѣло~и и черно~и восточно~и полуночно~и[6], и на
по~лдень лежащіи народы в хр~стиянско~и[7] вѣре под властию[8]
патриа~рха[9] констянтинополского~гω[10] и дѣиствами[11] греческими тве~рдо
і неколебимо пребываю~т, противъ р8скихъ[12] и греческихъ
лѣтописцо~в от сотворения мира .҂су~чз. в том сочислѣнïи лѣтъ
Жигимо~нтъ[13], и Герберштеин зѣло помѣшали~с[14], считая год о
Владимерове крещенïи на .҃з.м листу во описанïи Москвы .҂су~ѕ.и
противъ тѣхъ всѣхъ лѣтописцо~в руских, издателеи греческих[15] и
по~лскихъ ‖ яже азъ сие согласовахъ многажды[16], у Меховиѧ в книге
.в҃.и в главѣ .г҃.и листъ .к҃е.и Вапов҃ïи и Бѣлскïи из них год от Хр~ста
полагаетъ быти .цч҃.[17] от крещения Владимерова, а Кромеръ в книгах
.г҃. о вѣре[18] дре~внихъ словянъ[18,19] считаетъ, от сотворения мира по
греческом8 числ8 год сеи .҂су~чз.и а от Хр~ста .цп҃. и считая с
н~нешнимъ лѣтомъ г~сднимъ .҂афоѳ.и[20] и тогω б8детъ, .фчѳ. лѣтъ, а
Олга жена Игорева баба Владимерωва крестися в лѣто .҂су~ѕг.е,
прежде Владимера за .л҃д. лѣта,
Аще Зонаръ[21] греческïи лѣтωписецъ в лѣтописце кни~г[22] .г҃.[23] ‖
пишетъ яко напере~д сегω от кесаря констянтинополского[24] Василия
македонянина[25] посла~н бысть в Русь еп~скъ, (егоже елéнь 8би́
рогами[26])[27]. Р8сь же тщаниемъ[28] его вѣру християн‘ск8ю[29] прия, внегда
моляху его о чюдеси[30], какова[31] от г~да Хр~ста, сотворити[32]. еп~скпъ[33]
еv~глие[34], илѝ новыи завѣтъ вве~рже во огнь, вели́кïи[35], еже[36] в
цѣлости[37] и невредимо[37] с велиıмъ 8дивлениемъ всѣхъ россиянъ[38]
пребысть[39],
Но яко вскоре от приятыя вѣры[40] христианские[41] отст8пиша, отздѣ

---

[1] N се | [2] BGN стекаются | [3] E полками | [4] ER возрастет | [5] ERN времяни | [6] G полѹчнои
ER полуно~инои | [7] GR хр~стианскои | [8] G ad. под властию in ras. | [9] В по~триарха |
[10] B ad. почита~л in ras. G костянтинопω~лского~г ER костянтинополскаго | [11] В дѣıтвами
G дѣиствовами N действамъ | [12] N рузких | [13] ER Жимонтъ N Жигмонтъ | [14] GN
помѣшали | [15] N suprascr. | [16] ER многожды | [17] ER .ц҃е. | [18–18] B ante corr. дре~вностях |
[19] G словяны | [20] N .҂афчз. | [21] ER Занар | [22] N книга | [23] B ante corr. .е҃. |
[24] GR костянтинωпωлского~гω E костянтинополского N константинопольскагω |
[25] ER македонина | [26] E рагами | [27] G om. right parenthesis sign | [28] BER тшаниемъ |
[29] G хр~стианск8ю | [30] GN чюдеси | [31] В каковы ante corr. каковѣ GN какωвы |
[32] В сотворитис ante corr. сотвори~л N сотворитись | [33] E епскуп8 R еп~скопу |
[34] ER еваꞃгелие | [35] B ad. невреди in ras. | [36] B ante corr. яже G ѧже N юже | [37–37] B in
marg. | [38] G ро~сıанъ ER росıанъ | [39] B ante corr. быша; ad. отставка ER пребывати |
[40] N выры | [41] GN христианские ER християнския

[a] ER in marg. зриï [R зри] еще о новогородцах

является, когда Олга потомъ ко Иоанн$\breve{8}$[1] Цымисхию, а Владимеръ[2]
вн$\breve{8}$къ еѣ, х Костянтину[3] и Василисю[4] с͠номъ Цымисхиевым[5] ‖

цесаремъ греческимъ идоша прияти вѣру с͠втую хр͠стиянскую[6], о
семъ тойже Зонар в тѣхъж книгах пишет,
Воспоминает Лямберътъ саѳнабурскіи иже прежде .ф͠і. лѣтъ лѣтопис
немецкую писа лѣта от Хр͠ста .ц͠з. росіиские[7] народы ко Антону[8]
первому кесарю послы своя послаша, моля его да пошлеть к нимъ
еп͠скпа учения ради вѣры хр͠стиянские[9]. кесар же посла к ним еп͠скпа
Адалберта[10], онже от руку их насилу $\breve{8}$йде, хотящим[11] убити его,[12]
[13]но мнится[13, 14] истинно быти, яко Зонар, и іные лѣтописатели
гречестіи и руские[15] лѣтописателі свидѣтелств$\breve{8}$ютъ, яко прежде
Олга, потом внукъ еѣ[16] Вла́димиръ[17] кр͠стилися, и всѣ руские земли
восприялі[18] вѣру греческаго[19] sакона, по чинам греческим в Ц͠рѣграде

основателно[20], руские ‖ всѣ земли, в[21] познание, истинног[22] Б͠га и
Їс͠8са Хр͠ста с͠на его единороднагѡ[23], приведоша в лѣто от Хр͠ста .ц͠п. а
поляки н͠ши .ц͠s. при Мечеславе[24] Земомиславовиче[25] к͠нзе[26, a] вси[27]
кр͠стишася единомышленно, венгры[28] потому[29] ж в лѣто .п͠ч. аще их
к͠нзь Геиджа Стеѳана[30] с͠втаго с͠нъ[31] крещение[32] прия в лѣто .ц͠п. в то
время когда и Владимир[33], а чехи в лѣто от Хр͠ста г͠сда .о͠че. при
Боривое к͠нзе первом хр͠стиянском[34], однакож до лѣта .ц͠кѳ. году
чернь вѣру крѣпко егда[35] прия,
Чита́телю любезный опи́сание[36] дѣйствъ Владимировыхъ[37] немного
оставити їмам понеже вѣдати намъ потребно есть какими
мерзкими[38] к$\breve{8}$мирохваленіи діаволъ[39] прелстилъ было предковъ

н͠ших словяковъ русаковъ чеховъ. ‖ поляковъ, и проч[40]: и Литв$\breve{8}$
которыя[41] поганския[42] дѣйства от насъ с велімъ трудом собраны, и
глубокими доводы достигнуты[43], и їспытаны здѣ аки[44] в зерцале[45], ї
аки на древніи[46] вѣкъ предков своих зрѣти имаши,

---

[1] Е Ианн$\breve{8}$ | [2] G Владимиръ | [3] N Констянтину | [4] BGRN Василию Е Василю | [5] B ante
corr. Цымис{ийн}ымъ | [6] GR хр͠стианск8ю | [7] BG росіиские ER росиские N россіискіи
| [8] BGN Онтону | [9] GR хр͠стианския | [10] R Адарберта | [11] N хотяще | [12] [Text passage
untranslated] | [13-13] ER помнится | [14] G мнитца | [15] G рустіи | [16] BGN ея | [17] GERN
Владимеръ | [18] B возприялі | [19] G греческѡго | [20] ER соснователно | [21] BGN во | [22] GER
їстиннаго | [23] G единороднѡгѡ | [24] BGN Мичеславе | [25] N Земомиславиче | [26] G кнзи |
[27] Е всиі | [28] R венгеры | [29] G потом | [30] B ante corr. Стевана | [31] ER omm. | [32] N крещенїя
| [33] R Владимер | [34] G хр͠стианскѡмъ | [35] B едва ante corr. едда GERN едва | [36] B ante corr.
описанеи | [37] GER Владимеровыхъ | [38] GER мерзскими N мерскими | [39] N діяволъ |
[40] R прочиі | [41] Е которые N которая | [42] G пѡганские | [43] U ante corr. достигнути
BGN достигнути | [44] B ante corr. яки | [45] B ante corr. герцале | [46] Е дре͠вни

[a] G in marg. время крещения россиянъ полаковъ венгровъ и чеховъ

Illustration 1. Ms. U, Slav 26, fol. 1r.

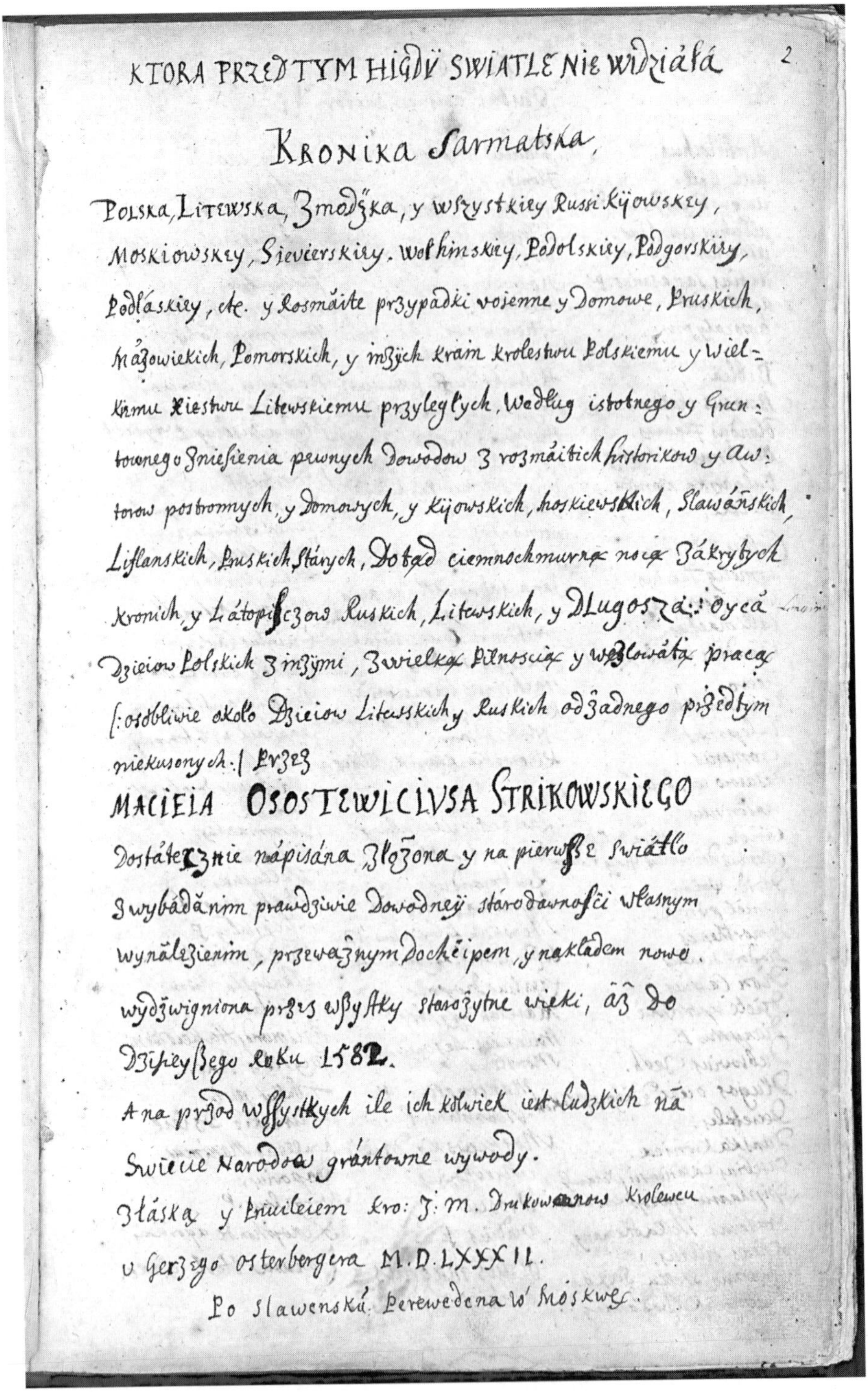

KTORA PRZEDTYM HIGDY ŚWIATŁE NIE WIDZIAŁA

Kronika Sarmatska,

Polska, Litewska, Zmodzka, y wszystkiey Russi Kijowskiey, Moskiowskiey, Sieverskiey. wołhinskiey, Podolskiey, Podgorskiey, Podlaskiey, etc. y rozmaite przypadki wojenne y Domowe, Pruskich, Mazowieckich, Pomorskich, y inszych kraim krolestwu Polskiemu y Wielkimu Xiestwu Litewskiemu przyległych, Według istotnego y Gruntownego Zniesienia pewnych dowodow z rozmaitich historikow y Awtorow postronnych, y Domowych, y Kijowskich, hoskiewskich, Sławańskich, Liflanskich, Ruskich starych, Dotąd ciemnochmurną nocą Zakrytych kronich, y Latopiszczow Ruskich, Litewskich, y Długosza: Oycá Dzieiow Polskich z inszymi, z wielką Pilnoscią y wązłowátą pracą [: osobliwie około Dzieiow Litewskich y Ruskich od zadnego przedtym niekusonych.] Przez

MACIEIA OSOSTEWICIVSA STRIKOWSKIEGO

Dostatecznie napisána złożona y na pierwsze świátło z wybádánim prawdziwie Dowodnej starodawnosci własnym wynalezienim, przeważnym dochcipem, y nakładem nowo wydzwigniona przez wszystky starozytne wieki, áż do Dziszyszego roku 1582.

A na przod wszystkych ile ich kolwiek iest Ludzkich ná Świecie Narodow grántowne wywody.

Z łáska y przwileiem kro: J. M. Drukowanow Kroleweu u Gerzego Osterbergera M.D.LXXXII.

Po Slawenską Perewedena w Moskwę.

Illustration 2. Ms. U, Slav 26, fol. 2r.

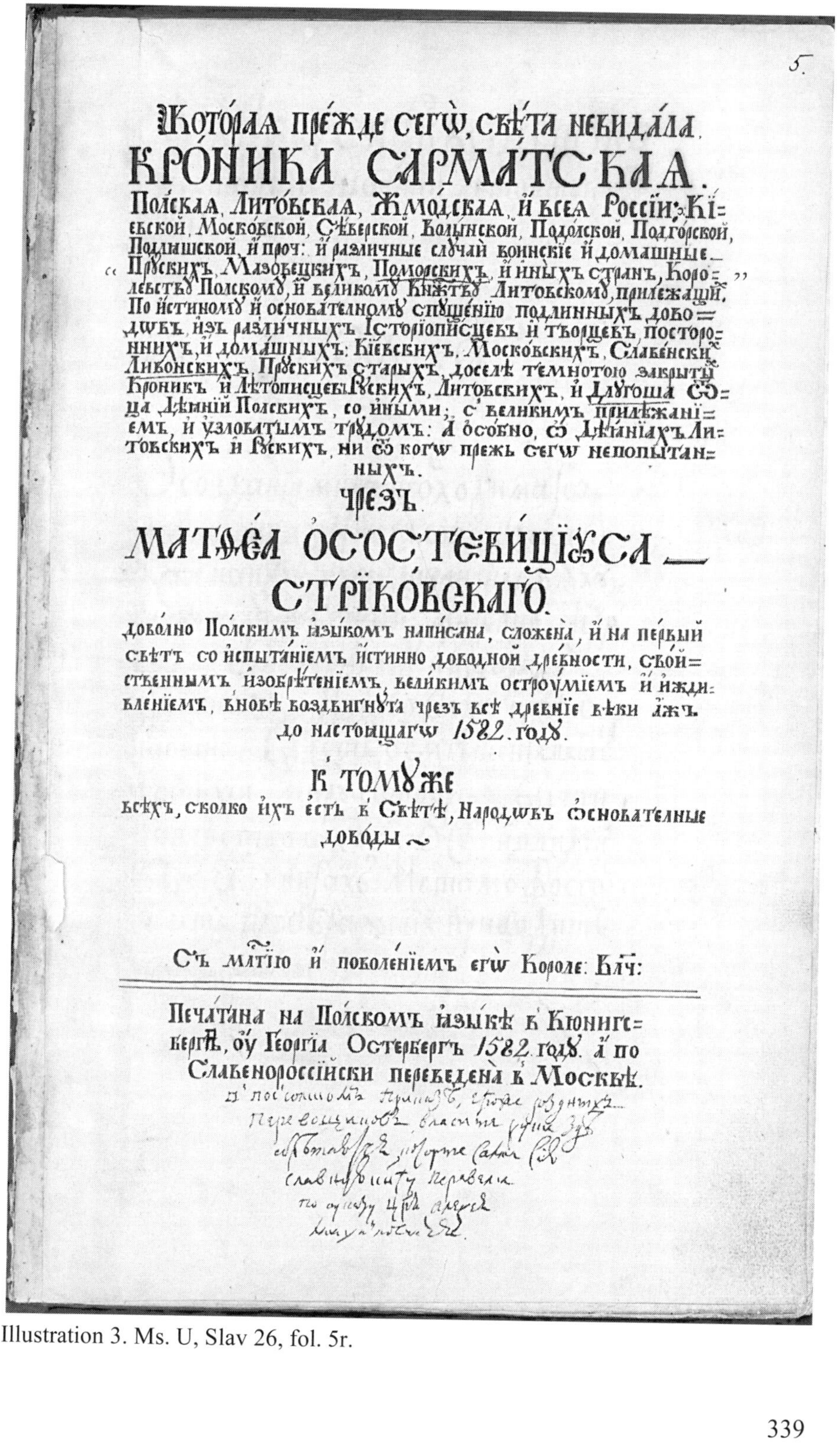

Которая прежде сегш, свѣта невидала.

КРОНИКА САРМАТСКАЯ.

Полская, Литовская, Жмодская, й всеѧ Россіи: Кі=
евской, Московской, Сѣверской, Волынской, Подолской, Подгорской,
Подляшской, й проч: и различные слѫчаи воинскіе й домашные
Прѫскихъ, Мазовецкихъ, Поморскихъ, й иныхъ странъ, Коро=
левствѣ Полскомъ, й великомꙋ Княжствꙋ Литовскому, прилежащи,
По истиномꙋ й основателномꙋ сношенію подлинныхъ дово=
дшвъ, изъ различныхъ Історіописцевъ и творцевъ, постороꙋ=
нныхъ, й домашныхъ: Кіевскихъ, Московскихъ, Славенски,
Лнвонскихъ, Прѫскихъ старыхъ, доселѣ темнотою закрыты
Кроникъ и Лѣтописцевъ Рѫскихъ, Литовскихъ, й Длꙋгоша Сѫ=
ца Дѣянїй Полскихъ, со иными, съ великимъ прилѣжанї=
емъ, й узловатымъ трꙋдомъ: А особно, со Дѣянїахъ Ли=
товскихъ й Рꙋскихъ, ни ш̑ кого прежъ сегш непопытан=
ныхъ.

ЧРЕЗЪ

МАТѲЕѦ ОСОСТЕВИЩꙊСѦ
СТРІКОВСКАГО

доволно Полскимъ языкомъ написана, сложена, й на первый
свѣтъ со испытанїемъ истинно доводной древности, свои=
ственнымъ изобрѣтенїемъ, великимъ остроꙋмїемъ й ижди=
вленїемъ, вновѣ воздвигнꙋта чрезъ всѣ древнїе вѣки ижъ
до настоѧщагш 1582. годꙋ.

К ТОМꙊЖЕ

всѣхъ, сколко ихъ есть к Свѣтѣ, Народшвъ ш̑снователные
доводы ~

Съ мѧтїю й поколенїемъ егш Короле: Влч:

Печатана на Полскомъ языкѣ к Кюниге=
кергѣ, ш̑ꙋ Геωргіа Остеркергъ 1582. годꙋ. а̑ по
Славенороссійски переведена к Москвѣ.

[рукописные строки, частично неразборчивы]

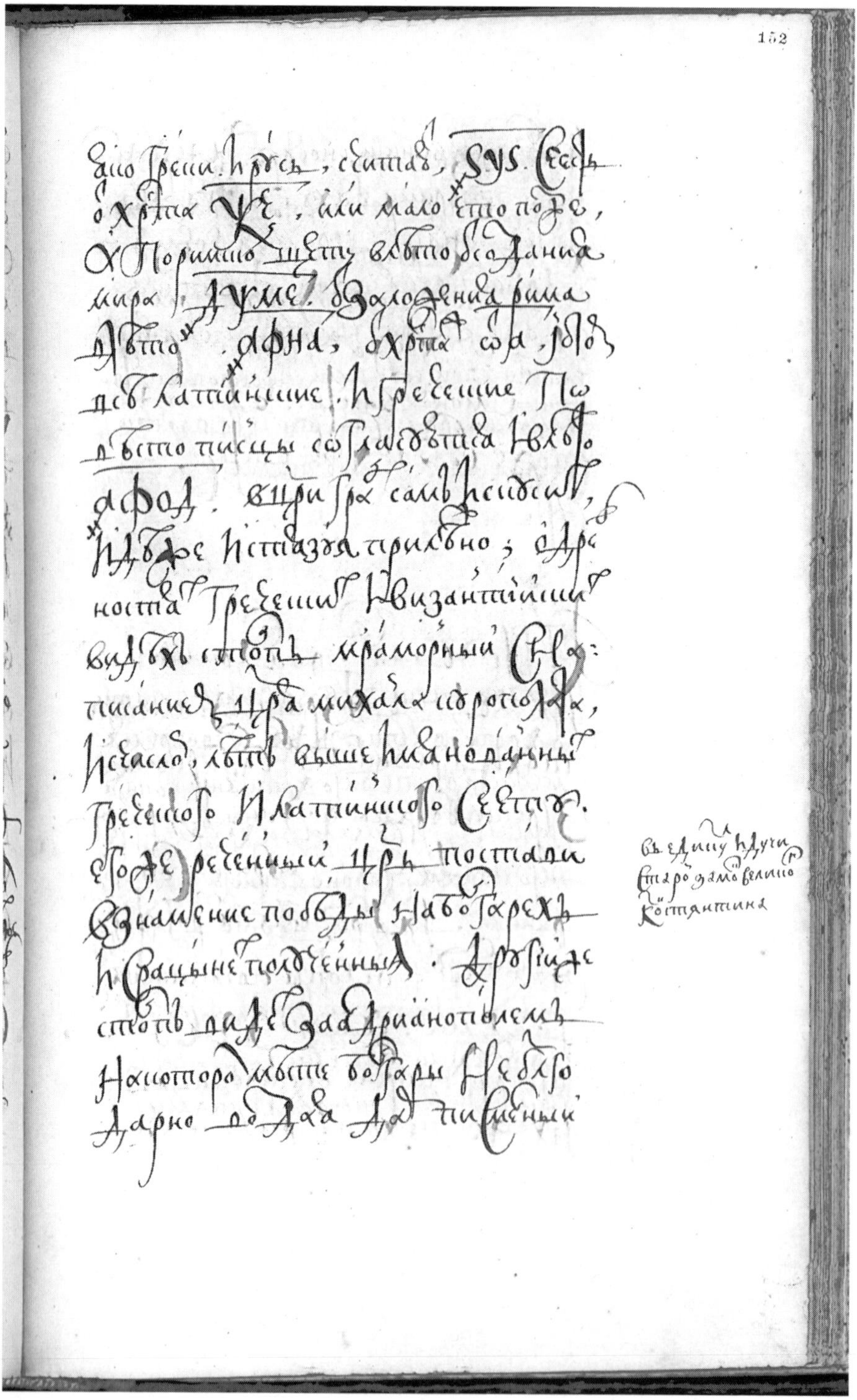

Illustration 4. Ms. U, Slav 26, fol. 152r. Hand U1.

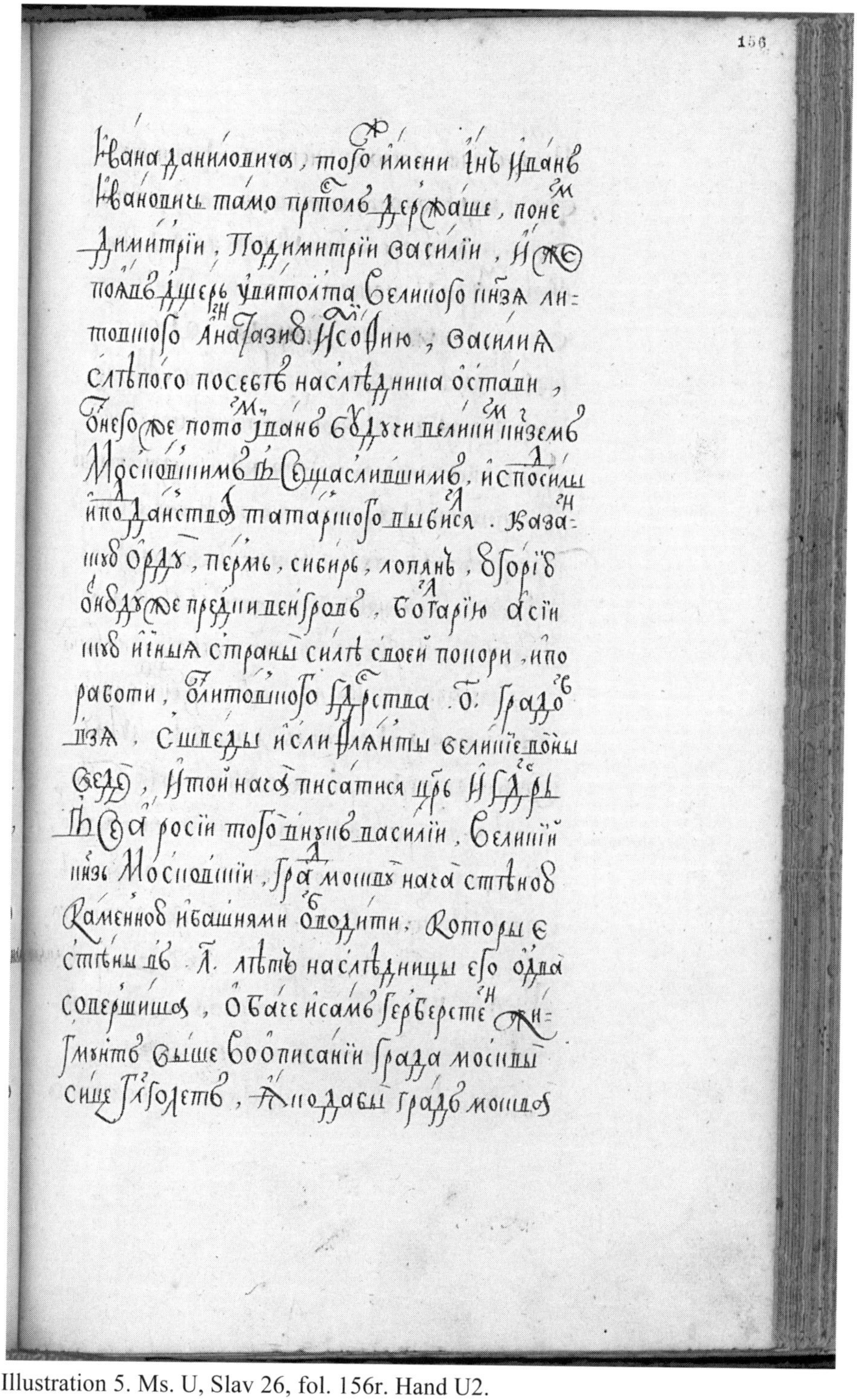

Ивана Даниловича, того имени Инъ Иванъ

Ивановичь тамо пртолъ держаше, понеже

Димитрїй, по Димитрїи Василїй, иже

поялъ дщерь у Литолта Великого кнѕа ли-

товского Анастазїю и со брню, Василїа

слѣпого по себѣ наслѣдника остави,

онего же пото Иванъ бѧ учинели ни кнѕемъ

московскимъ и всщаслившимъ, и споди

и по данство татарщого избися. Каза-

нию Орду, пермь, сибирь, лопань, Югорѣ

ондахъ же предиписенгролъ. Ботарїю и сїи

иныа страны силѣ своей покори, ипо

работи, Онитонного цртва о. градо

иѕа. Сшеды и слифланты великїе поны

велю, И той началъ писатися цръ И цадрь

и во росїи того кнѕвъ Василїй. Великїй

кнѕь московскїй. Градъ мошхъ на са стѣнов

каменнои ибашнями ополдити. Которыѥ

стѣны до Л. лѣтъ наслѣдницы его одна

совершиша, о вагеи самъ герберсте кни-

гмѣнтъ выше во описанїи града москвы

сице глаголетъ, Ано даби градъ мошва

Illustration 5. Ms. U, Slav 26, fol. 156r. Hand U2.

совершилось , а иже барашихъ иные
кнзи о иг[о]ря да доннешнаго единого
кнза мос[ко]пикого нопимъ родословие
зачелись ,

и де потомъ споимомъ бле на дрепла=
ны соборенъ и деднша таиоде
народа рекшего , и понорилъ и попла=
ти спод дань нани пологи попо=
еде ра додиа пишетъ попе[р]венъ
прилеспи нона его же болши пебхъ
ле баше прислалъ поихпопъ поиро=
еи ихъ , сто отиоемъ нонъ чаали
еле , иде приниe решаша , дисъ
тии вдинии инаде о сего нонъ
отреши , того да поимбъ есъ ,
оседа отъ еспи , пособъ храниши ,
и обрапъ болши поисчъ и ре спихъ
в диеиъ иде водяны народомъ
грегорное море пигрь гра , его же
сило отъ единоe достапаше бепресда
но морень и земеу дрошина лехтена

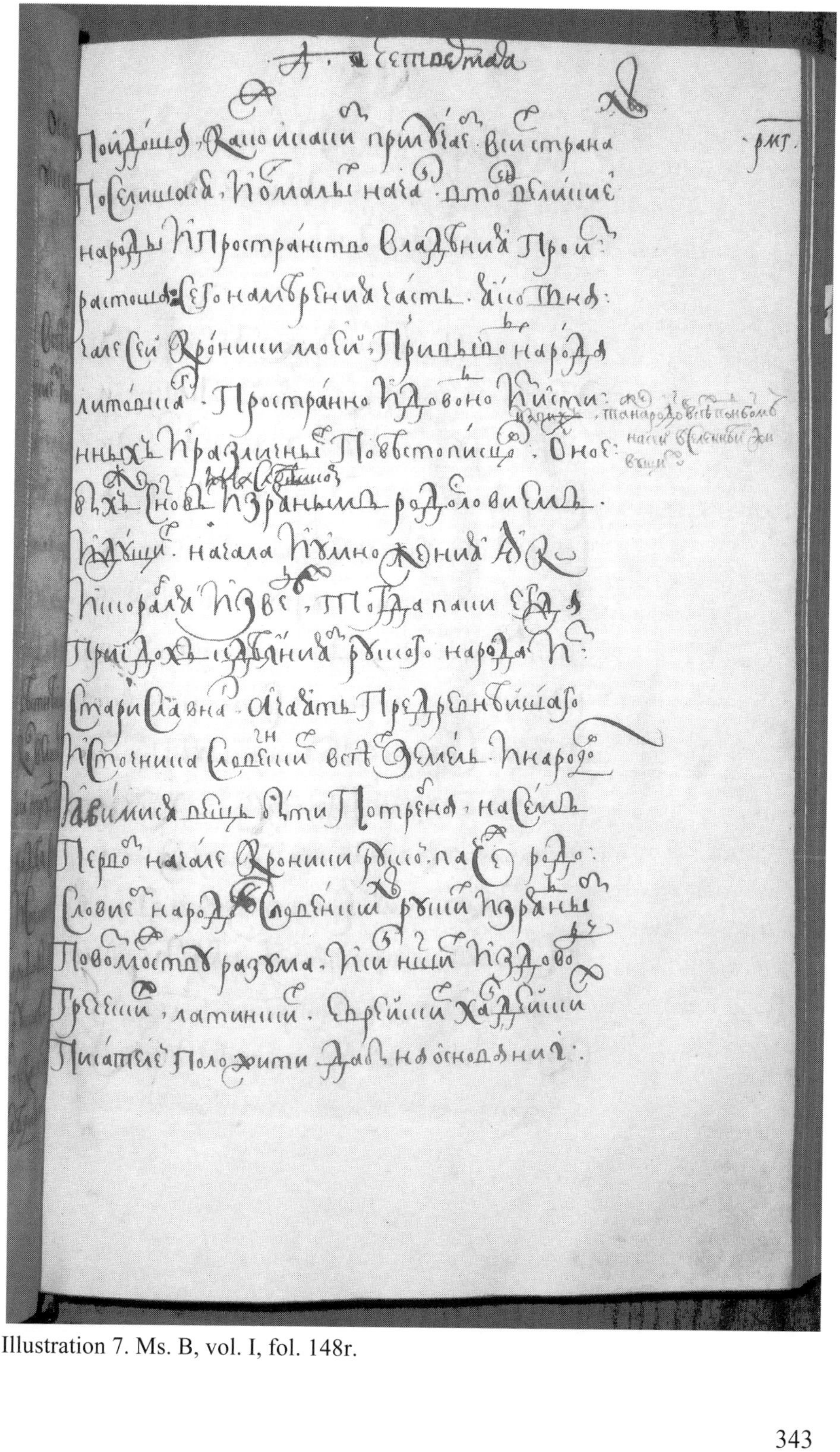

Illustration 7. Ms. B, vol. I, fol. 148r.

которые постели единаго краля быль
щедро каменiем драгимъ сребромъ
шиталми также Изрядными рядами
и обиталнаго сыровища на дели .

Основа ж король а сеи июда храма .
Ситабу картина вверхней твердыни
виленскои, которыи также потребными
вещми Инаданиемъ трапезны на дели
нике яко видимъ да престъ юда же тописе
знаменiа былыа горы писанаго зданiа
удавлены стоятъ содовъ, о которомъ
нике гляти пореме домъ божiи и ж ..
тре ж де сотники почитаемъ об дiи ..
нике ж пресилиш .... ж ... жилище
... плаче въ благо драгу ханi ..
а нет разорi гд арi дн станна ф ранктiа замiа Iо ... прiе и ра ...
та же а сеи з братиевъ своевъ сикнзi ями старочнiи ...
нато же виленскомъ ситу де, даде тра благосовнед пл ...
мотъ зданъ на виленское бишъ ство , разорнiа поирибо,
в которой то преж де з запони, да бы
рюмъ греческаго закона сiа домiалми
вимши в отеры в утру ж еитъ о не достоише ор ... ф имiаны
входитеи, да ж е бы пре дерзновенна по ... становленiе
при пргiанiа яко слышанiе вмишанiе постела

Bibliography

Manuscript sources
BAN 31.4.32
CGIA SPb no. 58922
GIM Muz. 1391
JaGPU B-596
RGADA f. 5, op. 1, no. 1
RGADA f. 138, op. 1, no. 20
RGADA f. 159, op. 1, no. 825
RGADA f. 181, no. 58
RGADA f. 181, no. 59
RGADA f. 181, no. 365
RGB Egor., f. 98, no. 243
RNB Ėrm. 551
RNB F.IV.103
RNB F.IV.131
RNB F.IV.172
RNB F.IV.688
UUB Bibl. Ark. K 52:3
UUB Bibl. Ark. A 7
UUB Slav 26, 27, 28

Dictionaries and encyclopedias
Brockhaus, Efron: Брокгаузъ, Ефронъ, *Энциклопедический словарь*, 1–82. Санкт-Петербург 1890–1904.
Estreicher: Estreicher, Karol, *Bibliografia polska*, 1–33. Kraków 1872–1939.
HSBM: *Гістарычны слоўнік беларускай мовы*, 1–31–. Мінск 1982–2011–.
Lexicon Slavonicum: Sparwenfeld, Johan Gabriel, *Lexicon Slavonicum*. Edited and commented by Ulla Birgegård, I–IV. Uppsala 1987–1990.
Linde: Linde, Samuel, *Słownik języka polskiego*, 2nd ed., I–VI. Lwów 1854–1860.
Nowy Korbut: Bibliografia literatury polskiej Nowy Korbut, 1–. Warszawa 1963–.
PSB: *Polski Słownik Biograficzny*, 1–47–. Wrocław – Warszawa – Kraków 1935–2011–.
SDJa: *Словарь древнерусского языка (XI–XIV вв.)*, I–VIII–. Москва 1988–2008–.
SKK 1988: *Словарь книжников и книжности древней Руси, вторая половина XIV–XVI в. Часть 1: А–К*. Ленинград 1998.
SKK 1989: *Словарь книжников и книжности древней Руси, вторая половина XIV–XVI в. Часть 2: Л–Я*. Ленинград 1989.
SKK 1992: *Словарь книжников и книжности древней Руси, XVII в. Часть 1: А–З*. Санкт-Петербург 1992.
SKK 1993: *Словарь книжников и книжности древней Руси, XVII в. Часть 2: И–О*. Санкт-Петербург 1993.

SKK 2004: *Словарь книжников и книжности древней Руси, XVII в. Часть 4: Т–Я.* Санкт-Петербург 2004.

SP XVI: *Słownik polszczyzny XVI wieku*, I–XXXV–. Wrocław – Warszawa – Kraków 1966–2011–.

Sreznevskij: Срезневский, И. И., *Материалы для словаря древне-русскаго языка по писменным памятникам*, I–III. Санкт-Петербург 1893–1903.

SRJa: *Словарь русского языка XI–XVII вв.*, 1–29–. Москва 1975–2011–.

SSP: *Słownik staropolski*, 1–11. Wrocław – Warszawa – Kraków 1953–2002.

SUM: *Словник української мови XVI–першої половини XVII ст.*, 1–15–. Львів 1994–2010–.

Vasmer: Фасмер, Макс, *Этимологический словарь русского языка. Перевод с немецкого и дополнения О. Н. Трубачева*, I–IV. Москва 1964–1973.

Literature

Avanesaŭ 1961: Аванесаў, Р. І. (рэд.), *Хрэстаматыя па гісторыі беларускай мовы. Частка I.* Мінск.

Aleksandrov & Volodichin 1993: Александров, Д. & Д. Володихин, «Русская хроничка» Стрыйковского. *Вестник МГУ. Серия 8: История* 2, 70–74.

Alekseev 1987: Алексеев, А. А., Participium activi в русской летописи: особенности функционирования. *Russian Linguistics* 11, 187–200.

Al'šic 1968: Альшиц, Д. Н., *Историческая коллекция Эрмитажного собрания рукописей. Памятники XI–XVII вв. Описание.* Москва.

Bardach 1970: Bardach, Juliusz, *Studia z ustroju i prawa Wielkiego Księstwa Litewskiego XIV–XVII w.* Warszawa.

Belokurov 1906: Белокуров, С. А., *О Посольском приказе.* Москва.

Beljakov 2002: Беляков, А. В., *Служащие Посольского приказа второй трети XVII века.* Дис. ... канд. ист. наук. Москва.

Bergman 1964: Bergman, Gun, *The Melusina Saga. The text in UUB Slav 34 and a study in 17th century literary language in Russia.* Uppsala (Acta Universitatis Upsaliensis, Studia Slavica Upsaliensia 2).

Besters-Dilger 1997: Besters-Dilger, Juliane, Модальность в польском и русском языках. Историческое развитие выражения необходимости и возможности как результат вне- и межславянского влияния. *Wiener Slavistisches Jahrbuch* 43, 17–31.

Besters-Dilger 2005: Besters-Dilger, Juliane, Modalität im Sprachkontakt. Die ukrainische „Prosta mova" (2. Hälfte 16. Jh). Hansen, Björn & Petr Karlík (eds.), *Modality in Slavonic languages. New perspectives.* München, 239–258.

Birgegård 1985: Birgegård, Ulla, *Johan Gabriel Sparwenfeld and the Lexicon Slavonicum. His contribution to 17th century Slavonic lexicography.* Uppsala (Acta Bibliothecae R. Universitatis Upsaliensis 23).

Birgegård 2002: Birgegård, Ulla, *J. G. Sparwenfeld's diary of a journey to Russia 1684–87.* Stockholm (Slavica Suecana, Series A: Publications 1).

Bjørnflaten 2010: Bjørnflaten, Jan Ivar, Grammaticalization theory and the formation of gerunds in Russian. Hansen, Björn & Jasmina Grković-Major (eds.), *Diachronic Slavonic syntax. Gradual changes in focus.* München/Berlin/Wien (Wiener slawistischer Almanach, Sonderband 74), 19–28.

Borkovskij & Kuznecov 1963: Борковский, В. И. & П. С. Кузнецов, *Историческая грамматика русского языка.* Москва.

Brogi Bercoff 2003: Броджи Беркофф, Дж., Аспекты русской историографии XVII – начала XVIII в. в европейском контексте. *ТОДРЛ* 54, 211–219.

Burzywoda et al. 2002: Burzywoda, Urszula, Danuta Ostaszewska, Artur Rejter & Mirosława Siuciak, *Polszczyzna XVII wieku. Stan i przeobrażenia*. Katowice.

The Cambridge History 2006: *The Cambridge History of Russia. Volume I: From Early Rus' to 1689*. Cambridge.

Čerepnin 1956: Черепнин, Л. В., *Русская палеография*. Москва.

Charlampovič 1914: Харлампович, К. В., *Малороссийское влияние на велико-русскую церковную жизнь. Том I*. Казань.

Churchill 1935: Churchill, W. A., *Watermarks in paper in Holland, England, France, etc., in the XVII and XVIII centuries and their interconnection*. Amsterdam.

Čistjakova 1963: Чистякова, Е. В., «Скифская история» А. И. Лызлова и труды польских историков XVI–XVII вв. *ТОДРЛ* 19, 348–357.

Čiževskij 1960: Čiževskij, Dmitrij, *History of Russian literature. From the eleventh century to the end of the baroque*. 'S-Gravenhage (Slavistic printings and re-printings 12).

Cocron 1962: Cocron, Friedrich, *La langue russe dans la seconde moitié du XVIIe siècle (morphologie)*. Paris (Bibliothèque russe de l'Institut d'études slaves 33).

Corin 1995: Corin, Andrew R., The Dative Absolute in OCS and OES. *Die Welt der Slaven* 40:2, 251–284.

Crummey 1983: Crummey, Robert O., *Aristocrats and servitors. The boyar elite in Russia, 1613–1689*. Princeton.

Daniłowicz [1846] 1985: Daniłowicz, Ignac, Wiadomość o właściwych litewskich latopisach. Stryjkowski, Maciej, *Kronika polska, litewska, żmódzka i wszystkiéj Rusi*, Wydanie nowe. I. Warszawa, 31–63.

Das 1986: Das, David, The margin is the message: Andrej Lyzlov's translation of Stryjkowski's *Kronika. Europa Orientalis* 5, 345–350.

Das 1992: Das, David, History writing and the quest for fame in late Muscovy: Andrei Lyzlov's *History of the Scythians. The Russian Review* 51:4, 502–509.

Davidsson 1975: Davidsson, Carin, Den slaviska handskriftssamlingen i Uppsala universitetsbibliotek. *Kring den svenska slavistikens äldsta historia*. Lund (*Slavica Lundensia* 3), 53–82.

Deržavina 1963: Державина, О. А., Работа русских переводчиков над сборником «Великое зерцало». *Славянска филология. Т. IV: Доклади, съобщения и статии по литературознание. Материали за V Международен конгрес на славистите*. София, 325–342.

Deržavina 1965: Державина, О. А., *«Великое зерцало» и его судьба на русской почве*. Москва.

Dianova 1997: Дианова, Т. В., *Филиграни XVII–XVIII вв. «Голова шута». Каталог*. Москва.

Djačok 1990: Дячок, О. А., Анализ рукописных переводов «Хроники Европейской Сарматии» А. Гваньини на русский и украинский языки. *Исследования по археографии и источниковедению отечественной истории XVI–XX вв*. Днепропетровск, 19–31.

Długosz-Kurczabowa & Dubisz 2006: Długosz-Kurczabowa, Krystyna & Stanisław Dubisz, *Gramatyka historyczna języka polskiego*. Warszawa.

Eckhoff 2006: Eckhoff, Hanne Martine, *Old Russian possessive constructions: A construction grammar account*. Oslo.

Erusalimskij 2009: Ерусалимский, К. Ю., *Сборник Курбского. Том I: Исследование книжной культуры*. Москва.

Filigrani XVII veka 1988: *Филиграни XVII века по рукописным источникам ГИМ. Каталог*. Москва.

Florus 1984: Florus, Lucius Annaeus, *Epitome of Roman History*. Cambridge, Mass./London (Loeb Classical Library 231).

Gardiner 1963: Gardiner, S. C., Translation technique in 17th-century Russia. *The Slavonic and East European Review* 42:98, 110–135.

Geraklitov 1963: Гераклитов, А. А., *Филиграни XVII века на бумаге рукописных и печатных документов русского происхождения*. Москва.

Gippius 2001: Гиппиус, А. А., Рекоша дроужина Игореви... К лингвотексто-логической стратификации Начальной летописи. *Russian Linguistics* 25, 147–181.

Gippius 2006: Гиппиус, А. А., Новгородская владычная летопись XII–XIV вв. и ее авторы (История и структура текста в лингвистическом освещении). *Лингвистическое источниковедение и история русского языка 2004–2005*. Москва, 114–252.

Glubokovskij 1918: Глубоковский, Н., *Описание «славянскихъ» рукописей, хранящихся в Королевской библиотеке Упсальского Университета, составленное профессором Петроградской Духовной Академии Николаем Глубоковским в октябре–ноябре 1918 года* (UUB Bibl. ark. M 40r:2).

Glubokovskij 1919: *Les manuscrits slaves de la Bibliothèque de l'Université d'Upsal par N. N. Gloubokovski, professeur de l'Académie Ecclésiastique de Pétrograde. Traduit du russe en français, avec des commentaires détaillés et des suppléments d'après les études de l'original, par Alexandre de Roubetz* (UUB Bibl. Ark. M 40r:4).

Golicyn 1892: Голицын, Н. Н., *Род князей Голицыных. Том I: Материалы родословные*. Санкт-Петербург.

Gorškova & Chaburgaev 1997: Горшкова, К. В. & Г. А. Хабургаев, *Историческая грамматика русского языка*. 2-е изд., испр. Москва.

Graham, Hirst & Marthi 2005: Graham, Neil, Graeme Hirst & Bhaskara Marthi, Segmenting documents by stylistic character. *Natural Language Engineering* 11, 397–415.

Grybosiowa 1973: Grybosiowa, Antonina, O spójnikowym połączeniu imiesłowu nieodmiennego z orzeczeniem w dawnej polszczyźnie. *Prace językoznawcze II*. Katowice (Prace naukowe Uniwersytetu Śląskiego w Katowicach 35), 83–93.

Günther-Hielscher 1995: Günther-Hielscher, Karla et al., *Real- und Sachwörterbuch zum Altrussischen*. 2. Aufl., neu bearb. von Ekkehard Kraft. Wiesbaden.

Hansen 2000: Hansen, Björn, The German modal verb *müssen* and the Slavonic languages – the reconstruction of a success story. *Scando-Slavica* 46, 77–92.

Haspelmath 1995: Haspelmath, Martin, The converb as a cross-linguistically valid category. Haspelmath, Martin & Ekkehard König (eds.), *Converbs in cross-linguistic perspective. Structure and meaning of adverbial verb forms – adverbial participles, gerunds*. Berlin – New York, 1–55.

Helander 2004: Helander, Hans, *Neo-Latin literature in Sweden in the period 1620–1720. Stylistics, vocabulary and characteristic ideas*. Uppsala (Acta Universitatis Upsaliensis, Studia Latina Upsaliensia 29).

Hüttl-Folter 1996: Hüttl-Folter, Gerta, *Syntaktische Studien zur neueren russischen Literatursprache. Die frühen Übersetzungen aus dem Französischen*. Wien – Köln – Weimar.

Iordanidi & Krys'ko 2000: Иорданиди, С. И. & В. Б. Крысько, *Историческая грамматика древнерусского языка. Том I: Множественное число именного склонения*. Москва.

Isserlin 1961: Иссерлин, Е. М., *Лексика русского литературного языка XVII века*. Москва.

Istorija russkogo dramatičeskogo teatra 1977: История русского драматического театра в семи томах. *Том I: От истоков до конца XVIII века.* Москва.

Izotova 2004: Изотова К. А., Русско-польские отношения во 2-й половине XVII-го века. Переговоры в Андрусово. 1674 г. (По материалам статейных списков русских послов). *Исследования по источниковедению истории России (до 1917 г.). Сборник статей.* Москва, 150–164.

Juola 2006: Juola, Patrick, Authorship attribution. *Foundations and trends in information retrieval* 1:3, 233–334.

Kamiński 1993: Kamiński, Andrzej Sulima, *Republic vs autocracy. Poland-Lithuania and Russia 1686–1697.* Cambridge, Mass. (Harvard Series in Ukrainian Studies).

Karplukówna 1977: Karplukówna, Maria, *O języku Macieja Stryjkowskiego historyka i poety z drugiej połowy XVI wieku.* Kraków (Prace komisji językoznawstwa PAN, oddział w Krakowie 45).

Karplukówna 1985: Karplukówna, Maria, Cechy regionalne oraz rutenizmy morfologiczne i składniowe w języku Macieja Stryjkowskiego (2. połowa XVI w.). *Studia z filologii polskiej i słowiańskiej* 25, 23–47.

Keenan 1971: Keenan, Edward, *The Kurbskii-Groznyi apocrypha.* Cambridge, Mass. (Russian Research Center Studies 66).

Kijanova 2006: Киянова, О. Н., *Язык памятников позднего русского летописания. Особенности грамматической нормы.* Москва.

Kijanova 2007: Киянова, О. Н., *Проблемы языковой нормы русских летописных текстов конца XVI–XVIII вв.* Дис. ... д-ра филол. наук. Москва.

Kijanova 2010: Киянова, О. Н., *Поздние летописи и истории русского литературного языка. Конец XVI – начало XVIII веков.* Санкт-Петербург.

Klemensiewicz et al. [1955] 1981: Klemensiewicz, Z., T. Lehr-Spławiński & S. Urbańczyk, *Gramatyka historyczna języka polskiego.* Warszawa.

Klepikov 1958: Клепиков, С. А., Бумага с филигранью «Герб города Амстердама». *Записки отдела рукописей* 20, 315–352.

Klepikov 1959: Клепиков, С. А., *Филиграни и штемпели на бумаге русского и иностранного производства XVII–XX вв.* Москва.

Klepikov 1963: Клепиков, С. А., Бумага с филигранью «голова шута (foolscap)». *Записки отдела рукописей* 26, 405–478.

Kloss 1980: Клосс, Б. М., *Никоновский свод и русские летописи XVI–XVII веков.* Москва.

Knjaz'kov 1984: Князьков, Ю. П., *Украинский хронограф как источник по отечественной истории.* Дис. ... канд. ист. наук. Днепропетровск.

Kochman 1975: Kochman, Stanisław, *Polsko-rosyjskie stosunki językowe od XVI do XVIII w.* Opole.

Kohut 2004: Когут, З., От Иафета до Москвы: процесс создания библейской родословной славян в польской, украинской и русской историографии (XVII–XVIII вв.). *Украина и соседние государства в XVII веке. Материалы международной конференции.* Санкт-Петербург, 59–82.

Koller 2004: Koller, Werner, *Einführung in die Übersetzungswissenschaft.* 7., aktualisierte Aufl. Wiebelsheim.

Kosta 1982: Kosta, Peter, *Eine russische Kosmographie aus dem 17. Jahrhundert. Sprachwissenschaftliche Analyse mit Textedition und Faksimile.* München (Specimina philologiae Slavicae 40).

Kozlov 2011: Козлов, С. А., *Русские пленные Великой Северной войны 1700–1721.* Санкт-Петербург.

Krys'ko 1994: Крысько, В. Б., *Развитие категории одушевленности в истории русского языка*. Москва.

Kudrjavcev 1963: Кудрявцев, И. М., «Издательская» деятельность Посольского приказа. (К истории русской рукописной книги во второй половине XVII века.). *Книга. Исследования и материалы* 8, 179–244.

Kulicka 1980: Kulicka, Elżbieta, Legenda o rzymskim pochodzeniu Litwinów i jej stosunek do mitu sarmackiego. *Przegląd historyczny* 71:1, 1–21.

Larsen 2005: Larsen, Karin, *The evolution of the system of long and short adjectives in Old Russian*. München (Slavistische Beiträge 439).

Laucevičius 1967a: Laucevičius, Edmundas, *Popierius Lietuvoje XV–XVIII a.* Vilnius.

Laucevičius 1967b: Laucevičius, Edmundas, *Popierius Lietuvoje XV–XVIII a. Atlasas.* Vilnius.

Leeming 1968: Leeming, Henry, Polonisms in a 17th-century Ruthenian text. *The Slavonic and East European Review* 46, 282–314.

Leeming 1973: Leeming, Henry, Polish-Latin influences in pre-Petrine East Slavonic: some observations. *The Slavonic and East European Review* 51, 344–357.

Leeming 1976: Leeming, Henry, *Rola języka polskiego w rozwoju leksyki rosyjskiej do roku 1696. Wyrazy pochodzenia łacińskiego i romańskiego.* Kraków (Prace komisji językoznawstwa PAN, oddział w Krakowie 44).

Leskien 1886: Leskien, A., *Handbuch der altbulgarischen (altkirchenslavischen) Sprache. Grammatik. Texte. Glossar.* 2., völlig umgearb. Aufl. Weimar.

Lichačëv 1947: Лихачев, Д. С., *Русские летописи и их культурно-историческое значение.* Москва – Ленинград.

Lichačëv 2001: Лихачев, Д. С., *Текстология на материале русской литературы X–XVII веков.* 3-е изд., перераб. и доп. Санкт-Петербург.

Lukičev 2004: Лукичев, М. П., *Боярские книги XVII века. Труды по истории и источниковедению.* Москва.

Luk'janov 1955: Лукьянов, В. В., Рукописные собрания Ярославского областного архива и Ярославского педагогического института им. К. Д. Ушинского. *ТОДРЛ* 11, 464–470.

Luppov 1970: Луппов, С. П., *Книга в России в XVII веке.* Ленинград.

Lyzlov 1990: Лызлов, Андрей, *Скифская история.* Москва.

Maier 2008: Майер, Ингрид, *Вести-Куранты 1656 г., 1660–1662 гг., 1664–1670 гг. Часть 2: Иностранные оригиналы к русским текстам.* Москва.

Maier & Pilger 2003: Maier, Ingrid & Wouter Pilger, Polnische Fabelzeitung über Sabbatai Zwi, übersetzt für den russischen Zaren (1666). *Zeitschrift für Slavische Philologie* 62:1, 1–39.

Malevanov 1957: Малеванов, Н. А., Рукописи XVI–XVIII вв. Государственного исторического архива Ленинградской области. *ТОДРЛ* 13, 574–576.

Malinowski [1846] 1985: Malinowski, Mikołaj, Wiadomość o życiu i pismach Macieja Stryjkowskiego. Stryjkowski, Maciej, *Kronika polska, litewska, żmódzka i wszystkiéj Rusi.* Wydanie nowe. I. Warszawa, 1–30.

Mathauserová 1976: Матхаузерова, Светла, *Древнерусские теории искусства слова*, Praha (Acta Universitatis Carolinae Philologica, Monographia 63).

Mathiesen 1984: Mathiesen, Robert, The Church Slavonic language question: An overwiew (IX–XX centuries). Picchio, Riccardo & Harvey Goldblatt (eds.), *Aspects of the Slavic language question. Volume I: Church Slavonic – South Slavic – West Slavic.* New Haven (Yale Russian and East European Publications 4a), 45–65.

Matthews 1995: Matthews, David, Preterites in direct discourse in three Old East Slavic chronicles. *Russian Linguistics* 19, 299–317.

Moiseeva 1970: Моисеева, Г. Н., Русская историческая проза первой половины XVIII в. и польские историки. *Польско-русские литературные связи.* Москва, 83–106.

Moiseeva 1973: Моисеева, Г. Н., Литературно-общественные и научные связи России и Польши конца XVII – середины XVIII в. *История, культура, этнография и фольклор славянских народов. VII международный съезд славистов, Варшава, август 1973 г. Доклады советской делегации.* Москва, 438–451.

Moiseeva 1980: Моисеева, Г. Н., «Собрание российских древностей» профессора Баузе. *ТОДРЛ* 35, 301–344.

Moser 1998: Moser, Michael, *Die polnische, ukrainische und weißrussische Interferenzschicht im russischen Satzbau des 16. und 17. Jahrhunderts.* Frankfurt am Main (Schriften über Sprachen und Texte 3).

Moser 2000: Moser, Michael, Seltene Nebensatztypen in polnisch-russischen Übersetzungen aus dem 17. Jahrhundert – die „Povest' ob astrologe Mustaeddyne". *Studia Russica (Budapest)* 18, 186–191.

Moser 2007: Moser, Michael, Zur Genese des allrussischen Geschichts- und Sprachmythos in der Kiewer „Synopsis". *Wort – Geist – Kultur. Gedenkschrift für Sergej S. Averincev.* Frankfurt am Main (Русская культура в Европе 2), 219–285.

Mosteller & Wallace 1964: Mosteller, Frederick & David L. Wallace, *Inference and disputed authorship: The Federalist.* Reading, Mass. – Palo Alto – London.

Myl'nikov 1996: Мыльников, А. С., *Картина славянского мира: взгляд из Восточной Европы. Этногенетические легенды, догадки, протогипотезы XVI – начала XVIII века.* Санкт-Петербург (Slavica Petropolitana 1).

Myl'nikov 1999: Мыльников, А. С., *Картина славянского мира: взгляд из Восточной Европы. Представления об этнической номинации и этничности XVI – начала XVIII века.* Санкт-Петербург (Slavica Petropolitana 4).

Nandriş 1965: Nandriş, Grigore, *Handbook of Old Church Slavonic. Part I: Old Church Slavonic grammar.* London.

Narbutt 1846: Narbutt, Teodor, *Pomniki do dziejów litewskich pod względem historycznym, diplomatycznym, geograficznym, statystycznym, obyczajowym, orcheograficznym i t. p.* Wilno.

Nida 1964: Nida, Eugene A., *Toward a science of translating. With special reference to principles and procedures involved in Bible translating.* Leiden.

Niendorf 2006: Niendorf, Mathias, *Das Großfürstentum Litauen. Studien zur Nationsbildung in der Frühen Neuzeit (1569–1795).* Wiesbaden (Veröffentlichungen des Nordost-Instituts 3).

Nikolaev 1989: Николаев, С. И., *Польская поэзия в русских переводах. Вторая половина XVII – первая треть XVIII века.* Ленинград.

Nikolaev 2004: Николаев, С. И., *От Кохановского до Мицкевича. Разыскания по истории польско-русских литературных связей XVII – первой трети XIX в.* Санкт-Петербург.

Nikolaev 2008: Николаев, С. И., *Польско-русские литературные связи XVI–XVIII вв. Библиографические материалы.* Санкт-Петербург.

NPL 1950: *Новгородская первая летопись старшего и младшего изводов.* Москва – Ленинград.

Opisanie 1959: *Описание Рукописного отдела БАН. Том 3, вып. 1.* Москва – Ленинград.

Otten 1973: Otten, Fred, *Die finiten Verbalformen und ihr Gebrauch in der Stepennaja kniga carskogo rodoslovija*. Berlin (Veröffentlichungen der Abteilung für slavische Sprachen und Literaturen des Osteuropa-Instituts (Slavisches Seminar) an der freien Universität Berlin 42).

Pennington 1980: Kotošixin, Grigorij, *O Rossii v carstvovanie Alekseja Mixailoviča. Text and commentary*. Ed. by A. E. Pennington. Oxford.

Perepiska 1979: *Переписка Ивана Грозного с Андреем Курбским*. Текст подготовили Я. С. Лурье и Ю. Д. Рыков. Ленинград (Литературные памятники).

Petruchin 1996: Петрухин, П. В., Нарративная стратегия и употребление глагольных времен в русской летописи XVII века. *Вопросы языкознания* 4, 62–84.

Petruchin 2003: Петрухин, П. В., *Лингвистическая гетерогенность и употребление прошедших времен в древнерусском летописании*. Дис. ... канд. филол. наук. Москва.

Pisarkowa 1984: Pisarkowa, Krystyna, *Historia składni języka polskiego*. Wrocław etc. (Prace instytutu języka polskiego 52).

Plokhy 2006: Plokhy, Serhii, *The origins of the Slavic nations. Premodern identities in Russia, Ukraine, and Belarus*. Cambridge.

Poslanija 1951: *Послания Ивана Грозного*. Подгот. текста Д. С. Лихачева и Я. С. Лурье, перевод и комм. Я. С. Лурье. Москва – Ленинград (Литературные памятники).

Pravila 1961: *Правила лингвистического издания памятников древнерусской письменности*. Москва.

Prozorovskij 1879: Прозоровский, Д., *Опись древних рукописей, хранящихся въ музее Императорскаго русскаго археологическаго общества*. Санкт-Петербург.

PSRL XIV: *Полное собрание русских летописей. Том XIV. Никоновская летопись*. Москва 2000.

PSRL XVII: *Полное собрание русских летописей. Том XVII. Западно-русские (литовские) летописи*. Санкт-Петербург 1907.

PSRL XXXI: *Полное собрание русских летописей. Том XXXI. Летописцы последней четверти XVII в.* Москва 1968.

PSRL XXXII: *Полное собрание русских летописей. Том XXXII. Хроники: Литовская и жмоймтская, и Быховца. Летописи: Баркулабовская, Аверки и Панцырного*. Москва 1975.

PSRL XXXIV: *Полное собрание русских летописей. Том XXXIV. Постниковский, Пискаревский, Московский и Бельский летописцы*. Москва 1978.

PSRL XXXV: *Полное собрание русских летописей. Том XXXV. Летописи белорусско-литовские*. Москва 1980.

Ptašickij 1905: Пташицкий, С., Западно-русские переводы хроник Бельскаго и Стрыковскаго. *Новый сборник статей по славяноведению*. Санкт-Петербург, 372–384.

Pugh 1996: Pugh, Stefan M., *Testament to Ruthenian. A linguistic analysis of the Smotryc'kyj variant*. Cambridge, Mass. (Harvard Series in Ukrainian Studies).

PVL 2007: *Повесть временных лет*. Подгот. текста, перевод, статьи и комментарии Д. С. Лихачева. Под ред. В. П. Адриановой-Перетц. 3-е изд. Санкт-Петербург (Литературные памятники).

Radziszewska 1978: Radziszewska, Julia, *Maciej Stryjkowski. Historyk-poeta z epoki Odrodzenia*. Katowice (Prace naukowe Uniwersytetu Śląskiego w Katowicach 208).

Robinson 1963: Робинсон, А. Н., *Историография славянского возрождения и Паисий Хилендарский.* Москва.

Rogov 1963: Рогов, А. И., Древнерусские переводы «Хроники» Стрыйковского. *Археографический ежегодник за 1962 год.* Москва, 206–214.

Rogov 1965: Rogow, Aleksander, Maciej Stryjkowski i historiografia ukraińska XVII wieku. *Slavia Orientalis* 14:3, 311–329.

Rogov 1966: Рогов, А. И., *Русско-польские культурные связи в эпоху возрождения. Стрыйковский и его кроника.* Москва.

Rogov 1967: Рогов, А. И., Стрыйковский и русская историография первой половины XVIII в. *Источники и историография славянского средневековья.* Москва, 145–157.

Rogožin 2003: Рогожин, Н. М., *Посольский приказ. Колыбель российской дипломатии.* Москва.

Rothe 1983: Rothe, Hans (Hrsg.), *Sinopsis, Kiev 1681. Facsimile.* Köln – Wien (Bausteine zur Geschichte der Literatur bei den Slaven 17).

Ruposova 1982: Рупосова, Л. П., Лексика перевода «Римских деяний» (на материале списков конца XVII – начала XVIII вв.). *Проблемы лексикологии и словообразования русского языка. Сборник научных трудов.* Москва, 32–40.

Ruposova 1985: Рупосова, Л. П., Лексика повести о Петре и Магилене (по спискам XVII – начала XVIII вв.). *Проблемы истории русской лексики и терминологии. Межвузовский сборник научных трудов.* Москва, 12–19.

Sablina 1982: Саблина, Н. П., Полонизмы в «Проблемате Аристотеля» – переводном памятнике XVII в. *Проблемы лексикологии и словообразования русского языка. Сборник научных трудов.* Москва, 100–107.

Sablina & Sacharovskaja 1982: Саблина, Н. П. & М. И. Сахаровская, Лексика переводного памятника русской письменности XVII в. «Селенография» И. Гевелия. *Проблемы лексикологии и словообразования русского языка. Сборник научных трудов.* Москва, 48–59.

Sazonova 2006: Сазонова, Л. И., *Литературная культура России. Раннее Новое время.* Москва (Studia philologica).

Ščepkin 1967: Щепкин, В. Н., *Русская палеография.* Москва.

van Schooneveld 1959: van Schooneveld, Cornelis H., *A semantic analysis of the Old Russian finite preterite system.* 'S-Gravenhage (Slavistic printings and reprintings 7).

Sedov 2006: Седов, П. В., *Закат Московского царства: Царский двор конца XVII века.* Санкт-Петербург.

Shevelov 1974: Shevelov, George Y., Belorussian versus Ukrainian: Delimitation of texts before A.D. 1569. *The journal of Byelorussian studies* 3:2, 145–156.

Sielicki 1965: Sielicki, Franciszek, Kronikarze polscy w latopisarstwie i dawnej historiografii ruskiej. *Slavia Orientalis* 14:2, 143–178.

Skinner 2009: Skinner, Barbara, Khmelnytsky's shadow: the confessional legacy. Friedrich, Karin & Barbara M. Pendzich (eds.), *Citizenship and identity in a multinational commonwealth. Poland-Lithuania in context, 1550–1772.* Leiden – Boston (Studies in Central European histories 46), 149–169.

Sobolevskij 1903: Соболевский, А. И., *Переводная литература московской Руси XIV–XVII вековъ. Библиографические материалы.* Санкт-Петербург (Сборник отделения русскаго языка и словесности императорской Академии наук 74:1).

Sokołowska 1976: Sokołowska, Teresa, *Funkcje składniowe imiesłowów nieodmiennych w języku polskim XVII wieku*. Wrocław etc. (Prace instytutu języka polskiego 18).

Steensland 1997: Стенсланд, Ларс, *Русская акцентография. Правила и тенденции в употреблении надстрочных знаков в русских рукописях, преимущественно XV и XVI веков*. Lund (Slavica Lundensia 17).

Stone 2001: Stone, Daniel, *The Polish-Lithuanian state, 1386–1795*. Seattle – London (A history of East Central Europe 4).

Stroev 1825: Строев, П., *Обстоятельное описание славяно-российских рукописей, хранящихся в Москве в библиотеке тайнаго советника, сенатора, двора его императорскаго величества действительнаго каммергера и кавалера графа Федора Андреевича Толстова*. Москва.

Stryjkowski 1582: Stryjkowski, Maciej, *Ktora przedtym nigdy swiácłá nie widziáłá Kronika Polska Litewska/ Zmodźka/ y wszystkiey Rusi Kijowskiey/ Moskiewskiey/ Siewierskiey/ Wołhińskiey/ Podolskiey/ Podgorskiey/ Podláskiey/ etć.*. Krolewiec.

Stryjkowski 1766: Stryjkowski, Maciej, *Kronika Macieia Stryikowskiego, niegdyś w Krolewcu drukowana, teraz znowu z przydaniem historyi panstwa rossyiskiego przedrukowana*. Warszawa (Zbior dzieiopisow polskich we czterech tomach zawarty 2).

Stryjkowski 1978: Stryjkowski, Maciej, *O początkach, wywodach, dzielnościach, sprawach rycerskich i domowych sławnego narodu litewskiego, żemojdzkiego i ruskiego, przedtym nigdy od żadnego ani kuszone, ani opisane, z natchnienia Bożego a uprzejmie pilnego doświadczenia*. Warszawa.

Stryjkowski [1846] 1985: Stryjkowski, Maciej, *Kronika polska, litewska, żmódzka i wszystkiéj Rusi*. Wydanie nowe. I–II. Warszawa.

Šustova 2008: Шустова, Ю. Э., Упсальский список перевода Хроники Мачея Стрыйковского. *Очерки феодальной России* 12, 181–204.

Sørensen 1958: Sørensen, Hans Christian, Zum russischen Genitiv auf -*a* und -*y* im 17. Jahrh. *Scando-Slavica* 4, 210–238.

Thomson 1993: Thomson, Francis J., The corpus of Slavonic translations available in Muscovy. *Christianity and the Eastern Slavs. Vol. I: Slavic cultures in the Middle Ages*. Berkeley (California Slavic studies XVI), 179–214.

Tichonravov 1874: Тихонравов, Н., *Русския драматическия произведения 1672–1725 годов. Том I*. Санкт-Петербург.

Timberlake 1995: Timberlake, Alan, Avvakum's aorists. *Russian Linguistics* 19, 25–43.

Toločko 1996: Толочко, О., Український переклад «Хроніки...» Мацея Стрийковського з колекції О. Лазаревського та історіографічні пам'ятки XVII століття (Український Хронограф і «Синопсис»). *Записки Наукового товариства імені Шевченка* 231, 158–181.

Toury 1995: Toury, Gideon, *Descriptive Translation Studies and beyond*. Amsterdam – Philadelphia (Benjamins translation library 4).

Tromonin 1965: *Tromonin's watermark album. A facsimile of the Moscow 1844 edition*. Hilversum (Monumenta chartæ papyraceæ historiam illustrantia 11).

Ulaščik 1968: Улащик, Н. Н., «Литовская и жмоитская кроника» и ее отношение к хроникам Быховца и М. Стрыйковского. *Славяне и Русь*. Москва, 357–365.

Ulaščik 1985: Улащик, Н. Н., *Введение в изучение белорусско-литовского летописания*. Москва.

Ul'janovs'kyj & Jakovenko 1993: Ульяновський, В. І. & Н. М. Яковенко, Український переклад Хроніки Стрийковського кінця XVI – початку XVII століття. *Рукописна та книжкова спадщина України* 1, 5–12.

Uspenskij 1969: Успенский, Б. А., *Из истории русских канонических имен.* Москва.

Uspenskij 2002: Успенский, Б. А., *История русского литературного языка (XI–XVII вв.).* 3-е изд., испр. и доп. Москва.

Uspenskij & Živov 1983: Успенский, Б. А. & В. М. Живов, Выдающийся вклад в изучение русского языка XVII века. *International journal of Slavic linguistics and poetics* 28, 149–180.

Vaillant 1951: Vaillant, André, Deux notules. *Revue des études slaves* 27, 288–292.

Večerka et al. 1996: Večerka, Radoslav, Felix Keller & Eckhard Weiher, *Altkirchenslavische (Altbulgarische) Syntax, III. Die Satztypen: Der einfache Satz.* Freiburg i. Br. (Monumenta linguae Slavicae dialecti veteris, Fontes et dissertationes 36 (27: 3)).

Venuti 2008: Venuti, Lawrence, *The translator's invisibility. A history of translation.* 2nd ed. London – New York.

Vesti-Kuranty 2009: *Вести-Куранты 1656 г., 1660–1662 гг., 1664–1670 гг. Часть I: Русские тексты.* Москва.

Vovina-Lebedeva 2004: Вовина-Лебедева, В. Г., *Новый летописец. История текста.* Санкт-Петербург.

Walczak-Sroczyńska 1976: Walczak-Sroczyńska, Barbara, Wielkie zwierciadło przykładów – dzieje tekstologiczne. *Slavia Orientalis* 25:4, 493–508.

Watson 2010: Watson, Christine, Den ryska översättningen av Maciej Stryjkowskis *Kronika Polska*: en del av den ryska kröniketraditionen? *Slovo. Journal of Slavic languages and literatures* 51, 83–93.

Weiss 1995: Weiss, Daniel, Russian converbs: A typological outline. Haspelmath, Martin & Ekkehard König (eds.), *Converbs in cross-linguistic perspective. Structure and meaning of adverbial verb forms – adverbial participles, gerunds.* Berlin – New York, 239–282.

Witkowski 1978: Witkowski, Wiesław, Einige Bemerkungen über polnische Einflüsse auf die Satzbildung der russischen Schriftsprache. *Biuletyn polskiego towarzystwa językoznawczego* 36, 33–42.

Wojtkowiak 1990: Wojtkowiak, Zbysław, *Maciej Stryjkowski, dziejopis Wielkiego Księstwa Litewskiego. Kalendarium życia i działalności.* Poznań (Uniwersytet im. Adama Mickiewicza w Poznaniu, Seria historia 169).

Wojtkowiak 2010: Wojtkowiak, Zbysław, *Odnaleziony tekst Macieja Stryjkowskiego o bitwie z Moskwą 1564 roku i inne rewelacje w zbiorach rosyjskich i nie tylko.* Poznań (Biblioteczka Źródłoznawcy 2).

Worth 1975: Worth, Dean S., Was there a "literary language" in Kievan Rus? *Russian Review* 34:1, 1–9.

Zabelin 1915: Забелин, И., *Домашний быт русских царей в XVI и XVII ст. Часть II.* Москва.

Zachara-Wawrzyńczyk 1963: Zachara-Wawrzyńczyk, Maria, Geneza legendy o rzymskim pochodzeniu litwinów. *Zeszyty historyczne Uniwersytetu Warszawskiego* 3, 5–35.

Zaliznjak 2004: Зализняк, А. А., *Древненовгородский диалект. 2-е изд., переработанное с учетом находок 1995–2003 гг.* Москва (Studia philologica).

Zaliznjak 2008: Зализняк, А. А., *Древнерусские энклитики.* Москва.

Živov 1995: Живов, В. М., Usus scribendi. Простые претериты у летописца-самоучки. *Russian Linguistics* 19, 45–75.

Živov 1996: Живов, В. М., *Язык и культура в России XVIII века.* Москва.

Živov 1998: Живов, В. М., Автономность письменного узуса и проблема преемственности в восточнославянской средневековой письменности. *Славянское языкознание. XII международный съезд славистов, Краков, 1998 г. Доклады российской делегации.* Москва, 212–247.

Živov 2004: Живов, В. М., *Очерки исторической морфологии русского языка XVII–XVIII веков.* Москва (Studia philologica).

Živov 2009: Zhivov, Victor, *Language and culture in eighteenth-century Russia.* Boston (Studies in Russian and Slavic literatures, cultures and history).

Živov 2011: Zhivov, Viktor, On the language of the Book of Degrees of the Royal Genealogy. Lenhoff, G. & A. Kleimola (eds.), *The Book of Royal Degrees and the genesis of Russian historical consciousness*, Bloomington (UCLA Slavic Studies, New Series 7), 141–153.

Zoltán 2003: Золтан А., Легенда о святой Урсуле в старой польской и восточнославянской письменности (XVI–XVII вв.). *Studia Slavica Academiae Scientiarum Hungaricae* 48:1–3, 323–334.

Zoltán 2006: Золтан А., Миграция одного текста: Легенда о святой Урсуле в составе русских переводов Хроники М. Стрыйковского. *ТОДРЛ* 57, 197–208.

Ågren 1995: Огрен, Ирина, К вопросу о теоретическом и практическом базисе древнейших славянских переводов, *Подобаетъ память сътворити. Essays to the memory of Anders Sjöberg.* Stockholm (Acta Universitatis Stockholmiensis, Stockholm Slavic Studies 24), 157–172.

Öberg 1992: Öberg, Jan, Det trots allt möjligas konst. Textutgivning ur en latinists perspektiv. Carlquist, Jonas (utg), *Föreläsningar i medeltidsfilologi.* Stockholm (Meddelanden från Institutionen för nordiska språk vid Stockholms universitet 38), 57–111.

Digital resources

www.dbc.wroc.pl
www.korpus.uni-r.de/diakorp
www.krotov.info/acts/17/azaryin/b61.htm
www.litopys.org.ua/novglet/novg.htm
www.litopys.org.ua/psrl3235/lytov15.htm
www.litopys.org.ua/psrl3235/lytov16.htm
www.lrc-lib.ru/rus_letopisi/Laurence/lavrfrm.htm
www.obc.opole.pl
www.pbi.edu.pl
http://rhssl1.uni-regensburg.de:8080/OCS

ACTA UNIVERSITATIS UPSALIENSIS
Studia Slavica Upsaliensia

1. Studia Slavica Gunnaro Gunnarsson sexagenario dedicata. 1960.
2. *Gun Bergman*: The Melusina Saga. The text in UUB Slav 34 and a Study in 17th Century Literary Language in Russia. 1964.
3. *Jurij Semjonow*: ”Das Häuschen in Kolomna” in der poetischen Erbschaft A. S. Puškins. 1965.
4. *Andreas Ådahl*: Rysk civilrättsterminologi i Sovjetunionen. (With a Summary in English: Russian Civil Law Terminology in the Soviet Union.) 1966.
5. *Karin Pontoppidan-Sjövall*: Categories of Content and Form in Language. A Study of the Personal and Impersonal Constructions in Russian. 1968.
6. *Gun Bergman*: Turkisms in Ivo Andrić's *Na Drini Ćuprija* examined from the points of view of Literary Style and Cultural History. 1969.
7. *Józef Trypućko*: O języku *Wspomnień dzieciństwa* Franciszka Mickiewicza. (Sur la langue des *Réminiscences de ma jeunesse* de Franciszek Mickiewicz.) 1970.
8. *Леннарт Лённгрен* (Lennart Lönngren): Употребление краткой формы страдательного причастия прошедшего времени в современном русском языке. (With a Summary in English: The Use of the Short Form of the Past Passive Participle in Modern Russian.) 1970.
9. *Nils B. Thelin*: On Stress Assignment and Vowel Reduction in Contemporary Standard Russian. 1971.
10. *Andreas Ådahl*: Öststatsforskning – en tvärvetenskaplig disciplin. (With a Summary in English: Soviet and East European Studies – an Interdisciplinary Science.) 1971.
11. *Lennart Stenborg*: Studien zur Erzähltechnik in den Novellen V. M. Garšins. 1972.
12. *Lars Steensland*: Die Distribution der urindogermanischen sogenannten Gutturale. 1973.
13. *Józef Trypućko*: Dziesięć lat językoznawstwa polskiego 1956–1965. Próba bibliografii. Ten years of Polish linguistics 1956–1965. A bibliography. 1973.
14. *Józef Trypućko*: Łacińska końcówka w polskim systemie fleksyjnym. Przyczynek do zagadnienia interferencji językowej. 1974.
15. *Nils B. Thelin:* Notes on General and Russian Morphology. 1975.
16. *Lennart Stenborg*: Die Zeit als strukturelles Element im literarischen Werk (mit Illustrationen aus der Novellistik V. M. Garšins). 1975.
17. *Nils B. Thelin*: Towards A Theory of Verb Stem Formation and Conjugation in Modern Russian. With an excursus on so-called *e-o* alternations and mobile vowels. 1975.
18. *Nils B. Thelin*: Towards A Theory of Aspect, Tense and Actionality in Slavic. 1978.
19. *Леннарт Лённгрен* (Lennart Lönngren): Русские деривационные суффиксы. (With a Summary in English: Russian Derivational Suffixes.) 1978
20. *Józef Lewandowski*: Swedish Contribution to the Polish Resistance Movement during World War Two (1939–1942). 1979.
21. *Lars Steensland*: A Method for Measuring Perceptual Distances between Different Vowel Qualities. Some Identification Tests Using Russian /e/ Variants and Swedish Subjects. 1981.
22. *Józef Trypućko*: Pięć lat językoznawstwa polskiego 1966–1970. Próba bibliografii. Five Years of Polish Linguistics 1966–1970. A Bibliography. 1984.
23. *Małgorzata Szulc Packalén*: Pokolenie 68. Studium o poezji polskiej lat siedemdziesiątych. (With a Summary in English: Generation 68. Studies in Polish Poetry of the '70s.) 1987.

24. *Jerzy Bralczyk*: O języku polskiej propagandy politycznej lat siedemdziesiątych. (With a Summary in English: On the Language of Polish Political Propaganda of the 1970s.) 1987.

25. *Jerzy M. de Kamiński*: „…Nápred i Názad se ogledát”. *Razgówori ob wladátelystwu* (1663–1666) Juraja Križanicia i ich spójność tematyczno-argumentacyjna. (With a Summary in English: '…to look forward and back'. Juraj Križaniç's *Razgówori ob wladátelystwu* ['Discourses on government'] and its Thematic and Argumentative Coherence.) 1987.

26. *Ирина Огрен* (Irina Ågren): Паренесис Ефрема Сирина. К истории славянского перевода. (With a Summary in English: Ephrem the Syrian's Paraenesis. A Contribution to the History of the Slavic Translation.) 1989.

27. *Людмила Ферм* (Ludmila Ferm): Выражение направления при приставочных глаголах перемещения в современном русском языке. К вопросу префиксально-предложного детерминизма. (With a Summary in English: Expression of Direction with Prefixed Verbs of Motion in Modern Russian. A Contribution to the Study of Prefixal-Prepositional Determinism.) 1990.

28. *Erik Fält*: Compounds in Contact. A Study in Compound Words with Special Reference to the Old Slavonic Translation of Flavius Josephus' Περὶ τοῦ Ἰουδαϊκοῦ πολέμου. 1990.

29. *Ingrid Maier*: Verben mit der Bedeutung "benutzen" im Russischen. Untersuchung einer lexikalisch-semantischen Gruppe. 1991.

30. *Roger Gyllin*: The Genesis of the Modern Bulgarian Literary Language. 1991.

31. *Ирина Огрен* (Irina Ågren): К проблеме использования печатных изданий греческих текстов при исследовании древних славянских переводов. На примере славянского перевода Паренесиса Ефрема Сирина. (With a Summary in English: On the Problem of Using Printed Editions of Greek Texts for Studying Old Slavonic Translations: With the Example of the Slavonic Translation of Ephrem the Syrian's *Paraenesis*.) 1991.

32. *Леннарт Лённгрен* (Lennart Lönngren), red.: Частотный словарь современного русского языка. (With a Summary in English: A Frequency Dictionary of Modern Russian.) 1993.

33. *Людмила Ферм* (Ludmila Ferm): Особенности развития русской лексики в новейший период (на материале газет). (With a Summary in English: Some Distinctive Features of the Development of Russian Vocabulary following Perestroika [based on news-paper language].) 1994.

34. *Тамара Лённгрен* (Tamara Lönngren): Лексика русских старообрядческих говоров (на материале, собранном в Латгалии и на Житомирщине). (With a Summary in English: The Lexicon of Russian Old-Believers [based on Material from Latgale and the Žitomir Area].) 1994.

35. *Maria Zadencka*: W poszukiwaniu utraconej ojczyzny. Obraz Litwy i Białorusi w twórczości wybranych polskich pisarzy emigracyjnych. Florian Czarnyszewicz, Michał Kryspin Pawlikowski, Maria Czapska, Czesław Miłosz, Józef Mackiewicz. (With a Summary in English: Searching for the Lost Homeland. The Image of Lithuania and Byelorussia in the Works of Selected Polish Emigré Writers.) 1995.

36. *Ирина Люсен* (Irina Lysén): Греческо-старославянский конкорданс к древнейшим спискам славянского перевода евангелий (codices Marianus, Zographensis, Assemanianus, Ostromiri). (With an Introduction in English: Greek-Old Church Slavic Concordance to the Oldest Versions of the Translation of the Gospel Texts.) 1995.

37. *Madlena Norberg*: Sprachwechselprozeß in der Niederlausitz. Soziolinguistische Fallstudie der deutsch-sorbischen Gemeinde Drachhausen/Hochoza. 1996.

38. *Ingrid Maier*: Verbalrektion in den „Vesti-Kuranty" (1600–1660). Eine historisch-philologische Untersuchung zur mittelrussischen Syntax. 1997.

39. *Thomas Rosén*: The Slavonic Translation of the Apocryphal Infancy Gospel of Thomas. 1997.

40. *Elisabeth Marklund Sharapova*: Implicit and Explicit Norm in Contemporary Russian Verbal Stress. 2000.

41. *Ирина Люсен* (Irina Lysén): Книга Есфирь. К истории первого славянского перевода. (With a Summary in English: The Book of Esther. A Contribution to the History of the First Slavonic Translation.) 2001.

42. *Eva Gruszczyńska*: Linguistic Images of Emotions in Translation from Polish into Swedish: Henryk Sienkiewicz as a Case in Point. 2001.

43. *Małgorzata Anna Packalén*: Under två kulturers ok. Allmogeskildringar i den polska och svenska 1800- och 1900-talslitteraturen. (With a Summary in English: Under the yoke of two cultures. Peasant portrayals in Polish and Swedish literature of the 19th and 20th centuries.) 2001.

44. *Larisa Dubrovina*: Вариативное глагольное управление в русском языке первой трети XIX века. (With a Summary in English: Variations in Russian Verbal Government 1800–1840.) 2002.

45. *Ingrid Maier*: Verbalrektion in den „Vesti-Kuranty" (1600–1660). Teil 2: Die präpositionale Rektion. 2006.

46. *Christine Watson:* Tradition and Translation: Maciej Stryjkowski's Polish Chronicle in Seventeenth-Century Russian Manuscripts. 2012.